www.oxfordshire.gov.uk

Working for you

Not For Loan

THE
WHO'S
WHO
OF
OXFORD UNITED

DEDICATION

For all those U's who are no longer with us, including Harry Thompson, Arthur Turner, Gerry Summers, Peter Houseman, Martin Aldridge, Maurice Evans, Ken Fish and last, but decidedly not least, Ken Ridley. RIP.

THE
WHO'S
WHO
OF
OXFORD UNITED

MARTIN BRODETSKY

Oxford United

First published in Great Britain in 2011 by The Derby Books Publishing Company Limited,
3 The Parker Centre, Derby, DE21 4SZ.

ISBN 978-1-85983-990-4

Printed and bound in Poland.
www.polskabook.co.uk

CONTENTS

FOREWORD

I am writing this in June 2011. The fixtures for the new season have just come out and we start against Rotherham United at the Don Valley Stadium in Sheffield from where I have presented many athletics programmes for ITV. Binoculars will be handy when it comes to watching football there!

It is not the most glamorous of starts but it is much better than going to some of the clubs visited in the four seasons out of the Football League. We're back where we belong and moving in the right direction.

Whatever club you support you will get highs and lows, but following Oxford United over the years has been a supreme test of loyalty and patience. I am old enough to have seen the U's play at the highest level. We were the first team to beat Alex Ferguson's Manchester United...we have beaten Chelsea, Arsenal and Everton.

Sadly memories of recent defeats at Eastbourne and by the part-timers of Hayes & Yeading are a painful reminder of how far the club fell because of a grim lack of care.

In the past couple of seasons that trend has been reversed by a clever and progressive chairman, Kelvin Thomas, and a bright, enthusiastic and hard-working manager, Chris Wilder. But we all know there's still a long way to go and problems remain. Owning the stadium would take the club to another level and remains a work in progress.

With our facilities and fan base my belief is that we should be a Championship club. Oxford fans are a special breed who give fantastic support both home and away. We took 33,000 to Wembley for the Blue Square Premier Play-off Final against York City in May 2010, showing just how important the club is to the wider community.

Getting promoted via the Play-offs is nerve-wracking, but there's no better way of going up than putting on a show at Wembley. Get in Alfie Potter!

Supporting Oxford has been a lifetime experience. I nearly lost my job for putting on my United hat while presenting the television coverage of the Milk Cup Final in 1986. Trust me, I was much more nervous when United returned to Wembley, we just HAD to win that one. Back in '86 we were talking about Cup glory – in 2010 the prize was the long-term future of OUFC.

Joining the players and staff on the bus tour through Oxford after we had returned to the League last year was a wonderful experience – especially when we finished in Broad Street where my dad had an antiquarian bookshop. Seeing the street jam-packed with joyous fans bought a lump to my throat.

A year ago Kelvin asked me to sit on the board. It is an honour, but it means I have to keep my emotions under control while watching with the opposition directors. I would much rather be with the fans behind the goal where I have shouted my way through hundreds of United matches.

Like me, Martin Brodetsky has been a dedicated, long-term Oxford fan. Martin has an unrivalled knowledge of the club and also has the writing skills and dedication required to compile this type of book. Last season he quietly and efficiently took over the duties of programme editor. Typically the standard of the programme was not maintained – it was enhanced.

I'm delighted that the prolific Martin has produced this *Who's Who* and I am looking forward to finding out a lot more about our club and the characters who have been part of it.
Come on you Yellows!

Jim Rosenthal
June 2011

INTRODUCTION AND ACKNOWLEDGEMENTS

Welcome to the *Who's Who of Oxford United*. This book should provide a great complement to the *Complete Record*, published in 2009, while also working well as a stand-alone record of all the players who have played for the club since 1949, when the side turned professional and records effectively began.

As with any team, there has been a great variety of players to have seen service with the U's. Some of their careers spanned many seasons, with Ron Atkinson leading the way with 561 appearances, while others lasted just a few minutes: Abdou Sall's entire Oxford career lasted fewer than six minutes spread over two games, while Scot Gemmill played 17 minutes at Mansfield and Tony Obi managed 15 minutes of a top-flight encounter at Watford.

This book documents the careers of all of these players and many hundreds more, but I have only included players who made a first-team competitive appearance for the club, so sadly there's no mention of players such as Bruce Grobbelaar, David Icke, Roy Pack or, more recently, Dexter Blackstock and Simon Eastwood.

Obviously, due to the nature of the beast, this book includes players who are still in the current Oxford squad (marked with a * in the text), and therefore their tales are as yet incomplete. Indeed, transfer activity in the few weeks since the end of the 2010–11 season has been frenetic, meaning that there are already half a dozen new signings who do not feature in these pages.

This volume would not have been anything like as comprehensive as it is without the help of numerous others – far too many to mention individually. Those who I will name include Jim Rosenthal, who interrupted a much-needed break in the USA to pen the foreword; Ian Pearce, whose technical expertise has ensured that the Rage Online database (www.rageonline.co.uk) continues to be the number one online resource for all OUFC statistical information; Chris Byrne, the Oxford City historian whose almost instantaneous responses to my many emails helped fill several gaps in my research; Ralph Sheppard, who provided an identical service for all my Barrow-related queries, with help from Phil Yelland, an all-the-more impressive feat considering he lives in New Zealand; and Leigh Edwards for his incomparable knowledge of lower League and non-League players' histories.

It would be remiss of me not to give a shout out to Steve Daniels, Dave Fleming, Darrell Fisher, Tony Bailey and all the other photographers who have captured images of United's players and games, usually for no monetary reward. Also to the many other photographers whose work has been reproduced in this book. Wherever possible I have sought permission to reproduce the images, but if I have inadvertently published a photo without permission please accept my sincere apologies.

Finally, my greatest thanks go to the dozens of United players past and present who have given their time to chat to me about their careers either in person, on the phone, or by email – they have all been very happy and willing to talk and to give me insights (occasionally unprintable) into their time at the club.

On a more prosaic note I would like to thank Derby Publishing, in particular Alex Morton and my editor Dean Rockett for helping move this project along and bringing it to life, and especially for their patience and lack of swearing for missed deadlines and pedantic last-minute amendments. Needless to say, any errors in the text are mine and no fault should be attached to anyone else.

A quick note about terminology: players' positions are often fairly arbitrary (goalkeepers notwithstanding) with programmes right up to the 1960s often having teams line up in the old 2–3–5 formation, long after it had stopped being used. Therefore some journalistic licence has gone into determining where a player played. I have used the term 'centre-back' rather than 'centre-half' to refer to central-defenders and I use 'striker' and 'forward' almost interchangeably, although there's probably a subtle difference. I have also, inevitably, got some wrong.

Martin Brodetsky
June 2011

A

ABBEY, Ben

Forward
Born: 13 May 1978, Westminster
United debut: 2 October 1999 v Bristol City (sub)
Final United game: 18 March 2000 v Notts County (sub)
Appearances: 0+13
Goals: 1
Clubs: Osterley, Maidenhead United, Crawley Town, Oxford United, Aldershot Town (loan), Southend United, Stevenage Borough, Crawley Town, Woking, Macclesfield Town, Gravesend & Northfleet, St Albans City, Northwood, Farnborough Town, Hampton & Richmond Borough, Metropolitan Police, Tooting & Mitcham, Wealdstone, Slough Town

Benjamin Charles Abbey was signed by Malcolm Shotton from Crawley Town for £35,000 on 29 September 1999, despite Crawley, who were in administration, receiving a higher bid from Exeter City. The 5ft 7in striker was reluctant to join the Grecians so he moved to the Manor instead because United were in a higher division. He had previously, in March, had a trial with Reading. On his first day of training he hit himself between the eyes with a cricket bat and had to visit casualty. He never made a start for Oxford and he scored just one goal; a last-minute winner against Morecambe in the FA Cup first round. While at Oxford he had a loan spell at Aldershot Town in August 2000, scoring one goal in six appearances, before signing for Southend United in October 2000. He started his career with Osterley, managed by Alan Devonshire, who took him to Maidenhead with him. In September 2007 he joined Crawley, scoring 46 goals in 97 games before his move to the Manor. At Roots Hall, Abbey played 31 games and scored nine goals, making him the Shrimpers' top scorer that season. A short spell at Stevenage in November 2001, when he made just one substitute appearance, was followed by a return to Crawley, before he moved to Woking in August 2002. He scored seven goals in 26 games before Macclesfield signed him on non-contract forms on transfer deadline day in March 2003, although he failed to make an appearance for the Silkmen. The following season Abbey joined Gravesend, where he made 26 appearances and scored eight goals, and in September 2004 he moved to St Albans, for whom he played three games and scored once. In November, Abbey joined Northwood and although he scored four goals in 18 games the crowd failed to warm to him. At the start of 2005–06 Abbey made two substitute appearances for Farnborough before he joined his mentor Alan Devonshire at Hampton & Richmond in October 2005. He moved to Metropolitan Police in March 2006 before his next stop at Tooting & Mitcham. He scored 13 goals in 77 games for the Terrors, easily Abbey's longest spell at one club, while working as a foreign currency trader in the City. He had an unsuccessful pre-season trial with Wealdstone in August 2009, and in October 2010 he joined Slough Town. Abbey has also coached at the Chelsea Academy and has a degree in business and administration.

ADAMS, Don

Forward
Born: 15 February 1931, Northampton
Died: March 1993
United debut: 27 October 1956 v Bath City
Final United game: 16 March 1957 v Kettering Town
Appearances: 6
Goals: 1
Clubs: Northampton Town, Bedford Town, Headington United

Donald Frederick Adams was a centre-forward. He joined Bedford Town from Northampton Town, where he made 23 Division Three South appearances for the Eagles. He scored seven goals, but because he was based in Oxford he found the travelling too difficult and in October 1956 he joined Headington United.

ADAMS, Eddie

Inside-left
United debut: 20 August 1955 v Gloucester City
Final United game: 22 April 1957 v Chelmsford City
Appearances: 78
Goals: 20
Clubs: Newtongrange Star, Queen of the South, Headington United

Edward Adams joined Headington from Queen of the South, where he made three League appearances, coming to England shortly after being demobbed from the Army. His first recorded appearance for his first club, Newtongrange Star, was in February 1951, when he scored once in a record 11–2 win. It was not until 1952–53 that Adams began to feature more in the first team; Newtongrange Star won three Cups that season (Thornton Shield, Brown Cup, and Murray Cup) and Adams scored in both the Thornton Shield and Brown Cup Finals. When not playing for Headington he worked as a plumber.

ADAMS, Graham

Full-back
Born: 1 March 1933, Torrington
United debut: 14 February 1959 v Barry Town
Final United game: 21 January 1961 v Dartford
Appearances: 85
Goals: 1
Clubs: RAF, Chippenham Town, Bath City, Plymouth Argyle, Headington United, Montreal Olympic

Graham Wallace Adams joined Plymouth Argyle after playing for the RAF. He made one League appearance before Arthur Turner signed him for a fee of £750 in February 1959. Adams' career was ended after he broke his leg while filling in for the United A team, and his contract was mutually terminated in September 1961. After finishing at United he coached abroad briefly and then spent a season as manager of Wycombe Wanderers in 1961–62. In 1970 Adams was the chief coach to the Bermuda World Cup squad, and in 1972 he was a coach with Montreal Olympic, where he also played four games.

ALDOUS, Stan

Centre-back
Born: 10 February 1923, Northfleet
Died: October 1995
United debut: 10 September 1958 v Cheltenham Town
Final United game: 1 November 1958 v Wealdstone
Appearances: 5
Clubs: Erith & Belvedere, Bromley, Gravesend & Northfleet, Leyton Orient, Headington United

Stanley Elvey Reginald Aldous was a central-defender. He joined Orient from Gravesend in July 1950 and captained them to promotion to Division Two. He signed for Headington as player-coach but he played just five games before injury ended his career. In 1967–68 he briefly managed Gravesend for no pay, having been a playing favourite there before his move to Orient. He once scored four in a game for Erith & Belvedere while deputising at centre-forward.

ALDRIDGE, John

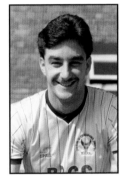

Forward
Born: 18 September 1958, Liverpool
United debut: 7 April 1984 v Walsall (sub)
Final United game: 24 January 1987 v Watford
Appearances: 138+3
Goals: 90
Clubs: South Liverpool, Newport County, Oxford United, Liverpool, Real Sociedad (Spain), Tranmere Rovers

John William Aldridge was signed by Jim Smith from Newport County for £78,000 after Sunderland had failed to meet Newport's asking price. The Ian Rush lookalike went on to become an Oxford legend, breaking the club's League goalscoring record with 34 goals as United won the Second Division title in 1984–85 when he forged an unforgettable partnership with Billy Hamilton. He was also leading scorer the following season, with 31 top-flight goals, and had scored 21 goals, making him leading scorer for the third consecutive season, when Liverpool paid £750,000 for him as a replacement for Rush in January 1987. This was the first time that one player had been top scorer for United three seasons running. Aldo won the first seven of his 69 Ireland caps while with United, going on to score 19 international goals. Aldridge started his career with South Liverpool, moving to Newport in1979 and turning professional aged 21. He played 198 times for County, scoring 78 goals. Real Sociedad paid Liverpool £1 million for him in September 1989 and he scored an impressive 40 goals in 63 games for the Basque club, becoming the first non-Basque to play for them. Two years later he joined Tranmere Rovers for £250,000 and in his first season at Prenton Park he scored a club record 40 goals, with the 40th coming in the final game of the season, a 2–1 defeat by Oxford that saved the U's from relegation. In 1996 he became player-manager of Tranmere, retiring from playing two years later, having scored 138 goals in 242 games, and he resigned as manager in March 2001 just before the Rovers were relegated to the third tier. He later became a pundit with various media outlets, summarising Liverpool games for Radio City, and he part-owned a bar called Aldo's in Liverpool. He was also a patron for fans' club AFC Liverpool. In total, Aldridge scored a post-war record of 474 goals in 882 career appearances.

ALDRIDGE, Martin

Forward
Born: 12 June 1974, Northampton
Died: 30 January 2000
United debut: 26 December 1995 v Bournemouth (sub)
Final United game: 7 February 1998 v Sheffield United (sub)
Appearances: 56+32
Goals: 22
Clubs: Northampton Town, Dagenham & Redbridge (loan), Oxford United, Southend United (loan), Blackpool, Port Vale (loan), Rushden & Diamonds (loan)

Martin James Aldridge joined Oxford on a free transfer from Northampton Town in December 1995. He seemed to specialise in scoring last-minute goals, but despite being prolific he found it difficult to hold down a regular starting place. His best moment came when he scored a hat-trick against Sheffield United. The striker started with Northampton, where in 82 games he scored 22 goals. Before coming to the Manor, in the same month, he had a brief loan spell with Dagenham & Redbridge. Shortly before leaving Oxford he had a three-month loan at Southend in February 1998, scoring once in 11 games, before joining Blackpool on a free transfer in August. He played 30 games for the Tangerines and scored 10 goals. He had a one-month loan at Port Vale at the end of September 1999, where he made three substitute appearances. Aldo joined Rushden & Diamonds on loan in January 2000. He played one game for the Diamonds before he was involved in a car crash following a game in which he was an unplayed substitute. He later died from his injuries in the JR Hospital in Oxford.

ALDRIDGE, Norman

Right-back
Born: 23 February 1921, Coventry
United debut: 20 August 1949 v Hastings United
Final United game: 8 March 1952 v Weymouth
Appearances: 86
Goals: 1
Clubs: Foxford, West Bromwich Albion, Northampton Town, Headington United

Norman Hubert Aldridge was a right-back. He was a model of consistency, missing just one game in his first season with United and was regarded by many as the finest right-back in the Southern League. He lived in Coventry and had to drive to Headington to play and train. Before his arrival at the Manor he made just one League appearance for West Brom in his three seasons at the Hawthorns, during the 1946–47 season, and he played twice for Northampton before he signed for Headington. He made his debut in the side's first Southern League match.

ALEKSIC, Milija

Goalkeeper
Born: 14 April 1951, Newcastle-under-Lyme
United debut: 14 August 1976 v Cambridge United
Final United game: 17 August 1975 v Cambridge United
Appearances: 2

Clean Sheets: 1
Clubs: Port Vale, Eastwood Town, Stafford Rangers, Plymouth Argyle, Oxford United (loan), Ipswich Town (loan), Luton Town, Tottenham Hotspur, Sheffield United (loan), Luton Town (loan), Bidvest Wits (South Africa)

Milija Anthony Aleksic was a goalkeeper whose father was from Yugoslavia. He joined Oxford on loan from Plymouth Argyle, playing two League Cup games against Cambridge United which Oxford lost 2–1 on aggregate. He earned an FA Cup winners' medal with Spurs when they beat Manchester City 3–2 after a replay in the 1981 Final. He started at Port Vale in 1969, then managed by Sir Stanley Matthews, making two appearances, but was released and he moved to local side Eastwood Town. In February 1970 he had a trial at Torquay United, where he played three games for the reserves. He joined Stafford Rangers, with whom he won an FA Trophy winners' medal after they beat Barnet 3–0 in 1972. Aleksic played for Stafford against Yeovil in the semi-final, played at the Manor. He joined Plymouth, making his debut as a second-half substitute in a friendly against Santos, conceding his first goal for the Pilgrims from a Pele penalty. He had loan spells at Oxford and Ipswich, before leaving for Luton for £20,000 in January 1976; at Luton he was on the receiving end of a two-fingered salute from Cardiff's Robin Friday in April 1977, a photo of which was later used on the cover of Super Furry Animals' 1996 single *The Man Don't Give a Fuck*. From Luton he joined Spurs for £100,000 in 1979, after 77 League appearances. Aleksic, nicknamed 'Elastic', had a non-playing loan spell at Sheffield United from which he was recalled in time to help Spurs to Wembley. He lost his place to Ray Clemence after playing 25 League games and returned to Luton on loan for four games in 1982. He then moved to South Africa where he played for Wits University and became a coach. Aleksic later worked at the Golfers Club in Johannesburg.

ALLEN, Chris

Left-winger
Born: 18 November 1972, Oxford
United debut: 1 October 1991 v Swindon Town (sub)
Final United game: 16 April 1996 v Notts County (sub)
Appearances: 131+48
Goals: 17
Clubs: Oxford United, Nottingham Forest (loan), Nottingham Forest, Luton Town (loan), Cardiff City (loan), Port Vale, Stockport County, Slough Town, Dover Athletic, Aldershot Town, North Leigh

Christopher Anthony Allen was a product of the Oxford United youth system. The Blackbird Leys youngster was a very fast winger who forged an exciting wing partnership with Joey Beauchamp. He was signed by Nottingham Forest for £500,000 in July 1996 following a brief loan spell at the City Ground the previous season. Following loans to Luton Town and Cardiff City, he moved to Port Vale on a free transfer in March 1999. After just five games he moved to Stockport County in October, but was released the following May. He signed for Slough before the 2000–01 season, scoring on his debut against Gravesend & Northfleet, but after a succession of injuries he left the club in February 2001 having scored twice in 15 games. In March 2001 he trained with Brighton, but left two months later without signing for them. Allen joined Dover Athletic, initially on non-contract terms, in October 2001, but in March 2002 he moved to Aldershot Town, where he stayed until the end of that season, scoring one goal in nine matches. Allen signed for North Leigh in 2006 and remained there until he returned to Oxford as youth team coach in July 2010.

ALSOP, Julian

Forward
Born: 28 May 1973, Nuneaton
United debut: 19 August 2003 v Lincoln City
Final United game: 18 September 2004 v Yeovil Town (sub)
Appearances: 31+5
Goals: 5
Clubs: Nuneaton Borough, VS Rugby, Racing Club Warwick, Tamworth, Halesowen Town, Bristol Rovers, Swansea City (loan), Swansea City, Cheltenham Town, Oxford United, Northampton Town, Forest Green Rovers, Tamworth, Forest Green Rovers (loan), Forest Green Rovers, Newport County, Cirencester Town, Bishops Cleeve, Cheltenham Town, Bishops Cleeve

Julian Mark Alsop signed from Cheltenham Town in June 2003, having been the Robins' leading scorer for the previous two seasons. The 6ft 3in target man was sent off three times in his first season for United, and he was eventually sacked by the club in October 2004 for gross misconduct following an incident involving a youth team player that became known as 'Bananagate'. He started his career at his home-town club, Nuneaton Borough, and played non-League football for a few seasons. While at Tamworth he became the fastest hat-trick scorer in history, notching three goals in just over a minute against Armitage in February 1995. He was signed by Bristol Rovers in March 1997 for £15,000 from Halesowen. He was at Rovers for almost exactly one year, but the last couple of months were spent at Swansea City, who paid the Pirates £30,000 to sign him in March 1998. He moved to Whaddon Road in June 2000, spending three seasons with Cheltenham before moving to Oxford. After his dismissal from United he was banned from football for six months. He then joined Northampton for a couple of months and thence to Forest Green Rovers, where he played just three games in seven months before joining Tamworth again. Tamworth loaned him back to Forest Green almost immediately, with Rovers signing him permanently again in January 2006. He spent two years at Newport County, joining in July 2006, before he returned to Cheltenham in July 2009, via Cirencester and Bishops Cleeve. He lasted for one season back in the League, winning the Supporters' Player of the Season award and scoring four goals, which made him Cheltenham's all-time top League goalscorer with 39 goals in total, before returning to Bishops Cleeve in July 2010. He started a company called Footballers Careers, offering advice and help to footballers once their playing days were over. In April 2011 he announced his retirement from playing by burning his football boots in a field in Gloucestershire. Alsop won five England C caps.

AMPHLETT, Ray

Left-back
Born: 25 September 1922, Manchester
Died: February 2004

United debut: 4 March 1950 v Exeter City Reserves
Final United game: 5 April 1950 v Gillingham
Appearances: 7
Clubs: Cardiff City, Newport County, Headington United, Newport County, Stockport County

Raymond Henry Amphlett signed for Headington from Newport County in March 1950, where he had played in 13 League games. He returned to Newport shortly afterwards. The following season he made four appearances for Stockport County's reserves. He was described as a bit on the small side, but was very good at tracking back.

ANDREWS, Keith

Midfielder
Born: 13 September 1980, Dublin
United debut: 11 November 2000 v Swansea City
Final United game: 16 December 2000 v Northampton Town
Appearances: 5
Goals: 1
Clubs: Wolverhampton Wanderers, Oxford United (loan), Stoke City (loan), Walsall (loan), Hull City, Milton Keynes Dons, Blackburn Rovers

Keith Joseph Andrews joined United from Wolverhampton Wanderers on loan in November 2000. He started his career at Molineux and spent five seasons there, becoming their youngest captain in over 100 years when he led them out against QPR in the final match of the 2000–01 season. He spent most of 2003–04 out on loan, first at Stoke City and later at Walsall before joining Hull City on a free transfer in May 2005. He spent one season at Hull before joining Milton Keynes Dons where he spent two years, mostly as captain. Andrews won the League Two Player of the Year award and was voted into the PFA Team of the Year in 2008. Blackburn Rovers signed him for £1.3 million in August 2008. He has won 16 caps for Ireland so far.

ANGEL, Mark

Left-winger
Born: 23 August 1975, Newcastle-upon-Tyne
United debut: 12 August 1995 v Chesterfield (sub)
Final United game: 11 April 1998 v Swindon Town (sub)
Appearances: 50+41
Goals: 5
Clubs: Walker Central, Sunderland, Oxford United, West Bromwich Albion, Darlington, Queen of the South (loan), Boston United, King's Lynn, Cambridge United (loan), Wisbech Town, Stamford Town, Diss Town, Bourne Town, Newmarket Town, Holbeach United

Mark Angel was a nippy little winger. He was signed from Sunderland on a free transfer by Denis Smith and spent three seasons at the Manor, where he frustrated and thrilled in more-or-less equal measure. He moved to West Brom on a free transfer in July 1998 where he made just five first-team starts in two seasons. He joined Darlington in the summer of 2000, and in January 2001 he had a four-month loan with Queen of the South. Boston United signed him in June 2001 and after three seasons at York Street he joined King's Lynn. He went to Cambridge United on loan for three months in

August 2005. Angel joined Wisbech Town from the Linnets and went on to play for various other East Anglian clubs, before joining Bourne Town in March 2008. His last proper side was Newmarket Town, after which he ran soccer schools in East Anglia for Arsenal. He won three England C caps.

ANSELL, Jack

Goalkeeper
Born: 4 August 1921, Newport Pagnell
Died: 22 April 2008
United debut: 23 August 1952 v Kidderminster Harriers
Final United game: 20 April 1955 v Gloucester City
Appearances: 149
Clean sheets: 51
Clubs: Bletchley Brickworks, Northampton Town, Headington United, Bletchley Town

William John Ansell was a poultry farmer by trade, playing for Bletchley Brickworks when Derby County made an offer for him. Instead, in January 1947, Northampton Town offered him a contract and the chance for him to remain in his home-town, and he soon took over as the club's number one 'keeper. He played 105 consecutive League and Cup games before breaking his leg in February 1951, and when he returned to full fitness he had lost his place to the more experienced Alf Wood. He made 147 first-team appearances for Northampton before joining Headington United after being released in 1952. In three seasons at the Manor, Ansell helped the club win the Southern League Championship in 1952–53 and the Southern League Cup in 1953 and 1954. He starred in Headington's 1953–54 FA Cup run, and almost single-handedly ensured that the team drew 0–0 at Stockport County to earn a third-round replay, which United won 1–0. After leaving Headington, Jack went back to his roots and signed for Bletchley Town. He was also a keen cricketer and played into his sixties.

ANTHROBUS, Steve

Forward
Born: 10 November 1968, Lewisham
United debut: 7 August 1999 v Stoke City
Final United game: 17 April 2001 v Reading (sub)
Appearances: 50+19
Goals: 4
Clubs: Millwall, Wimbledon, Southend United (loan), Peterborough United (loan), Chester City (loan), Shrewsbury Town, Crewe Alexandra, Oxford United, TNS, Hednesford Town

Stephen Anthony Anthrobus joined Oxford from Crewe Alexandra on a free transfer in June 1999. After the striker performed well in pre-season friendlies and scored the winner on his debut at Stoke, he then failed to score in any of his next 22 appearances and his total of four goals in almost 70 games for Oxford makes him statistically one of the club's poorest forwards. Nevertheless, thanks to having a Barbadian father, 'Bus' was called-up for Barbados in July 2000; however, because his registration papers could not be sorted in time, he returned to England without playing for them. He started his career at Millwall's youth team, signing professionally in 1986, and in February 1990 Wimbledon paid £150,000 for him. He failed to hold down a regular place for the Dons, and had unsuccessful loan spells with Peterborough, Chester and Southend, where he stayed for less than a day before being recalled. Shrewsbury paid £25,000 for Anthrobus in August 1995 and he had his most successful spell with the Shrews, scoring 18 goals in 94 appearances, prompting Crewe to pay £75,000 for him in March 1997. However, Anthrobus scored just nine goals in 64 games for the Alex before his move to Oxford. After his release by the U's he moved to Welsh Premier League side Total Network Solutions (called Llansantffraid before their sponsorship deal) where he remained for two seasons before joining Hednesford Town as assistant player-manager, where he won the FA Trophy. Anthrobus became player-manager in December 2005, but was unable to prevent Hednesford's relegation from the Conference North to the Unibond Premier and he was sacked in May 2006. In November 2006 he was fined £500 for outraging public decency after being caught having sex in a public place.

ARENDSE, Andre

Goalkeeper
Born: 27 June 1967, Cape Town (South Africa)
United debut: 7 August 1999 v Stoke City
Final United game: 7 March 2000 v Reading
Appearances: 18+1
Clean sheets: 3
Clubs: Cape Town Spurs (South Africa), Fulham, Oxford United, Santos Cape Town (South Africa), Mamelodi Sundowns (South Africa), SuperSport United (South Africa)

Andre Leander Arendse joined Oxford from Fulham for £30,000 in July 1999. As a youngster he played as a striker, but he turned to goalkeeping and was signed by Cape Town Spurs, winning the National Soccer League in 1995. He won the African Nations Cup with South Africa in 1996, and set an African record for keeping eight successive clean sheets for his country. In 1997 Arendse represented Africa against Europe in an exhibition match, and also played in the FIFA Allstars team against an Asia select team in Hong Kong, joining Fulham immediately afterwards. He played 11 times in two seasons at Craven Cottage before he joined Oxford, where he shared goalkeeping duties with Pål Lundin, but he never appeared entirely confident. At the end of the season he was released and he returned to South Africa, where he played for Santos Cape Town and Mamelodi Sundowns before finishing his career in 2009 with SuperSport United (formerly Pretoria City). Arendse went on to become a pundit with South African sports television station SuperSport and in March 2011 he joined Mpumalanga Black Aces as their goalkeeping coach, linking up with Mark Harrison, who was Malcolm Shotton's assistant manager when Arendse was at Oxford. Arendse was capped 67 times for South Africa, for whom he appeared at the World Cup finals in South Korea in 2002 and was also occasionally captain.

ARIES, Eddie

Centre-forward
Born: 7 November 1941, Oxford
United debut: 5 September 1959 v Kettering Town
Final United game: 3 March 1960 v Kettering Town

Appearances: 2
Clubs: Headington United

Edward Aries played for Oxford and Worcester Boys' Club in the Oxfordshire Youth League, where he was spotted by Bristol Rovers. He played for the Pirates' youth team, but when Arthur Turner offered him the chance to join Headington he opted to forgo the travelling to Bristol and became the skipper of United's youth team. He also played for the Oxfordshire Youth team and the National Association of Boys' Clubs. After failing to make the breakthrough with United he became a professional accountant and still practises in Wheatley. His son Steve was also a professional with Oxford, but never played for the first team.

ASHTON, Jon

Centre-back
Born: 4 October 1992, Nuneaton
United debut: 9 August 2003 v Lincoln City
Final United game: 17 April 2006 v Boston United
Appearances: 98+5
Goals: 1
Clubs: Leicester City, Notts County (loan), Oxford United (loan), Oxford United, Rushden & Diamonds, Grays Athletic, Stevenage Borough

Jonathan James Ashton joined Oxford from Leicester City on loan in August 2003. He was a trainee at Filbert Street, signing professionally in August 2000, but he made just three starts (and seven substitute appearances) for the Foxes. Ashton had a brief loan spell at Notts County in November 2002. After his very successful loan period with Oxford, United signed him permanently in September 2003. He was a regular in the Oxford defence until a calamitous game at Stockport in March 2006. He was released at the end of that relegation season and signed for Rushden. Ashton was at Nene Park for one season before being transfer-listed and moving to Grays Athletic, where he was the Player of the Year at the end of his first season. He joined Stevenage Borough in January 2009 and won the Conference with them in 2010. He won four England C caps, and scored one goal for the non-League international side.

ASHTON, Roger

Goalkeeper
Born: 16 August 1921, Llanidloes
Died: July 1985
United debut: 27 October 1951 v Gloucester City
Final United game: 26 April 1952 v Cheltenham Town
Appearances: 31
Clean sheets: 12
Clubs: Wrexham, Cardiff City, Bath City, Merthyr Tydfil, Newport County, Headington United, Milford United, Barry Town

Roger William Ashton joined Headington from Newport County, where he had played 11 League matches, to replace Burnley's Colin McDonald. He had joined Newport from Cardiff, where he played just one League game. During World War Two, Ashton played four games for Wrexham in the 1943–44 season, three in 1944–45 and 21 the following season. After leaving Headington, Ashton returned to Wales.

ATKINSON, Graham

Forward
Born: 17 May 1943, Birmingham
United debut: 2 September 1959 v Chelmsford City
Final United game: 13 April 1974 v Preston North End
Appearances: 394+4
Goals: 107
Clubs: Aston Villa, Oxford United, Cambridge United (loan), Kettering Town

Graham James Atkinson was signed by Arthur Turner at the same time as his older brother Ron, in the 1959 close season, and signed professionally on his 17th birthday. He holds a number of United records, including the youngest player to play for the club during the professional era, aged just 16 years 108 days when he made his debut, and he became the club's youngest goalscorer in the same period as he scored in his first game. He scored Oxford's first goal in the Football League in the 3–2 defeat at Barrow and his 77 League goals makes him United's top League goalscorer. He was leading scorer in both the 1965–66 season with 19 goals and the following season with 15 goals. The 107 goals he scored in his United career make him the club's top goalscorer in the professional era. He started on the ground staff of Aston Villa, playing at junior level for both Villa and Birmingham City as an amateur, before his move to Oxford. He was selected several times for the Southern League representative side and he represented Oxfordshire in the County Youth Championship. He joined Cambridge United on loan in March 1963, returning to the Manor in December 1964. His achievements include being the first Oxford player to score against Swindon and he was one of the few players who was with the club throughout their climb from the Southern League to the Second Division. He left at the end of the 1973–74 season to join Kettering Town, who were managed by his brother Ron. He played 26 games for the Poppies, scoring four goals.

ATKINSON, Ron

Centre-half/Centre-back
Born: 18 March 1939, Liverpool
United debut: 22 August 1959 v Weymouth
Final United game: 12 October 1971 v Fulham
Appearances: 561+1
Goals: 21
Clubs: Aston Villa, Oxford United, Witney Town, Kettering Town

Ronald Frederick Atkinson is probably Oxford's most famous old boy. In the summer of 1959 Arthur Turner signed Big Ron from Aston Villa, who he joined in 1956 after serving on the ground staff at Wolverhampton Wanderers, where he spent six months. He was a part-time professional with Villa, where he spent three years after serving an apprenticeship with BSA Tools in the Birmingham Works League. He joined United as a full-time professional and the half-back was soon made captain, a position he held throughout the club's rise from the Southern League to the Second Division. During that time he broke the club's appearance record and earned himself the nickname 'The Tank'. In 1971 Atkinson joined the Witney Town coaching staff, his first coaching position, as player-coach. He left Oxford in December 1971 to become player-manager of Kettering Town, leading them to the Southern League Division One North title in his first season. The following season they won the Southern League Premier Division and in December 1974, after 142 appearances and 10 goals, he left to manage Cambridge United, where he won the Fourth Division in 1977. In January 1978 he was appointed manager of West Bromwich Albion, where he stayed until June 1981 when Manchester United made him their manager. In 1983 he led them to an FA Cup Final win over Brighton, and the following season he was Manchester United's manager when Oxford beat them in a League Cup fourth-round second replay. He took them to another FA Cup Final victory in 1985 when they beat Everton, but the lack of a League title led to his dismissal in November 1986. In September 1987 he returned to manage West Brom, saving them from relegation to the Third Division, but in October 1988 he left for a brief three-month spell as manager of Atletico Madrid. Atkinson returned to England to manage Sheffield Wednesday from February 1989 until June 1991, during which time the Owls were relegated to the Second Division and then promoted back to the First. His next post was at Aston Villa, where he won the League Cup in March 1994 before being sacked in November. In February 1995 he took over at Coventry City where he had little success, and in November 1996 he was made director of football, with Gordon Strachan taking over managerial duties. Atkinson returned to Sheffield Wednesday in November 1997, staying until May the following year. In January 1999 he briefly managed Nottingham Forest, in a rather unsuccessful spell, before giving up management to concentrate on his punditry. His enigmatic comments were termed 'Ronglish'. In April 2004 he was sacked by ITV and lost his column in the *Guardian* because of making a racist comment about Marcel Desailly live on air, believing his microphone was switched off. However, he still continued with some media work, notably for Sky, and he featured in *Big Ron Manager* as a troubleshooter at Peterborough United, causing manager Steve Bleasdale to resign, with Atkinson taking over for the final three games of the season. In January 2007 Atkinson was appointed director of football at Kettering, but he stood down in April after a disagreement with owner Imraan Ladak. He was briefly a consultant at Halesowen Town before retiring and becoming an after-dinner speaker.

ATTLEY, Brian

Full-back
Born: 27 August 1955 in Cardiff
United debut: 16 March 1983 v Lincoln City
Final United game: 2 April 1983 v Newport County
Appearances: 5
Clubs: Cardiff City, Swansea City, Derby County, Oxford United (loan), Gresley Rovers, Stapenhill

Brian Robert Attley was a versatile full-back who joined Oxford on loan from Derby County in March 1983. He started his career at his home-town club Cardiff City in 1974, playing 79 League games and scoring once before joining Swansea City for £20,000 in February 1979. He was at the Vetch for three seasons, scoring six goals in his 89 League games, before his £25,000 move to Derby, where he played until the summer of 1984. He made 55 League appearances for the Rams, scoring once. He joined Gresley Rovers in August 1984, playing his final game for them in March 1986, after which he moved to Stapenhill.

AYLOTT, Steve

Centre-back
Born: 3 September 1951, Ilford
United debut: 9 October 1971 v Middlesbrough
Final United game: 19 April 1976 v Southampton
Appearances: 155+12
Goals: 9
Clubs: West Ham United, Oxford United, Brentford, Witney Town

Stephen John Aylott started his career at West Ham, but failed to make a first-team appearance. He was spotted by United when playing for West Ham reserves at the Manor, and the central-defender turned midfielder replaced Ron Atkinson as captain when the Tank left for Kettering in 1974. Aylott stayed with United for five seasons, but after the club was relegated to the Third Division he was forced out by budgetary constraints, and he went on to join Brentford. Two years later, having played just seven League games, he left Griffin Park and went to play for Witney Town. He played for Quarry Nomads in the 1987–88 season.

AYLOTT, Trevor

Forward
Born: 26 November 1957, Bermondsey
United debut: 14 September 1991 v Millwall
Final United game: 2 May 1992 v Tranmere Rovers
Appearances: 38+2
Goals: 6
Clubs: Fisher Athletic, Chelsea, Barnsley, Millwall, Luton Town, Crystal Palace, Barnsley (loan), AFC Bournemouth, Birmingham City, Oxford United (loan), Oxford United, Gillingham, Wycombe Wanderers (loan), Bromley

Trevor Keith Charles Aylott joined United from Birmingham City in September 1991, initially on a one-month loan deal, but then signing until the end of the season. He is remembered more for his white headband and his two-handed 'Aylott wave' than for his striking prowess. He started his career at Fisher Athletic, joining Chelsea in 1975, where he scored in his first start, against Bristol City. He moved to Barnsley four years later where he was leading scorer and consolidated his reputation as a striker. He joined Millwall for £150,000 in June 1982 and in March 1983 Luton paid £55,000 for him. He was at Kenilworth Road for one season before moving to Crystal Palace, succeeding Andy McCulloch, where he remained for the next two seasons, scoring 14 goals in 61 games, returning briefly for a nine-game loan spell at Barnsley in 1986. Aylott moved to Bournemouth in August 1986 for £15,000, earning legend status by scoring twice in the Cherries' 3–1 win over Fulham in May 1987 to win promotion to the Second Division for the first time. Aylott spent four seasons with Bournemouth before joining Birmingham, where he was generally regarded as a flop. After leaving Oxford, Aylott moved to Gillingham, but he played just 10 games for the Gills, plus a further three on loan to Conference side Wycombe Wanderers, before dropping out of the professional game and joining Bromley. He became a London black cab driver in 1995.

B

BAILEY, Stefan

Midfielder
Born: 10 October 1987, Brent
United debut: 11 October 2007 v Torquay United
Final United game: 10 November 2007 v Northwich Victoria
Appearances: 6
Clubs: Queen's Park Rangers, Oxford United (loan), Grays Athletic, Farnborough Town (loan), Ebbsfleet United, AFC Telford United, Kettering Town

Stefan Kyon Lloyd Bailey was a combative midfielder signed on a one-month loan from QPR. He made his Rangers debut in 2005 aged 17 and, although he played well, he failed to hold down a regular first-team place, making 22 appearances in three years. After his loan with Oxford had finished he was released by QPR at the end of that season and in June 2008 he joined Grays Athletic. Financial constraints led to him being transfer-listed in January 2009, and in March he went to Farnborough on loan. Following a trial he joined Ebbsfleet in August, where he spent a season before being released, joining Conference North side Telford, initially for one month but this was extended. In April 2011 Bailey joined Kettering Town on non-contract terms, playing without pay to try and earn a contract. He won a single England C cap, coming on as a substitute in a 6–2 defeat by Bosnia & Herzegovina in September 2008.

BAIN, Jimmy

Left-winger
Born: 14 December 1919, Blairgowrie
United debut: 21 August 1954
Final United game: 28 April 1956
Appearances: 80
Goals: 7
Clubs: Gillingham, Chelsea, Swindon Town, Headington United

James Alistair Bain was signed by Headington from Swindon in July 1954. He had played 255 games for Swindon, scoring 43 goals. He started his career with Gillingham, moving to Chelsea in 1945 (he played for the Blues in their 2–1 defeat by Bolton in June 1945 in the Cup Winners' game and in their friendly 3–3 draw against Dynamo Moscow in November 1945). He spent two seasons at Stamford Bridge, scoring four goals in his 39 appearances, before joining Swindon in May 1947.

BAKER, Richie

Midfielder
Born: 29 December 1987, Burnley
United debut: 7 August 2010 v Burton Albion (sub)
Final United game: 30 October 2010 v Bradford City (sub)
Appearances: 1+7
Clubs: Preston North End, Bury, Oxford United, Barrow

Richard Peter Baker joined Oxford on a six-month contract in July 2010 after being released by Bury. He started at Preston, for whom he signed professionally in July 2005, but moved to Bury in May 2006 without having played a first-team game for North End. He made 129 appearances for the Shakers, scoring eight goals, and was a regular while future Oxford manager Chris Wilder was assistant manager at Gigg Lane in the first half of the 2008–09 season. He left Oxford when his contract expired in January 2011, joining Barrow on non-contract terms the following month and signing a longer-term deal in May 2011.

BANGER, Nicky

Forward
Born: 25 February 1971, Southampton
United debut: 9 August 1997 v Huddersfield Town
Final United game: 24 August 1999 v Oldham Athletic (sub)
Appearances: 50+25
Goals: 9
Clubs: Southampton, Oldham Athletic (loan), Oldham Athletic, Oxford United, Dundee, Scunthorpe United (loan), Plymouth Argyle, Merthyr Tydfil, Torquay United, Andover, Woking, Eastleigh, AFC Newbury, Brockenhurst, Lymington & New Milton

Nicholas Lee Banger joined Oxford on a free transfer from Oldham Athletic in August 1997. He started as a trainee with his home-town club, Southampton, signing as a professional in April 1989. He scored a hat-trick on his debut against Rochdale in the League Cup and went on to make 62 appearances for the Saints, scoring 11 goals. He joined Oldham, initially on loan, in October 1994, the Latics paying Southampton £250,000 for him a month later. He played 70 games for the Boundary Park club, scoring 11 goals, before arriving at the Manor. His time at Oxford was steady if unspectacular, and there was little surprise when he left for Dundee on a free transfer. He played just nine games in almost two years at Dens Park, plus one substitute appearance in a loan spell at Scunthorpe, before moving all the way down south to Plymouth in August 2001. He was at Home Park for just three months, playing 10 games and scoring twice (including against Oxford at the Kassam Stadium) before his short-term contract expired. A back injury caused him to rest for a few months before he joined Merthyr Tydfil in February 2002. Banger was with the Welsh club for just one month before he joined Torquay United, but after only one appearance he requested a release from his contract as he was still struggling for fitness. He joined Andover for the final game of the 2001–02 season, which the Hampshire club drew to win the Wessex League, and by the start of the following season he was a Woking player, before moving to Eastleigh in February 2003. He continued playing for the Spitfires until February 2005, having in the meantime been appointed corporate manager and coach. He played for AFC Newbury while maintaining his corporate post at the Silverlake Stadium, and in November 2005 he became Brockenhurst's player-coach, leaving for a similar post at Lymington a month later. In February 2006 he resigned from Eastleigh and in June he stepped down at Lymington. He became Romsey Town's commercial manager in December 2006, but after 17 days he was dismissed amid rumours, strongly denied by Banger, that he was touting himself as their next manager and tapping up players. In February 2007 he joined Havant & Waterlooville as corporate sales manager, and in June 2008 he moved to take up a similar post at Aldershot.

BANNISTER, Gary

Forward
Born: 22 July 1960, Warrington
United debut: 21 March 1992 v Portsmouth (sub)
Final United game: 2 May 1992 v Tranmere Rovers
Appearances: 7+3
Goals: 2
Clubs: Coventry City, Sheffield Wednesday, Queen's Park Rangers, Coventry City, West Bromwich Albion, Oxford United (loan), Nottingham Forest, Stoke City, Hong Kong Rangers, Lincoln City, Darlington

Gary Bannister joined Oxford on loan from West Brom to help the U's avoid relegation from Division Two. He started as an apprentice at Coventry City, signing as a professional in May 1978, but after failing to get a regular first-team place he moved to Sheffield Wednesday for £100,000 in August 1981. In three years at Hillsborough he played 143 games and scored 59 goals, earning him a £200,000 transfer to QPR. He was at Loftus Road until March 1988, playing against Oxford in the 1986 Milk Cup Final, and he made a total of 172 appearances, notching 72 goals, before Coventry signed him back for £300,000. His second spell with the Sky Blues was not much more successful than his first; in his two years at Highfield Road he played just 48 games, scoring 16 goals. West Brom paid £250,000 for him in March 1990, and in his 81 games for the Baggies he managed 20 goals. His loan to Oxford took him to the end of the 1991–92 season, and he played in the final game of the season at Tranmere, which Oxford won to avoid the drop to Division Three. At the end of the season he moved to Nottingham Forest on a free transfer, remaining at the City Ground for one season, making 37 appearances and scoring 10 goals, before he moved on to Stoke, where he played 18 games and scored twice in his three months with the Potters. He followed this by moving to Hong Kong Rangers for a year, returning in September 1994 to play for Lincoln City. His 34 games for the Imps resulted in eight goals before the final move of his playing career, in August 1995, to Darlington as player-coach. In 51 appearances for Darlo he scored 10 goals before moving with his family to Cornwall, where he coached Porthleven FC while indulging in property development. He moved back to the Midlands after 10 years, working in Birmingham doing hotel maintenance. He won one England Under-21 cap.

BARDSLEY, David

Right-back
Born: 11 September 1964, Manchester
United debut: 19 September 1987 v QPR
Final United game: 2 September 1989 v Blackburn Rovers
Appearances: 94
Goals: 7
Clubs: Blackpool, Watford, Oxford United, Queen's Park Rangers, Blackpool, Northwich Victoria

David John Bardsley was an attacking right-back who joined Oxford from Watford for a club record £265,000. He started his career with Blackpool, where he signed professionally in November 1982. He made 50 appearances for the Tangerines before moving to Watford for £150,000 in November 1983. He played 151 games for the Horns, including the FA Cup Final defeat to Everton in May 1984, scoring nine goals, before his move to Oxford, signing at the same time as his teammate Richard Hill in September 1987. Although he started his career as a full-back, at Watford Graham Taylor put him on the right wing, but Oxford signed him to play in defence. He left United for QPR in a deal valued at £500,000 (of which Mark Stein was valued at £300,000) in September 1989, and he went on to spend almost nine years at Loftus Road. He played 296 games for the Hoops, finding the net six times, despite an Achilles tendon injury keeping him out for almost two years. It was while he was with QPR that he won his two England caps, bestowed by his former Watford manager Taylor. In May 1998 he was released by QPR and returned to Blackpool, where he spent the next two seasons, playing 74 games. Injury kept him out of the game for a while, and he signed for Northwich Victoria in August 2001, playing three games for them. He then ran his own soccer schools for a couple of years before moving to the USA to manage the Ajax America schools in Florida. As well as his two England caps, Bardsley was an England youth international.

BARKER, Bobby

Winger
Born: 1 December 1927, Kinglassie, Fife
United debut: 18 August 1951 v Worcester City
Final United game: 26 December 1951 v Kettering Town
Appearances: 22
Goals: 5
Clubs: Kelty Rangers, West Bromwich Albion, Shrewsbury Town, Headington United, Worcester City

Robert Campbell Barker joined West Brom in 1949 from Kelty Rangers, a small village side just north of Cowdenbeath, about six miles from his birthplace. He made 14 League appearances for the Throstles, scoring twice, before leaving for Shrewsbury in 1950. He played 25 League games for the Shrews, scoring one goal, before joining up with Headington United. Midway through the season he moved on to Worcester City, where he scored 10 goals (including one against Headington in the Southern League Cup, when the U's beat Worcester 5–1 in October 1952).

BARLEY, Jack

Centre-forward
Born: 20 March 1932, Highbury
Died: March 1994
United debut: 5 September 1955 v Worcester City
Final United game: 31 March 1956 v Tonbridge
Appearances: 13
Goals: 1
Clubs: Maidenhead United, Arsenal, Queen's Park Rangers, Aldershot, Headington United

Charles Derek Barley was an England youth international. The son of Arsenal player Charles Barley, he left Maidenhead in 1951 for the Gunners to turn professional, playing for the reserve and youth sides, before joining QPR in May 1953. He played four games for Rangers before joining Aldershot in July 1954. He played just two League matches for the Shots before signing for Headington.

BARNES, Ashley

Forward
Born: 31 October 1989, Bath
United debut: 24 November 2007 v Kidderminster Harriers (sub)
Final United game: 29 December 2007 v Kidderminster Harriers (sub)
Appearances: 4+4
Goals: 1
Clubs: Paulton Rovers, Plymouth Argyle, Grays Athletic (loan), Oxford United (loan), Salisbury City (loan), Eastbourne Borough (loan), Torquay United (loan), Brighton & Hove Albion (loan), Brighton & Hove Albion

Ashley Luke Barnes was a striker who came to Oxford on a one-month loan from Plymouth Argyle. He scored on his debut when he came off the bench at Kidderminster. However, it was downhill thereafter, and Barnes failed to score in any of his other appearances. He started his career with Somerset side Paulton Rovers, making his debut in September 2005 aged 16, and joined Plymouth for an extended trial in March 2007. Barnes went on loan to Grays, making one substitute appearance, before his loan to Oxford. After returning to Home Park he went out on loan again to Salisbury, where he played five games; this was followed by further loans to Eastbourne Borough (eight games, five goals), Torquay (six games), and Brighton (eight games, four goals). At the end of the 2009–10 season Barnes joined Brighton, having played 25 times for Argyle, scoring twice. In 2011 he won the League One title with Brighton. Barnes has been capped once by Austria Under-20s, qualifying for Austria by virtue of his father's mother.

BARNETT, Gary

Winger
Born: 11 March 1963, Stratford-upon-Avon
United debut: 14 August 1982 v Reading
Final United game: 7 September 1985 v Manchester United (sub)
Appearances: 51+10
Goals: 10
Clubs: Coventry City, Oxford United, Wimbledon (loan), Fulham (loan), Fulham, Huddersfield Town, Leyton Orient, Evesham United, Barry Town, Kidderminster Harriers

Gary Lloyd Barnett was signed from Coventry City by Jim Smith in August 1982. He was with United throughout their rise from the Third to the First Divisions, although his participation was interrupted by loan spells to Wimbledon for a month in February 1983 (where he scored once in five games) and Fulham in December 1984 (one goal in two games). In December 1985 he moved to Craven Cottage permanently as a makeweight in the deal that brought Ray Houghton to the Manor. He remained with the Cottagers until May 1990, scoring 30 goals in 180 League appearances. From there Barnett moved to Huddersfield where he played 100 League games in three years, scoring 11 goals, followed by a couple of seasons at Orient (seven goals in 63 League games). From East London, Barnett moved to the Welsh seaside, joining Barry Town in August 1995, and being appointed player-manager in July the following year. He played 132 games and scored 13 goals for Barry, and made history by leading them to become the first League of Wales club to progress in Europe, as they reached the first round proper of the UEFA Cup. He also led them to three consecutive League of Wales titles, earning three successive Welsh Premier League Manager of the Year honours, before stepping down in July 1999 and joining Kidderminster as Jan Molby's player-assistant manager. He helped lead the Harriers into the Football League, playing 10 games and scoring twice, before moving with Molby to Hull after three years at Aggborough. After four months they were sacked by the Tigers and returned to Kidderminster in 2004, having coached and played for Evesham United in the interim, but failure to gain success resulted in a termination of his contract in February 2006. Barnett then became a personal trainer.

BARNEY, Vic

Inside- forward
Born: 3 April 1922 in Stepney
Died: 26 May 2006
United debut: 19 August 1950 v Bedford Town
Final United game: 26 April 1952 v Cheltenham Town
Appearances: 93
Goals: 26
Clubs: Fanshawe Old Boys, Napoli (Italy), Morris Motors, Reading, Bristol City, Grimsby Town, Headington United, Guildford City, Pressed Steel

Victor Charles Barney played youth football for Fanshawe Old Boys, in the same team as Alf Ramsey. During World War Two he served in Italy as an infantryman, and in 1945 he was sent to Naples to recover from a battlefield injury. Immediately after the war he played one season for Napoli, who spotted him playing in their stadium for an Army team. He was Napoli's first English player, and possibly the first Englishman to play in Serie A. On his return to England he asked Reading for a trial and went on to score 16 goals in 80 games for the Biscuitmen, including on his debut in Reading's record victory, 10–2 versus Crystal Palace. Barney moved to Bristol City at the start of the 1948 season, scoring four goals in 28 League matches, and thence to Grimsby in 1949. He played seven League games without scoring before joining Headington in 1950, becoming captain the following year. He was the club's leading scorer with 14 goals in the 1951–52 season. Following a disagreement over the terms offered to him for the 1952–53 season he was given a free transfer and signed for Guildford. He returned to Oxford to work for Pressed Steel, where he played for and coached the works' football team. At 5ft 5in he was one of the shortest players to have played for the club.

BARRON, Jim

Goalkeeper
Born: 19 October 1943, Tantobie, County Durham
United debut: 8 April 1966 v Hull City
Final United game: 18 April 1970 v Blackpool
Appearances: 165
Clean sheets: 51
Clubs: Newcastle West End, Wolverhampton Wanderers, Chelsea, Oxford United, Nottingham Forest, Swindon Town, Connecticut Bicentennials, Peterborough United

James Barron joined Oxford from Chelsea at the start of March 1966 to replace Harry Fearnley. He made seven appearances for the reserves before making his first-team debut, immediately ousting Brian Sherratt as first-choice 'keeper. He was United's regular goalkeeper for four years, but an impressive display against Nottingham Forest in the League Cup fourth round in October 1969 led to Forest paying Oxford £30,000 for his services. Barron's father, also called Jim, had been a professional goalkeeper with Blackburn Rovers. Young Jim started his career as a youth with Newcastle West End, and he played for England Boys' Clubs against Ireland. He had the chance to sign for Newcastle United, but instead joined Wolves in 1961. He played eight League games for Wanderers, and also played 20 minutes for Chelsea against Wolves during a tour of the West Indies in 1964 after Chelsea's regular 'keeper John Dunn was injured and their second choice, Peter Bonetti, was ill. Barron joined Chelsea in May 1965, before the Blues' tour to Australia, but he made just one appearance for them, a 2–1 home defeat by Stoke, before his move to Oxford. Barron went on to make 180 appearances for Forest before his career nosedived with a move to Swindon in August 1974. He played 93 games for the Robins, then fled to the USA in March 1977 to join the Connecticut Bicentennials, Swindon agreeing to cancel his contract. Connecticut was formed in 1975 as the Hartford Bicentennials before their move to New Haven in 1977; they became the Oakland Stompers when relocating to California in 1978, thence to Canada to become the Edmonton Drillers one season later, folding in 1982. Barron played 10 games for them before returning to Blighty to play for Peterborough, helping Posh to a club record of just 33 goals conceded in 1977–78. Twenty-one games later Barron retired from playing. He became assistant manager at Wolves, and he was caretaker manager for three games in May 1984 following Graham Hawkins' dismissal. In 1986 Barron was coach with Íþróttabandalag Akraness, winning the Icelandic Cup, and two years later he took charge of Cheltenham Town for one season, while at the same time acting as personal goalkeeping coach to Wales 'keeper Neville Southall. He went to Birmingham City as reserve team coach, and in October 2001 Barron, along with Mick Mills, was appointed caretaker manager following the sacking of Trevor Francis. The pair were in charge for 12 games until Steve Bruce was appointed manager in December. Francis took Barron to Crystal Palace where he was reserve team and goalkeeping coach until September 2003. In 2005 he became goalkeeping coach at Wycombe Wanderers, and was also part of a temporary managerial team when John Gorman was placed on compassionate leave for the last five fixtures of the season. He left to become goalkeeping coach at Northampton Town in June 2006, almost simultaneously with Gorman. In December Gorman resigned and Barron and Ian Sampson were appointed joint caretaker managers. They were in charge for four games before Stuart Gray was appointed permanently and Barron became first-team coach. In October 2009 Sampson, now the Cobblers' manager, appointed Malcolm Crosby as his assistant and Barron left to become goalkeeping coach at Cheltenham, returning to Northampton as first-team coach in the summer of 2010. Barron was part of the FA squad that toured Ireland and Australia in May and June 1971.

BASHAM, Steve

Forward
Born: 1 December 1977, Southampton
United debut: 10 August 2002 v Bury (sub)
Final United game: 1 January 2007 v Exeter City

Appearances: 157+32
Goals: 49
Clubs: Southampton, Wrexham (loan), Preston North End (loan), Preston North End (loan), Preston North End, Oxford United, Exeter City, Luton Town, Hayes & Yeading United (loan), Brackley Town, Oxford City

Steven Brian Basham joined Oxford on a free transfer from Preston North End in August 2002. He was leading scorer for United in both the 2003–04 and 2005–06 seasons, but suffered from injuries which meant he missed the second half of Oxford's first season in the Conference, at the end of which he was released. He started as a trainee with Southampton, his home-town club, signing professionally in May 1996. He made 20 appearances for the Saints, but just one start, and scored once. He had a five-game loan spell with Wrexham in February 1998 and another loan at Preston in December, during which he did not play. In February 1999 he returned to Deepdale on loan and had a far more productive time, scoring 10 goals in 17 appearances. This led Preston to pay Southampton a tribunal-determined £200,000 for him in June 1999. However, a serious leg break meant that he played only 62 games, mostly as substitute, for North End in three seasons, scoring just five goals. After his release from Oxford he joined Exeter, where he spent two seasons and made 58 appearances, scoring nine goals. While with the Grecians, Basham won promotion from the Conference via the Play-offs and immediately won promotion to League One, preceding his release in August 2009. He immediately signed for Luton Town, also in the Conference, but played just six games for the Hatters, scoring twice. In November he was loaned to Hayes & Yeading where he scored twice in a 2–1 win over Oxford at the Kassam Stadium. In May 2010 Basham refused a longer-term contract with Hayes and was almost immediately released by Luton. Later that summer he signed for Brackley Town, but after suffering a serious leg injury, he left at the end of the season and joined Oxford City in June 2011.

*BATT, Damian

Right-back
Born: 16 September 1984, Hoddesdon
United debut: 24 January 2009 v Crawley Town
Final United game: 7 May 2011 v Shrewsbury Town
Appearances: 84+8
Goals: 1
Clubs: Norwich City, Redbridge, Barnet, St Albans City, Stevenage Borough, St Albans City (loan), Woking, Fisher Athletic, Grays Athletic, Oxford United

Damian Alexander Nathaniel Batt joined Oxford from Grays Athletic in January 2009. In 2001 he joined the Norwich City academy despite interest from a number of London clubs, and in 2003 he was the club's second-choice right-back, although he never made a first-team appearance. In February 2004 Batt had trials with Wycombe (playing for their reserves against Oxford), Cheltenham (also playing against Oxford's reserves), and Bournemouth. In the summer of 2004 he joined Conference South side Redbridge but played just one game before being released after two weeks. In September 2004 he joined Barnet, who won the Conference title that season, and by the time he moved to St Albans in August 2006 he had made 44 appearances for the Bees, three in the Football League, scoring once. He made his St Albans debut in a 2–1 defeat at Oxford in September and played

23 games, scoring twice, before leaving for Stevenage Borough in January 2007. He played nine games for Stevenage before being loaned back to St Albans for three months in September, when he played eight games and scored once. In February 2008 Batt joined Woking, playing 13 games and scoring once before moving to Fisher Athletic in August 2008. Fisher had just sold Damian's brother Shaun to Peterborough. He joined Grays on non-contract terms in October 2008, but was at the Recreation Ground for fewer than three months, playing 10 games, before Chris Wilder stepped in to sign him for Oxford. Batt was selected for the 2010–11 PFA League Two Team of the Year at right-back.

BEAUCHAMP, Joey

Left-winger
Born: 13 March 1971, Oxford
United debut: 13 May 1989 v Watford (sub)
Final United game: 23 February 2002 v Exeter City
Appearances: 375+53
Goals: 77
Clubs: Oxford United, Swansea City (loan), West Ham United, Swindon Town, Oxford United (loan), Oxford United, Abingdon Town, Didcot Town, Abingdon Town

Joseph Daniel Beauchamp is possibly Oxford's favourite son. The winger played for Summertown Stars as a youth, and was a part of the Oxford youth set-up before he signed as a YTS trainee in September 1987. He was chosen to act as a ball-boy for the 1986 Milk Cup Final. Beauchamp started in the reserves, but still attracted enough attention to be selected to play for the Football League Under-18s against the USSR in Moscow on 22 April 1989 in a match organised to link with the British-Soviet Trade Fair, which the League won 2–1. Beauchamp signed professional terms later that week. Joey, who was voted United's Player of the 1990s, had two spells with the club, his first coming to an end on the final day of the 1993–94 season when he scored in a 2–1 win against Notts County, but could not prevent the club's relegation from Division Two. By the time that West Ham paid £1 million for him on 22 June 1994 he had played 145 games for the club, scoring 25 goals. He had also had a loan spell at Swansea in November 1991 in which he played six games, scoring twice, and Oxford rejected a bid from the Swans to take him permanently. Beauchamp had already turned down a million-pound bid from West Ham in March, but managing director Keith Cox told him that if he turned down this second bid then United might have to fold. His time at the Hammers was an unhappy one, with Beauchamp playing just one game, a friendly at Oxford City, before he was moved on to Swindon Town in a deal worth £800,000 (a Swindon record, which included Adrian Whitbread moving to Upton Park). Beauchamp had just bought a house in Oxford and did not want to move, despite West Ham manager Harry Redknapp insisting upon it. His time at the County Ground was not much happier, despite playing 56 games and scoring three goals for the Robins in his first season under John Gorman. But when Steve McMahon took over in the summer of 1995 after Swindon's relegation, Beauchamp played just four more games, scoring once, before Denis Smith brought him back to the Manor, initially on loan for a week before paying Town just £75,000 for his signature. Despite his time in Swindon, Beauchamp soon endeared himself to most Oxford fans by scoring the third goal in a 3–0 win over their fiercest rivals, as Oxford went on to finish runners-up to the Robins as both sides were promoted to Division One. Beauchamp's 35-yard volley against Blackpool in the promotion run-in was later voted the 'Best Goal at the Manor'. With Oxford still in financial turmoil in 1998, Beauchamp turned down £800,000 offers from both Nottingham Forest and Southampton, meaning Swindon missed out on their 20 per cent sell-on clause. He was the leading goalscorer in the 1997–98 season with 19 goals, despite playing as a winger. He later turned down another big-money offer from Reading. Beauchamp scored a spectacular volley against Exeter in his last game for United before his career was cut short by an injury to his big toe that failed to heal properly, and in July 2002 the club chairman Firoz Kassam invoked a clause in Beauchamp's contract that enabled them to cut it short by one season. He played a few games for Abingdon Town in a bid to keep fit prior to an operation on his toe, and in March 2003 he joined Abingdon Town properly, moving to Didcot Town in December 2004. He rejoined Abingdon in July 2005 for one season, and rejoined them again for a couple of games in March 2007, while playing regularly for Sunday League side Oxford Yellows. He later appeared in the Oxfordshire Senior League with Bletchingdon and also turned out for Kidlington Old Boys Reserves.

BEAVON, Cyril

Full-back
Born: 27 September 1937 in Barnsley
United debut: 21 September 1959 v Gravesend & Northfleet
Final United game: 20 April 1969 v Sheffield United
Appearances: 461+3
Goals: 11
Clubs: Wolverhampton Wanderers, Headington United, Banbury United

Cyril Beavon joined Headington United from Wolves in January 1959, becoming Arthur Turner's first signing for the club. While with Wanderers he played for the England youth team against Hungary at White Hart Lane in 1956. He signed for Wolves from their nursery side, Wath Wanderers, in November 1954, and during his National Service he represented the RAF. Beavon was with United through two Southern League titles and the club's rise to the Second Division. Turner claimed that Beavon could have played at a much higher level and would have taken him with him to First Division Leeds had he accepted their job offer in April 1959. After leaving Oxford, Beavon joined Banbury United for one season, and from there went on to manage Bicester Town. Cyril's son Michael Stuart Beavon was an Oxford youth team player and a professional player with Northampton, Reading, and Spurs, and his grandson Stuart Beavon had a trial with Oxford before joining Weymouth and then Wycombe Wanderers.

BEEBY, Olly

Full-back
Born: 2 October 1934, Whetstone, Leicestershire
United debut: 3 October 1961 v Cambridge City
Final United game: 18 November 1961 v Romford
Appearances: 7
Clubs: Cosby United, Enderby Town, Whitwick Colliery, Leicester City, Notts County, Oxford United, Burton Albion

Oliver Beeby joined Oxford from Notts County. He started his career playing for local sides in Leicestershire before joining Leicester City in 1955. He played just one game for the Foxes, a 6–2 defeat against Doncaster Rovers in his first season with the club, and in 1959 he moved to Notts County. Beeby made his debut in October in a 4–0 win over Hartlepool and made 13 starts for County in their promotion season before his move to the Manor. After leaving Oxford, Beeby joined Burton Albion where he made three appearances in the 1962–63 season.

BEECHERS, Billy

Forward
Born: 1 June 1987, Oxford
United debut: 5 February 2005 v Lincoln City (sub)
Final United game: 16 January 2007 v Halifax Town (sub)
Appearances: 0+7
Clubs: Oxford United, Oxford City (loan), Abingdon United, Oxford City, Abingdon United

Billy Junior Beechers came up through the ranks at Oxford, making his first-team debut before he signed as a professional in June 2006. He joined Oxford City on a one-month loan, extended for a further month, in November 2006, but was released by United at the end of that season, having failed to start a first-team game. In July 2007 Beechers signed for Abingdon United, rejoining City in June 2010. However, he rejoined Abingdon in October 2010.

BENJAMIN, Declan

Midfielder
Born: 4 February 1991, Oxford
United debut: 17 November 2007 v Ebbsfleet United (sub)
Final United game: 20 January 2008 v Exeter City (sub)
Appearances: 0+2
Clubs: Oxford United, Abingdon United (loan), Banbury United (loan), Banbury United, Oxford City

Declan Rousseau Benjamin signed as a scholar in May 2007, having previously played for Garsington Youth. When he made his Oxford first-team debut he became the third-youngest professional player to do so, aged 16 years 286 days. In December 2008 he joined Abingdon United on work experience, followed by a similar deal at Banbury United. In April 2009 Benjamin scored the winning goal for Oxford against Banbury in the Oxfordshire Senior Cup Final. After his scholarship ended the midfielder was offered an extended deal until Christmas 2009, having broken his leg with six months of his original scholarship remaining. However, in January 2010 he was released by United and he returned to Banbury. As well as being a solid midfielder, at Banbury Benjamin also earned a reputation as a stand-in goalkeeper; following sendings-off of the usual incumbents, Benjamin twice saved penalties. He joined Oxford City in June 2011.

BENNETT, Ken

Inside-left
Born: 2 October 1921, Wood Green
Died: February 1994

United debut: 6 December 1954 v Gloucester City
Final United game: 28 December 1954 v Tonbridge
Appearances: 5
Clubs: Wood Green Town, Tottenham Hotspur, Southend United (guest), Southend United, Bournemouth & Boscombe Athletic, Guildford City, Brighton & Hove Albion, Crystal Palace, Tonbridge, Headington United

Kenneth Edgar Bennett joined Headington from Tonbridge. He started with his local club, Wood Green Town (which became Haringey Borough in 1976) before World War Two, during which he played four games for Spurs in 1941–42. In June 1946 he joined Southend United, having guested for them for 11 games the previous season. He played 54 games and scored 16 goals in the next two years before moving to Bournemouth. He spent one season at Dean Court, scoring once in 19 League games, before dropping out of the League to join Guildford. In 1950 he returned to League action with Brighton, where he spent three years and played 101 League games, scoring 37 goals. He left the Goldstone in May 1953 and joined Crystal Palace, where he scored twice in 17 appearances. His next stop was Tonbridge in June 1954, but he was there for just five months before he moved to the Manor.

BERRY, Paul

Forward
Born: 8 April 1958, Oxford
United debut: 26 March 1977 v Bury (sub)
Final United game: 23 March 1982 v Doncaster Rovers
Appearances: 108+13
Goals: 20
Clubs: Norwich City, Oxford United, Banbury United, Witney Town

Paul Alan Berry was a local player who signed non-contract forms with Oxford after a two-month trial at Norwich City (although he did not play a game for the Canaries). On his return to the Manor in 1974 he was given a job in the Pools Promotions Department while he completed his apprenticeship, and was a member of the side that won the Midlands Youth League. In April 1976 he signed on professionally. He was United's leading scorer in the 1979–80 season with 14 goals. Berry was released at the end of the 1981–82 season, rejoining the club on non-contract terms in October 1982. After leaving Oxford he spent seven years with Witney Town, becoming assistant manager of the Blanketmen in 1989. He moved on to become Bicester Town's manager in 1991 for a season. Berry joined United's Centre of Excellence coaching staff in 1998, and in May 2002 he was appointed as Carterton Town's manager. In December 2003 he moved on to manage Abingdon Town and in October 2004 he became joint manager at Ardley United with Ian Feaver, but they resigned a year later. In June 2008 Feaver brought in Berry as a coach at Easington Sports. In June 2009 Berry was reappointed as Bicester manager but he resigned in September after a perceived lack of commitment by certain players, going on to manage Abingdon Town.

BIDOIS, David

Right-half
Born: 4 December 1932, Oxford
Died: November 2005

United debut: 5 April 1950 v Gillingham
Final United game: 26 March 1958 v Dartford
Appearances: 29
Goals: 1
Clubs: Headington United

David Frederick Bidois joined Headington as an amateur. He was an England youth international and took part in the International Youth Tournament in Cannes in March 1951, in which England finished fifth after beating the Netherlands 2–1 and Switzerland 3–1, and drawing 1–1 with Belgium, who were awarded the match on the toss of a coin. Despite being at the Manor for eight years (two of which consisted of his National Service until January 1956), Bidois failed to hold down a regular first-team place.

BIGGINS, Steve

Forward
Born: 20 June 1954, Lichfield
United debut: 14 August 1982 v Reading
Final United game: 13 October 1984 v Brighton & Hove Albion (sub)
Appearances: 62+19
Goals: 28
Clubs: Hednesford Town, Shrewsbury Town, Oxford United, Derby County, Wolverhampton Wanderers (loan), Port Vale (loan), Trelleborgs FF, Exeter City, Telford United, Worcester City, Ludlow Town

Steven James Biggins joined Oxford from Shrewsbury Town. He scored 24 goals in the 1983–84 season, including the extra-time winner against Manchester United in the League Cup fourth-round second replay. Biggins was a maths teacher at Shire Oak Grammar School and joined Hednesford Town in 1976 before moving to Shrewsbury for £6,000 in December 1977. He scored on his debut against Hereford and went on to make 146 League appearances for the Shrews, scoring 41 goals, being their leading scorer in both 1979–80 with 13 goals and the following season with 10, before Jim Smith brought him to Oxford on a free transfer. After losing his place to John Aldridge, Biggins moved to Derby in October 1984, having scored the winning goal in his final appearance for the U's against Brighton. However, he failed to make an impression at the Baseball Ground and spent time on loan with Wolves in March 1985 and Port Vale in March the following year, playing four games at each without scoring. After netting just one goal in 10 appearances for the Rams, Biggins moved to Swedish side Trelleborgs FF in the summer of 1986 for the second half of the season; he was signed to keep them out of the relegation places and his five goals in 12 games helped Trelleborgs to a mid-table finish. He joined Exeter City on a semi-pro basis in October 1986, where he played 14 League games, scoring twice. In March 1987 he moved to Telford United, scoring 20 goals the following season while teaching at the Old Hall Preparatory School in Wellington. In 1988-89 he played for Telford in the FA Trophy Final at Wembley against Macclesfield, which they won 1–0 after extra-time. His next stop was Worcester City, where he scored once, in 1989. In 1990–91 he featured for Ludlow Town, where he was voted the Midland League Player of the Year. Biggins returned to Shrewsbury as a part-time youth team coach, later taking control of the Under-17s, leaving the Centre of Excellence in February 2007, and in December that year he started to train with Ellesmere Rangers to keep fit, occasionally coaching and advising them. In 2009 he left the Old Hall School to become the master in charge of football at Shrewsbury School.

BIGGINS, Wayne

Forward
Born: 20 November 1961, Sheffield
United debut: 12 August 1995 v Chesterfield
Final United game: 7 November 1995 v Barnet (sub)
Appearances: 11+4
Goals: 2
Clubs: Lincoln City, King's Lynn, Matlock Town, Burnley, Norwich City, Manchester City, Stoke City, Barnsley, Celtic, Stoke City, Luton Town (loan), Oxford United, Wigan Athletic, Leek Town, Stocksbridge Park Steels, Buxton Town

Wayne Biggins was signed by Denis Smith from Stoke City. Biggins' time at Oxford was fairly unsuccessful and Smith later admitted that signing him had been a mistake and in November 1995 he moved to Wigan on a free transfer. Biggins, nicknamed 'Bertie', started as an apprentice at Lincoln City in 1979 for whom he made eight League appearances, scoring once, before being released in 1981. He worked as a hod carrier while playing for King's Lynn for six months and then Matlock Town for a couple of years. He was signed by Burnley for £7,500 in February 1984, where he scored 37 goals in 94 appearances, many alongside Billy Hamilton, leading to Norwich paying £40,000 for him in October 1985. After 97 appearances and 21 goals, Manchester City bought him for £150,000 in July 1988 where he played just 39 games, scoring nine goals, before Lou Macari's Stoke paid £250,000 for him. He became a crowd favourite at the Potters, partnering Mark Stein in attack, where he played 148 games and scored 53 goals, but in October 1992 he joined Barnsley for £200,000. He was with the Tykes for just over a year, playing 51 games and scoring 16 goals, before Macari came in for him again to take him to Celtic in November 1993. His four months north of the border yielded just 10 games without scoring and Stoke were quick to take him back to Staffordshire for a fee of £125,000. His 13 months back in the Potteries were far less prolific than his first spell, and he made just 33 appearances, scoring eight goals. Before his move to Oxford, Bertie had a loan spell at Luton in January 1995, where he scored twice in nine games. Biggins contributed five goals in his 50 games at Wigan, during which time the Latics won the Division Three title in 1997. He was released in the summer of that year and joined Leek Town. One year later he moved to Stocksbridge Park Steels, where in 2001 he became player-assistant manager, stepping up to manager in April 2002. In November 2003 poor results led to him vacating that position, and in March 2004 he became player-coach at Buxton Town, where he remained until January 2005. While in non-League football Biggins also set up a pallet business.

BILLINGTON, Wilf

Goalkeeper
Born: 28 January 1930, Blackburn
United debut: 23 August 1958 v Hereford United
Final United game: 14 February 1959 v Barry Town
Appearances: 32

Clean sheets: 4
Clubs: Blackburn Rovers, Workington, Headington United

Wilfred Francis Billington was on Blackburn Rovers' books from 1947 until 1954 without featuring in the first team. He then moved to Workington, managed at that time by Bill Shankly, where he played 55 games prior to his move to Headington. He later emigrated to Australia.

BLACKWOOD, Michael

Left-winger
Born: 30 September 1979, Birmingham
United debut: 9 February 2008 v Histon
Final United game: 29 March 2008 v Northwich Victoria (sub)
Appearances: 5+2
Clubs: Aston Villa, Chester City (loan), Wrexham, Worcester City, Stevenage Borough, Halesowen Town, Telford United, Lincoln City, Kidderminster Harriers, Oxford United (loan), Mansfield Town, Tamworth (loan), Tamworth, Brackley Town, Solihull Moors (loan)

Michael Andrew Blackwood joined Oxford on loan from Kidderminster in January 2008. However, his loan was cut short by an injury just before the end of the season. His career began at Aston Villa, where he was a trainee, but he failed to appear for the Villains and was loaned to Chester for two months in September 1999. He scored two goals in nine games before returning to Villa Park. He joined Wrexham in June 2000, playing 50 games in just over two years, scoring twice. He had a brief seven-game spell with Worcester before, in September 2002, he moved to Stevenage. He scored two goals in 21 games for Boro before he joined Halesowen in March 2003. After seven games and two goals he moved to Telford in August, making 42 appearances and scoring five goals in the 2003–04 season, at the end of which he signed for Lincoln City. Blackwood was with the Imps for one season and played just 10 games before moving to Kidderminster in July 2005. He played 112 games for the Harriers, scoring six goals, before his move to the Kassam. He returned to Aggborough, but was released at the end of the season and signed for Mansfield in July 2008. Blackwood scored three goals in 25 games, before moving to Tamworth on loan in March 2009, making the move permanent in the summer. He scored twice in 31 matches for the Lambs. In June 2010 Blackwood joined Brackley Town and in October he was loaned to Solihull Moors.

BLAKE, Henry

Outside-right
Born: 1924, Oxford
United debut: 20 August 1949 v Hastings United
Final United game: 27 December 1949 v Chelmsford City
Appearances: 9
Goals: 1
Clubs: Headington United

Henry Percy Blake was born in Headington. He played for United in the Oxfordshire Senior League during 1942 and again in the Spartan League after the war. Blake turned professional with the club in 1949, just after the club's first game in the Southern League. He showed exceptional promise, but injury and ill health prevented him from progressing.

BLIZZARD, Les

Left-half
Born: 13 March 1923, Acton
Died: December 1996
United debut: 8 December 1956 v Guildford City
Final United game: 1 May 1957 v Tonbridge
Appearances: 12
Clubs: Queen's Park Rangers, Bournemouth & Boscombe Athletic, Yeovil Town, Leyton Orient, Headington United

Leslie William Benjamin Blizzard joined QPR in 1944, playing five games during the war and then normal League football, making his proper debut in March 1947. He played five League games for Rangers before moving to Bournemouth. He made just one League appearance for the Cherries and then joined Yeovil in the summer of 1948. He scored four goals in two years at the Huish and then signed for Orient. He made 212 League appearances for the O's, scoring 12 goals, before moving to Headington United in December 1956.

BODEL, Andy

Centre-half
Born: 12 February 1957, Clydebank
United debut: 9 September 1975 v Charlton Athletic
Final United game: 1 May 1980 v Colchester United
Appearances: 141
Goals: 11
Clubs: Oxford United, Oxford City

Andrew Cunningham Bodel was a central defender who became an apprentice at Oxford in 1972. In February 1975 he was promoted to the seniors and was one of the members of the squad that won the Midlands Youth League in 1975. He became a first choice after Dave Roberts was sold to Hull, but his contract was cancelled in August 1980 and he moved to Oxford City.

BOLLAND, Phil

Centre-back
Born: 26 August 1976, Liverpool
United debut: 11 August 2001 v Rochdale
Final United game: 1 December 2001 v Hull City
Appearances: 23
Goals: 1
Clubs: Altrincham, Salford City, Trafford, Knowsley United, Southport, Oxford United, Chester City (loan), Chester City, Peterborough United, Chester City, Wrexham, Cambridge United, Barrow

Philip Christopher Bolland was signed by Mark Wright in June 2001 from Wright's former club, Southport, where he had been the most booked player in the Conference in 2000–01. He made his Oxford debut in the first game to be played at the Kassam Stadium, but when Ian Atkins replaced Wright and brought in Andy Crosby, Bolland followed Wright to Chester, initially on loan for six games in January 2002 before the move was made permanent for a fee of £15,000 in March. Bolland started at Altrincham in 1995 and during the following two years he played for Salford, Trafford, and the now defunct Knowsley United. He joined Southport in July 1997 and went on to make 75 appearances for the Sandgrounders, scoring 10 goals, before his move to Oxford. After joining Chester permanently, he was at the Deva Stadium for almost four years, playing 145 games and scoring eight goals. In January 2006 Bolland again linked up with Wright when he moved to Peterborough. He made just 17 appearances in his five months at London Road before returning to Chester where he made a further 35 appearances, scoring twice, before moving on to Wrexham in January 2008 after a brief trial. He was at the Racecourse for just six months, playing 18 games, before he joined Cambridge United following Wrexham's relegation to the Conference. He spent one season at the Abbey, playing 44 games and scoring once, before moving to Barrow in July 2009, where he was installed as captain. He signed a new contract with the Barrovians in May 2011.

BOOTH, Colin

Inside-forward
Born: 30 December 1934, Manchester
United debut: 22 August 1964 v Crewe Alexandra
Final United game: 20 November 1965 v Gillingham
Appearances: 52
Goals: 23
Clubs: Wolverhampton Wanderers, Nottingham Forest, Doncaster Rovers, Oxford United, Cambridge United

Colin Booth joined Oxford from Doncaster Rovers for £7,500. In his first season at the Manor, Booth set the club's League goalscoring record with 23 goals, including a hat-trick in United's record League win, 7–0 v Barrow. Booth's record would stand for 19 seasons until Steve Biggins went one better. In his second season with the club Booth suffered badly with injuries and had to undergo an operation. He was advised to stop playing and at the end of the season he was released, going on to make a couple of appearances for Cambridge United. Booth started as an apprentice in 1950 with Wolves, where he won two Football League winners' medals. His debut came in April 1955. He scored 28 goals in 76 League appearances for Wolves before joining Nottingham Forest in October 1959. He scored 41 goals in 98 games for Forest before moving to Doncaster at the end of the 1960–61 season. He was leading scorer in both his seasons at Belle Vue, grabbing a total of 57 goals in his 88 League games. On his retirement from the game he became a healthcare professional. He won one England Under-23 cap.

BOTTOMS, Mickey

Inside-left
Born: 11 January 1939, Fulham
United debut: 17 February 1962 v Gravesend & Northfleet
Final United game: 28 April 1962 v Yeovil Town
Appearances: 4
Clubs: Harrow Town, Queen's Park Rangers, Oxford United

Michael Charles Bottoms joined QPR from Harrow Town (who changed their name to Harrow Borough in 1967) in July 1960, making his debut in October. He played mostly in QPR's London Combination League team, plus twice for Rangers' first team during 1960–61 before leaving for Oxford on a free transfer in January 1962.

BOULTON, John

Outside-left
Born: 18 May 1935, Church Gresley, Derbyshire
Died: 6 December 2006
United debut: 28 February 1959 v Gloucester City
Final United game: 30 March 1959 v Kidderminster Harriers
Appearances: 6
Goals: 1
Clubs: Gresley Rovers, Burton Albion, Gresley Rovers, Chesterfield, Burton Albion, Matlock Town, Headington United, Gresley Rovers

John Boulton joined Headington from Matlock Town. He was the youngest ever player for South Derbyshire Schoolboys, aged 11, and he made his Gresley Rovers debut aged 15 in September 1952. A year later he signed professionally for Burton Albion before his two years' National Service. He returned to Gresley in 1956 before being called-up as a result of the Suez crisis. After his return he joined Chesterfield, but in his one season there he failed to play for the first team and he returned to Burton. In 1959 he joined Matlock Town before his brief spell with Headington, but he returned to Gresley for the 1962–63 season.

BOUND, Matthew

Centre-back
Born: 6 November 1972, Melksham
United debut: 26 December 2001 v Luton Town
Final United game: 8 May 2004 v Rochdale
Appearances: 107+4
Goals: 2
Clubs: Southampton, Hull City (loan), Stockport County, Lincoln City (loan), Swansea City, Oxford United (loan), Oxford United, Weymouth, Eastleigh

Matthew Terence Bound was signed by Ian Atkins from Swansea, initially on loan. He formed a strong partnership with Andy Crosby, but towards the end of his time with Oxford age and injuries caused his mobility to desert him. He started with the team he supported as a child, Southampton, but played just five games for the Saints, plus a further seven on loan to Hull in August 1993, before Stockport paid £100,000 for him in October 1994. He made 50 appearances for the Hatters and scored seven goals for them, plus he also had a five-game loan spell at Lincoln in September 1995, before a broken foot curtailed his appearances and he moved to Swansea for £50,000 in November 1997. After being transfer-listed for rejecting a new contract offer, he joined Oxford on loan in December 2001, making the move permanent in February 2002. After his release by United in 2004 the left-sided defender signed for Weymouth. He was made captain and at the end of his first season he won the Player of the Year award. In May 2006 he was released by the Terras after they won promotion to the Conference Premier and he joined Eastleigh. In September 2009 he briefly returned to Weymouth on non-contract terms. Bound was managing director of a holiday cottage business in South Wales.

BOWIE, Jim

Inside-forward
Born: 9 August 1924, Aberdeen
Died: August 2000

United debut: 23 February 1957 v Gravesend & Northfleet
Final United game: 1 May 1957 v Tonbridge
Appearances: 12
Goals: 1
Clubs: Park Vale (Aberdeen), Chelsea, Fulham, Brentford, Watford, Bedford Town, Headington United, Fulham, March Town, Wisbech Town

James Duncan Bowie joined Chelsea in September 1944 from Park Vale in Aberdeen, after having been spotted in wartime football while he was serving in the Navy. His military duty prevented him from playing very often during the war, but he was a member of the Chelsea team that was defeated 3–1 by Charlton at Wembley before 85,000 spectators in the 1943–44 League South Cup Final. He played 13 games, scoring once, for Chelsea. He also played 12 games for Middlesbrough in 1943–44, and played for Hounslow (which is probably where he was originally spotted by Chelsea). He was described as a typical Scottish inside-forward: energetic, temperamental and full of ball-playing tricks. He made 84 appearances, scoring 22 goals, before he was transferred to Fulham, also in the top division at the time, in exchange for Wally Hinshelwood. He was transferred to Brentford in March 1952 just before the club was relegated. During the close season he was sold to Watford of the Third Division South. He began to suffer from knee injuries which kept him out of the side and, in January 1956, after 131 games and 39 goals, he slipped out of League football by signing for Bedford Town for £500. He moved on to Headington United in February 1957 and amazingly returned to Fulham just three months later. He did not, however, figure in the first team, and was soon on his way again when he joined March Town during the 1958 close season. His final destination was Wisbech Town, in December 1959.

BOWSTEAD, Peter

Inside-forward
Born: 10 May 1944, Cambridge
United debut: 13 October 1962 v Crewe Alexandra
Final United game: 8 October 1963 v Bradford Park Avenue
Appearances: 8
Goals: 2
Clubs: Cambridge United, Oxford United, King's Lynn, Brentwood

Peter Edward Bowstead was signed from Cambridge United in October 1962. He was described as small in stature, but adding punch up front. He featured 28 times, scoring seven goals, for the side that finished second to Arsenal in the Metropolitan League in 1962–63, but he was unable to displace either Graham Atkinson or Arthur Longbottom and at the end of the 1963–64 season he moved on to King's Lynn.

BRADBURY, Lee

Forward/Midfielder
Born: 3 July 1975, Cowes
United debut: 7 August 2004 v Boston United
Final United game: 7 January 2006 v Shrewsbury Town
Appearances: 65+8
Goals: 10
Clubs: Cowes Sports, Portsmouth, Exeter City (loan), Manchester City, Crystal Palace, Birmingham City (loan), Portsmouth, Sheffield Wednesday

(loan), Derby County (loan), Walsall, Oxford United, Southend United, AFC Bournemouth

Lee Michael Bradbury joined Oxford in June 2004 on a free transfer from Walsall, who were unable to afford to renew his contract after being relegated. He was signed by Graham Rix, who knew him from their time together at Portsmouth. Bradbury started with Oxford as a forward, but it was after Ramon Díaz converted the club captain to a midfielder that he began to shine. His departure was controversial, as he was dropped after his 29th appearance of the season so as not to invoke a clause in his contract that would have automatically given him a further year at the club, and he eventually moved to Southend on a free transfer, gaining promotion to the second tier with them at the end of his first season there. In the late 1980s Bradbury reached the FA Schools Cup Final with his Cowes school and played amateur football for Cowes Sports and also played for the Army, where he impressed Portsmouth in a game against them enough for Pompey to offer him a trial, which led to him earning a professional contract in August 1995. A loan to Exeter in December 1995 saw him score five goals in 14 games, and in his two seasons with Portsmouth he played 61 games and scored 17 goals, earning him a club record £3 million move to Manchester City. His season at Maine Road was not a success, with City getting relegated at the end of it, and in October 1998 he joined Crystal Palace for £1.5 million, having scored 11 goals in 46 games. His time at Selhurst Park was interrupted by a two-month loan to Birmingham in March 1999, during which he made nine appearances without scoring, and just one year after joining Palace he returned to Portsmouth for just £300,000, having scored eight goals in 38 games. Bradbury's career started to recover back at Fratton Park until he lost his first-team place in December 2001. After a year without a first-team game Bradbury joined Sheffield Wednesday on loan, playing three games before returning to Pompey. He was back on loan at Hillsborough two months later, this time scoring three goals in eight games. At the start of the following season he had a one-game loan spell at Derby, rejoining them on loan for six games without scoring in November 2003. In March 2004 Bradbury moved to Walsall on a free transfer, scoring once in his eight games, before his move to the Kassam. After leaving Oxford Bradbury played 55 games for Southend United, scoring nine goals, before he joined Bournemouth on a four-month loan which was made permanent after just one game. At Bournemouth, Bradbury converted to right-back and played almost 150 games before becoming caretaker manager and then manager in January 2011. He was also nominated as the Isle of Wight's manager for the 2011 Island Games tournament.

BRADLEY, Jimmy

Left-winger
Born: 21 March 1927, Greenock
Died: 2008
United debut: 12 September 1953 v Gloucester City
Final United game: 16 April 1954 v Tonbridge
Appearances: 11
Goals: 5
Clubs: Port Glasgow Rangers, Hibernian, Third Lanark, Shrewsbury Town, Headington United, Gravesend & Northfleet, Dumbarton, New Jersey (USA)

James Bradley joined Headington United from Shrewsbury, for whom he made just one League appearance. He rarely featured for United and played just one game in the momentous 1953–54 FA Cup run, against Harwich & Parkeston. Bradley started with Port Glasgow Rangers, moving to Hibernian where he made just one, albeit significant, appearance. He was called into the Hibs team to deputise for the injured Eddie Turnbull for the 1950 Scottish Cup Final, but Bradley froze on the big occasion as Motherwell won 3–0. Between 1950 and 1952 Bradley played nine games for Third Lanark, scoring twice, before moving to Shrewsbury. After leaving Headington, Bradley spent two years with Gravesend, after which he returned to Scotland to play twice and score once for Dumbarton.

BRAY, Geoff

Forward
Born: 30 May 1951, Chatham
United debut: 9 September 1972 v Huddersfield Town (sub)
Final United game: 18 January 1975 v Aston Villa (sub)
Appearances: 24+12
Goals: 7
Clubs: Gillingham, Erith & Belvedere, Oxford United, Swansea City, Torquay United, Dartford

Geoffrey Charles Bray started his career with Gillingham, for whom he was leading scorer in the South East Counties League for two successive seasons between 1967 and 1969. He moved to Erith & Belvedere, from where he joined Oxford a season later. He was never able to oust the regular first-team strikers and spent most of his time in the reserves. He joined Swansea in July 1975, scoring 20 times in 46 League games, before Jeremy Charles took his place and he moved to Torquay in November 1976 for £3,000. After seven games yielded just two goals, Bray was released at the end of the season and moved to Southern League Dartford. In 1977–78 he was the Darts' leading scorer, after which he moved into the motor trade, opening dealerships in Southend and Rayleigh.

BREVETT, Rufus

Left-back
Born: 24 September 1969, Derby
United debut: 9 September 2006 v Morecambe
Final United game: 4 May 2007 v Exeter City (sub)
Appearances: 24+3
Clubs: Doncaster Rovers, Queen's Park Rangers, Fulham, West Ham United, Plymouth Argyle, Leicester City (loan), Oxford United

Rupis Emanuel Brevett, a tough-tackling and dreadlocked left-back, was signed by Jim Smith in September 2006 to provide cover for the injured Gavin Johnson. He joined initially on a month-by-month contract after the transfer deadline had passed, but as he had been released by Plymouth in the close season this was allowed. His first club was Doncaster Rovers, who he joined as a trainee in 1988. He played 129 games for Doncaster, scoring three goals, before moving to QPR for £275,000, a record sale for Donny. Brevett made 172 appearances in almost seven years at Rangers, finding the net just once, and suffering relegation from the top flight in 1996, before a £375,000 move back to the Premiership with Fulham in January 1998. He was at

Craven Cottage for five years, playing 217 games and scoring twice, after which he signed for West Ham, with whom he suffered relegation at the end of his first season at the Boleyn Ground. In June 2005, after 29 games and one goal with the Hammers, Brevett joined Plymouth on a free transfer. He played just 13 times for Argyle, and made one substitute appearance on loan at Leicester, before his move to the Kassam. After his release by Oxford, Brevett announced his retirement from the game and in June 2007 he joined the coaching staff at Camberley Town, but a month later he was named as Swindon Town's sporting director. However, he soon realised the error of his ways and he left the club in October, immediately joining Bedfont Town as assistant manager while owning a tanning salon. In 2010 he coached at Badshot Lea in the Combined Counties League.

BRIGGS, Gary

Centre-back
Born: 8 May 1959, Leeds
United debut: 11 January 1978 v Cambridge United
Final United game: 15 April 1989 v Shrewsbury Town
Appearances: 506+2
Goals: 22
Clubs: Middlesbrough, Oxford United (loan), Oxford United, Blackpool, Chorley

Gary Briggs is widely regarded as one of the best central-defenders ever to have played for Oxford, and certainly one of the toughest, earning the nickname 'Rambo' for his no-nonsense approach and his hard, but occasionally fair, tackling. Briggs started at Middlesbrough but did not make their first team. United signed him on a four-month loan in January 1978, and his performances led the U's to offer Boro a deal, initially offering £30,000. However, the Teessiders did not want to sell and the transfer went to the first ever tribunal, at which United lowered their offer to £12,500 which became the fee that the tribunal decided upon. Briggs was to be a rock in the Oxford defence for over a decade, forming a formidable partnership with Malcolm Shotton that saw the club earn successive promotions to reach the top flight and win the Milk Cup. In May 1989 Briggs' long association with Oxford came to an end when he moved to Blackpool on a free transfer. At the end of his first season at Bloomfield Road the Tangerines were relegated to the bottom division, with Briggs' season prematurely ended in January through injury. In 1991 Blackpool reached the Play-off Final, but Briggs missed their Wembley defeat by Torquay after being injured in the semi-final win over Scunthorpe. Blackpool reached the Play-off Final again the following season, and again Briggs missed the final through injury, although this time they were triumphant against Scunthorpe. In May 1995 Briggs retired from the professional game after 137 League games, and four goals, for Blackpool. He briefly joined Chorley and became a civil servant, playing for his local side, Bispham Juniors, in 2006.

BRIGGS, Max

Midfielder
Born: 9 September 1948, Bramerton, Norfolk
United debut: 23 February 1974 v Portsmouth
Final United game: 5 November 1977 v Exeter City

Appearances: 102+3
Goals: 1
Clubs: Norwich City, Oxford United

Maxwell Francis Briggs was a right-sided midfielder who started his career with Norwich. Under Ron Saunders he won promotion with the Canaries to the First Division in 1972 and played in the 1–0 League Cup Final defeat to Spurs in 1973. He played 170 games and scored two goals for Norwich before joining United for £10,000 in February 1974. However, his time with Oxford was blighted by injury and his absence was crucial during the 1975–76 relegation season. Injuries continued to interrupt his career and Oxford cancelled his contract in October 1978.

BRINE, Albert

Left-back
United debut: 20 August 1949 v Hastings United
Final United game: 27 December 1949 v Chelmsford City
Appearances: 19
Clubs: Wolverhampton Wanderers, Guildford City, Headington United

Albert Brine joined Headington United from Guildford as one of the club's first professionals, having previously spent three seasons with Wolves. Nicknamed 'Son', he made his debut in United's first Southern League match, having performed outstandingly in the club's pre-season trial matches.

BROCK, Kevin

Left-midfielder
Born: 9 September 1962, Bicester
United debut: 1 September 1979 v Barnsley (sub)
Final United game: 9 May 1987 v Leicester City
Appearances: 283+22
Goals: 32
Clubs: Oxford United, Queen's Park Rangers, Newcastle United, Cardiff City (loan), Stockport County, Stevenage Borough, Yeovil Town, Rushden & Diamonds, Bath City, Cirencester Town, Oxford City, Banbury United, Bicester Town, Banbury United

Kevin Stanley Brock is an Oxford United legend. Brock was taken on as an apprentice at United in March 1979, and was promoted to the seniors the following January, making his debut aged 16 years and 357 days, turning down a £200,000 move to First Division Brighton shortly afterwards. Playing mostly on the left wing, Brock was a mainstay of the side that won two successive Championships to reach the top flight and then win the Milk Cup at Wembley in the Glory Years of 1983–86. He also weighed in with some important goals, such as the direct free-kick at Old Trafford that earned the Yellows a 1–1 draw against Manchester United in the League Cup fourth-round replay in 1983. While at Oxford he became the first Third Division player to be voted Player of the Month, in December 1983, and at the end of the season he was selected for the PFA Third Division Team of the Season. Brock also won three England Under-21 caps, the most for a Division Three outfield player, when England won the European Championship in 1984, and he received a fourth Under-21 cap in a 1–1 draw against Italy just three days after winning the Milk Cup in April 1986. In August 1987 Jim Smith signed Brock for QPR for £260,000 and while at Rangers he won an England B cap in a 2–0 win in Malta in October 1987. Brock played 40 League games for QPR, scoring twice, before following Smith to Newcastle for £300,000 in December 1988. Newcastle were relegated at the end of his first season on Tyneside, but they won promotion back to the top flight three seasons later, although by this time Brock rarely featured in the first team. He was at St James' Park until September 1994, making 145 League appearances and scoring 14 goals, but he did not feature at all during 1993–94 apart from a 14-game loan spell at Cardiff, where he scored twice. He left Newcastle for Stockport in September 1994 but did not play for the Hatters before joining Stevenage Borough, for whom he made his debut in November 1994. Brock then followed Graham Roberts to Yeovil, where he made his debut in February 1995 and he played 17 games, scoring once, in the remainder of that season. After Yeovil, Brock played for Rushden, Bath City, Cirencester, and as player-manager for Oxford City in October 1997, but he was sacked after seven months when City were relegated from the Isthmian League Premier Division. He briefly joined Banbury from July until October 1998 and then played for Bicester. He returned to Banbury in August 1999 as player-manager. He was with the Puritans for six years, leading them to the Hellenic League Premier Division title in his first season and in May 2004 they won promotion to the Southern League Premier Division via the Play-offs, but in May 2007 Brock resigned following budget cuts. He had a brief spell as assistant manager of Woodford Town before taking over at Ardley United in April 2008.

BROOKS, Jamie

Forward
Born: 12 August 1983, Oxford
United debut: 8 October 2000 v Swindon Town (sub)
Final United game: 6 May 2006 v Leyton Orient (sub)
Appearances: 33+20
Goals: 13
Clubs: Oxford United, Maidenhead United (loan), Tamworth (loan), Slough Town (loan), Brackley Town (loan), Didcot Town, Abingdon United, Oxford City, Abingdon United

Jamie Paul Brooks came up through the Oxford youth ranks, joining on a three-year scholarship in 1999. He made his Oxford debut under Mike Ford while still a scholar, and was promoted to the seniors in 2001. He scored Oxford's first competitive goal at the Kassam Stadium in a 2–1 defeat by Rochdale in August 2001 and at the end of that season Brooks swept the board by winning all of the available Player of the Season trophies (Players' Player of the Year, Supporters' Player of the Year, Young Player of the Year, and Media Writers' Player of the Year). In May 2002, just hours after the last game of the season and six days before he was due to have a medical at Highbury with a view to signing for Arsenal, he went down with Guillain–Barré syndrome, a rare disorder affecting the peripheral nervous system. Brooks was hospitalised for almost five months and spent 14 weeks in intensive care, totally paralysed for much of that time and losing a lot of weight. In December 2002 he won the BBC South Young Sports Personality of the Year award. He did not return to first-team action, aside from a few cameo substitute appearances in pre-season friendlies, until a substitute appearance against Rochdale in November 2004, over 30 months after his previous game. In the meantime he had loan spells at Maidenhead in December 2003 and Tamworth in February 2004. However, he never fully recaptured either his pace or his stamina, and he did not play a first-team game because of injuries (he required a hip operation in April 2005) between February 2005 and December 2005, when he joined Brackley on loan, although he did play 12 games on loan to Slough in August 2005, scoring twice. He saw out the end of United's 2006 relegation season, mostly as a substitute, and he was released in May 2006. Two months later he turned down the option of a two-year contract with Chester City in order to sign for Didcot, because he wanted to remain in the area as he was about to become a father. In July 2007 he moved to Abingdon United, and from there he joined Oxford City in September 2008. Brooks left City in August 2010, rejoining Abingdon United, for whom he played just one game before stepping down for personal reasons.

BROWN, Danny

Left-midfielder
Born: 12 September 1980, Bethnal Green
United debut: 9 August 2003 v Lincoln City
Final United game: 28 August 2004 v Shrewsbury Town
Appearances: 18+1
Clubs: Watford, Leyton Orient, Barnet, Oxford United, Crawley Town, Cambridge United, Eastbourne Borough (loan), Eastbourne Borough, Harlow Town (loan)

Daniel Brown joined Oxford from Barnet in the summer of 2003. He started his career in the Watford youth team, moving to Orient in August 1997. He made just one appearance for the O's, in a Football League Trophy game. In June 1999 Barnet paid Orient £40,000 for Brown and he spent four years with the Bees, making 102 appearances and scoring eight goals. At Oxford, Brown started well, but he lost his place in September 2003 and only made sporadic appearances thereafter, his final season blighted by injury. He was released in May 2005 and in August he signed for Crawley, where he was made captain and scored once in 37 games. In November 2006 he was released due to financial problems at the club, and Cambridge United signed him. Brown was at the Abbey for almost two and a half years, making 49 appearances and notching two goals, although in November 2008 he joined Eastbourne Borough on a two-month loan, which was made permanent in January 2009. In October 2010 Brown joined Harlow on a three-month loan deal.

BROWN, David

Goalkeeper
Born: 28 January 1957, Hartlepool
United debut: 20 October 1979 v Sheffield Wednesday
Final United game: 26 August 1980 v Chesterfield
Appearances: 24
Clean sheets: 3
Clubs: Horden Colliery Welfare, Middlesbrough, Plymouth Argyle (loan), Oxford United, Bury, Preston North End, Scunthorpe United (loan), Halifax Town

David James Brown signed from Middlesbrough for £40,000 in October 1979 as competition for Roy Burton. He played five games on loan from Boro to Plymouth, where he was spotted by United, and he joined Oxford after Argyle were unable to afford Middlesbrough's asking price. He had started his career with Horden Colliery, signing for Boro in February 1977, and he made 10 appearances for the Reds before his move to Oxford. He was described as agile, and with a long, accurate goal-kick, but this was not enough for him to displace Burton and in September 1981 he moved to Bury for £5,000. Brown made 146 League appearances in his five years with the Shakers, which included promotion to Division Three in 1985. In June 1986 he moved to Preston, who won the Fourth Division title at the end of his first season. In January 1989 Brown played five games on loan to Scunthorpe. He played 74 League games for Preston before moving to Halifax in July 1989, playing 38 games in two seasons with the Shaymen, including against Manchester United in the Carling Cup when Halifax were bottom of the League. He subsequently moved to Italy with his family.

BROWN, Keith

Centre-back
Born: 24 December 1979, Edinburgh
United debut: 11 November 2000 v Swansea City
Final United game: 9 December 2000 v Chester City
Appearances: 6
Clubs: Blackburn Rovers, Barnsley (loan), Barnsley, Oxford United (loan), Falkirk, Portadown, Berwick Rangers, The City (Australia), ECU Joondalup (Australia), Sunshine Lions (Australia), Mandurah City (Australia)

John Keith Brown was a versatile defender who joined Oxford on loan from Barnsley in November 2000. He started as a trainee with Blackburn Rovers but did not feature for them. In September 1999 he spent four games on loan to Barnsley, whose attempts to buy him were met with a £500,000 asking price. However, once Brian Kidd left Blackburn, Dave Bassett was able to buy the Scottish Under-18 international for £100,000 in December 1999. Brown made just 14 appearances for the Tykes over the next 15 months, however, including the Play-off Final defeat against Ipswich in May 2000. His loan spell at the Manor was the one bright spot in that period, and in March 2002 he moved to Falkirk after being released from his contract. In August 2002 Brown moved to Portadown in Northern Ireland after just five games and one goal for Falkirk, but he was the victim of a mugging in Edinburgh shortly after his debut and was released after just one week without being paid. He played for Berwick as a trialist in October 2002 despite still being registered with Portadown, although the SFA and Irish FA later gave Berwick permission to sign him. He played 19 games for Berwick, scoring one goal, before being released in July 2003. Brown then moved to Western Australia, playing for The City. He was selected for the WA squad to play Iraq in the World Peace Game in November 2003, which Iraq won 4–0, and he also played in WA's 3–0 defeat by Perth Glory two weeks earlier. In the 2004 close season he moved to Perth side ECU Joondalup. By 2007 he was playing for Sunshine Lions, and in the 2008 close season he moved on to Mandurah City. Brown was one of the Dolphins' stand-out performers in their inaugural Premier League season, but in July 2008 visa complications forced him to return to the UK.

BRYAN, Peter

Half-back
Born: 30 April 1944, Ashbourne, Derbyshire
United debut: 12 April 1963 v Bradford City
Final United game: 5 March 1966 v Workington
Appearances: 20
Clubs: Oxford United, Waterford

Peter Bryan represented Oxford Boys while a youth with Botley Minors. He joined Oxford in 1960 and in December 1966 he moved to Waterford in Ireland. He played for the Blues in their first-round European Cup tie against holders Manchester United, writing himself into Waterford folklore. He owned an athletics store in the city centre and played for Lismore Cricket Club. Bryan even played in goal for the inaugural Irish League Cup 2–1 win against Finn Harps in 1974 after the regular custodian was injured before the game. Bryan won five League of Ireland titles with Waterford and played Inter League games for the Irish League against the Ulster League and managed Clonmel Town during that club's early days. He later moved to the United States.

BUCHANAN, Peter

Right-winger
Born: 13 October 1915, Denistoun
Died: 26 June 1977
United debut: 15 September 1949 v Worcester City
Final United game: 11 October 1950 v Exeter City Reserves
Appearances: 49
Goals: 18
Clubs: Wishaw Juniors, Chelsea, Aldershot (guest), Portsmouth (guest), Southampton (guest), Millwall (guest), Crystal Palace (guest), Fulham (guest), West Ham (guest), Clapton Orient (guest), Fulham, Brentford, Headington United, Guildford City

Peter Symington Buchanan was a right-winger who joined Headington from Brentford. Although from Glasgow, Buchanan played all his senior football in southern England, despite becoming homesick first time around and returning to Scotland to play for Wishaw Juniors in December 1934 for a year, after which he signed for Chelsea. In December 1937 Buchanan won his only Scotland cap, scoring in a 5–0 win over Czechoslovakia. He would almost certainly have played more games for his country but for the intervention of World War Two. Buchanan played 40 matches for Chelsea, scoring six goals, plus a further 42 games and 14 goals during the war. He remained at Stamford Bridge until 1946, although during the war he also guested for Aldershot (four games), Portsmouth (28 games, three goals), Southampton (10 games, two goals), Millwall (two games, one goal), Crystal Palace (one game), Fulham (26 games, nine goals), West Ham (one game), and Clapton Orient (one game). He rejoined Fulham in 1946, scoring one goal in 20 League appearances, and in July 1947 he joined Brentford, where he played 74 League games and scored 13 goals before his move to Headington. He later moved to Guildford where he managed a pub.

BUCK, Tony

Forward
Born: 18 August 1944, Chesterfield, Derbyshire
United debut: 3 October 1962 v Stockport County
Final United game: 16 September 1967 v Peterborough United
Appearances: 32+6
Goals: 7
Clubs: Oxford United, Newport County, Rochdale, Bradford City (loan), Northampton Town, Bedford Town

Anthony Rowland Buck began his career as an apprentice with Oxford, joining the seniors in 1962 on election to the Football League. He was the first teenager to play League football with Oxford, and made history as United's first scoring substitute in a 2–1 League Cup defeat at Peterborough on 24 August 1966. Between 1966 and 1973 Buck also played Minor Counties cricket for Oxfordshire. In December 1967 he moved to Newport, where he played 49 League games and scored 16 goals, prompting Rochdale to make a bold bid of £5,000 for him in February 1969, paid for out of the directors' own money. Buck's goals helped Rochdale to a third-place finish and promotion to Division Three in his first season. In the four years he was with Dale, Buck played 103 games and scored 33 goals. During that time he had a three-game loan spell at Bradford City in 1970. On leaving Rochdale, Buck joined Northampton where he scored three goals in 17 League games over two seasons, after which he moved into non-League football with Bedford.

BULLOCK, Mick

Forward
Born: 2 October 1946, Stoke-on-Trent
United debut: 19 August 1967 v Shrewsbury Town
Final United game: 19 October 1968 v Charlton Athletic
Appearances: 64+1
Goals: 18
Clubs: Birmingham City, Oxford United, Leyton Orient, Halifax Town

Michael Edwin Bullock joined Birmingham as an apprentice, having previously played for Stoke Schools, Staffordshire Schools and the England Schools XI. The striker made his debut at just 16 years of age, scoring the winning goal in a 2–1 victory over Manchester United. Despite that auspicious start Bullock found a regular first-team place hard to come by, and in the summer of 1967 Oxford paid the Blues a United club record £10,000 for Bullock's signature. Bullock was United's leading scorer in his first season, helping to fire Oxford to the Third Division title. His goals dried up in Division Two and in October United sold him to Orient for £10,000, another Oxford club record. Bullock was particularly successful with the O's, spending eight years at Brisbane Road in which he played 277 League games and scored 65 goals. He was leading scorer in 1973–74 with 16 goals. In 1976 Bullock moved to Halifax, where he played 106 League games and scored 19 goals before, in July 1981, he was appointed manager. He remained in the Shay hot seat until October 1984, having taken charge of 148 League matches. In 1986 he was appointed manager of Goole Town, who won the West Riding County Cup under his charge, and in 1987 he moved on to manage Ossett Town. In 1989 he led Ossett to the Northern Counties East

League Division Two title, and the following season they won promotion to the Premier Division and won the League Cup. In 1991 Bullock left Ossett and became a scout.

BULMAN, Dannie

Midfielder
Born: 24 January 1979, Ashford, Surrey
United debut: 8 August 2009 v York City
Final United game: 11 September 2010 v Hereford United (sub)
Appearances: 58+3
Clubs: Ashford Town (Middlesex), Wycombe Wanderers, Stevenage Borough, Crawley Town (loan), Crawley Town, Oxford United, Crawley Town (loan), Crawley Town

Dannie Mark Bulman was a combative player, signed on a free transfer by Chris Wilder from Crawley in May 2009. In his first season with Oxford he won the Players' Player of the Season award and, despite his lack of goals, was considered a key component of the team that won promotion from the Conference. In September 2010 he returned to Crawley on a three-month loan that ended with him joining the club permanently. His career started with his local club Ashford Town in 1997. A year later he moved to Wycombe for a Combined Counties League record fee of £10,000, scoring on his debut with his first touch, the ball going in off his posterior. He played 243 games for the Chairboys, scoring 16 goals, before his move to Stevenage in June 2004. He made 90 appearances for Borough, scoring three goals, and was Supporters' Player of the Season in 2005. His contract was cancelled by mutual consent in December 2006, following a three-month loan to Crawley in which he played 37 games and scored four times. After signing permanently for the Red Devils, Bulman played 90 games and scored five goals. As at Wycombe and Stevenage, his battling style and tough tackling endeared him to the supporters, and there was much disquiet when he left for Oxford. This turned to joy on his loan return.

BURGE, Ryan

Midfielder
Born: 12 October 1988, Cheltenham
United debut: 19 March 2011 v Crewe Alexandra
Final United game: 16 April 2011 v Accrington Stanley
Appearances: 5
Clubs: Cadbury Athletic, Birmingham City, Coventry City, Birmingham City, Barnet, Oita Trinita (Japan), Machida Zelvia (Japan), Worcester City, Jerez Industrial (Spain), Doncaster Rovers, Oxford United (loan), Hyde, Port Vale

Ryan James Burge joined United on loan from Doncaster in March 2011. As an eight-year-old he played for Cheltenham YMCA, where he spent two years before joining West Bromwich Albion for a year. He played for Cadbury Athletic in the Birmingham League before joining Birmingham City, and he was offered contracts by both Manchester City and Manchester United when he was 15. He played for Coventry, and had two-week trials with both Ajax and Manchester United, but he returned to Birmingham City, where he was offered a three-year deal, aged 17. He made one appearance for the Blues before his contract was cancelled by mutual consent in March 2008. Following trials with Hereford United and Cheltenham Town he joined Barnet in November 2008, making two appearances for the Bees. Burge was invited to

Japan in February 2009 to trial with a couple of clubs, and he signed a professional contract with Oita Trinita and later Machida Zelvia. He returned to England in July 2009 and played a pre-season friendly for Forest Green Rovers, but he rejected their contract offer and instead moved to Spain to join the Glenn Hoddle Academy. While with the Academy he scored the quickest goal in their history, netting after just 11 seconds against San Fernando. In March 2010 Burge played once for Worcester City by arrangement with the Academy, going on to play for the Academy's Spanish League development side Jerez Industrial the following season, where he played alongside former United striker Alex Fisher. Burge scored two goals in 13 games for Jerez before joining Doncaster Rovers on deadline day at the end of January 2011. He played just one game for Doncaster before his loan spell with Oxford, who he joined after impressing in a trial with the reserves. Burge was recalled by Doncaster in April 2011, along with their other loaned-out players, for the Rovers to assess. At the end of the 2010–11 season Burge was released by Doncaster and the registration of all Glenn Hoddle Academy players was taken over by Hyde, with Burge almost immediately signing for Port Vale.

BURGESS, Andy

Midfielder
Born: 10 August 1981, Bedford
United debut: 14 January 2006 v Macclesfield Town (sub)
Final United game: 8 May 2007 v Exeter City
Appearances: 48+11
Goals: 7
Clubs: Rushden & Diamonds, Oxford United, Rushden & Diamonds, Luton Town, Mansfield Town (loan), Mansfield Town, Chester FC, Fleetwood Town, Corby Town, Droylsden, Woking, Corby Town

Andrew John Blakemore Burgess joined Oxford in January 2006 at the same time as his Rushden & Diamonds teammate John Dempster. He was signed by Brian Talbot, his former manager at Rushden and, at the time, his prospective father-in-law. In Oxford's first season in the Conference, Burgess was widely regarded as that League's best midfielder, despite his tendency to drift out of games. In May 2007 Burgess played three games for England C, scoring in a 3–0 win over Scotland as England won the Four Nations Tournament. In August 2007 he rejoined Rushden on a free transfer. In his first spell at Nene Park, Burgess played 232 games and scored 23 goals between 1999 and 2006. His second spell lasted two seasons and saw him play 86 matches and score eight times, winning Player of the Year for the 2007–08 season. In May 2008 he won further England C caps and scored in a 3–0 win over Wales as England retained the Four Nations trophy; he won eight caps in total. In May 2009 Burgess joined Luton, the team he had supported as a child, but he made just eight appearances for the Hatters due to injury. In November 2009 he joined Mansfield on loan and after five matches and one goal he joined the Stags permanently in January 2010. He played just 12 more games, scoring one more goal, before his contract was terminated by mutual consent at the end of the season. In July 2010 he joined the newly-formed Chester FC, in the Evo-Stik First Division North. However, he struggled to adapt to the lower level and, after a niggling hamstring injury, he was transfer-listed, joining Conference side Fleetwood on an emergency basis in November 2010, moving to Corby later that same month. He was released by Corby in January 2011 because of budgetary constraints and joined

Droylsden almost immediately afterwards. Just two months later Burgess was on the move again, joining Woking in March 2011. In June 2011 Burgess returned to Corby as player-coach. Burgess was also involved in women's football, coaching Nottingham Forest Ladies, Leeds Carnegie Ladies, Sheffield Wednesday Women and Preston North End Women.

BURNELL, Joe

Midfielder
Born: 10 October 1980, Bristol
United debut: 8 August 2008 v Barrow
Final United game: 29 January 2009 v Cambridge United
Appearances: 24+1
Goals: 1
Clubs: Bristol City, Wycombe Wanderers, Northampton Town, Oxford United, Exeter City, Bath City

Joseph Michael Burnell was a midfielder signed from Northampton in July 2008, becoming Darren Patterson's third signing in the Conference. He was steady rather than spectacular, and when Chris Wilder took over it was clear that Burnell's days at Oxford were numbered. In July 2009 his contract was cancelled by mutual consent with a year still left to run, and he joined Exeter later that month after a successful trial. Burnell started with Bristol City, becoming an established figure in the Robins' midfield. In six years at Ashton Gate he made 161 appearances and scored three goals. He joined Wycombe in July 2004 as a replacement for Dannie Bulman, with City waiving their right to a fee as Burnell was aged under 24. He played 62 games for Wycombe, scoring one goal, before following manager John Gorman to Northampton in July 2006. He played 67 games for the Cobblers, scoring twice, before being released and arriving at the Kassam on a free transfer. After United, Burnell's time at Exeter was not a success, and because of a long-term groin injury he played just eight games for the Grecians before being released in May 2010. He joined Conference new boys Bath City in July 2010 and signed a one-year extension to his contract in May 2011.

BURTON, Paul

Midfielder
Born: 30 November 1985, Enfield
United debut: 25 August 2004 v Reading (sub)
Final United game: 7 May 2005 v Chester City (sub)
Appearances: 0+2
Clubs: Peterborough United, Oxford United, Wealdstone, Ware, Harlow Town, Brimsdown Rovers, Ware, Cheshunt, Broxbourne Borough

Paul David Burton was a midfielder who joined United as a second-year scholar after Peterborough scrapped their youth set-up, which he had joined from Tottenham. An industrious player who could pick out a decent pass, he was never able to establish himself in the first team, making just two substitute appearances before his release in July 2005. Burton briefly appeared for Wealdstone, making four appearances in August 2005. He joined Ware, where he was a key component in the side's run to the FA Cup first round in 2007. He then moved to Harlow and in July 2009 he joined Brimsdown before rejoining Ware. In December 2009 Burton moved from Ware to Cheshunt and in July 2010 he signed for Broxbourne Borough.

BURTON, Ron

Centre-forward
United debut: 7 April 1954 v Merthyr Tydfil
Final United game: 18 December 1954 v Bedford Town
Appearances: 13
Goals: 1
Clubs: Derby County, Headington United, Burton Albion, Matlock Town

Ronald Burton joined Headington from Derby in April 1954, while still serving in the Forces. He was released at the end of the 1954–55 season.

BURTON, Roy

Goalkeeper
Born: 13 March 1951, Wokingham
United debut: 20 November 1971 v Portsmouth
Final United game: 28 December 1982 v Newport County
Appearances: 449
Clean sheets: 132
Clubs: Milton United, Oxford United, Witney Town

Royston Burton was spotted while playing for Milton United and taken on as an apprentice by United in 1969 and promoted to the seniors the following summer. The goalkeeper remained with Oxford for over a decade, making him easily the longest-serving custodian the club has ever had. He had an agility that belied his short stature (he was just 5ft 9in) and was an immensely popular figure with the Oxford supporters. Burton was first-choice 'keeper almost from making his League debut, losing his place briefly to John Milkins at the start of the 1974–75 season, but winning it back in December 1974 and then playing virtually every game until October 1982 when John Butcher took over. Steve Hardwick's arrival from Newcastle spelt the end for Burton and he was released in the summer of 1983. He joined Reading on a non-contract basis but did not play for them, and he signed for Witney Town. By this time his property investment was beginning to take off and he concentrated on this full-time after leaving Witney.

BUSBY, Hubert

Goalkeeper
Born: 18 June 1969, Kingston (Canada)
United debut: 8 August 2000 v Wycombe Wanderers
Final United game: 8 August 2000 v Wycombe Wanderers
Appearances: 0+1
Clubs: Detroit Wheels (USA), SC Telstar (Netherlands), Montreal Impact (Canada), Toronto Lynx (Canada), Caldas Sport Clube (Portugal), Oxford United, Crystal Palace, Vancouver Whitecaps (Canada)

Hubert Busby Junior was a Canadian goalkeeper whose Oxford career lasted just 45 minutes. He arrived at the Manor from second division Portuguese side Caldas SC in August 2000, but his playing time was limited to the second half of a game at Wycombe. He almost had the distinction of saving a penalty after keeping out Chris Vinnicombe's effort, but the linesman deemed that he had moved too early and Steve Brown converted the retake. Despite a lack of games, Busby stayed with United until his release in December 2000, joining Crystal Palace the following month. He did not play for Palace and in March 2001 he signed for Vancouver Whitecaps. Busby, a sociology graduate from Queens University, Ontario, began his career in 1994 with the Detroit Wheels, playing in the USISL (United Systems of Independent Soccer Leagues). He then moved to Dutch second division side Telstar before returning to Canada with Montreal Impact in 1996. Two years later Busby played for Toronto Lynx in the North American A League, where he played 16 games before joining Caldas. While on Palace's books Busby was called into the Jamaica national side, being an unplayed substitute for the Reggae Boyz in their 1–0 win over Trinidad & Tobago in the World Cup qualifiers. In 2003 Busby was appointed head coach of Ottawa Wizards, now defunct, in the CPSL (Canadian Professional Soccer League) and the following year he was appointed the Canadian youth team coach for the National Training Centre in Eastern Canada and the technical director of the Kanata Soccer Club. In 2005 he was appointed head coach of Toronto Lynx, but the side finished bottom of the league and he left after just one season. Busby moved on to coach AFC (African) Leopards and the following year he became technical coordinator of the Whitecaps Academy. In 2009 he signed with LA Sol of Women's Professional Soccer as an assistant coach for the inaugural WPS season, although the club folded in January 2010 because of low crowds. However, Busby had already moved on, becoming head coach of the Vancouver Whitecaps women's team in December 2009 and in September 2010 he was named USL W-League Coach of the Year.

BUTCHER, John

Goalkeeper
Born: 27 May 1956, Newcastle upon Tyne
United debut: 17 August 1982 v Aldershot
Final United game: 22 February 1984 v Swindon Town
Appearances: 23
Clean sheets: 6
Clubs: Blackburn Rovers, Oxford United, Halifax Town (loan), Bury (loan), Chester City, Bury (loan), Altrincham, Macclesfield Town

John Melvin Butcher was a goalkeeper who joined Oxford from Blackburn in July 1982. He made 104 League appearances for Blackburn, winning promotion to Division Two in 1978. In September 1982 he joined Halifax on loan, playing five games, and on his return in October he went straight into the first team to replace Roy Burton. However, Steve Hardwick's arrival saw him lose his place and in December 1983 he went on loan to Bury, where he displaced former Oxford 'keeper David Brown for 11 games. In August 1984 he moved to Chester on a free transfer, winning a Fourth Division runners'-up medal in 1986, having spent a second loan at Bury for five matches in October 1985. He played 84 League games for Chester in total. In 1987 Butcher was released and joined Altrincham, moving to Macclesfield Town in January 1988 but without getting a game for the Silkmen.

BUTLER, Ray

Inside-left
United debut: 12 March 1952 v Tonbridge
Final United game: 26 April 1952 v Cheltenham Town
Appearances: 7

Goals: 3
Clubs: Oxford City, Abingdon Town, Headington United, Abingdon Town, Oxford City, Wycombe Wanderers, Abingdon Town

Butler joined Headington at the same time as his friend from Abingdon, Sammy Chung. He played for United's reserves during their Metropolitan League Cup-winning season in 1951. He later played for Wycombe, where they used to pay their players by slipping money into their shoes during the second half of matches. He finished back at Abingdon, where he eventually became manager.

BUTTERS, Guy

Centre-back
Born: 30 October 1969, Hillingdon
United debut: 5 November 1994 v Stockport County
Final United game: 26 November 1994 v AFC Bournemouth
Appearances: 4
Goals: 1
Clubs: Tottenham Hotspur, Southend United (loan), Portsmouth, Oxford United (loan), Gillingham, Barnet (loan), Brighton & Hove Albion, Lewes FC, Winchester City

Guy Butters joined Oxford on loan from Portsmouth. He started out as a trainee at Spurs, making his debut in the League Cup at Blackburn in November 1988, during which he scored an own-goal. He made his League debut in his next game, when he scored in a 3–2 win over Wimbledon. He started looking assured and confident, and won three England Under-21 caps as a result, but as the season wore on he began to look more shaky and nervous and was dropped. In January 1990 he was loaned to Southend United where he scored three goals in 18 games. In September 1990, after 39 games and one goal for Tottenham, he moved to Portsmouth for £375,000. Butters' first League goals for Pompey came in November 1991, when he scored twice against Oxford. He was at Fratton Park for over six years, including his loan spell at the Manor, playing 186 games and scoring seven goals, before he moved to Gillingham for a club record £225,000 in October 1996. Butters spent a further six years with the Gills, playing 193 games and scoring 17 goals, before a free transfer in August 1982 took him to Brighton, where he played for almost six more years. He did not enjoy a brilliant start with the Seagulls and, after Steve Coppell replaced Martin Hinshelwood, Butters was loaned to Barnet for seven games in March 2003. He was even put up for sale on eBay by disgruntled Brighton fans. However, after his return from Underhill, he became a favourite with Brighton supporters, being voted Player of the Season in 2004. He made a total of 212 appearances for Brighton, scoring nine goals, before he was released and signed for Havant & Waterlooville on a free transfer in May 2008. He made eight appearances for the Hawks, and had a seven-game loan spell with Lewes in January 2009, but after being unable to agree a new contract with Havant he left in August 2009 and signed for Winchester. He was made assistant manager in April 2010, becoming caretaker manager at the start of the 2010–11 season after Glenn Cockerill's departure, taking on the role permanently in September 2010.

BYRNE, John

Forward
Born: 1 February 1961, Manchester
United debut: 6 November 1993 v Millwall
Final United game: 21 February 1995 v Rotherham United
Appearances: 63+3
Goals: 19
Clubs: York City, Queen's Park Rangers, Le Havre (France), Brighton & Hove Albion, Sunderland, Millwall, Brighton & Hove Albion (loan), Oxford United, Brighton & Hove Albion, Crawley Town

John Frederick Byrne, nicknamed 'Budgie', was a stylish, flamboyant striker who was signed for Oxford from Millwall for £50,000 by Denis Smith in November 1993, making his debut against his former club. He started with York City, where he played alongside and was later managed by Smith. He played 198 games for York, scoring 63 goals, before joining QPR for £115,000 in October 1984, after impressing Jim Smith while playing against Rangers in a League Cup tie. At Loftus Road, Byrne played alongside Gary Bannister and was in the side when they lost the Milk Cup Final to Oxford. He played 149 games for QPR and scored 36 goals before he moved to Le Havre for £175,000 in May 1988. After over two years in France, Byrne returned to England in September 1990, signing for Brighton for £125,000. He was at the Goldstone Ground for just over a year, appearing 58 times and scoring 18 goals, before Denis Smith signed him for Sunderland for £225,000 in October 1991. Almost exactly a year later, after 44 games and 15 goals, Millwall paid £250,000 for Byrne. He played just 17 games, scoring once, for the Lions in his year at the Den, part of which was spent on loan back at Brighton in March 1993, where he scored twice in seven appearances, before he again joined up with Denis Smith at the Manor. In February 1995 he joined Brighton for a third time, this time on a free transfer, as personal reasons took him back to the south coast. He played until the end of the following season, making 45 appearances and scoring eight goals, before joining Crawley in August 1996. In August 2001 he joined the Whitehawk team. In 2000 Byrne gained a degree in podiatry and worked both privately and for the NHS as a podiatrist, while he has also been an expert summariser on Brighton games for BBC Southern Counties Radio and a lecturer on clinical podiatry at Brighton University. Byrne won 23 caps and scored four goals for the Republic of Ireland.

BYRNE, Paul

Midfielder
Born: 30 June 1972, Dublin
United debut: 21 October 1989 v Barnsley (sub)
Final United game: 24 August 1991 v Grimsby Town (sub)
Appearances: 4+2
Clubs: Bluebell United (Ireland), Oxford United, Bangor (Ireland), Celtic, Brighton & Hove Albion (loan), Southend United, Glenavon, Bohemians, Philadelphia Union (USA), St Patrick's Athletic, Bohemians, Kilkenny City, Dundalk, St James' Gate, Newbridge Town, Dublin Bus

Paul Peter Byrne graduated through Oxford's youth ranks, having joined from Irish side Bluebell. He became a father aged just 15, and was rejected by Oxford for his drinking, smoking, and gambling habits. He tried out for

Arsenal, who also rejected him, before he returned to Ireland to play for Bangor, with whom he won the Irish Cup and where he won both the Irish League's Young Player and Player of the Year awards. This success prompted Liam Brady to take him to Celtic in 1993, where he scored two goals against Rangers within a few weeks of each other. He left Celtic after 33 games and four goals, plus a loan spell at Brighton where he scored once in eight games, having been told by Tommy Burns that he could not be guaranteed a first-team place. He joined Southend for £80,000 in August 1995, but in the summer of 1998, after 96 games and eight goals, his contract was cancelled and he returned to Ireland. Byrne signed for Glenavon, with whom he won the Irish Cup again, and the following season he moved to Bohemians, following a few reserves outings with Shelbourne. After narrowly avoiding relegation at the end of his first season, they reached the Irish Cup Final with Byrne as captain the following season, but lost to Shelbourne. In the summer of 2000 Byrne played 10 games and scored four goals for Philadelphia Union before returning to Ireland with St Patrick's Athletic. He rejoined Bohemians a few months later, and once more was on the losing side in the Irish Cup Final. After leaving Bohemians in 2002 he had a spell with Kilkenny City, and also played for Dundalk, St James' Gate, and Newbridge Town. In November 2004 he had a trial with Carlisle. After leaving Newbridge in 2006 he became player-manager of Leinster Senior League side Dublin Bus. In February 2009 he was appointed manager of Hemel Hempstead Town, who he guided to the Southern League Premier Division Play-offs before being relieved of his post in May 2009. Byrne was capped for Ireland at Under-15, Under-16, Under-17, Under-18, and Under-21 levels, and also for Ireland B. He was also selected for the full Ireland squad, but failed to make the team.

C

CAIN, Ashley

Winger
Born: 27 September 1990, Nuneaton
United debut: 20 February 2010 v Kidderminster Harriers (sub)
Final United game: 9 March 2010 v Hayes & Yeading United (sub)
Appearances: 0+2
Clubs: Coventry City, Luton Town (loan), Oxford United (loan), Mansfield Town, Tamworth

Ashley Thomas Cain was a lightning-quick winger who joined Oxford from Coventry on a one-month loan in February 2010, after scoring twice against United in a training match. He returned to Coventry early after picking up an injury during training. Cain turned professional with Coventry in July 2009 and made eight appearances for the Sky Blues (seven of them as substitute). He had a one-month loan with Luton in November 2009, but made just one substitute appearance. After being released by Coventry he joined Mansfield in July 2010 but after one goal in 20 appearances Cain was released by the Stags in May 2011 and joined Tamworth.

CAIRNEY, Chic

Wing-half
Born: 21 September 1926, Blantyre
Died: 25 March 1995
United debut: 24 August 1955 v Guildford City
Final United game: 8 October 1955 v Cheltenham Town
Appearances: 2
Clubs: Cambuslang Rangers, Glasgow Celtic, Leyton Orient, Barry Town, Bristol Rovers, Headington United, Worcester City, East Stirlingshire

Charles Cairney joined Headington United from Bristol Rovers in August 1955. After leaving the Forces he joined Cambuslang in 1947 and was signed by Celtic in March 1949. He played just one game for Celtic, against Raith Rovers in October 1949, moving to Orient in May 1950. He made four League appearances for the O's before moving to Barry in 1951. In July 1953 Cairney moved to Bristol Rovers, where he played in 14 matches, scoring one goal, before his move to Headington. Cairney then joined Worcester, for whom he played two games in 1956, before returning north of the border to play three times for East Stirling in 1957–58.

CALDER, Bill

Centre-forward
Born: 28 September 1934, Glasgow
United debut: 23 November 1963 v Gillingham
Final United game: 29 October 1966 v Peterborough United
Appearances: 78+1
Goals: 39

Clubs: Port Glasgow, Leicester City, Bury, Oxford United, Rochdale, Macclesfield Town

William Carson Calder joined Oxford from Bury in November 1963 for a club record £8,000. Calder started with Port Glasgow, moving to Leicester in 1958. He played three times for Leicester in his one season at Filbert Street before signing for Bury in May 1959. Calder was a member of the Shakers' Third Division Championship side of 1961. While at Bury he changed from being a right-winger to a centre-forward, and it was as a central-striker that he joined United, scoring on his debut against Gillingham. Calder also scored United's first goal against Blackburn Rovers in the FA Cup fifth-round win that set the side up to be the first Fourth Division club to reach the quarter-finals. In September 1964 Calder scored four against Walsall in the League Cup as Oxford won in that competition for the first time. Calder completed a successful time with the U's when scoring against Peterborough in his final appearance for the club. In November 1966 he joined Rochdale, playing eight games and scoring one goal before a transfer to Macclesfield.

CAMPBELL, Andy

Forward
Born: 18 April 1979, Stockton
United debut: 2 September 2005 v Shrewsbury Town (sub)
Final United game: 14 October 2005 v Northampton Town (sub)
Appearances: 3+2
Clubs: Middlesbrough, Sheffield United (loan), Bolton Wanderers (loan), Cardiff City (loan), Cardiff City, Doncaster Rovers (loan), Oxford United (loan), Dunfermline, Halifax Town, Farsley Celtic, Bradford Park Avenue, Whitby Town (loan), Whitby Town

Andrew Paul Campbell joined Oxford on loan for three months from Cardiff in September 2005. He failed to live up to his promise, and his below-par performances led to him failing even to make the bench towards the end of his three-month loan spell. Campbell started at Middlesbrough, where he turned professional in 1995. Although he was on Teesside for almost seven years, he managed just 71 appearances and seven goals before Cardiff paid £950,000 for him in March 2002, having scored six goals in five loan appearances at Ninian Park. Before his move to Wales, Campbell had two separate loan spells with Sheffield United: initially moving to Bramall Lane for two months in December 1998 he played five games and scored once, before returning to Sheffield just five weeks after his first loan had ended, playing six games and scoring twice. In March 2001 he went to Bolton on loan until the end of the season, making six appearances. While with Cardiff, Campbell scored in the Bluebirds' Play-off Final win over QPR to earn them promotion to the Championship, but this proved to be the highlight of his career. He played 88 games for Cardiff after his permanent move, scoring just 11 goals. Before his loan with Oxford he joined Doncaster on loan from January 2005, playing three games for them. After leaving Wales, Campbell tried his luck in Scotland, joining Dunfermline in January 2006, but in eight months he played just six games and failed to score. He joined Halifax in August 2006 where he played 53 games and scored 14 goals before the club folded, and in July 2008 he signed for Farsley Celtic. He played 19 games and scored 8 goals in six months before leaving for Bradford Park Avenue. He scored the first of his six goals for them in the first of his 22 games. In

November 2009 he joined Whitby on loan, with the move being made permanent three months later. Campbell scored seven goals in his 17 appearances for Whitby that season.

CAPPER, Jack

Centre-back
Born: 23 July 1931, Wrexham
Died: 10 March 2009
United debut: 20 August 1955 v Gloucester City
Final United game: 26 November 1955 v Cheltenham Town
Appearances: 11
Clubs: Wrexham, Headington United, Lincoln City, Chester City

John Capper joined Headington United from Wrexham in the summer of 1955. He turned professional with Wrexham in November 1949, playing initially in their Welsh National League and Cheshire League sides. He returned from National Service to make his debut against Grimsby Town on the opening day of the 1952–53 season. He played 48 League games for the Robins before joining Headington, following a benefit game for him. In January 1956 Capper left the Manor for Lincoln. After 21 League games for the Imps he was sold to Chester for £1,500 in September 1959. He played 37 League games for the Seals before retiring through injury in the summer of 1961. After quitting the game, Capper joined the Lincolnshire police force, being promoted to detective sergeant in 1971. He remained a policeman until his retirement, after which he became head of security at a holiday camp in Prestatyn.

CARPENTER, Tommy

Goalkeeper
Born: 11 March 1925, Carshalton
United debut: 12 March 1952 v Tonbridge
Final United game: 20 March 1952 v Bedford Town
Appearances: 2
Clean sheets: 1
Clubs: Harrow Town, Watford, Headington United

Thomas Albert Edward Carpenter was a goalkeeper who joined Headington United from Watford, where he had made four appearances in 1950–51.

CARR, Hughie

United debut: 24 February 1951 v Gloucester City
Final United game: 14 April 1951 v Lovell's Athletic
Appearances: 3
Clubs: Headington United

CARR, Jack (left)

United debut: 1 September 1949 v Worcester City
Final United game: 27 December 1949 v Chelmsford City
Appearances: 3
Clubs: Headington United, Kidlington

CARRUTHERS, Chris

Left-back
Born: 19 August 1983, Kettering
United debut: 8 August 2008 v Barrow
Final United game: 15 August 2009 v Histon
Appearances: 38+5
Clubs: Northampton Town, AFC Hornchurch (loan), Kettering Town (loan), Bristol Rovers (loan), Bristol Rovers, Oxford United, Crawley Town (loan), York City (loan), York City, Gateshead

Christopher Paul Carruthers joined Oxford from Bristol Rovers in July 2008. He looked more assured going forwards than defensively, and after Chris Wilder signed Kevin Sandwith to shore up the defence his appearances were limited. At the end of the 2008–09 season Carruthers was told that he was free to look for another club, and in September 2009 he had a six-game loan spell with Crawley, for whom he scored once. Immediately upon the end of that loan he moved to York on another loan, where he scored once in his 13 appearances. In January 2010 he was released from his Oxford contract and he signed permanently for York, scoring the goal at Luton in the Conference Play-off semi-finals that took the Minstermen to Wembley, where Carruthers played in his side's 3–1 defeat by Oxford. In July 2011 he signed a one-year contract with Gateshead. Carruthers started as a Northampton trainee, making his first-team debut in April 2001. In December 2003 he played twice for England Under-20s in the World Youth Championships as England finished bottom of their group. In November 2004 he had a four-game loan spell at Hornchurch, followed in January 2005 by another loan to Kettering. In March 2005 he joined Bristol Rovers on loan for five games. At the end of that season he was given a free transfer by Northampton and was set to join Wycombe Wanderers on a two-year deal, but changed his mind at the last minute and opted to sign for Ian Atkins' Bristol Rovers instead. Carruthers spent three years at the Memorial Ground, playing 123 games and scoring once, before he was released and he signed for Oxford.

CARTER, Jimmy

Midfielder
Born: 9 November 1965, Hammersmith
United debut: 26 March 1994 v Grimsby Town
Final United game: 2 January 1995 v York City (sub)
Appearances: 8+1
Clubs: Crystal Palace, Queen's Park Rangers, Millwall, Liverpool, Arsenal, Oxford United (loan), Portsmouth, Millwall

James William Charles Carter had two loan spells at Oxford, both times joining from Arsenal. In his first loan he joined in March 1994, playing five games and proving a positive presence on the right wing. His second spell, in December 1994, was less successful and there was little disagreement when he returned to Highbury. Carter started as an apprentice with Crystal Palace, but it was after his move to Millwall from QPR for £15,000 that he made his League debut. He played 130 games at the Den, scoring 12 goals, and was in the side that won promotion to the top flight in 1988, before an £800,000 move to Liverpool in January 1991. Carter's time at Anfield was not a positive one, and he rarely featured after Kenny Dalglish's resignation. He made just eight appearances for the Reds before he returned to London,

Arsenal paying £500,000 for him in October 1991. His time with Arsenal was not particularly any more rewarding than his period at Liverpool, as Carter played 30 games for the Gunners up to his move to Portsmouth in July 1995. Carter stayed with Pompey for almost three years, playing 80 games and scoring six goals, before returning to Millwall, now playing at the New Den, in June 1998. He featured 19 times for the Lions before suffering a back injury that forced him to retire at the end of the season.

CARTER, Tim

Goalkeeper
Born: 5 October 1967, Bristol
Died: 19 June 2008
United debut: 12 August 1995 v Chesterfield
Final United game: 14 October 1995 v Wrexham
Appearances: 17
Clean sheets: 6
Clubs: Bristol Rovers, Newport County (loan), Sunderland, Carlisle United (loan), Bristol City (loan), Birmingham City (loan), Hartlepool United, Millwall, Blackpool, Oxford United, Millwall, Halifax Town

Timothy Douglas Carter joined Oxford on a free transfer from Blackpool, but because of his physique he failed to impress, and he returned to Millwall fewer than four months later. Carter started as an apprentice with Bristol Rovers, playing 53 games in two years before moving to Sunderland for £50,000 in December 1987, having earlier that month played one game on loan to Newport County. While he was at Roker Park, Sunderland won promotion to the top flight and reached the FA Cup Final in 1992, but Carter was mostly second-choice goalie behind Tony Norman. In March 1988 Carter spent two months on loan to Carlisle, playing four games, and in September he played three games on loan to Bristol City. A three-game loan spell to Birmingham followed in November 1991. In August 1992, he moved to Hartlepool on a free transfer, but again chances were limited and he played just 25 games before moving to Millwall in January 1994. Carter managed just five games for Millwall before his move to Blackpool on a free transfer in July 1995. However, he played in just two pre-season friendlies before announcing that he was leaving Bloomfield Road and he joined Oxford in August 1995. After he left the Manor and moved to the New Den in December 1995 he cemented a regular place in Millwall's side, playing 68 games before his move to Halifax in August 1998. After playing 10 games for the Shaymen, Carter retired from playing in the summer of 1999 and he became a goalkeeping coach at Sunderland. On 19 June 2008 Carter was reported missing from his home in Durham, and his body was found under a bush in Stretford later that afternoon, the former 'keeper having apparently taken his own life.

CASLEY, Jack

Goalkeeper/Forward
Born: 27 April 1926, Torquay
United debut: 27 August 1949 v Colchester United
Final United game: 10 May 1951 v Dartford
Appearances: 19
Goals: 3

Clean sheets: 1
Clubs: Torquay United, Headington United

Jack Edward Casley joined Headington United from Torquay in July 1949, becoming the club's first full-time professional player. He joined initially on a one-month trial at a rate of £6 per week plus bonuses, which was increased to £7 a week plus £1 a week groundsman's fees after signing permanently. His first game for Headington was as a goalkeeper, and in his second match he played as a striker. Casley's only goals for United saw him score the club's first Southern League hat-trick in a 4–2 win over Guildford City on 22 September 1949. The club initially decided to refrain from offering Casley a new contract at the end of the 1949–50 season, but after he agreed to reduce his winter wages to £3 a week they relented and he was re-signed. After his early retirement, Casley stayed on at United in a variety of roles, eventually becoming chief scout. In 2002 the club recognised his long service, presenting him with a special award. He started in June 1947 with Torquay, his home-town club. His final game for the Plainmoor outfit had seen him play in goal because of an injury crisis although he was nominally a midfielder.

CASSELLS, Keith

Forward
Born: 10 July 1957, Islington
United debut: 12 November 1980 v Exeter City
Final United game: 13 March 1982 v Southend United
Appearances: 58+3
Goals: 25
Clubs: Wembley, Watford, Peterborough United (loan), Oxford United, Southampton, Brentford, Mansfield Town

Keith Barrington Cassells joined Oxford from Watford for £5,000 in November 1980 as a makeweight in the deal that took Les Taylor to Vicarage Road. He joined Watford from Wembley, signed by Graham Taylor for £500. However, Cassells was down the pecking order at Vicarage Road, and in three years he made just a dozen League appearances without scoring, and he failed to make an impression during an eight-game loan spell with Peterborough. It was at the Manor that Cassells started to get noticed. A sharp and nimble player who began scoring regularly, he was steady rather than spectacular and he established himself in the side that was on the fringes of the Third Division promotion places, scoring in United's famous 3–0 FA Cup win at First Division Brighton. It came as a surprise when, just before the transfer deadline in March 1982, Southampton stepped in to sign Cassells and Mark Wright for a combined fee of £230,000, with Trevor Hebberd also moving to the Manor as £80,000-worth of the fee. Although the price was never formally divided between the two players, it has generally been considered that it was an even split, making both players worth a club record £115,000. Cassells had an early run in the Saints side, but after the return to fitness of Steve Moran his appearances became more sporadic and in February 1983, after playing 19 League games and scoring four goals, he moved on to Brentford for £25,000. At Griffin Park, Cassells became an important part of the Brentford side, playing regularly and scoring consistently. In the summer of 1985 Cassells moved on to Mansfield for £17,000. In his first game the balding, moustachioed striker scored a hat-trick in a 4–0 thrashing of Hereford. His goals were instrumental in taking Mansfield to promotion in his first season at Field Mill, where he starred alongside Neil Whatmore. The Stags also reached the Freight Rover Trophy Final at Wembley in 1987, and although he missed a spot-kick in the penalty shoot-out he did earn a winners' medal. In the penultimate game of the 1988–89 season Cassells, who was Mansfield's leading scorer with 14 goals, had to deputise in goal after an injury to Andy Beasley. This turned out to be Cassells' last game as a professional footballer as he retired injured, having scored 52 goals in 163 League games for Mansfield. Upon retirement, Cassells joined the police service.

CASSIDY, Jim

Full-back
Born: 1 December 1943, Glasgow
United debut: 24 August 1963 v Chester City
Final United game: 16 November 1963 v Folkestone Town
Appearances: 6
Clubs: Woodburn Athletic, Stirling Albion, Oxford United, Barrow, Banbury United

James Cassidy joined Oxford United from Stirling, where he scored three goals in 30 League appearances. He occasionally deputised for Pat Quartermain, but was never able to oust him from the side and spent most of his time playing for the reserves in the Metropolitan League. He moved to Barrow on transfer deadline day in March 1964. He spent one season at Holker Street, again failing to trouble the first team too much, making just five League appearances, before returning to Oxfordshire with Banbury United. In the 1967–68 season Cassidy was an ever-present, making 73 appearances.

CASSIDY, Nigel

Forward
Born: 7 December 1945, Sudbury
Died: 19 May 2008
United debut: 21 November 1970 v Swindon Town
Final United game: 26 January 1974 v Millwall
Appearances: 132+3
Goals: 34
Clubs: Norwich City, Lowestoft, Norwich City, Scunthorpe United, Oxford United, Cambridge United, Denver Dynamos (USA)

Nigel Cassidy joined Oxford United from Scunthorpe for £20,000, a record fee for both clubs, in November 1970. Cassidy's first club was Norwich, for whom his father had played before the war. In 1962 he was released and joined Lowestoft, making his first-team debut in 1964–65. Cass was initially a left-back, but in a post-season friendly in May 1965 he played up front and scored four goals against FA Vase winners Diss Town, and from then onwards he played in attack. In 1966 Lowestoft reached the FA Cup first round for the first time since the war, losing 2–1 to Orient with Cassidy scoring the goal. That season they won the Eastern Counties League for the third year in succession. Cassidy played a total of 94 games for Lowestoft, scoring an incredible 103 goals, before he joined Norwich in July 1967. He played three games for the Canaries before moving to

Scunthorpe in December 1968. He played 88 League games and scored 35 goals for the Iron before Oxford came in for him in a bid to reverse their ailing fortunes in Division Two. Cassidy quickly became popular with the United supporters, enamoured of his swashbuckling approach and his drooping Mexican-style moustache. In the summer of 1973 Cassidy almost left the club to return to Lowestoft Town as player-coach, but they failed to agree terms. He was a regular first-choice striker at the Manor until Keith Gough joined in January 1974, after which his appearances became rarer. In March 1974 he was bought by Cambridge United for £28,000, a record for the club from the Abbey Stadium. Unfortunately his arrival came too late to save Cambridge from relegation to Division Four. The following season Cassidy's former teammate Ron Atkinson arrived as manager, and he made Cass team captain. In the summer of 1975 Cassidy played 20 games, scoring once, for Denver in the North American Soccer League, where he was nicknamed Walrus. In November 1975 Cassidy suffered an Achilles injury that forced him to retire. He returned to Oxfordshire where he managed Bicester Town for four years, followed by two seasons with Banbury United. Over the next 13 years he ran a couple of pubs in Bicester before moving to Cornwall to manage a pub in Wadebridge. He died in May 2008 after a short illness brought on by an insect bite received while on holiday.

CATON, Tommy

Centre-back
Born: 6 October 1962, Liverpool
Died: 30 April 1993
United debut: 7 February 1987 v West Ham United
Final United game: 7 May 1988 v Nottingham Forest
Appearances: 62+3
Goals: 3
Clubs: Manchester City, Arsenal, Oxford United, Charlton Athletic

Thomas Stephen Caton joined Oxford from Arsenal for £180,000 in February 1987. He made his Manchester City debut as a 16-year-old in 1979 and featured for City in the 1981 FA Cup Final and replay against Spurs, where he was one of the defenders beaten by Ricky Villa's twisting run for the winning goal. Caton won 14 England Under-21 caps while at Maine Road and in 1982 he won the Manchester City Player of the Year award. He was also selected three times for England, but never got off the substitutes' bench. In December 1983, after 198 games and eight goals, he moved to Arsenal for £400,000. His first couple of years at Highbury were reasonably productive as he partnered David O'Leary, but the emergence of Martin Keown saw him lose his regular place. He played 95 games for the Gunners, scoring three goals, before his move to the Manor for a club record £180,000. Caton was captain of the Oxford side that fought unsuccessfully against relegation from the First Division, and after the inevitable was confirmed he moved on to Charlton in the summer of 1988 for £100,000. In three years with Charlton, Caton scored five goals in 67 games before a serious foot injury required repeated surgery and caused the player to suffer from depression. He announced his retirement in March 1993, just one month before he died of a heart attack, aged 30. Tommy's son Andy later had an unsuccessful trial with Oxford.

CHALMERS, Lewis

Midfielder
Born: 4 February 1986, Manchester
United debut: 9 March 2010 v Hayes & Yeading United (sub)
Final United game: 24 April 2010 v Eastbourne Borough
Appearances: 6+2
Clubs: Altrincham, Aldershot Town, Crawley Town (loan), Oxford United (loan), Macclesfield Town

Lewis John Chalmers joined Oxford United on loan from Aldershot in March 2010. He was a busy little player with an astonishingly powerful long throw-in. As a youth he played for Manchester City and Accrington Stanley, but it was Altrincham who gave him his chance. He joined them in 2002–03. He was made youth team captain before becoming a regular in the reserves in 2004–05 and a regular first-team player the following season. In June 2007 he became a full-time professional on signing for Aldershot, having scored six goals in his 96 games for Altrincham. Chalmers was an influential member of the Shots squad that won the Conference title and Setanta Shield in 2008, and was named in the Conference Select XI Team of the Year for that season. After falling out of the Aldershot squad, in January 2009 Chalmers had a four-game loan spell at Crawley, after which he cemented his place again in the Shots first team. After returning to the Recreation Ground from Oxford at the end of the 2009–10 season, Chalmers was released by Aldershot and he joined Macclesfield on a one-year deal, having played 99 times for the Shots, scoring four goals. In his time in the Conference, Chalmers won 10 England C caps.

CHAPMAN, Adam

Midfielder
Born: 29 November 1989, Belfast
United debut: 13 January 2009 v York City
Final United game: 16 May 2010 v York City
Appearances: 50+16
Goals: 5
Clubs: Sheffield United, Oxford United (loan), Oxford United

Adam Chapman joined Oxford from Sheffield United, initially on loan. The Blades were Chapman's first club, signing professionally with them in July 2007. Although he never played in their first team, he became captain of their reserves, playing as a full-back, and he won the first of his two Northern Ireland Under-21 caps in October 2007. He joined Oxford on a one-month loan in January 2009, the deal later being extended to the end of that season. He became a vital cog in the Oxford midfield, while also filling in at right-back, exhibiting an excellent range of passing and a deadly free-kick, and so it was with much joy that United supporters learned that he had signed permanently for £15,000 in June 2009. Chapman was a key component of the side that won promotion from the Conference, and was voted Man of the Match in the Play-off Final victory in May 2010. However, by that time it was public knowledge that Chapman was due to be convicted of causing death by dangerous driving, and in June 2010 he was sentenced to 30 months in a young offenders' institution in Doncaster and disqualified from driving for five years. The following season Oxford kept hold of Chapman's registration and kept his number-seven shirt unassigned.

CHARLES, Jeremy

Forward
Born: 26 September 1959, Swansea
United debut: 19 February 1985 v Fulham
Final United game: 24 September 1986 v Gillingham
Appearances: 50+6
Goals: 16
Clubs: Swansea City, Queen's Park Rangers, Oxford United

Jeremy Melvyn Charles joined Oxford from QPR in February 1985. The towering striker scored United's first home goal in the top flight in a 1–1 draw with Spurs, and he scored the third goal in Oxford's Milk Cup win at Wembley in April 1986, ensuring his place in United folklore. However, shortly after the start of the following season Charles was forced to retire through injury. He had started his career with his home-town club Swansea, making his debut in the first game of the 1976–77 season and signing as a professional in January 1977. Charles was an important member of the squad that rose from Division Four to Division One in successive seasons, and scored the Swans' first goal in the top flight. After the Welsh club's relegation in 1983, Charles moved to QPR in November 1983 for £100,000 having scored 53 goals in 247 League games for Swansea. Due to injuries Charles played just 12 League games for Rangers, scoring five goals, before his move to Oxford. Charles, whose uncle was the famous Wales striker John Charles, was capped 19 times by the Principality, for whom he scored once. After his retirement he coached for Oxford and then became football development officer at Swansea and then Southampton, before coaching at schools in Oxford.

CHARLES, R

Centre-forward
United debut: 10 February 1954 v Guildford City
Final United game: 1 May 1954 v Llanelly
Appearances: 6
Goals: 3
Clubs: Charlton Athletic, Headington United

Despite limited first-team appearances, Charles proved his goalscoring worth in the Metropolitan League, where he scored 20 goals in 38 games during the 1953–54 season.

CHUNG, Sammy

Left-winger
Born: 16 July 1932, Abingdon
United debut: 17 February 1951 v Worcester City
Final United game: 10 November 1951 v Exeter City Reserves
Appearances: 20
Goals: 11
Clubs: Headington United, Reading, Norwich City, Watford

Cyril 'Sammy' Chung was a nippy left-winger who joined Headington United from school. His first game was United's first floodlit friendly, against Banbury Spencer in December 1950. Chung, born of a Chinese father and English mother, had been captain of his school team before joining United.

In 1951 he joined Reading, despite United matching their offer, and after returning from his National Service he signed as a professional in 1953. Chung played 20 League games for the Biscuitmen, scoring 12 goals, until Norwich paid £6,000 for him. He scored nine goals in 47 League games for the Canaries before his move to Watford, where he really made his mark, playing 220 League games and scoring 22 goals over eight years, the last of which was under manager Bill McGarry, who made Chung player-coach. In October 1964 McGarry moved to Ipswich, taking Chung with him as his assistant, where they won promotion to Division One in 1968. McGarry then became Wolves manager, with Chung again following him as trainer-coach. In the summer of 1974 he spent two weeks as a guest coach with Swedish side IFK Västerås before taking over from McGarry as Wolves manager in June 1976, winning promotion back to the top flight at the end of his first season. After 97 games in charge Chung was sacked in November 1978 with Wanderers third from bottom, having lost 11 of their last 14 matches. He returned to Västerås, signing a three-year contract, and spent some time working in the Gulf, before returning to England in 1985 as assistant manager at Stoke City before helping with coaching at Colchester, Blackburn, and Sheffield Wednesday. Chung managed Tamworth for a year from January 1992, and in July 1994 he was appointed manager at Doncaster Rovers. After two promising seasons and 96 games in charge, he was dismissed for no apparent reason on the opening day of the 1996–97 season, with chairman Ken Richardson reneging on an agreed contract and failing to pay full compensation. Chung retired to Somerset, briefly becoming director of football in Barbados in 1999, before helping out with pre-season training with Minehead in 2005.

CLARK, Willie

Centre-forward
Born: 25 February 1932, Larkhall, Lanarkshire
Died: July 2006
United debut: 8 October 1958 v Tonbridge
Final United game: 4 April 1959 v Wisbech Town
Appearances: 2
Clubs: Petershill, Queen's Park Rangers, Berwick Rangers, Cheltenham Town, Headington United, Guildford City, Clacton Town, Romford, Bexley United, Hastings United

William Clark joined Headington United from Cheltenham Town at the start of the 1957–58 season. Clark joined QPR from Petershill in February 1954, playing 95 games and scoring 32 goals before moving to Berwick in July 1956. He played one season for Berwick, making 20 appearances and scoring six goals before moving to Whaddon Road. He later played against Oxford for Clacton in United's last two Southern League seasons. Clark died of Alzheimer's in July 2006.

CLARKE, Bradie

Goalkeeper
Born: 26 May 1986, Cambridge
United debut: 11 December 2004 v Cambridge United
Final United game: 15 April 2005 v Swansea City (sub)
Appearances: 3+1
Clubs: Reading, Oxford United

Bradie Jason Clarke joined United from Reading in 2003 to be Oxford's youth team 'keeper. However, due to injuries to regular goalies Chris Tardif and Simon Cox, he was thrown into the deep end by manager Ramon Díaz in his first game in charge, against Cambridge United. He was promoted to the seniors in 2005 and was released at the end of the following season. He later became a male model.

CLARKE, Colin

Centre-back
Born: 4 April 1946, Penilee, Glasgow
United debut: 11 February 1966 v Workington Town
Final United game: 1 March 1978 v Wrexham
Appearances: 496+1
Goals: 26
Clubs: Arthurlie Juniors, Arsenal, Oxford United, Los Angeles Aztecs (USA), Plymouth Argyle, Kettering Town

Colin Clarke joined Oxford from Arsenal. He joined the Gunners from Glaswegian side Arthurlie Juniors in October 1963, having played for Glasgow Schoolboys, and moved to Oxford on a free transfer in July 1965 without having appeared for Arsenal's first team, rejecting offers from Luton Town, York City and a number of Scottish clubs. Clarke was a tough, no-nonsense defender, having been converted from his original position as wing-half. He was an ever present in the side that won the Third Division in 1968, and played throughout most of United's first period in the Second Division. It was the arrival of Gary Briggs that saw Clarke lose his regular place, and after leaving United, where he became the fourth player in the all-time leading appearances chart, he spent the summer of 1978 playing 17 games for Los Angeles Aztecs in the North American Soccer League before joining Malcolm Allison's Plymouth Argyle. Clarke scored three goals in 36 matches in his one season with Argyle, after which he became Kettering's player-manager in June 1979, although he never actually played for the Poppies. In his second season with Kettering, Clarke led them to second place in the Alliance Premier League (now the Conference) and the Alliance Premier League Cup Final, losing out to Altrincham in both competitions. In February 1982, after five successive defeats, Clarke resigned from Kettering and shortly afterwards became manager of Corby Town. In 1985 he became youth team manager for Charlton Athletic, who reached the Finals of the National Youth Cup and won the Southern League Cup. He moved to take on the same role at Aston Villa in 1993, winning the Midland Purity League, the Midland Cup, and the Mito Cup in Japan, beating Ajax 7–1 in the Final. He also appeared as a guest coach for the England team. In the autumn of 1995 Clarke returned to the States as head men's soccer coach at the University of South Carolina at Aiken, moving on to become director of the Augusta Arsenal Gunners. In 2000 he became coach for the Stone Mountain, Georgia, Under-17 boys' team, before becoming consultant coach for Brookestone High School, Georgia, in 2002. Later that year he became assistant head men's soccer coach at the University of Tulsa, whose team is called the Golden Hurricane, and he was selected as the National Soccer Coaches' Association of America 2009 National Assistant Coach of the Year.

CLARKE, Derek

Forward
Born: 19 February 1950, Willenhall
United debut: 24 October 1970 v Sunderland
Final United game: 17 August 1976 v Cambridge United (sub)
Appearances: 187+8
Goals: 40
Clubs: Walsall, Wolverhampton Wanderers, Oxford United, Leyton Orient, Carlisle United (loan)

Derek Clarke was a striker who joined Oxford from Wolves for £11,500 in October 1972. Clarke was the middle of five famous footballing brothers. He started his career with Walsall, signing as a professional in December 1967 and playing six League games for the Saddlers, scoring twice, before moving to Wolves for £25,000 in May 1968. However, Clarke was unable to break into the Wolves first team and he played just five League games for the Wanderers and a handful of games in a tournament in America in the summer of 1969, before his move to the Manor. He was signed for United by Gerry Summers, who had worked with Clarke at Walsall and also been assistant manager at Wolves. It took Clarke a little time to establish himself in United's first team, especially with competition from Nigel Cassidy and, later, Hugh Curran, who had also kept him out of the Wolves side. However, like his older brother Allan, Derek scored some excellent goals and he was an important component of United's Second Division side of the early and mid-1970s. In August 1976 Clarke moved to Orient, with whom he played in the FA Cup semi-final defeat to Arsenal in 1978. He played 36 games for Orient, scoring six goals, and also had a one-game loan spell at Carlisle in 1978 before injury forced him to retire. After retiring he combined some coaching with working in the paving business in London before returning to the West Midlands in the mid-1980s. After 20 years with the same company he was made redundant in 2008; since then he has been a part-time cleaner and caretaker. Clarke was once called-up for the England youth squad, but did not get a game.

CLARKE, James

Full-back
Born: 17 November 1989, Aylesbury
United debut: 24 November 2007 v Kidderminster Harriers
Final United game: 13 January 2009 v York City
Appearances: 33+7
Clubs: Oxford United, Oxford City

James Anthony John Clarke was a defender who joined Oxford in 2004, having previously been with the Watford Academy from 2001–03. Clarke joined United's scholarship scheme in 2006, and in 2007 he won the Young Player of the Year award, signing professionally in December 2007. Clarke was a tough-tackling full-back, who was often on the receiving end of referees' cards. In January 2009 Clarke had to be cut free from his car after an accident on the A34, but he was released from hospital the following day and suffered no ill effects. He had a year of his contract still to run when he was surprisingly told that he could leave the club in February 2009, and he almost immediately signed for Oxford City, where he won the Players' Player of the Year, the Supporters' Player of the Year and the Manager's Player of the Year for 2010–11. Clarke left for South Africa, but returned to City in July 2011.

*CLARKE, Ryan

Goalkeeper
Born: 30 April 1982, Bristol
United debut: 8 August 2009 v York City
Final United game: 7 May 2011 v Shrewsbury Town
Appearances: 103
Clean sheets: 36
Clubs: Bristol Rovers, Southend United (loan), Kidderminster Harriers (loan), Forest Green Rovers (loan), Salisbury City, Northwich Victoria (loan), Oxford United

Ryan James Clarke joined Oxford from Salisbury City on a free transfer in May 2009. Although signed nominally to provide cover for Billy Turley, the giant and agile stopper started the new season in goal and immediately became the first-choice 'keeper. United won promotion from the Conference at the end of his first season, despite him scoring an own-goal in the Wembley Play-off Final, and Clarke was voted the Supporters' Player of the Season. Commanding in the air, a superb shot-stopper, and with a great kick, Clarke averaged a clean sheet every other game in his first season with the club, the 22 League shut-outs being a club record since 1949. At the end of the 2010–11 season Clarke was voted the Players' Player of the Year. Clarke started as a trainee at Bristol Rovers in 2000, making 26 appearances for the Pirates. In October 2004 he played one game on loan to Southend, and the following month he played six matches on loan at Kidderminster. He spent the whole of the 2005–06 season on loan at Forest Green Rovers, where he played 42 games, before moving to Salisbury on a free transfer in July 2006. Clarke immediately established himself as first-choice goalkeeper at Salisbury, playing 106 games over the next two seasons. He lost his first-team place after breaking a bone in his foot while on holiday in the summer of 2008. In November 2008 he went on loan to Northwich Victoria, playing 23 matches for the Cheshire side, including the last game of the season at Oxford in his last match before moving to the Kassam.

CLARKE, Tony

Born: 10 July 1935, North Buckinghamshire
United debut: 12 March 1955 v Tonbridge
Final United game: 12 March 1955 v Tonbridge
Appearances: 1
Goals: 1
Clubs: Headington United, Bedford Town, Bletchley Town

Anthony Clarke scored in his only appearance for Headington United. He started with Headington aged 18, driving from Bletchley and giving a lift to goalie Jack Ansell (another Bletchley lad), stopping in Thame to pick up Ron Eele. In the summer of 1955 he joined the Army, where he stayed for three years playing football and cricket (keeping wicket for the Army team). He then went to Bedford for a year before becoming player-manager of Bletchley Town. He was later involved with setting up the Bletchley Town youth teams.

CLAYTON, Roy

Forward
Born: 18 February 1950, Dudley
United debut: 20 December 1969 v Watford

Final United game: 9 September 1972 v Huddersfield Town
Appearances: 54+4
Goals: 10
Clubs: Warley Borough, Oxford United, Kettering Town, Barnet (loan), Barnet, Corby Town

Roy Charles Clayton joined Oxford from Warley Borough for £1,000 in the summer of 1969. He was unable to cement a regular place in the side, and despite showing a lot of promise his goalscoring record was not prolific. In November 1972 Ron Atkinson signed him for Kettering for a Southern League record fee of £8,000. At Kettering Clayton bloomed into an excellent marksman, and in his nine seasons at Rockingham Road he notched 184 goals from 462 games, becoming the Poppies' all-time top goalscorer. He left for Barnet in the summer of 1980, initially on a month's loan before signing permanently for £2,000. Clayton played 45 games for the Bees but scored just seven goals, after which he played for Corby.

CLINCH, Peter
Centre-back
Born: 15 October 1950, Coventry
United debut: 24 February 1970 v Huddersfield Town
Final United game: 4 April 1970 v Charlton Athletic
Appearances: 2
Clubs: Oxford United, Bedworth Town

Peter John Clinch joined Oxford as an apprentice in 1967. He was promoted to the seniors two years later and was released in the summer of 1971, having failed to make an impression on the first team.

CLINKABERRY, Les
Goalkeeper
Born: 1932, Reading
United debut: 28 February 1952 v Gravesend & Northfleet
Final United game: 16 October 1954 v Dartford
Appearances: 4
Clubs: Headington United

Leslie G. Clinkaberry joined Headington United as an amateur in 1952. He was released at the end of the 1954–55 season, having been a mainstay of the reserves in the Metropolitan League but failing to dislodge any of the first-team 'keepers.

*CLIST, Simon
Midfielder
Born: 13 June 1981, Shaftesbury
United debut: 14 February 2009 v Barrow
Final United game: 15 March 2011 v Stevenage
Appearances: 84+10
Goals: 9
Clubs: Bristol City, Torquay United (loan), Barnet, Forest Green Rovers, Oxford United

Simon James Clist joined Oxford from Forest Green Rovers for £5,000 in January 2009. The left-sided midfielder immediately slotted into the team, his short passing and vision giving the side the necessary balance. He played in the Conference Play-off winning side at Wembley in May 2010, although his League debut the following season was delayed because of an operation during the summer. At the end of the 2010–11 season Clist was transfer-listed. Although he began his career as a trainee at Spurs, it was at Bristol City that he turned professional, in July 1999. Clist played 91 games for the Gas and scored nine goals, but he was transfer-listed in April 2002. However, he remained at the Memorial Stadium until February 2003, when he joined Torquay on loan, playing 11 games and scoring twice. In August 2003 Clist was again transfer-listed, moving to Barnet on a free in January 2004. He was with the Bees as they won the Conference title in 2005, but was released at the end of the following season having scored twice in 73 games, although he spent much of that time at full-back. He signed for Forest Green in May 2006, going on to make 112 appearances and score 12 goals before Chris Wilder took him to the Kassam.

COLE, Jake

Goalkeeper
Born: 11 September 1985, London
United debut: 12 August 2008 v Weymouth
Final United game: 30 August 2008 v Ebbsfleet United
Appearances: 5
Clean sheets: 1
Clubs: Queen's Park Rangers, Hayes (loan), AFC Wimbledon (loan), Farnborough (loan), Oxford United (loan), Barnet (loan), Barnet

Jake S. Cole joined Oxford on loan from QPR at the start of the 2008–09 season. He initially joined for three months, but was injured just three weeks into the season and returned to Rangers. He was a product of the QPR youth system, and played much of the 2003–04 season on loan with Hayes, where he played 16 League matches. This was followed by seven games on loan for AFC Wimbledon in January 2005, where he saved a penalty on his debut, and in March that year he had a game on loan at Farnborough. Cole managed to make eight appearances for QPR before his loan to Oxford. After he returned to Loftus Road he had a ten-game loan spell at Barnet in March 2009. At the end of that season he was released by QPR and immediately signed for Barnet. Cole made 87 appearances for the Bees before he was released in May 2011. In July 2011 he signed for Plymouth Argyle.

COLE, Mitchell

Left-winger
Born: 6 October 1985, London
United debut: 14 August 2010 v Bury (sub)
Final United game: 16 October 2010 v Macclesfield (sub)
Appearances: 2+4
Clubs: Norwich City, West Ham United, Grays Athletic, Southend United, Northampton Town (loan), Stevenage Borough, Oxford United

Mitchell James Cole joined Oxford from Stevenage in June 2010. Cole started his career with the Norwich Centre of Excellence, moving to West Ham's Academy when the centre closed in 2003. He was signed by Grays where he was first selected for England C aged just 17, and where he won the Conference South and the FA Trophy in 2005. He made a total of 43 appearances for Grays, scoring six goals, before joining Southend in July 2005. In September 2006 he joined Northampton on loan, where he scored once in nine games, and on his return to Roots Hall he established himself in the Shrimpers' first team. He played 37 games and scored once for Southend before joining Stevenage in January 2007 for an undisclosed five-figure fee. While with Borough he won the FA Trophy, scoring Stevenage's first goal in the first game at the new Wembley Stadium in a 3–2 win over Kidderminster in May 2007, and this was followed by another FA Trophy success two seasons later. In 2010 he won the Conference title with Stevenage before his transfer to Oxford. He scored 22 goals in 140 matches for Stevenage. He also scored seven goals in 14 England C appearances, including a hat-trick against Ireland in May 2007. Cole was forced to retire from football in February 2011 after it was discovered that a low-risk heart condition, which was first diagnosed when he was 17 at West Ham, had become potentially life-threatening.

COLFAR, Ray

Winger
Born: 4 December 1935, Liverpool
United debut: 18 August 1962 v Barrow
Final United game: 31 August 1963 v York City
Appearances: 20
Goals: 4
Clubs: Sutton United, Crystal Palace, Cambridge United, Oxford United, Guildford City, Wimbledon

Raymond Joseph Colfar joined Oxford from Cambridge United in time to make his debut in Oxford's first game as a Football League club. Starting as an amateur with Sutton, Colfar joined Crystal Palace in November 1958, going on to score six goals in 44 appearances and winning promotion from Division Four in 1961 before his move to the Abbey. He joined Oxford one season later. Standing at just 5ft 4in, Colfar is the shortest United player on record. Despite making just one appearance in 1963–64, it was not until the end of that season that he moved to Guildford. Colfar joined Wimbledon in 1968, scoring 10 goals in 60 appearances over two seasons.

COLLINS, Brian

Inside-left
United debut: 3 September 1955 v Chelmsford City
Final United game: 1 May 1957 v Tonbridge
Appearances: 10
Goals: 4
Clubs: Headington United

Brian Collins joined Headington United in the summer of 1955.

COLLINS, Dave

Centre-back
Born: 30 October 1971, Dublin
United debut: 15 August 1992 v Bristol Rovers
Final United game: 8 May 1994 v Notts County (sub)
Appearances: 41+10
Clubs: Liverpool, Wigan Athletic (loan), Oxford United, Shelbourne, Athlone Town

David Dennis Collins joined Oxford United on a free transfer from Liverpool in the summer of 1992, having made 73 appearances and scored four goals for the Reds' reserves over the previous five seasons. He also appeared nine times while on loan to Wigan during the 1991–92 season. Collins' time at the Manor was not a particularly happy one, and he was often berated for his lack of speed and non-athletic physique. After United's relegation to Division Three in 1994 Collins returned to his native Ireland and joined Shelbourne, later moving to Athlone Town. Collins was an Irish youth international and also somehow won six Ireland Under-21 caps.

COLLINS, Patrick

Right-back
Born: 2 April 1985, Oman
United debut: 10 November 2007 v Northwich Victoria
Final United game: 17 November 2007 v Ebbsfleet United
Appearances: 2
Clubs: Sunderland, Sheffield Wednesday, Swindon Town (loan), Darlington, Oxford United (loan)

Patrick Paul Collins was a tall right-back or central-defender who joined Oxford United on loan from Darlington in November 2007, but the loan was cut short after Collins was injured. He started his career with the Sunderland Academy, and was promoted to the first-team squad by Mick McCarthy in the summer of 2003. However, he did not play for Sunderland and a year later he moved to Sheffield Wednesday. He was with the Owls for two seasons, playing 36 games and scoring once, but he never looked convincing in defence despite appearing in Wednesday's Play-off win over Hartlepool in 2005, and he was loaned to Swindon in August of that year. His 13 appearances for Swindon coincided with the club's worst ever run of defeats, and when Iffy Onuora replaced Andy King as manager Collins found himself relegated to the bench for much of the remainder of his loan, returning to Hillsborough in January 2006. He was released by Wednesday at the end of the season and joined Darlington. He made 34 appearances for Darlo, scoring once, before his release in January 2008, shortly after his return from the Kassam, after which he moved to Cyprus. While at Hillsborough, Collins played for England Under-19s in a friendly against Portugal, keeping Cristiano Ronaldo quiet and scoring a goal.

COMINELLI, Lucas

Midfielder
Born: 25 December 1976, Buenos Aires (Argentina)
United debut: 22 January 2005 v Kidderminster Harriers (sub)
Final United game: 30 April 2005 v Rochdale
Appearances: 11+5
Goals: 1
Clubs: Argentinos Juniors (Argentina), Platense (Argentina), Los Andes (Argentina), Sarmiento de Junin (Argentina), Granada (Spain), Newcastle United (loan), St Pauli (Germany), Avellino (Italy), Las Palmas (Spain), Pahang Darul Makmur (Malaysia), Oxford United, CD Ceuta (Spain), AO Ayia Napia (Cyprus), Ethnikos Achna (Cyprus), UD Vecindario (Spain)

Lucas Ariel Cominelli was a tough-tackling midfielder who joined Oxford from Pahang of Malaysia in January 2005. Before leaving Argentina,

Cominelli played for Argentinos, Platense, Los Andes, and Sarmiento. He then travelled to Spain in 1999 where he joined Granada. In 2000 Cominelli had a loan spell at Newcastle, making several appearances for their reserves but not impressing Sir Bobby Robson enough to earn a permanent contract, and he also had trials with Carlisle, Norwegian side Brann Bergen, and Fortuna Dusseldorf before returning to Granada. He very briefly was with St Pauli in Hamburg before playing for Italian side Avellino in 2002, and the following year he returned to Spain to play for Las Palmas. He was signed by Malaysian side Pahang, with whom he won the inaugural Malaysian Super League, before Ramon Díaz brought him to the Kassam in order to provide experience on the left of midfield. It took a while for Cominelli to find his feet with Oxford but eventually the supporters started to take to him, and he was looking to extend his contract before Díaz and Horacio Rodriguez left the club and Brian Talbot released him. Spanish Second Division B side Ceuta made Cominelli their first signing of the new season in July 2005, but after just one season he was on the move again, joining Cypriot side Ayia Napia. Before the end of the season he had moved across the border into Northern Cyprus to play for Achna, from where he returned to Spain to play for Vecindario. He later became a football agent. Cominelli's father Marcos played for Racing Club de Avellaneda when they beat Celtic in 1967 to become the first Argentine team to win the Intercontinental Cup.

*CONSTABLE, James

Forward
Born: 4 October 1984, Malmesbury
United debut: 8 August 2008 v Barrow
Final United game: 7 May 2011 v Shrewsbury Town
Appearances: 127+13
Goals: 69
Clubs: Cirencester Town, Chippenham Town, Walsall (loan), Walsall, Kidderminster Harriers (loan), Kidderminster Harriers, Shrewsbury Town, Oxford United (loan), Oxford United

James Ashley Constable joined Oxford from Shrewsbury in April 2009, having completed a very successful season-long loan in which he scored 26 goals. Constable, nicknamed 'Beano' as a child because of his alleged resemblance to a baked bean, started his career with Cirencester Town, playing in the same Academy side as Matt Green, and making his first-team debut during 2002–03. In December 2003 he moved to Chippenham Town, where he supplemented his income by working in an underwear factory. In almost three seasons with Chippenham, Constable made 70 appearances and scored 30 goals, prompting a number of League clubs to enquire about him. In November 2005 he joined Walsall on loan, scoring twice in six games, persuading the Saddlers to pay £4,000 for him in January 2006. He then made a further 29 appearances for Walsall, scoring five goals, before joining Kidderminster on loan in November 2006. In his 10 loan games at Aggborough, Constable scored five goals and the club signed him for a nominal fee in January 2007. Kidderminster reached the FA Trophy Final at Wembley at the end of the season, where Constable scored the first two goals of any English side at the newly rebuilt stadium, but they lost 3–2 to Stevenage. In January 2008 Constable joined Shrewsbury, having played a further 44 matches for Kiddy, scoring 18 goals. However, his time with the Shrews was not a happy one, with manager Paul Simpson feeling that

Constable did not have what it took to be a successful League striker, and in July 2008 he was allowed to return to the Conference on loan to Oxford. Constable's strength, both on the ground and in the air, his finishing ability, and his phenomenal work-rate combined to make him an almost instant fans' favourite, and his 26 goals in his first season made him the first player to score that many for Oxford since John Aldridge in 1985–86. In April he signed a three-year contract for an undisclosed fee, and he won both the Supporters' Player of the Year and the Conference Player of the Year. The following season he again scored 26 goals as United won promotion from the Conference, with Constable scoring United's second goal in the Wembley Play-off Final. At the end of the 2010–11 season he was again voted the Supporters' Player of the Year, the first person to win the award twice. Constable won the first of his three England C caps in November 2007 against Finland, and he scored his only England C goal in October 2008 against Italy.

COOK, Jamie

Left-winger
Born: 2 August 1979, Oxford
United debut: 23 August 1997 v Nottingham Forest (sub)
Final United game: 24 April 2010 v Eastbourne Borough
Appearances: 58+56
Goals: 11
Clubs: Oxford United, Boston United, Stevenage Borough, Bath City (loan), Maidenhead United, Witney United, Rushden & Diamonds, Havant & Waterlooville, Crawley Town, Oxford United, Crawley Town, Bath City

James Steven Cook had two separate spells with United. In his first period he came through the club's YTS programme, starting in 1995, and he was part of the youth side that won the Southern Junior Floodlit Cup in May 1996. He was promoted to the seniors in 1997, gradually becoming a more integral part of the first team, despite his wispy frame. In February 2001 he left United for Boston, having played 98 games (of which 52 were as a substitute) and having scored seven goals, including a winner at Maine Road against Manchester City. Boston won promotion to the Football League at the end of Cook's first season, and he remained with the Pilgrims until February 2003, when he moved to Stevenage after 61 games and seven goals for Steve Evans' side. Cook played 37 games for Borough, scoring two goals, but in February 2004 he moved to Bath on loan until the end of that season. In August 2004 he joined John Dreyer's Maidenhead after being released by Stevenage, and he remained with the Magpies until returning home to Witney United in July 2005, where he also continued to pursue his golfing career. In January 2007 he was signed by Rushden & Diamonds, for whom he made just nine appearances and scored one goal. He joined Havant & Waterlooville in March 2007 and signed for Crawley at the end of that season. It was under Steve Evans again that Cook blossomed into a striker, and he scored 32 goals in 78 appearances for the Red Devils, including a brace against Oxford in September 2008. It was this record that prompted Chris Wilder to pay £5,000 for him in August 2009 to bring him back to Oxford, the transfer being the first to be funded by the fans' 12th Man initiative. Unfortunately, despite a wonder-goal against Luton, Cook again failed to live up to his promise and there was little surprise when he was released at the end of his first season, going back to rejoin Crawley. The Red

Devils won the Conference in 2011, but Cook was released at the end of the season, joining Bath City on a one-year deal in May 2011.

COOKE, Joe
Centre-back/Forward
Born: 15 February 1955, Roseau (Dominica)
United debut: 25 August 1979 v Hull City
Final United game: 29 April 1981 v Millwall
Appearances: 78+1
Goals: 13
Clubs: Bradford City, Peterborough United, Oxford United, Exeter City, Bradford City (loan), Bradford City, Rochdale, Wrexham, Liversedge

Joseph Cooke is the only native-born Caribbean player to have played for Oxford. His first club was Bradford City for whom he signed associate schoolboy forms in July 1970, making his debut aged 16 in September 1971. He signed professionally in May 1972 and, as a striker, he scored prolifically. After 204 League games and 62 goals for the Bantams, he joined Peterborough in January 1979 for £45,000 but just eight months later, after 18 League games had brought five goals, Oxford paid £50,000 for his signature. Cooke scored on his debut against Hull and had four goals by mid-October, when he was converted into a centre-back. He still finished the following season as joint-leading scorer with just six goals. In June 1981 he moved to Exeter for £25,000. Cooke scored three goals for the Grecians in 17 League games before returning to Bradford in January 1982 on a one-month loan. This was made permanent a month later for £10,000. Injuries restricted his appearances, but he still managed 67 League games, in which he scored six goals, before he joined Rochdale on a free transfer in June 1984. He was made captain at Dale, and in two seasons he played 75 League games, scoring four goals, before moving to Wrexham for £8,000 in August 1986. He made 51 League appearances, scoring four goals for the Robins, after which he returned to Yorkshire to play for Liversedge in 1988.

COOMBES, Gregg
Midfielder
Born: 1 March 1988, Porth (Wales)
United debut: 29 January 2007 v Rushden & Diamonds
Final United game: 29 January 2007 v Rushden & Diamonds
Appearances: 1
Clubs: Cardiff City, Oxford United (loan), Carmarthen Town, Clevedon Town

Gregg Alexander Coombes was a highly promising midfielder who joined Oxford on a one-month loan from Cardiff in January 2007 at the same time as Michael Corcoran, later extended for a further month. Coombes' only first-team game for United was their first home defeat of the season, live on Sky TV, against Rushden & Diamonds. He did force the Rushden 'keeper into a save, but was taken off with 15 minutes remaining. At the end of the season he was released by Cardiff, having never played a first-team game for them. He joined Welsh Premier League side Carmarthen Town, playing 34 games and scoring three goals for them before taking a break from the game. In June 2009 he joined Clevedon Town.

CORBO, Mateo

Left-back
Born: 21 April 1976, Montevideo (Uruguay)
United debut: 15 January 2005 v Yeovil Town
Final United game: 7 May 2005 v Chester City
Appearances: 13
Clubs: CA River Plate (Uruguay), Real Oviedo (Spain), Barnsley, CA River Plate (Uruguay), Olimpia Asuncion (Paraguay), Oxford United, Newcastle United Jets (Australia)

Mateo Andrés Corbo Sottolano was a left-sided defender signed for Oxford by Ramon Diaz in January 2005 from Paraguayan side Olimpia Asuncion. Strong in the tackle and in the air, he was also able to pick out teammates with long cross-field passes. However he also suffered from a poor disciplinary record, picking up 10 bookings in his 13 games (including two in one match at Swansea). He walked out of United at the end of the 2004–05 season after new manager Brian Talbot failed to call him in to a team training session. Raised in Pocitos, an upmarket beach neighbourhood in Montevideo, Corbo's first club was River Plate, not to be confused with its more famous namesake across the Rio de la Plata in Buenos Aires, Argentina. He started with the reserves, but was promoted to the first team in 1994. In 1999 he switched to Oviedo in Spain where he stayed for one season, playing just six games, before transferring to Barnsley for £250,000 in August 2000. He stayed at Oakwell until June 2001, playing 20 games and scoring one goal, in the League Cup at Stoke, before returning to River Plate for six months. In 2004 he moved to Olimpia, who finished second in the final table, losing to Libertad on penalties in the Play-off. While playing for Oxford, Corbo was spotted by Richard Money, then manager of Australian A League side Newcastle Jets, and when he was released by United, Corbo moved Down Under to join the Jets. Corbo lasted one season with the Australian side, playing 18 games without scoring (although he did receive two red cards), before being released in July 2006.

CORCORAN, Michael

Midfielder
Born: 28 December 1987, Coalisland (Northern Ireland)
United debut: 3 February 2007 v Cambridge United
Final United game: 12 January 2008 v Salisbury City
Appearances: 33+2
Goals: 2
Clubs: Cardiff City, Oxford United (loan), Oxford United, Rushden & Diamonds

Michael Corcoran was a midfielder and defender who joined Oxford on a one-month loan from Cardiff City in January 2007, later extended to the end of the 2006–07 season, at the same time as Gregg Coombes. On his release by Cardiff at the end of the 2006–07 season he signed a one-year contract with Oxford. He was later placed on the transfer list by Darren Patterson and in January 2008 his contract was cancelled by mutual consent and he moved to Rushden. After six goals in 106 appearances, in June 2011 Corcoran left the Diamonds and signed for Dover Athletic. Corcoran started his career as a trainee with Cardiff, but he never appeared for their first team, although he was capped for the Northern Ireland youth team and Under-21s.

CORNWELL, Kevin

Inside-forward
Born: 10 December 1941, Birmingham
United debut: 17 March 1962 v Bexley Heath & Welling
Final United game: 25 April 1964 v Southport
Appearances: 28
Goals: 10
Clubs: Banbury Spencer, Oxford United (loan), Oxford United, Cambridge City, Cheltenham Town

Kevin John Cornwell was an inside-forward who joined Oxford United on loan from Banbury Spencer in March 1962, just before the U's were elected to the Football League, after which his transfer was made permanent. Cornwell played just two games in the Southern League and was in the Oxford side that played their first game in the Football League at Barrow in August 1963. After his release in the summer of 1964 he joined Cambridge City.

COTTON, Fred

Inside-forward
Born: 12 March 1932, Halesowen
Died: November 1994
United debut: 11 September 1957 v Chelmsford City
Final United game: 7 April 1958 v Yeovil Town
Appearances: 27
Goals: 6
Clubs: Crystal Palace, Headington United, Kidderminster Harriers

Frederick Joseph Cotton joined Headington United from Crystal Palace, for whom he made four appearances in the 1956–57 season. After the end of the following season he was released by Headington and joined Kidderminster, for whom he was the leading goalscorer in the Southern League in 1958–59.

COX, Simon

Goalkeeper
Born: 24 March 1984, Clapham
United debut: 27 March 2004 v Doncaster Rovers
Final United game: 30 October 2004 v Cheltenham Town
Appearances: 7+1
Clean sheets: 3
Clubs: Reading, Oxford United

Simon Peter Cox joined Oxford as a third-year scholar from Reading in the summer of 2002, winning promotion to the senior squad a year later. He was already a regular fixture in the Ireland Under-19 side. He was given his debut by Graham Rix, in his first game in charge, against Fourth Division leaders Doncaster Rovers, and Cox was named Man of the Match for his display in the goalless draw. After his release in the summer of 2005 he applied to join the Army, but injuries acquired as a footballer caused him to fail his medical, which was also the case when he tried to join the police force. He later became a plumber in Surrey.

*CRADDOCK, Tom

Forward
Born: 14 October 1986, Darlington
United debut: 4 September 2010 v Morecambe
Final United game: 7 May 2011 v Shrewsbury Town
Appearances: 37+3
Goals: 15
Clubs: Middlesbrough, Wrexham (loan), Hartlepool United (loan), Luton Town (loan), Luton Town, Oxford United

Thomas Michael Craddock was signed from Luton for an undisclosed fee in August 2010. Although he preferred to play centrally, Craddock nevertheless managed 15 goals in his first season with United playing on the left of a front three. He started his career with Middlesbrough, joining their Academy from Darlington Spraire Lads aged 11 and making his first-team debut for Steve McClaren on the final day of the 2005–06 season against Fulham. He played a total of five senior games for Boro, and had loan spells at Wrexham (one game) in October 2006, Hartlepool (four games) in February 2008, and Luton (nine games and four goals) in October 2008 before Luton paid £80,000 for him in January 2009. Before he left for Oxford, Craddock played 77 games for the Hatters, scoring an incredible 34 goals, including one when they won the Football League Trophy at Wembley in 2009, beating Scunthorpe 3–2 after extra-time.

CRAIG, Bobby

Left-back
Born: 16 June 1928, Consett, County Durham
United debut: 18 August 1951 v Worcester City
Final United game: 30 April 1955 v Lovell's Athletic
Appearances: 190
Goals: 10
Clubs: Sunderland, Headington United, Bedford Town, Quarry Nomads, Barton United

Robert Craig joined Headington United from Sunderland, for whom he made one appearance (a 2–1 home win over West Bromwich Albion). Craig was one of five players released at the end of the 1954–55 season after a dispute about non-payment of appearance money, with Craig and two others joining Bedford. Craig was at Bedford for five seasons, making 271 appearances and scoring two goals. He then returned to Oxford where he played for Quarry Nomads. Craig was a semi-professional with Headington, combining football with his work as a carpenter.

CREIGHTON, Mark

Centre-back
Born: 8 October 1981, Birmingham
United debut: 8 August 2009 v York City
Final United game: 7 November 2010 v Burton Albion
Appearances: 47+7
Goals: 2
Clubs: Kidderminster Harriers, Moor Green, Paget Rangers (loan), Halesowen Town, Bromsgrove Rovers, Redditch United, Bromsgrove Rovers, Causeway United, Willenhall Town, Redditch United, Kidderminster Harriers, Oxford United, Wrexham (loan), Wrexham

Mark Adam Creighton joined Oxford from Kidderminster for £7,500 in May 2009. Nicknamed 'Beast' by United supporters because of his hulking physique, Creighton scored the winning goal against York on his debut in the first game of the 2009–10 season, and became an integral part of the side, playing in the Wembley Play-off Final victory, also against York, in May 2010. However, he was unable to cement a regular place in the side at the start of the following season, and in November 2010 he joined Wrexham on a two-month loan which was made permanent in January 2011. Creighton started his career with Halesowen on their YTS, joining the Harriers as a trainee in August 1999; a year later he moved to Moor Green on a free transfer. In November 2000 Creighton joined Paget Rangers on loan and in February 2001 he was drafted in to help Halesowen through an injury crisis, before joining Bromsgrove in March 2001. In July he joined Redditch, but in December 2001 he was released and went back to Bromsgrove briefly before signing for West Midland League leaders Causeway United. This was another short stop in Creighton's peripatetic career, as in January 2002 he was on the move again, joining Willenhall. Creighton's stay at Willenhall was a lengthy one by his standards, playing for the Lockmen until August 2005, when his former club Redditch signed him for £1,000. While with the Reds he became club captain and won the Player of the Season award, prompting Kidderminster to take him back to Aggborough on a free transfer in July 2006. He played 146 games for Kiddy, scoring eight goals, before his move to the Kassam.

CRICHTON, Johnny

Inside-forward
Born: 1925, Scotstoun
United debut: 5 May 1951 v Hastings United
Final United game: 30 April 1955 v Lovell's Athletic
Appearances: 187
Goals: 22
Clubs: Greenock Morton, Dumbarton, East Stirling, Airdrie United, Headington United, Bedford Town, Banbury Spencer, Hinckley Athletic, Thame United

John David Grey Crichton joined Headington United from Airdrie, where he had played five games and scored one goal, in 1951. He started his career with Greenock Morton in 1947, playing five games before moving to Dumbarton in 1948. After four games and two goals he was off to East Stirling in 1949, scoring one goal in seven games before his move to Airdrie later that year. Crichton was released by Headington at the end of 1954–55, one of five players involved in a dispute about non-payment of appearance money. He moved to Bedford with two of his comrades-in-arms. He was with the Eagles for two seasons, making 79 appearances and scoring 12 goals, before returning to Oxfordshire with Banbury Spencer. After Banbury, Crichton had a short spell at Hinckley Athletic and then became player-coach with Thame. In 1967–68, after looking after Oxford United's reserves, he managed Oxford City. In April 1969, on the way back from a win at Maidstone City, he decided he had had enough of the lengthy pub breaks on the journeys back to Oxford from away matches and he phoned his resignation through to the committee from the pub where they had stopped; on the Monday he agreed to continue until the end of the season, after which he went to manage Banbury, by now sporting the United suffix.

CROKER, Ted

Left-back
Born: 13 February 1924, Kingston
Died: 25 December 1992
United debut: 19 August 1953 v Hastings United
Final United game: 8 April 1955 v Hereford United
Appearances: 91
Clubs: Dartford, Kingstonian, Charlton Athletic, Kidderminster Harriers, Headington United

Edgar Alfred Croker was at technical college in Surrey before joining the Royal Air Force aged 18, he joined Headington in 1953 after leaving the RAF. He was involved in a flying accident in the Pennines in 1945, breaking both his ankles but crawling away to get help for his colleagues, and subsequently being awarded the King's Commendation for Brave Conduct. His first football team was Dartford, with whom he won the Kent Senior Cup in 1947 before moving on to Kingstonian the following season. He made eight successive appearances for Charlton in 1950–51, converting from wing-half to defender, and was just starting to establish himself in the team when he was recalled by the RAF. He was stationed at Moreton-in-Marsh and captained the RAF football team, then joined Southern League Kidderminster in 1952, who finished third, their highest position in their history so far. In 1953 Croker opted not to continue in the RAF at the end of his 18-month recall and he signed for Headington while he ran a garage in Chipping Norton. He spent three 'enjoyable' years with United, but in 1956 he sustained a dislocated ankle and severe fracture of the leg in a Hospital Cup game against Oxford City, ending his playing career just after he had agreed to join Cheltenham Town. Croker was not insured, but Headington had insured him and gave him the £500 that they received. Croker regained fitness and started coaching youngsters at Cheltenham, while at the same time setting up in business, inventing the Croker Sno-Blo, a new type of snow blower. In September 1973, Croker was appointed FA secretary, succeeding Denis Follows, and he was almost immediately embroiled in controversy as he supported the appointment of Don Revie to succeed Sir Alf Ramsey. His lasting legacy came in 1974, when he proposed moving the Charity Shield to Wembley to be contested between the League Champions and FA Cup winners as the season's curtain raiser. In 1987 he was appointed president of Cheltenham Town, and he was also president of Kingstonian for many years. Croker, suffering from ill health, retired from the FA in 1989, to be succeeded by Graham Kelly. He published his autobiography, *The First Voice You Will Hear Is...*, in September 1987.

CROMBIE, Don

Inside-left
Born: 1932, Grimsby
United debut: 1 April 1954 v Guildford City
Final United game: 24 April 1954 v Weymouth
Appearances: 3
Goals: 1
Clubs: Huddersfield Town, Headington United (loan), Berwick Rangers, Duntochter Hibernian

Donald Crombie joined Headington on loan from Huddersfield while he underwent his National Service in the Oxford area, having made a good impression for the U's against an England Amateur XI at the Manor. Crombie failed to make the Huddersfield first team, and in 1956 he joined Berwick Rangers where he scored eight goals in 30 Scottish League appearances before his move to Duntochter Hibs, a now defunct Scottish Junior League club based in West Dunbartonshire.

CROOK, Les

Midfielder
Born: 26 June 1949, Manchester
United debut: 5 October 1968 v Portsmouth
Final United game: 5 October 1968 v Portsmouth
Appearances: 1
Clubs: Manchester Amateurs, Oxford United, Hartlepool United, Macclesfield Town

Leslie Ronald Crook joined United, initially on a trial basis, from Manchester Amateurs in the summer of 1968. After playing well for the reserves, he signed professionally in October 1968, but was substituted in the second half of his League debut and did not appear again for the first team. His second season at the Manor was blighted by injuries, and in July 1970 he was released, going to join Hartlepool. In his one season with the Pool he played 26 games and scored three goals, before moving on to Macclesfield.

CROSBY, Andy

Centre-back
Born: 3 March 1973, Rotherham
United debut: 15 December 2001 v Mansfield Town
Final United game: 8 May 2004 v Rochdale
Appearances: 120+2
Goals: 13
Clubs: Leeds United, Doncaster Rovers, Darlington, Chester City, Brighton & Hove Albion, Oxford United, Scunthorpe United

Andrew Keith Crosby joined Oxford on a free transfer from Brighton in December 2001. The commanding centre-back was Ian Atkins' first signing as manager and the player around whom Atkins built his team as captain. Crosby's penalty prowess was particularly prevalent, scoring 11 of his 13 goals from the spot and never missing. Towards the end of his time with United his pace was beginning to slow and on his release he was snapped up by Scunthorpe, with whom he enjoyed two promotions to reach the Championship. Crosby's career started as a junior with Leeds, with whom he signed his first contract in August 1990. He failed to make the first team at Elland Road and joined Doncaster on a free transfer in July 1991. He played 50 games for the Belle Vue outfit, scoring one goal, before moving to Darlington in December 1993. Crosby was with Darlo until joining Chester in July 1998; in that time he played 211 games and scored four goals, and was a runner-up in the Division Three Play-off Final in 1996. His stay with Chester lasted exactly a year before his £10,000 move to Brighton. He played 46 games for the Seals, scoring four goals, and while with Brighton he made 85 appearances and scored five goals. At Scunthorpe, Crosby played 191 games and scored 17 goals; the Iron were League Two runners-up in 2005 and

League One champions in 2007. Although relegated from the Championship in 2008, they won the League One Play-offs in 2009. In September 2010, Crosby was appointed assistant manager to Ian Adkins at Southampton.

CROSS, Jack

Centre-forward
Born: 5 February 1927, Bury
Died: 2006
United debut: 24 August 1957 v Cheltenham Town
Final United game: 7 April 1958 v Yeovil Town
Appearances: 40
Goals: 27
Clubs: Blackpool, Hendon, Guildford City, Bournemouth & Boscombe Athletic, Northampton Town, Sheffield United, Reading, Headington United, Weymouth, Poole Town

John Cross joined Headington United from Reading in February 1957, although injuries prevented him making his debut until the start of the following season. He left United for Weymouth when his work as a higher executive officer for the United Kingdom Atomic Energy Authority (UKAEA) at Harwell took him to Winfrith. A talented all-round sportsman, he joined Blackpool as an amateur in 1944, making his debut against Rochdale aged 17 as a replacement for Stanley Matthews, who was on duty with England. He had made four first-team appearances for Blackpool before being called-up for National Service. He represented the Army and played for Hendon and Guildford while on National Service, after which he joined Bournemouth. Cross earned a degree in economics while with the Cherries, for whom he played 216 games and scored 110 goals, but in 1953 Bournemouth rejected a bid for him from Division One side Blackpool without telling him and, Cross by name and nature, he put in a transfer request. The outcome was a club record £6,000 move to Northampton, where he scored 11 goals in 13 games before signing for Sheffield United for another record fee of £15,000. He played 54 games, scoring 26 goals, before breaking his ankle against Wolves in April 1955. While recuperating, in 1956 Cross applied for and was offered a job at Harwell, necessitating a move to Reading, who paid Sheffield United £3,000 for him. He played just 16 games for the Biscuitmen, scoring eight goals, before his move to the Manor. After leaving United he played 11 games for Weymouth, scoring twice, but his injuries were starting to tell and after a brief spell with Poole he retired from football in 1959. He continued to work for the UKAEA at Winfrith, Risley, and London before returning to Winfrith where he retired.

CROSS, Jimmy

Right wing-half
Born: 3 December 1929, Liverpool
Died: December 1999
United debut: 23 August 1958 v Hereford United
Final United game: 31 March 1959 v Nuneaton Borough
Appearances: 32
Clubs: Everton, Swindon Town, Headington United

James Keith Cross started his career with his home-town club Everton. In July 1953 he joined Swindon without having played for the Toffees' first team. He played 163 matches for the Robins, scoring six goals, before his move to Headington United. He was with the U's for one season, but was released in the summer of 1959.

CULLEN, John

Goalkeeper
Born: 13 August 1940, Dublin
Died: September 2010
United debut: 2 December 1961 v Chelmsford City
Final United game: 7 February 1962 v Clacton Town
Appearances: 9
Clean sheets: 2
Clubs: Ormeau Athletic, Wolverhampton Wanderers, Oxford United, Wolverhampton Wanderers (loan), Stafford Rangers, Kidderminster Harriers, Hednesford Town

John Cullen joined Oxford United from Wolves in 1961. He never played a first-team game for the Molineux club, but he was a member of their FA Youth Cup-winning side of 1958 (Wolves lost the first leg 5–1 to Chelsea, but won the second leg 6–1 to capture the trophy). He arrived at Molineux from Dublin side Ormeau Athletic. Before playing his first game for United he was loaned back to Wolves to help cover their goalkeeping problems. After leaving Oxford he had spells with Stafford and Kidderminster before joining Hednesford, where he became manager. He later played in the Wolverhampton Works Premier League and ran a garage in the town.

CURRAN, Hugh

Forward
Born: 25 September 1943, Carstairs, South Lanarkshire
United debut: 16 September 1972 v Millwall
Final United game: 4 October 1978 v Nottingham Forest
Appearances: 115+6
Goals: 43
Clubs: Home Farm (Ireland), Shamrock Rovers, Manchester United, Third Lanark, Corby Town, Millwall, Norwich City, Wolverhampton Wanderers, Oxford United, Bolton Wanderers, Oxford United, Banbury United

Hugh Patrick Curran joined Oxford initially from Wolves in September 1972 for £50,000, a huge sum for United at that time. The money was well spent as Curran was the side's leading scorer in 1972–73 with 17 goals, and again the following season with 14 goals. In September 1974 he moved to Bolton for £40,000 where he played 47 League games, scoring 13 goals, before returning to Oxford in 1977. In his second spell at the Manor, Curran was far less prolific, and after playing his last game he was forced to retire through injury in 1979. Curran's first club was Home Farm, who he joined as a youth in 1954 after his family moved to Dublin. He joined Shamrock in 1960 and then served time as an apprentice with Manchester United in 1962. He was released the following year and returned to Scotland to play for Third Lanark. He played nine League games for the now-defunct club, scoring four goals, before returning to England with Corby. His 34 goals in 32 League games brought him to the attention of Millwall, for whom he signed professionally in March 1964. In his first full season Curran was Millwall's leading scorer with 19 goals as the Lions finished in second place, two places and one point ahead of also-promoted Oxford. The following season, with Millwall at the top of Division Three, in January 1966 Curran was sold to Norwich for £12,500, and he scored on his debut in a 2–0 win over Carlisle. After a slow start, Curran started to find his form for the Canaries and became a cult hero when scoring a hat-trick in a derby game against Ipswich. In January 1969 Wolves bought Curran for £60,000 after the striker had scored 53 goals in 124 games for City. In November 1969 Curran won the first of his five Scotland caps (scoring one international goal, in a 3–1 defeat to England) and in 1972 he came on as a substitute in the second leg of the UEFA Cup Final defeat by Spurs. Curran scored 47 goals in 98 games before his first sojourn at the Manor. After leaving Oxford for the second time Curran joined Banbury, later becoming the Puritans' manager. He returned to his native Carstairs where he ran a hairdressing business before coming back to Oxfordshire to run pubs in Islip and Horton-cum-Studley and then working for the local bus company at a park-and-ride car park.

CUSACK, Nick

Forward
Born: 24 December 1965, Maltby, South Yorkshire
United debut: 15 August 1992 v Bristol Rovers
Final United game: 22 October 1994 v Wrexham (sub)
Appearances: 57+16
Goals: 13
Clubs: Long Eaton United, Alvechurch, Leicester City, Peterborough United, Motherwell, Darlington, Oxford United, Wycombe Wanderers (loan), Fulham, Swansea City

Nicholas John Cusack joined Oxford from Darlington for £95,000 in July 1992. He was not the most prolific of strikers, and despite his six-foot height his aerial ability was often questioned. In March 1994 United loaned him to Wycombe for four games, in which he scored once, and in November 1994 he left for Fulham on a free transfer. He was at Craven Cottage for almost three years, captaining the side to the Third Division Championship while making 141 appearances and scoring 19 goals, before moving to Swansea for £50,000 in October 1997. Cusack started with Long Eaton and Alvechurch, while graduating with a degree in politics, before joining Leicester in June 1987. He scored one goal in 19 appearances for the Foxes, but this was enough to tempt Peterborough into parting with £40,000 for him in July 1988. After scoring 12 goals in 54 games he joined Motherwell for £100,000 in August 1989. He played 88 games north of the border, finding the net on 24 occasions, and winning the Scottish Cup, which prompted Darlington into paying £95,000 for him in January 1992. He scored six goals in 21 games for Darlo before moving to the Manor. It was at Swansea that he was successfully converted into a defender, captaining them to the Third Division title in 2000. In March 2002 Cusack was appointed caretaker manager of the Swans, with a permanent appointment as player-coach following in April. He was released from his contract in September 2002 with Swansea sitting at the foot of the Football League. Cusack, who was chairman of the Professional Footballers' Association (PFA) since his election in November 2001, decided to retire from football and became a full-time executive with the PFA. Cusack had played 224 games for the Swans, scoring 17 goals.

CUTLER, Neil

Goalkeeper
Born: 3 September 1976, Perton, Staffordshire
United debut: 16 December 2000 v Northampton Town
Final United game: 24 February 2001 v Millwall
Appearances: 11
Clubs: Tamworth, West Bromwich Albion, Coventry City (loan), Chester City (loan), Crewe Alexandra, Chester City (loan), Stalybridge Celtic (loan), Leek Town (loan), Cheltenham Town (loan), Chester City, Aston Villa, Oxford United (loan), Stoke City, Swansea City (loan), Stockport County, Rotherham United, Bury

Neil Anthony Cutler joined United on loan from Aston Villa in December 2000. He failed to keep a clean sheet in his 11 games, of which just two were won, as the U's plummeted towards the basement division. Cutler's first team was Tamworth, where he was spotted and signed by West Brom, but he failed to break into the Baggies' first team. He had a loan spell with Coventry in October 1995, where again he did not make a first-team appearance, and another loan to Chester in March 1996, where he played once. He was signed by Crewe in July 1996 and a month later was loaned out to Chester again, where he played four games. He then had a two-month loan with Stalybridge Celtic, another month at Leek, who won that season's Northern Premier League, and a non-playing spell with Cheltenham before he joined Chester permanently in May 1998, without him having played a game for Crewe. Cutler played 26 games for Chester before Premiership side Aston Villa signed him in October 1999. In addition to his loan with Oxford, Cutler made just one substitute appearance for the Villains before he joined Stoke in July 2001. In his first season Stoke won promotion to the Championship and he went on to make 82 appearances for them, plus a 13-game loan spell with Swansea in March 2003 which included playing in the game that ensured their League survival. In June 2004 Cutler moved to Stockport, where he made 27 appearances before continuing on to Rotherham in August 2005. Cutler played 80 games for the Millers before a back injury forced his retirement from the game in September 2007 and in March 2008 he joined Bury as their goalkeeping coach. Bury re-registered Cutler as a player on non-contract terms in November 2010 to provide goalkeeping cover, but he moved to Scunthorpe with manager Alan Knill in March 2011. Cutler was capped at both England Schoolboy and England Youth levels.

D

DAVIDSON, David

Centre-half
Born: 25 March 1920, Lanark
Died: 1954
United debut: 7 April 1950 v Yeovil Town
Final United game: 27 September 1950 v Kidderminster Harriers
Appearances: 16
Clubs: Douglas Water Thistle, Bradford Park Avenue, Leyton Orient, Headington United

David Blyth Logie Davidson joined Headington from Orient after being released from his contract. At the end of the 1949–50 season he was being talked about as the defensive lynchpin United so desperately needed, but he played just nine games the following season before being relegated to the reserves, where he remained until the end of the 1950–51 season. Davidson had played 84 League games for Orient, scoring once, after signing for them from Bradford Park Avenue in 1946, having played 13 games for BPA earlier in the year. He had joined the Yorkshire club from Douglas Water Thistle, a now-defunct village team from Douglasdale, about 30 miles south-east of Glasgow. Davidson died aged just 33 in the first quarter of 1954, still residing in Hackney.

DAVIES, Craig

Forward
Born: 9 January 1986, Burton-on-Trent
United debut: 30 August 2004 v Notts County (sub)
Final United game: 7 January 2006 v Shrewsbury Town (sub)
Appearances: 26+29
Goals: 8
Clubs: Manchester City, Oxford United, Hellas Verona (Italy), Wolverhampton Wanderers (loan), Oldham Athletic, Stockport County (loan), Brighton & Hove Albion, Yeovil Town (loan), Port Vale (loan), Chesterfield, Barnsley

Craig Martin Davies joined United's youth scheme from Manchester City, having previously been on Shrewsbury's books. After half-a-dozen substitute appearances, Ramon Díaz, in his opening game in charge, gave the youngster his first start, and he was rewarded with a fine individual goal. Five more goals followed during the season, which brought him to the attention of Brian Flynn, who gave Davies a couple of games for Wales Under-21s, for whom he became one of just four players to have scored a hat-trick. John Toshack then invited Davies to join the senior Wales squad for their post-season training camp in Spain. Davies was also allegedly the subject of a transfer bid from Premiership Charlton Athletic during the summer of 2005, but chairman Firoz Kassam spurned their offer. In August 2005 Davies won his first senior Wales cap, coming on as a substitute in a friendly international against Slovenia. Davies was unable to maintain a regular first-team place with United, and in December 2005 he let it be known that he was not going to sign a new contract at the end of the season. He was sold to

Italian side Hellas Verona of Serie B for £85,000 in the January transfer window. He failed to shine in Italy, making just one League appearance, and was loaned out to Wolves for the whole of the 2006–07 season, where he played 27 games and scored three goals. In June 2007 he left Verona for a nominal fee to join Oldham, scoring a last-minute winner on his debut. However, poor form in the first part of the season led to him being loaned to Stockport, where he scored five goals in 14 games. In January 2009 Davies moved to Brighton for a fee believed to be £150,000, but in 17 months there he played in just 23 games, scoring only one goal, which was on his debut. In September 2009 he played four games on loan to Yeovil, and in January 2010 he joined Port Vale on loan, initially for one month but that was extended to the end of the season after he impressed in his opening games, including scoring his first goals in a year. In July 2010 Davies' contract with Brighton was cancelled and he immediately signed for Chesterfield, becoming the first player to score at their new B2Net Stadium, in a pre-season friendly against Derby. After scoring 23 goals as Chesterfield won League Two, he signed for Barnsley in June 2011. Davies was capped eight times by Wales Under-18s (scoring twice), seven times by the Under-19s, eight times for Wales Under-21s (three goals), and has won five full Wales caps.

DAVIES, Rob

Midfielder
Born: 24 March 1987, Tywyn, Gwynedd
United debut: 8 August 2008 v Barrow
Final United game: 8 August 2008 v Barrow
Appearances: 1
Clubs: Wrexham, West Bromwich Albion, Kidderminster Harriers (loan), Barakaldo CF (Spain), Hednesford Town, Oxford United, Worcester City

Robert John Davies joined United as a free agent, initially on a trial, in July 2008. The central-midfielder was then offered a short-term deal until the end of August, but was released after the contract expired. Davies started with Wrexham, joining West Brom in 2006 for £30,000, the highest fee yet paid for a youth player. In November 2006 he was loaned out to Kidderminster for four games and in March 2007 he had an unsuccessful trial with Colchester United. After making just one substitute appearance for the Baggies, coming on in the final minute of normal time in an extra-time FA Cup defeat at Reading in January 2006, he was released at the end of the 2006–07 season. Davies was offered a contract by Spanish side Barakaldo, but after 11 games and one goal he returned to England and in February 2008 he joined Hednesford. He was released at the end of the season, having scored three goals in 10 games and having refused the offer of a contract with the Pitmen. Following his release by Oxford he signed for Worcester City. He left Worcester in the summer of 2009, but signed for them again in September that year.

DAVIS, Steve

Centre-back
Born: 26 July 1965, Birmingham
United debut: 17 February 1998 v West Bromwich Albion
Final United game: 6 May 2000 v Millwall
Appearances: 43+5
Goals: 3

Clubs: Stoke City, Crewe Alexandra, Burnley, Barnsley, York City (loan), Oxford United (loan), Oxford United, Macclesfield Town, Northwich Victoria, Nantwich Town

Steven Peter Davis joined United from Barnsley, initially on loan for one month before signing permanently. He was a strong defender, but it was clear that he was nearing the end of his career as he suffered from lack of pace. It came as little surprise that after finishing at Oxford he dropped out of the League to join Macclesfield. Davies started his career in 1982 as a junior with Stoke but he failed to make their first team and he signed for Crewe in August 1983. Over the next four years, Davis made 166 appearances for the Alex, scoring once, before Burnley signed him for £15,000 in October 1987. He played 183 games for the Clarets, finding the net 11 times, after which Barnsley paid £180,000 for him in July 1991. In his time at Oakwell, Davis played 119 games and scored 10 goals; he also had a three-game (one goal) loan spell at York in September 1997 before his move to Oxford. After leaving the Manor, Davis was with Macclesfield for less than a month before he joined Northwich Victoria. At the end of his first season with the Vics, Davis was appointed assistant manager to Jimmy Quinn, taking over permanently in June 2003, by which time he had stopped playing for the club after 24 games for them, taking over the youth team. With the Vics second-bottom of the Conference in September 2003, Davis resigned and returned to managing the youth team. In December 2003 he joined Nantwich, becoming player-manager in May 2004. Davis led Nantwich to two promotions to reach the Northern Premier League in 2008, and also won the FA Vase in 2006. Davis played 71 League games for Nantwich, scoring twice, before being appointed assistant manager at Crewe in May 2009. Davis was an England youth international.

DAY, Matt

Defender
Born: 24 March 1987, Hungerford
United debut: 12 August 2006 v Halifax Town
Final United game: 7 March 2009 v Forest Green Rovers
Appearances: 86+25
Goals: 7
Clubs: Portsmouth, Oxford United, Oxford City, Hungerford Town, Eastleigh, Hungerford Town

Matthew James Day was signed by Jim Smith from Portsmouth in July 2006 after impressing on trial, and he made his debut in Oxford's first game in the Conference, against Halifax. Day came through the ranks at Pompey but never played for their first team. He could play at both right-back and centre-back, and earned a reputation for scoring from powerful long-range shots. Day was released by United in August 2009 after he returned from close season out of condition, and he immediately signed for Oxford City. However, in September he was released by new manager Mike Ford and he joined Hungerford. He was signed by Eastleigh in November 2009 to replace Warren Goodhind, but in February 2010, after just six appearances, he was released and he returned to Hungerford.

DAY, Rhys

Centre-back
Born: 31 August 1982, Bridgend
United debut: 15 August 2009 v Histon (sub)
Final United game: 16 May 2010 v York City (sub)
Appearances: 19+4
Clubs: Manchester City, Blackpool (loan), Mansfield Town (loan), Mansfield Town, Aldershot Town, Oxford United, Mansfield Town (loan), Mansfield Town

Rhys Day joined Oxford from Aldershot in July 2009, although he was mainly used as cover and failed to get a regular first-team place. He came on as a substitute in United's Play-off Final win over York City in May 2010 and was instrumental in setting up Oxford's third goal. He did not play for United in the Football League and in October 2010 he joined Mansfield on loan for three months, and was immediately made their captain. The loan was made permanent in January 2011. Day started as a youth with Manchester City in June 2000 but did not play for City's first team. He had a 13-game loan with Blackpool in December 2001 and played a further nine games on loan with Mansfield in November 2002. This was made permanent in March 2003 and Day went on to make a further 112 appearances for the Stags, scoring 14 goals, before joining Aldershot in July 2006. He was made captain in his second season and led the Shots to the Conference title, but he was released at the end of their first season in the League whereupon he joined Oxford. Day has won two Wales Under-19 caps and 11 Wales Under-21 caps.

DEAN, Brian

Inside-forward
Born: 1933
Died: December 2006
United debut: 31 March 1956 v Tonbridge
Final United game: 22 March 1958 v Kettering Town
Appearances: 33
Goals: 11
Clubs: Oxford City, Headington United, Witney Town

Brian W Dean, nicknamed Dixie, played for Oxford City for 10 years before signing as a professional with Headington in 1956. After completing his National Service he had the chance to join either Bolton or Tottenham, but decided to stay loyal to Headington. He eventually quit the full-time game due to a bad knee injury. Dean later coached Marston FC and had a spell at Witney Town. He also played bowls for Oxfordshire.

DEEGAN, Mark

Goalkeeper
Born: 12 November 1971, Liverpool
United debut: 17 September 1994 v Brighton & Hove Albion
Final United game: 14 January 1995 v Bristol Rovers
Appearances: 5
Clean sheets: 1
Clubs: Crewe Alexandra, Droylsden, Stockport County, Wigan Athletic, Holywell Town, Oxford United, Bangor City, Barrow, Bangor City, Stafford Rangers, Caernarfon Town, TNS Llansantffraid, Colwyn Bay

Mark Deegan joined Oxford from Holywell in the League of Wales. He had spells with Liverpool and Everton as a junior before joining Crewe, but Droylsden was where he made his first-team debut. He joined Stockport in the summer of 1993 and Wigan in September 1993 but did not play for either of them before he moved to Holywell Town, where he played 27 games before his move to the Manor. While at Holywell he won his only Wales semi-professional cap in a 2–1 defeat by England in February 1994. He left Oxford in the summer of 1995 and returned to Wales with Bangor, for whom he appeared in the UEFA Cup in a 4–0 defeat by Wizdew Lodz. He moved to Barrow in August 1995, playing 85 games in two seasons, before returning to Bangor to make 13 appearances for them before the end of the 1996–97 season. His next stop was with Conference side Stafford Rangers in 1997–98 before he returned to Wales with Caernarfon Town, where he played 64 games over two seasons, moving to TNS in 1999. He played 34 games for the Llansantffraid club, including four European ties, before joining Colwyn Bay in March 2001.

DEERING, Sam

Midfielder
Born: 26 February 1991, Tower Hamlets
United debut: 12 August 2008 v Weymouth (sub)
Final United game: 22 January 2011 v Northampton Town (sub)
Appearances: 29+36
Goals: 4
Clubs: Oxford United, Newport County (loan), Barnet (loan)

Sam Deering joined United in May 2007 as a 16-year-old scholar, having previously spent time with both Chelsea and Charlton Athletic. The 5ft 5in midfielder caught the eye during pre-season friendlies in the summer of 2008, making his debut shortly afterwards. He broke his leg at Salisbury on Boxing Day 2008 in manager Chris Wilder's first game in charge and while in hospital he was in trouble for making racist remarks on a social networking website. As part of his recovery he spent time on loan at Newport in August 2009, making four appearances. Deering was a substitute in United's Conference Play-off win over York City at Wembley in May 2010, setting up Alfie Potter for the club's third goal. He struggled to make an impact on Oxford's return to the League, and had to be disciplined for turning up late to both training and an away game at Wycombe Wanderers, for which he was dropped. He returned to Newport on loan in November 2010, playing three games, and in February 2011 he went on loan to Barnet until the end of the season, winning the club's Goal of the Season and Young Player of the Season awards after his 16 games and two goals. He signed a two-year deal with the Bees in May 2011. Deering won two England C caps in May 2010, in wins against the East of Scotland and the Republic of Ireland Under-23s.

DEMPSTER, John

Centre-back
Born: 1 April 1983, Kettering
United debut: 29 January 2006 v Rushden & Diamonds
Final United game: 23 January 2007 v Woking (sub)
Appearances: 16+10

Clubs: Rushden & Diamonds, Oxford United, Kettering Town (loan), Kettering Town, Darlington

John Dempster joined Oxford from Rushden & Diamonds in January 2006, signed by his former manager Brian Talbot at the same time as Andy Burgess. Dempster was sent off on his debut against his former club, with whom he played 79 games, scoring four goals, and won a Division Three Championship medal in 2003. By the time that he left the Kassam for Kettering on loan in February 2007, Dempster had lost his first-team place, along with his pace, and his loan was made permanent on its completion. In his first full season with the Poppies he captained them to the Conference North title and won the Players' Player of the Year, the Supporters' Player of the Year, and the President's Player of the Year, and he won the supporters' award again in 2010. In January 2011 Dempster joined Darlington on a free transfer. Dempster won caps for Scotland Under-20s and Under-21s while with Rushden, and while with Oxford he played for England C.

DENIAL, Geoff

Forward
Born: 3 January 1932, Sheffield
United debut: 29 September 1956 v Exeter City Reserves
Final United game: 1 December 1962 v Workington
Appearances: 199
Goals: 51
Clubs: Sheffield United, Headington United, Rugby Town

Geoffrey Denial joined Headington from Sheffield United in 1955 but his debut was delayed after he was called-up for service during the Suez Crisis. As a part-time professional, Denial supplemented his income by working as a heating engineer. Denial set several records in his time at United, becoming the first player since the club turned professional to score three hat-tricks in a season in 1959–60, in which he was the club's leading scorer with 32 goals, including scoring in a club-record seven games in a row. He also set a club record of scoring in nine consecutive away games that season. Denial started as a goalkeeper for Sheffield Boys and at the age of 16 he played for Oaksfold, the nursery side of Sheffield Wednesday, and was selected to play for the county at centre-half. He signed professional forms for Sheffield United at 17, and had played 16 games for the Blades before he arrived at Headington, for a moderate fee, at left-back. After leaving United he had a spell at Rugby.

DENTON, Eddie

Midfielder
Born: 18 May 1970, Oxford
United debut: 30 April 1988 v Newcastle United (sub)
Final United game: 2 May 1988 v Manchester United (sub)
Appearances: 0+2
Clubs: Oxford United, Witney Town, Watford, Newbury Town, Chesham United, Abingdon Town, Aylesbury United, Oxford City, Slough Town

Edward John Denton joined Oxford's YTS in 1986. In the summer of 1988, having already played twice for the first team in the top flight and being named United's Young Player of the Year, he was promoted to the senior squad, but in the summer of 1989 he was released without playing any further matches. After a spell with Witney he joined Watford where he made just two League appearances before returning to the non-League with Newbury, Chesham, and Abingdon Town. In February 1997 he joined Aylesbury, for whom he scored two goals in 17 games, before leaving for Oxford City. He moved to Slough in the summer of 1998 and went on to make 75 appearances for the Rebels, scoring four goals, becoming manager of their reserves in June 1999, and then becoming manager in June 2003. Under his charge Slough beat League One Walsall in the FA Cup and won the Ryman League Cup in 2005. He left in September 2006 after his work for the Oxford & County Newspaper Group became more demanding.

DÍAZ, Emiliano

Right-winger
Born: 22 June 1983, Naples (Italy)
United debut: 5 March 2005 v Grimsby Town (sub)
Final United game: 23 April 2005 v Southend United (sub)
Appearances: 2+5
Clubs: Avellino (Italy), River Plate (Argentina), Talleres Córdoba (Argentina), Deportivo Colonia (Uruguay), Oxford United, Defensores de Belgrano (Argentina), Defensa y Justicia (Argentina), Platense (Argentina), San Lorenzo (Argentina), San Luis de Puebla (Mexico), All Boys (Argentina), Guaraní Asunción (Paraguay)

Ramon Emiliano Díaz was the son of manager Ramon Díaz, who brought him to Oxford from Uruguayan side Colonia. Nominally a right-winger, it is doubtful that Emiliano would have been given an opportunity at United if his father was not the manager, as he appeared to lack the basic skills required of a professional footballer, as did his brother Michael, who also signed for Oxford but who did not get to grace the Kassam pitch. Emiliano's career started at Avellino in Italy; he later joined River Plate, where Ramon was such a successful coach for many years. He made just one appearance for them in 2001–02 before joining Talleres, for whom he failed to make any appearances. He did manage four games for Colonia during the same season that he played for Oxford. After leaving the Kassam in May 2005 he returned to Argentina, where he played twice for Defensores. The following season he made one appearance for Defensa, and in 2007–08, after leaving Platense, he played nine games for San Lorenzo. He then joined San Luis, a subsidiary club of Mexico's America, where Ramon was coincidentally the coach. He had unsuccessful trials with Major League Soccer clubs DC United and New York Red Bulls, as well as with Italian side Benevento. He returned to Argentina to play for All Boys, but in 2010 he moved on without playing for them to join Paraguayan side Asunción.

DICKSON, Joe

Inside-forward
Born: 31 January 1934, Liverpool
Died: November 1990
United debut: 30 August 1958 v Boston United
Final United game: 7 December 1960 v Tonbridge
Appearances: 101
Goals: 39
Clubs: Liverpool, Headington United, Cambridge United

Joseph James March Dickson joined Headington from Liverpool in the summer of 1958. He joined the Reds as an 18-year-old in June 1952 and turned professional the following year, but had to wait almost four years for his first game. When it eventually arrived he scored four goals in his six Liverpool appearances at the end of the 1955–56 season. While at Anfield Dickson won three England Youth caps, having previously been selected as a reserve for England Schoolboys. Before joining Headington Dickson had scored 33 goals in 75 reserve matches at Anfield. Dickson lost his Headington first-team place at the end of 1960 and in the 1961 close season he was released, moving on to join Cambridge United.

DOBLE, Ryan

Forward
Born: 1 February 1991, Abergavenny
United debut: 2 April 2011 v Bury (sub)
Final United game: 16 April 2011 v Accrington Stanley
Appearances: 1+2
Clubs: Southampton, Oxford United (loan), Stockport County (loan)

Ryan Alan Doble joined Oxford in March 2011 on loan until the end of the season from Southampton. He was unable to participate in the first game of his loan spell because he was in Andorra on international duty with Wales Under-21s, for whom the Andorra match was his fifth cap. Doble joined the Southampton Academy aged eight, and he progressed through the ranks with the Saints, signing as a professional on his 17th birthday. In February 2011 Doble played three games on loan with Stockport County, where he both scored and was sent off in his second appearance at Bradford City. Doble had already won three Wales Under-17 caps and three Wales Under-19 caps to add to his Under-21 appearances.

DOBSON, James

Left-winger
Born: 13 October 1991, Abu Dhabi
United debut: 25 October 2008 v Hayes & Yeading United (sub)
Final United game: 8 November 2008 v Dorchester Town (sub)
Appearances: 0+2
Clubs: Oxford United, Oxford City

James Edward Dobson became a first-year scholar in 2008. After just two substitute appearances for United he was released when his scholarship expired in the summer of 2010 and he moved to neighbours Oxford City. He played for City and City Nomads while coaching with United's Centre of Excellence.

DOBSON, Tony

Centre-back
Born: 5 February 1969, Coventry
United debut: 17 December 1994 v Hull City
Final United game: 2 October 1995 v York City
Appearances: 5
Clubs: Coventry City, Blackburn Rovers, Portsmouth, Oxford United (loan), Peterborough United (loan), West Bromwich Albion, Gillingham, Northampton Town, Forest Green Rovers

Anthony John Dobson joined Oxford on loan from Portsmouth in December 1994. He started as a trainee at Coventry, signing professionally in July 1986. He played 63 games for Coventry, scoring once, before Blackburn signed him for £300,000 in January 1991. Over two seasons he played 49 games for Rovers, moving to Portsmouth for £150,000 in September 1993. In addition to his loan with Oxford, Dobson also made four appearances on loan with Peterborough in January 1996. Apart from those hiatuses, Dobbo played 76 games for Pompey, scoring three goals. He was released in May 1997, joining West Brom in August on a monthly contract. In the next 13 months he made 15 appearances for the Baggies before moving to Gillingham for £25,000 in September 1998. He played just two games for the Gills before Northampton paid Gillingham the same amount later that month to take him to Sixfields. Although he was with the Cobblers until May 2000, he played just 13 matches in that time, leaving for Forest Green Rovers in August 2000. He played three games for Rovers before becoming manager of Rugby Town in February 2001. He was at the Valley for four years, winning promotion to the Southern League Premier Division. He resigned in May 2005 to take over at Solihull Borough where he stayed for one season, returning to Rugby in September 2008. Dobson was capped four times by England Under-21s.

DOHERTY, Sam

United debut: 20 August 1955 v Gloucester City
Final United game: 28 April 1956 v Merthyr Tydfil
Appearances: 33
Goals: 2
Clubs: Headington United

DONALDSON, O'Neill

Forward
Born: 24 November 1969, Birmingham
United debut: 31 January 1998 v Nottingham Forest
Final United game: 28 February 1998 v Stockport County
Appearances: 6
Goals: 2
Clubs: Hinckley United, Shrewsbury Town, Doncaster Rovers, Mansfield Town (loan), Sheffield Wednesday, Oxford United (loan), Stoke City, Torquay United, Halesowen Town

O'Neill McKay Donaldson was a forward who joined Oxford on loan from Sheffield Wednesday in January 1998. United tried to sign him permanently, but allegedly his agent blocked the deal. He started with Hinckley United in 1990, moving to Shrewsbury on a free transfer in November 1991. He played 28 games for the Shrews and scored four goals, before joining Doncaster in August 1994. He played 12 games and scored two goals, and in December 1994 he had a five-game loan spell with Mansfield in which he scored seven goals, before Sheffield Wednesday paid £50,000 for him in January 1995. Before his time at the Manor, Donaldson managed just 14 games for the Owls, and after his return from Oxford in March 1998 he moved to Stoke on a free transfer. He was with them for just two matches before his release at the end of the season. In September 1998 he joined Torquay where he made 33 appearances, scoring three goals, in just under three years, but was hampered by a broken leg. In July 2001 he stepped down from League football to sign for Halesowen before retiring from football. In November 2010 he joined Team United Birmingham for the season to play futsal.

DONNELLY, Ron

United debut: 24 October 1959 v Yeovil Town
Final United game: 24 October 1959 v Yeovil Town
Appearances: 1
Goals: 1
Clubs: Headington United

Signed before the start of the 1959-60 season, released at the end of it.

DONOVAN, Terry

Forward
Born: 27 February 1958, Liverpool
United debut: 1 February 1983 v AFC Bournemouth
Final United game: 12 February 1983 v Cardiff City
Appearances: 3
Clubs: Louth United, Grimsby Town, Aston Villa, Portland Timbers (USA) (loan), Oxford United (loan), Burnley, Rotherham United, Blackpool (loan)

Terence Christopher Donovan joined Oxford on loan from Aston Villa in February 1983. His career started with Lincolnshire side Louth juniors in 1972, graduating to the senior side in 1975 after trials with Everton, Nottingham Forest, and Derby County. From Louth he made the short move to Grimsby as an amateur in 1975, signing professionally the following year, where he scored 28 goals in 75 appearances. He joined Aston Villa in July 1979 for £75,000, scoring six goals in 17 League games, and where he also spent April to August 1982 playing 15 games and scoring one goal for Oregon side Portland Timbers, in addition to his loan spell at the Manor. Burnley signed him for £25,000 from Villa in February 1983. Donovan played alongside Billy Hamilton initially, but after six goals in 20 games he moved to Rotherham in September 1983 for £10,000 less than Burnley had paid for him. The following season he played two games on loan with Blackpool, but a bad knee injury put paid to his career in May 1986 after 11 League matches with the Millers. He retired to Grimsby and became a mortgage adviser. Donovan won one full Ireland cap, in 1979 against Czechoslovakia, and in 1981 he was capped for Ireland B against West Germany B. He also won one Ireland Under-21 cap and was an England Schoolboy international.

DOUDOU

Winger
Born: 11 September 1980, Kinshasa (DR Congo)
United debut: 3 January 2005 v Bury (sub)
Final United game: 3 January 2005 v Bury (sub)
Appearances: 0+1
Clubs: AS Monaco (France), Queen's Park Rangers, Farnborough Town, Oxford United, Racing Club Paris (France)

Aziana Doudou Ebeli Mbombo was the first player signed by Ramon Díaz for Oxford United, but the diminutive winger just played half a game before having to return to his native Democratic Republic of the Congo for domestic reasons after a member of his immediate family had been killed in the DR Congo civil war, the deadliest conflict since World War Two. He returned to Oxford a few weeks later, but he had already been replaced in the squad. His European football career started as a schoolboy trainee with Monaco, where he played for six years before joining QPR in August 2001 after impressing in two pre-season trial matches. His first year's wages and accommodation were paid for by two Rangers fans. He played 39 games for QPR over two seasons, scoring three goals, but was released in 2003. The following season he played eight games for Farnborough, scoring one goal. He was with Racing Club Paris in 2006 but failed to make an appearance for them. In 2002 he was called-up for the DR Congo squad for a friendly against Belgium, but he did not play.

DOUGHTY, Eric

Left-back
Born: 9 April 1932, Radstock, Somerset
United debut: 12 March 1960 v Yeovil Town
Final United game: 12 March 1960 v Yeovil Town
Appearances: 1
Clubs: Peasedown, Arsenal, Plymouth Argyle, Headington United (loan), Bristol City

Eric Doughty played one game for Headington on loan from Plymouth to allow manager Arthur Turner to assess him. His lack of further matches implies that he failed to impress. Doughty began his working life as a coal miner in Somerset. He joined Arsenal but did not play a game for them. He was signed for Plymouth in 1958 by Jack Rowley, who had never seen Doughty play but who needed a left-back. However, he made just one appearance for Argyle. He later joined Bristol City, but again failed to appear for them, retiring with an injury and becoming a foreman at a factory in Bath, becoming secretary of the Working Mens' Club in 1971. In 2002 he was appointed as a specialist skilled director of the Norton Radstock Regeneration Company.

DOUGLAS, Stuart

Forward
Born: 9 April 1978, Enfield
United debut: 23 October 2001 v Carlisle United
Final United game: 20 November 2001 v Leyton Orient (sub)
Appearances: 1+3
Clubs: Luton Town, Oxford United (loan), Rushden & Diamonds (loan), Boston United, Rovaniemen Palloseura (Finland), Dagenham & Redbridge, Crawley Town, Eastleigh, Lymington & New Milton (loan), Weymouth, Bath City, Newport County (loan), Dorchester Town, Poole Town

Stuart Anthony Douglas joined Oxford on loan from Luton in October 2001. Although fast, Douglas was never prolific and often found it difficult to find new clubs. The dreadlocked striker started as a trainee with the Hatters in 1995, making 183 appearances for them and scoring 23 goals, including on his debut. He followed his experience at the Kassam with a loan to Rushden in January 2002, playing nine games for the Diamonds. In August 2002, following an unsuccessful trial with Gillingham, he joined Boston on a free transfer, going on to score eight goals in 63 games for them in two years. After leaving Boston he played 10 games, scoring three goals, for Finnish side RoPS before returning to England to sign for Dagenham in November 2004. He played just five games for the Daggers, moving to Crawley at the end of the season. His spell with the Red Devils was hardly more successful, playing just eight games and scoring once before his contract was terminated following a row with the manager. He signed for Eastleigh where he scored six goals in 18 appearances, and for a while combined playing with being the club's commercial manager, and had a brief loan spell with Lymington. After two years with Eastleigh, during which he qualified as a sports therapist, he joined Weymouth in July 2007 as player-physiotherapist. He played 18 games, scoring once, for the Terras before moving to Bath in July 2008, where he played 50 League games, scoring 11 goals, before having to undergo surgery in the summer of 2009, after which he failed to regain his place in the side. In February 2010 he had a six-game loan with Newport, scoring one goal, before leaving Bath to sign for Dorchester in August 2010. He was released by Dorchester in October 2010 after eight games, and joined nearby Poole Town the following month. Meanwhile, Douglas started a four-year physiotherapy degree at Brunel University in 2009.

DOYLE, John

Right-back
Born: 8 February 1960, Oxford
United debut: 3 December 1977 v Shrewsbury Town
Final United game: 15 May 1982 v Wimbledon
Appearances: 80
Clubs: Oxford United, Torquay United, Oxford City

John Joseph Doyle signed for Oxford as an apprentice in 1976. He was initially a winger with Oxford Boys before dropping back into defence at United. He retired in the summer of 1979, but recanted in October and returned to the side. After the arrival of Jim Smith, Doyle was released and in the summer of 1982 he moved to Torquay. He played 41 League games, scoring three goals in the 1982–83 season before moving back to Oxford to join City.

DREYER, John

Midfielder/Centre-back
Born: 11 June 1963, Alnwick
United debut: 7 October 1986 v Gillingham
Final United game: 7 May 1988 v Nottingham Forest
Appearances: 72+4
Goals: 2
Clubs: Wallingford Town, Oxford United, Torquay United (loan), Fulham (loan), Luton Town, Stoke City, Bolton Wanderers (loan), Bradford City, Cambridge United, Stevenage Borough, Long Melford

John Brian Dreyer, nicknamed 'Tumble', was a midfielder and later a defender who joined Oxford in January 1985 from nearby Wallingford. He had a five-game loan spell with Torquay in December 1985 and in March 1986 he joined Fulham on loan until the end of the season, scoring twice in 12 games. It was after his return from Craven Cottage that he broke into the United team, playing regularly in the top flight until his £140,000 move to Luton in June

1988. He scored 15 goals in his 250 appearances for the Hatters in six years at Kenilworth Road, after which he joined Stoke on a free transfer in July 1994. His 60 games for the Potters (four goals) sandwiched a four-match loan spell at Bolton in March 1995, prior to his £25,000 transfer to Bradford in November 1996. He played 93 games for the Bantams, scoring five times, and was part of the side that won promotion to the Premiership in 1999. In July 2000 he joined Cambridge after rejecting a new deal at Valley Parade and made 40 appearances and scored one goal in his one season at the Abbey. In July 2001 he had a brief trial back with Oxford but despite Mark Wright wanting to sign him, chairman Firoz Kassam refused to sanction it, believing the club already had enough central-defenders, so in August Dreyer joined Stevenage instead. In January 2003 Dreyer had a spell as caretaker manager of Borough, and in May 2003 he left to manage Maidenhead United, with whom he reached the quarter-finals of the FA Trophy and achieved promotion to the Conference South. He left Maidenhead in November 2004, joining Long Melford as a player while being assistant manager of Hemel Hempstead Town. He joined Rushden & Diamonds as assistant manager in December 2006, returning to Stevenage as assistant manager in May 2008.

DRUCE, Mark

Forward
Born: 3 March 1974, Oxford
United debut: 30 October 1991 v Southend United (sub)
Final United game: 16 March 1996 v Notts County (sub)
Appearances: 21+37
Goals: 4
Clubs: Oxford United, Rotherham United (loan), Rotherham United, Hereford United, Kidderminster Harriers, Woking, Oxford City

Mark Andrew Druce joined Oxford as a YTS trainee in 1990. In December 1991 he was promoted to the senior squad and remained with the club until his move to Rotherham in September 1996, initially on loan. After scoring four goals in six games the Millers paid United £50,000 to sign Druce in October 1996, but he made just 32 appearances and scored just one goal in the next 19 months before leaving for Hereford in July 1998. Druce scored three goals in 19 League games for the Bulls and in January 1999 Kidderminster paid £10,000 to sign him. He scored seven goals in 22 games for the Harriers and in June 2000 he joined Woking. He played just nine games for the Cards, scoring twice, before ending back in Oxford at Court Place Farm with City.

DRYSDALE, Brian

Left-back
Born: 24 February 1943, Wingate, County Durham
United debut: 13 August 1977 v Shrewsbury Town
Final United game: 25 February 1978 v Hereford United
Appearances: 18
Clubs: Lincoln City, Hartlepool United, Bristol City, Reading (loan), Oxford United, Frome Town, Clevedon Town, Shepton Mallet

Brian Drysdale joined Oxford from Bristol City in the summer of 1977, his experience leading to him being given the captaincy. He started his career with Lincoln, making his debut in April 1960. He played 24 games for the

Imps before joining Hartlepool in the summer of 1965. He was a member of Pool's 1968 promotion-winning squad and was named the club's Player of the Decade for the 1960s. Drysdale scored twice in 182 appearances before joining Bristol City in 1969. He played 282 League games for the Robins, scoring three goals, before a 16-game loan spell with Reading impressed Oxford manager Mick Brown enough to sign him for United on his release from Bristol City. He was released by Oxford at the end of the 1977–78 season and joined Frome as player-manager. He continued playing in the non-League in the West Country, before becoming a carpenter in Bristol.

DUFFY, Rob

Forward
Born: 2 December 1982, Swansea
United debut: 12 August 2006 v Halifax Town
Final United game: 20 January 2008 v Exeter City
Appearances: 55+12
Goals: 27
Clubs: Rushden & Diamonds, Stamford (loan), Cambridge United, Kettering Town, Gainsborough Trinity, Stevenage Borough, Oxford United, Wrexham (loan), Newport County, Mansfield Town, Grimsby Town

Robert James Duffy joined Oxford in August 2006 after impressing Jim Smith on trial. He scored a penalty on his debut against Halifax in Oxford's first game in the Conference and ended his first season as United's leading scorer with 21 goals. His penalty-taking was exemplary, missing just once from 15 attempts (including in a penalty shoot-out in United's Play-off semi-final defeat by Exeter in May 2007). In his second season with United he failed to capture his previous form after breaking his arm in September 2007. He was sent off just 20 seconds after coming on as a substitute in his first match back. He was loaned to Wrexham in January 2008, making six substitute appearances as they were relegated from the Football League. He was released by Oxford at the end of the season and signed for Newport after an unsuccessful trial with Mansfield. He scored three goals in 16 appearances for the Welsh club before Mansfield decided that they did want him after all. He moved permanently to Field Mill in January 2009, scoring on his debut, after Newport manager Dean Holdsworth released him so that his brother David Holdsworth could sign him for the Stags. In January 2010 Duffy moved to Grimsby but in May 2011 he was told that he was free to find another club after scoring two goals in 17 games for the Mariners. After playing for Swansea side Garden City as a youngster, Duffy played his youth football for Charlton Athletic. When they decided not to take him on he followed Graham Westley, former Charlton youth team manager, to Rushden in December 2000. He played 37 games for the Diamonds, scoring four goals, but a broken kneecap saw him miss out between August 2003 and the following January, and he failed to regain his previous form. He was loaned to Stamford, where he scored twice in two games. After another brief loan spell with the Daniels he then had a short period with Cambridge, playing nine games, and made a handful of appearances for Kettering, before he was released and joined Gainsborough Trinity in January 2006. He ended the season with Stevenage, where he played just one game and which is where he was playing when Malcolm Elias, United's former youth development officer, recommended him to Smith. Duffy was capped for Wales Youth and Wales Under-21s.

DUNCAN, Ben

Inside-left
United debut: 18 November 1950 v Weymouth
Final United game: 30 April 1955 v Lovell's Athletic
Appearances: 187
Goals: 30
Clubs: Distillery (Northern Ireland), Airdrieonians, Headington United

Irishman Ben Duncan joined United from Airdrieonians in November 1950, having played 58 games and scored 10 goals over the previous four seasons since joining from Distillery. His Headington career was a distinguished one, playing for the Southern League double-winners in 1953 and in the famous FA Cup run the following season, but it had an ignominious end as he was one of five players who refused to sign new contracts in a protest over non-payment of appearance fees, and in May 1955 he returned to Scotland.

DUNCAN, Colin

Midfielder
Born: 5 August 1957, Plymstock
United debut: 9 November 1974 v Portsmouth
Final United game: 26 January 1980 v Barnsley
Appearances: 206+1
Goals: 7
Clubs: Oxford United, Gillingham, Reading, Aldershot, Fleet Town, Basingstoke Town

Colin John Duncan joined Oxford as an apprentice in December 1973, having been with Reading as a schoolboy, and was promoted to the senior squad in December 1974. He was a member of the squad that won the Midlands Youth League in 1975 and his terrier-like midfield qualities earned him an extended run in the first team at just 17 years old after Gerry Summers had handed him his debut. Summers was manager of Gillingham when they paid their record fee of £60,000 for Duncan in January 1980. He moved to Reading in September 1983, where he scored three goals in 62 games, and thence to Aldershot in the summer of 1985. After playing 15 League games for the Shots, Duncan moved to Fleet Town, later joining Southern League outfit Basingstoke in January 1987. He later set up as a self-employed painter and decorator in Thatcham.

DURNIN, John

Forward
Born: 18 June 1965, Bootle
United debut: 11 February 1989 v Portsmouth
Final United game: 1 May 1993 v Notts County
Appearances: 158+22
Goals: 47
Clubs: Waterloo Dock, Liverpool, West Bromwich Albion (loan), Oxford United, Portsmouth, Blackpool (loan), Carlisle United (loan), Carlisle United, Kidderminster Harriers, Rhyl, Port Vale, Accrington Stanley

John Paul Durnin was signed for Oxford from Liverpool by Brian Horton in February 1989 for £225,000. He had joined the Reds from Waterloo Dock for just £500 in 1986 and failed to get into the first team, making just three appearances plus scoring 60 goals in 84 games in the Central League. In October 1988 he played five games on loan at West Brom, scoring two goals, before his move to the Manor. At Oxford he quickly became a fans' favourite, as much for his off-field antics as for his goalscoring exploits, earning the nickname 'Johnny Lager'. In July 1993 he moved to Portsmouth for £200,000 and made 207 appearances for the Fratton Park club, scoring 33 goals. He played six games on loan to Blackpool in October 1999, scoring twice, and in December 1999 he scored once in a seven-game loan with Carlisle, who he then joined permanently in February 2000. He played a further 16 games, scoring two goals, at Brunton Park before the end of the season. He joined Kidderminster in October 2000 where he scored nine goals in 32 games, and he then moved to Rhyl as player-coach in July 2001. He signed for Brian Horton's Port Vale in December 2001 and he played 50 games for the Valiants, scoring just twice. In August 2003 he joined Accrington where he scored four goals in 15 games and at the end of that season he retired from playing. In the summer of 2006 he joined Southport as a coach, but other commitments led to him resigning in October 2006.

DYER, Alex

Forward

Born: 14 November 1965, Forest Gate
United debut: 14 August 1993 v Portsmouth
Final United game: 15 April 1995 v Wycombe Wanderers
Appearances: 76+14
Goals: 8
Clubs: Watford, Blackpool, Hull City, Crystal Palace, Charlton Athletic, Oxford United, Lincoln City, Barnet, FC Maia (Portugal), Huddersfield Town, Notts County, Kingstonian, Hayes, Dulwich Hamlet

Alexander Constantine Dyer was a forward who Brian Horton signed for Oxford from Charlton in the summer of 1993. Dyer was an apprentice with Watford, but it was with Blackpool that he turned professional in October 1983. He played 129 games for the Tangerines, scoring 21 goals, before Hull signed him for £37,000 in February 1987. After 66 games and 15 goals he joined Crystal Palace for £250,000 in November 1988. In two years with Palace he played just 27 games, scoring five goals. Charlton then signed him for £100,000 in November 1990. Dyer made 86 appearances for Charlton and scored 14 goals before his move to the Manor. He left Oxford for Lincoln in August 1995, but made just two appearances for the Imps before his move to Barnet the following month. He completed the season at Underhill, playing 37 games and scoring two goals, before spending a season with Portuguese side Maia. He then linked up with Brian Horton again when he signed for Huddersfield in August 1997 on a short-term contract, playing 13 games and scoring two goals. Dyer moved on to Notts County in March 1998, making 92 appearances and scoring six goals before dropping out of the Football League in December 2000 to play for Kingstonian. He played just one match, against Rushden & Diamonds in the Bob Lord Trophy, and after an unsuccessful trial with Reading he signed for Hayes in January 2001, where he again made just one appearance, before joining Dulwich Hamlet in March 2001. By this time he was already coaching a youth side at Reading, but in April 2004 he joined West Ham as an assistant to the sports scientist, becoming reserve team coach in September 2008.

E

E'BEYER, Mark

Midfielder
Born: 21 September 1984, Stevenage
United debut: 18 September 2004 v Yeovil Town (sub)
Final United game: 18 February 2006 v Cheltenham Town
Appearances: 11+9
Goals: 2
Clubs: Watford, Wimbledon, Stevenage Borough (loan), Oxford United, Crawley Town, Hayes, Cambridge City, Wivenhoe Town, Hitchin Town, Wealdstone

Mark Edward E'Beyer joined Oxford from Wimbledon in July 2004, following a successful pre-season trial. In February 2005 E'Beyer was diagnosed with testicular cancer and required an operation to remove the tumour, returning to action in August 2005. In May 2006 Jim Smith gave E'Beyer permission to train with other clubs and after an unsuccessful trial with Northampton Town he joined Conference side Crawley. E'Beyer started as an apprentice with Watford, but was not offered a contract at Vicarage Road and so moved to Milton Keynes in 2003 to join the Dons, who were still calling themselves Wimbledon until becoming MK Dons on 7 August 2004. He did not play a game with the Dons' first team, and in March 2004 he had a loan spell with Stevenage, but again did not make it on to the pitch. E'Beyer, who was of Maltese descent, left Crawley for Hayes, where he played 11 games. He joined Cambridge City in December 2007, but was released in October 2008 and signed for Wivenhoe. He was with them for just one month before joining Hitchin, for whom he was sent off on his debut. In August 2009 he moved to Wealdstone, where he remained until November 2010.

EDWARDS, Bill

United debut: 15 September 1949 v Worcester City
Final United game: 15 September 1949 v Worcester City
Appearances: 1
Clubs: Headington United, Stamford

William Edwards was injured on his United debut, which therefore also became his final appearance for the club. He was transferred from Headington to Stamford in November 1949, scoring on his debut for the United Counties League side.

EDWARDS, Christian

Centre-back
Born: 23 November 1975, Caerphilly
United debut: 26 February 2000 v Wrexham
Final United game: 8 February 2003 v Rochdale
Appearances: 10+1
Goals: 1

Clubs: Swansea City, Nottingham Forest, Bristol City (loan), Oxford United (loan), Crystal Palace (loan), Tranmere Rovers (loan), Oxford United (loan), Bristol Rovers, Swansea City (loan), Forest Green Rovers, Aberystwyth Town

Christian Nicholas Howells Edwards had two separate loan spells at Oxford, both from Nottingham Forest. Edwards joined Forest from Swansea, where he began his career as a trainee, going on to play 134 games for the Swans, scoring four goals, before Forest paid £275,000 for him in March 1998. His first loan from Forest came later that year, when he played three games for Bristol City in December, and it was not until February 2000 that he played five games for United, which is when he scored his only goal for the club, in a 4–1 home defeat by Wrexham. A nine-game loan spell with Crystal Palace followed in November 2001, and he played 17 games on loan to Tranmere in September 2002 before he returned for his second spell with United in January 2003. In between all these loan deals, Edwards managed to play 56 times for Forest, scoring three goals, but he moved to Bristol Rovers shortly after his second loan with Oxford expired. He was with the Pirates for three seasons, playing 110 games and scoring three goals, and had a three-game loan back at his original club, Swansea, before being released in the summer of 2006. He joined Forest Green Rovers in August, going on to play nine games for them. In January 2007 Edwards signed for League of Wales side Aberystwyth. In September 2009 he was briefly their caretaker manager, becoming the assistant to new manager Alan Morgan. In April 1996 Edwards won his only full Wales cap, to add to his two Wales B caps and seven Under-21 caps. In July 2009 Edwards was awarded a first-class honours degree in sports development from the University of Wales Institute, Cardiff.

EELE, Ron

Outside-right
Born: 1935, Ploughley, Bucks
Died: February 1998
United debut: 24 August 1955 v Guildford City
Final United game: 7 April 1958 v Yeovil Town
Appearances: 27
Goals: 8
Clubs: Thame United, Headington United, Banbury Spencer

Ronald Thomas Eele played for Headington United while living in Thame.

ELLIOTT, Jack

Outside-right
Born: 23 March 1929, Tonypandy, Mid-Glamorgan
United debut: 14 October 1950 v Chelmsford City
Final United game: 26 April 1952 v Cheltenham Town
Appearances: 43
Goals: 8
Clubs: Woking, Millwall, Gloucester City, Headington United, Hastings United, Bognor Regis Town, Gravesend & Northfleet, Grantham, Bourne Town, Chobham

Raymond John Elliott, also known as 'Young' Jack, was a tall, strong, fast outside-right who joined Headington United from Gloucester, where he had played for just 11 weeks after completing his National Service. During his conscription he had played in the same Army team as Cliff Nugent while they were based in Aldershot. As a schoolboy he played for the YMCA and Farnborough Grammar School before joining his local side Woking. He was spotted by Millwall and moved to the Den, making his debut against West Ham. He played just two League games for the Lions before his call-up. In 1952 Elliott left United for Hastings, where he converted to a defender, because they offered him the opportunity to pursue a career as a PE teacher in a local school. He played for Bognor Regis simultaneously while studying at college there and he also played cricket for Bognor. He then joined Gravesend before teaching PE while playing for Grantham, Bourne Town and Chobham. Elliott then moved into management with Camberley and Woking and later did some scouting work for Maurice Evans before retiring in Sandhurst.

ELLIOTT, Matt

Centre-back
Born: 1 November 1968, Wandsworth
United debut: 6 November 1993 v Millwall
Final United game: 11 January 1997 v Bradford City
Appearances: 181
Goals: 25
Clubs: Epsom & Ewell, Charlton Athletic, Torquay United (loan), Torquay United, Scunthorpe United (loan), Scunthorpe United, Oxford United, Leicester City, Ipswich Town (loan)

Matthew Stephen Elliott was arguably one of the best centre-backs to have played for Oxford in the Football League. Commanding in the air, he also showed a deft touch with the ball at his feet and his return of 25 goals is astonishing for a defender. He joined Oxford from Scunthorpe for £150,000 in November 1993 and left for Leicester for a club record £1.6 million in January 1997. Although Oxford had already slipped out of the Division One Play-offs by the time he left, his departure is for many the turning point that led to United's decade-long decline. Elliott started his career playing for his local club in Epsom. Charlton's physio helped out at Epsom and managed to get Elliott a trial with the Addicks, who eventually paid Epsom £5,000 for him. He made just one appearance for Charlton before joining Torquay, initially on loan, for £10,000 in March 1989. He stayed with the Gulls for over three years, playing 158 games and scoring 20 goals before a loan move to Scunthorpe in March 1992 turned into a £50,000 transfer. He made 79 appearances for the Iron, scoring eight goals, before Denis Smith brought him to the Manor and made him the bedrock of United's 1996 promotion-winning defence. Martin O'Neill had been thinking of buying Elliott for Leicester for some time, but had concerns about his lack of pace. However, he took the plunge and signed the 28-year-old defender, who went on to earn 18 caps for Scotland courtesy of a Scottish grandmother, and score one international goal. Elliott spent eight seasons at Filbert Street, scoring 33 times in 290 games and captaining them to a 2–1 League Cup Final win over Tranmere in February 2000, in which Elliott also scored both City's goals. In March 2004 Elliott had a 10-game loan to Ipswich, before retiring from playing in January 2005. Three years later, in June 2008, he was persuaded out of retirement to become assistant manager of Hednesford Town by his former Torquay teammate Dean Edwards, the club's manager. He left in May 2009, becoming co-manager of Oadby Town the following month, but in May 2010 he stepped down following a cut in the playing budget. In October 2010 Elliott was appointed assistant manager of Stafford Rangers by his former Leicester teammate Tim Flowers, becoming caretaker manager in December after Flowers' departure, and appointed manager of Stafford in January 2011. However, Stafford were relegated from the Conference North at the end of the season and in May 2011 Elliott resigned.

EVANS, Bernard

Forward
Born: 4 January 1937, Chester
United debut: 8 December 1962 v Mansfield Town
Final United game: 8 October 1963 v Bradford Park Avenue
Appearances: 14
Goals: 3
Clubs: Wrexham, Queen's Park Rangers, Oxford United, Tranmere Rovers, Crewe Alexandra, Guildford City, Rhyl

Bernard Evans joined Oxford from QPR, where he had scored 47 goals in 114 games. United paid a club joint-record £5,000 for the striker, who had set a Football League record when scoring for Wrexham against Bradford City after just 25 seconds. Wrexham was Evans' first club, where he scored 56 goals in 125 games before his move to QPR for £2,000. Described as being as mobile as a fridge but with a lethal shot and a bullet header, Evans scored in his final game for Oxford, a 5–2 defeat, before his move to Tranmere in October 1963. He scored five goals in 12 League matches for Rovers before his move to Crewe the following season. He left for Guildford without making the Alex first team.

EVANS, Ceri

Centre-back
Born: 2 October 1963, Christchurch (New Zealand)
United debut: 1 April 1989 v Leicester City
Final United game: 17 April 1993 v Charlton Athletic
Appearances: 132+3
Goals: 3
Clubs: Nelson United (New Zealand), Christchurch United (New Zealand), Dunedin Technical (New Zealand), Christchurch United (New Zealand), Oxford United, Marlow

Ceri Lee Evans signed for Oxford after asking for a trial while a Rhodes Scholar at the University of Oxford, where he gained a first-class honours degree in experimental psychology at Worcester College. Evans was already an established New Zealand international when he arrived in Oxford, having twice won the National League with Christchurch, and he was named Footballer of the Year in New Zealand. He was described by New Zealand defender Garry Lund as 'probably New Zealand's premier centre-back'. Before signing for Oxford Evans won a Blue in 1989 by playing for the University of Oxford in the Varsity match against the University of Cambridge at Craven Cottage, in which Evans scored Oxford's second goal in a 3–2 win. He was selected for the following year's Varsity match, but by this time he had signed professional forms with United, who refused to release him. After playing at Marlow under Peter Foley while studying psychiatry at the Maudsley Hospital in south London, Evans retired from football and became a forensic psychiatrist in Christchurch, New Zealand. Evans' first club was Nelson United in 1980–81, after which he played for Christchurch in 1982. He moved to Dunedin the following year and played again for Christchurch from 1984–87. He won 85 New Zealand caps, seven of them while at the Manor. Evans' father, Gwyn Evans, played for Crystal Palace at centre-half between 1958 and 1963, after which he emigrated to Christchurch, New Zealand.

EVANS, Paul

Midfielder
Born: 1 September 1974, Oswestry
United debut: 13 September 2008 v Kidderminster Harriers
Final United game: 1 January 2009 v Salisbury City (sub)
Appearances: 2+2
Clubs: Shrewsbury Town, Brentford, Bradford City, Blackpool (loan), Nottingham Forest (loan), Nottingham Forest, Rotherham United (loan), Swindon Town, Bradford City, Oxford United, FC Halifax Town, Farsley Celtic

Paul Simon Evans joined Oxford on a short-term contract in September 2008 but he was released in January 2009 after Chris Wilder took over, having failed to make an impact on the first team. He started in 1993 as a trainee with Shrewsbury, making 238 appearances and scoring 36 goals for the Shrews before Brentford paid £110,000 for him in March 1999. Evans played 155 games for the Bees, scoring 34 goals, and won the first of his two Wales caps. In August 2002 he moved to Bradford City for the first time, going on to play 45 games and score five goals for the Bantams. He had a 10-game loan spell with Blackpool in January 2003, during which he scored one goal, and in March 2004 he moved to Nottingham Forest, after a brief loan spell, for £25,000. He played 53 games for Forest, scoring four goals, before he was dropped by Gary Megson. He had a four-game loan at Rotherham in November 2005 in a bid to regain fitness, but was injured and did not play again until moving to Swindon in July 2006, after a trial with Halifax. He played 18 games for the Moonrakers, scoring three goals, before returning to Bradford. He featured in 28 games for the Bantams without scoring and was released in June 2008, failing to find another club, despite trials with Darlington and Morecambe, before Oxford signed him. After his release by the U's he joined Halifax, and in August 2009 he moved to Farsley Celtic.

EVANSON, John

Midfielder
Born: 10 May 1947, Newcastle-under-Lyme
United debut: 20 August 1966 v Bournemouth & Boscombe Athletic
Final United game: 17 February 1974 v Crystal Palace
Appearances: 168+11
Goals: 11
Clubs: Towcester, Oxford United, Blackpool, Miami Toros (USA), Fulham, AFC Bournemouth, Poole Town

John Michael Evanson was a no-nonsense midfielder who joined Oxford as an amateur after his father requested that Arthur Turner give him a trial in the summer of 1964. He had previously played for Towcester while a trainee manager of a boot and shoe firm in Northampton. After a handful of Hellenic League appearances, Evanson was given a professional contract in February 1965. He came through the reserves, where Gerry Summers converted him from an inside-forward, and became a regular first-team player in 1970–71. He moved to Blackpool for what was then United's record sale of £40,000 in February 1974. He played 67 League games for Blackpool without scoring and was released in April 1976, going to play for North American Soccer League outfit Miami Toros in the summer, playing 16 games and scoring one goal. On his return to England, Evanson joined Fulham, where he played in midfield alongside George Best and Rodney Marsh. Evanson scored five goals in 95 League games for the Cottagers before moving to Bournemouth in 1979. He was at Dean Court for two years, playing 53 League games and scoring two goals, before joining Poole and entering the pub and food trade. In November 2010 he became landlord of the Black Horse in Cherhill, Wiltshire.

F

FAHY, John

Centre-forward
Born: 13 May 1943, Paisley
United debut: 18 April 1964 v Bradford City
Final United game: 18 March 1966 v York City
Appearances: 25
Goals: 14
Clubs: Luton Town, St Neots Town, Letchworth Town, Bedford Town, Oxford United, Cambridge United, Bedford Town, Margate, Germiston Callies (South Africa), Toronto Metros (Canada), Toronto Hungaria (Canada)

John Joseph Fahy was a tall, bustling centre-forward who joined Oxford United from Bedford in January 1964 for £2,500. It took Fahy some time to establish himself in the United side, not getting a regular run of games until March 1965, when his goals helped earn the U's promotion from the Fourth Division. He started regularly in the Third Division until mid-September, but then made only a handful of appearances before he was released at the end of the 1965–66 campaign, whereupon he moved to Cambridge United. Although born in Scotland, Fahy's family moved to England when he was young and his first club was Luton in 1960, where he played as an amateur in their youth team, during which time he was also selected to represent Bedfordshire. He played a few games for St Neots at the end of the 1960–61 season before moving to Letchworth for the start of the following season. In September 1961 he impressed Bedford when playing against them in the FA Cup and they signed him shortly afterwards. In January 1964 he scored Bedford's first as they beat Newcastle United 2–1 in the FA Cup third round, moving to Oxford almost immediately afterwards. He had scored 30 goals in 52 games for the Eagles. After playing for Cambridge, Fahy briefly returned to Bedford in March 1967, scoring four goals in 17 games, before joining Margate in October 1967. He scored a hat-trick within 33 minutes of his debut, his first goal coming after 10 seconds, and he went on to score 53 goals in 82 games, including four against Gravesend, and a hat-trick of headers within three minutes against Tonbridge. Fahy also scored a hat-trick in his last Margate match, against Ramsgate in a Southern League Cup Final replay win. At the end of 1967–68 Fahy was released (not surprisingly with reluctance) as he emigrated to South Africa, where he joined Germiston Callies for £350. He was there for four years, surviving a knee injury that could have ended his career, before moving to Canada in 1972 to play for Toronto Metros in the NASL, scoring three goals in 10 games. He then joined Toronto Hungaria of the Canadian League as he went part-time for three seasons, becoming the League's leading scorer in two of them. In 1986 Fahy moved to Australia to run a McDonald's franchise, and in 2003 he was a local councillor in New South Wales.

FARR, Tony

United debut: 22 January 1955 v Merthyr Tydfil
Final United game: 5 March 1955 v Dartford
Appearances: 4
Clubs: Headington United

Tony Farr was a local lad who joined Headington United at the start of the 1954–55 season, and was released at the end of it.

FARRELL, Craig

Forward
Born: 5 December 1982, Middlesbrough
United debut: 1 February 2009 v Lewes
Final United game: 26 April 2009 v Northwich Victoria (sub)
Appearances: 7+8
Goals: 2
Clubs: Leeds United, Carlisle United (loan), Carlisle United, Exeter City, York City, Oxford United (loan), Rushden & Diamonds, AFC Telford

carlotti

Craig Wayne Farrell joined Oxford from York at the end of January 2009, on loan until the end of the season. Farrell started as a junior with Middlesbrough, having a successful trial with Leeds when he was 15, signing professionally in August 2002 and representing England Under-17s almost immediately. Failure to get into the first team led to a 10-game loan spell with Carlisle, during which he scored six goals, leading to a permanent contract in November for a fee of around £50,000 dependent on appearances. Farrell went on to play a further 85 games for the Cumbrians, notching 18 goals, before Paul Simpson released him in May 2005. He signed for Exeter in August, scoring eight goals in 39 games, before being released, joining York in June 2006. Farrell played 101 games for the Minstermen prior to his loan with Oxford, scoring 21 goals. After he returned to York he joined Rushden in June 2009 in an exchange deal for Michael Rankine, with £10,000 also going York's way. After 12 goals in 71 games Farrell left the Diamonds and signed for AFC Telford in June 2011.

FEAR, Peter

Midfielder
Born: 10 September 1973, Sutton
United debut: 11 September 1999 v Gillingham
Final United game: 21 April 2001 v Bristol Rovers
Appearances: 35+12
Goals: 3
Clubs: Wimbledon, Oxford United, Kettering Town, Crawley Town, Sutton United, Havant & Waterlooville, Carshalton Athletic, Sutton United

Peter Stanley Fear joined Oxford from Wimbledon on a free transfer in July 1999. Fear joined Wimbledon as an apprentice in July 1990, turning professional two years later. Fear played 88 games for the Premiership club, scoring four goals, before moving to the Manor. At the time Oxford were struggling both financially and on the pitch, and Fear's performances failed to aid the situation, providing little in the way of Premiership quality. After United's relegation to the basement Fear was released and he joined Kettering in August 2001. Fear was highly influential during the Poppies'

Southern League Championship season in which they won promotion back to the Conference National, but at the end of the season, after 24 League games for Kettering, he unexpectedly signed for Crawley. In his two seasons with Crawley he captained them to the Southern League title, scoring six goals in 49 League games. In 2004 he joined Sutton for the first time, playing 23 League games and scoring three goals before moving to Havant & Waterlooville in February 2005. He played 13 games for the Hawks, scoring once, but in the summer of 2005 he failed to reappear for training and despite being under contract he refused to return to Havant, eventually signing for Carshalton. In December 2006, after five League appearances for Carshalton, he returned to Sutton, making 25 League appearances and scoring twice before retiring at the end of the 2006–07 season.

FEARNLEY, Harry

Goalkeeper
Born: 16 June 1939, Penistone, Yorkshire
United debut: 5 October 1963 v Newport County
Final United game: 5 February 1966 v Shrewsbury Town
Appearances: 104
Clean sheets: 34
Clubs: Penistone Juniors, Huddersfield Town, Oxford United, Doncaster Rovers

Henry Perry Fearnley joined Oxford from Huddersfield in October 1963 for £4,000. He had spent 11 years as a professional with Huddersfield, making 90 League appearances, and because of problems finding accommodation in Oxford, Fearnley continued to live and train up north. Fearnley starred in United's FA Cup run to the quarter-finals in 1964 and is generally considered one of the better 'keepers to have played for United. In February 1966 he suddenly moved back north to Doncaster, leaving United short of goalkeeping cover. He played 32 League games for Rovers, winning a Division Four Championship medal in his first season. In 1969 Fearnley was appointed manager of Emley (now Wakefield) for their first season in the Yorkshire League, in which they finished runners-up in the second division (but were denied promotion) and won the Yorkshire Cup.

FEEHAN, Iggy

Goalkeeper
Born: 17 September 1926, Dublin
Died: 11 March 1995
United debut: 2 September 1959 v Chelmsford City
Final United game: 5 December 1959 v Boston United
Appearances: 19
Clean sheets: 4
Clubs: Bohemians (Ireland), Waterford (Ireland), Manchester United, Northampton Town, Brentford, Headington United

John Ignatius Feehan, nicknamed 'Sonny', joined Headington from Brentford in the summer of 1959. He started as an amateur with Dublin side Bohemians in 1942, turning professional when he signed for Waterford two years later. In November 1948 he joined Manchester United as understudy for Jack Crompton. He made his League debut a year later and played 14 games for the Red Devils before he was sold to Northampton for £525 in

August 1950. Feehan made 39 League appearances for the Cobblers over the next two seasons, but in 1952 he dropped out of sight for two years, before re-emerging at Brentford. He played just 30 League games over five years with the Bees before he joined Headington, who he left in the summer of 1960.

FISHER, Alex

Forward
Born: 30 June 1990, Wycombe
United debut: 14 October 2007 v Farsley Celtic (sub)
Final United game: 28 December 2008 v Ebbsfleet United (sub)
Appearances: 1+17
Goals: 2
Clubs: Oxford United, Brackley Town (loan), Bognor Regis Town (loan), Oxford City (loan), Oxford City, Jerez Industrial (Spain)

Alex Paul Fisher scored prolifically for United's youth team and reserves. The tall, curly-haired striker was fast and clever and in March 2008 he had a loan spell with Brackley on work experience, scoring on his debut, but he was recalled after just one week. He joined Bognor Regis in September 2008, also on a work experience loan deal, but was told by United in January 2009 that he could find another club. He immediately joined Oxford City on loan, signing permanently in June 2009. In October 2009 he won a scholarship to the Glenn Hoddle Academy in Jerez, Spain, from where he played for Jerez Industrial in 2010.

FITZGERALD, Scott

Forward
Born: 18 November 1979, Hillingdon
United debut: 26 November 2005 v Grimsby Town
Final United game: 21 December 2005 v Mansfield Town (sub)
Appearances: 2+1
Goals: 1
Clubs: Northwood, Watford, Swansea City (loan), Leyton Orient (loan), Brentford (loan), Brentford, Oxford United (loan), Walsall (loan), AFC Wimbledon (loan), Basingstoke Town, Hayes & Yeading United, Wealdstone

Scott Peter Fitzgerald joined Oxford on loan from Brentford in November 2005, scoring on his debut in a home defeat by Grimsby. His career started with Northwood, for whom he made his debut in 1998, going on to score 95 goals in 220 games before signing for Watford in February 2003. He scored on his debut and the following season he was the Horns' top scorer, but thereafter he lost his place and found himself on loan to Swansea for four games in September 2004, followed by one loan appearance with Orient in February 2005 in which he was sent off. The following month he enjoyed a more successful four games at Brentford, which returned two goals and led to a permanent contract. Fitzgerald scored four goals in his further 22 games for the Bees, but fell out of favour, leading to his loan with Oxford. In February 2006 he spent two months with Walsall, playing five games without scoring, and at the start of the 2006–07 season Fitzgerald scored eight goals in 19 games on loan at AFC Wimbledon. His contract with Brentford was terminated in January 2007 and he moved to Basingstoke. He was with Basingstoke for one season, scoring 12 goals in 58 League games, before moving on to Hayes & Yeading in August 2008. After 25 goals in 70 appearances he signed for Wealdstone in June 2010.

FLAY, Steve

Full-back
Born: 2 October 1954, Poole
United debut: 16 October 1973 v Fulham
Final United game: 19 October 1974 v Notts County
Appearances: 4
Clubs: Oxford United, Yeovil Town, Salisbury City (loan)

Stephen Flay was taken on as an apprentice by United in 1971 and was promoted to the seniors in the summer of 1972. His brother Dick had also been an apprentice at the club, but was released at the end of his apprenticeship, just before Steve was signed on. Three years later, after failing to dislodge John Shuker from the first team, he left the club and signed for Yeovil. In January 1979 he joined Salisbury on loan, having scored three goals for the Glovers.

FLEMING, John

Midfielder
Born: 1 July 1953, Nottingham
United debut: 30 October 1971 v Carlisle United
Final United game: 15 March 1975 v West Bromwich Albion
Appearances: 76+8
Goals: 2
Clubs: Oxford United, Lincoln City, Port Vale (loan), Wollongong City (Australia)

John Joseph Fleming came to Oxford aged 17, too old to be taken on as an apprentice. He was offered a full-time contract in September 1970 but never really cemented a regular first-team place and was released at the end of the 1974–75 season. He was part of the Imps squad that won the Fourth Division title in his first season. He went on to play 141 games for Lincoln, scoring 18 goals before joining Port Vale on a three-game loan in March 1980. After emigrating to Australia he played for and coached Wollongong. He was later head coach at Kemblawarra in New South Wales and in the 2006–07 season he joined Illawarra Premier League side Port Kembla as head coach, but he was sacked in May 2009 after a dismal start to the season. At the start of the 2010 season he was appointed coach of Wollongong United.

FLOOD, John

Winger
Born: 21 October 1932, Southampton
United debut: 22 August 1959 v Weymouth
Final United game: 22 August 1959 v Weymouth
Appearances: 1
Clubs: Southampton, Bournemouth & Boscombe Athletic, Headington United

John Ernest Flood joined Headington from Bournemouth at the start of the 1959–60 season. He played just one game for the U's, and was released at the end of his first season. He started as a junior with Southampton, becoming professional in 1952 and going on to play 122 League games for the Saints, scoring 28 goals. He joined Bournemouth in 1958, scoring three goals in 17 League games before his move to the Manor.

FOGG, David

Full-back
Born: 28 May 1951, Dingle, Merseyside
United debut: 17 August 1976 v Cambridge United
Final United game: 15 February 1985 v Crystal Palace
Appearances: 331+5
Goals: 21
Clubs: Wrexham, Oxford United

David Fogg was a full-back who joined Oxford from Wrexham on a free transfer in the summer of 1976 after his release by Wrexham. He joined Wrexham from Belvedere aged 21 in May 1970 after finishing his apprenticeship as a toolmaker, going on to play 176 games for the Welsh outfit. Although he did not score for the Red Dragons, at Oxford he was made penalty taker and found the net regularly. He also played in both full-back positions and could fill in well at centre-back. He played with Oxford until his late thirties, after which he joined United's coaching staff and managed the reserves. He became Everton's youth team coach and then helped set up Chester City's youth system before he was illegally approached by Shrewsbury to become their assistant manager. After working for Blackpool as head of youth development until 2004, Fogg then became a scout for Everton.

FOLEY, Dominic

Forward
Born: 7 July 1976, Cork (Ireland)
United debut: 25 March 2003 v Bury (sub)
Final United game: 19 April 2003 v Exeter City
Appearances: 4+2
Clubs: St James's Gate (Ireland), Wolverhampton Wanderers, Watford (loan), Notts County (loan), Ethnikos Piraeus (Greece) (loan), Watford, Queen's Park Rangers (loan), Swindon Town (loan), Queen's Park Rangers (loan), Southend United (loan), Oxford United (loan), Sporting Braga (Portugal), Bohemians (Ireland), KAA Gent (Belgium), Cercle Brugge (Belgium)

Dominic Joseph Foley joined Oxford on loan from Watford in March 2003. However, he failed to score for United and returned to Vicarage Road. His career started in 1994 as a youth with north Cork outfit Charleville AFC and then with Leinster side St James's Gate, from where he joined Wolves in 1995. His 27 games for Wanderers yielded three goals, and he also had an eight-game and one goal loan spell with Watford in February 1998 followed by a three-game loan to Notts County in December 1998. His first spell abroad came later that season, with a seven-game loan to Athens side Ethnikos Piraeus, for whom he scored three goals. On his return to England he joined Watford on a free transfer in July 1999. His first season with the Hornets ended with relegation, but that year he won his six Republic of Ireland caps, scoring two international goals. His lack of goals for Watford led to him falling down the pecking order and he was loaned to QPR in October 2001, making just one appearance, and Swindon the following month where he scored once in five games. A second loan to QPR followed in March 2002, during which he scored once in four games, and then he had a five-game loan to Southend in February 2003, again without scoring, before his unsuccessful loan with Oxford. Overall he played 40 matches for Watford, scoring six goals, before he was released in the summer of 2003 and he tried his luck overseas. His first port of call was Portugal's oldest city, Braga, where he stayed for one season, playing 12 games and scoring one goal. After leaving Braga he returned to Ireland to join Bohemians, where an impressive performance against KAA Gent in an Intertoto Cup game prompted the Belgians to enquire about him. Bohemians' dire financial straits meant that they had failed to pay Foley some bonuses, an excuse he used to cancel his contract and move to Belgium with Gent in 2005. His time with Gent saw him become more settled and he was handed the captaincy in his third season, but new manager Michel Preud'homme dropped him before selling him controversially to rivals Cercle Brugge in January 2009, after 103 games and 27 goals for Gent.

FOLEY, Peter

Forward
Born: 10 September 1956, Bicester
United debut: 22 March 1975 v Oldham Athletic
Final United game: 5 February 1983 v Huddersfield Town (sub)
Appearances: 306+15
Goals: 90
Clubs: Oxford United, Gillingham (loan), Bulova (Hong Kong), Aldershot, Oxford United, Iggesund HIF (Sweden), Witney Town, Iggesund HIF (Sweden), Swansea City, Exeter City, Oxford City

Peter James Foley joined Oxford as an apprentice in 1973 after being spotted by manager Gerry Summers playing for Bardwell Boys. He was part of the squad that won the Midlands Youth League in 1975, having already been promoted to the seniors in September 1974. Foley also played for Marston Saints, which at the time was used by Oxford as a youth development club. He became the only United player to be top scorer in four different seasons, with 13 goals in 1976–77, 21 goals the following season, 11 in 1978–79 and seven goals in 1980–81 (joint with Malcolm Shotton). His 90 goals for Oxford make him the club's joint-third leading scorer of all time. While with Oxford he played four times as an Ireland Youth international and won six Ireland Under-21 caps. Foley was also selected for the full Ireland side for a friendly in Malta, but because Oxford needed him for a vital League game he was forced to withdraw. United also turned down a £100,000 bid for him from Ron Atkinson's West Bromwich Albion. In February 1983 he played five games on loan with Gillingham but failed to score. In the summer of 1983 Foley left United and joined the now defunct Bulova FC in Hong Kong for 15 months. On his return to England he joined Aldershot for whom he scored twice in nine league games before he returned to Oxford on non-contract terms. He joined Swedish side Iggesund HIF in 1985, returning in the winter to become player-coach of Witney Town. He returned to Iggesund for the following season, where he was player-manager, after which he joined Swansea City on non-contract terms for three months but did not play for the first team. Foley made a cameo appearance for Exeter in March 1987 on a one-month contract but was released after Exeter ensured their safety from relegation. He then became manager of Thame United, later managing and playing for Oxford City after their reformation in July 1990, making 19 appearances, his last being against Bedford Town in May 1993. He managed City until the end of the following season, going on to take charge of Marlow, managing them to their FA Cup giant-killing over Oxford United in November 1994, which did not save him from the sack in 1995. In 2000–01 Foley managed Brackley Town, taking charge of Didcot Town in September 2002. He won two successive Hellenic League Division One titles with Ardley Town after joining them in October 2005, before his appointment as caretaker manager of Banbury side Easington Sports in December 2008, a role he combined with managing his son's Brackley youth team, and in 2010 he took over at Easington as manager.

FOLLAND, Rob

Midfielder
Born: 19 June 1979, Swansea
United debut: 7 August 1999 v Stoke City (sub)
Final United game: 16 November 2001 v Leyton Orient (sub)
Appearances: 28+24
Goals: 3
Clubs: Oxford United, Port Talbot Town, Aberystwyth Town, Maesteg Park, Pontardawe Town, Neath Athletic, Goytre United

Robert William Folland joined Oxford's Youth Training Scheme in 1996, joining the senior squad two years later. In June 2002 he was released by United and joined Port Talbot. Folland made two appearances for Aberystwyth in 2004–05, playing for Maesteg Park on joint-registration terms the same season. He joined Pontardawe Town before moving to Neath Athletic in August 2006. Folland played 18 games for the Eagles until the summer of 2010 when he joined Port Talbot-based side Goytre United. Folland was a Wales Youth international and also won one Wales Under-21 cap while with Oxford.

FORAN, Richie

Forward
Born: 16 June 1980, Dublin
United debut: 10 January 2004 v Lincoln City (sub)
Final United game: 17 February 2004 v Leyton Orient
Appearances: 3+1
Clubs: Shelbourne (Ireland), Home Farm (Ireland) (loan), Carlisle United, Oxford United (loan), Motherwell, Southend United, Darlington (loan), Inverness Caledonian Thistle

Richard Foran was a forward who joined Oxford on loan from Carlisle in January 2004. Foran started with St Patrick's Athletic, but failed to make an appearance and moved to Shelbourne, where he played just over 30 League games, scored 14 goals as the Shels' top scorer, and won the PFAI Young Player of the Year award. He also won the first of his two Ireland Under-21 caps. Foran scored seven goals in 24 games on loan to Home Farm and in August 2001 he moved to Carlisle for £20,000, winning the Supporters' Player of the Year award in his first season. This successful start was not maintained and in his third season with the Cumbrians came his loan to Oxford. He returned to Carlisle in time for their relegation to the

Conference, after which he was released. In June 2004 he was signed by Motherwell where he played 105 games and scored 35 goals before Southend came in with a £200,000 bid for him in January 2007. In November 2007 he had a loan spell with Darlington, scoring three goals in 12 games, and this was followed by a second loan with Darlo in November 2008, this time playing 13 games and netting three goals. After scoring two goals in 23 games for the Shrimpers, Foran moved on a free transfer to Inverness Caledonian Thistle in January 2009.

FORD, Bobby

Midfielder
Born: 22 September 1974, Bristol
United debut: 4 September 1993 v Bristol City
Final United game: 3 May 2003 v York City
Appearances: 170+20
Goals: 12
Clubs: Oxford United, Sheffield United, Oxford United, Bath City

Robert John Ford had two separate spells with Oxford United, initially joining United's Youth Training Scheme in 1991, joining the seniors in October 1992. He became a fine creative playmaker and made 148 appearances, scoring 11 goals, before Sheffield United took advantage of Oxford's precarious financial situation by signing him for £400,000 in November 1997. Ford played 185 games for the Blades, scoring seven goals (the first coming against Oxford in February 1998) before he was released in the summer of 2002. After appearing in some pre-season friendlies he was unveiled as a new signing for Oxford in August 2002. However, he failed to fit into Ian Atkins' system and at the end of his first season he was released, joining Bath City in January 2004 while working as a plumber in his native Bristol. He retired from the game in November 2005.

FORD, Mike

Midfielder/Left-back
Born: 9 March 1966, Bristol
United debut: 7 January 1989 v Sunderland (sub)
Final United game: 30 September 2000 v Bristol City
Appearances: 321+18
Goals: 22
Clubs: Leicester City, Devizes Town, Cardiff City, Oxford United, Cardiff City, Oxford United, Thame United, Didcot Town, Brackley Town

Michael Paul Ford was a midfielder before converting to a left-back who joined the club twice, both times from Cardiff, and went on to become one of the most consistent and popular players of recent times. After turning professional with Leicester, for whom he did not make a first-team appearance, he joined Devizes where, aged 18, he played in the same team as his father Tony, who was 40. In September 1984 he joined Cardiff, where he established himself, playing 167 games and scoring 13 goals as he helped them to win the Welsh Cup and earn promotion from Division Four in 1988 and where he was voted Player of the Season just before Oxford signed him for £150,000 in June 1988. He was signed by Mark Lawrenson, but an injury sustained while on his honeymoon meant that he did not play his first game until Brian Horton had taken over. He played almost all his Oxford games in his first spell with the club, which lasted a full decade. Fordy rejoined Cardiff in August 1988, playing 65 games and grabbing one goal as the Bluebirds won promotion from Division Three in 1999, before returning to the Manor as reserve and youth team coach in September 2000, playing just one match for the U's in this second spell. That was Denis Smith's final game as Oxford manager, and Ford was appointed caretaker manager. In his six games in charge United earned just one point and Ford returned to coach the youth team after David Kemp's appointment. After Kemp's dismissal Ford was caretaker again for the last two games of the 2000–01 season, including Oxford's last game at the Manor, in which Oxford earned one point. In November 2001 Ford was made assistant manager to Ian Atkins but he was sacked in December 2003, joining Thame United. In August 2003 he moved to Didcot, managed by Peter Foley, and in the summer of 2004 he joined Brackley as player-coach, becoming player-manager in October 2004. In November 2006 he became assistant manager and coach at Oxford City, becoming manager in August 2009.

FORRESTER, George

Wing-half
Born: 28 June 1927, Cannock
Died: 25 September 1981
United debut: 18 August 1956 v Yeovil Town
Final United game: 30 March 1957 v Cheltenham Town
Appearances: 6
Clubs: West Bromwich Albion, Gillingham, Reading, Headington United, Ashford Town

George Larmouth Forrester joined Headington United from Reading in the summer of 1956. His career started a decade earlier with West Brom, but he joined Gillingham in 1947 without having played a game for the Baggies. He scored three goals for Gillingham in 100 League appearances before his move to Reading in 1955. He scored two in six games for the Biscuitmen before his move to the Manor, where he was released at the end of his first season.

FOSTER, Luke

Centre-back
Born: 8 September 1985, Mexborough
United debut: 11 March 2007 v Kidderminster Harriers
Final United game: 28 December 2009 v Salisbury City
Appearances: 112+5
Goals: 3
Clubs: Sheffield Wednesday, Scarborough (loan), Alfreton Town (loan), Lincoln City, York City (loan), Stalybridge Celtic, Oxford United, Mansfield Town, Stevenage, Rotherham United

Luke James Foster joined Oxford after the club had put in a seven-day approach to Stalybridge after he had impressed during a trial, United having been alerted to his availability by a letter from his father. In 2008 he won both the Players' Player of the Year and the Supporters' Player of the Year awards and the following season he won his only England C cap, in a 2–0 defeat by Finland. After being told he was free to talk to other clubs, he left Oxford for Mansfield in January 2010. Foster started as a trainee with

Sheffield Wednesday in 2004, and although he did not make a first-team appearance for the Owls he did have loan spells with Scarborough for eight games in September 2004 and Alfreton, where he scored three goals in 18 Conference North matches, in February 2005. Foster was released by Wednesday at the end of the 2004–05 season and moved to Lincoln, where he scored one goal in 17 appearances. In October 2006 he had a six-game loan spell at York and in January 2007 his contract with Lincoln was cancelled and he joined Stalybridge, where he scored an own-goal on his debut. He scored one goal in six games for Stalybridge before his move to Oxford, where he became the mainstay of a very mean Conference defence, despite receiving rather too many red cards. Upon signing for Mansfield, Foster was immediately made club captain but he was released in May 2010 after just 16 games following a falling-out with manager David Holdsworth. He joined newly-promoted Stevenage later that month. After Stevenage won promotion to League One, Foster was released and joined Rotherham United in June 2011.

FOSTER, Martin

Midfielder
Born: 29 October 1977, Rotherham
United debut: 3 February 2007 v Cambridge United
Final United game: 8 May 2007 v Exeter City
Appearances: 15
Clubs: Leeds United, Blackpool (loan), Greenock Morton, Doncaster Rovers (loan), Doncaster Rovers, Ilkeston Town (loan), Forest Green Rovers, Halifax Town, Oxford United (loan), Rushden & Diamonds, Tamworth, Eastwood Town, Harrogate Town

Martin Foster was a midfielder who joined Oxford on loan from Halifax in January 2007 until the end of the season, playing in the Play-off semi-final defeat to Exeter before a move to Rushden in the summer. He started as a trainee with Leeds, but made just one senior appearance on loan to Blackpool before moving to Scotland to play for Morton in August 1998. He played 19 games for the Scottish side before moving to Doncaster in March 1999, initially on loan. Foster scored two goals in 32 games for Doncaster, and in September 2000 he had a four-game loan spell with Ilkeston before joining Forest Green Rovers in January 2001. He played 143 games for Rovers, including the 2001 FA Trophy Final, scoring five goals, before his move to Chris Wilder's Halifax in July 2004. He amassed 10 goals in 105 games for the Shaymen prior to his loan to Oxford, but was released on his return to Halifax. Foster played 21 games for the Diamonds, moving to Tamworth in January 2008, where he was made captain. He helped the Lambs to promotion to the Conference Premier Division, but for financial reasons he quit the club in June 2009 after one goal in 65 games and signed for Eastwood. In January 2009 the Eastwood skipper joined Conference North rivals Harrogate, where he was again installed as captain.

FOSTER, Steve

Centre-back
Born: 24 September 1957, Portsmouth
United debut: 19 August 1989 v Plymouth Argyle
Final United game: 5 February 1992 v Sunderland

Appearances: 112
Goals: 13
Clubs: Portsmouth, Brighton & Hove Albion, Aston Villa, Luton Town, Oxford United, Brighton & Hove Albion

Stephen Brian Foster joined Oxford from Luton for £175,000 in the summer of 1989. Foster was an associate schoolboy at Southampton, but he turned professional with Portsmouth in 1973, initially as a centre-forward. He was converted into a defender by Ian St John and went on to play 130 games for Pompey, scoring eight goals, before joining Brighton for £150,000 in July 1979. Foster appeared 202 times for the Seagulls, scoring eight goals, and won his three England caps in that time, including in the Spain 1982 World Cup squad. He also played for Brighton in their FA Cup Final defeat to Manchester United in 1983. In March 1984 Aston Villa paid £200,000 for him, but he was at Villa Park for just eight months, scoring three goals in 17 games, before he joined Luton for £150,000. His 212 appearances for the Hatters included him captaining them to the 1988 League Cup win over Arsenal after Luton beat Oxford in the semi-finals. Foster left Oxford in August 1992 after his performances had deteriorated and he returned to Brighton on a free transfer, going on to play another 129 games and score seven goals for them before retiring in May 1996 after relegation to the basement.

FOWLER, Lee

Midfielder
Born: 10 June 1983, Cardiff
United debut: 19 January 2010 v Woking
Final United game: 19 January 2010 v Woking
Appearances: 1
Clubs: Coventry City, Cardiff City (loan), Huddersfield Town (loan), Huddersfield Town, Scarborough, Burton Albion, Newport County (loan), Newport County, Forest Green Rovers, Kettering Town, Oxford United, Cirencester Town, Halesowen Town, Forest Green Rovers, Wrexham

Lee Anthony Fowler joined Oxford from Kettering in December 2009 after leaving the Poppies by mutual consent. However, he failed to make an impression with United and was released at his own request in March 2010 after playing just one FA Trophy game. His career started as a trainee with Coventry, for whom he played 16 games and scored one goal. Following a trial on loan with Cardiff in March 2003, a 19-game loan to Huddersfield in August 2003 turned into a permanent move in November, and Fowler went on to play a further 34 games for the Terriers, scoring once. After an unsuccessful trial with Grimsby in June 1995, followed by a few months out of the game, in November 1995 Fowler joined Scarborough, where he scored three goals in 25 games. Financial problems led to Boro's relegation from the Conference at the end of the season and Fowler left to join Burton, where he played 23 games and scored once before falling out with manager Nigel Clough. This led to a loan move to Newport from March 2007 until the end of the season, when it was made permanent. In July 2008 Fowler returned to the Conference with Forest Green Rovers, where he was made captain. He played 46 games and scored once before joining Kettering after one year. While at Rockingham Road he claimed homesickness, leading to the club releasing him, believing him to be about to rejoin Newport. Instead he turned up at the Kassam Stadium, albeit briefly. In March 2010 he joined Cirencester, but after just one game he left for Halesowen, making his debut against Oxford City. Fowler left Halesowen in May 2010 and returned to Forest Green Rovers. In October 2010 Fowler admitted that he was an alcoholic and, with the support of his club, he was seeking treatment. In January 2011 Fowler joined Wrexham, and he signed a new two-year contract in May 2011. He was a Wales Youth international and won nine Wales Under-21 caps.

FOYLE, Martin

Forward
Born: 2 May 1963, Salisbury
United debut: 28 March 1987 v Sheffield Wednesday (sub)
Final United game: 11 May 1991 v Leicester City
Appearances: 144+7
Goals: 44
Clubs: Southampton, IFK Munkfors (Sweden) (loan), Blackburn Rovers (loan), Aldershot, Oxford United, Port Vale

Martin John Foyle joined Oxford from Aldershot for £140,000 in March 1987. He was an intelligent footballer, who arguably failed to score as many goals as his ability suggested he should. Foyle started as an apprentice with Southampton, for whom he scored three goals in 14 appearances over four years. He spent the summer of 1982 on loan to Swedish side Munkfors, where his 30 goals in 22 games helped them win promotion from Division Five Central, in which he was the top scorer. In March 1984 he had a brief loan with Blackburn, where he failed to play for the first team. In August 1984 Foyle joined Aldershot for £10,000, going on to play 122 games for the Shots, scoring 45 goals. After he joined Oxford he took a little while to oust Billy Whitehurst from the starting line up, but after relegation in 1988 he became a regular alongside Dean Saunders. In June 1991 Port Vale paid a club record £375,000 for Foyle, who scored both goals on his debut in a 2–1 win over Oxford. He was a prolific scorer with the Valiants, being their leading marksman in four seasons and finding the net 107 times, a post-war record for Vale, in his 356 games. After his retirement through injury in 2000 he became manager of Vale's youth team, taking over as first-team manager in February 2004 after Brian Horton's departure. He left Vale by mutual consent in September 2007 and in January 2008 he became assistant manager at Wrexham. He became joint caretaker manager with Brian Carey in September 2008 after Brian Little's departure, but Foyle left Wrexham in October after Dean Saunders was made manager. In November 2008 he was appointed manager of York City, and he took them to the FA Trophy Final in his first season, losing to Stevenage. In May 2010 he took York to the Conference Play-off Final, where Oxford won 3–1 to deny the Minstermen promotion back to the League. He resigned as manager in September 2010 and in January 2011 was appointed first-team coach at Bristol Rovers under David Penney. However, they were both dismissed in March 2011 when Foyle was approached by Tamworth to work as Des Lyttle's assistant, although they did not pursue this as Foyle was on gardening leave, while Lyttle resigned from Tamworth because he was not consulted about the approach for Foyle.

FRANCIS, Kevin

Forward
Born: 6 December 1967, Moseley
United debut: 17 February 1998 v West Bromwich Albion
Final United game: 7 March 2000 v Reading (sub)
Appearances: 27+13
Goals: 8
Clubs: Redditch United, Mile Oak Rovers, Derby County, Stockport County, Birmingham City, Oxford United, Stockport County, Castleton Gabriels, Exeter City, Hull City, Hednesford Town, Studley

Kevin Michael Derek Francis was a 6ft 7in striker who joined Oxford from Birmingham in February 1998 for £100,000. The lanky forward was a popular figure and once joined the crowd in the London Road to lead the singing when out of the side through injury. He started with Redditch, who released him to Mile Oak Rovers before he joined Derby in February 1989. After 15 games, during which he scored one goal, Stockport paid £45,000 for him in February 1991. In the next four years Francis made himself a cult hero with the Hatters, scoring 117 goals in 198 games; he was later voted Stockport's Player of the Century. His form brought him to the attention of Barry Fry at Birmingham, who took him to St Andrew's for £800,000 in January 1995. However, Fry had assembled a huge squad and Francis found opportunities irregular, playing 94 games and scoring 21 goals in three years before his move to the Manor. At Oxford he was famously penalised by referee Mike Read to concede a late penalty in United's 1–1 FA Cup game against Chelsea. Francis left the Manor in March 2000, returning to Stockport on a free transfer, but after just four appearances he suffered a bad injury and was released at the end of the season, following a recuperative spell with non-League outfit Castleton Gabriels in April 2000. He joined Exeter on a non-contract basis in November 2000, playing nine games and scoring one goal for the Grecians, and then joined Hull in December 2000. After scoring five goals in 24 games Francis left the Football League and joined Hednesford for a couple of seasons. In February 2005 he signed for Studley until the end of the season before emigrating to Canada to drive monster trucks, then becoming a police officer in Calgary in 2008. While with Oxford, Francis was capped twice for St Kitts and Nevis.

FRANKS, Leigh

Centre-back
Born: 7 March 1991, Hunmanby, North Yorkshire
United debut: 28 September 2010 v Cheltenham Town (sub)
Final United game: 2 November 2010 v Torquay United
Appearances: 4+1
Clubs: Bridlington Town, Fleetwood Town, Huddersfield Town, Oxford United (loan), Alfreton Town

Leigh David Franks joined Oxford on a six-month loan from Huddersfield in July 2010. Franks started with Hunmanby Juniors, joining Scarborough's School of Excellence aged 10. Although Scarborough were keen to keep him, Franks opted to join his friends at Bridlington, for whom he made his debut on Boxing Day 2006. By the end of the season at least five Football League clubs had enquired about him, and in March 2007 he had a trial with Huddersfield, signing in May 2007. In January 2010 he joined Fleetwood on loan, but he was recalled in March after Huddersfield manager Lee Clark found that he was only playing for the reserves rather than gaining Conference North experience. He joined Oxford still without having made his senior Huddersfield debut and returned in December 2010 after picking up an injury. He was released by Huddersfield in May 2011 and joined Alfreton Town the following month.

FRASER, John

Centre-forward
United debut: 1 October 1956 v Kidderminster Harriers
Final United game: 30 March 1957 v Cheltenham Town
Appearances: 3
Clubs: Headington United

John Fraser was an amateur player who joined the club in the 1956 close season, mostly playing for the reserves in the Metropolitan League.

FURSDON, Alan

Full-back
Born: 16 October 1947, Grantham
United debut: 18 December 1967 v Chelmsford City
Final United game: 7 December 1968 v Preston North End
Appearances: 1+1
Clubs: Swindon Town, Oxford United, Dover Town, Tonbridge (loan), Witney Town, Wealdstone, Hendon, Banbury United

Alan Harry Fursdon joined Oxford from Swindon as a part-timer in May 1967. At the start of 1968 he turned full-time, and was converted into an inside-left at the start of 1968–69, but he was released at the end of the season having made just one substitute appearance in his new position. He left for Dover in 1969, staying five years at the Crabble, and he had a brief loan spell at Tonbridge before he joined John Shuker's Witney Town. However, due to suffering a broken ankle, he did not play for Witney and, despite new manager Maurice Kyle's entreaties, Fursdon moved to Wealdstone where he had already played a couple of games. He stayed five years at Wealdstone, scoring five goals in 175 games, becoming Hendon's player-coach in 1980, although he played just one game in his two seasons there. The last club that Fursdon played for was Banbury, where he spent a year and a half. He then managed Eynsham in the Oxfordshire Senior League, earning them promotion to the Premier Division, and was then involved in various boys' teams with Yarnton until 2010. He also refereed locally.

FUTCHER, Ben

Centre-back
Born: 4 June 1981, Bradford
United debut: 13 November 2010 v Rotherham United
Final United game: 1 January 2011 v Southend United
Appearances: 6
Clubs: Oldham Athletic, Stalybridge Celtic (loan), Stalybridge Celtic, Doncaster Rovers, Lincoln City, Boston United, Grimsby Town, Peterborough United, Bury, Oxford United (loan)

Benjamin Paul Futcher was a 6ft 7in centre-back who joined Oxford on loan from Bury in November 2010. He signed professionally with his first club, Oldham, in July 1999. In August 2001 he spent three months on loan with Stalybridge, managed by his father Paul, where he scored once in 17 appearances. He joined Stalybridge permanently in January 2002 because his Oldham contract was cancelled after 11 appearances for the Latics. He played a further 10 games before moving to Doncaster in March 2002. He played just two games for Doncaster before manager Dave Penney released him at the end of the season and he joined Lincoln, where he was to have his most successful spell. He finished his first season as top scorer and was voted the Supporters' Player of the Year as he helped the Imps reach the Play-off Final. After 142 games and 17 goals Futcher surprisingly left Lincoln for Boston in the summer of 2005, having appeared in three Play-offs, losing twice in the final and once in the semi-finals. He lasted just six months with the Pilgrims, making 19 appearances and scoring one goal, before joining Grimsby in January 2006. He remained at Blundell Park until the end of the season, playing 23 games and scoring three goals, after which he moved to Peterborough, having once more appeared in a losing Play-off Final side. Futcher played 30 games over the season, scoring three goals, before he moved to Bury in June 2007. By the time that he moved to the Kassam on loan, Futcher had played 128 games for the Shakers and scored four goals, but he had lost his regular first-team place. He returned to Bury in January 2011 and in May 2011 he signed a one-year extension to his contract with the newly-promoted Shakers.

G

GABBIADINI, Marco

Forward
Born: 20 January 1968, Nottingham
United debut: 2 February 1997 v Manchester City
Final United game: 1 March 1997 v Crystal Palace
Appearances: 5
Goals: 1
Clubs: York City, Sunderland, Crystal Palace, Derby County, Birmingham City (loan), Oxford United (loan), Panionios (Greece), Stoke City, York City, Darlington, Northampton Town, Hartlepool United

Marco Gabbiadini joined Oxford on loan from Derby in February 1997, but his performances failed to live up to his reputation and after just one goal in five games he returned to the Baseball Ground. Born to an English mother and Italian father, Gabbiadini joined York City straight from school, signed by Denis Smith. Fast and with an imposing physique, he was at the back of a long list of strikers and did not make his first appearance until 1985. He went on to play 71 games, in which he scored 18 goals, before Sunderland, by then managed by Denis Smith, came in with an £80,000 offer for him in September 1987. In his first season with the Rokerites they won the Third Division and he was awarded two caps for England Under-21s. The first red card of his career came in an FA Cup defeat to Oxford, but he still won the North East Player of the Year award in 1989. Sunderland were promoted to the top flight the following season despite losing the Play-off Final to Swindon, who were relegated for gambling offences, but Gabbiadini struggled at the higher level and Sunderland were relegated after just one season. After 185 games and 85 goals, Gabbiadini was sold to Crystal Palace for a club record £1.8 million in October 1991. He was with Palace for just four months, scoring seven goals from 25 games, before Derby paid £1 million for him. He scored on his debut and won the Player of the Year award in his first season, and in 1996 the club won promotion to the Premiership. Troubled by knee injuries, Gabbiadini was loaned to Birmingham for two substitute appearances in October 1996, followed by his spell at the Manor. He returned to Derby, but at the end of the season, after 227 games and 68 goals for the Rams, he moved to Greece to play for Panionios. By the end of the year he had returned to England and in December 1997 he joined Stoke on a month-by-month contract. In nine games he managed just one goal and Stoke soon moved him on. Another spell with York followed in February 1998, where he managed one goal in seven appearances, but it was when he moved to Darlington in July 1998 that his career revived. Injury free, Gabbiadini helped Darlington to the Play-off Final and was later voted as the club's greatest ever player. Despite this, after 53 goals in 96 games, Gabbiadini joined Northampton in June 2000. He stayed at Sixfields for the next three seasons and was the club's leading scorer in his final season with 14 goals. He played 131 games for the Cobblers, scoring 30 goals, before he was released and signed for Hartlepool in July 2003. After suffering a recurrence of his knee injury Gabbiadini retired in January 2004, having scored seven goals in 18 games for the Pools. He restored and ran a hotel in York, which won the Guest House of the Year award in 1999, while also co-presenting a sports show on BBC Newcastle.

GARDNER, Lee

Midfielder
Born: 11 July 1970, Ayr
United debut: 10 April 1991 v Newcastle United (sub)
Final United game: 11 May 1991 v Leicester City (sub)
Appearances: 2+5
Clubs: Aberdeen Lads' Club, Aberdeen, Oxford United (loan), Ayr United, Meadowbank Thistle, Arbroath, Albion Rovers, Clydebank, Alloa Athletic, Brechin City (loan), Airdrieonians, Airdrie United

Robert Lee Gardner joined Oxford on loan from Aberdeen in April 1991. He joined the Dons from Aberdeen Lads' Club in January 1987. He played just two games before his loan to Oxford, after which he joined Ayr in the summer of 1991. In 1992 he was in the Ayr side that finished runners-up to Hamilton Academical in the Scottish Challenge Cup Final and in August 1993, after 23 games for Ayr, he joined Meadowbank. He played 17 games for Thistle before joining Arbroath in October 1994. Gardner was with the Red Lichties for two years, playing 54 games and scoring three goals, before a move to Albion in October 1996. He scored 16 goals in 48 matches before his next move took him to Clydebank in August 1998. In two seasons with the Bankies, Gardner scored eight goals in 83 appearances before his tour of the Scottish lower divisions took him to Alloa in July 2000. He managed just 10 games for the Wasps, plus a seven-game loan with Brechin in October 2000, before leaving for Airdrieonians in March 2001. He played 37 games for the Diamonds, scoring once, and won a Scottish Challenge Cup winners' medal in 2002 before the club was wound up on 1 May 2002. After an attempt to revive the club failed, local businessman Jim Ballantyne bought financially-troubled Clydebank, moved it to Airdrie and changed its name to Airdrie United; Gardner went on to play 28 games for the new club. Eventually his injuries took their toll and he left Airdrie in 2004.

GASTON, Ray

Forward
Born: 22 December 1946, Belfast
United debut: 18 September 1968 v Blackburn Rovers
Final United game: 8 February 1969 v Cardiff City
Appearances: 12+1
Goals: 2
Clubs: Coleraine, Wolverhampton Wanderers, Coleraine, Oxford United, Lincoln City (loan), Coleraine, Ballymena United, Coleraine, Finn Harps

Raymond Gaston joined Oxford from Coleraine for a United record fee of £12,500 in September 1968, the day after making his only full Northern Ireland appearance as a substitute against Israel, in the same game that David Sloan won his first cap. He started as a youth at Coleraine in 1964, winning the Intermediate Cup with the reserves and playing two games for the first team, scoring on his debut in February 1965. He then tried his luck with Wolves but did not get to play for them and returned to Coleraine, where he initially dropped out of football to become a concrete worker. After being restored to the Coleraine side he won the Ulster Cup and became a club legend. Overall, in his four spells with the Bannsiders, he scored 63 goals in 127 games. His time at the Manor was altogether less successful, with many supporters deriding his fitness and attitude, and he spent much of his second season at the club playing in the reserves. He scored one goal in a four-game loan with Lincoln in February 1970, after which he returned to Coleraine on a free transfer that summer. He also won one Northern Ireland Under-23 cap.

GEMMILL, Scot

Midfielder
Born: 2 January 1971, Paisley
United debut: 1 April 2006 v Mansfield Town (sub)
Final United game: 1 April 2006 v Mansfield Town (sub)
Appearances: 0+1
Clubs: Nottingham Forest, Everton, Preston North End (loan), Leicester City, Oxford United, New Zealand Knights

Scotland Gemmill's Oxford career lasted just 27 minutes, the midfielder coming on as a substitute for Liam Horsted in a 1–0 defeat at Mansfield as Oxford plummeted towards the Football Conference. He joined Oxford as a player-coach from Leicester in March 2006 on Jim Smith's first day in his second spell in charge. However, in April, just two days after his only United appearance, he left to pursue a career with the New Zealand Knights. Gemmill is the son of Scotland legend Archie, and he won 26 Scotland caps himself, scoring once for his country, although he was a non-playing substitute at the World Cup finals in 1998 in France. He started as a trainee with Nottingham Forest in 1987, spending 12 years at the City Ground and playing 302 games and scoring 35 goals for Forest before his move to Everton for £250,000 in March 1999. While with Forest, Gemmill scored twice to help them win the ZDS Cup against Southampton at Wembley, and the following week they lost the League Cup Final to Manchester United. He played 110 games for the Toffees, scoring five goals, but found his chances restricted after David Moyes replaced Walter Smith as manager, and he spent seven games on loan to Preston in March 2004, during which he scored once. In August 2004 he moved to Leicester where he played 18 games before his move to the Kassam. Gemmill had already been in discussions with the Knights before he joined Oxford, and the offer to join them came a week later. He played 20 games for the Knights before retiring and he returned to Scotland to help coach the national Under-19 side.

GEORGE, Ricky

Winger
Born: 28 June 1946, Barnet
United debut: 27 August 1966 v Swansea Town
Final United game: 24 March 1967 v Leyton Orient
Appearances: 7
Clubs: Tottenham Hotspur, Watford, Bournemouth & Boscombe Athletic, Oxford United, Hastings United, Barnet, Hereford United, Cambridge City, Boreham Wood, Corinthian Casuals

Richard Stuart George was best known for his giant-killing FA Cup exploits while with Hereford, where he scored the winning goal against Newcastle

United in January 1971. He joined Oxford in July 1966 but after failing to earn a regular place he was released at the end of the season. He began his career with Spurs after leaving school, and he signed as a professional after a two-year apprenticeship, but he left for Watford in August 1964 without having played a senior game for Tottenham. He had one season at Vicarage Road, playing four League games, and the following summer he joined Bournemouth, where he made three appearances in the season before his move to the Manor. After his release from Oxford he dropped into the Southern League with Hastings, where he earned an 'international cap', playing for 'Old England' against 'Old Scotland' in a charity match in Ayr. However, Hastings then became the latest club to release George, whose work rate failed to match his talent, and he joined his home-town club, Barnet. He had a more productive time with the Bees under Dexter Adams, but left for Hereford in January 1971 after they offered a small fee for him. After a slow start George found his feet at Hereford and wrote himself into their history with his FA Cup goal and performances. At the end of the season he returned to Barnet and wound down his career in the non-League. He started a successful sportswear business in 1976 and in 1992 he bought a share in a horse called Earth Summit, which won the Grand National in April 1998. In 2001 his autobiography *One Goal, One Horse* was published, after which he wrote a weekly non-League column for the *Daily Telegraph* and co-presented a Radio 5 show with John Motson, who he knew from Motty's time as a Barnet supporter in the early 1960s.

GERRARD, Paul

Goalkeeper
Born: 22 January 1973, Heywood, Rochdale
United debut: 19 December 1998 v Stockport County
Final United game: 26 March 1999 v Sheffield United
Appearances: 16
Clean sheets: 5
Clubs: Oldham Athletic, Everton, Oxford United (loan), Ipswich Town (loan), Sheffield United (loan), Nottingham Forest (loan), Nottingham Forest, Sheffield United, Blackpool (loan), Stockport County, Oldham Athletic

Paul William Gerrard joined Oxford on loan from Everton in December 1998. He began as an apprentice with Oldham in 1991, playing 136 games for the Latics before Everton paid £1 million for him in July 1996. He took over from Neville Southall as first-team 'keeper for a while, but after Southall regained his place Gerrard found opportunities limited, hence his loan to Oxford. His performances for the U's had United wanting to offer Gerrard a permanent deal, but he was recalled by Howard Kendall, albeit mainly as cover for Southall. Gerrard's former manager Joe Royle took him to Ipswich for a five-game loan spell in November 2002, and in August 2003 he joined Sheffield United on loan for 16 games, followed in March 2004 by an eight-game loan to Nottingham Forest. At the end of the season this became a permanent deal as he joined Forest on a free transfer, although they were relegated at the end of his first season, in which he won the Player of the Year award. After an injury, Gerrard was released by Forest at the end of the 2005–06 season, having played 73 games for them. He rejoined Sheffield United in September 2006 as goalkeeping cover and he played just three games for the Blades before being released at the end of the season, although new manager Bryan Robson re-signed him in August 2007. In January 2008 he joined

Blackpool on loan until the end of the season, but did not play a first-team game for them as he required surgery on a knee injury. He was released again by the Blades at the end of the season and joined Stockport County as cover and goalkeeping coach. He made two appearances for the Hatters before becoming Oldham's goalkeeping coach in June 2010 on a part-time basis, joining Shrewsbury in the same capacity the following month. In August 2010 he signed a pay-as-you-play contract with Oldham in order to provide them with goalkeeping cover and continue acting as coach. In July 2011 he left Shrewsbury to become full-time goalkeeping coach with the Latics.

GIBBINS, Roger

Midfielder
Born: 6 June 1955, Enfield
United debut: 16 August 1975 v Carlisle United
Final United game: 24 April 1976 v Leyton Orient
Appearances: 16+3
Goals: 2
Clubs: Tottenham Hotspur, Oxford United (loan), Oxford United, Norwich City, New England Tea Men (USA), Hayes (loan), Cambridge United, Cardiff City, Swansea City, Newport County, Torquay United, Newport County, Cardiff City, Cwmbran Town, Weston-super-Mare

Roger Graeme Gibbins joined Oxford from Tottenham in August 1975, initially on loan before signing permanently. He was a Spurs apprentice, winning caps for England Schoolboys and turning professional in December 1972, but never playing a senior game for them. He did not have the best of starts for United and, despite being fast, his strike rate was poor and he soon lost his first-team place. He came back into the side briefly, but after relegation in 1976 he moved to Norwich on a free transfer. He played 48 League games and scored 12 goals for the Canaries before a £60,000 move to Boston, Massachusetts in March 1978 to play for the New England Tea Men in the NASL. In his two years in Foxboro, Gibbins played 59 games and scored eight goals before returning to England to join Cambridge United in September 1979. While with the Tea Men he had a loan spell at Hayes which lasted for 14 games until March 1979, in which he scored four goals. At Cambridge, Gibbins played exactly 100 League games, scoring 12 goals, before moving on a free transfer to Cardiff in August 1982. Cardiff won promotion from Division Three in Gibbins' first season, and he went on to score 17 goals in 139 appearances before moving to Swansea in exchange for Chris Marustik in October 1985. He did not stay long at the Vetch and, after scoring six goals in 39 League games, he joined Newport, who were on the verge of going out of business, in August 1986. Despite their problems, Gibbins remained with Newport until March 1988, playing 79 games and scoring eight goals, when he moved to Torquay. He scored five goals in 33 matches for the Gulls before a surprise £10,000 transfer in January 1989 back to Newport, by then in the Conference. However, County's troubles caught up with them before the end of the season and they were forced to fold in March 1989, their record being expunged, and Gibbins returned to Cardiff, where he was made captain. After a further 142 games and seven goals for the Bluebirds, Gibbins joined the Ninian Park coaching staff while playing for Cwmbran, for whom he scored 11 goals in 101 games. In 1998 Gibbins was assistant manager to Colin Addison at Merthyr Tydfil, leaving to become player-manager at Weston-super-Mare in August 1998. In March 1999 he was appointed manager of Merthyr, but he resigned in September 1999 when the board stipulated that they wanted a full-time manager and Gibbins did not want to give up his job as regional merit officer for the PFA. In 2000 he became coach at Cwmbran, later becoming assistant manager and then manager before resigning in June 2003. In 2010 he was the League Football Education (LFE) regional officer for the South West and Wales.

GIBBS, Alan

Inside-right
Born: 7 February 1934, Orpington
United debut: 24 August 1957 v Cheltenham Town
Final United game: 30 November 1957 v Worcester City
Appearances: 8
Goals: 1
Clubs: Cardiff City, Swindon Town, Headington United, Cheltenham Town

Alan Martin Gibbs was one of three players who joined Headington United from Swindon in the summer of 1957. He lasted just one season at the Manor before leaving for Cheltenham the following summer. Gibbs started with Cardiff in 1954, but left for Swindon in May 1956 without having played for the Bluebirds. He played 17 games and scored five goals for Swindon before his move to Headington. He scored 13 goals in his first season for Cheltenham, but managed only two the following year.

GIBSON, Dave

Right-winger
Born: 18 March 1931, Runcorn
United debut: 24 August 1957 v Cheltenham Town
Final United game: 30 April 1960 v Gravesend & Northfleet
Appearances: 97
Goals: 31
Clubs: Everton, Swindon Town, Headington United, Bedford Town

David James Gibson was one of three players who joined Headington from Swindon in the summer of 1957. He started with Everton in 1950, playing three games for the Toffees and winning England Youth honours, before his move to the County Ground in November 1954. In the next three seasons he scored seven goals in 76 matches before escaping to the Manor. Gibson played regularly for the U's over the next three seasons but was not retained in the summer of 1960 and he moved to Bedford, where he scored twice in 11 games.

GIBSON, Stuart

Midfielder
Born: 22 July 1963, Nottingham
United debut: 22 February 1984 v Swindon Town (sub)
Final United game: 22 February 1984 v Swindon Town (sub)
Appearances: 0+1
Clubs: Birmingham City, Oxford United, Yeovil Town, Oddevold (Sweden), BK Häcken (Sweden), Trelleborg FF (Sweden), IFK Holmsund (Sweden), Elfsborg (Sweden), IFK Uddevalla (Sweden), Smögen (Sweden)

Alexander Stuart Gibson joined Oxford from Birmingham as an apprentice in 1980. He never played a senior game for the Blues, but he did gain

England Youth honours. In the summer of 1982 he joined the Oxford senior squad, but Gibson made just one substitute appearance for United, when he came on for Gary Barnett in the 72nd minute of an Associate Members' Cup tie against Swindon, and after 21 appearances for the reserves he moved to Yeovil in April 1984. After scoring three goals for the Glovers, Gibson moved to Sweden in 1985 and joined Oddevold, a third-tier outfit. He was successful enough for Gothenburg-based Häcken to offer him a decent contract, but he broke his ankle there. He joined Trelleborg, where he began to earn his coaching badges and, after playing for a series of different sides in Sweden, he became player-manager of Smögen, followed by being appointed manager of Hunnebostrand. After 12 years in Sweden, Gibson returned to England to take charge of the youth and reserves coaching at Darlington. He then became head of youth at Plymouth Argyle, but after public criticism by manager Tony Pulis he left in October 2006 to return to Scandinavia as manager of Norwegian side Steinkjer FK. In August 2009 Gibson became head of development at Barnsley. However, in October 2009 he joined Torquay as head of recruitment, but shortly afterwards he returned to Sweden to become manager of Umeå. In December 2010 it was announced that he would share that role with training at Division Two side Marie Hem SK.

GILCHRIST, Phil

Centre-back
Born: 25 August 1973, Stockton-on-Tees
United debut: 18 February 1995 v Bristol Rovers
Final United game: 1 November 2007 v Rushden & Diamonds
Appearances: 245+4
Goals: 12
Clubs: Nottingham Forest, Middlesbrough, Hartlepool United, Oxford United, Leicester City, West Bromwich Albion, Rotherham United (loan), Rotherham United, Oxford United, Anstey Nomads, Quorn

Philip Alexander Gilchrist was a left-sided central-defender who had two spells with Oxford United. He initially joined the club from Hartlepool for £100,000 in February 1995, going on to forge a solid partnership with Matt Elliott. His pace and tackling was the perfect complement to the more composed play of Elliott, and his long throw was a useful attacking weapon. The partnership was largely responsible for United's promotion in 1996 and there was little surprise when he rejoined Elliott at Leicester after the first game of the season in August 1999 for £500,000. Gilchrist's first club was Nottingham Forest, but he played no senior games for them or for Middlesbrough before his move to Hartlepool in November 1992. He played 96 games for the Monkeyhangers before his move to the Manor. In his first spell with Oxford, Gilchrist played 205 games and scored 11 goals before moving to Filbert Street. He played 51 games for Leicester, scoring one goal for the Premiership side, before joining West Brom for £500,000 in March 2001. The Baggies won promotion to the Premiership at the end of Gilchrist's first season, keeping a club record 27 clean sheets. He played 105 games for West Brom before joining Rotherham on loan in March 2004. He played 10 games before the end of the season and in the summer the move was made permanent. Over the next two years Gilchrist made 41 appearances for the Millers, scoring one goal, before he rejoined Oxford in June 2006 for their first season in the Conference, his wages being covered by a competition run by *Coca Cola* in which an Oxford fan won £50,000 for the club. In his second spell with United Gilchrist played 44 games, scoring once, before hanging up his boots after United lost 5–0 at Rushden & Diamonds, which was also Jim Smith's last game as manager in that spell. At the end of that season Gilchrist became assistant manager of Woking, becoming manager in September 2008. He was sacked in April 2009 and started playing for Anstey Nomads while setting up a soccer academy in Leicester, and in August 2009 he joined Quorn.

GILLIES, Bill

United debut: 24 August 1955 v Guildford City
Final United game: 5 September 1955 v Worcester City
Appearances: 2
Clubs: Celtic, Headington United

William Gillies joined Headington from Celtic in the summer of 1955.

GLADWIN, Robin

Full-back
Born: 12 August 1940, Harlow
United debut: 10 August 1968 v Bolton Wanderers
Final United game: 18 March 1973 v Bristol City
Appearances: 48
Clubs: Harlow Town, Cambridge City, Leyton, Chelmsford City, Norwich City, Oxford United

Robin Gladwin joined Oxford from Norwich in July 1968 on a free transfer. His first club was Harlow Town, after which he joined Cambridge City in the Southern League as an amateur. He was with City for two years before a spell with Leyton. He moved to Chelmsford where he turned professional in 1964. Norwich signed Gladwin in January 1966 but injuries led to him making just 16 appearances before he moved to the Manor. Gladwin's debut was Oxford's first match in the Second Division and he made regular appearances at both left- and right-back.

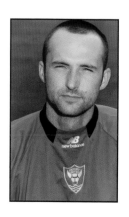

GLASS, Jimmy

Goalkeeper
Born: 1 August 1973, Epsom
United debut: 13 September 2000 v Stoke City
Final United game: 5 December 2000 v Brentford
Appearances: 2
Clubs: Crystal Palace, Dulwich Hamlet (loan), Carshalton (loan), Portsmouth (loan), Gillingham (loan), Burnley (loan), AFC Bournemouth, Swindon Town, Carlisle United (loan), Cambridge United, Brentford, Oxford United, Crawley Town, Kingstonian, Brockenhurst, Salisbury City, Lewes

James Robert Glass joined Oxford from Brentford at the tail-end of his career, having already made a name for himself as the 'keeper whose last-minute goal for Carlisle against Plymouth kept the Cumbrians in the Football League at Scarborough's expense. Glass turned professional with Crystal Palace in 1991, but he did not play for them. His first loan was to Dulwich in January 1990, followed by a move to Carshalton later in 1990. He had another loan with Portsmouth in February 1995, where he made three appearances, although loans to Gillingham in December 1995 and Burnley in February 1996 failed to bring any further games for Glass. He joined Bournemouth in March 1996, going on to play 111 games for the Cherries and scoring an own-goal in the final of the Football League Trophy at Wembley in 1998, until his career nosedived in June 1998 with a free transfer to Swindon. He played 12 games for the Robins until manager Jimmy Quinn dropped him and in April 1999 he made his famous three-game loan move to Carlisle, replacing Richard Knight. In February 2000 Glass moved to Cambridge United on non-contract terms, where he played in five reserve games, but he was behind second-choice goalie Arjan Van Heusden in the pecking order and the club could not afford to offer Glass a contract, so they released him. At the end of March he joined Brentford where he played twice, but Ron Noades recalled Andy Woodman from his loan at Peterborough to deny Glass any further appearances. After training with Wimbledon and having a trial with Exeter, Glass played a friendly for Crawley against Oxford in July 2000, after which Denis Smith offered him a contract as reserve goalie, behind Knight. However, after David Kemp took over from Smith and Glass conceded four goals against Brentford in an LDV Trophy game, he was given no more chances and United signed Neil Cutler on loan from Aston Villa, leaving Glass training with the youth team. After ringing around trying to find a club, Glass was eventually offered a job at Crawley, playing four games while their regular 'keeper recovered from injury. This was followed by a spell with Kingstonian until July 2001, after which he had a trial with Yeovil before joining Brockenhurst in August 2001. In September he signed for Salisbury but played two games before giving up and joining a Sunday League side as a striker. In July 2004 Glass played two pre-season games for Lewes before they withdrew their offer of a contract. Later in 2004 Glass published his autobiography *One Hit Wonder*, in which he details his career and his problems with gambling. Glass became a taxi driver in Bournemouth.

GNOHÉRÉ, Arthur

Centre-back
Born: 20 November 1978, Yamassoukro (Côte d'Ivoire)
United debut: 11 August 2007 v Forest Green Rovers
Final United game: 6 October 2007 v Droylsden
Appearances: 7+1
Clubs: AS Cannes (France), Caen (France), Burnley, Queen's Park Rangers (loan), Queen's Park Rangers, FC Istres Ouest Provence (France), Oxford United, FC Bulle (Switzerland), FC Monthey (Switzerland)

David Arthur Gnohéré was a central-defender who joined Oxford, initially on trial, in July 2007. He missed pre-season through injury, but Jim Smith still offered him a monthly contract. However, his exotic origins failed to confer on him the necessary talent to prosper and he was released in October 2007. Gnohéré's career started with Cannes in 1997, but after just two appearances he joined Caen in 1999. In August 2001, after two goals in 48 games, he signed for Burnley where he became a fans' favourite and earned the nickname 'King Arthur'. He played 92 games for the Clarets, scoring six goals, before a six-game loan spell with QPR in September 2003. He returned to Turf Moor the following month, but in February 2004 he joined the Hoops permanently on a free transfer. He played just 16 games in his second period with Rangers, but was released at the end of the 2004–05 season, returning to France to play for Istres, for whom he made 12 appearances before his release and subsequent signing for Oxford. After leaving Oxford, Gnohéré had a brief spell out of the game before joining Swiss side Bulle, after which he dropped into the Swiss second tier with Monthey.

GOODHIND, Warren

Right-back
Born: 16 August 1977, Johannesburg (South Africa)
United debut: 25 February 2006 v Wycombe Wanderers (sub)
Final United game: 1 April 2006 v Mansfield Town (sub)
Appearances: 4+2
Clubs: Barnet, Cambridge United, Rochdale, Oxford United (loan), Dagenham & Redbridge, Ebbsfleet United, Eastleigh, Harrow Borough, Eastleigh, Hemel Hempstead Town

Warren Ernest Goodhind joined Oxford on loan from Rochdale in January 2006 initially for one month, but it was later extended until the end of the season. Although it took Brian Talbot a while to give him his debut, once he played he looked like the solid defender that United had required. However, at the end of the season, after Oxford's relegation to the Conference, Jim Smith decided against signing him and sent him back to Spotland. Goodhind began his career with Barnet, who he joined in 1995 as a trainee, and for whom he played 114 games and scored five goals. In September 2001 Cambridge United paid £80,000 for him and he spent four years at the Abbey, making 122 appearances without finding the net. He joined Rochdale in September 2005, having been released by Cambridge in May. Goodhind did not have the best of times at Dale, and in September 2006 he was placed on the transfer list and told he could leave on a free transfer. In fact, he played just 12 games for Dale before leaving at the end of his contract in the summer of 2007. After spending pre-season with Dagenham, he signed for Ebbsfleet United in August 2007. He played just eight games for Fleet before moving to Eastleigh in November 2007. At the end of that season he rejected a new contract offer and joined Harrow, but he failed to make an appearance for Borough and he rejoined Eastleigh in September 2008. At the end of November 2009 Goodhind left for Spain to start a coaching career, but the South African returned to Eastleigh in February 2010. He was released at the end of the 2010–11 season and joined Hemel Hempstead Town.

GORDON, Gavin

Forward
Born: 24 June 1979, Manchester
United debut: 28 September 2002 v York City (sub)
Final United game: 6 November 2002 v Aston Villa (sub)
Appearances: 3+4
Goals: 1
Clubs: Hull City, Lincoln City, Cardiff City, Oxford United (loan), Notts County, Crawley Town, Histon

Sir Kenyatta S Gordon (Sir is his given first name) was a striker who joined Oxford on loan from Cardiff in September 2002. He scored on his debut for the U's after coming on as a substitute for David Oldfield at York, but thereafter he failed to set the place alight and his loan was not extended. He joined Hull as a youth and became their second-youngest ever player when he made his debut in September 1995 aged 16 years and 88 days. He played 45 games in total for the Tigers, scoring 10 goals, before he moved to Lincoln for £30,000 in November 1997. After featuring mainly for the reserves, it was not until his second year at Sincil Bank that he was given a sustained run in the first team. However, his potential made it unlikely that he would remain with the Imps in the long term and in December 2000, having just signed a new three-year contract, he joined Cardiff for £275,000. The deal could have been worth £550,000, but Gordon failed to play enough games for the Bluebirds to activate the necessary clauses, making just 56 appearances and scoring 13 goals. Controversially, Cardiff chairman Sam Hammam insisted that Gordon give up his right to play international football for Jamaica in order to sign for them. In June 2004 he moved to Notts County on a free transfer, playing 39 games for the Magpies and scoring eight goals before joining Crawley in February 2006. After just four games Gordon was seriously injured and did not feature again for Crawley, joining Histon in July 2007, but his injuries meant that he did not get to play for them and he retired after one season.

GOUGH, Keith

Winger
Born: 4 February 1953, Willenhall, West Midlands
United debut: 23 December 1972 v Burnley
Final United game: 22 April 1975 v Fulham
Appearances: 37+7
Goals: 6
Clubs: Walsall, Oxford United, Cheltenham Town, Willenhall

Keith Gough was a former England Schoolboy international winger who joined Oxford from Walsall in July 1972. He played for South-East Staffs Schools, Staffordshire Schools and the England Schoolboys Under-15 team. He made 15 Division Three appearances for the Saddlers. After being released by Oxford in the summer of 1975 Gough joined Cheltenham before returning to his home town of Willenhall, where he played for the local club.

GRANT, David

Left-back
Born: 2 June 1960, Sheffield
United debut: 14 August 1982 v Reading
Final United game: 2 January 1984 v Exeter City
Appearances: 29
Goals: 1
Clubs: Sheffield Wednesday, Oxford United, Chesterfield (loan), Crystal Palace (loan), Cardiff City, Rochdale, Macclesfield Town, Mossley (loan), Boston United

David Grant joined Oxford on a free transfer from Sheffield Wednesday in the summer of 1982. He joined Wednesday as an apprentice in July 1976 and turned professional in February 1978. He scored four goals in 133 League games before his move to the Manor. After establishing a first-team place for himself with Oxford, the arrival of Bobby McDonald in September 1983 saw him lose it again. He played seven games on loan for Chesterfield before moving to Cardiff in March 1984. He also had a spell on loan with Crystal Palace, but he was unable to appear for their first team because of problems with his registration. Grant made 25 League appearances for Cardiff before moving to Rochdale, where he scored twice in 97 League games. He joined Macclesfield in 1987 and in the autumn of 1988 he played four games on loan with Mossley, where he scored once. In December 1988 he joined Boston for a small fee and went on to play 43 games and score three goals for them.

GRANT, John

Forward
Born: 9 August 1981, Manchester
United debut: 23 February 2010 v AFC Wimbledon (sub)
Final United game: 27 March 2010 v Gateshead (sub)
Appearances: 3+4
Clubs: Crewe Alexandra, Rushden & Diamonds (loan), Northwich Victoria (loan), Hereford United, Telford United, Shrewsbury Town, Halifax Town, Hyde United, Aldershot Town, Oxford United, Barrow

John Anthony Carlton Grant joined Oxford on loan from Aldershot in February 2010. He arrived with a reputation as a goalscorer, having notched 51 goals for the Shots in 143 games as he helped fire them to the Conference title in 2008. However, he failed to live up to this billing while at Oxford, where he was signed in a bid to arrest a slump in form as Oxford fell away from the title race, and he returned to Aldershot at the end of the season, without having scored for the U's, when he was released. After a move to Wimbledon collapsed, he joined Barrow in November 2010 but left by mutual consent two months later, rejoining the club in June 2011. Grant started his career with Crewe, playing 11 games for them before joining Rushden on loan in November 2001, playing two games. He also had a loan spell with Northwich in February 2002, where he scored four goals in 12 games. In June 2002 he moved to Hereford, scoring four goals in 26 matches, and a year later he signed for Telford United. Grant scored eight goals in 40 matches for the Bucks before signing for Shrewsbury in July 2004. Chances were limited at Gay Meadow, and in March 2005, after two goals in 21 games, he moved to Halifax, managed by Chris Wilder. It was at the Shay that Grant started to live up to his potential, scoring 14 goals in 54 games and being the side's top scorer in 2005–06, when he scored for the Shaymen in their Conference Play-off Final defeat by Hereford. In that summer he moved to Aldershot, scoring twice on his debut and becoming their top scorer with 23 goals and winning the Supporters' Player of the Year at the end of his first season. He was top scorer with 25 goals the following season and was named in the Conference Team of the Year. Grant, who has only nine fingers as the result of a DIY accident, also won four England C caps, scoring one goal.

GRAY, Martin

Midfielder
Born: 17 August 1981, Stockton-on-Tees
United debut: 2 April 1996 v Wrexham
Final United game: 9 May 1999 v Stockport County
Appearances: 126+6
Goals: 4

Clubs: Ferryhill Athletic, Sunderland, Aldershot (loan), Fulham (loan), Oxford United, Darlington, Whitby Town, Bishop Auckland

Martin David Gray joined Oxford from Sunderland for £100,000 in March 1996. He joined Sunderland in 1990 as a trainee after playing for Trimdon United Juniors, and in his six years at Roker Park he played 79 games and scored one goal. In his time there he also had loan spells with Aldershot in January 1991 (six games) and Fulham in October 1995 (seven games). It was at Oxford that he really established himself, linking up with David Smith during and after Oxford's promotion in 1996. He was released by Oxford in May 1999 and returned up north to sign for Darlington. After 84 games for the Quakers, Gray moved to Whitby in August 2002 while continuing as youth team coach at Feethams. In 2003 he became assistant manager and in 2006 he was made joint caretaker manager with Neil Maddison following David Hodgson's suspension. Two weeks later David Penney was appointed manager with Gray as his assistant. When Penney left for Oldham in May 2009 Gray was again made caretaker for the final game of the season, after which he moved to Oldham to become Penney's assistant again. In May 2010 Penney left Oldham and Gray was appointed caretaker, but after failing to get the manager's job he left the club and instead concentrated on his football academy business.

GRAY, Phil

Forward
Born: 2 October 1968, Belfast
United debut: 11 November 2000 v Swansea City
Final United game: 1 April 2002 v York City
Appearances: 39+9
Goals: 13
Clubs: Tottenham Hotspur, Barnsley (loan), Fulham (loan), Luton Town, Sunderland, AS Nancy (France), Fortuna Sittard (Netherlands), Luton Town, Burnley, Oxford United, Boston United (loan), Chelmsford City, Stevenage Borough (loan), Maidenhead United, Stotfold

Philip Gray joined Oxford from Burnley in November 2000 on a free transfer. He started with Ballyclare Comrades before joining Spurs, signing professionally in August 1986. He played just 10 matches for Tottenham without scoring, and had a four-game loan spell with Barnsley in January 1990 followed by a five-game loan with Fulham in November 1990 in which he scored once. In August 1991 he joined Luton for £275,000, going on to play 65 games and score 26 goals over the next two years. This prompted Sunderland to pay £800,000 for Gray in July 1993. He was released by the Rokerites in May 1996 after playing 134 games and scoring 41 goals, and he joined French side Nancy, for whom he scored four goals in 16 games. Gray moved from France to the Netherlands to sign for Fortuna Sittard, scoring one goal in 12 Eredivisie appearances, returning to England in September 1997 to rejoin Luton, who this time paid £400,000 for him. Gray played 94 games in his second spell at Kenilworth Road, scoring 27 goals before being released in July 2000 and joining Burnley. He played just eight games for the Clarets, scoring once, before moving to the Manor. At Oxford he showed intelligence and an eye for goal, despite being in the twilight of his career. He had a three-game loan with Boston before leaving Oxford and joining Chelmsford. He played two games on loan to Stevenage before leaving

Chelmsford to become player-assistant manager to John Dreyer at Maidenhead in May 2003. In February 2005 he signed for Stotfold in Bedfordshire. Gray also played 26 games for Northern Ireland, scoring six goals.

GRAY, Stuart

Left-winger
Born: 18 December 1973, Harrogate
United debut: 6 August 2005 v Grimsby Town
Final United game: 25 February 2006 v Wycombe Wanderers
Appearances: 11
Clubs: Celtic, Giffnock North AFC (loan), AFC Bournemouth (loan), Greenock Morton (loan), Reading, Rushden & Diamonds, Oxford United, Guiseley Town

Stuart Edward Gray was signed by Brian Talbot from his former side Rushden & Diamonds in May 2005, but after an injury in February 2006 he failed to regain his first-team place and was released at the end of the 2005–06 season. Gray was the son of Scottish international Eddie Gray and he joined Celtic as a youngster, going on work experience to Glasgwegian side Giffnock North in August 1991. While with Celtic Gray won seven Scotland Under-21 caps and played 30 games, scoring one goal. He was loaned to Bournemouth in 1994 but did not get to play for the Cherries and on his return to Celtic he signed a monthly deal. After injuries he was loaned to Morton in October 1997, scoring one goal in 15 appearances. Afterwards he was unable to get back into Celtic's first team and in January 1998 he moved to Reading for £100,000. Despite spending three years with the Royals, Gray made just 64 appearances and scored two goals and in March 2001 he left on a free transfer for Rushden & Diamonds. While he was with the Diamonds the club won the Division Three title, although they were relegated in 2004 and he left the club at the end of the following season, having made 145 appearances in which he scored 15 goals. After his season with the U's Gray retired from full-time football and joined Guiseley Town, where he became assistant manager and coach of their reserves side. In the 2009 film *The Damned United*, about Brian Clough's time with Leeds United, Gray played the part of his father.

GRAYDON, Ray

Winger
Born: 21 July 1947, Bristol
United debut: 18 November 1978 v Swansea City
Final United game: 4 April 1981 v Brentford (sub)
Appearances: 40+7
Goals: 10
Clubs: Bristol Rovers, Aston Villa, Coventry City, Washington Diplomats (USA), Oxford United

Raymond Jack Graydon joined Oxford from Washington Diplomats for £30,000 in November 1978. In April 1981, after playing his final game, he joined United's coaching staff, later becoming assistant manager to Jim Smith and then Maurice Evans. He was sacked when Mark Lawrenson took over, becoming youth team coach at Watford. Graydon later coached at Southampton before going into management at Walsall in 1998. At the end of his first season he took Walsall up to Division One and finished second, behind Sir Alex Ferguson, in the League Managers' Association's Manager of the Season poll. Although Walsall were relegated after just one season, Graydon took them up again the following season via the Play-offs. This time, the disappointing results were too much for the board, who sacked Graydon in January 2002. In April 2002 he was appointed as manager of Bristol Rovers, but he was sacked in January 2004, after which he went to manage in China for a few months. He became first-team coach at Leicester in February 2006, but left the Foxes at the end of the season, going on to become a Premiership referees' assessor. Graydon's first club was Bristol Rovers, for whom he played 133 League games and scored 33 goals before he joined Aston Villa for £23,000 and a player exchange in June 1971. He was capped for the England Youth side while with the Gas. Villa won promotion from Division Three in Graydon's first season, and in 1973 they finished third in Division Two, with Graydon as top scorer. The following season Graydon scored 27 goals as Villa were promoted to the top flight and won the League Cup, with Graydon scoring the winning goal against Norwich City at Wembley. In July 1977, after Graydon had won a second League Cup winners' medal and had scored 68 goals in 192 League games, he joined Coventry. He scored five goals in 20 League games for the Sky Blues before a transatlantic move to Washington Diplomats in the NASL. He played 26 games without scoring before his return to England with Oxford.

GREBIS, Kristaps

Forward
Born: 13 December 1980, Liepija (Latvia)
United debut: 20 January 2007 v Grays Athletic
Final United game: 10 February 2007 v Aldershot Town (sub)
Appearances: 3+1
Clubs: FHK Liepijas Metalurgs (Latvia), FK Riga (Latvia), FHK Liepijas Metalurgs (Latvia), Oxford United, FK Ventspils (Latvia), FHK Liepijas Metalurgs (Latvia), AEL Limassol (Cyprus), FK Gäncä (Azerbaijan)

Kristaps Grebis was a Latvian international signed by Jim Smith, who had not seen him play, from Liepijas Metalurgs in January 2007. Unfortunately, Grebis was unable to replicate the form that had made him such a prolific scorer in the Latvian League and he was released from his contract in March 2007 without even managing a shot on goal in his four appearances. Grebis had scored 82 goals in 188 starts for Metalurgs and had won four caps for Latvia before he joined United. After leaving the Kassam, Grebis returned to Latvia with Ventspils, but he soon returned to Metalurgs, which was the team where he began his career. In 2009 he was the Latvian League's leading scorer with 30 goals in 28 games, having scored 12 goals the season before and another 12 from 23 games in 2010. He then had a trial with FC Tobol of Kazakhstan before, in February 2011, Grebis joined Cypriot side AEL Limassol. He was, however, released just a few days later with the club falsely claiming that Grebis had a heart problem, whereas in fact their new coach wanted an excuse to release him. Shortly afterwards he joined Azerbaijani side FK Gäncä.

GREEN, Francis

Forward
Born: 25 April 1980, Nottingham
United debut: 24 November 2009 v Forest Green Rovers
Final United game: 13 April 2010 v Cambridge United
Appearances: 13+4
Goals: 2
Clubs: Ilkeston Town, Peterborough United, Lincoln City (loan), Lincoln City, Boston United (loan), Boston United, Macclesfield Town, Kettering Town, Oxford United (loan), Oxford United, Brackley Town

Francis James Green joined Oxford from Kettering in November 2009, initially on loan. Unfortunately Green failed to impress and, despite scoring a spectacular goal at Chelmsford City in the FA Trophy, he was too far off the pace to challenge for a regular first-team place and he was released in May 2010, eventually signing for nearby Brackley. Green started his career as a youth with Ilkeston, where Keith Alexander was manager. In March 1998 he joined Peterborough for £25,000, where he scored 16 goals in 126 appearances, before linking up with Alexander again at Lincoln in September 2003, initially on loan, for £75,000. He played 106 games for the Imps, scoring 20 goals, and in November 2005 he had a six-game loan spell at Boston, during which he scored once. Green moved permanently to Boston in May 2006 where he stayed for a year, scoring four goals in 40 games before rejoining Alexander again in June 2007 when he moved to Macclesfield. In his two seasons at Moss Rose, Green scored 16 goals in 72 matches. In July 2009 he dropped into the Conference, joining Kettering Town, where he scored four goals in 21 games before signing for Oxford.

*GREEN, Matt

Forward
Born: 2 January 1987, Bath
United debut: 24 November 2007 v Kidderminster Harriers
Final United game: 3 January 2011 v Torquay United
Appearances: 61+30
Goals: 25
Clubs: Newport County, Cardiff City, Darlington (loan), Oxford United (loan), Torquay United, Oxford United (loan), Oxford United, Cheltenham Town (loan), Mansfield Town (loan)

Matthew James Green had three spells with Oxford, initially joining United on a one-month loan from Cardiff in November 2007. He scored on his debut at Kidderminster, but he broke his collarbone three minutes into his third game and returned to Wales. Following his recovery Oxford signed him again in January 2008 on loan until the end of the season. His excellent performances, allied with his pace and eye for goal, led United to try and sign him permanently after his loan expired, and he agreed to the deal but, on the day he was due to sign, with his agent and United manager Darren Patterson waiting for him at the Kassam, he instead travelled to Torquay and signed for them. In his first season at Plainmoor, Torquay won promotion from the Conference via the Play-offs, but Green was only a bit-part player, making 32 appearances (mainly as substitute) and scoring five goals. Despite his previous about-turn, Oxford re-signed Green from the Gulls on a season-long loan in July 2009, and Green played a significant role in United's promotion from the Conference, playing 46 games and scoring 12 goals, including Oxford's first in the Wembley

Play-off Final. He also made the second goal for James Constable, his teammate when they were both with the Cirencester Academy, where Green went after being released by Bristol City. In June 2010 Green signed a two-year contract with Oxford, but in the Football League he lost his scoring touch and in January 2011 he joined Cheltenham on loan until the end of the season, failing to find the net in 19 appearances, after which he was transfer-listed. In July 2011 he moved to Mansfield on loan until 31 December. After leaving Cirencester, Green joined Newport County in the summer of 2005 and after scoring eight goals in 48 Conference South matches, Cardiff paid £10,000 for him. He made just seven substitute appearances for the Bluebirds, plus a five-game loan spell with Darlington in October 2007, before his first arrival at the Kassam. Green won an England C cap in September 2009.

GREENALL, Colin

Centre-back
Born: 30 December 1963, Billinge, Lancashire
United debut: 5 March 1988 v West Ham United
Final United game: 11 November 1989 v Oldham Athletic
Appearances: 74
Goals: 2
Clubs: Blackpool, Gillingham, Oxford United, Bury (loan), Bury, Preston North End, Chester City, Lincoln City, Wigan Athletic, Rossendale United

Colin Anthony Greenall became United's record signing when he joined from Gillingham for £235,000 in February 1988. He made his debut for his first club, Blackpool, aged 16 years 238 days, becoming their youngest ever player at the time. He won his England Youth caps at that time and in 1984 Greenall was voted the PFA's Fourth Division Player of the Year. Greenall played 206 games for Blackpool, scoring 11 goals, before joining Gillingham for £40,000 in September 1986. He played 80 games for the Gills, scoring eight times, before his move to the Manor. Oxford was Greenall's only experience of top-flight football, and although he was named club captain he never truly convinced at the heart of the defence. United were relegated at the end of Greenall's first season but he remained with the U's until July 1990, when he joined Bury for £100,000 after a four-game loan spell at Gigg Lane. He made 80 appearances for the Shakers, grabbing six goals, before moving to Preston for £50,000 in March 1992. At the end of the following season North End were relegated and Greenall moved on again, this time joining Chester on a free transfer after scoring one goal in 29 games for the Deepdale club. He spent one season with Chester, during which they won promotion and Greenall was voted Player of the Season, and after 52 games and two goals he moved to Lincoln. He scored four times in 52 games for the Imps before moving, in September 1995, to Wigan for £45,000. While with the Latics he was made captain and guided them to promotion from Division Three in 1997. In 1999 he captained Wigan to a Wembley win over Millwall in the Auto Windscreens Trophy and to a Play-off semi-final defeat against Manchester City. He retired at the end of the season having played 228 games for Wigan, for whom he scored 21 goals. He stayed with Wigan as reserve team manager, and had a six-game spell as caretaker manager in February 2001, after which he became first-team coach. He left Wigan in November 2001, joining Rossendale on a match-by-match basis. He became head of youth development at Rochdale in June 2002 and two years later he became Dale's Centre of Excellence director. In August 2005 Greenall became the coach education manager at the Lancashire FA.

GREGORY, Peter

Full-back
United debut: 12 November 1949 v Exeter City Reserves
Final United game: 11 February 1950 v Merthyr Tydfil
Appearances: 4
Clubs: Headington United

Peter E. Gregory was a regular member of the reserves and played three games 'of exceptional merit' for the first team. He was considered an excellent prospect for the future who was urged to give all his time to training and take all opportunities of further coaching. His lack of future appearances suggests that he failed to heed this advice.

GRIEVE, David

Right-winger
Born: 15 February 1929, Selkirk
Died: 2004
United debut: 28 December 1959 v Barry Town
Final United game: 9 April 1960 v Bedford Town
Appearances: 10
Goals: 4
Clubs: Dalry Thistle, Reading, Crystal Palace, Worcester City, Headington United

David Grieve joined Headington from Worcester and left in the summer of 1960. He had played 20 games and scored one goal for Reading between 1951 and 1954 before moving to Crystal Palace, for whom he played 22 matches and scored three goals. He moved to Worcester City in 1955, scoring 44 goals before his move to the Manor.

GRIFFIN, Adam

Left-winger
Born: 26 August 1984, Salford
United debut: 12 November 2005 v Wrexham (sub)
Final United game: 14 January 2006 v Macclesfield Town
Appearances: 12+1
Clubs: Oldham Athletic, Chester City (loan), Oxford United (loan), Stockport County (loan), Stockport County, Darlington, Stockport County

Adam Griffin was a left-winger who joined Oxford on loan from Oldham in November 2005. His pace and trickery made him instantly popular, but his loan was not extended and he returned to Boundary Park. Oldham was Griffin's first side and he made his debut in April 2002. He played 74 games for the Latics, scoring four goals, and in addition to his spell at the Kassam he also made one appearance on work experience with Chester in January 2003. After returning to Oldham from Oxford in January 2006 he immediately went on loan to Stockport until the end of the season, where he played 21 games and scored twice. After the loan ended he joined Stockport on a permanent deal, playing 78 games over the next two years, in which he scored four goals. After Stockport's promotion in 2008 Griffin was released and signed for Darlington, where he made 22 appearances before rejoining Stockport in July 2009. Griffin made 69 appearances for the Hatters, scoring three goals, but after their relegation to the Conference in May 2011 he was released by the club.

GROVES, Richard

Midfielder

Born: 4 January 1991, Hillingdon
United debut: 4 November 2008 v Forest Green Rovers
Final United game: 28 December 2008 v Ebbsfleet United (sub)
Appearances: 1+2
Clubs: Plymouth Argyle, Oxford United, Banbury United (loan), Tiverton Town (loan), Weymouth

Richard David Groves joined Oxford from Plymouth as a youth, having previously been with the Torquay United Centre of Excellence and, before that, the Fulham Academy. While with Oxford he had a spell on work experience with Banbury in October 2008 and in February 2010 he spent a month on loan at Tiverton. He was released by Oxford and signed for Weymouth in August 2010.

GUATELLI, Andrea

Goalkeeper

Born: 5 May 1984, Parma (Italy)
United debut: 25 March 2006 v Peterborough United
Final United game: 29 April 2006 v Wrexham
Appearances: 4
Clean sheets: 1
Clubs: Parma (Italy), Unione Sportiva Fiorenzuola 1922 (Italy) (loan), Portsmouth, Oxford United (loan), FC Zürich (Switzerland)

Andrea Guatelli was a 6ft 4in goalkeeper signed on loan by Jim Smith in March 2006 as one of five players brought in on transfer deadline day after Smith was appointed manager for the second time. Despite keeping a clean sheet in a win over Peterborough in his first game, Guatelli failed to impress and his presence added a nervousness to United's defence as Oxford plummeted from the Football League into the Conference. Guatelli returned to Portsmouth at the end of the season, when he was released without having played for the first team. He had signed for Pompey from Parma on a free transfer in August 2004, having established a reputation with the Italian side as an up-and-coming future star. He had a 34-game loan spell with Serie D side Fiorenzuola in 2004, just before his move to Portsmouth. In January 2007 he signed for Zürich as a back-up 'keeper.

GUNN, Andrew

Centre-back

Born: 22 February 1988, Oxford
United debut: 1 January 2007 v Exeter City (sub)
Final United game: 10 February 2007 v Aldershot Town (sub)
Appearances: 1+2
Clubs: Oxford United, Didcot Town (loan), Oxford City, Didcot Town

Andrew Peter Gunn was a centre-back who became an Oxford United scholar in 2004, progressing to the senior squad two years later. In May 2006 he was voted the Young Player of the Year, and he had a month's loan at Didcot in October 2006. Gunn was released by United at the end of the 2006–07 season and joined neighbours Oxford City. He returned to Didcot in July 2010.

GUY, Jamie

Forward
Born: 1 August 1987, Barking
United debut: 25 August 2008 v Woking
Final United game: 1 January 2009 v Salisbury City
Appearances: 21+5
Goals: 5
Clubs: Colchester United, Tiptree United (loan), Gravesend & Northfleet (loan), Cambridge United (loan), Oxford United (loan), Dagenham & Redbridge (loan), Port Vale (loan), Grays Athletic, Braintree Town

James Leslie Guy moved to Oxford from Colchester on a season-long loan in the summer of 2008, bringing with him the reputation as a bit of a bad boy. He showed a lot of promise in the pre-season games, but was recalled by Colchester in January 2009 without having lived up to that early potential. Guy started at Colchester as a trainee and spent a month on loan at Tiptree in August 2004 before making his Colchester debut in February 2005, coming on for Sam Stockley. In October 2005 he joined Gravesend on loan, but made just one substitute appearance for the Kent club. His next loan was to Cambridge in February 2006, where he scored twice in 12 games. His loan at Oxford was blighted by a hamstring injury he received in a pre-season friendly against Portsmouth and his United career was thereafter somewhat spasmodic. When Chris Wilder became manager in December 2008 Guy returned to Layer Road and almost immediately went out on loan again, this time to Dagenham, where he scored once in nine matches. His final loan move was to Port Vale in July 2009, but he made just six appearances in four months due to a torn knee cartilage keeping him out until October. In January 2010 his contract with Colchester was cancelled by mutual consent and he joined Grays, having played 59 games for them, but making just four starts, and scoring three goals. He scored three goals in 15 games for Grays before being released at the end of the season, whereupon he moved to Braintree. In February 2011 Guy suffered an open double leg fracture in a collision with the Eastleigh goalkeeper.

GUYETT, Scott

Centre-back
Born: 20 January 1976, Ascot
United debut: 11 August 2001 v Rochdale
Final United game: 13 April 2002 v Cheltenham Town (sub)
Appearances: 23+2
Clubs: Brisbane City (Australia), Taringa Rovers (Australia), Gresley Rovers, Southport, Oxford United, Chester City, Yeovil Town, Aldershot Town (loan), AFC Bournemouth, Dorchester Town

Scott Barry Guyett was signed by Mark Wright from his former club Southport. Although he was an Australian national, he was born in Ascot and represented England for the semi-professional side. He started with Brisbane and also captained Queensland. While playing for Taringa he was spotted by Paul Futcher who brought him back to England to play for Gresley, with whom he won the Southern League Premier Division. Gresley were denied promotion to the Conference because of ground grading issues and in August 1988 Futcher paid Gresley £5,000 to sign Guyett for Southport. At the end of his first season he won both the Players' Player of the Year and the Supporters' Player of the Year awards as he formed a solid central-defensive partnership with Phil Bolland. He played 108 games and scored 12 goals for Port before joining Wright and Bolland at Oxford, making his debut in the first game at the Kassam Stadium. After Wright's dismissal in November 2001 Guyett's opportunities became more limited and he was released from his contract by Ian Atkins after claiming that he wanted to return to Australia. Days later he rejoined Wright and Bolland at Chester. In his second season he was voted the Supporters' Player of the Year as the club won the Conference title, with Guyett voted the best defender in the Conference. In the summer of 2004 he joined Yeovil on a free transfer after 69 games and one goal for Chester. Guyett spent four years at the Huish, interrupted by a 13-game (one goal) loan with Aldershot in August 2005. He played 102 games for the Glovers, scoring two goals, before joining Bournemouth on a free transfer in August 2008. He played 40 matches for the Cherries, leaving in May 2010. He then joined Dorchester in September 2010, but left at the start of November to become a fitness and conditioning coach at Crystal Palace.

H

HACKETT, Chris

Right-winger
Born: 1 March 1983, Oxford
United debut: 8 April 2000 v Wigan Athletic (sub)
Final United game: 7 January 2006 v Shrewsbury Town
Appearances: 79+63
Goals: 9
Clubs: Oxford United, Heart of Midlothian, Millwall

Christopher James Hackett was a local boy from Sandford-on-Thames. He was a former Oxfordshire sprint champion and came through the Oxford youth system, becoming a scholar in 1999 and joining the senior squad the following season. He is one of the fastest players to have appeared in an Oxford shirt, but his crossing was often rather haphazard. In January 2006 he moved to Hearts, managed by Graham Rix, for £20,000. In his seven months in Edinburgh, Hackett made just two appearances and in August 2006 he joined Millwall on a free transfer. At Millwall he was successfully converted to a right-back.

HACKNEY, Simon

Left-winger
Born: 5 February 1984, Manchester
United debut: 2 February 2011 v Southend (sub)
Final United game: 2 April 2011 v Bury (sub)
Appearances: 2+9
Clubs: Nantwich Town, Woodley Sports, Carlisle United, Colchester United, Morecambe (loan), Oxford United (loan), Rochdale

Simon John Hackney joined Oxford on loan from Colchester on transfer deadline day in January 2011 until the end of the season. He started his career as a semi-professional with Nantwich before joining Woodley Sports. He became the first player that Woodley sold to a professional club when he joined Carlisle in February 2005. In January 2009 he moved to Colchester, having played 138 times for the Cumbrians, scoring 17 goals and helping Carlisle climb from the Conference to League One. In March 2010 Hackney spent eight games on loan with Morecambe, scoring one goal. Hackney had played 41 games and scored three goals for Colchester before his loan to Oxford. Unfortunately, a hamstring injury led to his loan being cut short and he returned to Colchester in April 2011. The following month he was told that he would not be offered a new deal by Colchester when his current contract expired in the summer and he was signed by Rochdale in June 2011.

HALDANE, Lewis

Left-winger
Born: 13 March 1985, Trowbridge
United debut: 8 August 2008 v Barrow
Final United game: 26 April 2009 v Northwich Victoria

Appearances: 40+10
Goals: 3
Clubs: Bristol Rovers, Clevedon Town (loan), Forest Green Rovers (loan), Oxford United (loan), Port Vale (loan), Port Vale

Lewis Oliver Haldane joined United on a season-long loan from Bristol Rovers. He started as a youth with Southampton Academy, where he was a prolific goalscorer, and after he was released by the Saints he was invited to join Rovers on a scholarship. At the beginning of the 2003–04 season he went on work experience to Clevedon Town. Haldane had a six-game loan spell with Forest Green Rovers in March 2005, and he returned to the New Lawn for seven appearances in August 2005. After he returned to the Memorial Stadium from Oxford, Haldane joined Port Vale on loan for the 2009–2010 season, playing 43 games and scoring three goals. He joined Vale permanently in January 2010, having competed in 177 games and scored 17 goals for the Pirates.

HALE, Graham

Full-back
United debut: 29 September 1949 v Cheltenham Town
Final United game: 21 January 1950 v Hereford United
Appearances: 10
Clubs: Pressed Steel, Headington United

Graham Hale was an amateur during United's first season in the Southern League.

HALE, Ken

Midfielder
Born: 18 September 1939, Blyth
United debut: 5 March 1966 v Workington
Final United game: 20 January 1968 v Peterborough United (sub)
Appearances: 70+2
Goals: 13
Clubs: Newcastle United, Coventry City, Oxford United, Darlington, Halifax Town

Kenneth Oliver Hale joined Oxford from Coventry for £8,000 in March 1966. He started as a junior with Newcastle United in 1957 and by the time that he moved to the Sky Blues in the 1962–63 season he had scored 15 goals in 30 League appearances for the Toon. He played 99 League games for Coventry, scoring 27 goals before his move to Oxford. The following season Hale was briefly made United's captain, but this honour soon reverted to Ron Atkinson. He moved to Darlington in May 1968 where he made 173 League appearances, scoring 25 goals, and in January 1972 he had a four-month spell as caretaker manager there. He joined Halifax as a player in April 1972, playing 52 League games and scoring four goals, before joining Hartlepool United as manager in June 1974, taking charge of over 100 games before leaving in October 1976. He later became a newsagent owner on Wearside.

HALL, Alan

Full-back/Winger
United debut: 29 April 1950 v Guildford City
Final United game: 26 December 1956 v Bedford Town
Appearances: 30
Clubs: Oxford City, Headington United

Alan J Hall spent two seasons with Oxford City before he joined Headington United. His first-team appearances were rare, and he was as likely to feature on the right wing as he was in either full-back position. His career was interrupted by National Service, and he did not play between April 1952 and August 1955.

*HALL, Asa

Midfielder
Born: 29 November 1986, Sandwell, West Midlands
United debut: 7 August 2010 v Burton Albion
Final United game: 7 May 2011 v Shrewsbury Town
Appearances: 36+8
Goals: 4
Clubs: Birmingham City, Boston United (loan), Ashford Town (Kent) (loan), Shrewsbury Town (loan), Luton Town, Oxford United

Asa Philip Hall joined Oxford from Luton in the summer of 2010. He joined Birmingham City after coming through the youth ranks at Wolverhampton Wanderers. He was capped for England at Under-19 and Under-20 levels and had loan spells with Boston United, Ashford Town and Shrewsbury Town, for whom he scored three goals in 15 appearances between January and May 2008. He joined Luton on a free transfer in July 2008, having failed to break into Birmingham's first team, and he starred for the Hatters as they won the Johnstone's Paint Trophy Final in April 2009, as Luton were relegated to the Conference. He joined Oxford on a free transfer after playing 89 games and scoring 17 goals for Luton.

HAMILTON, Billy

Forward
Born: 9 May 1957, Belfast
United debut: 25 August 1984 v Huddersfield Town
Final United game: 11 October 1986 v Coventry City
Appearances: 41
Goals: 20
Clubs: Linfield (Northern Ireland), Queen's Park Rangers, Burnley, Oxford United, Limerick (Ireland), Coleraine (Northern Ireland), Sligo Rovers (Ireland), Distillery (Northern Ireland)

William Robert Hamilton was at Oxford for just a short time, but he became a Manor legend for his goals and the partnership that he forged with John Aldridge. He joined United from Burnley for £95,000 plus Neil Whatmore. He started with Belfast Scots, but was spotted by Linfield, with whom he won the Ulster League and Cup double in 1978. In March that year QPR signed him for £25,000 and it was while with Rangers that Hamilton won his first Northern Ireland cap. He joined Burnley from Loftus Road for £55,000 in November 1979. In 1982, Billy played in the World Cup finals in Spain, and he scored both goals in the 2–2 draw with Austria. He won 41 caps for Northern Ireland, of which six were earned while he was at the Manor, and he scored five international goals. He was forced to retire through injury in October 1986 after hurting himself during a pre-match warm-up. After doing a couple of months' scouting for United, Hamilton went on to become player-manager of Limerick. Following spells with Sligo Rovers and Coleraine, he was signed by Distillery as player-manager in 1989 before eventually retiring in 1995.

HAND, Jamie

Midfielder
Born: 7 February 1984, Uxbridge
United debut: 28 August 2004 v Shrewsbury Town
Final United game: 26 April 2008 v Ebbsfleet United
Appearances: 25
Goals: 2
Clubs: Watford, Oxford United (loan), Livingston (loan), Peterborough United (loan), Huddersfield Town (loan), Fisher Athletic, Northampton Town (loan), Chester City, Lincoln City, Oxford United (loan), Ebbsfleet United, Chelmsford City, Woking, Hemel Hempstead Town, Hayes & Yeading United

Jamie Hand started with Watford as a trainee and made 61 senior appearances for the Horns without scoring. During his time at Vicarage Road he had several loan spells, the first of which was with Oxford in August 2004. During this first loan at the Kassam, Hand played 12 games and scored twice. He went on to play nine games for Livingston in January 2005, two for Peterborough in September 2005 and one for Huddersfield the following month. He left for Fisher Athletic in February 2006 but moved straight to Northampton on loan for 11 games the same month. Without having played a game for Fisher, in May 2006 Hand joined Chester on a free transfer, spending the full season at the Deva Stadium before moving on to Lincoln in August 2007. It was while at Sincil Bank that Hand returned to Oxford for a second loan, making 13 appearances. A year after arriving at Lincoln he moved to Ebbsfleet United, but he had to leave for personal reasons in February 2009. He joined Chelmsford for the rest of the season, and in September 2009 he signed for Woking. In March 2010 Hand joined Hemel Hempstead where he stayed until he signed for Hayes & Yeading in the August.

HANSON, Mitchell

Defender
Born: 2 September 1988, Derby
United debut: 23 April 2011 v Chesterfield (sub)
Final United game: 7 May 2011 v Shrewsbury Town (sub)
Appearances: 0+2
Clubs: Derby County, Port Vale (loan), Notts County (loan), Oxford United

Mitchell Gene Ben Hanson joined Oxford in March 2011 until the end of the season, having impressed on trial with the reserves the previous month. Hanson played well in both right-back and central-defensive positions, but he was unable to break into the United first team and was released at the end of the season. He had been released by Derby County in January 2011 after a career disrupted by injury. This trend was continued on his Oxford debut against League Two leaders Chesterfield in April 2011; after coming on as a substitute he suffered a head wound that required seven stitches just 12 minutes later. Hanson graduated through the Derby Academy and signed professionally in June 2007. He joined Port Vale on loan in March 2008, but because of injury he returned to Derby the following month without having played for the Valiants. In November 2008 Hanson made his only appearance for the Rams, as a substitute in a Coca-Cola Cup tie against Brighton, and later that month he joined Notts County on loan, managing five games for the Magpies. In January 2009 Hanson signed a two-year deal with Derby, but in September 2009 he suffered a dislocated kneecap, ruling him out for a whole year. He did not play another game for Derby before he was released.

HARDWICK, Steve

Goalkeeper
Born: 6 September 1956, Mansfield
United debut: 26 February 1983 v Walsall
Final United game: 6 February 1988 v Luton Town
Appearances: 196
Clean sheets: 57
Clubs: Chesterfield, Newcastle United, Detroit Express (USA) (loan), Oxford United, Crystal Palace (loan), Sunderland (loan), Huddersfield Town, Emley, Boston United

Steven Hardwick was an England Youth and amateur international before signing professional papers for his first club Chesterfield in 1974. In December 1976 he moved to Newcastle for £80,000 and was called-up to the England Under-21 squad. Hardwick made 101 appearances for the Magpies and had a 34-game loan spell with Detroit during the summer of 1978. Unusually for a goalkeeper, Hardwick scored eight goals while with Newcastle. In February 1983 United paid £15,000 for him and he immediately displaced John Butcher. Hardwick was virtually an ever present as the U's won the Third and Second Division titles, and he also played the first half of United's maiden top-flight season until he lost his place to Alan Judge. He was recalled for Oxford's game at Liverpool in which he conceded six goals – before that he had a loan with Crystal Palace in January 1986, playing three games. He also played most of the second half of the 1986–87 season and in August 1987 he had an eight-game loan to Sunderland. Hardwick moved to Huddersfield in the summer of 1988, where he stayed for three seasons before dropping into local football. Hardwick joined Hoylandswaine Cricket Club (between Barnsley and Penistone) as wicketkeeper in the 1990s (when he was playing for Huddersfield), and also became their groundsman, a role that he still performs.

HARGREAVES, Chris

Midfielder
Born: 12 May 1972, Cleethorpes
United debut: 6 August 2005 v Grimsby Town
Final United game: 24 April 2010 v Eastbourne Borough
Appearances: 83+12
Goals: 6

Clubs: Grimsby Town, Scarborough (loan), Hull City, West Bromwich Albion, Hereford United (loan), Hereford United, Plymouth Argyle, Northampton Town, Brentford, Oxford United, Torquay United, Oxford United

Christian Hargreaves had two spells with Oxford. He initially signed from Brentford in the summer of 2005, was installed as club captain and scored on his debut against his first club, Grimsby. However, Oxford were relegated to the Conference at the end of that season, during which Hargreaves was badly injured. He left United for Torquay at the end of the 2006–07 season and he played 121 games, scoring 10 goals, before rejoining the U's in January 2010 because the club required his experience of winning the Conference Play-offs with the Gulls as they sought their own promotion, successfully. After being released by United in the summer of 2010, Hargreaves retired from football and wrote his autobiography *Where's Your Caravan?* Hargreaves began his career with Grimsby in 1989, but was used mainly as a substitute. He had a three-game loan with Scarborough in March 1993 before moving to Hull in July 1993. After two years on Humberside, Hargreaves made an ill-fated move to West Brom, where he made just two appearances, both as substitute, in 13 months. He joined Hereford on loan in February 1996 and was so successful that the Bulls signed him in August that year. Hargreaves spent two years at Edgar Street before joining Plymouth, where he played for a further two seasons. In June 2000 he signed for Northampton where he played for four years, his longest spell at any club. He played 170 games for the Cobblers before his move to Brentford in June 2004.

HARPER, Tony

Wing-back
Born: 26 May 1925, Horspath, Oxford
Died: 1982
United debut: 17 September 1955 v Yeovil Town
Final United game: 26 September 1959 v Cheltenham Town
Appearances: 138
Goals: 6
Clubs: Oxford City, Brentford, Headington United

Antony Frederick Harper was a local wing-back who played for Headington in the Spartan League aged just 14 years. He was spotted by Brentford scouts while playing against Chelsea Mariners in the Spartan League in March 1948 and joined the Bees at the end of that season, thereby becoming the first Headington player to join the Football League. Harper made 173 League appearances for the West London club and scored six goals in those games before returning to the Manor in 1955. Back in Oxford, Harper played for a further four years before a knee injury ended his career.

HARRINGTON, Colin

Winger
Born: 3 April 1943, Bicester
United debut: 19 April 1963 v Workington
Final United game: 10 March 1971 v Leyton Orient
Appearances: 254+6
Goals: 32
Clubs: Wolverhampton Wanderers, Oxford United, Mansfield Town, Kettering Town

Colin Andrew Harrington, nicknamed 'Flash' because of his speed, was widely regarded as one of the fastest players ever to play for the club. He joined United as an apprentice while they were still in the Southern League, having had a spell with Wolves' youth team, and earned promotion to the seniors in 1962. He signed for Mansfield in 1971, making just 13 League appearances before linking up with his former playing colleague Ron Atkinson, who took him to Kettering. Harrington scored 18 goals in 81 games for the Poppies.

HARRIS, Andy

Midfielder
Born: 17 November 1972, Birmingham
United debut: 26 October 1991 v Leicester City
Final United game: 26 October 1991 v Leicester City
Appearances: 1
Clubs: Birmingham City, Oxford United (loan), Exeter City, Nuneaton Borough

Andrew Harris had a brief career at Oxford. He arrived on loan from Birmingham in October 1991 and started against Leicester. His performance was so poor that he was substituted at half-time and never played for the club again. The following month, after just one substitute appearance for the Blues, he moved to Exeter, where he spent two and a half years. After 38 League games for the Grecians, Harris moved to Nuneaton.

HARRIS, Bernard

Outside-left
United debut: 10 December 1960 v Wisbech Town
Final United game: 25 February 1961 v Bath City
Appearances: 4
Goals: 1
Clubs: Oxford City, Oxford United, Oxford City

Bernard Harris played for Oxford City from 1955 until joining United during the 1960–61 season, but he left for Australia shortly afterwards. He briefly returned to City after a three-year absence. During the 1958–59 season Harris was chosen for the South v North England Trial, where he scored the South's only goal.

HARTLAND, Mick

Midfielder
Born: 7 January 1944, Dunfermline
United debut: 12 October 1963 v Halifax Town
Final United game: 28 November 1964 v Wrexham
Appearances: 20
Goals: 6
Clubs: Birmingham City, Nuneaton Borough, Oxford United, Barrow, Crewe Alexandra, Southport, Fleetwood

Michael Leo Hartland joined Oxford from Nuneaton Borough in June 1963. He secured a regular first-team place at the end of his first season, and continued until Graham Atkinson ousted him on his return from his loan at Cambridge United. In July 1965 he moved to Barrow on a free transfer, becoming a regular for the Bluebirds and earning the captaincy and a hard-man reputation. In almost six years Hartland played 200 senior games for Barrow, scoring 22 goals, before moving briefly to Crewe. He managed just three League appearances for Alex, scoring two goals, but was soon on his way to Southport. In two seasons with the Sandgrounders Hartland scored four goals in 37 League appearances, before moving to Fleetwood in 1973.

HATCH, Peter

Left-midfielder
Born: 22 October 1949, Wargrave, Berkshire
United debut: 25 March 1968 v Colchester United (sub)
Final United game: 20 April 1973 v Burnley
Appearances: 16+4
Goals: 2
Clubs: Oxford United, Exeter City, Hamrun Spartans (Malta), Bideford Town, Taunton Town

Peter Derek Hatch was an apprentice at United, earning promotion to the senior squad on his 17th birthday in October 1966. Over the following seven years Hatch was unable to cement a regular first-team place, and in December 1973 he moved to Exeter for £8,000. Hatch became a regular with the Grecians, where his long throw-ins were used to good effect. His versatility meant that he was played in all left-sided positions, including defence. In 1981, after 367 appearances and 23 goals, Hatch joined Maltese side Hamrun in a move that caused a number of disputes with the island's Immigration Division, who initially refused to issue work permits, as he became one of the first foreigners to play in Malta for some time. He then returned to Devon to play for Bideford, and after a spell with Taunton he returned to Exeter to become a postman.

HATSWELL, Wayne

Centre-half
Born: 8 February 1975, Swindon
United debut: 2 December 2000 v Oldham Athletic (sub)
Final United game: 2 February 2002 v Bristol Rovers
Appearances: 51+1
Clubs: Trowbridge, Cinderford Town, Witney Town, Forest Green Rovers, Oxford United, Chester City, Kidderminster Harriers, Rushden & Diamonds, Cambridge United, Dundalk FC (Ireland), Newport County

Wayne Mervin Hatswell worked as a printer while playing for a succession of non-League clubs, but it was at Forest Green Rovers that he began to attract the attention of bigger clubs, and not just for scoring an own-goal against Morecambe in the FA Cup that made him famous. After 57 games for Forest Green in little over a year, plus seven goals at the right end of the pitch, United paid £35,000 to bring him to the Manor. His time at Oxford was characterised by struggles against relegation (unsuccessfully in the third tier, successfully in the basement) and although he failed to score this was the highest level at which Hatswell played. In the summer of 2002 he was signed by Mark Wright at Chester, but after just 42 games he moved to Kidderminster on a free transfer after a personal incident involving Wright. He was with the Harriers until January 2006, playing 108 games, scoring seven goals and winning the Player of the Year award in 2004–05, although he was stripped of the club captaincy for his poor disciplinary record. Hatswell was given a transfer by Kidderminster, who were trying to cut their costs, and joined Rushden for an undisclosed fee. He was with the Diamonds for two years, which included relegation from the Football League in the same season that Oxford went down; he made 80 appearances and scored five goals, before joining Cambridge United for £20,000. He was in the Cambridge side that lost successive Conference Play-off Finals in 2008 and 2009 before moving to Dundalk as player-coach in July 2009 after 92 games for the U's. In December 2010 Hatswell moved to Newport in a similar role. He won four England C caps.

HAVENHAND, Keith

Inside-forward
Born: 11 September 1937, Dronfield
United debut: 21 December 1963 v York City
Final United game: 26 October 1964 v Darlington
Appearances: 16
Goals: 4
Clubs: Chesterfield, Derby County, Oxford United, King's Lynn

Keith Havenhand was a centre lathe turner when he signed professionally for Chesterfield, where he made his debut at the end of the 1953–54 season, aged 16 years. He was a member of their successful 1955–56 FA Youth Cup side and won England Youth international honours, playing alongside Cyril Beavon. By the end of that season he had become established in the first team, despite starting National Service in February 1956, having turned down Wolves and Sheffield Wednesday to sign for the Spireites. In October 1961 he was sold to Derby for £10,000 but after a season he picked up a cartilage injury. He joined Oxford for £4,000 in December 1963 and scored on his United debut, but he was never able to establish a first-team place and in the summer of 1965 he moved to King's Lynn on a free transfer. He was with the Linnets for 18 months before retiring, becoming a driving instructor in Chesterfield in 1968.

HAYNES, Arthur

Right-winger
Born: 23 May 1924, Birmingham
Died: July 1990
United debut: 5 January 1952 v Hereford United
Final United game: 22 March 1952 v Chelmsford City
Appearances: 9
Goals: 2
Clubs: Aston Villa, Walsall, Weymouth, Worcester City, Headington United

Arthur Edwin Thomas Haynes started his career with Aston Villa before moving to Walsall in May 1948. He played two games for the Saddlers before joining Weymouth in July 1949. Haynes was a member of Weymouth's great FA Cup run of 1949–50 when they progressed from the FA Cup preliminary round to the third round proper, at which point they lost 4–0 to Manchester United at Old Trafford. In the preliminary round Haynes bagged a double hat-trick against Totton & Ryde Sports, and he was also on the score sheet in the Terras' second-round victory over Hereford. During the Cup run Weymouth played 10 games, with Haynes and fellow striker Stan Northover scoring 21 goals between them. In 1950 Haynes moved to Worcester, where he scored 12 goals before his brief stint with Headington. After playing for United Haynes moved back to Birmingham, where he resided until his death.

HEATH, Phil

Left-winger
Born: 24 November 1964, Stoke-on-Trent
United debut: 27 August 1988 v Leeds United
Final United game: 7 April 1990 v West Ham United
Appearances: 29+15
Goals: 1
Clubs: Stoke City, Oxford United, Cardiff City, Aldershot, Aylesbury United, Chipping Norton Town

Philip Adrian Heath started his career with Stoke, with whom he was an apprentice. In his six years at the Victoria Ground, Heath scored 19 goals in 166 appearances. In 1987–88 he was joint top goalscorer with eight goals, joining Oxford before the following season for £80,000. Heath's only goal for United came in his third appearance, a 3–2 win over Brighton. However, he never really convinced on the wing and his appearances became more sporadic. In the summer of 1990 he was released and joined Cardiff, where he spent one season, scoring one goal in 11 League appearances. The following season he played for Aldershot in their final League season before being wound up, scoring one goal in his 24 League games. He joined Aylesbury in February 1992, scoring seven goals in 68 games over two seasons with the Ducks. Heath later played for Chipping Norton Town and Chippy Old Boys and was manager of Chipping Norton.

HEBBERD, Trevor

Midfielder
Born: 19 June 1958, New Alresford, Hampshire
United debut: 27 March 1982 v Chesterfield
Final United game: 7 May 1988 v Nottingham Forest
Appearances: 326
Goals: 43
Clubs: Southampton, Washington Diplomats (USA) (loan), Bolton Wanderers (loan), Leicester City (loan), Oxford United, Derby County, Portsmouth (loan), Chesterfield, Lincoln City, Grantham Town

Trevor Neal Hebberd is a true Oxford legend; he scored the opening goal in the 1986 Milk Cup Final win, set up Ray Houghton for the second goal, and was involved in the move that led to Jeremy Charles scoring the third. Hebberd was also named Man of the Match. Hebberd joined Oxford from Southampton in March 1982 as a makeweight in the deal that took Mark Wright to the Dell. He joined the Saints in 1974 as a schoolboy, making his debut two years later. In 1981 he had a 28-game loan with Washington Diplomats, where he finished the season as the team's second-highest scorer with nine goals. On his return to England he played six games on loan to Bolton in September 1981, and in December he had a further four games on loan, this time at Leicester, where he found the net once. Hebberd, nicknamed 'Nijinsky' after the famous racehorse because of his phenomenal stamina, moved to Derby from Oxford for £300,000 in the summer of 1988. He made 81 League appearances for the Rams, scoring 10 goals, and he had a four-game loan with Portsmouth in 1991 before he moved to Chesterfield. At Saltergate, Hebberd played 78 League games over a three-year period, scoring just the once, before joining Lincoln in the summer of 1994. He was at Sincil Bank for one season, playing 33 games, before retiring as a professional and joining Grantham. He later worked in a warehouse in Leicester.

HERON, Brian

Left-winger
Born: 19 June 1948, Dumbarton
United debut: 17 August 1974 v Cardiff City
Final United game: 9 April 1977 v Reading
Appearances: 44+3
Goals: 9
Clubs: Baillieston, Rangers, Motherwell, Dumbarton, Oxford United, Scunthorpe United

Brian Heron's first professional club was Rangers, where he played nine games, including two in European ties, during 1969–70. Although he started as an outside-left and played there for most of his career, Rangers' manager Davie Whyte converted him into a left-back. At the end of that season Heron and Bobby Watson left for Motherwell with goalkeeper Peter McCloy going to Ibrox. After three seasons with Well, in which he scored 20 goals in 75 appearances, he left for Dumbarton. He played 36 games for the Sons, scoring 10 goals, before his move to Oxford for £20,000 in the summer of 1974. Although he scored on his United debut, Heron's time at the Manor was blighted by injury. In October 1975 he broke his leg against Notts County, and in his comeback match for the reserves he broke it again after just five minutes, leading to a total of 17 months out of the game. After his return he played just four more games for United before joining Scunthorpe on a free transfer in July 1977. Heron was a regular with Scunthorpe for the first part of the 1977–78 season, but fell out of favour after Christmas and he quit professional football at the end of the season, having made 25 appearances for the Iron, scoring one goal. At the end of 2007 Heron suffered a stroke, leaving him partially paralysed.

*HESLOP, Simon

Midfielder
Born: 1 May 1987, York
United debut: 7 August 2010 v Burton Albion
Final United game: 16 April 2011 v Accrington Stanley
Appearances: 32+8
Goals: 5
Clubs: Barnsley, Kidderminster Harriers (loan), Tamworth (loan), Northwich Victoria (loan), Halifax Town (loan), Grimsby Town (loan), Kettering Town (loan), Luton Town (loan), Oxford United

Simon James Heslop joined Oxford on a three-year deal in June 2010, having been released by Barnsley. He came through the youth ranks at Oakwell and signed professionally in 2003, playing for the reserves in his first season. In August 2005 he joined Kidderminster for a season on work experience, playing 23 games for the Conference club and scoring one goal. On his return to Barnsley he signed a new two-year deal before a loan to Tamworth in November 2006 for four months. He played 28 games for the Lambs, scoring once, and on his return to Barnsley he made his Tykes debut in the final game of the 2006–07 season. In September 2007 Heslop had a six-game loan with Northwich and immediately on his return to Oakwell he went to Halifax on loan for the remainder of the season, scoring five goals in 33 games. At the start of the following season he joined Grimsby on loan for two months, making 11 appearances, and then he immediately left for Kettering for a further two-month loan, again playing 11 games. His Barnsley career ended with him playing 13 games on loan to Luton, scoring once before his departure, having made just one substitute appearance for the Tykes.

HIGGINS, Peter

Centre-back
Born: 1 August 1944, Blidworth, Notts
United debut: 6 April 1963 v Chesterfield
Final United game: 20 April 1969 v Sheffield United (sub)
Appearances: 36+5
Clubs: Blidworth YC, Oxford United, Crewe Alexandra

Peter Higgins was promoted to Oxford's senior squad at the same time that the club was promoted to the Football League, in 1962, making two first-team appearances in his first season as a pro. After playing for the Blidworth Colliery Boys' Club and winning the Newark Youth League and the Notts Inter-League Cup, Higgins arrived at the Manor in 1960, following a trial with Derby County. He signed for United the day before he received a letter from the Rams offering him a contract. He flitted around the edges of the side as backup to Maurice Kyle until his final season, when he had a more sustained run in the side. He left Oxford for Crewe in the summer of 1969 and went on to play 59 League matches for the Alex before leaving Gresty Road in 1972.

HILL, Charles

Goalkeeper
United debut: 30 March 1956 v Dartford
Final United game: 28 April 1956 v Merthyr Tydfil
Appearances: 5
Clubs: Headington United

Hill played in five of the last six games of the 1955–56 season.

HILL, Danny

Midfielder
Born: 1 October 1974, Enfield
United debut: 15 August 1998 v Wolverhampton Wanderers (sub)
Final United game: 7 November 1998 v Watford (sub)
Appearances: 1+9
Clubs: Tottenham Hotspur, Birmingham City (loan), Watford (loan), Cardiff City (loan), Oxford United, Cardiff City, Dagenham & Redbridge, Hornchurch, Heybridge Swifts, Billericay Town, Harlow Town

Big things were expected of Daniel Ronald Louis Hill after he joined Oxford from Spurs, but sadly he failed to live up to the hype. He only lasted five months at the Manor, making just one start, before he left for Cardiff on a free transfer. Hill played 13 times for Tottenham, where he came up through the ranks, signing professionally in September 1992. In November 1995 he had a seven-game loan at Birmingham and on his return to White Hart Lane in February 1996 he went out again immediately to Watford, where he played just once. He played seven games on loan to Cardiff in February 1998 before he left Spurs for United on a free transfer in June 1998. Hill's second spell at Cardiff was far more successful than his time with Oxford and he spent two and a half seasons at Ninian Park, playing 69 games and scoring four goals there. He eventually left for Conference side Dagenham & Redbridge in July 2001, spending three and a half years in the East End and scoring seven goals in 88 appearances. In October 2004 Hill left Victoria Road and signed for Hornchurch until the end of that season, after which he became a full-time plumber while playing for a succession of Essex-based semi-professional sides.

HILL, Richard

Forward
Born: 20 September 1963, Hinckley
United debut: 19 September 1987 v Queen's Park Rangers
Final United game: 13 May 1989 v Watford (sub)
Appearances: 58+20
Goals: 17
Clubs: Leicester City, Nuneaton Borough, Christchurch United (New Zealand), Nuneaton Borough, IFK Grankulla (Finland), Nuneaton Borough, Northampton Town, Watford, Oxford United, Kettering Town, Witney Town

Richard Wilfred Hill joined Oxford for £235,000 from Watford at the same time as David Bardsley in September 1987. Hill scored on his United debut and on Boxing Day 1988 he scored four goals as the U's won 5–1 at Walsall. He left Oxford for Kettering at the end of that season. He went on to be assistant manager at Reading, and then joined John Gregory at Wycombe Wanderers. He was appointed manager of Stevenage Borough in 1998, guiding them to sixth in the Conference, but he was sacked in March 2000, after which he had spells as assistant at Gillingham and Northampton. He was assistant boss to Brian Little at Tranmere Rovers from 2003 until 2005, where he was linked briefly with the managerial vacancy at Oxford following Graham Rix's departure. Instead he joined QPR as assistant to John Gregory again. He was suspended by QPR and arrested in February 2007 for his part in an on-pitch brawl during a friendly with the Chinese Under-23 side, after which Hill was banned from football for three months. He was dismissed by Rangers in the summer of 2007 as a result of the brawl. Hill later coached at Didcot Town until June 2010, after which he joined the Ethiopia national team as technical coach for the African Nations Cup qualifying games. In November 2010 Hill returned to coach at Didcot and in January 2011 he was appointed manager of Witney United, resigning from the post in March 2011 but changing his mind a week later after an individual within the club wrote an apology. In May 2011 Hill finally left Witney because there was no budget for squad strengthening. Hill started his career with Leicester at the same time as Mike Ford, leaving to join Nuneaton Borough in December 1982. In March 1983 he went to New Zealand where he played for Christchurch United, returning to Nuneaton in September 1983, after the New Zealand season finished. The following summer Hill played for Grankulla in Finland because at that time non-League players did not receive any payment during the close season. He returned to Nuneaton after the Finnish season was completed. The following year he was spotted by Northampton and joined the Cobblers, helping them to a record-breaking promotion from the Fourth Division in 1987 with his 29 goals. Hill became Northampton's record sale when Watford paid £265,000 for him in July 1987, but played only four games for Graham Taylor's side before he moved to Oxford two months later.

HINCHLIFFE, Ben

Goalkeeper
Born: 9 October 1988, Preston
United debut: 8 August 2008 v Barrow
Final United game: 22 November 2008 v Histon (sub)
Appearances: 4+2
Clubs: Preston North End, Kendal Town (loan), Tranmere Rovers (loan), Derby County, Oxford United, Worcester City, Kendal Town, Bamber Bridge, Northwich Victoria

Ben Hinchliffe started his career with his home-town club of Preston North End, signing professionally in August 2006. He played 10 games for Unibond League side Kendal Town on loan in August 2006, and had a two-game loan spell with Tranmere in February 2007, but he was released by Preston in May of that year without having played for North End's first team. He was signed for Derby two months later by Billy Davies, his former manager at Preston. Hinchliffe spent one season at Pride Park without playing a first-team game and was released at the end of that season, whereupon he joined Oxford on non-contract terms after impressing in a pre-season trial. He was then handed a contract until the end of the season, after which he was released. He joined Worcester, where he played 17 games before returning to Kendal in November 2009. In January 2010 Hinchliffe moved to Bamber Bridge, and joined Northwich Victoria in June 2011.

HINSHELWOOD, Paul

Right-back
Born: 14 August 1956, Bristol
United debut: 27 August 1983 v Lincoln City
Final United game: 13 October 1984 v Brighton & Hove Albion
Appearances: 64
Goals: 1
Clubs: Crystal Palace, Oxford United, Millwall, Colchester United, Dartford

Paul Alexander Hinshelwood was playing for Croydon Schools in the 1969 Final of the London FA Schools' Cup when he was scouted by Crystal Palace. Originally a striker, Paul converted to a full-back in November 1976 and was an integral part of the Palace defence as they rose from Division Three to Division One and also won two England Under-21 caps. He was Palace's Player of the Year in both 1980 and 1981 and he made 321 appearances for the Eagles, scoring 28 goals, before he joined Oxford in the summer of 1983. Hinshelwood was a regular in the side that won the Division Three title in 1984, but he managed just one goal for United, in the 4–1 defeat at Everton in the Milk Cup quarter-finals. He left for Millwall in January 1985 after losing his first-team place to David Langan, and helped Millwall to promotion from the Third Division that season. In September 1986, after 61 League games for the Lions in which he scored two goals, he moved to Colchester for a nominal fee. He spent two seasons at Layer Road, playing 81 League games and scoring six goals, before joining Dartford in the summer of 1988. He later became assistant manager to Steve Kember at Whyteleafe, and in July 1993 he had a brief spell as manager following Kember's departure. Paul's sons, Adam and Paul, also both became professional footballers.

HODGSON, Gordon

Midfielder
Born: 13 October 1952, Newcastle upon Tyne
Died: April 1999
United debut: 30 September 1978 v Hull City
Final United game: 2 May 1980 v Colchester United
Appearances: 70+1
Goals: 3
Clubs: Newcastle United, Mansfield Town, Oxford United, Peterborough United, King's Lynn

Gordon Henry Hodgson joined his local club Newcastle United aged 18. He was a member of Newcastle's 1974 FA Cup Final squad, but did not play in the Toon's 3–0 defeat by Liverpool. While with Newcastle, Hodgson earned England Youth international honours. He joined Mansfield in May 1974 and by the time he left for Oxford in September 1978 he had missed just two games, both due to suspensions. He played 184 League games and scored 24 goals. In his first season with the Stags the club won the Division Four Championship, with a record points and goals total and Hodgson was selected for the Fourth Division PFA Team of the Season. Two seasons later Mansfield won the Division Three title, with Hodgson made team captain midway through the season. After two seasons with Oxford, Hodgson moved to Peterborough for £10,000, where after 94 games and five goals he ended his League career and joined the police service, while playing for King's Lynn.

HOLDER, Alan

Inside-forward
Born: 10 December 1931, Oxford
United debut: 23 August 1958 v Hereford United
Final United game: 31 January 1959 v Merthyr Tydfil
Appearances: 2
Clubs: Nottingham Forest, Lincoln City, Tranmere Rovers, Headington United

Alan Maurice Holder began his football career in the Army, from where he joined Nottingham Forest in October 1954. He made three League appearances for Forest before moving to Lincoln in July 1955. He made just one appearance for the Imps, in a Division Two defeat at Fulham in March 1956, before joining Tranmere midway through the following season. He played 13 games for Rovers, scoring one goal, before he returned to the city of his birth in the summer of 1958 to play for Headington.

HOLDER, Jorden

Forward
Born: 22 October 1982, Oxford
United debut: 1 May 2001 v Port Vale (sub)
Final United game: 5 May 2001 v Notts County (sub)

Appearances: 0+2
Clubs: Oxford United, Oxford City (loan), Oxford City, St Louis Steamers (USA)

Jorden Andrew Holder joined United on a three-year scholarship in 1999 but at the end of it, in March 2002, he was released and joined neighbours Oxford City, with whom he had previously played on a work experience loan deal in December 2001. In his two substitute appearances for United, Holder totalled 20 minutes of football. In August 2002 he moved to the Central Connecticut State University on a four-year sports scholarship, being voted Men's Soccer Rookie of the Year in November 2002. In February 2006 Holder was selected to play in the New England Intercollegiate Soccer League Senior All-Star game, having set a new university record for assists. In March 2006 he was chosen by St Louis Steamers in the third round of the Major Indoor Soccer League draft, becoming the first former Central Connecticut University player to be drafted.

HORSTED, Liam

Left-winger
Born: 28 October 1985, Portsmouth
United debut: 25 March 2006 v Peterborough United (sub)
Final United game: 17 April 2006 v Notts County (sub)
Appearances: 1+3
Clubs: Portsmouth, Dunfermline Athletic (loan), Oxford United (loan), Cirencester Town, Gosport Borough, Paulsgrove, Chichester City

Liam Anthony Horsted joined United on loan from Portsmouth as one of a number of players brought in by new manager Jim Smith on transfer deadline day in March 2006. This was his second loan from Pompey, having already played 13 games for Dunfermline in August 2005. After his return to Fratton Park from Oxford, Horsted was released by Portsmouth having failed to play a first-team game for them. He had a trial with Havant & Waterlooville in the 2006 pre-season but signed instead for Cirencester Town. In June 2008 he signed for Gosport Borough, and Horsted moved to Paulsgrove in June 2009 before joining Chichester City a year later.

HOUGHTON, Bud

Forward
Born: 1 September 1936, Madras (India)
Died: May 1994
United debut: 4 March 1961 v Cambridge City
Final United game: 8 October 1963 v Bradford Park Avenue
Appearances: 114
Goals: 75
Clubs: St Wilfred's, Bradford Park Avenue, Birmingham City, Southend United, Oxford United, Lincoln City, Chelmsford City, Cambridge United, Wellington Town, Cheltenham Town, Morris Motors

Harry Brian Houghton was an Anglo-Indian who moved to England in 1947 upon India's independence. He first played football at school in Surrey, and was selected for Godalming School Association. When he left school he signed for St Wilfred's, a youth team in Bradford, and he joined Bradford Park Avenue as an amateur in 1955. He had played 28 times and scored seven goals when Arthur Turner signed him for Birmingham City in 1957 for

£5,250. He played only four games for Birmingham, scoring once, before joining Southend United in 1959. At Roots Hall he scored an astonishing 32 goals from 68 games before Turner signed him again, this time for Oxford for a club record £2,000 in March 1961. Houghton became the first professional player to score four hat-tricks for United, and in April 1961 he scored five goals in a 7–2 win over Boston United. Houghton was United's joint top Southern League goalscorer with 52 goals (along with Billy Rees) and in the 1961–62 season he scored 43 goals, a club record for a single season. He scored in each of United's first three games as a Football League club. In order to supplement his income he set up a window-cleaning business with Ron Atkinson. Houghton joined Lincoln City in October 1963 for £6,000, playing 54 games for the Imps over two seasons, and scoring 22 goals. He left Lincoln for Chelmsford City, for whom he scored 73 goals in two seasons until 1967, when he moved to fellow Southern Leaguers Cambridge United, remaining in that League thereafter with Wellington and Cheltenham before returning to Oxford with Hellenic League side Morris Motors.

HOUGHTON, Ray

Midfielder
Born: 9 January 1962, Glasgow
United debut: 14 September 1985 v Liverpool
Final United game: 17 October 1987 v West Ham United
Appearances: 105
Goals: 14
Clubs: West Ham United, Fulham, Oxford United, Liverpool, Aston Villa, Crystal Palace, Reading, Stevenage Borough

Scottish-born Raymond James Houghton started his career with West Ham United, signing as a professional in 1979, but he only made one substitute appearance in three years at Upton Park, and he moved to Fulham in July 1982. Houghton made an impression as a hard-working midfielder at Craven Cottage, where he played 129 first-team games and scored 16 goals in three seasons. Houghton wrote himself into the Oxford record books with the second goal in United's 3–0 Milk Cup Final win over QPR in April 1986, capping a superb passing move with Trevor Hebberd, and he also scored a vital goal in Oxford's 3–0 win over Arsenal in the final game of the season which saw the club avoid relegation. He left Oxford to join Liverpool for £825,000. While at Oxford, Houghton won the first 12 of his 73 Republic of Ireland caps, often featuring alongside Dave Langan and John Aldridge in Jackie Charlton's side. His first Ireland goal was against England in the 1988 European Championships in West Germany. He also scored the winning goal against Italy in the 1994 World Cup finals in New York. He scored six international goals altogether. In five seasons with Liverpool Houghton played 202 games, scoring 38 goals, and won the League Championship in 1988 and 1990, and an FA Cup winners' medal in 1989 and 1992. In July 1992 Aston Villa paid £900,000 for Houghton, and he was an unused substitute when the Villains won the League Cup in 1994. Houghton played 117 games for Villa, scoring 11 goals, before Crystal Palace paid £300,000 for him in March 1995. In two seasons with Palace he played 87 games, scoring eight goals. He then joined Reading in July 1997, playing 56 games and scoring once in his only season there. His final club before retiring to take up TV and radio punditry was Stevenage Borough, where he played just three games.

HOUSEMAN, Peter

Midfielder
Born: 24 December 1945, Battersea
Died: 20 March 1977
United debut: 16 August 1975 v Carlisle United
Final United game: 19 March 1977 v Crystal Palace
Appearances: 72
Goals: 2
Clubs: Chelsea, Oxford United

Peter Houseman is arguably one of the most famous players to have played for Oxford. Having joined Chelsea as an apprentice and signing professional forms in 1963, he scored in the 1970 FA Cup Final against Leeds United, and he won the European Cup Winners' Cup with the Blues the following season when they beat Real Madrid in the final. After Chelsea were relegated to Division Two in 1975 Oxford paid £35,000 for Houseman, who had played 343 games and scored 39 goals for the Stamford Bridge side. Houseman was a left-sided midfielder who made 72 appearances for Oxford, starting with a 1–1 draw at Carlisle United on 16 August 1975. Houseman was one of the three players sent off at Blackpool in February 1976, equalling a League record, the only dismissal of his career. His last game for Oxford was a 1–0 home defeat by Crystal Palace on 19 March 1977. The following day Houseman, his wife Sally, and their friends Alan and Janice Gillham were all killed in a car crash on the A40, near Oxford, on his way home to Witney. Both couples left three parentless children and a fund was established to raise funds for the six orphans. A youth league in Oakley, Hampshire, where Houseman set up and coached a youth team, has been named after him.

HOWARD, Michael

Left-back
Born: 2 December 1978, Birkenhead
United debut: 26 January 2008 v Grays Athletic
Final United game: 26 April 2008 v Ebbsfleet United
Appearances: 17
Goals: 1
Clubs: Tranmere Rovers, Swansea City, Morecambe, Oxford United (loan), Llanelli, Aberystwyth Town

Michael Anthony Howard was initially on Liverpool's books as a youth in 1994 before crossing the Mersey to join Tranmere as a trainee two years later. In February 1998 Howard joined Swansea without having played in Tranmere's first team. He was to stay with the Swans for almost six years, playing 261 games and scoring two goals. He moved to Morecambe in July 2004 and played 110 games for the Lancashire side without scoring. He joined Oxford on loan in January 2008, remaining until the end of the season, but United opted not to sign him and he was released by the Reds at the end of the following season. In June 2009 he joined Llanelli, playing 13 Welsh Premier League games in his season at Stebonheath Park before he was released in July 2010, whereupon he moved to Aberystwyth Town.

HOWLETT, Arthur

Born: September 1933, Ploughley, Bucks
Died: 11 September 2010

United debut: 17 April 1954 v Dartford
Final United game: 17 April 1954 v Dartford
Appearances: 1
Clubs: Thame United, Headington United, Oxford City, Aylesbury United, Chesham United, Thame United, Oxford City, Thame United, Aylesbury United

Arthur G Howlett started with Thame United before joining Headington, where he was unable to break out of the reserves. He moved on to Oxford City where he became a prolific centre-forward, becoming the first player to score 100 goals for the first team, notching 137 in three seasons from 1957–60. He represented the Isthmian League, and played for the Oxfordshire and Berks & Bucks FA representative teams and he also had a trial for the England Amateur team. He moved to Aylesbury and then to Chesham United, signing forms that also allowed him to play for Thame, before returning to Oxford City. Howlett became player-manager at Thame for two seasons in 1964, and he also played 17 games for Aylesbury, scoring 12 goals in 1966–67 before retiring aged 35. He refereed locally before managing Thame again. He spent his early working life as a hide and skin merchant before becoming a lorry driver for butchers' waste.

HOWSE, Doug

Centre-forward
Born: December 1929, Headington
United debut: 4 February 1950 v Colchester United
Final United game: 6 May 1950 v Weymouth
Appearances: 7
Goals: 3
Clubs: Oxford City, Headington United

Douglas WJ Howse was easily top scorer for the reserves in the Metropolitan League in the 1949–50 season and, but for injury, may well have held his place in the first team.

HUCKER, Peter

Goalkeeper
Born: 28 October 1959, Hampstead
United debut: 20 April 1987 v Wimbledon
Final United game: 21 October 1989 v Barnsley
Appearances: 75
Clean sheets: 18
Clubs: Queen's Park Rangers, AFC Bournemouth (loan), Dagenham (loan), Oxford United, West Bromwich Albion (loan), Manchester United (loan), Millwall, Aldershot, Farnborough Town, Enfield, Purfleet, Fisher Athletic, Thurrock

Ian Peter Hucker came through the ranks at QPR, making his debut in May 1981. He was voted Man of the Match in the following season's FA Cup Final replay as Rangers lost to Spurs and he also won the first of his two England Under-21 caps. Hucker was due to play against Oxford in the 1986 Milk Cup Final, but due to a dispute with Rangers chairman Jim Gregory he was dropped, and United signed him for £100,000 in February 1987. He had played 160 League games for QPR. It took some time before Hucker could make his Oxford debut because of the good form of Steve Hardwick, but he eventually managed a regular first-team place. He had a seven-game loan with West Brom in January 1988 and in October 1989 he spent three weeks with Manchester United, without playing for them. He joined Millwall on a free transfer in November 1989 and exactly a year later he moved to Aldershot, without having played for the Lions. He turned out for 27 League games in his time at the Rec, moving to Farnborough in February 1992 where he made 12 appearances in two months. His next stop was Enfield, followed by sojourns at Purfleet and Fisher. He then stopped playing regularly, became goalkeeping coach at Spurs and set up his soccer schools, although he did turn out occasionally for Thurrock.

HUDSON, Ernie

Half-back
Born: 1926, Carlisle
United debut: 1 November 1952 v Dartford
Final United game: 1 May 1957 v Tonbridge
Appearances: 117
Goals: 1
Clubs: Edinburgh Waverley, East Fife, Headington United

Ernest Hudson was an electrician by trade who joined Headington from East Fife, for whom he made three Scottish League appearances in three seasons. He was a strong, well-built player, good in the air and powerful in the tackle.

HUGHES, Rob

Midfielder
Born: 6 September 1980, Wallington
United debut: 6 August 2005 v Grimsby Town (sub)
Final United game: 18 October 2005 v Brentford
Appearances: 2+3
Clubs: Fulham, Farnborough Town, Yeading, Oxford United, Sutton United, Maidenhead United, Ashford Town, Bromley, Sutton United, Welling United, Fisher Athletic, Croydon Athletic, Oxford City

Robert Albert Hughes joined Oxford after asking manager Brian Talbot for a trial following a United friendly against Yeading in July 2005. He started his career as a Fulham youth player, moving to Farnborough in July 2004. He joined Yeading in May, but begged his move to Oxford before appearing in a competitive game for the Ding. He joined United on non-contract terms, but was released in November 2005, joining Sutton. He made his Maidenhead debut in August 2006, making 16 appearances for the Berkshire side. After a brief spell at Ashford he moved to Bromley and thence back to Sutton. He was due to rejoin Bromley in the summer of 2008, but while holidaying in the resort of Malia in Crete he was brutally attacked by five English holidaymakers and left in a coma. Hughes, who suffered brain damage and was told he would never play football again, made a miraculous recovery, although he lost a lot of his memory. After recuperating he joined Welling and had a spell with Fisher and, in February 2010, Croydon Athletic before joining Oxford City in February 2011.

HUMPSTON, Ron

Goalkeeper
Born: 14 December 1923, Derby
United debut: 26 April 1954 v Llanelly
Final United game: 2 October 1954 v Llanelly
Appearances: 5
Clean sheets: 3
Clubs: Portsmouth, Huddersfield Town, Headington United

Ronald Humpston's first club was Portsmouth, for whom he made nine appearances, two in January 1948 and then seven in August and September 1950. In the intervening years Humpston was backup to regular 'keeper Ernie Butler. After Pompey he played five League games for Huddersfield before signing for Headington in the 1953–54 season. Humpston next turns up in 1960 as manager of Gravesend & Northfleet, who started well under his charge but ended up narrowly avoiding relegation on goal average at the end of his first season. Humpston was sacked midway through the following season and applied unsuccessfully for the vacant Romford job in March 1962. Humpston then relocated to Czechoslovakia to become the trainer to the national side, after which he returned to England to manage Moreton Town. He became manager of Oxford City in June 1968 but in May 1971 he resigned due to ill health.

HUNT, James

Midfielder
Born: 17 December 1976, Derby
United debut: 10 August 2002 v Bury
Final United game: 8 May 2004 v Rochdale
Appearances: 82+5
Goals: 4
Clubs: Notts County, Northampton Town, Oxford United, Bristol Rovers, Grimsby Town (loan), Grimsby Town, Gainsborough Trinity

James Malcolm Hunt joined Oxford in the 2002 close season, rejoining his former manager from Northampton, Ian Atkins. He became a professional with Notts County in July 1994, having come up through their youth ranks. He played 19 games for the Magpies and scored one goal before being signed by Atkins at Northampton in August 1997. Hunt spent five years at Sixfields, becoming an established player with 205 appearances in which he scored 10 goals. After his two years at Oxford, Hunt joined Bristol Rovers, where he was given the captaincy. However, he had a disagreement with coach Paul Trollope and was transfer-listed, joining Grimsby on loan for 15 games in January 2007, during which he scored twice. At the end of his loan spell he moved to Grimsby permanently, having played 108 games for the Gas and scoring six goals. At Blundell Park Hunt went on to complete 73 games, scoring once in the League Cup before being released in May 2009. He joined Gainsborough Trinity where he was again made captain and although Trinity initially released Hunt at the end of his first season, he continued to skipper the side the following season.

HUNTER, Roy

Midfielder
Born: 29 October 1973, Saltburn, Yorkshire
United debut: 22 October 2002 v AFC Bournemouth
Final United game: 19 April 2003 v Exeter City
Appearances: 14+5
Goals: 1
Clubs: West Bromwich Albion, Northampton Town, Nuneaton Borough, Oxford United, Northwich Victoria, Hucknall Town, Harrogate Town, Teesside Athletic

Roy Ian Hunter began his career as a trainee with West Brom, for whom he played 14 games and scored one goal before moving on to Northampton in August 1995. He spent more than seven years with the Cobblers, amassing 208 appearances and 20 goals. Like James Hunt, he was brought to Oxford by his former manager at Sixfields, Ian Atkins, having played three games for Nuneaton in October 2002 in the interim. His time at Oxford was not a happy one, and he failed to distinguish himself in an unadventurous midfield. Hunter was released in June 2003 and after interest in him from Tamworth he eventually signed for Northwich. He spent just one month with the Vics before joining Hucknall in September 2003. In his first season Hucknall won the Northern Premier League and, after a poor start to the following season, Hunter was appointed player-assistant manager as the team reached the Final of the FA Trophy, losing on penalties to Grays Athletic after a 1–1 draw at Villa Park. In July 2005 Hunter signed for Harrogate and three years later he moved to Teesside Athletic. In May 2010 the club changed its name to Redcar Athletic.

HUSBANDS, Michael

Forward
Born: 13 November 1983, Birmingham
United debut: 8 August 2008 v Barrow (sub)
Final United game: 12 August 2008 v Weymouth (sub)
Appearances: 0+2
Clubs: Aston Villa, Hereford United (loan), Southend United, Bristol Rovers, Walsall, Port Vale, Macclesfield Town, Telford United (loan), Oxford United, Royal Marines

Michael Paul Husbands had a bright start to his football career, winning the FA Youth Cup with Aston Villa in 2002 with a 4–2 aggregate win over an Everton side that included Wayne Rooney. Although he failed to play a first-team game for Villa, he did have a five-game loan with Hereford in December 2002 before leaving for Southend in July 2003. He played just 16 games for the Shrimpers in two seasons at Roots Hall because of injuries, and in August 2005 he was released and joined Bristol Rovers on non-contract terms for a month. He was signed by Walsall, where he made four appearances in just over a month before Port Vale took him on in October 2005. In just under two seasons at Vale Park Husbands made 57 appearances and scored six goals, including one in 14 seconds against Nottingham Forest. After being released in July 2007 he joined Macclesfield where he played just three games before joining Telford United on loan in November 2007 for a month, which was later extended until the end of the season. He scored three times in 25 games for Telford but he struggled with a knee injury and the

Bucks opted not to sign him at the end of the season, when he had trials with Spanish side CD Javea and with Cheltenham Town. He signed a short-term deal with Oxford in August 2008 but was released when the deal expired. In May 2010 he made his debut for the Royal Navy, scoring eight goals in seven games up to November 2010.

HUTCHINSON, Eddie

Midfielder
Born: 23 February 1982, Kingston
United debut: 12 August 2006 v Halifax Town
Final United game: 17 April 2009 v Burton Albion (sub)
Appearances: 54+33
Goals: 4
Clubs: Sutton United, Brentford, Oxford United, Crawley Town, Sutton United, Eastbourne Borough

Edward Stephen Hutchinson will be forever associated by Oxford supporters with the episode that they dubbed 'Hutchgate', when United were docked five points for fielding Hutchinson at the start of the 2008–09 season when he had not been properly registered with the Football Conference. The season concluded with the U's missing out on the Play-offs by four points. Hutch had arrived at Oxford from Brentford, where he started his career as an 18-year-old, having joined from Sutton, signing professionally in June 2000. He went on to make 136 appearances for the Bees, scoring nine goals, before Jim Smith signed him for the start of Oxford's first season in the Conference; the player allegedly turned down an offer from Swindon to sign for the U's. Hutchinson was initially a mainstay of the United midfield, but he fell out of favour and when Darren Patterson became manager Hutchinson was transfer-listed in December 2008. After allegedly turning down opportunities to move to other sides Patterson forced Hutchinson to train with the youth team and had no intention of including him in the first team, hence his non-registration, until injuries forced his hand. Hutchinson played in 11 matches before his non-registration came to light, but the Conference deducted points just from games in which the midfielder had started. At the end of the Hutchgate season Hutchinson did eventually leave United, joining Crawley. He played 39 games for the Red Devils, scoring twice, before leaving in November. He was without a club for a couple of months, but signed for Eastbourne Borough in January 2011.

HYDE, Steve

Left-winger
Born: 18 December 1943, High Wycombe
United debut: 31 October 1964 v Doncaster Rovers
Final United game: 26 February 1966 v Brentford
Appearances: 10
Clubs: Wycombe Wanderers, Oxford United, Bedford Town

Stephen Leslie Hyde was Wycombe's youngest ever player when he made his debut aged 16 years and nine months in September 1960. He attracted interest from Crystal Palace, Fulham and Oxford and played for United reserves shortly before a bad injury in May 1962 against Wimbledon looked like ending his career as doctors advised him to give up playing. He never fully recovered and played just a few Metropolitan League appearances for the U's before the club joined the Football Combination, after which he started to play more regularly. He signed as a full professional in January 1965 but was released at the end of the season. He joined Bedford for the start of the 1966–67 season and made 10 appearances for the Eagles, scoring once, before retiring at the end of that season.

HYND, Roger

Centre-back
Born: 2 February 1942, Falkirk
United debut: 4 October 1975 v Leyton Orient
Final United game: 1 November 1975 v Hull City
Appearances: 5
Clubs: Glasgow Rangers, Crystal Palace, Birmingham City, Oxford United (loan), Walsall

John Roger Shankly Hynd, the nephew of Bill Shankly, joined Rangers in 1961 from Lanark Grammar School, having just won the Scottish Schools' Under-18 Cup, making his Gers debut in October 1963. While at Ibrox he played in the 1967 UEFA Cup Winners' Cup Final, which Rangers lost 1–0 to Bayern Munich in Nuremberg. He played 48 senior games for Rangers and scored five goals (although he did miss a sitter against Bayern), supplementing his income by teaching part-time. He joined Crystal Palace in 1969, playing 38 games and cementing his reputation as one of football's hard men. He moved to Birmingham in 1970 and made 197 first-team starts. In October 1975 Mick Brown signed him on loan from the Blues with the intention of signing him permanently as United's player-coach, but the Oxford board refused to sanction the move. After returning to St Andrew's he joined Walsall in December 1975 where he played 89 games, scoring once. In December 1977 he was appointed as manager of Motherwell but shortly into the following season he resigned his post and became a PE teacher at Wishaw School, where he remained until his retirement in 2003.

J

JACKSON, Darren

Midfielder
Born: 24 September 1971, Keynsham
United debut: 5 May 1990 v Port Vale
Final United game: 18 December 1993 v Portsmouth (sub)
Appearances: 15+3
Clubs: Oxford United, Reading (loan), Bath City

Darren William Jackson joined Oxford's Youth Training Scheme in 1988, graduating to the senior squad in the summer of 1990. However, in October of that year Jackson's leg was badly broken and he never fully recovered, making just two appearances in the whole of 1991. He played five games on loan with Reading in 1992. Jackson was released in the summer of 1994, joining Bath for whom he made nine Conference appearances. In 1998 he relocated to Thailand where he trained schoolchildren and started the Darren Jackson Can U Kick It Soccer Clinic.

JACKSON, Elliott

Goalkeeper
Born: 27 August 1977, Swindon
United debut: 1 October 1996 v Tranmere Rovers
Final United game: 3 February 1999 v Chelsea
Appearances: 13
Clean sheets: 1
Clubs: Oxford United, Bath City, Stevenage Borough (loan), Cirencester Town, Swindon Supermarine, Hungerford Town, Pewsey Vale, Swindon Supermarine, Highworth, Cricklade Town, Malmesbury Victoria, Cricklade Town

Elliott Jackson joined Oxford's YTS in 1994, joining the senior squad in December 1995. He played for the side that won the Junior Floodlit Cup in May 1996. He made sporadic first-team appearances, but was never able to dislodge the almost impeccable Phil Whitehead. Jackson's final match was an FA Cup replay at Stamford Bridge against Chelsea. He had starred in the first game at the Manor, which was a 1–1 draw, and was only beaten by a controversial late penalty by Franck Leboeuf. In July 1999 he joined Bath City where he made 54 appearances and he had a loan with Stevenage in March 1999. After a loss of form he was released by Bath in May 2000, and following a spell with Cirencester he joined Swindon Supermarine in September 2001. After a period with Hungerford he moved to Pewsey Vale and then Supermarine again in December 2002. His next stop was Highworth in 2003 and then Cricklade, followed by Malmesbury. After a few seasons he returned to Cricklade in September 2010.

JACKSON, Fred

Right-half
Born: 15 October 1932
United debut: 9 April 1955 v Hastings United

Final United game: 3 September 1955 v Chelmsford City
Appearances: 6
Clubs: Headington United, Oxford City

Frederick Arthur Edward Jackson played for Headington United as an amateur until he left to join the RAF. The club had offered him a professional contract, but his father refused to allow him to sign it. After leaving Headington Jackson played for Oxford City for several years, making his debut in August 1956. He was a member of the team that beat Pegasus 3–0 after a replay to win the Oxfordshire Senior Cup Final in 1960. He left City the following season after scoring seven goals in 158 matches for them.

JACKSON, Jimmy

Centre-forward
Born: 26 March 1931, Glasgow
United debut: 23 March 1958 v Hereford United
Final United game: 27 April 1959 v Kettering Town
Appearances: 43
Goals: 23
Clubs: Mapperley Celtic, Notts County, Canada, Notts County, Headington United, Sutton Town, Arnold St Mary's

James Jackson was with Notts County for 10 seasons before moving to Headington. In his two spells at Meadow Lane, punctuated by a period in Canada, Jackson played 122 games, in which he scored 50 goals. Jackson was the Magpies' leading scorer in both 1954–55, when he scored 17 goals in 20 games which included four against Sheffield Wednesday on New Year's Day, and the following season with a more modest eight goals. He had a decent goalscoring record with United, who let him go at the end of the 1958–59 season.

JACQUES, Tony

Wing-half
Born: 10 October 1942, Oddington
United debut: 28 September 1961 v Bedford Town
Final United game: 18 May 1963 v Southport
Appearances: 8
Clubs: Oxford United, Hereford United, Gloucester City, Banbury United, Nuneaton Borough, Kettering Town

Anthony Jacques signed for United from Kingham All Blacks. He served his apprenticeship with United before joining the seniors upon the club's election to the Football League in 1962. He was released in the summer of 1963. In 1967–68 Jacques scored a club record 62 goals in all competitions as Banbury won the prestigious Midland Floodlit Cup before he joined Nuneaton, for whom he went on to score over 100 goals. Jacques made his debut for Kettering in August 1971, going on to score 38 goals in 50 appearances before he was released by manager Ron Atkinson in the summer of 1972. Jacques was also a useful cricketer, and had a trial with Gloucestershire.

JARMAN, Lee

Centre-back
Born: 16 December 1977, Cardiff
United debut: 12 August 2000 v Peterborough United

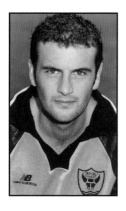

Final United game: 30 January 2001 v Peterborough United
Appearances: 19+5
Goals: 1
Clubs: Cardiff City, Merthyr Tydfil, Exeter City, Oxford United, Merthyr Tydfil, Barry Town, Weston-super-Mare, Newport County, Haverfordwest County, Llanelli, Haverfordwest County

Lee Jarman began his career with his home-town club Cardiff City, coming up through the juniors and the club's YTS before making his debut in 1995. He played 110 times for the Bluebirds and scored two goals, and was also capped for and later captained Wales Under-21s, before he was released in October 1999. After trials with various clubs he briefly signed for Merthyr Tydfil before returning to the League on non-contract terms with Exeter in March 2000. In July 2000, after eight appearances for the Grecians, he joined Oxford on a monthly contract, eventually staying until the end of the season. He never particularly impressed while with United and after being released by the U's he returned to Merthyr. In October 2001 he moved to Barry where he scored four goals in 52 Welsh Premier League appearances over two seasons before moving to Weston-super-Mare in September 2003. In May 2007 he moved to Newport but was released by the Exiles at the end of his first season, whereupon he signed for Haverfordwest in June 2008. After 30 League appearances and two goals in his first season, Llanelli put in seven days' notice of approach in May 2009 to make Jarman new manager Andy Legg's first signing. He made 21 League appearances and scored three goals before rejoining Haverfordwest.

JEANNIN, Alex

Left-back
Born: 30 December 1977, Troyes, France
United debut: 11 August 2007 v Forest Green Rovers
Final United game: 20 January 2008 v Exeter City (sub)
Appearances: 32+1
Goals: 2
Clubs: Troyes AC (France), Racing Club Paris (France), Troyes AC (France), Darlington, RCS La Chapelle (France), Exeter City, Bristol Rovers, Hereford United, Oxford United, Kidderminster Harriers (loan), Mansfield Town, Truro City

Alexandre Jeannin joined United in July 2007, having been released by Hereford the previous April. Although he played well going forward, he was suspect defensively and he was transfer-listed by Darren Patterson in January 2008, joining Kidderminster on loan later that month, where he made 18 appearances. After his loan at Aggborough finished, Jeannin was signed by Mansfield in August 2008. He played 27 games for the Stags, leaving for Truro in May 2009. However, he suffered a broken leg while on trial with the Cornish outfit and he did not sign for them until July 2010. Jeannin began his career with his local club Troyes AC (Espérance Sportive Troyes Aube Champagne) before joining Racing Paris (proper name: Racing Club de France – Levallois 92) in 1999. He played 31 games in Le Championnat National before returning to Troyes in 2000. In March 2001 he signed for Darlington, but after 24 appearances for the Quakers he was released in November 2001 after breaking the club's drinking curfew. He returned to France to play in the fifth tier with Reunion des Cheminots et des Sportifs de la Chapelle Saint-Luc. In July 2003 he came back to England to sign for Exeter, where he played 82 games and scored five goals before being released because of budgetary constraints after the Grecians' relegation to the Conference. He signed for Bristol Rovers for the final game of the 2004–05 season and then moved to Hereford. He made 64 appearances, scoring four goals, before he was signed by Oxford.

JEFFERIES, Ray

Inside-left
Born: June 1929, Oxford
United debut: 6 September 1951 v Bedford Town
Final United game: 14 April 1952 v Guildford City
Appearances: 29
Goals: 5
Clubs: Oxford City, Brentford, Dartford, Headington United

Raymond J Jefferies started his career with Oxford City before following his goalkeeping brother Alf to Brentford in the summer of 1948. Unlike Alf, who later joined Torquay, Ray never played for Brentford's first team and he later moved to Dartford before returning to Oxford to play for Headington.

JEFFREY, Billy

Midfielder
Born: 25 October 1956, Clydebank
United debut: 26 September 1973 v Fulham
Final United game: 11 May 1982 v Bristol Rovers
Appearances: 353+3
Goals: 26
Clubs: Oxford United, Blackpool, Northampton Town, Kettering Town, Blacktown City (Australia)

William Greenwood Jeffrey joined Oxford as a schoolboy, becoming an apprentice in 1972. He was promoted to the seniors in October 1973 and was a member of the squad that won the Midlands Youth League in 1974–75. When Jeffrey made his debut against Fulham he was, at 16 years and 336 days, the youngest player to have represented United in the Football League until Jason Seacole came on for him in September 1976. Jeffrey was made club captain following Les Taylor's departure for Watford in November 1980 and he won caps for Scotland Youth. After amassing over 350 appearances he finally left the U's for Blackpool in the summer of 1982, playing 14 League games for the Tangerines and scoring one goal before moving on to Northampton. He was at the County Ground for two seasons, scoring five goals in 54 League appearances, after which he joined Kettering. He was the Poppies captain and leading scorer with 20 goals in his first season and he became player-coach before leaving for Australia, where he held a similar role at Blacktown City in New South Wales for a year. Jeffrey returned to England to manage Irthlingborough Diamonds, becoming assistant manager to Roger Ashby when Irthlingborough merged with Rushden Town to become Rushden & Diamonds in 1992, where he was later assistant to Brian Talbot. In 1998 he became manager at Stamford, where he remained for six and a half years before becoming manager of Rugby United in May 2005 (the club reverted to its previous name of Rugby Town that summer). In December 2007 he resigned from his post. He spent some time as a scout while working as a sales and production manager with a publishing company, Dram Good Books, who produce books on whisky, before being appointed as Banbury United's manager in March 2009. He resigned in July 2011 due to ill health.

JEMSON, Nigel

Striker

Born: 10 August 1969, Preston
United debut: 17 August 1996 v Queen's Park Rangers
Final United game: 6 May 2000 v Millwall (sub)
Appearances: 95+5
Goals: 33
Clubs: Preston North End, Nottingham Forest, Bolton Wanderers (loan), Preston North End (loan), Sheffield Wednesday, Grimsby Town (loan), Notts County, Watford (loan), Coventry City (loan), Rotherham United (loan), Oxford United, Bury, Ayr United, Oxford United, Shrewsbury Town, Ballymena United (Northern Ireland), Ilkeston Town, FC Halifax Town, Arnold Town, Rainworth Miners' Welfare

Nigel Bradley Jemson had two spells with United. He initially joined the U's in the summer of 1996 for £60,000 from Notts County, who he had joined for £300,000 from Sheffield Wednesday in September 1994. At the end of his first season he was the side's leading scorer with 23 goals and in February 1998 he moved to Bury for £100,000. He played 33 games and scored one goal before he moved to Ayr on a free transfer in September 1999. Jemson scored five goals in 13 games for the Honest Men, returning to Oxford on a free in January 2000. His second period with United was far less successful than his first, as he played just 18 games and did not score. He left for Shrewsbury in July 2000 and in three seasons at Gay Meadow he played 127 games and scored 43 goals. Jemson started his career with his home-town club, Preston, scoring 14 goals in 40 games before his £150,000 move to Nottingham Forest in March 1988. He was at the City Ground until September 1991, playing 61 games and scoring 20 goals, including the only goal of the 1990 League Cup Final against Oldham, and this period included a five-game loan at Bolton in December 1988 followed by an 11-game loan in which he scored twice back at Preston in March 1989. Jemson left Forest for Sheffield Wednesday for £800,000, but in three years he played just 68 games and scored 11 goals. He scored twice in a seven-game loan with Grimsby in September 1993 and a year later he moved to Notts County for £300,000. However, Jemson spent most of his time at Meadow Lane out on loan and played just 19 games for the Magpies, scoring once. His loans included four appearances for Watford in January 1995, no games at Coventry in March 1995 and 19 matches for Rotherham, in which he scored nine goals, in February 1996, immediately before his first move to Oxford. Jemson left Shrewsbury after they were relegated to the Conference in 2003 and he joined Northern Irish side Ballymena, where he scored eight goals in 26 games before returning to England to play for Ilkeston in 2004, going on to become their player-manager in October 2005 after a spell as caretaker boss. In May 2008 he left his post after the club changed ownership and in July 2008 he became player-assistant manager at FC Halifax and in April 2009 he was made caretaker manager. He joined Arnold Town in the summer, but in October he left to play for North East Counties League side Rainworth, where he stayed until January 2010. He coached part-time for a while at Castle College in Nottingham and in November 2010 he played alongside Jim Magilton for Royale Asia in the International 7s Tournament in Tenerife, having registered for HKDC Mobsters in the Hong Kong Yau Yee amateur football league.

JENKINS, Alf

Midfielder
United debut: 4 March 1950 v Exeter City Reserves
Final United game: 23 April 1952 v Bath City
Appearances: 44
Goals: 2
Clubs: Bury, Headington United, Mossley

Signed from Bury, where he did not play a first-team game, in March 1950, Alfred Jenkins was the first player in local football to wear contact lenses, which he bought after his glasses were broken on his United debut. After leaving Headington he signed for Mossley, where he scored two goals in nine appearances in the 1953–54 season. While with Headington, Jenkins worked as a scientist at Harwell.

JOHNSON, Gavin

Left-back
Born: 10 October 1970, Eye, Suffolk
United debut: 12 August 2006 v Halifax Town
Final United game: 8 May 2007 v Exeter City (sub)
Appearances: 26+9
Goals: 2
Clubs: Ipswich Town, Luton Town, Wigan Athletic, Dunfermline Athletic, Colchester United, Boston United, Northampton Town, Oxford United, Bury Town, Walsham-le-Willows

Gavin Johnson joined United from Northampton and made his debut in Oxford's first match in the Conference. An injury in September saw him lose his place to Rufus Brevett, but after his recovery in November the pair shared the left-back position until both were released at the end of the season. Johnson began his career at Ipswich, where he played 158 games and scored 15 goals before he moved to Luton on a free transfer in July 1995. He had made just five appearances for the Hatters before Wigan paid £15,000 for him in December 1995. In his two and a half seasons at Springfield Park Johnson played 109 games and scored 10 goals. In July 1998 he moved north of the border to Dunfermline, but after just 19 games he returned to England in November 1999 to play for Colchester. Johnson spent over five years at Layer Road, making 166 appearances and scoring 14 goals before leaving for Boston in June 2005. He was at York Street for just over a month, playing in four matches, signing for Northampton at the end of August. In his season at Sixfields Johnson scored one goal in 26 games before he moved to Oxford. After leaving the Kassam he played for Bury Town, signing in August 2007 and winning the Supporters' Player of the Year award in his first season at Ram Meadow. After helping the club from Bury St Edmunds to promotion from the Zamaretto League Midlands Division One, Johnson joined Walsham-le-Willows in July 2010.

JOHNSTON, David

Inside-forward
United debut: 11 February 1950 v Merthyr Tydfil
Final United game: 26 April 1951 v Worcester City
Appearances: 10
Goals: 2
Clubs: Headington United, Scarborough

David Johnston joined United as an amateur during the club's first season in the Southern League. He was described as having 'exceptional promise' but was unfortunately unable to live up to that billing and after leaving Headington he went on to play for Scarborough in the Midland League.

JOHNSTON, Peter

Right-half
United debut: 19 April 1954 v Tonbridge
Final United game: 12 January 1957 v Kidderminster Harriers
Appearances: 56
Goals: 3
Clubs: Headington United

Peter Johnston played for Headington as an amateur.

JOHNSTON, Ron

Centre-forward
Born: 3 April 1921, Glasgow
United debut: 19 August 1950 v Bedford Town
Final United game: 7 October 1950 v Guildford City
Appearances: 13
Goals: 9
Clubs: Glasgow Perthshire, Rochdale, Exeter City, Weymouth, Headington United, Brighton & Hove Albion

Ronald Johnston moved from Glasgow Perthshire, a club from Possilpark in the north of Glasgow, to Rochdale during the 1947–48 season. He played 17 League games for Dale, scoring seven goals, before leaving for Exeter the following season. After 10 League games and two goals Johnston left for Weymouth, from where he joined Headington in the summer of 1950. However, he was at the Manor for just a couple of months before returning to the Football League with Brighton, where he played just one game.

JOHNSTONE, Gordon

Inside-right
United debut: 16 December 1961 v Weymouth
Final United game: 16 December 1961 v Weymouth
Appearances: 1
Clubs: Oxford United

Gordon Johnstone played just one game for the first team and one Metropolitan League game for the reserves.

JONES, Davy

Midfielder
Born: 18 May 1950, Brixham
United debut: 9 October 1968 v Carlisle United
Final United game: 27 March 1971 v Leicester City
Appearances: 20+4
Goals: 1
Clubs: Arsenal, Oxford United, Torquay United, Witney Town, Oxford City, Aylesbury United, Hungerford, Oxford City

David Frederick Jones is considered to be Oxford's first black player, although his mother was white. He joined Oxford after an unsuccessful trial with Middlesbrough, having previously been on Arsenal's books. After losing his first-team place to John Shepherd, Jones starred for the reserves as they finished second in the Football Combination in 1971–72, after which he joined Torquay United on a free transfer. He made just one substitute appearance for the Gulls before returning to Oxfordshire to play for Witney Town. Jones then played 128 games, scoring 21 goals, for Aylesbury United between 1978 and 1983. After playing for Hungerford he joined Oxford City as player-manager in 1986, having played for them three years previously. He went on to become a police officer.

JONES, GH

United debut: 26 April 1954 v Llanelly
Final United game: 26 April 1954 v Llanelly
Appearances: 1
Clubs: Headington United

JONES, Mark

Midfielder
Born: 26 September 1961, Berinsfield
United debut: 29 March 1980 v Exeter City (sub)
Final United game: 5 May 1986 v Arsenal
Appearances: 120+38
Goals: 7
Clubs: Oxford United, Swindon Town (loan), Swindon Town, Cardiff City, Farnborough Town

Mark K Jones became an Oxford apprentice in 1978, becoming a professional the following summer. In September 1986, after playing in United's first season in the top flight, he left for Swindon, initially on loan before United's rivals paid the U's £30,000 for him in October 1986. After scoring 10 goals in 50 games for the Robins, Jones was released and signed for Cardiff in May 1990. In two seasons Jones played 36 League games and scored two goals for the Bluebirds, joining Farnborough in the summer of 1992. He made 92 appearances, scoring twice, before his final game in February 1995. In 2003, after coaching for Oxford's soccer schools, Jones left to form Premier Soccer Centres.

JONES, Tony

Inside-forward/Right-half
Born: 12 November 1937, Birmingham
Died: April 1990
United debut: 10 October 1959 v Poole Town
Final United game: 18 December 1967 v Chelmsford City (sub)
Appearances: 355+1
Goals: 100
Clubs: Birmingham City, Headington United, Newport County, Cheltenham Town, Merthyr Tydfil, Witney Town

Anthony Peter Jones' career started after leaving school, when he joined Birmingham from Tower United, signing for the Blues as an amateur in

1954. Jones failed to progress to the Birmingham first team so he contacted Arthur Turner, who signed him as a part-time professional in the summer of 1959; he turned full-time after four months. In his eight years at the Manor Jones scored exactly 100 goals, elevating him to second place in the club's post-1949 goalscoring chart. Five of those goals came in United's 9–0 win over Wisbech in December 1960, and he hit four against Newport County in September 1962. Jones also scored a brace in the FA Cup triumph over Blackburn Rovers in February 1964. He was United's leading scorer when the club won the Southern League in 1960–61 with 38 goals. In December 1967 Jones moved to Newport, where he scored nine goals in 54 games before he joined Witney in 1969.

JUDGE, Alan

Goalkeeper
Born: 14 May 1960, Kingsbury
United debut: 17 December 1985 v Chelsea
Final United game: 6 November 2004 v Southend United
Appearances: 102
Clean sheets: 21
Clubs: Luton Town, Reading (loan), Reading, Oxford United, Lincoln City (loan), Cardiff City (loan), Hereford United, Bromsgrove Rovers, Chelsea, Kettering Town, Brackley Town, Banbury United, Swindon Town, Oxford United, Didcot Town, Slough Town, Oxford United, Chipping Norton Town, Banbury United, Ardley United, Oxford City, Woodford United

Alan Graham Judge played in United's Milk Cup-winning side of April 1986 and in November 2004 he broke his own record as Oxford's oldest League player, playing at Southend at the age of 44 years and 176 days. This made him the seventh-oldest player to have appeared in the Football League at that time. Judge started his career as a junior at Luton, having been a schoolboy at Crystal Palace. He signed professionally for the Hatters in January 1978 and went on to make 11 League appearances for them, plus three during a loan spell at Reading, who he then joined permanently in January 1982. He played 74 League games for the Biscuitmen before signing for Oxford on Christmas Eve 1984. Judge had to wait almost a year for his United debut as he was unable to dislodge the excellent Steve Hardwick. When he finally made the team, after two games on loan to Lincoln in November 1985, he quickly became first choice until an injury in October 1986 saw him out of the first team for over a year, although he played eight games on loan to Cardiff in October 1987. Judge moved to Hereford in July 1991, playing 105 games in three seasons. He sat on the bench as cover for an injury-struck Chelsea for their Cup Winners' Cup quarter-final second leg against Club Bruges in March 1995 while at Bromsgrove, where he played three games during 1994–95. Judge signed for Kettering in the summer of 1995, spending two seasons at Rockingham Road before moving to Brackley for a couple of years. His next stop was at Banbury United where he played until 2002, at which point he became goalkeeping coach for both Swindon and Oxford, while also working as a driving instructor. In 1999 Judge was diagnosed with bowel cancer and he underwent an operation in May 2000. In 2002 Swindon registered him as a player to provide goalkeeping cover, but he did not play for them. He became Oxford's oldest player in March 2003 at home to Cambridge United after an injury to regular 'keeper Andy Woodman, and broke his own record 18 months later. In the meantime Judge signed for Didcot Town to provide goalkeeping cover, and appeared three times for Slough in March 2004. He played some games for Chipping Norton during the 2004–05 season. He later played for Banbury again during the 2006–07 season and in May 2007 he played for Ardley in the final of the Direct Sports & Trophies Supplementary Cup against AFC Wallingford. In November 2008 Judge answered an emergency call from Oxford City after their regular 'keepers were injured and later that season he turned out for Woodford.

K

KARAM, Amine

Midfielder
Born: 3 January 1984, Besançon (France)
United debut: 9 April 2005 v Notts County (sub)
Final United game: 15 April 2005 v Swansea City (sub)
Appearances: 0+2
Clubs: Sochaux (France), Oxford United, Saint Paulienne (France), Vannes Olympique Club (France), Ittihad Zemmouri de Khémisset (Morocco), Ornans AS (France), Chabab Rif Al Hoceima (Morocco)

Amine Karam was Ramon Díaz's final signing. The midfielder of French Moroccan descent arrived having gone through the ranks at Sochaux and, after impressing in a series of reserves fixtures, he was signed on a short-term professional contract in March 2005. Unfortunately the Díaz experiment ended before Karam could be signed on permanently and he returned to France where he signed for Saint Paulienne. After two years he moved to Vannes, but in December 2007, after making three appearances, he left for Moroccan side Ittihad Khémisset on a free transfer. Karam failed to break into the first team and found himself back in France, with Ornans, in July 2009. He played just one first-team game in a year and a half in the CFA 2 Groupe D before returning to Morocco in January 2011, when he signed for CR Al Hoceima.

KAY, Bert

Inside-right
United debut: 20 August 1949 v Hastings United
Final United game: 7 April 1951 v Cheltenham Town
Appearances: 44
Goals: 15
Clubs: Bury, Headington United, Peterborough United

Albert Kay joined Headington from Bury for a club record £1,000 in August 1949, making his debut in the club's first Southern League fixture at Hastings. After leaving Headington Kay joined Midland League side Peterborough United.

KEARNS, Mick

Goalkeeper
Born: 26 November 1950, Banbury
United debut: 27 March 1970 v Leicester City
Final United game: 22 January 1972 v Queen's Park Rangers
Appearances: 78
Clean sheets: 25
Clubs: Banbury United, Oxford United, Swindon Town (loan), Plymouth Argyle (loan), Charlton Athletic (loan), Walsall, Wolverhampton Wanderers

Michael Joseph Kearns was the oldest of five brothers, the youngest of whom (Ollie) later also played for United. Mick became an Oxford United

apprentice in 1966, joining the professional staff two years later. It was almost a further two years before he made his debut because of the good form of Jim Barron. Before he made the breakthrough he had a loan with Swindon to act as Peter Downborough's understudy in the May 1970 Anglo-Italian Cup, but he did not play for them. Towards the end of his time at the Manor he had a one-game loan spell with Plymouth in October 1972, followed by a four-game loan at Charlton Athletic in February 1973, who refused to pay United's asking price of £20,000 for him. He joined Walsall in July 1973. Kearns spent six years at Fellows Park, being an ever present for three seasons between 1974 and 1977. It came as a surprise to Walsall fans when he was allowed to leave for Wolves in July 1979 as cover for Paul Bradshaw after 293 competitive games, having missed only five matches for the Saddlers. Kearns managed just five League games in three years for Wanderers before returning to Walsall in August 1982, playing in 26 League games up to May 1985, the last five of which were as a non-contract player while he worked in a working men's club. He became Walsall's community liaison officer in 1990, a role he still held when this book was published.

KEARNS, Ollie

Forward
Born: 12 June 1956, Banbury
United debut: 19 August 1981 v Watford
Final United game: 4 May 1982 v Swindon Town (sub)
Appearances: 11+12
Goals: 4
Clubs: Banbury United, Reading, Oxford United, Walsall, Hereford United, Wrexham, Kettering Town, Rushden Town, Worcester City, Rushden & Diamonds, Racing Club Warwick

Oliver Anthony Kearns was Mick Kearns' youngest brother. He started his career with Banbury United, where he played alongside Tony Jacques, moving to Reading early in 1977. The Royals were relegated at the end of his first season, but they won the Fourth Division title in 1979. Kearns scored 40 goals in 86 League games for Reading before moving to Oxford in August 1981, some eight years after his brother Mick had left. Ollie scored in new manager Jim Smith's first game but that did not save him from the end-of-season clear-out, when he moved to Walsall to play with his brother Mick. Ollie spent one season with the Saddlers, scoring 11 goals in 38 League appearances, before moving to Hereford in June 1983. In his four and a half years at Edgar Street Kearns played 170 League games in which he scored 58 goals. He moved to Wrexham where he found the net 14 times in 46 League appearances over two seasons, after which he dropped out of the League to join Kettering, playing the first of his two games with the Poppies in August 1990. Kearns' next stop was Rushden Town, and he played for Worcester City for the 1991–92 season. He joined the newly-amalgamated Rushden & Diamonds in July 1992, scoring the team's first goal in their inaugural fixture against Bilston Town. However, he was released at the end of that season and joined Racing Club Warwick, with whom he played for one season before retiring and becoming a property developer in Oxfordshire.

KEE, Paul

Goalkeeper
Born: 8 November 1969, Belfast
United debut: 25 November 1989 v Middlesbrough
Final United game: 14 September 1993 v Portsmouth
Appearances: 68
Clean sheets: 13
Clubs: Ards (Northern Ireland), Oxford United, Wimbledon (loan), Ards (loan), Reading (loan), Ards, Linfield (Northern Ireland), Cobh Ramblers (Ireland), Carrick Rangers (Northern Ireland), Bangor (Northern Ireland), Crusaders (Northern Ireland), Glentoran (Northern Ireland)

Paul Victor Kee won Northern Ireland caps at Under-15, Under-16 and Under-18 levels. He started his career as a youth player with Ards, graduating to their Irish League side in 1987 and making 22 appearances before Oxford paid £15,000 for him in June 1988. He won his first full Northern Ireland cap in March 1990 in a friendly against Norway, playing for the Under-21s against Israel the following month. Although Kee was never particularly highly regarded by Oxford supporters he played an integral role in keeping the side in Division Two in 1992, when he made several outstanding saves in the season's final game at Tranmere, which United won 2–1 to avoid relegation. In April 1993 Kee went on loan to Wimbledon, but he did not make a first-team appearance for the Dons and in December 1993 he had an eight-game loan spell back at Ards. He had another non-playing loan spell, this time with Reading, in March 1994 before returning to Ards again, this on a free transfer, in July 1994. He stayed with Ards until October 1997, making 54 League appearances, before joining Linfield where he remained for two months, moving on to Cobh Ramblers. Kee joined Carrick Rangers in August 1998, making 53 appearances before moving to Bangor in July 2000, where he played 11 games. In August 2001 he moved to Crusaders where he played 70 games before finally moving to Glentoran in July 2003. After stopping playing he became a goalkeeping coach with Glentoran and then Bangor, returning to Ards in August 2010 to fulfil the same role. Kee won nine full Northern Ireland caps in total.

KEEBLE, Matthew

Forward
Born: 8 September 1972, Chipping Norton
United debut: 13 March 1993 v Southend United
Final United game: 23 October 1993 v Luton Town (sub)
Appearances: 1+1
Clubs: Oxford United, Abingdon Town, Hailey

Matthew Edwin Keeble joined Oxford's YTS from school in 1989, having previously played for West Witney Boys, Clanfield Youth, Mid Oxon and Oxfordshire. He joined the senior squad in 1991 but was released in January 1994. Keeble later played for Abingdon Town and then Hailey FC.

KEELEY, John

Goalkeeper
Born: 27 July 1961, Plaistow
United debut: 6 November 1991 v Watford
Final United game: 7 December 1991 v Blackburn Rovers

Appearances: 6
Clubs: Southend United, Chelmsford City, Brighton & Hove Albion, Oldham Athletic, Oxford United (loan), Reading (loan), Chester City (loan), Colchester United, Chelmsford City, Stockport County, Peterborough United, Brighton & Hove Albion, Chelmsford City, Canvey Island, Havant & Waterlooville, Worthing, Crawley Town

John Henry Keeley joined United on loan from Oldham in November 1991 as cover for the injured Ken Veysey and Paul Kee. He started with Southend as an apprentice, having been on West Ham's books as a youth, playing 76 games for the Shrimpers between July 1979 and November 1985, when he moved to Chelmsford. At the end of the season he joined Brighton for £1,500, spending four years there and making 138 League appearances, before leaving for Oldham in August 1990 for a Latics record fee of £240,000. However, because of injury he made just four first-team appearances for Oldham before joining Colchester on a free transfer in August 1993. In the meantime he had his loan spell at the Manor, followed by a six-game loan at Reading in February 1992 and a four-game loan to Chester in August 1992. Keeley made just 15 League appearances for Colchester, in one of which he helped set an unwanted record when the Essex side became the first club to have two goalkeepers sent off in a League match when Keeley and Nathan Mumford were both dismissed for professional fouls. After another spell with Chelmsford, Keeley moved to Stockport where he appeared in the 1994 Second Division Play-off Final for the Hatters as they lost 2–1 to Burnley. After 20 League appearances for Stockport, he joined Peterborough in February 1995 where he played just three games before going to Chelmsford for the third time. At the start of the following season Keeley played part-time for Canvey Island while earning his living as a taxi driver. Keeley played six games for Havant & Waterlooville in April 1999 and a further two for the Hawks in October that year. In 2001 he returned to Brighton as goalkeeping coach, and was also registered as a player. In 2003 he turned out for Worthing a few times and in January 2004 he signed for Crawley. In May 2007 Keeley moved from Brighton to become goalkeeping coach at Portsmouth.

KELLY, Marcus

Left-winger
Born: 16 March 1986, Kettering
United debut: 8 August 2009 v York City
Final United game: 14 November 2009 v Kidderminster Harriers (sub)
Appearances: 2+1
Clubs: Rushden & Diamonds, Oxford United, Kettering Town (loan), Kettering Town

Marcus Philip Kelly started with Rushden & Diamonds as a trainee, making his debut in March 2004 after impressing for both the youth and reserve teams. He became a first-team regular the following season and apart from a few spells out with a troublesome shoulder injury he became an established player until he left Rushden for Oxford in May 2009, having made 175 appearances for the Diamonds, scoring 12 goals, including a brace against United in January 2006. Unfortunately he was unable to replicate his good form for the U's and in November 2009 he joined Kettering on loan, making two Conference appearances before joining the Poppies permanently in

January 2010, following his release by Oxford. At Kettering he was converted to left-back and in 2011 he won the Supporters' Player of the Year. Kelly won an England C cap against Northern Ireland in 2007.

KENNET, Josh

Midfielder
Born: 27 September 1987, Camden
United debut: 1 January 2007 v Exeter City (sub)
Final United game: 1 January 2007 v Exeter City (sub)
Appearances: 0+1
Clubs: London Maccabi Lions, Oxford United, Didcot Town (loan), Maccabi Herzliya (Israel), Hapoel Bnei Lod (Israel) (loan), London Maccabi Lions

Joshua Simon Kennet was a stylish young midfielder who came up through the United youth team ranks. Prior to that, he spent time at Millwall and Spurs, and it was after the latter opted not to sign him that he went for a trial at Oxford who, impressed with what they saw, offered him a scholarship in 2004. Kennet also made a few appearances for London Maccabi Lions in the Maccabi Southern Football League. He made his United debut on New Year's Day 2007, away to Exeter. However, that was a rare opportunity and in March 2007 he joined Didcot Town on a month's loan. He was released by Oxford at the end of that season and left to play for Maccabi Herzliya in Israel. In February 2010 Kennet joined Hapoel Bnei Lod on a six-month loan, and at the start of the following season he found himself back in England playing for the London Lions again, with a proposed move to Rushden & Diamonds in November 2010 falling through following an injury.

KERR, George

Inside-forward
Born: 9 January 1943, Alexandria, West Dunbartonshire
United debut: 10 September 1966 v Shrewsbury Town
Final United game: 16 September 1967 v Peterborough United (sub)
Appearances: 43+1
Goals: 6
Clubs: Vale of Leven, Barnsley, Bury, Oxford United, Scunthorpe United

George Adams McDonald Kerr joined United from Bury for £8,000 in the summer of 1966, having scored two goals in 15 League appearances for the Shakers, who he had joined from Barnsley in the previous March. Having started the Vale of Leven Academy, Kerr was signed by Barnsley in 1961, while still at school. In his four seasons with the Tykes, he scored 40 goals in 166 appearances. Despite his fee, a large one for the U's at the time, he was never a regular starter for Oxford and in February 1968 he joined Scunthorpe as part of the deal that took David Sloan to the Manor. Kerr played with the Iron for six seasons, playing 157 games and scoring 32 goals before hanging up his boots in 1973. Kerr became a coach at Lincoln City, briefly becoming manager for 18 games between June and December 1977. In July 1979 he became manager of Grimsby Town, taking them to the Third Division title in his first season. He was sacked, though, in January 1982 and in March 1983 he was appointed Rotherham United's manager, where he remained until May 1985. Kerr returned to Lincoln in December 1985, and left in March 1987 as the Imps were on their way to relegation from the

Football League. He managed non-League Boston United between 1987 and 1990 before becoming an expert summariser with BBC Radio Humberside. His younger brother was Bobby Kerr, Sunderland's captain when they won the FA Cup in 1973.

KEY, Lance

Goalkeeper
Born: 13 May 1968, Kettering
United debut: 28 January 1995 v Shrewsbury
Final United game: 25 February 1995 v Chester City
Appearances: 6
Clean sheets: 2
Clubs: Histon, Sheffield Wednesday, Oldham Athletic (loan), Oxford United (loan), Lincoln City (loan), Hartlepool United (loan), Rochdale (loan), Dundee United, Tranmere Rovers, Sheffield United, Rochdale, Northwich Victoria (loan), Northwich Victoria, Altrincham (loan), Kingstonian, Histon, Wivenhoe Town, Rushden & Diamonds

Lance William Key started his career with his home-town club, Histon, in the Eastern Counties League, joining Sheffield Wednesday for £10,000 in April 1990. In his six years at Hillsborough Key made just one substitute appearance, in an FA Cup tie against Gillingham, spending much of his time on loan. His first loan spell was with Oldham in October 1993, where he played two games. This was followed by his period with Oxford and then five games with Lincoln in August 1995, one match with Hartlepool in December 1995 and 14 appearances for Rochdale in March 1996. He finally left Wednesday in July 1996 when he joined Dundee United where, despite remaining at Tannadice until March the following year, he played just three games before moving back to Sheffield to join United. Key was not at Bramall Lane for long, and did not play a game for the Blades, before moving back to Rochdale in August 1997. He managed 22 games for Dale before losing his place and eventually going on loan to Northwich Victoria in December 1998. The loan was made permanent in February 1999 and he went on to play 51 games for the Vics, plus 15 during a loan spell with Altrincham in February 2000. In June 2001 Key moved to Kingstonian where he played 136 games and was made club captain just a few weeks before Histon came in for him in September 2004. While with Histon the team was promoted twice to return to the Conference, and he made 124 appearances with the Stutes during four years. Key had a brief spell with Wivenhoe, playing once in the FA Vase, before dropping out of the game, but he returned with Rushden & Diamonds in July 2010, registering as a player while performing goalkeeping coach duties.

KILLIP, John

United debut: 20 August 1955 v Gloucester City
Final United game: 17 September 1955 v Yeovil Town
Appearances: 2
Goals: 1
Clubs: Headington United

KILLOCK, Shane

Centre-back
Born: 12 March 1989, Huddersfield
United debut: 13 January 2009 v York City
Final United game: 24 January 2009 v Crawley Town
Appearances: 4
Clubs: Ossett Albion, Huddersfield Town, Hyde United (loan), Harrogate Town (loan), Oxford United (loan), Oxford United, AFC Telford United (loan), AFC Telford United

Shane Adam Killock joined United on loan from Huddersfield in January 2009. Despite being injured in what was to be his final appearance, United extended his contract until the end of the season following his release by Huddersfield and then offered him a new contract for the following season. He joined Telford on loan at the start of the 2009–10 campaign and the move was made permanent in November 2009. He was made captain for the 2010–11 season, at the end of which he was voted Telford's Player of the Season. Killock started his career with Huddersfield, but was released by the Terriers as a youth, going on to play for Ossett Albion as a 15-year-old schoolboy. His impressive performances for Albion earned him a recall by Huddersfield and he played for their Academy side while still on Ossett's books. Killock signed a professional deal in January 2008 at the same time as future United goalkeeper Simon Eastwood, going on loan to Hyde United the following month. He made 14 appearances for the Ewen Field outfit and in September 2008 he spent six weeks with Harrogate Town. Killock made just one appearance for Huddersfield before his move to Oxford.

KING, Simon

Left-back
Born: 11 April 1983, Oxford
United debut: 1 May 2001 v Port Vale
Final United game: 20 April 2002 v Darlington
Appearances: 3+1
Clubs: Oxford United, Barnet, Gillingham

Simon Daniel Roy King became an Oxford United scholar in 1999, making his first-team debut in the last competitive game to be played at the Manor when Oxford drew 1–1 with Port Vale. He became a professional at the start of the following season but was released by Ian Atkins in the summer of 2003, when he signed for Barnet, then in the Conference. While with the Bees he won three England C caps and a Conference Championship medal in 2005. In the 2006–07 season King was named Barnet's Player of the Year. He was transfer-listed at the end of that season and in June 2007 Gillingham paid £200,000 for him. King was named Gillingham's Player of the Year for the 2008–09 season, in which they won the League Two Play-offs, when he was also named in the PFA League Two Team of the Season.

KINGSTON, Andy

Centre-back
Born: 21 February 1959, Oxford
United debut: 14 May 1977 v Sheffield Wednesday (sub)
Final United game: 23 March 1982 v Doncaster Rovers (sub)
Appearances: 51+7

Clubs: Oxford United, Corby Town, Nuneaton Borough

Andrew Keith Kingston came up through the ranks at United and was in the squad that won the Midlands Youth League in 1975, signing as an apprentice the following season. He won England Youth and Schoolboy honours, but after turning professional during the 1976–77 season his appearances for United were limited and he was released by Jim Smith in April 1982. Kingston later moved to Nuneaton.

*KINNIBURGH, Steve

Left-back
Born: 13 June 1989, Glasgow
United debut: 31 August 2009 v Forest Green Rovers
Final United game: 7 May 2011 v Shrewsbury Town
Appearances: 26+1
Goals: 1
Clubs: Rangers, Queen of the South (loan), St Johnstone (loan), Oxford United (loan), Oxford United

Steven Steel Kinniburgh joined Oxford on loan from Rangers in August 2009, but he had to return to Glasgow earlier than anticipated after receiving an ankle injury. However, he impressed enough during his time with United that when Rangers released him in May 2010 Kinniburgh was signed by Oxford. Unfortunately he struggled to make an impact and in March 2011 he was told that he was free to look for another club. Kinniburgh signed for Rangers from East Kilbride side Burgh United and was a member of the Under-19s side that won the Scottish Youth League and Cup in both 2006–07 and the following season. In December 2008 he played two games on loan for Queen of the South and in April 2009 he joined St Johnstone on loan until the end of the season, but he did not get to play for the Saints.

KNIGHT, Peter

Outside-right
Born: 26 December 1937, Ilford
United debut: 20 August 1960 v Worcester City
Final United game: 17 October 1964 v Notts County
Appearances: 200
Goals: 33
Clubs: Southend United, Nottingham Forest, Oxford United, Reading, Guildford City

Peter Robert Knight played for Essex County while still at school and later was selected to play twice for the England Amateur XI. During his National Service he represented the RAF Command at both football and athletics. In August 1958 he signed professionally with Southend but left for Nottingham Forest the following season without having played for the Shrimpers' first team. He made seven appearances for Forest, including in the Charity Shield against Wolves, before joining Oxford at the start of the 1960–61 season. He made the right-wing berth his own because of his outstanding crossing ability that created numerous goals. It came as a surprise when Knight left Oxford for Reading during the 1964–65 season, and he went on to make 26 League appearances for the Biscuitmen over the next two seasons before moving to Guildford.

KNIGHT, Richard

Goalkeeper
Born: 3 August 1979, Burton-on-Trent
United debut: 22 January 2000 v Bristol Rovers
Final United game: 23 March 2002 v Carlisle United
Appearances: 52+1
Clean sheets: 8
Clubs: Burton Albion, Derby County, Carlisle United (loan), Birmingham City (loan), Hull City (loan), Macclesfield Town (loan), Oxford United (loan), Oxford United, Colchester United (loan), Didcot Town, Brackley Town, Oxford City

Richard Knight joined United initially on loan from Derby County in January 2000. He played just two games before returning to Derby, but United brought him back in March and in his 11 appearances he made a significant contribution to United avoiding relegation. He was signed permanently that summer but, despite winning Supporters' Player of the Year at the end of his first season, United were relegated to the basement division and the U's conceded 100 League goals. Knight, however, failed to impress new manager Mark Wright, and his card was marked when United lost 3–2 at non-League Chester City in the FA Cup, having been 2–0 up, with Knight feigning injury to cover up an error for the equalising goal. Knight lost his place to Ian McCaldon and when Andy Woodman arrived it was only a matter of time before Knight was on his way. He had a one-game loan to Colchester in March 2002 and was released by United at the end of that season. Knight dropped out of the game briefly until he was signed by Didcot Town in January 2004 and moved to Brackley in the summer. In July 2009 Knight moved to Oxford City. Knight's career began with Burton Albion, but he was signed by Derby County in June 1997. In March 1999 he played six games on loan to Carlisle and then made one substitute appearance for Birmingham City in August 1999. He then played one game for Hull in October and completed a peripatetic 1999 at Macclesfield, where he played three loan games.

KYLE, Maurice

Centre-back
Born: 8 November 1937, Darlington
Died: January 1981
United debut: 14 February 1959 v Barry Town
Final United game: 18 October 1969 v Bolton Wanderers
Appearances: 448
Goals: 4
Clubs: Wath Wanderers, Wolverhampton Wanderers, Headington United, Southend United (loan), Worcester City, Bath City, Oxford City

Maurice Kyle was a part-timer at Wolves, playing for their nursery side Wath Wanderers and for Wolves' Central League side after being spotted by a scout playing for a youth side in Darlington. He turned down a professional contract, however, so that he could continue with his apprenticeship as an electrician. He joined United on loan initially, but when Stan Cullis expressed no interest in taking him back he stayed at the Manor. When Oxford joined the Football League in 1962 his transfer had to be properly registered, and Oxford paid Wolves a then club record £5,000 for him. Kyle's nickname at Oxford was 'King' and he stayed at the Manor despite interest in him from clubs higher up the Football League. Kyle coached the Oxford University team for two seasons from 1968. He was loaned to Southend United in March 1970, playing eight games for the Shrimpers, and was released at the end of the season. After spells with Worcester City and Bath City Kyle became manager of Oxford City in September 1972 and he even played a few games in the Premier Midweek Floodlit League, becoming the first ex-professional 'permit' player ever to represent the City. He resigned in September 1976, to be succeeded by Geoff Denial, and a week later was appointed manager of Witney Town. In January 1981 Kyle died from cancer.

L

LAMBERT, Jamie

Winger
Born: 14 September 1973, Henley on Thames
United debut: 30 August 1999 v Blackpool (sub)
Final United game: 4 December 1999 v Stoke (sub)
Appearances: 10+6
Goals: 2
Clubs: Reading, Walsall (loan), Watford, Checkendon, Oxford United, Barry Town, Slough Town, Basingstoke Town

Christopher James Lambert started his career with Reading, for whom he made 151 appearances and scored 20 goals over six years. At the age of 17 he was invited for a trial with Monaco. In October 1998 he had a six-game loan spell with Walsall and in April 1999 he played several reserves games for Watford. He dropped out of the professional game and played for his local village team, Checkendon, before joining Oxford on non-contract terms. While with United he scored a goal against Colchester United after just 17 seconds to set a Manor record for the fastest goal at the ground. After leaving Oxford Lambert had an unsuccessful trial with Port Vale, after which he returned to Checkendon. He signed for Barry in August 2000, playing against Boavista in the UEFA Cup, before moving to Slough Town in September 2000. Lambert scored two goals in 19 appearances for the Rebels before he moved to Basingstoke Town, where he played until August 2003, scoring one goal in eight appearances.

LANGAN, David

Right-back
Born: 15 February 1957, Dublin
United debut: 25 August 1984 v Huddersfield Town
Final United game: 5 September 1987 v Luton Town
Appearances: 134+2
Goals: 3
Clubs: Cherry Orchard, Derby County, Birmingham City, Oxford United, Leicester City (loan), AFC Bournemouth, Peterborough United, Holbeach United, Ramsey Town, Rothwell Town, Mirlees Blackstone

David Francis Langan can truly be considered an Oxford United legend. Signed from Birmingham City on a free transfer by his former Blues boss Jim Smith, Langan proved to be an inspirational attacking full-back, bringing the crowd to its feet with his surging overlapping runs. He only scored three goals for United, but two of them were of great significance; his first Oxford goal was a 30-yard strike that beat Pat Jennings for United to record a 3–2 win over Division One leaders Arsenal in the League Cup, and his second goal was the one that beat Shrewsbury Town 1–0 to confirm Oxford's place in the top flight for the first time in the club's history. Langan went on to be an important component of United's First Division squad, and played in the club's Milk Cup Final victory over Queen's Park Rangers in April 1986. Langan began his career with Dublin-based side

Cherry Orchard, moving to Derby in 1974 and turning professional the following year. He made his debut for the Rams in 1977 and in 1977–78 he was voted the Player of the Year and won his first Ireland cap in February. After making 155 appearances Langan was sold to Jim Smith's Birmingham City for a then club record £350,000. However, at St Andrew's injuries began to take their toll and he missed over a year, leading Smith's successor Ron Saunders to release him. Aware of his ability and his commitment, Smith acted immediately to bring Langan to Oxford, where his form was such that he won a deserved recall to the Ireland side, winning 11 of his 26 caps while with United. In January 1987 Langan had a five-game loan spell with Leicester City and in December that year he moved to AFC Bournemouth. He played 20 League games for the Cherries before joining Peterborough United for £25,000 in the summer of 1988. He managed 22 games for the Posh before he was advised to give up playing on medical grounds after requiring a second spinal fusion. He joined Holbeach United in 1989 and went on to play for a succession of lower-league clubs. His knee and back injuries finally took their toll and Langan was forced to eke out a living as a porter for Peterborough Town Council while claiming disability benefit. United awarded Langan a long-overdue benefit game in July 2011.

LAWRENCE, George

Right-winger
Born: 14 September 1962, Kensington
United debut: 27 March 1982 v Chesterfield
Final United game: 26 December 1984 v Cardiff City
Appearances: 101
Goals: 27
Clubs: Southampton, Oxford United (loan), Oxford United, Southampton, Millwall, AFC Bournemouth, Mikkelin Palloilijat (Finland), Weymouth, Portsmouth, Hibernians (Malta), Halesowen Town, Rushden & Diamonds

George Randolph Lawrence, nicknamed 'Chicken' George after a character in Alex Haley's novel *Roots*, joined United from Southampton, initially on loan. He arrived at the Saints as a trainee in August 1979 and made his debut in October 1981, playing in four Division One games before joining Oxford on loan in March 1982. He played 15 games for the U's and scored four goals, including one in Oxford's 5–0 win over Swindon Town in April 1982, before returning to Southampton. Lawrence played a further six games, scoring once, before his transfer to United in November 1982. A player of power, speed and flair, Lawrence often caused panic among opposition defences, although he too often neglected to take the ball with him on his charges down the wing. He returned to Southampton in January 1985 and spent two and a half seasons with the Saints, playing 68 League games in which he scored 11 goals before his £160,000 transfer to Millwall in July 1987. The Lions won the Second Division title at the end of Lawrence's first season, but he played just 28 League matches, scoring four goals, before his £65,000 transfer to Bournemouth in August 1989. Lawrence scored five goals in 75 League games, with his first coming against Oxford, before joining Finnish side Mikkelin Palloilijat in the summer of 1992. He returned to England to play for Weymouth, from where Jim Smith signed him for Portsmouth in March 1993 on a non-contract basis. He made 14 non-scoring appearances for Pompey, all except the Play-off semi-final against Leicester City as substitute, before leaving for Malta. Lawrence played one game for Sliema Wanderers but, despite impressing with his skill and strength, Sliema did not offer him a contract and Hibernians stepped in to sign him instead. Lawrence was a major factor behind Hibs winning the Championship in 1994 and 1995, but his injury midway through the 1995–96 season derailed their bid for a third successive title and he was released. On his return to England Lawrence joined Halesowen Town before ending his playing days with Rushden. He became a players' agent after his retirement.

LEACH, Brian

Wing-half
Born: 20 July 1932, Reading
United debut: 24 August 1957 v Cheltenham Town
Final United game: 7 February 1959 v Cheltenham Town
Appearances: 77
Goals: 11
Clubs: Reading, Headington United, Tunbridge Wells, Thorneycrofts, Henley Town, Fleet Town, Henley Town, Mapledurham

Brian Ernest Leach joined Headington in the summer of 1957 after being released by Reading. He joined the Biscuitmen in 1951 and went on to play 118 games, in which he scored one goal. Leach, who could also play at fullback or up front, moved from Headington to Tunbridge Wells, then played for Thorneycrofts, before moving to Henley. While with Henley he became captain and led his team to win two important Cup competitions on successive evenings, and the next season they did better still when they won the First Division of the Hellenic League. When he returned after playing for Fleet he again won the Hellenic League First Division. Leach made his final appearance for Henley aged 44, after which he played for Mapledurham. He became a bricklayer until his retirement in July 1997.

LEDGISTER, Joel

Left-winger
Born: 29 September 1987, London
United debut: 11 August 2007 v Forest Green Rovers
Final United game: 20 January 2008 v Exeter City (sub)
Appearances: 9+4
Clubs: Southend United, Gravesend & Northfleet (loan), Oxford United, Hayes & Yeading United (loan), Woking, Kingstonian, Carshalton Athletic

Joel Sebastian Ledgister started as a trainee with Southend United and in January 2007 he started a 13-game loan spell with Gravesend during which he scored two goals. In August 2007 Ledgister signed for Oxford, but injury and poor form limited his appearances and in January 2008 he was transfer-listed, subsequently joining Hayes & Yeading on loan until the end of the season, scoring four goals in 13 appearances. He had his contract cancelled in July 2008 and was immediately snapped up by Woking, managed by Phil Gilchrist. He went on to play 40 games for the Cards, scoring six goals, after which he joined Kingstonian. In November 2009 Ledgister was released by the K's at his own request and had a trial with Crystal Palace. In July 2010 he had a trial with Derby County before joining Carshalton. In March 2011 Wealdstone made a seven-day approach for Ledgister, but he decided to stay with Carshalton.

LEWIS, Brian

Midfielder
Born: 26 January 1943, Woking
Died: 14 December 1998
United debut: 17 January 1970 v Norwich City
Final United game: 14 November 1970 v Hull City (sub)
Appearances: 12+2
Goals: 4
Clubs: Crystal Palace, Portsmouth, Coventry City, Luton Town, Oxford United, Colchester United, Portsmouth, Hastings United

Brian Lewis was a versatile player who during his career played in every outfield position. He started with Crystal Palace in 1960, playing 32 League games in which he scored four goals before moving to Portsmouth, the team he supported, in 1963. In his four seasons with Division Two Pompey, Lewis made 134 League appearances and scored 24 goals. He then spent a season in the top flight with Coventry City, scoring twice in 34 League games, before moving to Luton in 1968. He played 43 games in Division Three with the Hatters, scoring 22 goals, before joining the U's at the very start of 1970. Lewis stayed with Oxford throughout the calendar year before his move to Colchester, where he played an integral part in their FA Cup fifth-round giant-killing over Leeds United in February 1971. After two seasons at Layer Road he returned to Portsmouth before joining Hastings United in 1975. Lewis died in Bournemouth in December 1998.

LEWIS, Fred

Full-back
Born: 26 July 1923, Broughton Gifford, Wiltshire
Died: 1975
United debut: 20 August 1955 v Gloucester City
Final United game: 23 April 1956 v Dartford
Appearances: 19
Clubs: Aylesbury Town, Chelsea, Colchester United, Headington United

Frederic Arthur Lewis played 26 matches for Chelsea from August 1946 until August 1953, when he joined Colchester United. He stayed at Layer Road for two seasons before leaving in May 1955, whereupon he signed for Headington.

LEWIS, Mickey

Midfielder
Born: 15 February 1965, Birmingham
United debut: 27 August 1988 v Leeds United
Final United game: 19 February 2000 v Chesterfield (sub)
Appearances: 319+32
Goals: 7
Clubs: West Bromwich Albion, Derby County, Oxford United, Banbury United, Oxford City, Des Moines Menace (USA)

Michael Lewis started his playing career with the West Bromwich Albion youth team, winning the Baggies' Young Player of the Year award in 1984 and collecting seven England Youth caps. After making 33 appearances for West Brom he moved to Derby County in November 1984 for £25,000. Lewis was with the Rams for just under four years, scoring one goal in 50 games, before joining Oxford in August 1988 as part of the deal that took Trevor Hebberd to the Baseball Ground. In over a decade with United Lewis played successfully both in central midfield and central defence; he was a model of reliability and an integral member of the 1996 promotion-winning side. After that promotion season Lewis stopped playing and became the U's youth team coach. However, injury problems saw Lewis recalled to the first team in August 1999 and he made his first start in over three years in a Worthington Cup tie against Everton, which United won 2–1 on aggregate. In October 1999 Lewis was made caretaker manager following the departure of Malcolm Shotton and held the position until the appointment of Denis Smith in February 2000, after which he returned to coaching the youth team while acting as Smith's assistant. After Smith's resignation in October 2000 Lewis became assistant to caretaker manager Mike Ford, having recently left United to play for Banbury United on a non-contract basis. He made one appearance for the Puritans before he was sacked by Oxford in November 2000 and he became player-coach at Oxford City before giving up playing to become assistant manager to Paul Lee, having spent the summer of 2001 as player-coach with Des Moines Menace, who he took to second place in the Premier Development League. While with City, Lewis also became coach to the Oxford University football team, who he led to three consecutive Varsity victories. Lewis left Oxford City in December 2003, becoming coach at Slough Town the following month. He remained at Slough until July 2005, at which point he was appointed David Penney's assistant manager at Doncaster Rovers, where he won the reserves League. In August 2006 Lewis and Penney both left Doncaster and Lewis returned to Oxford where he became a van driver while coaching Abingdon Town and Oxford United Under-11s, and returning to coach the University side alongside Phil Heath. In May 2007 he replaced new manager Darren Patterson as youth team coach and in November 2007 he became Patterson's assistant. Lewis continued as assistant manager following the appointment of Chris Wilder in December 2008.

LEWORTHY, Dave

Forward
Born: 22 October 1962, Portsmouth
United debut: 26 December 1985 v Southampton
Final United game: 29 April 1989 v Manchester City (sub)
Appearances: 31+16
Goals: 9
Clubs: Portsmouth, Fareham Town, Tottenham Hotspur, Oxford United, Shrewsbury Town (loan), Reading, Colchester United (loan), Farnborough Town, Dover Athletic, Rushden & Diamonds, Kingstonian, Havant & Waterlooville

David John Leworthy started his career with his home-town club of Portsmouth in September 1980. He made just one appearance for Pompey, his 12 minutes as a substitute earning him the dubious distinction of having the shortest Portsmouth first-team career. Portsmouth released Leworthy in April 1982 and he joined Fareham, where he became a prolific goalscorer. His goals brought him to the attention of First Division Tottenham Hotspur, who paid £5,000 for him. He spent two years with Spurs, scoring three goals in 11 games before his move to Oxford for a club record £200,000. Leworthy scored a brace on his debut, but thereafter the goals dried up somewhat and he was mainly used as an understudy for John Aldridge and Jeremy Charles. Once United had signed Billy Whitehurst and then Dean Saunders and Martin Foyle, Leworthy's opportunities were even scarcer and he spent a six-game loan spell with Shrewsbury in October 1987, scoring three goals. In the summer of 1989 Leworthy joined Reading on a free transfer, scoring eight goals in 54 appearances in three seasons, plus a loan spell at Ian Atkins' Colchester in 1991 in which he scored four goals in nine games as they finished second in the GM Vauxhall Conference. In February 1992 Leworthy moved to Farnborough where he rediscovered his scoring touch, scoring 61 goals in 74 games before Dover Athletic smashed the non-League transfer record when they paid £50,000 for Leworthy in the summer of 1993. In his 152 appearances for Dover, Leworthy scored 86 goals before moving to Rushden & Diamonds in January 1997, where his goals helped save them from relegation from the Conference. In the summer of 1997 Kingstonian paid a club record £18,000 to sign Leworthy, the move paying off as the K's won the Ryman League Premier Division in his first season there. Leworthy scored 66 goals in 146 appearances before moving to Havant & Waterlooville in August 2000, just after he had won the FA Trophy with Kingstonian. During the 2002–03 season Leworthy gained his first coaching experience as he took charge of the Hawks' Under-18s, who won all four Hampshire youth trophies in his first season. He was then put in charge of the reserves before, in January 2004 after an unbeaten 18-game run, he was promoted to be first-team manager. In November 2004 Leworthy was relieved of his position and he retired from the game. He returned in March 2006, however, as manager of Kingstonian. In July 2007 Leworthy was appointed as manager of Croydon Athletic, and in December 2007 he became manager of Banstead Athletic, returning to Croydon in January 2008, but he was forced to step down due to work commitments in January 2009.

LIGHT, Jimmy

Right-back
Born: 13 January 1954, Oxford
United debut: 24 April 1973 v Preston North End
Final United game: 12 September 1975 v Bristol City
Appearances: 68
Goals: 1
Clubs: Oxford United, Witney Town

Having been on Tottenham's books as a youth, James Power Light became a United apprentice in 1969, rejecting a similar offer from Spurs at the same time. He joined the professional ranks in January 1972, taking over defensive duties from Dick Lucas. In the summer of 1976 he was released by United and joined Witney Town. In 1988 Light became manager of Headington Amateurs after they were accepted into the Hellenic League, remaining in charge for six seasons, when they achieved their highest ever placing of fourth in the Premier Division and reached the semi-finals of the Oxfordshire Senior Cup in April 1991, when they lost to Oxford United. Light eventually became the Amateurs' general manager.

LILLEY, Derek

Forward
Born: 9 February 1974, Paisley
United debut: 7 August 1999 v Stoke City
Final United game: 2 December 2000 v Oldham Athletic
Appearances: 61+16
Goals: 10
Clubs: Everton Boys' Club, Greenock Morton, Leeds United, Heart of Midlothian (loan), Bury (loan), Oxford United, Dundee United, Livingston, Boston United, Livingston, Greenock Morton, St Johnstone, Stirling Albion, Forfar Athletic

Derek Symon Lilley joined Oxford from Leeds United for £75,000 in August 1999 after a disappointing two years at Elland Road. He had joined Leeds for £500,000 from Greenock Morton in March 1997, but made only 26 appearances, including just four starts, and scored one goal. He had joined Morton in August 1991 from Paisley-based Everton Boys' Club and played 210 games, in which he scored 80 goals, for the Cappielow club. In December 1998 Leeds loaned him to Hearts, where he scored once in five appearances, and this was followed by a five-game loan to Bury in March 1999, where he again scored one goal, against Oxford. Lilley's time at Oxford was more successful, and he had regular first-team football, his form earning him a £100,000 move to Dundee United in December 2000, where he scored on his debut in a 1–1 draw with Rangers. Lilley ended that season as Dundee United's top scorer with six goals, including another against Rangers in a 2–0 win at Ibrox and the winner against St Johnstone that preserved their Premier League status. However, his goalscoring record dropped off and he was released in July 2003, whereupon he signed for Livingston. Lilley rediscovered his scoring form and his tally included a goal in the Scottish League Cup Final 2–0 win over Hibernian. In his 81 games for Livingston, sandwiching a non-playing spell at Boston in July 2004, he scored 21 goals before his return to Morton in June 2005. He played a further 65 games for Morton, scoring 22 goals, before his contract was terminated in January 2007. He joined St Johnstone but all of his 14 appearances were as substitute, and after failing to find the net in any of them, he was released at the end of the season. Lilley then spent a season with Stirling Albion, playing 25 games and again failing to score. He joined Forfar Athletic in July 2008, scoring three goals in 30 games, before his release at the end of the season, when he gave up playing and started providing statistical analysis of St Johnstone's home matches for the Press Association.

LINIGHAN, Andy

Centre-back
Born: 18 June 1962, Hartlepool
United debut: 17 October 2000 v Luton Town
Final United game: 28 April 2001 v Swansea City (sub)
Appearances: 14+1
Clubs: Smith's Dock, Hartlepool United, Leeds United, Oldham Athletic, Norwich City, Arsenal, Crystal Palace, Queen's Park Rangers (loan), Oxford United, St Albans City

Andrew Linighan's first club was Smith's Dock FC, who represented the South Bank-based shipyard whose Smith's Dock Park home was actually at nearby Normanby. In September 1980 he was signed by Hartlepool United and after making 127 appearances in almost four years, in which he scored six goals, the solid defender joined Leeds United for £20,000. Linighan played 78 games for Leeds, scoring four goals, before a £65,000 move to Oldham Athletic in January 1986. He played 102 times, scoring six goals, before he joined Norwich City for £350,000 in March 1988. Linighan helped shore up the Canaries defence and he helped them to fourth place in the Premiership in 1989, when they also reached the FA Cup semi-finals. His success prompted Arsenal to pay £1.25 million for him in July 1990. Although his first-team appearances for the Gunners were initially limited, he scored the winning goal in the 1992 FA Cup Final against Sheffield Wednesday, helping Arsenal to become the first team in England to win the League Cup and the FA Cup in the same season. Linighan remained a backup defender, managing a total of 156 appearances and eight goals before his £110,000 transfer to Crystal Palace in January 1997. With Palace he won promotion to the Premiership and was made club captain but because of the club's financial problems he was loaned to QPR for seven games in March 1999 to help reduce Palace's wage bill. After his return to Palace he was voted the Supporters' Player of the Year in 2000, but he had a disagreement with club owner Simon Jordan and in October 2000 he was given a free transfer to Oxford. By this time Linighan was at the tail-end of his career and his movement was cumbersome. He became United's oldest outfield player in professional times, aged 38 years and 114 days when making his final appearance as a substitute against Swansea City. With the U's relegated to the basement division at the end of the season Linighan left United and signed for St Albans City in June 2001. He played just twice for the Ryman League side before leaving to concentrate on his plumbing business.

LINNEY, David

Full-back
Born: 5 September 1961, Birmingham
United debut: 14 August 1982 v Reading
Final United game: 5 March 1983 v Wrexham
Appearances: 35+2
Clubs: Birmingham City, Oxford United, Yeovil Town, Basingstoke Town, Weymouth, Chard

David William Linney began as an apprentice with Birmingham City, turning professional in 1979. Linney was David Langan's understudy for much of his time at St Andrew's. He made just one appearance for Birmingham, deputising for the injured Neil Whatmore, before Ron Saunders released him in the summer of 1982, whereupon his former Birmingham manager, Jim Smith, picked him up for Oxford. He was a regular choice in his first season before joining Alliance Premier League side Yeovil Town on a free transfer. He was the Supporters' Player of the Year in 1984 and a regular first-team player until his move to Basingstoke Town in September 1988. By the end of the season Linney had moved to Weymouth and he later also played for Chard. In November 2002 Linney was appointed commercial manager at Yeovil.

LLOYD, John

Left-back
Born: 10 December 1944, Hitchin
United debut: 2 April 1966 v Watford
Final United game: 15 February 1969 v Huddersfield Town

Appearances: 70+4
Clubs: Swindon Town, Oxford United, Aldershot, Margate, Ramsgate, Southwood

John David Lloyd was a member of the East London Schools XI which reached the Final of the 1960 English Schools' Trophy, losing to Manchester in the final. Lloyd joined Swindon Town as an apprentice after leaving school but he never played for their first team. He was released in October 1964 when Arthur Turner offered him a one-month trial, followed by a second month before he signed for United in December 1964. He did not get a regular first-team place until the 1967–68 season and in February 1969 he moved to Aldershot. Lloyd failed to feature regularly for the Shots, making just 13 appearances, and in July 1970 he moved to Margate. He scored one goal in 55 appearances but was released in the summer of 1971. He joined Ramsgate for the following season, and in 1972–73 and 1973–74 he also played for Southwood. In December 1973 he was sent off in two consecutive games for the Rams.

LONGBOTTOM, Arthur

Inside-forward
Born: 30 January 1933, Leeds
United debut: 31 August 1963 v York City
Final United game: 26 September 1964 v Bradford City
Appearances: 42
Goals: 16
Clubs: Methley United, Queen's Park Rangers, Port Vale, Millwall, Oxford United, Colchester United, Scarborough

Arthur Longbottom first came to prominence with Leeds-based Methley United. He signed for Queen's Park Rangers in March 1954, playing 202 games and netting 62 goals while supplementing his income by working as a barber. He then joined Port Vale for £2,000 in May 1961, for whom he was an ever present the following season, scoring on his debut and finishing as joint top scorer with 20 goals. In total Longbottom scored 18 League goals in 52 League appearances for Vale. In January 1963 he returned briefly to London to play for Millwall, who paid £2,000 for his services for which they were rewarded with one goal in 10 appearances. In August that year he then moved to Oxford United where he finished the 1963–64 season as top scorer with 14 goals. Longbottom stayed at the Manor until October 1964 when he was transferred to Colchester United. He scored 12 goals in 33 games for the Layer Road outfit and at the end of the season he left for Scarborough, where he ended his career. He later changed his surname to Langley by deed poll.

LOUIS, Jefferson

Forward
Born: 22 February 1979, Harrow
United debut: 20 April 2002 v Darlington (sub)
Final United game: 7 August 2004 v Boston United (sub)
Appearances: 22+42
Goals: 10
Clubs: Aylesbury West Indies, Risborough Rangers, Thame United, Aylesbury United, Thame United, Oxford United, Woking (loan), Gravesend & Northfleet (loan), Forest Green Rovers, Woking, Bristol Rovers, Hemel

Hempstead Town, Lewes, Worthing, Stevenage Borough, Eastleigh, Yeading, Havant & Waterlooville, Weymouth, Maidenhead United, Mansfield Town, Wrexham, Crawley Town, Rushden & Diamonds (loan), Gainsborough Trinity, Darlington (loan), Weymouth, Hayes & Yeading United, Maidenhead United, Brackley Town

Jefferson Lee Louis has played for more clubs in his career than any other United player. Maidenhead United became his 29th club when he joined them in March 2011. Louis started his career at Aylesbury West Indies before joining Risborough Rangers. While there he was incarcerated for dangerous driving. After he was released from prison Risborough manager Bob Raynor recommended him to Lee Sinnott, then manager of Thame. He moved to Aylesbury United in December 2000 but was allowed to return to Thame the following summer, after scoring five goals in 15 appearances. Sinnott recommended him to Oxford, for whom he signed in March 2002. Louis' first claim to fame was scoring the winning penalty against Charlton Athletic in the shoot-out after the sides had drawn 0–0 at the Valley in the League Cup. He then scored the only goal against Swindon Town in the FA Cup and was captured on TV dancing naked around the United dressing room on hearing that Oxford had been drawn to play his boyhood favourites Arsenal in the next round. In August 2003 he had an eight-game loan at Woking, where he scored five goals, and in August 2004 he played five games, scoring twice, on loan to Gravesend. Louis spent two years with Oxford (longer than anywhere else during his entire career), before leaving for Forest Green Rovers in September 2004. He scored twice in eight appearances before rejoining Woking, where he managed four goals in 25 games. Louis then had a 10-game spell at Bristol Rovers in 2005, during which year he also appeared for Hemel Hempstead (three games, one goal), Lewes (two games), and Worthing (six games, two goals) before joining Stevenage Borough on non-contract terms in December 2005. He scored six goals in 18 games at Broadhall Way before leaving for Eastleigh in July 2006 after an unsuccessful trial with Exeter City. After one goal in six appearances Louis' contract was terminated and he signed for Yeading, with whom he had played during the pre-season, in September 2006, scoring four goals in eight games. He was with the Ding until his contract was cancelled in December 2006, when he found himself at Havant & Waterlooville, from where he joined Weymouth in June 2007. His time with the Terras ended in January 2008 when their manager Jason Tindall vowed that Louis would never play for them while he was in charge, and after scoring eight goals in 22 matches he rejoined another of his ex-bosses, Johnson Hippolyte, at Blue Square South Maidenhead United. After a three-game spell at Maidenhead he briefly returned to the Football League with Mansfield in January 2008, but they were relegated that season with Louis scoring four goals in 18 appearances. Louis remained in the Conference, joining Wrexham in June 2008, where he managed to stay for a whole season, playing 44 games and scoring 15 goals, including one against Oxford live on Setanta TV. His next stop was Crawley Town in July 2009, where he scored four goals (including another against Oxford) in 17 appearances. In November 2009 he moved on loan to Rushden & Diamonds, initially for two months, but that was later extended until the end of the season. While at Nene Park Louis scored seven goals in 26 games. In June 2010 he joined Gainsborough Trinity under former manager Brian Little, where he scored two goals in 10 appearances, although one goal was expunged after Ilkeston Town went out of business, but he failed to settle and in October 2010 he went to Darlington on loan. After six games without a goal a proposed deal to sign Louis permanently fell through and he returned to Gainsborough, who released him in January 2011. Louis made one substitute appearance for Weymouth before signing for Hayes & Yeading later that month. He was with Hayes for 10 games before he asked to be released from his contract in March 2011, whereupon he returned to Maidenhead. In March 2008 Louis won his only international cap, representing Dominica in a World Cup qualifier against Barbados. In July 2011 Brackley became Louis' latest club.

LOVE, Johnny

Left-winger
Born: 11 March 1937, Eynsham
Died: 19 November 2010
United debut: 15 March 1955 v Barry Town
Final United game: 20 September 1963 v Carlisle United
Appearances: 309
Goals: 45
Clubs: Eynsham, Oxford City, Wolverhampton Wanderers, Headington United, Wellington Town

An Eynsham boy, Love played for Oxford City and the Wolves youth team before joining Headington United. After his first game for the club he went overseas to the West Indies on National Service, gaining experience by playing in Army games, and earning England Youth caps at outside-left against Wales and Scotland. He returned for one game on 21 September 1955, scoring in a 3–1 win at Guildford City, but it was not until August 1957, when he left the Forces after the Suez Crisis, that Love started to feature regularly for the team. He played 219 games before United's election to the Football League, setting a Southern League record for the club. After leaving United he moved to Wellington Town (later Telford United) in October 1963, where he played 14 games for the first team and nine for the reserves, although he did not feature for them in future seasons. Love represented Oxfordshire at both football and boxing, and was also the Oxfordshire youth table-tennis champion. After finishing his football career, Love became a painter and decorator and worked for Smiths Industries Ltd.

LOWE, Nick

Centre-back
Born: 28 October 1952, Oxford
United debut: 21 February 1973 v Bologna (sub)
Final United game: 2 April 1977 v Peterborough United
Appearances: 79+1
Goals: 4
Clubs: Oxford City, Oxford United, Halifax Town (loan), Oxford City, Mooroolbark (Australia), Frankston City (Australia), Sunshine City (Australia), Doveton (Australia)

Nicholas Paul Lowe joined United from Oxford City as an apprentice in 1969, signed by Ron Saunders on the same day that the U's manager resigned. Lowe joined the senior ranks in July 1970. In August 1974 Lowe played nine games on loan to Halifax and after Dave Roberts' departure Lowe became a regular in the first team. In the summer of 1977 Lowe was given a free transfer by United and he returned to Oxford City but by July he had emigrated to Australia, where he joined the police force while playing for

Mooroolbark in the outer suburbs of east Melbourne, in the National Soccer League. By 1980 Lowe had moved down the Mornington Peninsula to join Frankston City in the Victoria State League and the following year he moved across to the west of the city to play for Sunshine City, also in the VSL. In 1983 City amalgamated with neighbours Sunshine George Cross, which was largely the football club of Melbourne's Maltese community, but the following year, after Sunshine George Cross joined the NSL, Lowe moved to the Dandenongs to play for Doveton.

LUCAS, Dick

Full-back
Born: 22 January 1948, Witney
United debut: 19 August 1967 v Shrewsbury Town
Final United game: 22 February 1975 v Blackpool
Appearances: 218+1
Goals: 4
Clubs: Oxford United, Kettering Town

Richard John Lucas joined United as a schoolboy, signing professionally in the summer of 1965. He became one of United's most consistent full-backs, playing for the club throughout its period in the Second Division in the early 1970s. Unfortunately injury took its toll and he was released by the U's in the summer of 1975, whereupon he joined Kettering Town of the Southern League Premier Division. He returned to Oxford with Kettering as Derek Dougan's side knocked the U's out of the FA Cup with a 1–0 win at the Manor in November 1976.

LUKE, George

Centre-forward
Born: 20 October 1932, Esh Winning, Durham
Died: December 2001
United debut: 15 October 1960 v Cambridge United
Final United game: 9 September 1961 v King's Lynn
Appearances: 24
Goals: 9
Clubs: Esh Winning, Sheffield United, Scunthorpe United, King's Lynn, Oxford United

George Baron Luke began his career with Waterhouse Juniors, winning the Mid-Durham Senior League three seasons running. He was signed by Sheffield United, where he played alongside Geoff Denial and made seven League appearances between 1953 and 1955. He spent the 1956–57 season with Scunthorpe, where he scored six goals in 17 League games, after which he moved to King's Lynn. Luke joined United for £300 in October 1960, scoring on his debut against Cambridge United. However, injuries cost him his place and after his final first-team game in September 1961 he played a number of Metropolitan League games for the reserves before being released at the end of United's final Southern League season.

LUNDIN, Pål

Goalkeeper
Born: 21 November 1964, Osby (Sweden)
United debut: 3 April 1999 v Bolton Wanderers

Final United game: 11 March 2000 v Colchester United
Appearances: 36+1
Clean sheets: 11
Clubs: Östers IF (Sweden), Oxford United, Umeå (Sweden), Trelleborgs FF (Sweden)

Pål Michael Lundin arrived at Oxford United from Östers in March 1999 after his former teammate Mark Watson arranged for him to have a trial at United. Upon signing his contract Lundin celebrated rather wildly and ended up in police custody, spending his first night as an Oxford player behind bars. As a youngster Lundin represented Sweden for the national youth wrestling team, but he gave up wrestling aged 16. He was also a First Division handball player, getting into trouble with his manager at Östers for playing handball without permission. Lundin was a popular goalkeeper at Oxford, albeit prone to errors. He achieved a rare distinction for a goalkeeper by scoring a goal, converting a penalty against Wycombe Wanderers in a shoot-out in the LDV Vans Trophy second round in January 2000. In June 2000 United failed to offer Lundin a new contract and he returned to Sweden to sign for Umeå in the north-east of the country. However, he soon returned back south to play for Trelleborgs FF in the Allsvenskan, making 34 appearances before joining his home-town club of Osby IK as goalkeeping coach in 2003, later becoming their manager until 2006. Lundin then ran a bricklaying company and a golf ranch near Osby, returning to Östers as goalkeeping coach in 2008.

LYTHGOE, Phil

Midfielder
Born: 18 December 1959
United debut: 20 August 1980 v Exeter City (sub)
Final United game: 20 March 1982 v Lincoln City
Appearances: 31+5
Goals: 5
Clubs: Norwich City, Bristol Rovers (loan), Oxford United, Witney Town, Cardiff City, Rangers (Hong Kong)

Philip Lythgoe joined Oxford from Norwich City for £15,000 in August 1980. He joined the Canaries as an apprentice after leaving school and made 14 appearances in Division One, scoring one goal, against Manchester United. He had a six-game loan to Bristol Rovers in September 1978; however, he was mostly confined to Norwich's reserves, which is where Bill Asprey spotted him, playing in a friendly at Oxford City. Lythgoe had a decent run in the first team initially, but lost his place. Jim Smith then became manager and he was released in April 1982, going on to join Witney Town. Lythgoe was only at Witney for a few weeks before he spent a month at Cardiff City in April 1982. The Bluebirds were struggling at the foot of Division Two and Lythgoe was not allowed to play in any League matches for them, but he did feature in the Welsh Cup Final against Swansea City, which was over two legs, City losing 2–1 on aggregate. In June 1982 Lythgoe signed for Rangers FC in Hong Kong. He was there for three months before returning to Norwich, where he played local football for about 10 years. He later worked at Norwich City in the advertising and sponsorship department.

M

MACKAY, Dave

Right-back
Born: 2 May 1980, Rutherglen
United debut: 7 August 2004 v Boston United
Final United game: 7 May 2005 v Chester City
Appearances: 47
Clubs: Benburb Thistle, Dundee, Brechin City (loan), Arbroath (loan), Oxford United, Livingston, St Johnstone

David Mackay joined United on a free transfer from Dundee. He came with a good reputation as someone who could play at either right-back or centre-back, and in his first few months at the club he impressed with his consistency. After his wife's alleged homesickness he returned to Scotland to play for Livingston. He began his career with Benburb Thistle before Jocky Scott signed him for Dundee in August 1999. In February 2001 Mackay had a 16-game loan spell with Brechin City, scoring once, and in July that year he spent two months on loan to Arbroath, where he featured in seven games before being recalled for his Dundee debut; he went on to make 105 appearances and score two goals before his move to Oxford. After leaving United Mackay became a mainstay of the Livingston side, appearing 154 times and even contributing 22 goals. In May 2009 he was transferred to Scottish Premier League newcomers St Johnstone, along with Murray Davidson, for a combined fee of £50,000, a week after his former manager at Dundee, Scott, had made a bid for the two players.

MACLEAN, Steve

Forward
Born: 23 August 1982, Edinburgh
United debut: 13 November 2010 v Rotherham United
Final United game: 7 May 2011 v Shrewsbury Town
Appearances: 26+5
Goals: 5
Clubs: Rangers, Scunthorpe United (loan), Sheffield Wednesday, Cardiff City, Plymouth Argyle, Aberdeen (loan), Oxford United (loan)

Steven George MacLean joined United from Plymouth Argyle in November 2010, initially on a one-month loan that was later extended until the end of the season. He started with Rangers, where he made just three substitute appearances, and had a successful loan spell with Scunthorpe for the 2003–04 season, where he scored 25 goals in 52 games. On his return to Ibrox he was immediately sold to Sheffield Wednesday for a fee believed to be around £125,000. MacLean spent three years at Hillsborough, making 90 appearances and scoring 35 goals, before moving to Cardiff City after failing to agree a new deal with Wednesday. MacLean started as the Bluebirds' first-choice striker, but the return to fitness of Robbie Fowler and the arrival of Jimmy Floyd Hasselbaink saw him lose his place and in his six months at Ninian Park he made just 18 appearances, scoring one goal, before his former manager from Sheffield, Paul Sturrock, paid an Argyle record fee of £500,000 to take him to

Plymouth in January 2008. However, financial problems at Home Park meant that the club looked to move MacLean on and in December 2009 he had a trial at Hearts, but this was scuppered as their chairman refused to finance a deal. He did get a loan to Scotland when he joined Aberdeen until the end of the season in February 2010, where he scored five goals, including a brace against Celtic, in his 18 games. He returned to Plymouth briefly before his move to Oxford, bringing his Argyle tally to 53 games and six goals, but at the end of his loan with Oxford MacLean was released by relegated Plymouth Argyle and in July 2011 he signed a one-year deal with Yeovil Town.

MACPHEE, Doug

Inside-forward
United debut: 5 November 1949 v Bedford Town
Final United game: 26 April 1950 v Cheltenham Town
Appearances: 20
Goals: 7
Clubs: Banbury Spencer, Headington United

Douglas MacPhee joined Headington from Banbury Spencer after the start of United's first Southern League season. However, he received a knee injury in February 1950 from which he never really recovered and in April he was forced to retire on medical advice. Described as 'one of the most popular Scotsmen to play football in Oxfordshire', MacPhee was United's third-highest scorer at the time of his retirement.

MADDISON, Lee

Left-back
Born: 5 October 1972, Bristol
United debut: 5 February 2002 v Rushden & Diamonds
Final United game: 1 April 2002 v York City
Appearances: 11
Clubs: Bristol Rovers, Bath City (loan), Northampton Town, Dundee, Carlisle United (loan), Carlisle United, Oxford United (loan), Gretna

Lee Robert Maddison joined Bristol Rovers as a trainee, signing professionally in July 1991. He had an impressive four-game loan with Bath City at the end of the 1992–93 season and played 86 games for the Gas before Northampton paid £25,000 for him in September 1995. He managed 60 appearances for the Cobblers before joining Dundee on a free transfer in July 1997. After 73 games, in which he scored the first two goals of his professional career, he joined Carlisle in October 2000 for a 14-game loan spell, which was made into a permanent deal in January 2001. It was while he was with Carlisle that he had his loan to Oxford. Maddison returned to Brunton Park and went on to play 61 games for the Cumbrians, scoring once, before returning to Scotland to play for Gretna in August 2003. After 35 appearances and one goal, club captain Maddison was diagnosed with non-Hodgkin's lymphoma, a rare form of leukaemia. This required extensive treatment and effectively ended his playing career.

MAGILTON, Jim

Midfielder
Born: 6 May 1969, Belfast
United debut: 3 October 1990 v West Ham United

Final United game: 9 February 1994 v Leeds United
Appearances: 173
Goals: 42
Clubs: Liverpool, Oxford United, Southampton, Sheffield Wednesday, Ipswich Town (loan), Ipswich Town

James Magilton joined Oxford for £100,000 from Liverpool, where he played in the same reserves side as John Durnin, making his debut in 1986–87. He made 130 appearances for the Reds' second string before his move to Oxford, where he established himself as one of the best central midfielders in the club's history and earned the nickname 'Magic'. He had an extensive range of passing coupled with an eye for goal and a deadly free-kick. He also scored 17 penalties, missing just one, and became United's most capped player, winning 18 of his eventual 52 Northern Ireland caps while at the Manor and scoring four of his five international goals while with the U's. His match-winning performance against Leeds in the FA Cup at Elland Road brought him to national attention and he was sold to Southampton for £600,000 soon afterwards in February 1994. Magilton played 156 games for the Saints, scoring 18 goals, before Sheffield Wednesday paid £1.6 million for him in September 1997. This proved not to be money well spent as Magilton made just 30 appearances for the Owls, scoring one goal, before his loan move to Ipswich Town in January 1999. He played 11 games and scored once before the deal was made permanent, Ipswich paying £682,500 for Magilton's services. While with Ipswich he scored the only hat-trick of his career in the 2000 Division One Play-off semi-final against Bolton Wanderers. Magilton totalled 309 games for Ipswich, notching 23 goals, before being appointed their manager in July 2006. He was in charge at Portman Road for 148 games before his dismissal in April 2009. In June he was appointed manager of Queen's Park Rangers where he was in charge for just 24 games before he left in December 2009. In addition to his 52 full Northern Ireland caps, Magilton also won five Under-15 caps (scoring one goal), one Under-16 cap, three Under-18 caps, one Under-21 cap, and two caps at Under-23 level.

MANSELL, Lee

Right-back/Midfielder
Born: 23 September 1982, Gloucester
United debut: 6 August 2005 v Grimsby Town
Final United game: 6 May 2006 v Leyton Orient
Appearances: 51
Goals: 2
Clubs: Luton Town, Nuneaton Borough (loan), Oxford United, Torquay United

Lee Richard Samuel Mansell joined United in June 2005 following his release by Luton Town, having played a trial game for United's reserves at the end of the previous season. Mansell became a professional with Luton in August 2000, playing 63 games and scoring 10 goals for the Hatters. He also scored twice during a five-game loan with Nuneaton Borough in March 2003. In his one season with United he won the Supporters' Player of the Year award, although this was tempered by the club's relegation to the Conference. Former United manager Ian Atkins paid a small fee to take Mansell to Torquay United in July 2006, where he was again relegated to the Conference in 2007.

MANSELL, Ray

Centre-forward
Born: 26 September 1923, Headington
Died: 23 February 1995
United debut: 20 August 1949 v Hastings United
Final United game: 10 September 1949 v Hereford United
Appearances: 2
Goals: 1
Clubs: Headington United, Oxford City, Headington United (loan)

Raymond James Mansell first played for Headington United in September 1946, scoring on his debut in a 3–2 win at Bicester in the FA Cup extra-preliminary round. In the next game Mansell scored an incredible seven goals as United beat Moreton RAF 12–2 in the Oxfordshire Senior League. Mansell scored United's first goal in the Spartan League (a 2–1 defeat at Marlow in August 1947) and he featured regularly throughout United's two seasons in the Spartan League. When Headington turned professional and joined the Southern League, Mansell remained an amateur, signing for neighbours and rivals Oxford City, although he joined United on loan for the start of the first Southern League campaign, scoring in United's first game at that level, a 5–2 defeat at Hastings United. He returned to City to make his debut in November 1949 against Kingstonian, playing 64 games and scoring 16 goals before his final game in April 1954.

MARSH, Simon

Left-back
Born: 29 January 1977, Ealing
United debut: 17 September 1994 v Brighton & Hove Albion
Final United game: 5 December 1998 v Bradford City
Appearances: 59+9
Goals: 3
Clubs: Oxford United, Birmingham City, Brentford (loan), Tamworth

Simon Thomas Peter Marsh was a member of Oxford's YTS intake in 1993. In the summer of 1995, having already made his senior debut, he was awarded a professional contract. Although he never established himself as first-choice left-back, he showed great potential until his sale to Birmingham City for £250,000 in December 1998 as the club tried to cash in on their assets in order to avoid administration. By this time Marsh had already won his only cap for England Under-21s when he was called-up for the Toulon Tournament in May 1998 against France. In November the same year he also played for the Football League Under-21s against Italy's Serie B equivalent. Marsh's debut for Birmingham was as a substitute in the Blues' 7–1 rout of United at the Manor in December 1998 but his time at St Andrew's was blighted by injury and he made just eight appearances for City. In September 2000 he went on loan to Brentford, where he played six games, but a permanent arrangement could not be reached and he returned to Birmingham. In April 2001, after Marsh had failed to feature for the first team since his loan return, a severance package with Birmingham was agreed and he left the club. In August 2002, after 18 months out of the game, Marsh signed for Tamworth but in February 2003 his back injury was deemed too serious for him to continue and he was forced to retire. In July 2010 Marsh was assistant manager at Penn & Tylers Green FC in the Hellenic League Division One East.

MASKELL, Dennis

Winger
Born: 16 April 1931, Mountain Ash (Wales)
United debut: 3 September 1952 v Hastings United
Final United game: 26 April 1954 v Llanelly
Appearances: 47
Goals: 6
Clubs: Watford, Headington United, Pressed Steel

Dennis Maskell joined Headington from Watford in 1952, having made five League appearances for the Hornets.

MASSEY, Stuart

Midfielder
Born: 17 November 1964, Crawley
United debut: 13 August 1994 v Hull City
Final United game: 7 March 1998 v Manchester City
Appearances: 102+26
Goals: 13
Clubs: Sutton United, Crystal Palace, Oxford United, Whyteleafe, Carshalton Athletic, Walton & Hersham, Sutton United, Chipstead, Whyteleafe

Stuart Anthony Massey started his playing career with Sutton United in the Diadora League Premier Division while an electrician's apprentice. In July 1992 Crystal Palace paid Sutton £20,000 for him, but he failed to make much of an impact at Selhurst Park, making just three appearances before he joined Oxford on a free transfer in July 1994. Massey proved an inspirational signing, playing a pivotal role in United's 1996 promotion team. However, a tackle by Peter Beardsley against Manchester City at Maine Road forced Massey to miss the remainder of the 1997–98 season with damage to both medial and cruciate ligaments in his knee, and United released Massey while he was still injured. Massey received a small insurance payment from the Professional Footballers' Association and started to build up his bespoke kitchens business. Eighteen months later he joined Whyteleafe and then played for Carshalton, Walton & Hersham and his first club Sutton before becoming player-manager of Chipstead in the Combined Counties League. He became Whyteleafe's player-manager on New Year's Day 2004, but resigned in October 2006. In May 2007 Massey was appointed assistant manager at Sutton United but he was back in charge of Whyteleafe for the start of the 2008–09 season.

MATHERS, David

Left-half
Born: 23 October 1931, Glasgow
United debut: 19 September 1959 v Chelmsford City
Final United game: 26 November 1960 v Bridgwater Town
Appearances: 56
Goals: 1
Clubs: Partick Thistle, Headington United, Partick Thistle, East Stirlingshire

David Cochrane Mathers was an intelligent and athletic left-half. He joined Partick Thistle from school in 1947 having represented both Glasgow Schools and Scottish Schools prior to that, and turned professional two years later aged 17. He remained with the Firhill club until September 1959, captaining them in his final season, when he joined Headington United and was with them when they changed their name to Oxford United the following summer. His arrival in Oxford was because of his wish to pursue his studies as a motor mechanic, and he remained a part-time professional throughout his career. He returned to Partick in December 1960 but did not make any more first-team appearances before joining East Stirlingshire the following summer. After one season at Firs Park he retired. He won his only cap for Scotland in their final preparation match for the 1954 FIFA World Cup finals against Finland. Although named in Scotland's 22-man squad for Switzerland, Scotland decided to take only 13 of the 22 to the finals. He also played for the Scottish League against the Irish League.

McALLISTER, Craig

Forward
Born: 28 June 1980, Glasgow
United debut: 5 January 2008 v Altrincham
Final United game: 26 April 2008 v Ebbsfleet United (sub)
Appearances: 9+8
Goals: 2
Clubs: Eastleigh, Basingstoke Town, Stevenage Borough, Eastleigh (loan), Gravesend & Northfleet (loan), Woking, Grays Athletic, Rushden & Diamonds (loan), Oxford United, Exeter City, Barnet (loan), Rotherham United (loan), Crawley Town, Newport County

Craig McAllister started his career at Eastleigh in March 2002 before joining Basingstoke Town in July 2003. In 92 games for Basingstoke McAllister scored 55 goals and was their leading scorer in the 2002–03 and 2003–04 seasons. After Basingstoke turned down an offer for McAllister from Queen's Park Rangers, where he had a week-long trial in January 2003, he had an unsuccessful trial with Stoke City in March 2003 and also attracted interest from Reading, Luton Town, and Southend United. He joined Stevenage in May 2004, but made just eight appearances for the Boro, who loaned him to Gravesend & Northfleet in December 2004 for five games, in which he scored twice. McAllister had a further loan to his first club, Eastleigh, in February 2005 where he managed four games. He joined fellow Conference side Woking in July 2005, spending two seasons at Kingfield. He made 90 appearances for the Cards, scoring 25 goals before he decided to move on and sign for Grays Athletic. After one goal in nine appearances McAllister went on loan to Rushden, where he played 11 games and scored once. Oxford signed McAllister from Grays in January 2008 but an injury in his second game meant his appearances were sporadic and he did not really get an opportunity to show his goalscoring form, and United released him in May. He immediately signed for Exeter City, who were just about to earn promotion to the Football League through the Conference Play-offs, but he featured mainly as a substitute for the Grecians. He made 10 starts and 27 appearances from the bench in his two years at St James' Park, punctuated by a five-game loan spell with Barnet in November 2009 and eight games with Rotherham at the end of his time with Exeter, in March 2010. Although he failed to score in either of these loans, he did manage seven goals for Exeter. In June 2010 he returned to the Conference when he signed for Crawley Town, who won promotion to the Football League in his first season at the Broadfield Stadium, but McAllister rejected the club's offer of a new contract in May 2011 and signed for Newport County.

McCALDON, Ian

Goalkeeper
Born: 14 September 1974, Liverpool
United debut: 18 August 2001 v Swansea City
Final United game: 1 April 2002 v York City
Appearances: 31
Clean sheets: 6
Clubs: Glenafton Athletic, Livingston, St Mirren (loan), Oxford United, Chester City (loan), Chester City, Ross County, Alloa Athletic (loan), Peterhead, Berwick Rangers

Ian Thomas McCaldon, nicknamed 'Eagle', came from Livingston having helped the former Meadowbank Thistle team achieve promotion to the Scottish Premier League. He displaced Richard Knight in goal and was United's number one until the arrival of Andy Woodman. Despite his height McCaldon was criticised for failing to dominate his area, but he was a good shot-stopper. In October 2002 he went on a two-game loan to Chester, where he rejoined manager Mark Wright and defenders Wayne Hatswell, Phil Bolland and Scott Guyett. He was released in July 2003, having failed to play a single game as Andy Woodman's deputy. McCaldon joined Livingston from junior club Glenafton Athletic and made 98 appearances for Livi, encompassing a nine-game loan with St Mirren in November 2000, before he joined United in August 2001. After his release by Oxford McCaldon signed permanently for Chester, playing 14 games before taking a break from football to work in Australia. He returned to Scotland in May 2005 and signed for Ross County, for whom he played 12 times. He also had a non-playing loan at Alloa Athletic, who tried to sign him, but McCaldon wanted to remain full-time. In January 2007 he joined Peterhead, where he played 14 games before a succession of injuries made him decide to retire from professional football in September 2008, and he became a fitness trainer. In late 2009 he was persuaded to sign for Berwick Rangers as cover during an injury crisis and in January 2010 he became their reserve 'keeper and goalkeeping coach.

McCALL, Tony

Winger
Born: 15 January 1936, Thatcham
United debut: 4 September 1957 v Chelmsford City
Final United game: 28 April 1958 v Gravesend & Northfleet
Appearances: 29
Goals: 9
Clubs: Reading, Headington United

Anthony Edward McCall came up through the Reading junior ranks, turning professional and playing eight Football League games and scoring one goal before he signed for Headington in the summer of 1957.

McCARTHY, Paul

Centre-back
Born: 4 August 1971, Cork (Ireland)
United debut: 28 March 2003 v Swansea City
Final United game: 8 May 2004 v Rochdale
Appearances: 34+1

Goals: 3
Clubs: Brighton & Hove Albion, Wycombe Wanderers, Oxford United (loan), Oxford United, Hornchurch, Gravesend & Northfleet

Paul Jason McCarthy arrived at United from local rivals Wycombe, initially on loan in March 2003, with a decent reputation as a commanding centre-back. Unfortunately, his time at Oxford was blighted by injury, and he failed to make too much of an impact. McCarthy started his career as a trainee with Brighton, making 217 appearances and scoring eight goals between April 1989 and July 1996, when he joined Wycombe for £100,000. While with the Chairboys McCarthy helped the side to the FA Cup semi-final against Liverpool in 2001. He played 259 games for them, in which he scored 19 goals prior to his loan move to Oxford, which lasted for six games (one goal) before he signed a permanent deal in the 2003 close season. One year later he was released by United and joined Hornchurch in the Conference South, where he was made captain, but after a wealthy benefactor withdrew his support their financial problems increased. This led to McCarthy leaving in November 2004 after 10 games and signing for Gravesend & Northfleet. He was made club captain and played in the team that won the FA Trophy against Torquay United in 2008. In June 2009 he was appointed as Ebbsfleet's assistant manager, while continuing to play in the heart of their defence. McCarthy was an Ireland Schoolboy international, an Ireland Youth international, and won 10 Ireland Under-21 caps.

McCLAREN, Steve

Midfielder
Born: 3 May 1961, Fulford, Yorkshire
United debut: 26 August 1989 v Watford
Final United game: 8 February 1992 v Leicester City
Appearances: 33+7
Clubs: Hull City, Derby County, Lincoln City (loan), Bristol City, Oxford United

Stephen McClaren is arguably more famous for his time after Oxford than for being a former United midfielder, although there is no denying that his time with United was influential to his future career path. McClaren played for York Boys and his school team and signed for Hull City immediately after leaving school. He played 178 League games, scoring 16 goals, for the Tigers before joining Derby in 1985. McClaren played 25 League games for the Rams and in February 1987 had an eight-game loan with Lincoln City. In 1988 McClaren moved to Bristol City where he scored two goals in 61 League games before he joined Oxford in a straight exchange for Gary Shelton. At the Manor McClaren was a solid, if unspectacular, midfielder but his career was ended early through injury and he joined the coaching staff, taking charge first of the youth team and then the reserves. In 1995 he joined Jim Smith as assistant manager at Derby County and in the pair's first season Derby won promotion to the Premier League. He moved to Manchester United to become Alex Ferguson's assistant in February 1999, at the end of which season the Red Devils won the treble of League, FA Cup and Champions League; they also won the League titles in the following two seasons. In June 2001 McClaren was appointed manager of Middlesbrough and they reached the FA Cup semi-final in his first season in charge. In 2004 Boro beat Bolton Wanderers in the League Cup Final and two years later they reached the semi-final of the FA Cup and the final of the UEFA Cup. Meanwhile, in October 2000 Peter Taylor had appointed McClaren as the England coach, a role he combined with his club commitments until stepping down in November 2002. In the summer of 2004 he returned to the England set-up as Sven-Göran Eriksson's assistant, remaining in the role until after the 2006 World Cup finals when he replaced Eriksson as England's new manager. This lasted until November 2007, when he was removed after England failed to qualify for the 2008 European Championships. In May 2008 McClaren made a brief cameo appearance as David Penney's coach at Darlington as the side prepared for the League Two Play-offs. In June 2008 McClaren was appointed as manager of Dutch side FC Twente, who finished in second place in the Eredivisie and were finalists in the KNVB Cup in his first season. In 2010 FC Twente won the Eredivisie for the first time in the club's history and McClaren was awarded the Rinus Michels Award as Dutch Manager of the Season. In May 2010 McClaren left the Netherlands to take up an appointment as manager of VfL Wolfsburg in the German Bundesliga, but in February 2011 he was sacked after a run of poor results. In June 2011 he was appointed manager of Nottingham Forest.

McCULLOCH, Andy

Forward
Born: 3 January 1950, Northampton
United debut: 17 August 1974 v Cardiff City
Final United game: 25 February 1976 v West Bromwich Albion
Appearances: 43
Goals: 9
Clubs: Walton & Hersham, Queen's Park Rangers, Cardiff City, Oxford United, Brentford, Oakland Stompers (USA) (loan), Sheffield Wednesday, Crystal Palace, Aldershot

Andrew McCulloch played for Fleet Town in the Hampshire League as a youngster, but after an unsuccessful trial with Tottenham Hotspur, where he played in the Metropolitan League alongside Steve Perryman, he signed for Walton & Hersham, with whom he won the Athenian League in 1969. Meanwhile he completed a degree in civil engineering. In October 1970 McCulloch signed for QPR and scored on his debut. After scoring 10 goals in 41 League appearances, McCulloch was sold to Cardiff City for £45,000 in October 1972. While with the Bluebirds McCulloch scored 30 goals in 68 games and won a Scotland Under-23 cap and he also featured in the side's UEFA Cup run following their triumphant Welsh Cup campaigns in 1973 and 1974. In July 1974 United paid a club record £70,000 to bring McCulloch to the Manor but the U's were relegated to Division Three at the end of his first season there. In March 1976, after his goals had apparently dried up and questions were raised over his fitness, he was sold to Brentford for £25,000. In 1978, after winning promotion with the Bees, McCulloch had an 18-game loan spell with Oakland Stompers where he scored three goals. In June 1979, after 48 goals in 127 League appearances, McCulloch joined Sheffield Wednesday for £70,000. There he enjoyed the best spell of his career, winning promotion to Division Two in 1980 and playing in the 1983 FA Cup semi-final. He scored a total of 44 goals in 125 League games for Wednesday before moving to Crystal Palace for £20,000 in August 1983. McCulloch scored three goals in 25 League games in his season at Selhurst Park, before moving to Aldershot for the following season. After scoring two goals in 16

League games for the Shots McCulloch suffered a knee injury that forced him to retire from the game in 1986. He worked for and later set up a business that specialised in upholstery cleaning. McCulloch later managed Esher United in the Kingston District League.

McDERMOTT, Brian

Winger
Born: 8 April 1961, Slough
United debut: 1 January 1985 v Middlesbrough
Final United game: 7 March 1987 v Nottingham Forest (sub)
Appearances: 18+8
Goals: 3
Clubs: Arsenal, Fulham (loan), IFK Norrköping (Sweden) (loan), Oxford United, Huddersfield Town (loan), Cardiff City, Exeter City, Yeovil Town, Slough Town

Brian James McDermott started as an apprentice with Arsenal, having been spotted playing for Slough Schools. After being released as a Queen's Park Rangers trainee aged 15, he signed professionally for the Gunners in February 1979, during the season in which he was the club's leading scorer in the London Combination. He also featured for the England Youth team that year, scoring three goals in a tournament in Austria. After breaking into Arsenal's first team that same season, he became a regular in 1981, but increasing competition saw him lose his place and in March 1983 he had a loan spell with Fulham where he made three substitute appearances. In April 1984 he played 17 games for IFK Norrköping in Sweden, scoring five goals and being named Player of the Year for 1984. After 13 goals in 71 appearances for Arsenal, McDermott was signed by Oxford for £40,000 in December 1984, making his debut in a 1–0 win at Middlesbrough on New Year's Day. He was a regular for the remainder of that promotion season, but once the U's reached the top flight McDermott faded and in October 1986 he had a four-game loan spell with Huddersfield. In August 1987 McDermott moved to Cardiff City where he scored eight goals in 51 League appearances, winning the Welsh Cup and helping the Bluebirds secure promotion to the Third Division before he joined Exeter in 1988. In two seasons with the Grecians McDermott played 68 League games, scoring four goals, before a £10,000 move to Yeovil in November 1990. McDermott played 85 games for the Glovers, scoring 19 goals before leaving in 1992. He became player-manager of Slough Town in February 1996 and was in charge until 1998 when the club were expelled from the Conference and McDermott was dismissed. He joined Woking as manager in September 1998, guiding them off the bottom of the Conference. However, after fortunes nosedived he was sacked in March 2000 and in September 2000 he became Reading's chief scout, taking over from the late Maurice Evans. McDermott then took over as manager of Reading's reserves, leading them to the title of the Pontin's Holidays Combination League in 2004. In December 2009 McDermott became caretaker manager of Reading, being appointed to the post permanently in January 2010.

McDONAGH, James

Centre-back
Born: 21 April 1962, Dublin
Died: November 2004

United debut: 13 January 1988 v Reading
Final United game: 13 January 1988 v Reading
Appearances: 1
Clubs: Derry City (Northern Ireland), Oxford United

James 'Jack' McDonagh joined Oxford in December 1987 with a contract until the end of the season, having previously played for Derry City. A regular for the reserves, McDonagh managed just one first-team appearance, a 1–0 Simod Cup defeat at Reading.

McDONALD, Bobby

Left-back
Born: 13 April 1955, Aberdeen
United debut: 10 September 1983 v Burnley
Final United game: 20 January 1987 v Blackburn Rovers
Appearances: 123+2
Goals: 21
Clubs: Aston Villa, Coventry City, Manchester City, Oxford United, Leeds United (loan), Leeds United, Wolverhampton Wanderers (loan), VS Rugby, Burton Albion, Nuneaton Borough, Worcester City, Sutton Coldfield, Armitage Town, Redditch United

Robert Wood McDonald joined Oxford from Manchester City in September 1983, his arrival coinciding with (or possibly prompting) a rise in United's fortunes that would see them reach the top flight within two seasons. The cultured left-back started with junior side King Street Sports Club in Aberdeen before joining Aston Villa as an apprentice in June 1971, signing professionally in September 1972, having been part of the Villa squad that won the FA Youth Cup. With McDonald in their side Villa won promotion to Division One in 1975, winning the League Cup the same season. He made 46 appearances for Villa, scoring five goals and winning Schoolboy and Youth caps for Scotland, before his £45,000 sale to Coventry City in August 1976. From his debut that month, McDonald was an ever present for the 161 League games that he played for the Sky Blues, in which he scored 14 goals, and he was voted the club's Player of the Year in 1979. In October 1980 Manchester City paid Coventry £270,000 for McDonald, his signing helping City to climb away from the First Division relegation zone, reach the League Cup semi-finals and the FA Cup Final, in which they lost a replay to Spurs 3–2 after a 1–1 draw. In August 1982 against Watford, McDonald took over from the injured Joe Corrigan in goal in the third minute, and his saves helped City to a 1–0 win to go top of the table. However, their form soon nosedived and City were relegated at the end of the season. McDonald's departure from City was an unhappy one, the defender being released after breaching the club's disciplinary policy, but it allowed Jim Smith to pick him up for free. The arrival of John Trewick and Neil Slatter saw McDonald drop down the pecking order in United's defence and he had a one-month loan with Leeds United in February 1987 before joining permanently for £25,000. Leeds reached the Division Two Play-off Final that season, but lost to Charlton Athletic and the following season McDonald's injuries cost him his first-team place and, after 24 games and one goal, he was loaned to Wolverhampton Wanderers for six matches in February 1988. McDonald was given a free transfer in May 1988 and he joined VS Rugby, playing for a year before moving to Burton Albion in the summer of 1989. In September

1989 he moved to Nuneaton Borough where he stayed for one month before moving to Worcester City. In January 1991 McDonald signed for Sutton Coldfield, joining Armitage Town later that year and Redditch United in 1992. After stopping playing McDonald returned to Aberdeen and worked for the ambulance service before becoming a TV rigger in Mansfield. He created his own coaching academies and worked as a freelance coach for a number of senior clubs and local authorities.

McDONALD, Colin

Goalkeeper
Born: 15 October 1930, Ramsbottom, Bury
United debut: 2 December 1950 v Yeovil Town
Final United game: 13 October 1951 v Wycombe Wanderers
Appearances: 37
Clean sheets: 12
Clubs: Burnley, Headington United (loan), Altrincham

Colin Agnew McDonald was arguably the greatest goalkeeper ever to play for United, going on to win eight England caps between May and November 1958. He started with Burnley, joining as an amateur in 1948 after a recommendation from former Blackburn Rovers manager Jack Marshall. He broke into the Burnley reserves team after completing his plumbing apprenticeship and was then called-up for his National Service, stationed at Moreton-in-Marsh. It was while here that, with Burnley's permission, McDonald signed to play for Headington United for the duration of his service. Unfortunately, Burnley had agreed only for McDonald to play in Southern League and Southern League Cup games, and they refused Headington's request to play him in the FA Cup. Undaunted, United registered McDonald as an amateur with the Oxfordshire FA and played him anyway in a 3–2 win over Wycombe Wanderers in the FA Cup second qualifying round. Wycombe complained, United sent a delegation to Burnley to plead for retroactive permission which was not forthcoming, and an FA commission found Headington guilty of fielding an ineligible player. Headington were expelled from that season's competition and fined five guineas, while McDonald returned to Burnley without playing again for United. In 1952 McDonald became a full-time professional but had to wait a further two years for his debut, when he conceded five goals to Aston Villa. In December 1956 McDonald broke his ankle just as he was tipped for international honours. He won his first England cap in May 1958 in a friendly against the USSR, having already played for the Football League in a 4–1 win over the Scottish League in Newcastle. McDonald's performance earned him a call-up to represent England in the 1958 World Cup in Sweden, where he was named as the tournament's best goalkeeper. Unfortunately McDonald broke his leg while appearing for the Football League against the League of Ireland in Dublin, and while recuperating he caught pneumonia and almost died. That game signalled the end of McDonald's professional playing career although he went on to become a coach initially, coincidentally, with Wycombe before working with Bolton, Bury, Oldham and Tranmere. He played briefly for Altrincham before becoming chief scout with both Bolton and Bury. In 1969 McDonald became general manager at Bury and then team manager, after which he became a youth coach at both Oldham and Tranmere.

McDONALD, Gordon

Full-back
Born: 7 February 1932, Hampstead
Died: February 1995
United debut: 23 August 1958 v Hereford United
Final United game: 11 April 1960 v Nuneaton Borough
Appearances: 30
Clubs: Eastbourne, Crystal Palace, Swindon Town, Headington United

Gordon McDonald joined Crystal Palace from Eastbourne in November 1954, playing 17 games before his transfer to Swindon in June 1957. He made 11 appearances for the Robins before his move to Headington in the summer of 1958.

McGARRITY, Tom

Winger
Born: 24 November 1922, Scotstoun
Died: 17 March 1999
United debut: 12 September 1953 v Gloucester City
Final United game: 1 May 1954 v Llanelly
Appearances: 13
Goals: 5
Clubs: Arthurlie, Morton, Southampton, Headington United, Banbury Spencer

Thomas Welsh McGarrity was a Scottish Schoolboy international. He played as an amateur for Arthurlie before joining the RAF as a navigator at the beginning of the war. He returned to play at inside-forward for Morton. He was a member of the team that won the Championship of the Scottish B Division in 1950. McGarrity was offered a chance to sign for Celtic but declined, at his mother's request, to avoid being caught up in sectarian rivalry. While at Morton he trained as a physiotherapist and worked at one of the first athletics and sports clinics in the country. In November 1952, after 128 League appearances in which he scored 34 goals, McGarrity joined Southampton and scored on his debut in a 5–1 home win over Hull City in the Second Division. He retired from playing as a professional at the end of that season after just five League games and one goal for the Saints, and moved to Oxford where he headed the Physiotherapy Geriatrics Department at the Radcliffe Hospital. He continued playing as an amateur for 10 more seasons after leaving Headington, had one more season in management and another 20 years coaching Oxford United. His three sons all represented Oxford at schoolboy level and just a few days before he died he accompanied one of his sons and a grandson to Oxford's League game against Watford.

McGOWAN, Neil

Left-back
Born: 15 April 1977, Glasgow
United debut: 21 August 1999 v Bristol Rovers (sub)
Final United game: 28 October 2000 v Reading
Appearances: 31+8
Clubs: Bonnyton Thistle, Stranraer, Albion Rovers, Oxford United, Stranraer, Clydebank, Knattspyrnufélag Akureyrar (Iceland), Airdrie United, Queen of the South, Stranraer (loan), Ayr United, Clyde

Neil William McGowan began his career in 1994 with Bonnyton Thistle in the Paisley & District Youth Football League, joining Stranraer for the first time in 1995. He made four appearances for the Blues before moving to Albion Rovers the following season. McGowan started to play regularly for Albion and was named their Player of the Year in 1999, earning a move to Oxford in August 1999 after 56 games. Unfortunately, McGowan struggled in the second tier of the English League and in March 2001 he returned to Stranraer. He made seven appearances in the final two months of the season and scored his first senior goal before joining Clydebank. He made 32 appearances for the Bankies and was named their Player of the Year for 2002, before joined Icelandic side Akureyri for the close season, scoring two goals in 11 games before returning to Scotland to sign for Airdrie in August 2002. In his five years with the Diamonds McGowan made 179 appearances, scoring two goals, winning the Scottish Second Division Championship in 2003–04 and Player of the Year for 2007, after which he joined Queen of the South. But, after just four appearances, he had an eight-game loan spell with Stranraer. McGowan moved to Ayr United in January 2008, making 62 appearances, scoring once and also acting as coach to the Under-19s. In January 2010 he joined Clyde.

McGROGAN, Hugh

Winger
Born: 1 March 1957, Dumbarton
Died: 2 September 1998
United debut: 8 February 1975 v Manchester United
Final United game: 2 May 1980 v Colchester United
Appearances: 115+26
Goals: 15
Clubs: Oxford United, Carlisle United, Witney Town, Banbury United

Hugh McGrogan became a United apprentice in 1972, despite having been offered schoolboy terms by Celtic, and was a member of the squad that won the Midlands Youth League in 1975, in the same season in which he signed a professional contract in March. McGrogan was the youngest of four brothers, of whom the oldest, James, played for Dumbarton, while brother Joe had featured for Hamilton Academical and Dumbarton, and his third brother Felix had played, also as a winger, for Raith Rovers and St Johnstone. Their father (also Felix, and also a winger) had played for Third Lanark, Dumbarton, Kilmarnock, Falkirk, Dunfermline Athletic, Blackburn Rovers and Brighton & Hove Albion; Felix senior's career was brought to a sudden halt when he broke his neck while playing for Durban City in South Africa. Hugh McGrogan's debut was a baptism of fire, playing in United's 1–0 win against Division Two leaders Manchester United at the Manor in February 1975. McGrogan did not win a regular starting place until he was switched from the left to the right wing, and even then his versatility meant that he was often preferred as a substitute. He was sold to Carlisle in May 1980 at the same time as Colin Duncan in a double deal worth £19,000. McGrogan spent only one season with the Cumbrians, making just two appearances, before returning to Oxfordshire to play for Witney Town. McGrogan was killed in a car crash outside Bicester in September 1998.

McGUCKIN, Ian

Centre-back
Born: 24 April 1973, Middlesbrough
United debut: 12 August 2000 v Peterborough United
Final United game: 30 January 2001 v Peterborough United (sub)
Appearances: 6+1
Clubs: Hartlepool United, Fulham, Oxford United, Hartlepool United (loan), Barrow, Oxford City, Durham City, Bishop Auckland

Thomas Ian McGuckin started his career with Hartlepool as an apprentice, signing professionally in June 1991, although he had already made his debut in a 6–1 friendly defeat against CSKA Moscow in November 1990. He played 179 games and scored nine goals for Pool before joining Fulham for £75,000 in the summer of 1997. However, he was injured before making his debut for the Cottagers and did not get to play a first-team game for them, although he did have an eight-game loan back with Hartlepool in December 1998. In June 2000 Oxford signed McGuckin on a free transfer from Fulham, but by this time his injuries had taken their toll and he proved not to be the defensive lynchpin that was required. Released by Oxford at the end of his first season with a compensation package from an insurance settlement because of his injuries, he joined Barrow in November 2001 but was unable to get a regular game, partly because he continued to live in Oxford and the travelling was too much. His final appearance for the Bluebirds was in February 2002 and he joined Oxford City, although he now required painkilling injections before each game because of recurring knee problems. In March 2005 McGuckin was named player-coach at Durham City and in July that year he joined Bishop Auckland. In July 2007 McGuckin joined Northallerton Town to help with the coaching. Two years later he was drafted in as assistant manager at West Auckland Town, but he only lasted until September. In the 2010 close season McGuckin was appointed assistant manager at Horden Colliery Welfare and in January 2011 he returned to Hartlepool as coach for the Under-16s.

McILVENNY, Eddie

Right-half
Born: 21 October 1924, Greenock (Scotland)
Died: 18 May 1989
United debut: 28 September 1957 v Chelmsford City
Final United game: 19 November 1958 v Dartford
Appearances: 39
Clubs: Greenock Morton, Wrexham, Philadelphia Nationals (USA), Manchester United, Waterford (Ireland), Headington United

Edward Joseph McIlvenney's first clubs were Klondyke Athletic Juniors and his school side, St Mungo's Roman Catholic School. He was selected for a Scottish Junior League side and played for Greenock Morton before joining Wrexham at the age of 22. He played seven games for them, scoring once, before he moved to the United States in 1949 to stay with his sister in New York. While there, he joined Philadelphia Nationals in the American Soccer League and his performances for them earned him a call-up to the US national side for the 1950 World Cup in Brazil. McIlvenny was the only full-time professional in the American ranks and therefore he coordinated their coaching sessions. Playing at right-half, he played all three games and was chosen as captain for the game against England in Belo Horizonte. The

United States shocked the world by beating England 1–0 with a goal from Joe Gaetjens. After the World Cup, McIlvenny joined Manchester United, having impressed Matt Busby with a display against them for a Kearny-Philadelphia All-Star team. He played twice for the Red Devils before joining Waterford in the Republic of Ireland in 1951, eventually captaining the side and leading them to the runners-up spot in the League of Ireland in 1955. He played for the League of Ireland representative team against the Northern Irish League in Dublin, the Hessen League of Germany in Frankfurt, and the Hessen League in Kassel. In 1957 he joined Headington United, playing 39 games for the U's. He retired in November 1958 and moved to Eastbourne to run a football school. McIlvenny was inducted into the US National Soccer Hall of Fame in 1976 and died in Eastbourne in May 1989.

McINNES, George

Centre-forward
United debut: 22 August 1959 v Weymouth
Final United game: 3 October 1959 v Worcester City
Appearances: 8
Goals: 2
Clubs: Inverness Clachnacuddin, Aberdeen, Headington United

George McInnes was the Highland League's top scorer with Inverness Clachnacuddin before he broke his ankle in 1957. After a swift recovery Aberdeen beat a number of clubs for his signature, but he never played for their first team. He joined Headington from Aberdeen at the start of the 1959–60 season. In his later life he became a ghillie (fishing guide) in Lower Ballathie on the River Tay.

McINTOSH, Ian

Inside-forward
Born: 14 September 1933, Glasgow
United debut: 20 August 1960 v Cambridge City
Final United game: 14 March 1962 v Cheltenham Town
Appearances: 59
Goals: 20
Clubs: Campsie Black Watch, Petershill, Partick Thistle, Bury, Weymouth, Oxford United, Hereford United, Gloucester City

John McGregor 'Ian' McIntosh joined Partick Thistle from Petershill aged 18, linking up with David Mathers, who also went on to play for United. McIntosh made 28 League appearances for the Firhill side, scoring 12 goals. After completing his National Service with the RAF in October 1956 he moved to Bury, where he played 29 League games in which he scored 13 goals over the next two seasons. He then played for Weymouth for one season before joining Oxford where he spent a further two campaigns, moving to Hereford just after United's election to the Football League was secured. McIntosh spent several seasons at Edgar Street, becoming a crowd favourite and helping them win promotion and the Merit Cup in 1964–65. He was voted the Bulls' Player of the Year in 1967 before moving to Gloucester in 1968 where, as player-manager, he won promotion to the Southern Premier League in his first season. His first managerial spell with the Tigers lasted two years, but he had a second spell in charge of Gloucester during the 1971–72 season.

McINTOSH, Malcolm

Full-back
Born: 6 July 1959, Oxford
United debut: 12 August 1978 v Cardiff City
Final United game: 9 April 1983 v Leyton Orient
Appearances: 61+4
Clubs: Oxford United, Kettering Town, Oxford United, Abingdon Town, Witney Town

Malcolm Patrick McIntosh joined United as an apprentice in 1975, becoming a professional two years later in July 1975. In the summer of 1981, after 59 games for the U's, he left for Kettering Town, where he played alongside Colin Clarke, but he returned a year later as a non-contract player to make two more appearances for United before being released in the summer of 1983. Meanwhile, McIntosh also played for Abingdon Town. After leaving Oxford he joined Witney Town where he eventually became manager, later becoming coach for Oxford United Under-16s.

McKEOWN, Joe

Centre-forward
United debut: 28 February 1952 v Gravesend & Northfleet
Final United game: 26 April 1952 v Cheltenham Town
Appearances: 13
Goals: 6
Clubs: Blairgowrie, Cowdenbeath, Headington United

Joe McKeown scored 12 goals in 13 Scottish League games for Cowdenbeath between 1950 and 1952 before he joined Headington United.

McLAIN, Tom

Right-half
Born: 19 January 1922, Morpeth
Died: December 1995
United debut: 18 August 1956 v Yeovil Town
Final United game: 30 March 1957 v Cheltenham Town
Appearances: 24
Goals: 6
Clubs: Ashington, Sunderland, Northampton Town, Headington United, Wellingborough Town

Thomas McLain was one of a number of Ashington players to make the grade in the Football League, joining Sunderland in 1946 and going on to play 67 League games for the Wearsiders, scoring one goal. He moved to Northampton in 1952 and was with the Cobblers for 96 League games in which he scored 11 goals before his move to Headington United in 1956.

*McLAREN, Paul

Midfielder
Born: 17 November 1976, High Wycombe
United debut: 3 January 2011 v Torquay United
Final United game: 7 May 2011 v Shrewsbury Town
Appearances: 24
Goals: 1

Clubs: Luton Town, Sheffield Wednesday, Rotherham United, Tranmere Rovers, Bradford City, Tranmere Rovers, Oxford United

Paul Andrew McLaren joined Oxford on New Year's Eve 2010, having been released from Tranmere Rovers the previous month because he wanted more first-team football. McLaren initially joined United until the end of the season, but his impressive performances as a central holding midfielder led the club to offer him a new contract for the following season. McLaren's career started with Luton Town in January 1994, where he played 198 games and scored six goals before he left for Sheffield Wednesday in June 2001. He spent three seasons at Hillsborough, playing 106 times and scoring nine goals, before being released and signing for nearby Rotherham United in July 2004. In two seasons at Millmoor McLaren played 76 matches and netted on six occasions before being released and following manager Ronnie Moore to Tranmere Rovers. He was with Tranmere for two years, making 96 appearances and scoring five goals, before turning down the offer of a new contract and joining Bradford City, where he played 37 games, scoring three goals in his one season at Valley Parade. McLaren then returned to Prenton Park for 51 games and one goal before leaving for Oxford.

McLAUGHLIN, Bob

Wing-half
Born: 6 December 1925, Dublin
Died: April 2003
United debut: 2 September 1959 v Chelmsford City
Final United game: 2 September 1959 v Chelmsford City
Appearances: 1
Clubs: Distillery (Northern Ireland), Wrexham, Cardiff City, Southampton, Headington United, Yeovil Town, Salisbury City

Robert McLaughlin was a left-sided forward who won an Irish League cap while with Distillery in 1947–48. In January 1950 Wrexham paid £3,000 for him. He played 17 League games for Wrexham before joining Cardiff City in the summer. Cardiff were promoted to Division One in 1952, but McLaughlin played just three top-flight games for them. In October 1953 he moved to Third Division South side Southampton as part of the deal that took Frank Dudley to Ninian Park, having played 48 League games for the Bluebirds in which he scored three goals. In his six seasons with the Saints McLaughlin played 169 League games and scored five goals. He was selected to represent the Northern Ireland B side in October 1957, but withdrew from the side that played Romania. He joined Headington in July 1959 but after just one appearance for the U's he moved to Yeovil where he was captain of the side that won the Southern League Cup in 1961, beating Chelmsford City 2–0 in the final. After a spell with Salisbury City he spent 31 years as a checker with Union Castle at Southampton Docks.

McNIVEN, Scott

Right-back
Born: 27 May 1978, Leeds
United debut: 10 August 2002 v Bury
Final United game: 8 May 2004 v Rochdale
Appearances: 95
Goals: 1

Clubs: Oldham Athletic, Oxford United, Mansfield Town, Chester City, Morecambe, Fleetwood Town, Guiseley, Farsley Celtic, AFC Fylde, Hyde United

Scott Andrew McNiven joined Oxford from Oldham Athletic, where he began his career as a trainee. He played 267 games for the Latics between October 1995 and his move to United in July 2002, scoring four goals. By the time he left the U's his best years were behind him and his move to Mansfield Town in July 2004 came as little surprise. McNiven played 26 times for the Stags, but his spell at Field Mill was blighted by him being diagnosed with testicular cancer. However, he made a full recovery and in June 2005 he moved to Chester City. After scoring one goal in 47 appearances for Chester he moved to Morecambe, then in the Conference, in August 2006 on non-contract terms. However, McNiven was unable to agree a longer-term deal and he left the Shrimps without making an appearance. He next joined Fleetwood in September 2006 and also joined Guiseley at the end of January 2007 before signing for Farsley Celtic in July 2007. After 30 games for the Leeds-based side, who were relegated from the Conference at the end of the season, McNiven joined Fylde in July 2008 and the following season he linked up with his twin brother David at Hyde. In October 2010 Scott was made assistant manager, becoming joint player-manager in April 2011. McNiven was a Scotland Youth international and also won a single Scotland cap at Under-21 level.

MEDLOCK, Owen

Goalkeeper
Born: 8 March 1938, Peterborough
United debut: 12 December 1959 v Gravesend & Northfleet
Final United game: 23 May 1965 v Newport County
Appearances: 133
Clean sheets: 38
Clubs: Chelsea, Swindon Town, Headington United, Chelmsford City

Owen Wilfred Medlock represented Northamptonshire and Midland Schoolboys before joining Bourne Town, aged 15. He joined the Chelsea ground staff in 1953 and played in the Chelsea youth team, including a tour of the Netherlands. Medlock signed professionally for the Pensioners at 17. After finishing his National Service he signed for Swindon, without having made the Chelsea first team, playing three League games for them before joining United in December 1959. Medlock was in goal for United in their first Football League game at Barrow in August 1962. After leaving the U's Medlock joined Chelmsford where he made 193 appearances and starred in successive Southern League title challenges. He helped the Clarets to the Southern League title in 1968, retiring the following year.

MELVILLE, Andy

Centre-back
Born: 29 November 1968, Swansea
United debut: 25 August 1990 v Port Vale
Final United game: 8 May 1993 v Watford
Appearances: 159
Goals: 15
Clubs: Swansea City, Oxford United, Sunderland, Bradford City (loan), Fulham, West Ham United, Nottingham Forest (loan)

Andrew Roger Melville joined Oxford from Swansea for £275,000 in July 1990. He started with the Swans as a midfielder before converting to centre-back. He had already won four Wales caps before he joined United, where he was capped a further 11 times. He eventually played 65 times for his country, putting him 10th in the list of most-capped Welsh players. Melville played 213 games for the Swans, scoring 29 goals, before his move to the Manor, where he established himself as one of the club's premier modern central-defenders, playing initially alongside Steve Foster. In August 1993 Sunderland paid £750,000 to take Melville to Roker Park where he played 236 games and scored 14 goals. In February 1998 he had a six-game loan spell with Bradford City, where he scored one goal, and in 1998–99 he was restored to the Sunderland team which went on to win promotion to the Premiership. Melville joined Fulham in June 1999 on a free transfer and he went on to play 193 times for the Cottagers, scoring four goals. He moved across London to West Ham in January 2004, playing 21 games for the Hammers, and in February 2005 he played 15 games on loan to Nottingham Forest, eventually retiring in August 2005. In July 2009 Melville returned to Oxford to help coach the side while studying for his coaching badges, earning a longer-term contract after United won promotion to the Football League in May 2010.

MIDDLETON, Jimmy

Inside-right
United debut: 31 October 1953 v Bedford Town
Final United game: 7 November 1953 v Wealdstone
Appearances: 3
Goals: 1
Clubs: Headington United, Dartford

MIDSON, Jack

Forward
Born: 12 September 1983, Stevenage
United debut: 8 August 2009
Final United game: 15 March 2011 v Stevenage
Appearances: 38+30
Goals: 15
Clubs: Stevenage Borough, Hayes (loan), Chelmsford City (loan), Hendon (loan), Arlesey, Dagenham & Redbridge, Hemel Hempstead Town (loan), Bishop's Stortford, Histon, Oxford United, Southend United (loan), Barnet (loan), AFC Wimbledon

Jack William Midson was a part-time footballer with Histon and a professional tennis coach before Oxford signed him in May 2009 after the Cambridgeshire club lost in the Conference Play-off semi-final. He rectified this by playing in United's May 2010 Conference Final win over York City, in which he made Oxford's first goal and later hit the post. In the Football League, Midson's appearances became less regular and he was loaned out to Southend in November 2010, where he scored two goals in six appearances. On his return to Oxford he scored a hat-trick in a 4–3 win at Torquay, but still found it difficult to get regular football and he was loaned out again, this time to Barnet, in March 2011. At the end of the season Midson was released and he signed for newly-promoted AFC Wimbledon in June 2011. Midson was a product of Stevenage's EFCO youth scheme, making his debut in December 2001. He scored once in 13 games for Borough before a loan spell with Hayes in September 2002. In December that year Midson joined Chelmsford on loan and in August 2003 he left Stevenage and joined Arlesey where he scored twice in five games before joining Dagenham & Redbridge at the start of the following season. In December 2004 he was loaned to Hemel Hempstead Town to gain more experience. He had played just 10 games for the Daggers but he was allowed to leave for Bishop's Stortford in July 2005 because he could not commit to daytime training. In 2006–07 Midson scored 14 goals as the Blues reached the Conference South Play-off Final for the first time in their history. In January 2008 Histon came in to sign Midson and he scored 25 goals in 70 games for the Stutes.

MIKE, Leon

Forward
Born: 4 September 1981, Manchester
United debut: 23 September 2000 v Millwall (sub)
Final United game: 8 October 2000 v Swindon Town (sub)
Appearances: 1+2
Clubs: Manchester City, Oxford United (loan), Halifax Town (loan), Aberdeen, Mossley, FC United of Manchester, Flixton, Bacup Borough

Leon Jonathan Mike joined Oxford on loan from Manchester City in September 2000 but, despite being an England Schoolboy at Under-15 and Under-16 levels and representing England at Under-18 level, he failed to impress. Mike made just two appearances for City, who he joined aged 13, and also had a seven-game loan with Halifax in February 2001 before Aberdeen paid £50,000 to take him to Pittodrie in February 2002. In his 15 months with the Dons Mike played 39 games and scored six goals before he was released in July 2003. Mike returned to the Manchester area and joined Mossley in the UniBond League Division One. Despite scoring 37 goals in 71 games for Mossley Mike was released with concerns about his fitness and in October 2005 he joined Leigh RMI. In December 2005 he was signed by FC United of Manchester in their inaugural season, playing six games for the Rebels before leaving in February 2007 to join Flixton and start studying law in Liverpool. Mike did not play a great deal for Flixton and exactly a year later he moved to Bacup Borough.

MILKINS, John

Goalkeeper
Born: 3 January 1944, Romford
United debut: 17 August 1974 v Cardiff City
Final United game: 5 May 1979 v Carlisle United
Appearances: 57
Clean sheets: 13
Clubs: Portsmouth, Oxford United, Waterlooville

In August 1974 Albert John Milkins joined Oxford for £10,000 from Portsmouth, where he is considered a legend. He joined Pompey from school and won England Youth honours in 1960–61. He signed professionally in May 1963 and clocked up 389 games before leaving for Oxford. Milkins won the first Portsmouth Player of the Season award in 1970, and in September 1973 he saved three penalties in a match against Notts County, the original kick having to be twice retaken, with Milkins stopping them all. After arriving at Oxford Milkins was preferred to Roy Burton, but after Burton regained his place Milkins' appearances became less frequent and he went part-time, training with Southern League side Waterlooville, now defunct, where he later became player-manager, and running a sports business in Portsmouth.

MILLS, Norman

Inside-left
United debut: 23 August 1952 v Kidderminster Harriers
Final United game: 1 May 1954 v Llanelly
Appearances: 73
Goals: 34
Clubs: Bath City, Cheltenham Town, Headington United

Norman Mills spent three seasons with Bath City shortly after World War Two before moving to Cheltenham Town, where he scored 42 goals in his two seasons at Whaddon Road. He joined Headington in the summer of 1952.

MILSOM, Paul

Forward
Born: 5 October 1974, Bristol
United debut: 26 September 1995 v Bristol City (sub)
Final United game: 26 September 1995 v Bristol City (sub)
Appearances: 0+1
Clubs: Bristol City, Clevedon Town (loan), Cardiff City, Stafford Rangers (loan), Oxford United (loan), Gloucester City, Trowbridge Town, Clevedon Town, Bath City, Forest Green Rovers (loan), Tiverton Town, Chippenham Town, Mangotsfield United, Almondsbury Town, Paulton Rovers

Paul Jason Milsom arrived in Oxford on trial after his release by Cardiff City, but his appearance record suggests that he failed to impress. He started his career at Ashton Gate where he spent two years as a Bristol City trainee, playing three games and having a loan spell at Clevedon before joining Cardiff in March 1995. Milsom managed four appearances with the Bluebirds and a loan spell at Stafford Rangers before his release in May 1995, leading to his solitary Anglo-Italian Cup substitute appearance for United. Milsom's next stop was Gloucester City, where he scored 13 goals in 44 games for the Tigers, followed by a brief stopover with Trowbridge Town, before moving back to Clevedon at the start of the 1997–98 season. He spent three seasons with the Seasiders before Bath City signed him for £3,000 in the summer of 2001, the money being raised by Bath supporters. Milsom scored 10 goals in 78 games for Bath and was a target for a number of sides, spending some time on loan at Forest Green Rovers, before joining Tiverton for around £3,000 at the start of the 2003–04 season. Milsom stayed with Tivvy for two seasons before agreeing a move to Chippenham in the summer of 2005, where he played for a further two years, moving to Mangotsfield in July 2007. In April 2008, after a brief stint as caretaker manager, Milsom was appointed Mangotsfield's player-manager, steering the club clear of relegation from the Southern League Premier Division. However, following a blackout in January 2008 Milsom was diagnosed with a heart condition and in July, having not played since his faint, he gave up playing on medical grounds, having made 30 appearances for Mangotsfield. In January 2009 Milsom was sacked and he moved to Almondsbury, where he took up playing again, scoring five goals in 19 games. In May 2009 he joined Paulton Rovers as player-assistant manager and in March 2011, after a spell as caretaker manager, he was appointed joint manager of Paulton.

MITCHELL, Bobby

Centre-forward
Born: 17 January 1927, Campbelltown
Died: April 2002
United debut: 23 August 1952 v Kidderminster Harriers
Final United game: 14 November 1953 v Kidderminster Harriers
Appearances: 44
Goals: 21
Clubs: Dunfermline Athletic, Third Lanark, Exeter City, Headington United, Chelmsford City, Bath City

Robert Barr Mitchell played just one Scottish League game for Third Lanark in 1950–51 after joining from Dunfermline, where he did not play a first-team game. He moved to Exeter where he managed three Football League appearances before his move to Headington. He was a mainstay of the side that won the Southern League double and was a regular until his transfer to Chelmsford in November 1953. He joined Bath in the summer of 1954 where he scored three goals in six games.

MOLYNEAUX, Lee

Midfielder/Right-back
Born: 16 January 1983, Portsmouth
United debut: 11 August 2004 v Mansfield Town (sub)
Final United game: 7 May 2005 v Chester City
Appearances: 7+10
Clubs: Selsey, Portsmouth, Derry City (Northern Ireland), Weymouth, Oxford United, Basingstoke Town, Cirencester Town, Forest Green Rovers, Clevedon Town, Gloucester City

Lee Alexander Molyneaux was one of a number of players with a connection to Portsmouth who were signed by Graham Rix. He began as a trainee at the south coast club, playing alongside Chris Tardif and Terry Parker, but moved to Derry City in the League of Ireland before making the Pompey first team. He also played one game for Weymouth before signing for the U's after impressing in a pre-season trial. Molyneaux was happiest at right-back, but he could play in most positions and his versatility counted against him as it meant he was more often than not on the bench. When Brian Talbot became the manager, Molyneaux never did enough to impress, and the writing was on the wall when he was a non-playing substitute for a very poor reserves side. He was eventually released from his contract in November 2005 and joined Basingstoke Town, where he made 26 appearances before his departure in May 2006. Molyneaux signed for Cirencester Town in August 2006 and found work as a personal trainer. He was at the Corinium Stadium for two seasons under manager Adi Viveash before moving to Forest Green Rovers in July 2008, while also captaining the first XI of Hartpury College at the same time, with whom he twice won the British Universities and Colleges Sport Cup while studying and winning England Universities caps.

Molyneaux played four games for Forest Green before moving to Clevedon Town in January 2009. In February 2010 Molyneaux signed for Gloucester City after his release by Clevedon, and he stayed with the Tigers until June 2010 when he relocated to Hampshire, having scored one goal in eight games, becoming player-assistant manager of Wessex League side Blackfield & Langley.

MONK, Garry

Centre-back
Born: 6 March 1979, Bedford
United debut: 13 January 2001 v Walsall
Final United game: 17 February 2001 v Bury
Appearances: 5
Clubs: Torquay United, Southampton, Torquay United (loan), Stockport County (loan), Oxford United (loan), Sheffield Wednesday (loan), Barnsley (loan), Barnsley, Swansea City

Garry Alan Monk started as a junior with Torquay United, playing five games for the Gulls and winning England Under-17 honours before his transfer to Southampton in July 1996. He signed professionally for the Saints before returning to Plainmoor on loan in September 1998 to help out with an injury crisis, playing six games. Despite breaking into the Southampton first team, appearances were hard to come by and Monk had to go out on loan again to Stockport for four games in September 1999 and to the Manor for five matches in January 2001 as Oxford struggled in vain against relegation to the basement, although it was clear from even these limited appearances that Monk was a classy defender. In December 2002 Monk had a further loan spell, playing 15 games for Sheffield Wednesday, followed by another loan, this time to Barnsley, in November 2003. Monk played 18 games for the Tykes and also registered his first senior goal before Barnsley made the deal permanent in February 2004, with Monk having played just 13 games for Southampton in his eight years at the Dell. However, Monk managed just three more appearances for Barnsley in the remainder of the season and in June 2004 he joined Swansea City on a free transfer. In his first season with the Swans the club won promotion from League Two and reached the League One Play-offs the following season, after which Monk was made club captain. In 2008 the club won promotion to the Championship and in May 2011 won promotion to the Premiership after beating Reading in the Play-off Final.

MOODY, Paul

Forward
Born: 13 June 1967, Portsmouth
United debut: 26 February 1994 v Nottingham Forest
Final United game: 20 April 2002 v Darlington
Appearances: 148+49
Goals: 75
Clubs: Challengers FC, Fareham Town, Waterlooville, Southampton, Reading (loan), Oxford United, Fulham, Millwall, Oxford United, Aldershot, Gosport Borough

When painter and decorator Paul Moody joined Waterlooville from Fareham Town in August 1989 for £4,000 he was the club's record signing. When he was sold to Southampton for £50,000 two years later he was their record sale. In his three years with the Saints Moody played just 14 games, coupled with a six-game loan spell to Reading in December 1992 in which he scored one goal. Given that record, when Denis Smith signed him for £60,000 in February 1994 it must have been considered a risky investment. However, it was one that paid off handsomely as Moody's goals shot United to promotion from Division Two in 1996. Moody scored 61 goals including four hat-tricks in his 161 games, despite struggling with a back injury at the end of his time with United, before Fulham paid £200,000 for him in August 1997. Moody scored 20 goals in 49 games for the Cottagers before he moved to Millwall for £140,000 in July 1999. By the time he returned to Oxford for £150,000 in September 2001, Moody had played 69 games and scored 27 goals for the Lions. He scored on his return to United in a 2–1 win against Southend United, and by the end of the season he had added a further 13 goals and 36 games to his Oxford total. He was released by the U's at the end of the season after he decided that the travelling and training was taking its toll on his back and after a trial match with Havant & Waterlooville he signed for Ryman League Premier Division outfit Aldershot Town in July 2002. He scored 10 goals for the Shots but his constant struggle to maintain his fitness led to his release in February 2003. In June he joined Gosport Borough, but because of a succession of injuries he managed just one substitute appearance, in which he broke his ribs. This signalled the end of Moody's playing career and he set up a tanning, fitness and holistic studio in Havant with his wife Tessa.

MOONEY, Tommy

Forward
Born: 11 August 1971, Billingham
United debut: 7 August 2004 v Boston United
Final United game: 7 May 2005 v Chester City
Appearances: 45
Goals: 15
Clubs: Aston Villa, Scarborough, Southend United, Watford (loan), Watford, Birmingham City, Stoke City (loan), Sheffield United (loan), Derby County (loan), Swindon Town, Oxford United, Wycombe Wanderers, Walsall, Unión Deportiva Marbella (Spain)

Thomas John Moody started his career with Aston Villa, but he failed to make the first team and was released in August 1990, joining Scarborough. He played 129 games for the Seadogs, scoring 40 goals, before his £100,000 transfer to Southend United in July 1993, although he managed just 21 appearances for the Shrimpers. His five goals for Southend include a hat-trick in a 6–1 win over Oxford. In March 1994 Mooney scored twice in a nine-game loan spell with Watford, who signed him permanently in the summer for £95,000. In 1999 Watford won the Championship Play-offs to win promotion to the Premiership, although they were relegated the following season, at the end of which Mooney was voted the Player of the Season. Mooney played 181 games for Watford (excluding his earlier loan) and scored 63 goals, earning him a place in the Watford Hall of Fame. In June 2001 he signed for Birmingham City after his contract with Watford expired, despite having an opportunity to join Premiership side Everton, although he spent most of his second season out on loan at various clubs; in September 2002 he scored three goals in 12 games for Stoke, followed by one goal in six games with Sheffield United in January 2003 and eight goalless games for Derby two months later. After 39 games for the Blues, in which he contributed 15 goals, Mooney signed for Swindon in July 2003. He spent exactly one year at the County Ground, scoring 20 goals in 49 appearances, including missing a penalty in the shoot-out as Swindon lost to Brighton in the Play-off semi-finals. His signing for Oxford in the summer of 2004 was considered something of a coup for manager Graham Rix, although it was under Ramon Díaz that Mooney came to life, ending the season as Oxford's leading scorer. Mooney failed to agree a new contract with new manager Brian Talbot and left for Wycombe Wanderers in June 2005. He managed two seasons with the Chairboys, scoring 32 goals (including against Oxford, naturally) in 101 games, before joining his final English club, Walsall. In his one season with the Saddlers Mooney played 40 games and scored 12 goals, earning himself a move to UD Marbella. After a handful of appearances Mooney retired just after Christmas 2008, but remained in Spain as his son Kelsey was offered a trial with Sevilla.

MORGAN, Danny

Forward
Born: 4 November 1984, Stepney
United debut: 23 August 2004 v Reading (sub)
Final United game: 27 August 2005 v Stockport County
Appearances: 2+6
Goals: 1
Clubs: Wimbledon, Oxford United, Brackley Town (loan), Basingstoke Town (loan), Bishop's Stortford, Billericay Town, St Albans City, Chesham United

Daniel Frederick Morgan joined Oxford from Wimbledon in May 2004 after scoring a hat-trick for the reserves while on trial. The move came shortly before the franchised Wimbledon changed their name to MK Dons, although Morgan never played a first-team game for them. After making only occasional appearances for the U's Morgan went on loan to Brackley in March 2005 and in November 2005, after being told he was free to leave United, he played seven games on loan to Basingstoke, scoring four goals before a broken jaw following an incident outside a nightclub led to his return to Oxford. In March 2006 Morgan moved to Bishop's Stortford and in July 2007 he joined Billericay but almost immediately he signed for St Albans City, where he scored three goals in 12 appearances and was criticised for his 'languid' performances. He left for Chesham in November 2007.

MORLEY, Dave

Centre-back
Born: 25 September 1977, St Helens
United debut: 15 December 2001 v Mansfield Town
Final United game: 13 April 2002 v Cheltenham Town
Appearances: 16+2
Goals: 3
Clubs: Manchester City, Ayr United (loan), Southend United, Carlisle United (loan), Carlisle United, Oxford United (loan), Oxford United, Doncaster Rovers, Macclesfield Town, Hyde United, Bangor City

David Thomas Morley began his career with Manchester City, scoring on his debut against Bury in September 1997, but he played just two more games for the Sky Blues before moving to Ayr for a four-game loan spell in March 1998. In August 1998 Morley joined Southend where he played 86 games without finding the net, joining Carlisle on loan in February 2001, playing six games and scoring once before the move was made permanent in March. Morley played a further 38 games for the Cumbrians before he joined Oxford on loan in December 2001. He scored once in his three loan games to earn himself a longer deal in January 2002 which took him to the end of the season. After his contract ran out he joined Doncaster, playing 74 games and scoring seven goals prior to his move to Macclesfield Town in January 2005. Morley spent almost three years at Moss Rose, becoming captain and scoring seven goals in 119 games, leaving in October 2007 after his contract was cancelled by mutual consent. He joined Hyde United the following month, scoring four goals in 66 games before he left for Welsh Premier League side Bangor City in June 2009.

MORRIS, Mike

Right-winger
Born: 20 January 1943, Plaistow
United debut: 22 August 1964 v Crewe Alexandra
Final United game: 22 April 1967 v Queen's Park Rangers
Appearances: 94+1
Goals: 15
Clubs: Barking, Grays Athletic, West Ham United, Faversham Town, Oxford United, Port Vale, Stafford Rangers, Leek Town

Michael John Morris grew up in the East End of London and played for Barking and Grays Athletic before briefly being on West Ham's books, although he never played for the Hammers. He joined Oxford as an amateur from Faversham, signing professionally for United in June 1964. Although a hard worker Morris was not prolific and despite a spell at centre-forward he gradually disappeared from the first team and joined Port Vale in August 1967, just days before their tour of Czechoslovakia, although Morris did not play as he burst a blood vessel in training. Morris played 200 games for the Valiants, scoring 25 goals; he missed just one game in their 1970 promotion season and was an ever present the following year. In 1972 Morris joined Stafford Rangers and in 1976 he played for them against Scarborough in the FA Trophy Final at Wembley, but was on the losing side as Scarborough won 3–2 after extra-time. Morris later played for Leek Town and Newcastle-under-Lyme side Jubilee Working Men's Club. After retiring he worked for Michelin and after undergoing heart surgery in 2002 he worked part-time at Barlaston Golf Club as assistant greenkeeper.

MULGREW, Andy

Left-winger
United debut: 27 August 1955 v Worcester City
Final United game: 24 March 1956 v Bath City
Appearances: 8
Goals: 1
Clubs: Merthyr Tydfil, Headington United

Andrew Mulgrew joined Headington from Merthyr Tydfil in the summer of 1955, but he was not able to displace Jimmy Bain from the left-wing berth.

MUMFORD, Percy

Inside-right
Born: June 1933, Headington
United debut: 28 April 1955 v Worcester City
Final United game: 28 April 1955 v Worcester City
Appearances: 1
Clubs: Headington United

MUNRO, Ken

Left-back
Born: 13 February 1940, Lancashire
United debut: 24 December 1960 v Bedford Town
Final United game: 24 December 1960 v Bedford Town
Appearances: 1
Clubs: Blackpool, Oxford United

Kenneth Munro was spotted by Blackpool playing for his local youth side. He was with the Seasiders for one and a half seasons without playing a first-team game before signing for United. He suffered an illness soon after joining, which set him back a bit. Munro made just one first-team appearance for United, but also featured 27 times for the reserves, scoring once in the Metropolitan League.

MURPHY, Matt

Midfielder
Born: 20 August 1971, Northampton
United debut: 6 May 1993 v Newcastle United
Final United game: 5 May 2001 v Notts County
Appearances: 196+92
Goals: 55
Clubs: Long Buckby, Cogenhoe United, Irthlingborough Diamonds, Corby Town, Oxford United, Scunthorpe United (loan), Bury, Swansea City, Kettering Town, King's Lynn, Ford Sports, Slough Town, Brackley Town, Wellingborough Town 2004, Northampton Sileby Rangers, Long Buckby

After spells in the United Counties League with Long Buckby, Cogenhoe United and Irthlingborough Diamonds, Matthew Simon Murphy joined Corby Town and became the Steelmen's record transfer in February 1993 when he joined Oxford United for a fee of £20,000. After a spell in the reserves Murphy began to appear with regularity and turned out to be a goalscoring midfielder, albeit frustratingly inconsistent. He was United's most used substitute, coming off the bench on 92 occasions, and was also substituted 57 times; in one game he was both a substitute and later substituted. He was the club's leading scorer in the 1999–2000 season with 17 goals from midfield. In December 1997 Murphy had a four-game loan spell with Scunthorpe. After United's relegation to the basement division Murphy moved to Bury where he played just 10 games, followed by a move to Swansea in June 2002, where he scored three goals in 14 appearances. In July 2003 he joined Kettering Town where he scored three goals in 10 appearances, but he was sacked in October 2003 for refusing to go on the bench. Murphy moved to King's Lynn, where he lasted just over a week before parting company with the Linnets and joining Ford Sports, where he was top scorer with 31 goals. Murphy's next stop was Slough Town, who he joined in August 2004, going on to be the Rebels' leading scorer that season before he left for Brackley in August 2005. In May 2007 he made the short journey to Banbury United before leaving for Spalding United in March 2008. After a brief spell with Wellingborough he joined Sileby Rangers in December 2008, before becoming player-assistant manager at Long Buckby in January 2009.

MURRAY, Adam

Midfielder
Born: 30 September 1981, Birmingham
United debut: 5 January 2008 v Altrincham
Final United game: 16 January 2010 v Tamworth
Appearances: 97+1
Goals: 11
Clubs: Derby County, Mansfield Town (loan), Kidderminster Harriers (loan), Notts County, Burton Albion, Notts County, Kidderminster Harriers, Mansfield Town, Carlisle United, Torquay United, Macclesfield Town, Oxford United, Luton Town, Mansfield Town (loan), Mansfield Town

Adam David Murray signed for Oxford during the January 2008 transfer window from Macclesfield Town on a one-and-a-half-year contract. He came with the reputation of someone with a troubled past, including drinking problems. However, none of this was in evidence as Murray proved to be an excellent central midfielder and he was made captain for the 2008–09 season. He left the club by mutual consent at the start of July 2010, and immediately signed for Luton. At the start of October 2010, after seven games for the Hatters, he rejoined Mansfield Town on a three-month loan deal, later made permanent after he had scored three goals in his 16 appearances. Murray started his career as a trainee with Derby County, turning professional in August 1998 and making his debut in the Premiership. While with the Rams Murray won England Youth and England Under-20 international honours. After a 13-game loan spell with Mansfield in February 2002, in which he scored seven goals, Murray became a regular in Derby's Championship side, albeit mostly as a substitute. He played three games on loan with Kidderminster Harriers in August 2003, but returned early because of an alcohol problem that needed treatment at the Priory Clinic, a private rehabilitation and mental health services provider. In November 2003 Murray left Derby for Notts County, but after just one game he moved to Burton Albion on non-contract terms, making two appearances before returning to the Magpies, again without a contract, where he made three substitute appearances. He signed for Kidderminster in January 2004 and scored three goals in his 19 games up to the end of the season. Murray joined Mansfield in June 2004 and in his season at Field Mill he scored five goals in 37 games before moving to Carlisle United in March 2005 for a nominal fee. He played 52 games and scored four goals and was a member of the side managed by Paul Simpson that won the Conference Play-offs in 2006, but in August he put in a transfer request and he joined Ian Atkins' Torquay United for £10,000. In January 2007, after 25 games for the Gulls, Macclesfield signed Murray for £17,500 on a two-and-a-half-year contract, but a year later, after 36 games for the Silkmen, Murray joined Oxford.

MURRAY, Tom

Inside-forward
Born: 5 February 1933, Airdrie
United debut: 27 August 1955 v Worcester City
Final United game: 10 December 1955 v Gravesend & Northfleet
Appearances: 14
Goals: 1
Clubs: Headington United, Darlington, St Johnstone, Alloa Athletic, Albion Rovers, Stranraer

Thomas Murray left Headington for Darlington, playing three Football League games for the Quakers before moving to St Johnstone, where he played three Scottish League games. His next stop was Alloa Athletic, where he made five Scottish League appearances, thence to Albion for two games and Stranraer for one match.

MUSTOE, Robbie

Midfielder
Born: 28 August 1968, Witney
United debut: 29 November 1986 v Norwich City (sub)
Final United game: 1 May 1990 v Oldham Athletic
Appearances: 85+13
Goals: 10
Clubs: Oxford United, Middlesbrough, Charlton Athletic, Sheffield Wednesday

Robin Mustoe became an apprentice with Oxford in 1984, signing professionally in the summer of 1986. After being a regular in the reserves he was handed his debut with United in the top flight, although it was only when he was in his last season with the club that he became a regular starter. His performances earned him a £375,000 transfer to Middlesbrough where, after a slow start, he was made club captain. In April 1997 he played for Boro in the Coca-Cola Cup Final at Wembley in a 1–1 draw with Leicester City and in the 1–0 defeat in the replay at Hillsborough; the following month he played in Boro's FA Cup Final defeat to Chelsea and in March 1998 he played as Chelsea again defeated Middlesbrough, this time in the Coca-Cola Cup Final. In 1999 Mustoe was Boro's joint Player of the Year, but in August 2002 he moved on a free transfer to Charlton, having played 454 games and scored 34 goals for the Boro, the last two seasons of which were under Steve McClaren's management. Mustoe was with Charlton for one season, but managed just seven appearances before he joined Sheffield Wednesday in July 2003. He scored one goal in 29 games before moving to the United States to take advantage of his UEFA B coaching badge that he earned in 2000. He spent the 2006 season as an assistant coach at Bentley College before joining Boston College. In January 2008 Mustoe also joined ESPN as an analyst.

MUTTOCK, Jon

Defender
Born: 23 December 1961, Oxford
United debut: 21 April 1990 v Wolverhampton Wanderers
Final United game: 21 April 1990 v Wolverhampton Wanderers
Appearances: 1

Clubs: Oxford United, Wycombe Wanderers (loan), Oxford City, Witney Town, Brackley Town, Abingdon Town, Chipping Norton Town, Abingdon United, North Leigh, Witney United

Jonathan Lee Muttock joined United's YTS from school in 1988, signing professionally in the summer of 1990, having previously played for Eynsham Boys and having represented Mid Oxon and Oxfordshire. He made just one appearance for the U's, a Division Two fixture at Wolves that Oxford lost 2– 0. Muttock was then out for five months with two broken bones in his foot. He had a week on loan at Conference side Wycombe Wanderers before he was released in the summer of 1992 and he spent much of the next decade and more playing for local non-League clubs. He signed for Oxford City in August 1992 and was in the City side that lost 2–1 to Arlesey at Wembley in May 1995 and captained them to the Oxfordshire Senior Cup in 1996, when they won 2–1 at Thame United. His last game for the Hoops was in November 1997 after scoring 19 goals in 224 games. In July 2000 Muttock made the move from Witney Town to Brackley Town, and he signed for Abingdon Town in August 2001. In October 2002 he moved from Abingdon Town to Chipping Norton Town and in September 2003 he joined Abingdon United. In October 2004 Muttock joined North Leigh and his next stop was Witney United.

N

NARBETT, Jon

Midfielder

Born: 21 November 1968, Birmingham
United debut: 25 August 1992 v Swansea City
Final United game: 14 September 1993 v Portsmouth
Appearances: 16+3
Clubs: Shrewsbury Town, Hereford United, Leicester City (loan), Oxford United, Kalmar FF (Sweden), Merthyr Tydfil, Chesterfield, Kidderminster Harriers, Worcester City

Jonathan Vellenzer Narbett started as an apprentice with Shrewsbury Town, scoring three goals in 31 games between September 1986 and October 1988, when he moved to Hereford United for £30,000. He made 181 appearances for the Bulls, scoring 36 goals, and was their leading scorer in 1990–91 with 12 goals. He joined Leicester City on loan in November 1991, but did not get to play for the Foxes. In July 1992 United paid £65,000 for Narbett, who turned out to be an expensive failure, and in March 1994 he joined Swedish second-tier side Kalmar. Narbett proved not to be what the Swedish side required and two months later he returned to Britain, or more accurately Wales, where he joined Merthyr Tydfil. He was at Penydarren Park until December, at which point he returned to League football with Chesterfield. Narbett scored one goal in 28 games for the Spireites, leaving for Kidderminster in May 1996. In the summer of 1998 he retired from full-time football due to injury, and in January 1999 he joined Worcester City. He joined the PFA financial management team, based in their Birmingham office, in January 2007. His brother Roger was chef for the England national team.

NELTHORPE, Craig

Left-winger

Born: 10 June 1987, Doncaster
United debut: 17 January 2009 v Altrincham
Final United game: 26 April 2009 v Northwich Victoria (sub)
Appearances: 14+2
Goals: 2
Clubs: Frickley Athletic, Doncaster Rovers, Hucknall Town (loan), Kidderminster Harriers (loan), Gateshead (loan), Halifax Town (loan), Darlington (loan), Gateshead (loan), Oxford United, York City, Barrow (loan), Luton Town (loan), Gateshead, Gainsborough Trinity

Craig Robert Nelthorpe joined Oxford on a free transfer after his release from Doncaster Rovers in January 2009. He had joined the Doncaster youth scheme from Frickley Athletic in May 2005. He scored one goal in 14 games for Rovers, but spent most of his time on loan, initially with Hucknall Town where he played five games in December 2005, scoring twice on his debut. In October 2006 he played five games at Kidderminster, and Nelthorpe joined Gateshead on loan for the first time in November 2006, playing 19 games in which he scored eight goals up to April 2007. In January 2008 Chris Wilder took Nelthorpe on loan at Halifax, where the winger scored two goals in his seven appearances, including one on his debut, and in March 2008 he played eight games for Darlington. In August 2008 he returned to Gateshead where he scored one goal in 15 games before his move to Oxford was finalised. Nelthorpe proved a creative outlet on the wing for the U's, but his temperament was suspect and he was sent off against Torquay. Nelthorpe was released at the end of the season and signed for York City, for whom he made eight appearances, all as substitute. In November 2009 he was loaned to Barrow where he scored two goals in six games and this was followed by a loan to Luton in January 2010, where he made eight substitute appearances. In the 2009–10 season Nelthorpe became the first player to appear against Oxford for three different clubs in the same season. In August 2009 Nelthorpe was arrested after an incident outside a York nightclub and he subsequently pleaded guilty to affray. In July 2010 Nelthorpe joined Gateshead following his release by York City, but after scoring five goals in 35 games he was released in May 2011 and signed for Gainsborough Trinity.

NEWTON, Eddie

Midfielder
Born: 13 December 1971, Hammersmith
United debut: 1 April 2000 v AFC Bournemouth
Final United game: 6 May 2000 v Millwall
Appearances: 7
Clubs: Chelsea, Cardiff City (loan), Birmingham City, Oxford United, Barnet, Hayes

Edward John Ikem Newton joined Second Division Oxford from First Division Birmingham City on his career's spectacular descent, having arrived at the Blues from Premiership Chelsea. The following season he joined Third Division Barnet, and thence to Conference club Hayes. Newton came through the youth system at Stamford Bridge and in January 1992 he went on loan to Cardiff, where he scored four goals in 18 games. On his return to Chelsea he became an established member of their Premiership side, winning two England Under-21 caps and playing in the 1994 FA Cup Final defeat by Manchester United. The following season he played in the UEFA Cup semi-final defeat against Real Zaragoza. In 1997 Chelsea reached the semi-finals of the FA Cup, and the next season Newton scored Chelsea's second goal as they beat Middlesbrough 2–0 in the FA Cup Final at Wembley. A year later Newton came on as a substitute as Chelsea beat VfB Stuttgart 1–0 in the European Cup Winners' Cup Final and was in the side that beat Middlesbrough 2–0 in the 1998 League Cup Final. After 213 games and 10 goals for Chelsea, Newton joined Birmingham City on a free transfer in July 1999, but persistent knee injuries restricted him to just nine games before his March 2000 move to the Manor. In his short spell with Oxford Newton appeared a decent midfielder, combative and with good vision, but his downward spiral continued in August 2000 when he joined Barnet on a monthly contract, playing just six games before signing for Hayes on non-contract terms in December 2000. After six games for the Missioners, Newton eventually retired in 2001 as his injuries got the better of him. After retirement Newton converted to Islam and ran New Vision Sports, offering multisport activities for children. He also coached at Chelsea and hosted Sky One's *Football Icon* with Jamie Redknapp. In July 2008 Newton was appointed assistant to Roberto Di Matteo at Milton Keynes Dons and he followed Di Matteo to West Bromwich Albion when the Italian was appointed manager at the Hawthorns in June 2009. However Newton left West Brom when Di Matteo was sacked in February 2011.

NICKLAS, Charlie

Centre-forward
Born: 26 April 1930, Sunderland
United debut: 25 September 1954 v Yeovil Town
Final United game: 30 April 1955 v Lovell's Athletic
Appearances: 14
Goals: 4
Clubs: Silksworth Colliery, Hull City, Darlington, Headington United

Charles Nicklas started out with Silksworth Colliery, Durham, joining Hull City in 1951 after demobilisation, having being discovered by Raich Carter while in the Forces. Nicklas made six appearances in the Football League for the Tigers, scoring one goal, before he moved to Darlington the following year. He played 17 League games for the Quakers in which he scored six goals prior to his move to Headington. Nicklas was also a professional sprinter.

NIELSON, Bill

Inside-right
United debut: 20 August 1955 v Gloucester City
Final United game: 17 December 1955 v Gloucester City
Appearances: 5
Goals: 1
Clubs: Headington United, Gravesend & Northfleet

After signing in the summer of 1955 William Nielson scored 21 goals in United's Metropolitan League side before his transfer to Gravesend & Northfleet in February 1956.

NOGAN, Lee

Forward
Born: 21 May 1969, Cardiff
United debut: 13 January 1988 v Reading (sub)
Final United game: 7 December 1991 v Blackburn Rovers
Appearances: 67+10
Goals: 12
Clubs: Oxford United, Brentford (loan), Southend United (loan), Watford, Southend United (loan), Reading, Notts County (loan), Grimsby Town, Darlington, Luton Town, York City, Harrogate Town, Pickering Town, Whitby Town, AFC Halifax

Lee Martin Nogan joined Oxford's Youth Training Scheme in 1985, turning professional in March 1987. After signing he immediately went out on loan to Brentford where he scored two goals in 11 appearances. Nogan had another loan spell at Southend United in September 1987 where he scored twice in nine games, after which he established himself as Dean Saunders' deputy, becoming United's first YTS recruit to figure in the club's first team when he made his debut in a 1–0 Simod Cup defeat at Reading in January 1988. Nogan figured three times for United in the First Division as they suffered relegation from the top flight. Even after Saunders was sold to Derby in October 1988,

Nogan had to wait until September 1990 for a sustained run in the first team, but he never really convinced as a first-choice striker and it came as a surprise to almost everybody when Watford paid £300,000 for him in December 1991. He scored 30 goals for the Hornets in 115 games, plus he had another loan spell at Southend in March 1994 in which he played five times, before he moved to Reading for £250,000 in January 1995. Reading finished runners-up in the Second Division in his first season at Elm Park but lost to Bolton in the Play-off Final at Wembley, in which Nogan scored the first goal. Nogan played 102 games for the Royals, scoring 29 goals, and had a six-game loan with Notts County in February 1997 before he was sold to Grimsby for £170,000 in August 1997. In his first season at Blundell Park the Mariners won the Division Two Play-offs and by the time Nogan moved to Darlington on a free transfer in July 1999 he had made 98 appearances and scored 16 goals for them. He played 68 games for the Quakers, finding the net eight times, and in November 2000 he joined Luton Town where he scored twice in 11 games before moving to his final professional club, York City, in February 2001. Nogan was at Bootham Crescent for over five years, playing 181 games, scoring 37 goals and becoming player-coach, but the Minstermen were relegated to the Conference in 2004 and in March 2005 he moved to Harrogate Town, scoring on his debut, having left York the previous month. In September 2005 he joined Pickering Town, playing in midweek while still registered with Harrogate, leaving in June 2006 to become player-manager of Whitby Town. However, in October 2007 Nogan resigned following some poor results but he remained registered as a player with Whitby and in March 2008 he rejoined them. He later turned up at AFC Halifax as a player in January 2011.

NORRIS, Eddie

United debut: 3 May 1958 v Yeovil Town
Final United game: 3 May 1958 v Yeovil Town
Appearances: 1
Clubs: Headington United

N'TOYA, Tcham

Forward
Born: 3 November 1983, Kinshasa (DR Congo)
United debut: 25 March 2006 v Peterborough United
Final United game: 6 May 2006 v Leyton Orient
Appearances: 7+1
Goals: 4
Clubs: Troyes (France), Chesterfield, York City (loan), Oxford United (loan), Notts County, Maccabi Herzliya (Israel), Maccabi Ahi Nazareth (Israel)

Tcham N'Toya-Zoa was signed by Jim Smith in March 2006 and scored on his debut, and Smith's first match on his return, at home to Peterborough. N'Toya also scored the fastest goal at the Kassam when he netted against Barnet after just 47 seconds. However, his goals were not enough to keep Oxford in the League and at the end of the season United went down to the Conference. N'Toya always looked threatening, and would probably have signed a permanent contract had Oxford not been relegated. Born in what was Zaire, N'Toya joined Troyes as a youth player in 2001 and played three Ligue 2 games for them before joining Chesterfield in March 2004 on the recommendation of Jim Smith. N'Toya played 53 games for the Spireites, mostly as a substitute, scoring eight goals. In January 2006 he played three games on loan with York City before his attempted rescue act at Oxford. In June 2006 he was released by Chesterfield and joined Notts County, where again he figured mainly from the bench, scoring two goals in 27 appearances. He was released at the end of the 2006–07 season and after a trial with St Mirren, in which he scored for the reserves against Rangers, he joined Israeli side Maccabi Herzliya, where he was to play alongside Josh Kennet. After two goals in 21 games he moved to Maccabi Ahi Nazareth in the north of the country in 2008. He was released two years later and had an unsuccessful trial with French side Chamois FC 79.

NUGENT, Cliff

Outside-forward
Born: 3 March 1929, Islington
United debut: 22 October 1949 v Weymouth
Final United game: 10 February 1951 v Barry Town
Appearances: 69
Goals: 15
Clubs: Woking, Oxford City, Headington United, Cardiff City, Mansfield Town, Weymouth, Portland United

William Clifford Nugent was one of United's first semi-professional players, along with Peter Sharman. Both were on Oxford City's books when, in August 1949, they approached Headington to sign as professionals. The board suggested that they think it over before making the step up from the Isthmian League, but both players returned to sign as part-time professionals in August 1949. The first that Oxford City heard of the matter was in the local press the following day. Nugent started badly, disappointing in the pre-season trials and then pulling a groin muscle that kept him out for seven weeks. He came back on the left wing for the reserves, but started his Southern League career on the right. After switching back to outside-left he became an automatic choice. The following season he was so successful that he had trials with Wolves, Fulham, Orient, West Brom, Aston Villa, West Ham, Leeds, and Cardiff, who he joined in February 1951 for £2,500, a Southern League record, after their initial bid of £2,000 was rejected. Nugent was born in London, moving to the Peak District as a child. When he was 16 he was on Sheffield United's books, but National Service took him initially to Aldershot where he played for Woking before coming to Oxford when he was posted to Cowley Barracks with the Royal Army Pay Corps, joining Oxford City after demobilisation. Nugent was a big success for Cardiff once he managed to get regular first-team football a couple of seasons after arriving at Ninian Park, although he missed almost all the 1955–56 season through injury. After scoring 20 goals in 122 games Nugent moved to Mansfield Town, where he made 52 League appearances in which he scored seven goals. Nugent moved to Weymouth in 1960 and after five years with the Terras, in which he scored 40 goals in 171 games, he joined Portland United as player-coach, returning to Weymouth as first-team coach in 1968. He later owned a hotel in the town before his retirement.

O

OBI, Tony

Winger
Born: 15 September 1965, Birmingham
United debut: 23 August 1986 v Watford (sub)
Final United game: 23 August 1986 v Watford (sub)
Appearances: 0+1
Clubs: Aston Villa, Walsall (loan), Plymouth Argyle (loan), Bristol Rovers, Oxford United, Brentford (loan), KV Oostende (Belgium)

Lloyd Anthony Obi played for 15 minutes at the end of United's first game of the 1986–87 season at Watford and never pulled on a Yellows shirt again. Obi started his career with Aston Villa, who he joined from Harborne Boys, and in 1983 he won an England Youth cap as a substitute although he did not get to play for Villa's first team. In December 1984 he had a two-game loan spell with Walsall, followed by a five-game loan at Plymouth in February 1985. After a brief spell training with Bromsgrove Rovers he joined Bristol Rovers in the summer of 1985 on a non-contract basis, where he played one game before his move to Oxford, as Rovers could not afford to take him on. Despite playing well and scoring lots of goals for United's reserves and in pre-season friendlies, Obi failed to make the breakthrough with the first team and immediately after his solitary substitute appearance in August 1986 he joined Brentford for a 10-game loan spell in which he failed to score. At the end of the 1986–87 season Obi was given a free transfer, at which point he moved to Belgium to play for Oostende. Obi played 174 games for the Belgian side, staying in the town after retiring to become part-owner of a restaurant called Valentientje.

ODELL, Bob

Centre-back
Born: 10 December 1934, Isle of Wight
United debut: 18 August 1956 v Yeovil Town
Final United game: 3 May 1958 v Yeovil Town
Appearances: 65
Goals: 3
Clubs: Reading, Headington United

Robert Edward Odell (also sometimes spelt O'Dell) played two League games for Reading, where he came through the juniors, in the 1953–54 season before his move to Headington.

ODHIAMBO-ANACLET, Eddie

Right-back/Right-winger
Born: 31 August 1985, Arusha (Tanzania)
United debut: 12 August 2006 v Halifax Town
Final United game: 26 April 2008 v Ebbsfleet United
Appearances: 79+6
Goals: 6

Clubs: Southampton, Chester City (loan), Yeovil Town (loan), Tamworth (loan), Oxford United, Stevenage Borough, Newport County, Gateshead

Edward Bahati Obara Odhiambo-Anaclet was a member of Oxford United's Academy, but it was at Southampton where he completed his football education. Although he did not play for the Saints he did make one substitute appearance on loan to Chester in December 2004. The pacey full-back had a non-playing loan with Yeovil before joining Tamworth on loan in July 2005, where he made eight appearances. He joined Oxford in the 2006 close season, making his U's debut in their first game as a Conference club, and featured regularly over the next two campaigns. Odhiambo-Anaclet was given a free transfer by United in May 2008, whereupon he joined fellow Conference outfit Stevenage, and in June 2009 he changed his surname to Anaclet in deference to his late father. He scored three goals in just 42 appearances for Borough, finding it difficult to displace the first-team regulars, and he was given a free transfer after the Broadhall Way side won promotion to the Football League. Anaclet joined Newport County in June 2010, playing 34 games without scoring and in June 2011 he moved to Gateshead.

O'DOWD, Adrian

Striker
Born: 16 September 1959, Solihull
United debut: 1 March 1980 v Sheffield Wednesday
Final United game: 20 August 1980 v Exeter City
Appearances: 9+2
Goals: 1
Clubs: Aston Villa, Oxford United, Alvechurch, Moor Green, Kidderminster Harriers, Aylesbury United, Bromsgrove Rovers, Banbury United

Adrian Gregory O'Dowd started his career with Aston Villa, with whom he played in the 1978 FA Youth Cup Final, in a 1–0 aggregate defeat by Crystal Palace. Although he failed to make the Villa first team, he was signed by Oxford in February 1980 but despite a few appearances he failed to set the Manor alight, scoring just one goal, and he was given a free transfer in October 1980. O'Dowd joined Alvechurch and in 1981 he was Moor Green's record signing when they paid £1,000 for him. He joined Kidderminster and played for them at Wembley in the FA Trophy against Burton Albion in May 1987. That game ended 1–1 but Kidderminster won the replay 2–1 at the Hawthorns. In 1988 O'Dowd moved to Aylesbury United, where he scored three goals in 22 games and the next season he was on Bromsgrove's books.

ODUBADE, Yemi

Forward
Born: 4 July 1984, Lagos (Nigeria)
United debut: 28 January 2006 v Rushden & Diamonds
Final United game: 26 April 2009 v Northwich Victoria
Appearances: 87+71
Goals: 31
Clubs: Yeovil Town, Eastbourne United, Eastbourne Borough, Oxford United, Stevenage Borough, Newport County (loan), Gateshead

Yemi Odubade was signed for Oxford by Brian Talbot in the January 2006 transfer window for £25,000 after impressing against United for Eastbourne

Borough in the first round of the FA Cup. His days looked numbered after Jim Smith became manager and declared himself distinctly unimpressed with Odubade, but hard work and his electric pace soon made the diminutive striker the first name on the team sheet. He was elected the Supporters' Player of the Season for 2006–07. However, his form dipped in the middle of the 2007–08 season, and he was placed on the transfer list. This gave him the necessary incentive, and he returned to the side revitalised, finishing the season as top scorer and one of the main sources of assists for his colleagues' goals. He was rewarded by being removed from the transfer list. The following season Odubade's inconsistency continued, with the result that he was released at the end of the 2008–09 season and signed for Stevenage Borough. He finished as Borough's top scorer in his first season and Stevenage won promotion to the Football League at the end of his second season. However, by this time his appearances were becoming more sporadic and in January 2011 he moved to Newport County on loan until the end of the season as part of the deal that took Craig Reid to Stevenage. Odubade played 59 games and scored 15 goals for Stevenage. In June 2011 Odubade moved north to sign for Conference side Gateshead having scored one goal in just 11 appearances. Odubade was born in Nigeria but brought up in Eastbourne, starting his career in 2002 with Eastbourne Town. He scored 70 goals in two seasons in the Sussex County League before Yeovil signed him in July 2004 after he impressed in a trial. However, he played just six games, scoring once, for the Glovers before returning to Eastbourne in February 2005 for personal reasons to sign for Borough and continue with his driving job. Odubade managed 20 goals in 40 games for Borough before his move to Oxford.

OLDFIELD, David

Forward
Born: 30 May 1968, Perth (Australia)
United debut: 10 August 2002 v Bury
Final United game: 30 August 2003 v Kidderminster Harriers
Clubs: Luton Town, Manchester City, Leicester City, Millwall (loan), Luton Town, Stoke City, Peterborough United, Oxford United, Stafford Rangers, Tamworth, Brackley Town

David Charles Oldfield joined United from Peterborough United in the summer of 2002 as a direct replacement for Paul Moody, although with the added extra of the coaching ability that he brought with him. He took up a player-coach role briefly after the departure of Mike Ford in February 2003, and in the summer of that year Oldfield was appointed as Ian Atkins' assistant. Oldfield was appointed caretaker manager following Atkins' departure, but his only game in charge, at Mansfield, was abandoned at half-time. He was retained as a coach by both Graham Rix and later Ramón Díaz, and was caretaker manager for the final game of the 2005–06 season against Chester City following the departure of Díaz. He had also taken charge of first-team affairs on a few occasions while Díaz and Horacio Rodriguez were unavailable during the preceding months. In March 2006 Brian Talbot informed Oldfield that his presence was no longer required at matches and he left the club, signing for Stafford Rangers in July 2006 as player-assistant manager, making 23 appearances before moving to Tamworth in November 2007. Four days later he became Brackley's manager. In 2008 he joined Peterborough as reserves and youth team manager, becoming caretaker for one game in January 2011. Oldfield started with Luton, signing professionally in 1986 and winning his one England Under-21 cap in 1988. In March 1989 Manchester City paid £600,000 for him, but 10 months later he moved to Leicester for £150,000. Apart from a spell on loan with Millwall in February 1995 he was with Leicester until July 1995, at which stage he returned to Luton for £150,000. In 1998 he joined Stoke and remained there until March 2000 when he moved to Peterborough.

OLDHAM, Eric

Full-back
Born: 27 June 1933, Newcastle upon Tyne
Died: February 1995
United debut: 20 September 1958 v Windsor & Eton
Final United game: 18 October 1958 v Maidenhead United
Appearances: 3
Clubs: Seaton Delaval, Bolton Wanderers, Gateshead, Headington United, Kidderminster Harriers, Hartlepools United

Eric Oldham started his football career with the Tyneside village team of Seaton Delaval. He was signed by Bolton Wanderers in 1953 but did not play in the Football League for them, and in 1956 he returned to the North East to play for Gateshead. He played 53 games in the Football League for the Heed before moving down south to play for Headington United. Oldham's next stop was Kidderminster, from where he joined Hartlepools United in 1959, where he played 12 games.

OMOYINMI, Manny

Forward
Born: 28 December 1977, Lagos (Nigeria)
United debut: 12 August 2000 v Peterborough United
Final United game: 1 May 2004 v Macclesfield Town (sub)
Appearances: 37+40
Goals: 9
Clubs: West Ham United, AFC Bournemouth (loan), Dundee United (loan), Leyton Orient (loan), Gillingham (loan), Scunthorpe United (loan), Barnet (loan), Oxford United, Margate (loan), Margate (loan), Gravesend & Northfleet (loan), Gravesend & Northfleet, Lewes, Worthing, Worthing, Plateau United (Nigeria)

Emmanual Omoyinmi earned fame for the wrong reasons, when he appeared for West Ham in a Worthington Cup quarter-final tie as a substitute against Aston Villa which the Hammers won on penalties after a 2–2 draw. However, Omoyinmi had played in a second-round tie against Bolton while on loan at Gillingham and was therefore ineligible to play for West Ham. The Football League ordered the tie to be replayed, with Villa winning; the error caused West Ham secretary Graham Mackrell to resign. Omoyinmi, a West Ham supporter, played for England Schoolboys in a 2–1 defeat by Scotland in March 1993 while at Newham. He joined West Ham as a trainee and in September 1996 he played seven games on loan to Bournemouth. Omoyinmi's next loan spell was with Dundee United in February 1998, when he made five appearances, and in March 1999 he scored one goal in four games for Leyton Orient. In September 1999 came his ill-fated loan to Gillingham, where he played 11 games and scored three goals, including one against Oxford at the Manor. As a result of the

Worthington Cup affair, Omoyinmi received death threats from West Ham fans, so the club loaned him to Scunthorpe in December 1999 where he scored once in seven matches. A six-game loan with Barnet in February 2000 yielded no goals and in June 2000 Omoyinmi joined Oxford on a free transfer, having made 13 appearances for West Ham, scoring twice. With Oxford Omoyinmi displayed electric pace although his inconsistency meant he was often a substitute. As he gradually faded from the first team, Omoyinmi went on loan to Margate in September 2003, scoring three goals in 11 games, and he returned to the Kent side in January 2004 for a further three matches, in which he scored twice. Gravesend & Northfleet was Omoyinmi's next port of call, joining on loan from Oxford in February 2004 to score twice in seven matches. After a brief return to the Kassam he joined Gravesend permanently in May 2004, going on to score six goals in 35 games. In December 2005 Omoyinmi's contract was cancelled and he signed for Lewes until the end of the season. In September 2006 he made the short move to Worthing where he played a couple of games. After a spell out of the game he rejoined Worthing in July 2008 and most recently he was back in Nigeria, playing for Plateau United.

OSBORNE, Karleigh

Centre-back
Born: 19 March 1988, Southall
United debut: 2 September 2008 v Northwich Victoria
Final United game: 27 September 2008 v Lewes
Appearances: 6
Clubs: Brentford, Hayes (loan), Oxford United (loan), Eastbourne Borough (loan)

Karleigh Anthony Jonathan Osborne joined Oxford on loan from Brentford, making some commanding performances in the centre of defence. As a youngster Osborne joined Hayes on loan in March 2006, having made his Brentford debut the previous May. On his return to Griffin Park he was occasionally made team captain before his loan to Oxford. Almost immediately that his Oxford loan expired Osborne joined Eastbourne Borough on loan, scoring one goal in his three matches, after which he returned to the Bees to help them to promotion to League One in 2009.

O'SULLIVAN, Cyril

Goalkeeper
Born: 22 February 1920, Lewisham
Died: March 2003
United debut: 17 October 1951 v Guildford City
Final United game: 20 October 1951 v Llanelly
Appearances: 2
Clubs: Crown Villa, Reading, Gillingham, Headington United

Cyril John O'Sullivan joined Reading in September 1946 and went on to play 41 games for the Biscuitmen. He later moved to Southern League Gillingham, where he played one game, in the 1948–49 season. O'Sullivan died in Oxford in March 2003.

OTTER, Peter

Goalkeeper
Born: 1935, Hendon
United debut: 11 April 1955 v Hereford United
Final United game: 30 March 1959 v Kidderminster Harriers
Appearances: 58
Clean sheets: 11
Clubs: Headington United

Peter F. Otter turned professional with Headington in 1956, having played locally.

P

PAGE, Malcolm

Right-back
Born: 5 February 1947, Knucklas, Wales
United debut: 21 February 1981 v Gillingham
Final United game: 24 October 1981 v Southend United
Appearances: 18
Goals: 1
Clubs: Birmingham City, Oxford United

Malcolm Edward Page was an apprentice with Birmingham City, where he arrived in 1964 having been spotted playing in Wales Schoolboy internationals. He was a regular in the side that reached the FA Cup semi-finals in 1968 and in 1972 Page was a member of the side that won promotion from Division Two and again reached the FA Cup semi-finals, an achievement matched three years later. Page was captain of both Birmingham City and Wales, for whom he won 28 caps (in addition to six Under-23 caps), making him Birmingham's most-capped player until 2005. His versatility meant that he played in every outfield position, but despite preferring to play in midfield he settled as right-back. After scoring 10 goals in 391 appearances for the Blues, Page moved to Oxford in February 1981, but a knee injury ended his career and in February 1982 he retired. He then moved into insurance before working for a civil engineering firm.

PARKER, Bernard

Full-back
Born: 1931, Abingdon
United debut: 31 October 1953 v Bedford Town
Final United game: 6 October 1956 v Hastings United
Appearances: 31
Clubs: Headington United

Bernard G.H. Parker, nicknamed Chick, was a local discovery.

PARKER, Terry

Midfielder
Born: 20 December 1983, Southampton
United debut: 7 August 2004 v Boston United (sub)
Final United game: 25 September 2004 v Bury
Appearances: 6+3
Clubs: Portsmouth, Oxford United, Farnborough (loan), Weymouth, Dorchester Town

Terence James Parker joined United from Portsmouth during the 2004 close season. He started as a trainee with Pompey in 2003, but had not featured in their first team by the time of his move. Parker rarely featured in the Oxford side and in March 2005 he joined Farnborough on loan, playing three games. In July 2005 Parker was convicted of assault following a brawl in a pub in Southampton. Although he pleaded not guilty a jury disagreed and Parker

was sentenced to 18 months in prison, it being his second offence. He became the first United player to be convicted while with the club and his contract at United was immediately terminated. Upon his release he joined Weymouth but his chances were limited and he was let go in May 2006. Parker then joined Dorchester Town where he played 21 games, but in September 2007 he required an operation on a hernia and when he failed to return to fitness he was released in January 2008.

PARKS, Tony

Goalkeeper
Born: 26 January 1963, Hackney
United debut: 11 October 1986 v Coventry City
Final United game: 8 November 1986 v Manchester United
Appearances: 5
Clean sheets: 3
Clubs: Tottenham Hotspur, Oxford United (loan), Gillingham (loan), Brentford, Queen's Park Rangers (loan), Fulham, West Ham United, Stoke City, Falkirk, Blackpool, Burnley, Doncaster Rovers (loan), Barrow (loan), Barrow, Scarborough, Halifax Town

Anthony Parks joined Spurs as a youngster and was a regular in the youth and reserves teams until a bad injury to Ray Clemence gave Parks his first-team debut in January 1984. A further injury to Clemence gave Parks the opportunity to play in the 1984 UEFA Cup Final against Anderlecht, in which the goalkeeper saved two penalties in the shoot-out to win the Cup for Tottenham. However, this was not enough to secure a regular first-team place and Parks went on loan, initially to Oxford who wanted to sign him permanently, but Spurs wanted Parks to replace Clemence until they signed Bobby Mimms. In September 1987 Parks spent two games on loan with Gillingham and after 48 games for Spurs he signed for Steve Perryman's Brentford in August 1988 for £60,000. Parks was with Brentford for almost three years, playing 91 games, and had a non-playing loan spell with QPR in August 1990. In March 1991 he moved to Fulham where he played just two games, but he stayed in London by signing for West Ham United in August 1991. Parks made just nine appearances for the Hammers in his season at the Boleyn, after which he moved to Stoke in August 1992 where he played three games. Parks' next move was to be the longest, both in time and distance, of his career as he signed for Falkirk in October 1992 and stayed with the Bairns for almost four years, making 128 appearances. He returned to England in September 1996, signing for Blackpool where he stayed for nine months without playing a first-team game. Parks signed a monthly contract with Burnley in August 1997, playing two games before a six-match loan spell with Doncaster Rovers in February 1998. Parks moved to Conference side Barrow on loan in September 1998, with the deal being made permanent the following month, and he played 23 times for them. He returned to the Football League with Scarborough in February 1999, playing 15 games before joining Halifax in July 1999 as player-coach, although he played just nine times. He also had two spells as caretaker manager at the Shay in 2000 and 2001 before leaving to become goalkeeping coach at Crewe Alexandra. After doing some part-time work at the FA, Parks joined the organisation in October 2002 as assistant national goalkeeping coach. In November 2008 Parks was appointed goalkeeping coach at Tottenham Hotspur.

PARSONS, Roy

Left-back
United debut: 9 March 1957 v Bath City
Final United game: 22 April 1957 v Chelmsford City
Appearances: 9
Clubs: Headington United

Roy Parsons was a local discovery.

PATON, Danny

Inside-forward
Born: 27 January 1936, Breich, Midlothian
Died: March 2011
United debut: 29 August 1964 v Barrow
Final United game: 7 November 1964 v Aldershot
Appearances: 2
Goals: 1
Clubs: Woodmuir Colliery, Newtongrange Star, Heart of Midlothian, Yeovil Town (loan), Oxford United, Bedford Town, Cambridge City, Washington Darts (USA), Atlanta Chiefs (USA)

Robert Simpson Reid Paton, known as Danny, was spotted by Heart of Midlothian while working and playing for Woodmuir Colliery. He was farmed out to Newtongrange Star and won the Edinburgh & District Junior League (Mid & East Division) in both 1952–53 and 1954–55 before turning professional in November 1956, for which Newtongrange received £200. Paton returned to Tynecastle in May 1957 and made his debut the following season, making three appearances as Hearts won the Scottish League title. In the summer of 1959 Paton was called-up for National Service, serving in the Army at Houndstone Camp near Yeovil, who he joined on loan. Over two seasons Paton scored 41 goals in 94 games and also played representative games for the Army. He returned to Hearts and was a key member of the side that won the Scottish League Cup Final against Kilmarnock in October 1962. After suffering a knee injury Paton was released in April 1964, having scored 34 goals in 81 games for Hearts. He joined Oxford but failed to make the breakthrough into the first team, and was released in January 1965, when he joined Bedford Town. After a number of years with the Eagles, Paton joined Cambridge City, after which he tried his luck in the United States, joining NASL side Washington Darts in 1970. He played 20 games for the Darts over two seasons before joining Atlanta Chiefs (later Apollos) for whom he made 25 appearances and scored two goals.

PATTERSON, Darren

Centre-back
Born: 15 October 1969, Belfast
United debut: 17 February 2001 v Bury
Final United game: 1 April 2002 v York City
Appearances: 20
Goals: 1
Clubs: West Bromwich Albion, Wigan Athletic, Crystal Palace, Luton Town, Preston North End (loan), Dundee Utd, York City, Oxford United

Darren James Patterson started his playing career at West Bromwich Albion, who he joined in July 1988, but he left for Wigan Athletic in April 1989 without playing a game for the Baggies. Patterson played 124 games for Wigan, scoring 10 goals, which earned him a £225,000 move to Crystal Palace in July 1992. Patterson played 32 games for the London club, including their FA Cup semi-final defeat by Manchester United. Patterson earned his first Northern Ireland cap in 1994 and scored one goal in his time at Selhurst Park before Luton Town paid £230,000 for him. In his three seasons at Kenilworth Road, Patterson made 66 appearances without getting on the score sheet. He also had a two-game loan spell at Preston North End. In July 1998 he joined Dundee United, where he played 38 games and scored one goal. In May 2000 he left Tannadice Park, and in December he signed a three-month contract with York City. Towards the end of his contract, on 14 February 2001, Patterson was David Kemp's first signing as Oxford boss. Patterson played his final game in April 2002. Injury had cut short his playing career, and at the end of the 2002–03 season he left the club. After featuring in a couple of pre-season friendlies, Patterson returned to Oxford in September 2002 as youth-team coach. In November 2004 Patterson was appointed caretaker manager after Graham Rix was relieved of his managerial duties. He was in charge for three games before Argentinian Ramón Díaz was announced as the new manager and Patterson returned to coaching the youth team. In March 2006, after David Oldfield's departure, Patterson looked after the reserve team, and just a week later, when Brian Talbot was sacked, he was placed in charge of the first team and given a contract until the end of the following season. When Nick Merry was installed as chairman and brought in Jim Smith as manager, Patterson returned to his former job as youth team coach. In 2006–07 he guided the youth team to the Puma Youth Alliance South West Conference title without losing a game, and in April 2007 Smith appointed him assistant manager following the departures of Andy Awford and Shaun North. In November 2007 Patterson was appointed manager again. A 2–0 defeat at Torquay United in the FA Cup in November 2008 led to Patterson's dismissal. Patterson was appointed head of the Bristol Rovers youth programme in May 2009 and he became assistant manager in May 2010. In December 2010 he was made caretaker manager for just under a month, until David Penney was appointed manager in January 2011, at which point Patterson returned to coaching the youth team. In June 2011 Patterson was appointed assistant manager to Andy Scott at Rotherham United.

*PAYNE, Josh

Midfielder
Born: 25 November 1990, Basingstoke
United debut: 31 August 2010 v Aldershot Town
Final United game: 7 May 2011 v Shrewsbury Town
Appearances: 25+4
Goals: 1
Clubs: West Ham United, Cheltenham Town (loan), Colchester United (loan), Wycombe Wanderers (loan), Doncaster Rovers, Oxford United

Joshua James Payne arrived on a one-month loan, later extended until January 2011, from Doncaster Rovers on 31 August 2010, which was transfer deadline day. In October 2010 the loan deal was made permanent. Payne started as a youth with Portsmouth and then Southampton before moving to West Ham in early 2007. He was made the captain of the Hammers' Under-18s and then promoted to the youth team, managed by Alex Dyer. In

September 2008 he joined Cheltenham on loan, scoring on his debut and getting sent off in his second game, going on to play 13 games for the Robins without scoring again. Payne made his West Ham debut in March 2009 and went on loan to Colchester in October 2009, where he played three games. In January 2010 Payne had a three-game loan with Wycombe, where he scored once before leaving for Doncaster in July 2010, having played three matches for the Hammers. Payne's Doncaster career was brief but successful, as he scored on his only appearance for the club in the Carling Cup against Accrington in August, just a fortnight before his move to Oxford.

PEART, Bob

Centre-forward
Born: 17 December 1926, Swindon
Died: 1966
United debut: 7 March 1953 v Merthyr Tydfil
Final United game: 26 April 1954 v Llanelly
Appearances: 38
Goals: 15
Clubs: Pinehurst, Burnley, Swindon Town, Yeovil Town, Headington United, Cheltenham Town

Robert Charles Peart joined Headington from Yeovil, where he scored 13 goals in his season at the Huish. Peart had joined the Glovers from Swindon in 1952, having scored five goals in 13 games for the Robins. He had previously been with Burnley, although he did not play any games for the Clarets and did not turn professional until his move to the County Ground.

PEMBERY, Gordon

Wing-half
Born: 10 October 1929, Cardiff
United debut: 24 August 1957 v Cheltenham Town
Final United game: 3 May 1958 v Yeovil Town
Appearances: 18
Clubs: Cardiff Nomads, Norwich City, Cardiff City, Torquay United, Charlton Athletic, Swindon Town, Headington United, Merthyr Tydfil, Nuneaton Borough

Gordon Denis Pembery joined Headington United from Swindon Town in the summer of 1957. He began his professional career with Norwich City in 1947, where he made just one League appearance before returning to Cardiff to join the Bluebirds. After just one League game he moved to Torquay in 1950, where he established himself in the side and played 55 games, in which he scored seven goals. Charlton bought him in 1952 and he scored one goal in his 18 Football League appearances before he joined Swindon in June 1956. Pembery scored twice in his 39 games for Swindon before his move to Headington.

PENNEY, David

Midfielder
Born: 17 August 1964, Wakefield
United debut: 19 August 1989 v Plymouth Argyle
Final United game: 12 February 1994 v Charlton Athletic
Appearances: 91+38

Goals: 16

Clubs: Pontefract Collieries, Derby County, Oxford United, Swansea City (loan), Swansea City, Cardiff City, Doncaster Rovers

David Mark Penney was a bricklayer for five years while playing for Pontefract before he signed for Derby County for £1,500 in September 1985. The busy midfielder made just 29 appearances in his four years at the Baseball Ground, scoring three goals, before his £175,000 move to Oxford, switching from father Robert Maxwell to son Kevin Maxwell. Penney spent over four years at the Manor, becoming an integral part of the midfield and moving to Swansea for £20,000 midway through Oxford's relegation season, in March 1994. He had already played 12 games on loan to the Swans in March 1991, in which he scored three goals, when he helped the side to win the Welsh Cup. In his second spell with the Swans Penney played 139 games in just over three years, scoring 23 goals. In July 1997 he moved to Cardiff for an undisclosed five-figure fee after Swansea had demanded £100,000 for his signature; he was immediately installed as team captain at Ninian Park. Penney was with Cardiff until August 1998, playing 44 games in which he scored five goals. He then joined Doncaster, in their first season in the Conference. Towards the end of the 1999–2000 season Penney was appointed joint caretaker player-manager and became Steve Wignall's assistant after saving Rovers from the threat of relegation. He became the reserve team coach and when Wignall left in January 2002 he became full-time manager, hanging up his boots at the end of the season having played 96 games for Doncaster, scoring 19 goals. Doncaster won the Conference Cup in 1999 and 2000, and in 2003 Penney guided Donny back to the Football League with a Play-off win; a David Morley goal helping Rovers beat Dagenham & Redbridge 3–2 after extra-time in the first season that Play-offs were used to decide the Conference's second promotion place. The following season Penney led Doncaster to the Third Division title and they remained in League One until Penney left in August 2006; in his final season he appointed Mickey Lewis, who played alongside at both Derby and Oxford, to be his assistant and was voted League One Coach of the Year. Penney took over the management of Darlington in October 2006, assisted by his former Oxford midfield partner Martin Gray, and in 2008 Darlington reached the League Two Play-offs but lost to Rochdale. In February 2009 Darlington went into administration and Penney left for Oldham in April 2009, taking Gray with him. In May 2010, with one game of the season remaining, Penney was sacked by Oldham and Gray took temporary charge. In January 2011 Penney took over from caretaker manager Darren Patterson as boss of Bristol Rovers, but in March 2011 he was dismissed after just two wins in 13 matches.

PERRY, Ross

Centre-back

Born: 7 February 1990, Falkirk
United debut: 29 August 2009 v AFC Wimbledon (sub)
Final United game: 8 December 2009 v Barrow
Appearances: 5+7
Clubs: Rangers, Oxford United (loan), Falkirk (loan)

Ross Perry joined Oxford on loan from Rangers in August 2009 at the same time as fellow Rangers youth player Steve Kinniburgh. At the time Perry had

yet to play for the Gers first team, although he had played for Scotland Under-17s against Armenia in September 2006. Although occasionally Perry looked the part, at times he also looked vulnerable and inexperienced. In September 2009 Perry was called-up for Scotland Under-21s and he won his first two Under-21 caps while with Oxford when he played against Belarus in October 2009 and in Azerbaijan the next month. He won a third Under-21 cap in March 2010. In February 2011 he joined Falkirk on loan.

PERRYMAN, Steve

Centre-back
Born: 21 December 1951, Ealing
United debut: 29 March 1986 v Queen's Park Rangers
Final United game: 11 October 1986 v Coventry City
Appearances: 17
Clubs: Tottenham Hotspur, Oxford United, Brentford

Stephen John Perryman had an illustrious career with Tottenham before his move to Oxford in March 1986. As a youth he played for the Ealing Schools' FA XI, Middlesex SFA, and the London Schools' FA. Perryman joined Spurs as an apprentice in July 1967 and turned professional in January 1969, making his League debut aged 17. He won four England Schools caps, four England Youth caps, and a record 17 England Under-23 caps. When he was just 20 years old Perryman was made captain of Spurs. At this stage he played mainly as a ball-winning midfielder, although his versatility allowed him to play in the centre of defence, as a sweeper, and also at right-back. In 1971 Perryman won the League Cup with the north London club, who beat Aston Villa 2–0 at Wembley, and in the following year Tottenham beat Wolves on aggregate in the two-legged UEFA Cup Final. In 1973 Tottenham won the League Cup again, beating Norwich 1–0, and in 1974 Spurs again reached the UEFA Cup Final, losing to Feyenoord 4–2 on aggregate. In 1981 Perryman captained Tottenham to the FA Cup Final, beating Manchester City 3–2 in a replay after a 1–1 draw. They won the FA Cup again the following season, beating QPR in the Final, again in a replay. In 1982 Perryman won his only full England cap, in a World Cup warm-up game in Iceland. That year the Football Writers' Association awarded Perryman the Footballer of the Year title. Also in 1982 Spurs reached the Milk Cup Final, in which they were beaten 3–1 by Liverpool, and two years later they beat Anderlecht in the UEFA Cup Final, winning the penalty shoot-out after both legs were drawn. By the time he joined Oxford Perryman had played 866 games for Spurs, scoring 39 goals, and he was awarded an MBE for services to football in 1984. His arrival at the Manor helped United avoid relegation in their first top-flight season, and at the start of the 1986–87 season Perryman was installed as captain, but in October 1986 he left to become player-assistant manager at Brentford. On New Year's Day 1987 Perryman became player-manager, completing 67 games for the Bees before hanging up his boots when he resigned as manager in August 1990. He did some scouting for Middlesbrough before becoming Watford's manager in December 1990, saving them from relegation. Perryman resigned in the summer of 1993 and became assistant manager to Ossie Ardiles at Tottenham, acting as caretaker manager for one game in November 1994 following Ardiles' dismissal, after which Perryman was also sacked. He had a brief spell as manager of Norwegian side IK Start in 1995 and in 1996 he rejoined Ardiles as his assistant at Japanese side Shimizu S-Pulse. In

September S-Pulse won the Nabisco Cup (the J League's equivalent of the League Cup), the club's first honour. In 1999 Ardiles left and Perryman was appointed manager. He took S-Pulse to the Final of the Emperor's Cup and later that season they won their first League title in Japan's split-league system, but lost to Jubilo Iwata in the Championship Play-off in a penalty shoot-out. Perryman was named the J League Manager of the Year for 1999 and the following year the side won the Asian Cup Winners' Cup. After five years in Japan Perryman returned to England in 2000 and helped out at Exeter City, returning to Japan to manage Kashiwa Reysol in 2001. He became Exeter's director of football in 2003.

PETERS, Peter

Goalkeeper
Born: Sydney (Australia)
United debut: 19 February 1958 v Gravesend & Northfleet
Final United game: 11 April 1960 v Nuneaton Borough
Appearances: 22
Clean sheets: 4
Clubs: Reading, Canterbury, Darlington, West Ham United, Margate, Headington United

A 6ft goalie who was born in Sydney, Australia and emigrated to England at the age of four. He started his football career with Reading, for whom he made two appearances during 1945–46 and also one appearance in the FA Cup. He joined Canterbury City in 1947 and in January 1949 he moved to West Ham United, where he spent several seasons but failed to make the first team. He joined Margate in the summer of 1952, going on to keep 52 clean sheets in 211 appearances while working as a carpenter before joining Headington in February 1958. At the time he was rated as Margate's best ever 'keeper. He returned to Australia in 1962.

PETTEFER, Carl

Midfielder
Born: 22 March 1981, Taplow
United debut: 12 August 2006 v Halifax Town
Final United game: 20 January 2006 v Exeter City
Appearances: 58+15
Goals: 1
Clubs: Portsmouth, Exeter City (loan), Southend United (loan), Southend United, Oxford United, AFC Bournemouth, Bognor Regis Town, AFC Totton

Carl James Pettefer arrived from Southend United in the summer of 2006, and rapidly established himself as a high-quality midfielder. Injury interrupted his season, and he failed to re-establish himself in the side. When Darren Patterson took over as manager from Jim Smith, Pettefer found himself on the transfer list, and he was then released in April 2008. He joined Bournemouth on a monthly contract in August 2008, but after just two substitute appearances he was released and signed for Bognor Regis in September 2008, at the same time as Chris Tardif. In January 2009 Pettefer was released because of Bognor's financial situation and he signed for AFC Totton. Pettefer started his career as a trainee with Portsmouth in 1999 and he had a lengthy loan spell with Exeter, starting in October 2002, where he played 37 games and scored one goal. He joined Southend on loan in February 2004 in a move which was made permanent in May when he was released by Portsmouth, after making just three appearances for Pompey, at the same time as Tardif and Terry Parker. In May 2006, after 84 games in which he scored one goal, Pettefer was released by Southend, joining Oxford shortly afterwards in time to play in the side's first match in the Conference.

PHILLIPS, Jimmy

Left-back
Born: 8 February 1966, Bolton
United debut: 27 August 1988 v Leeds United
Final United game: 13 March 1990 v Ipswich Town
Appearances: 89
Goals: 7
Clubs: Bolton Wanderers, Rangers, Oxford United, Middlesbrough, Bolton Wanderers

James Neil Phillips was Graeme Souness's first signing after he became manager of Rangers, paying £95,000 for the exciting left-back who had played 137 games and scored two goals for Bolton after coming through the youth ranks at his home-town club. In August 1988, after just 36 games for Rangers, Phillips was sold to Oxford for £150,000, and he quickly established himself as a top-quality full-back. In March 1990 Middlesbrough paid £250,000 for Phillips and he went on to play 170 games, scoring eight goals, before he returned to Bolton in another £250,000 move. Phillips was with the Trotters for almost eight years in his second spell with the club, making 274 appearances and scoring six goals before he hung up his boots in June 2001. He then worked as a coach with the club's youth academy before taking over the reserve team in the summer of 2005, while continuing as youth coach. In April 2008 Phillips became the director of the Bolton Academy.

PHILLIPS, Les

Midfielder
Born: 7 January 1963, Lambeth
United debut: 24 March 1984 v Plymouth Argyle (sub)
Final United game: 3 April 1993 v Brentford
Appearances: 208+16
Goals: 15
Clubs: Birmingham City, Oxford United, Northampton Town, Marlow, Oxford City, Banbury United

Leslie Michael Phillips joined Birmingham City in 1980, making his debut two years later. He scored three goals in 44 League games before moving to Oxford in March 1984. Phillips was an occasional player during the successive Championships of 1984 and 1985, but started to become a regular first-teamer in September 1985, becoming an essential component of the team that won the 1986 Milk Cup Final and scoring some vital goals that both took Oxford to Wembley and ensured their First Division survival. In the summer of 1993 Phillips joined Northampton Town, where he played 32 games before joining Marlow in 1994. He was a member of the Marlow side that beat Oxford in the FA Cup first round in November 1994. The following season Phillips played for Oxford City, making his debut at Wembley in the FA Trophy Final 2–1 defeat against Arlesey in March 1996, before he moved to Banbury United after scoring one goal in his 13 games for the Hoops. In February 2008 Phillips became a scout for Oxford United, and later became a matchday greeter at the Kassam Stadium.

PHILLIPS, Lionel

Centre-forward
Born: 13 December 1929, Much Dewchurch, Herefordshire
United debut: 26 December 1955 v Kettering Town
Final United game: 12 January 1957 v Kidderminster Harriers
Appearances: 48
Goals: 25
Clubs: Yeovil Town, Portsmouth, Tonbridge, Margate, Headington United, Margate, Hastings United, Ramsgate, Tonbridge

Lionel Arthur Raymond Phillips joined Portsmouth from Yeovil in February 1953, although he was with Pompey for just 10 days in which he played four games, all heavy defeats. Phillips was then dropped by new manager Eddie Lever and he returned to non-League football with Tonbridge. After a spell with Margate, Phillips joined Headington United for £250, where he led the line for just over a year. In January 1957 Phillips rejoined Margate, scoring twice in the opening nine minutes of his comeback game. He scored 11 goals in his 15 appearances that season before joining Hastings United in a part-exchange deal. He then moved to Ramsgate before returning to Tonbridge in 1959.

PHILLIPS, Marcus

Midfielder
Born: 17 October 1973, Bradford-on-Avon
United debut: 4 March 1997 v Huddersfield Town (sub)
Final United game: 4 March 1997 v Huddersfield Town (sub)
Appearances: 0+1
Clubs: Swindon Town, Cheltenham Town, Gloucester City, FC Utrecht (Netherlands), Witney Town, Oxford United, Sydney United (Australia), Marconi Stallions (Australia), Olympic Sharks (Australia), Canberra Cosmos (Australia), Sengkang Marine FC (Malaysia), Brunei, Northern Spirit (Australia), Brunei, Blacktown City Demons (Australia), Geylang United (Singapore), Albany United (New Zealand), Auckland City (New Zealand), Waitakere United (New Zealand), Central United FC (New Zealand)

Marcus Stuart Phillips came through Swindon Town's youth set-up, but his only first-team appearance for the Robins was as a substitute in a League Cup tie against Torquay United. He was released in 1995 and after a brief spell with Cheltenham he scored six goals in 12 games for Gloucester, after which he had a spell in the Netherlands with Utrecht. He was released by the Dutch side in June 1996 after 12 appearances, and then had a period with Witney prior to his arrival at the Manor on trial in January 1997. Phillips' Oxford career was as undistinguished as his time with Swindon, and he made just one substitute appearance before leaving England for Australia, where he made 17 appearances for Sydney United and scored two goals. The following season he played for another Sydney-based club, Marconi Stallions, where he scored one goal in 23 games, and Phillips remained in Sydney the following season with Sydney Olympic, playing 16 games. In

2000 he moved to Canberra Cosmos, where he made 24 appearances before the club folded due to financial difficulties and he moved to Brunei, who played in the Malaysia Premier League. After a season with Brunei Phillips returned to Australia where he signed a short-term deal with Northern Spirit, back in Sydney. However, after just four games for the Spirit he returned to Brunei in March 2003, although he was back in Australia three months later when he joined New South Wales Premier League side Blacktown City Demons, for whom he scored three goals in 14 appearances. He then joined Singapore League side Geylang United, for whom he scored one goal as the side finished second in the S-League. Phillips continued his career in the South Pacific, moving to Albany United in New Zealand and then Auckland City for the 2004–05 season. Phillips' next stop was Waitakere United, also based in Auckland, where he remained until March 2010, at which point he joined Central United, who also played in the Auckland Football Federation's Lotto NRFL Mens' Premier League.

PHILLISKIRK, Danny

Striker
Born: 10 April 1991, Oldham
United debut: 7 August 2010 v Burton Albion (sub)
Final United game: 7 August 2010 v Burton Albion (sub)
Appearances: 0+1
Clubs: Oldham Athletic, Chelsea, Oxford United (loan), Sheffield United (loan), Sheffield United

Daniel Philliskirk joined Chelsea from Oldham Athletic in the summer of 2007, after which he earned three England Under-17 caps. In 2008–09 he captained the Chelsea youth team, while at the same time making several appearances for Chelsea's reserves. He joined Oxford on a one-month loan at the start of August 2010 but apart from a few pre-season games his only appearance for the U's was as a substitute in their first game in the Football League after gaining promotion from the Conference. Philliskirk returned to Chelsea but without playing for the Blues he went on loan to Sheffield United in January 2011, joining them permanently in July 2011.

PITT, Courtney

Left-winger
Born: 17 December 1981, Westminster
United debut: 27 March 2004 v Doncaster Rovers
Final United game: 1 May 2004 v Macclesfield Town
Appearances: 5+3
Clubs: Chelsea, Portsmouth, Luton Town (loan), Coventry City (loan), Oxford United, Boston United, Cambridge United, York City (loan), Weymouth, AFC Telford United

Courtney Leon Pitt started his career as a trainee with Chelsea, but he moved to Portsmouth in June 2001 without having played a first-team game for the Blues. Graham Rix was Pompey manager at the time and he paid a tribunal-determined fee of £200,000 plus add-ons. Pitt made 41 appearances for Portsmouth, scoring three goals, all in his first season at Fratton Park. After falling out of favour he had a loan spell with Luton Town in August 2003 in which he played 14 games and scored once, followed by a one-game loan to Coventry in December 2003. In March 2004 Pitt became Rix's first signing for Oxford, joining from Portsmouth for an undisclosed fee. His time at the Kassam was not a particularly happy one, and he was released at the end of the season, joining Boston in August 2004. In his year with the Pilgrims Pitt played 34 games and scored two goals, but he was released and joined Cambridge United on a short-term deal in September 2005. Pitt stayed at the Abbey for almost five years, making 165 appearances and contributing 16 goals. After the club's defeat to Exeter City in the Conference Play-off Final in 2008 he was released by Jimmy Quinn, but Quinn himself was sacked and his successor, Gary Brabin, brought Pitt back to Cambridge, where he remained until going on loan to York in January 2010. Pitt scored one goal and made 12 appearances for York, including a substitute cameo in the Minstermen's 3–1 defeat by Oxford in the Conference Play-off Final. After a trial with Wrexham Pitt signed for Zamaretto Southern Premier League side Weymouth in September 2010, at the same time as Rob Wolleaston joined the Terras, both on non-contract terms. However, Weymouth were unable to afford to keep him, so in November 2010 Pitt joined AFC Telford, again on non-contract terms.

*POTTER, Alfie

Winger
Born: 9 January 1989, Islington
United debut: 8 August 2009 v York City (sub)
Final United game: 7 May 2011 v Shrewsbury Town (sub)
Appearances: 36+35
Goals: 8
Clubs: AFC Wimbledon, Millwall, Peterborough United, Kvinesdal IL (Norway) (loan), Grays Athletic (loan), Havant & Waterlooville (loan), AFC Wimbledon (loan), Kettering Town (loan), Oxford United (loan), Oxford United

Alfie James Potter signed for Oxford on a season-long loan from Peterborough United in July 2009. At the end of the season Potter scored United's third goal in their 3–1 win over York in the 2010 Conference Play-off Final, after which he joined United for an undisclosed fee, alleged to be £50,000, on a two-year contract. Potter started his career with Wimbledon's Academy, but was released at the age of 14 and joined Millwall, where he was a regular in their youth team. He joined Peterborough and played for their youth side before signing professionally in June 2007, becoming their first Centre of Excellence product to become a professional. He was immediately loaned to Norwegian fourth division side Kvinesdal, but left without playing for them after he got homesick. In September 2007 Potter joined Grays Athletic on loan, but he made just one substitute appearance for them and in November 2007 he joined Havant & Waterlooville on loan. It was while with the Hawks that Potter shot to national fame when he scored against Liverpool in front of the Kop to put Havant 2–1 up in the FA Cup fourth round; although Liverpool won 5–2 Potter was voted as the Player of the Round. Potter returned to Peterborough to sign a two-year deal and in February 2008 he rejoined Wimbledon on loan where he scored one goal in four games. He joined Kettering on loan in August 2008 and he played 45 games in his season at Rockingham Road, scoring just one goal. By the time he signed for Oxford he had made just two substitute appearances for Peterborough.

POTTER, Tom

Right-back
United debut: 10 January 1953 v Yeovil Town
Final United game: 19 April 1954 v Tonbridge
Appearances: 27
Clubs: Headington United, Banbury United

Thomas Potter was a Scottish right-back who was captain of Headington's reserves when not in the first team.

POTTS, Henry

Winger
Born: 23 January 1925, Carlisle
United debut: 23 March 1950 v Lovell's Athletic
Final United game: 1 April 1950 v Hastings United
Appearances: 3
Clubs: Pegasus, Headington United, Northampton Town, Kettering Town

Henry James Potts was an England Amateur international who played for Headington while studying at Oxford University. He won the first of his eight caps in February 1950 and he also played four times for the university's cricket team in 1949 and five times the following summer, including getting his Blue against Cambridge. Potts, who studied at Keble College, also won his football Blue when he was captain of Oxford in the Varsity match in December 1949 that ended 2–2. In addition, Potts played three times for Lancashire's second XI in the 1949 Minor Counties Championship. After his brief cameo with Headington Potts signed for Northampton Town, where he made 10 Football League appearances before leaving for Kettering in 1951, in which year he was in the Pegasus team that beat Bishop Auckland 2–1 to win the Amateur Cup at Wembley; Potts scored the first Pegasus goal.

POWELL, Paul

Left-winger/Left-back
Born: 30 June 1978, Wallingford
United debut: 7 November 1995 v Barnet (sub)
Final United game: 1 April 2003 v Carlisle United (sub)
Appearances: 160+42
Goals: 23
Clubs: Oxford United, Ards (loan), Tamworth, Didcot Town, Brackley Town, Didcot Town, Hungerford Town, AFC Wallingford, Didcot Casuals

Paul Powell came through the ranks at Oxford, joining the club's YTS in 1994. He was a member of the side that won the Junior Floodlit Cup in May 1996 and he had already made his first-team debut by the time that he signed professionally in the summer of 1996, shortly after being named the Young Player of the Year. He joined Ards on loan in March 1997 and the following season he was called-up for England Under-21s for the Toulon Tournament, but was unable to play because of illness. Powell started with Oxford as a winger, but he was converted to left-back by Ian Atkins, who recalled him to the side after he had fallen out of favour with previous manager Mark Wright. By the time he left Oxford for Tamworth in August 2003, having been released at the end of the previous season, Powell had lost much of his pace and could only manage five games for the Lambs, in which he scored one goal. In September 2003 Powell signed for his local club Didcot Town, and was there until he followed manager Mike Ford to Brackley Town in June 2004. He was with Brackley for just four months, playing nine games, before returning to Loop Meadow to rejoin Didcot. Powell was a member of Didcot's FA Vase-winning side that beat AFC Sudbury 3–2 at White Hart Lane in May 2006. He scored 49 times in 196 appearances for the Railwaymen before joining Hungerford with dual registration in February 2008, at which point Didcot manager Stuart Peace claimed that Powell would not play for them again, having made his last appearance in December 2007. Powell also played for Wallingford in August 2008, but shortly afterwards returned to the fold at Didcot. In the spring of 2010 Powell made the transition to the Didcot Casuals side in the North Berks League.

PUFFET, Geoff

Centre-half
Born: 1939, Ploughley
United debut: 30 March 1960 v Kettering Town
Final United game: 30 March 1960 v Kettering Town
Appearances: 1
Clubs: Headington United

Geoffrey R Puffet was a local lad who made just one appearance for the first team after appearing in the pre-season trial in August 1959.

PURDIE, Jon

Left-winger
Born: 22 February 1967, Corby
United debut: 3 September 1988 v Brighton & Hove Albion (sub)
Final United game: 28 January 1989 v Manchester United
Appearances: 7+7
Clubs: Arsenal, Wolverhampton Wanderers, Cambridge United (loan), Oxford United, Brentford, Shrewsbury Town, Worcester City, Cheltenham Town, Kidderminster Harriers, Telford United, Bromsgrove Rovers, Kidderminster Harriers, Worcester City, Bilston Town

Jonathon Purdie was a gifted ball player who started as a junior with Arsenal and won England Youth honours. Initially a centre-forward, he converted to the wing and went on to play 103 games for Wolves, scoring 13 goals, before he was released in May 1988, having previously spent time on loan with Cambridge United where he scored two goals in seven League appearances. After leaving Oxford, Purdie joined Brentford, where he played six games in April 1989. He made 12 appearances for Shrewsbury, in which he scored one goal, up to December 1989, after which he joined Worcester City and then Conference side Cheltenham, where he made nine appearances. Purdie was at Kidderminster Harriers in 1992–93 and the following season, which was when he shot to fame by scoring the winner as the Harriers beat Birmingham City 2–1 at St Andrew's in January 1994, the same season that Kidderminster won the Conference. Purdie was released by Kidderminster and joined Telford, from where he moved to Bromsgrove Rovers in April 1998. He had a brief spell back at Kidderminster before rejoining Worcester in February 1999. Purdie was released by Worcester at the end of that season and in June 1999 he signed for Bilston, where he remained until he hung up his boots in December 2000. In 2002 Purdie, who had been involved in telecoms since leaving the full-time game, started his own company, The Independent Choice. In September 2010 he was appointed to be a coach for Wolves Under-14s.

*PURKISS, Ben

Right-back
Born: 1 April 1984, Sheffield
United debut: 21 August 2010 v Wycombe Wanderers (sub)
Final United game: 30 April 2011 v Lincoln City (sub)
Appearances: 22+4
Clubs: Sheffield United, Gainsborough Trinity, York City (loan), York City, Oxford United

Benjamin John Purkiss signed for Oxford on a two-year contract from York City in May 2010. Purkiss left school aged 16 and became an apprentice with Sheffield United. However, Purkiss was unable to break through into the first team and in July 2004 he moved to Gainsborough Trinity to play part-time while studying for his degree in French and law. In December 2003 Purkiss had a trial with Scunthorpe United, but he remained with Gainsborough until March 2007, playing 117 games and scoring one goal, although much of the 2005–06 season was disrupted by his time spent in France as part of his studies. In March 2007 Purkiss had an eight-game loan spell with York after which he signed permanently for the Minstermen. He had finished his degree by now, but signing full-time meant having to defer his legal practice course. Purkiss played in York's 2–0 FA Trophy Final defeat by Stevenage Borough at Wembley in May 2009, and also played against Oxford in York's 3–1 defeat in the Conference Play-off Final at Wembley in May 2010, after which he refused the offer of a new contract with York before signing for Oxford. However, he found it difficult to establish himself in United's Football League side and he was transfer-listed at the end of his first season. Purkiss was selected to represent GB in the World University Games in Izmir, Turkey in 2005 and in Belgrade, Serbia in July 2009, where he won a bronze medal. He was also called-up for the England C squad in February 2009 against Malta Under-21s, but had to withdraw through injury. In addition, Purkiss represented England at futsal in January 2004 in a preliminary round tie against Cyprus that the Cypriots won 8–4 in Albania.

PURSE, Darren

Centre-back
Born: 14 February 1977, Stepney
United debut: 3 September 1996 v Norwich City (sub)
Final United game: 7 February 1998 v Sheffield United
Appearances: 64+8
Goals: 7
Clubs: Leyton Orient, Oxford United, Birmingham City, West Bromwich Albion, Cardiff City, Sheffield Wednesday, Millwall

Darren John Purse joined Oxford from Leyton Orient in July 1996 for £100,000 having made 66 appearances for the O's and having scored five goals. At Oxford Purse eventually replaced Matt Elliott and went on to become a sought-after and cultured ball-playing centre-back, attracting the attention of Birmingham City, whose offer of £700,000 in February 1998 was too tempting for cash-strapped United to refuse. While with Birmingham Purse played against Liverpool in the 2001 Worthington Cup Final at Wembley; Purse scored Birmingham's 90th-minute penalty equaliser to make the score 1–1, but despite Purse scoring in the shoot-out the Blues lost on penalties. In June 2004, after playing 202 games and scoring 11 goals, Purse was signed by West Brom for £750,000. He was with the Baggies for just one season, playing 24 games, before Cardiff paid a similar sum to take him to Ninian Park in a move that required five City players to take wage cuts. Purse spent four years with the Bluebirds, playing 123 games and scoring 12 goals, before being released in July 2009, when he joined Sheffield Wednesday and was immediately made club captain. Purse made 71 appearances for the Owls, scoring three goals, before joining Millwall in January 2011 on a free transfer.

Q

QUARTERMAIN, Pat

Full-back
Born: 16 April 1937, Garsington
United debut: 24 September 1955 v Exeter City Reserves
Final United game: 27 March 1967 v Leyton Orient
Appearances: 304+1
Clubs: Headington United, Cambridge United

Patrick George Quartermain supplemented his footballing income by working as an apprentice toolmaker, but in 1958 he had to give both up to report for his National Service in Cyprus. Two years later he returned to his work and to Oxford United. Having turned from an amateur to a part-time professional in 1956, he became a full-time professional when United joined the Football League in 1962. In his 305 games for the U's Quartermain failed to score; however, in his single season at Cambridge United, Quartermain broke his duck in September 1967, scoring in a 4–1 win over Guildford City, in which Bud Houghton also scored twice.

QUINLAN, Eddie

Winger
Born: 15 August 1931, Finsbury Park
Died: 10 March 2008
United debut: 27 August 1949 v Colchester United
Final United game: 26 March 1951 v Tonbridge
Appearances: 3
Goals: 1
Clubs: Romford, Headington United, Great Yarmouth Town, Tottenham Hotspur, Reading, Worcester City, Dartford

Maurice Edward Quinlan joined Headington United shortly after the club started its first Southern League campaign, but he failed to break into the first team and in March 1951 he moved to Great Yarmouth. He was spotted by Spurs and signed for them in March 1952, going on to play 59 games for Tottenham's reserve, A and B teams between March 1952 and May 1953. In June 1953 Quinlan moved to Reading for £850 and he went on to play 53 games for the Royals, scoring 11 goals. In 1956 Quinlan left Elm Park and joined Worcester City, where he spent three seasons and scored 23 goals. He had a brief spell with Dartford in 1959 before retiring. He then ran a fruit and vegetable business in Reading for a number of years, was a keen golfer, and a member of the Reading Bridge Club.

QUINN, Barry

Midfielder/Defender
Born: 9 May 1979, Dublin
United debut: 3 March 2004 v York City
Final United game: 15 November 2008 v Grays Athletic
Appearances: 204+4
Goals: 6

Clubs: Manortown United (Ireland), Coventry City, Rushden & Diamonds (loan), Oxford United (loan), Oxford United, Brackley Town

Barry Scott Quinn signed permanently for United from Coventry in the summer of 2004, following a successful loan spell at the end of the previous season. Quinn started with Dublin side Manortown United, moving to Coventry in August 1996. Quinn played for the Republic of Ireland Under-18 team which won the European Championship in 1998, and was also capped 17 times at Under-21 and four times at full international levels. Quinn was a creative midfielder who made 91 appearances for the Sky Blues before his move to Oxford, which was preceded by a four-game loan with Rushden & Diamonds in January 2004. Quinn struggled in midfield during the 2005–06 season, when United were relegated to the Conference, although when he played at right-back he shone. Quinn was one of just three players to be offered a new contract for the 2006–07 season, and he signed another year-long deal the following summer, having won the Players' Player of the Season award for 2006–07. Quinn was made captain for the 2007–08 season, and in January 2008 he signed a one-year extension to his contract. He was released in April 2009 and after a spell out of the game he joined Brackley Town in July 2010.

QUINN, Rob

Midfielder
Born: 8 November 1976, Sidcup
United debut: 13 January 2001 v Walsall
Final United game: 2 March 2002 v Southend United (sub)
Appearances: 23+6
Goals: 2
Clubs: Crystal Palace, Brentford, Oxford United, Bristol Rovers, Stevenage Borough, Gravesend & Northfleet, AFC Wimbledon, Welling United, Cray Wanderers, Sevenoaks Town

Robert John Quinn arrived from Brentford as the makeweight in the deal that also brought Andy Scott to United in January 2001 for a combined fee of £150,000. Quinn had made 132 appearances for the Bees, scoring five goals, following his £40,000 move from Crystal Palace, where he started his career. While with Palace Quinn appeared in the First Division Play-off Final against Leicester City in May 1996, which Leicester won 2–1 after extra-time. Quinn played 29 games for Palace, scoring twice. Quinn failed to make much of an impact at Oxford and after the club's relegation to Division Three and move from the Manor he lost his midfield place to the altogether more effective Dean Whitehead. Quinn left for Ray Graydon's Bristol Rovers on a free transfer in August 2002 and was virtually an ever present until Ian Atkins took over, whereupon he was released in May 2004 and joined Conference side Stevenage Borough after 88 games for the Gas, in which he scored three goals. Quinn scored twice in 69 games for Borough before his move to Gravesend in June 2006. In May 2007 Quinn moved from the newly-renamed Ebbsfleet United to AFC Wimbledon, where he played 47 games and scored three goals before leaving for Welling in May 2008. He was with Welling for one season, becoming a full-time coach with the Welling Academy as well as setting up his own coaching company before leaving for Cray Wanderers, where he remained until joining Sevenoaks Town in the Kent League as player-coach in June 2010. In April 2011 Quinn stated that he was 95 per cent certain that he was going to stop playing at the end of the season to concentrate on coaching.

R

RAMSHAW, Frank

Full-back
Born: 20 June 1925, Oxhill, County Durham
Died: October 2003
United debut: 19 August 1950 v Bedford Town
Final United game: 1 February 1958 v Bedford Town
Appearances: 361
Goals: 1
Clubs: Sunderland, Headington United

Frank Ramshaw was signed in the summer of 1950 by Harry Thompson after he made a special scouting trip to watch Sunderland's reserves. He was made club captain for the 1952–53 season, and led the club to its first Southern League Championship when Headington won the League and Cup double in 1953. He also captained the side to a second Southern League Cup win the following season and was skipper for the momentous FA Cup run, also in 1953–54. Described as 'the most consistent and reliable performer in the history of the club', he was also considered the club's hardest-working member. He eventually retired on the advice of a specialist, aged 33.

RAPONI, Juan Pablo

Midfielder
Born: 7 May 1980, Alvarez, Santa Fe, Argentina
United debut: 19 February 2005 v Cheltenham Town
Final United game: 23 April 2005 v Southend United (sub)
Appearances: 5+5
Clubs: Unión de Alvarez (Argentina), River Plate (Argentina), Universidad de Chile (Chile) (loan), Banfield (Argentina) (loan), Olimpo (Argentina) (loan), Oxford United (loan), Instituto de Córdoba (Argentina), SD Ponferradina (Spain), Racing de Ferrol (Spain), Lorca Deportiva CF (Spain), Club Sport Emelec (Ecuador), Ferro Carril Oeste (Argentina)

Juan Pablo Raponi was signed in February 2005 on loan from River Plate for three months, at a fee of £10,000, by his former River Plate manager Ramon Díaz. This was possible because Raponi had dual Argentine/Italian nationality. He suffered with the rough and tumble of English lower-league football, but when he was able to shine his quality was obvious. He began his career with Unión de Alvarez but joined River Plate in time for the Clausura Torneo in 2002. After playing five games he joined Universidad de Chile on loan for six months in January 2003. After suffering a knee injury that interrupted his season, he returned to Argentina to play the Apertura Torneo in 2003 for Banfield, but he played just one game, at Boca Juniors, in which he scored and was sent off. He did better in the following year's Clausura, playing 19 games, before joining Olimpo in July 2004 for the Apertura as River Plate wanted the player to gain further experience. He scored one goal in 12 games for the Bahía Blanca club before his move to Oxford. After Díaz left Oxford Raponi did not wait to see if new manager Brian Talbot would offer him a contract, but instead returned to Argentina to play for Instituto de Córdoba where he played just 13 games in both the Apertura Torneo of 2005 and the Clausura of 2006. He was released as a cost-cutting measure and travelled to Spain to join Second Division side Ponferradina in the El Bierzo region, scoring on his debut. He was with Ponferradina for a year before joining fellow Second Division side Racing de Ferrol. While with Ferrol Raponi was linked with a move to Argentinean side Newell's Old Boys in January 2008, but nothing came of it and instead he moved to Lorca Deportiva. In July 2009 Raponi returned to Latin America to sign for Ecuadorian side Emelec, for whom he played eight games before signing for Ferro Carril Oeste from Buenos Aires in July 2010. In December 2010 Raponi was linked with a move to Talleres, but he still had six months on his contract and nothing happened.

RAWLE, Mark

Striker
Born: 27 April 1979, Leicester
United debut: 25 August 2003 v Swansea City (sub)
Final United game: 11 December 2004 v Cambridge United (sub)
Appearances: 11+28
Goals: 8
Clubs: Rushden & Diamonds, Boston United, Southend United, Oxford United, Tamworth (loan), Kidderminster Harriers, Woking, Gravesend & Northfleet (loan), Alfreton Town, Kettering Town, Redditch United (loan), Tamworth, Brackley Town

Mark Anthony Rawle was on the verge of signing a new contract with Southend United when he did a u-turn and signed for Oxford instead, just before the 2003–04 season. He had been the Shrimpers' leading scorer the previous season. Rawle started his career with Rushden & Diamonds after playing junior football in Leicestershire, but after impressing in the Under-18s he made sporadic appearances, mainly as substitute, and after playing 16 games in which he scored once, he was released and moved to Boston United in June 1999. Rawle scored on his debut for the Pilgrims against Gresley Rovers in the Dr Martens League and went on to play 81 games for Boston, scoring 38 goals, before being sold for a club record £60,000 to Southend in February 2001. Rawle scored 20 goals in 89 appearances for the Shrimpers and had verbally agreed to sign a new contract before his sudden move to Oxford. Rawle was quick but with a bit of a reputation as being injury-prone. He scored within 17 seconds of his United debut against Swansea, and added to that tap-in with some spectacular goals. However, he was mainly used as an impact substitute, and his first six goals for Oxford were all from off the bench. He was loaned to Tamworth in January 2005, scoring one goal in the first of his three games for the Lambs. Rawle joined Conference side Kidderminster on a free transfer in February 2005 but, after scoring three goals in his 11 games for the Harriers, he refused to sign a new contract because he wanted to play in the Football League. At the end of July 2005 he signed for fellow Conference side Woking. Rawle played 21 games for the Cards, scoring three goals, but was placed on the transfer list after falling out with manager Glenn Cockerill and in January 2006 he joined Gravesend & Northfleet on loan until the end of the season, scoring one goal in his 11 games for the Fleet. Rawle signed for Alfreton in September 2006 having trained with Crawley in the interim, and in July 2007 he moved to Kettering Town. He was out for six months following a knee injury and had a spell on loan with Redditch United in November 2008 to recuperate. Rawle was released by Kettering in January 2009, at which point he returned to Tamworth but he was let go by the Lambs two months later and he signed for Brackley.

RECK, Sean

Midfielder
Born: 3 March 1967, Oxford
United debut: 4 October 1986 v Sheffield Wednesday (sub)
Final United game: 19 November 1988 v Plymouth Argyle
Appearances: 13+4
Clubs: Oxford United, Newport County (loan), Reading (loan), Wrexham, Cheltenham Town, Oxford City

Sean Mark Reck came through the ranks at the Manor, becoming an apprentice in 1983 and turning professional in April 1985. He joined Newport on loan in August 1985, playing 17 games in his three months at Somerton Park, while scoring seven goals in 13 Football Combination appearances for United's reserves. Reck later played one game on loan with Reading but he failed to make an impact on the Oxford first team and in July 1989 he moved to Wrexham for £25,000. Reck made 45 League appearances over two seasons for the Red Dragons, scoring twice, before moving to Cheltenham. He was at Whaddon Road for one season before returning to Oxford to spend three seasons with Oxford City.

REECE, Paul

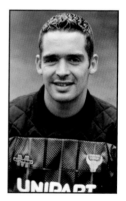

Goalkeeper
Born: 16 July 1968, Nottingham
United debut: 3 October 1992 v Birmingham City
Final United game: 5 October 1993 v Tranmere Rovers
Appearances: 45
Clean sheets: 12
Clubs: Stoke City, Kettering Town, Grimsby Town, Doncaster Rovers, Oxford United, Notts County, West Bromwich Albion, Ilkeston Town (loan), Cliftonville

Paul John Reece was generally considered a bit small for a goalkeeper at 5ft 11in, but he made up for his lack of height with some incredible agility that earned him great popularity with the supporters. Reece started his career with Stoke City, where he was coached by Gordon Banks, moving to Kettering Town after just two appearances for the Potters. Reece was Kettering's Player of the Year before his £10,000 move to Grimsby Town in 1988. Reece was mainly deputy for Steve Sherwood, making 66 appearances for the Mariners, and he won the Young Player of the Year award as well as two promotions before his move to Doncaster Rovers as cover for the injured Paul Crichton. He made just one appearance for Donny, in September 1992, before he joined Oxford. Despite a good start to his Oxford career, winning Man of the Match in a live TV performance at Derby in just his second League game, the arrival of Phil Whitehead saw Reece relegated from the first team and almost exactly a year after his arrival he left for Notts County. Reece played 15 games for the Magpies and was with the club when they became the last English side to win the Anglo-Italian Cup in March 1995, although he was not in the side for the Final, in the same season that

County were relegated from the First Division. In August 1995 Reece signed for West Bromwich Albion, but he played just one game in his two years at the Hawthorns before injury forced him to quit the professional game, and he spent some time on loan to Ilkeston Town before he joined Cliftonville in Northern Ireland. On his debut in the 1997 County Antrim Shield Reece became an instant hero when he made a Cup-winning save in the penalty shoot-out. Reece was with Cliftonville when the side won the Northern Ireland League in 1998. Reece later became a goalkeeping coach in the USA with Kickzsoccer training camps.

REES, Billy

Inside-forward
Born: 10 March 1924, Blaengarw
Died: March 1996
United debut: 26 December 1955 v Kettering Town
Final United game: 30 March 1959 v Kidderminster Harriers
Appearances: 131
Goals: 60
Clubs: Caernarvon Rovers, Cardiff City, Tottenham Hotspur, Leyton Orient, Headington United, Kettering Town

William Rees was a coal miner, playing as an amateur for Caernarvon Rovers when he was spotted by Cardiff City. Rees made 83 appearances in wartime fixtures for the Bluebirds, scoring 74 goals, and was a regular member of the Cardiff team who won the Third Division South Championship in 1946–47. He appeared in a wartime international for Wales against England in May 1945. At the end of the 1948–49 season Tottenham Hotspur signed him for £14,000, shortly after he had won the first of his four Wales caps, against Northern Ireland; he had scored 33 goals in 101 games for Cardiff. Rees suffered a number of injuries which caused him to lose form and he was dropped from the first team. Rees was bought by Leyton Orient for £14,500 in the summer of 1950. He spent six years with the O's before moving to Headington United, where he spent over three years and established a reputation as one of the best forwards to have played for the club. Rees joined Kettering Town from the U's before his retirement from football. He later worked as a plant operator before joining a Bridgend pharmaceutical company.

REID, Levi

Right-back/Winger
Born: 19 January 1983, Stafford
United debut: 8 August 2008 v Barrow (sub)
Final United game: 23 September 2008 v Cambridge United (sub)
Appearances: 6+4
Goals: 2
Clubs: Port Vale, Hinckley United, Stafford Rangers, Macclesfield Town, Oxford United, Stafford Rangers, AFC Telford United

Levi Stanley Junior Reid came to Oxford as a triallist in July 2008, and impressed enough to be offered a deal until the end of August to give him the chance to earn a longer contract, which he did, signing a month-by-month deal at the start of September. For family reasons he asked to be released from his contract at the end of September, and the club duly obliged. Reid came through the youth ranks at Port Vale, making his debut on the last day of the 2002–03 season when he came on as a substitute for John Durnin. He made 49 appearances for Vale, scoring one goal, before he was released in May 2005 and he joined Hinckley United, making his debut in September 2006. Reid's next stop was Conference North side Stafford Rangers, and it was Reid's goal in the Play-off Final penalty shoot-out that earned Stafford a place in the Conference National in May 2006. In August 2007 Reid signed for Macclesfield after impressing during a trial and he went on to play 33 games for the Silkmen, scoring two goals. After his release at the end of the season came his trial and subsequent contract with Oxford. He rejoined Stafford in August 2009 but in March 2011 he informed manager Matt Elliott that he wanted to move on after taking a 40 per cent pay cut and he joined AFC Telford United on non-contract terms.

REMY, Christophe

Right-back
Born: 6 August 1971, Besançon (France)
United debut: 9 August 1987 v Huddersfield Town
Final United game: 6 March 1999 v West Bromwich Albion (sub)
Appearances: 28+9
Goals: 1
Clubs: Senlis (France), Auxerre (France), Derby County, Oxford United

Christophe Phillipe Remy was a cultured defender who started his career with Senlis before joining AS Auxerre in 1986. Remy played in the same France Under-18 side as Zinedine Zidane and Emmanuel Petit. He played in the reserves for several seasons, making his Division One debut in May 1990, having already won the France Cadet League in 1987, the Division Three Championship in 1992 and the Division Two title in 1994 and again in 1996. His best season with Auxerre was in 1996, when the club won the French double. However, this was also his final season with the French side and in August 1996, after playing 24 Division One games for the French champions, plus four European Cup appearances, Remy earned a masters degree in sports management at the Audencia Nantes School of Management. Remy then moved to Derby County for a month but did not play any competitive first-team games for the Rams, and the following summer he moved to Oxford where he endeared himself to the fans with some impressive displays and an approachable manner. After leaving Oxford, where his first son was born, Remy returned to France and took a masters degree in e-business at the ESCP-EAP European School of Management before setting up his own web agency called Proxilog in Auxerre.

RHOADES-BROWN, Peter

Left-winger
Born: 2 January 1962, Hampton
United debut: 28 January 1984 v Blackpool
Final United game: 11 October 1988 v Bristol City
Appearances: 113+29
Goals: 16
Clubs: Chelsea, Oxford United, Abingdon Town, AFC Newbury, Marlow, Abingdon Town, Oxford City, Didcot Town, Weston-super-Mare

Peter Rhoades-Brown was a speedy left-winger with outstanding natural pace. He joined the Chelsea youth scheme and made his first-team debut in December 1979. He scored five goals in 109 games for the Blues before his £85,000 sale to Oxford in January 1984. Rosie was a regular in the side that won Division Two in 1985 and continued in the first team in the top flight the following season until an injury against Queen's Park Rangers robbed him of the chance to appear in the Milk Cup Final against the same opponents. Rhoades-Brown continued with United until he was forced to retire due to injury, after which he travelled around Australia for a month before returning to England when he had a pre-season trial with Conference side Wycombe Wanderers, playing against Nottingham Forest in the first game at Adams Park. Rhoades-Brown joined Abingdon Town where he played for a couple of years, meanwhile joining United's Centre of Excellence. A year later Rhoades-Brown was appointed as the club's community officer while playing for Newbury Town for a couple of years, winning promotion from the Diadora Division Two in 1994. He started playing for Peter Foley's Marlow in the summer of 1994 and played in the FA Cup win over Oxford in November that year, but when Foley left at the end of the season Rosie became player-manager for a season. He returned to Abingdon Town for a year and in October 1997 he became Kevin Brock's player-assistant manager at Oxford City, but he left after Brock was sacked in May 1998, but returned almost immediately as Paul Lee's assistant. Rosie's next club was Didcot Town and he then played a number of games for Weston-super-Mare in the second half of the 1998–99 season before hanging up his boots to concentrate on his community work with Oxford United.

RHODES, Alex

Left-winger
Born: 23 January 1982, Cambridge
United debut: 8 August 2009 v York City (sub)
Final United game: 22 August 2009 v Stevenage Borough (sub)
Appearances: 0+3
Clubs: Newmarket Town, Brentford, Swindon Town (loan), Grays Athletic (loan), Bradford City, Rotherham United, Woking (loan), Oxford United, Braintree Town, Grays Athletic, Canvey Island

Alexander Graham Rhodes signed for Oxford from Rotherham in May 2009. After just three substitute appearances he was released from his contract by mutual consent at the start of November 2009. Rhodes started his career with Newmarket Town aged 17, and after trials with Ipswich Town, Norwich City and Yeovil Town he joined Brentford in November 2003 for a fee believed to be £7,500. He was initially a regular for the Bees, but his appearances gradually became fewer and in October 2006 he had a loan spell with Swindon, for whom he made four substitute appearances. This was followed by a loan spell with Grays Athletic in March 2007 where he scored two goals in 14 games. After rejecting a new contract from Brentford Rhodes signed for Bradford City in August 2007. He played 30 games for the Bantams, scoring three goals, but was released at the end of the season and in June 2008 he signed for Rotherham United. Rhodes played most of the first half of the season, making 27 appearances and scoring three goals, but was loaned to Woking for three games, in which he scored once, before being released by the Millers, after which he was offered a contract by Oxford. After being released by United he joined Braintree until the New Year and in

January 2010 he rejoined Grays, where he made his debut in a 4–0 defeat by Oxford. He was released by Grays at the end of the season and had trials with AFC Sudbury and Hereford United before signing for Canvey Island in August 2010.

RHODES, Jordan

Striker
Born: 5 February 1990, Oldham
United debut: 11 October 2007 v Farsley Celtic (sub)
Final United game: 1 November 2007 v Rushden & Diamonds
Appearances: 4+1
Goals: 2
Clubs: Ipswich Town, Oxford United (loan), Rochdale (loan), Brentford (loan), Huddersfield Town

Jordan Luke Rhodes joined Oxford on loan from Ipswich Town in October 2007. Although he played just four games his class was obvious and he scored a phenomenal goal at Merthyr Tydfil in the FA Cup fourth qualifying round. Rhodes joined Ipswich in 2005 after playing for Barnsley's youth teams, but he was unable to break into the first team, making 10 substitute appearances in which he scored once before his transfer to Huddersfield Town in July 2009. His first loan from the Tractor Boys was to Oxford, where he made his first senior start, and in September 2008 he had a five-game loan spell with Rochdale, where he scored twice. This was followed by a lengthier loan spell with Brentford in January 2009 in which Rhodes scored seven goals in his 14 appearances, including becoming the Bees' youngest hat-trick scorer ever in a 3–1 win at Shrewsbury Town in the third game of his loan. He joined Huddersfield for an undisclosed fee and scored six goals in his first six games and in October 2009 he scored the quickest headed hat-trick on record in a 4–0 win over Exeter City, the goals all coming within 10 minutes. Rhodes played for Scotland Under-21s against Belgium in March 2011.

RICHARDS, Justin

Striker
Born: 16 October 1980, West Bromwich
United debut: 26 January 2008 v Grays Athletic
Final United game: 15 April 2008 v York City (sub)
Appearances: 10+5
Goals: 1
Clubs: West Bromwich Albion, Bristol Rovers, Newport County (loan), Colchester United (loan), Stevenage Borough (loan), Stevenage Borough, Woking, Peterborough United, Grays Athletic (loan), Boston United (loan), Kidderminster Harriers, Oxford United (loan), Cheltenham Town, Port Vale

Justin Donovan Richards arrived on a loan deal from Kidderminster Harriers during the January 2008 transfer window until the end of the season. Richards started his career with West Bromwich Albion, where he turned professional in 1999. He made just two substitute appearances for the Baggies before his £75,000 transfer to Bristol Rovers in January 2001. However, just a week later manager Ian Holloway left Rovers and Richards found it difficult to get into the side, making just 17 appearances for Rovers in two years at the club. In October 2002 he had a loan spell with Colchester United during which he made three substitute appearances and in December

2002 he joined Stevenage Borough on loan, scoring six goals in 13 appearances before joining Borough permanently in March 2003. Richards scored three goals in his 30 games for the Broadhall Way club, although he suffered with injuries during his season there and left for Woking in May 2004. In his two seasons with the Cards Richards scored 36 goals in his 89 games, prompting Peterborough United to sign him in May 2006. In his one season with the Posh Richards played 16 games, scoring one goal, but he did go out on loan twice, first to Grays Athletic in November 2006, playing five games, and next to Boston United in January 2007 where he made three appearances. In June 2007 Richards joined Kidderminster on a free transfer and it was midway through his time at Aggborough that he was loaned to Oxford. Although his time at United was less than successful, on his return to Kidderminster Richards hit a rich scoring vein and by the time he left for Cheltenham Town in July 2009 he had scored 23 goals in 70 games for the Harriers. In his first season with the Robins he ended as the club's leading scorer, with 15 goals from 47 matches, after which he rejected Cheltenham's offer of a new contract to join League Two rivals Port Vale.

RICHARDS, Mike

Goalkeeper
Born: 26 May 1939, Codsall
United debut: 8 September 1962 v Southend United
Final United game: 1 October 1963 v Brighton & Hove Albion
Appearances: 30
Clean sheets: 6
Clubs: Wolverhampton Wanderers, Wellington Town, Oxford United, Shrewsbury Town, Telford United

Michael James Richards was an amateur with Wolverhampton Wanderers, but had not made a first-team appearance before he joined Wellington Town as a professional. Richards played for United in their first season as a Football League side, but despite playing more games than Oxford's other custodian Owen Medlock, he was unable to get a regular run in the side and was displaced by new signings Vic Rouse and then Harry Fearnley. In November 1963 Richards joined Shrewsbury Town, but he did not feature in their first team and he later played for Wellington again, under their new name of Telford United.

RICHARDSON, Jon

Centre-back
Born: 29 August 1975, Nottingham
United debut: 12 August 2000 v Peterborough United
Final United game: 5 March 2002 v Kidderminster Harriers
Appearances: 62+2
Goals: 2
Clubs: Exeter City, Oxford United, Forest Green Rovers, Exeter City, Worcester City, Solihull Moors

Jonathan Derek Richardson began his career as a trainee with Exeter City, playing his first game for the Grecians in 1994. In six years at St James' Park Rico played 286 games and scored 11 goals, but the commanding central-defender was allowed to leave for Oxford in August 2000 for a nominal fee. However, Richardson was part of a defence that conceded 100 goals in his first season, with United relegated to the bottom tier at the end of it as they moved from the Manor to the Kassam Stadium. The following season saw new manager Mark Wright bring in his preferred central-defenders, followed by his successor Ian Atkins bringing in his own players, with Richardson's opportunities correspondingly limited. In the summer of 2002 Richardson was released by Atkins and in August he joined Conference side Forest Green Rovers. He spent four years at the New Lawn, playing 127 games and scoring seven goals, before he was released and he rejoined his first club Exeter City after a trial. Rico played 41 games in his second spell with the Grecians before joining Worcester City in June 2008. At the end of the season Richardson decided to concentrate on studying for a degree in physiotherapy. However, the lure of playing football proved too strong and in November 2009 he joined Solihull Moors, who were coached by Paul Wanless, with whom Richardson had played at both Oxford and Forest Green Rovers.

RICKETTS, Sam

Full-back
Born: 11 October 1981, Aylesbury
United debut: 8 October 2000 v Swindon Town
Final United game: 14 December 2002 v Bristol Rovers (sub)
Appearances: 35+13
Goals: 1
Clubs: Oxford United, Nuneaton Borough (loan), Telford United, Swansea City, Hull City, Bolton Wanderers

Samuel Derek Ricketts is the son of 1978 showjumping champion Derek Ricketts and the nephew of National Hunt champion jockey John Francombe. Ricketts' versatility was probably his greatest asset, being able to play anywhere in defence or midfield, with varying degrees of success. He joined the Oxford United YTS in 1998 and turned professional in 2000. After an alleged training ground fight with Jefferson Louis he was loaned out to Nuneaton Borough in the Vauxhall Conference in October 2002, having only made one substitute appearance so far that season. He played 11 games for Nuneaton, scoring one goal. Ricketts was released in the summer of 2003 and signed for Conference side Telford United. Ricketts impressed enough to win four England Semi-Pro caps, scoring one goal at that level. He scored six goals in his 51 games for Telford, and after they went bust at the end of the 2003–04 season he was snapped up by Swansea. While with the Swans he won the first of his 64 Wales caps (so far), against Hungary. After 105 games and three goals for Swansea, Hull City paid £300,000 for Ricketts in July 2006. In May 2008 Ricketts played in Hull's 1–0 Championship Play-off Final victory over Bristol City, in which Dean Windass scored the goal, to earn promotion to the Premiership. Ricketts played 129 games for the Tigers, scoring just one goal, before he moved to Bolton Wanderers for a fee believed to be £2 million.

RIVERS, Ron

Outside-right
Born: 1939, Oxford
United debut: 19 September 1959 v Chelmsford City
Final United game: 30 April 1960 v Gravesend & Northfleet
Appearances: 6
Goals: 5
Clubs: Headington United

ROACH, Neville

Striker
Born: 29 September 1978, Reading
United debut: 26 November 2005 v Grimsby Town (sub)
Final United game: 28 January 2006 v Rushden & Diamonds
Appearances: 2+5
Clubs: Reading, Kingstonian (loan), Slough Town (loan), Wycombe Wanderers (loan), Southend United (loan), Southend United, Kingstonian, Eastern Pride (Australia), St Albans City, Frickley Athletic, Oldham Athletic, Torquay United, Stevenage Borough, Slough Town, Basingstoke Town, Eastleigh, Oxford United (loan), Maidenhead United (loan), Basingstoke Town, Maidenhead United (loan), Maidenhead United, Harrow Borough (loan), Farnborough (loan), Farnborough, Uxbridge, Didcot Town, North London Raiders, Hungerford Town, Hartley Wintney

Neville Ivan Roach had a peripatetic career, travelling around mainly non-League clubs. He started with Reading, his home-town team, where he managed just 23 games and two goals in his three years as a professional with the Royals, although he did score on his debut against Oldham. He did have an 11-game loan spell with Kingstonian in January 1998 and in August 1998 he played 12 games on loan with Slough Town, scoring twice. In February 1999 Roach had a final loan from Reading, joining Wycombe Wanderers, but he did not play for the Chairboys' first team and a few days later he joined Southend United, initially on loan for five games, in which he scored once, before the move was made permanent for £30,000 in March 1999. However, Roach managed just two goals in 18 appearances and in August 2000 he was told he was free to leave. In March 2000 Roach had been called-up by the Cayman Islands for their World Cup qualifier against Cuba, but the move was blocked by FIFA, who ordered the tiny island nation to travel without their imported players, although he did manage to play one friendly game against DC United. In August 2000 Roach travelled to Morwell in Victoria to play for Eastern Pride – formerly Gippsland Falcons – in the National Soccer League, where he scored five goals in 12 games. In February 2001 Eastern Pride disbanded and Roach returned to England, where he joined St Albans City and scored two goals in seven games. In March 2001 Roach joined Frickley Athletic and after just one appearance he signed for Oldham Athletic after impressing in a reserves game, although he made just one substitute appearance for the Latics before being released at the end of the season. In August 2001 Roach signed for Torquay United where he scored one goal in 14 games before leaving for Stevenage in November 2001 and then Slough Town on a match-by-match basis in December 2001. He scored 14 goals in 23 appearances for the Rebels before leaving for Basingstoke Town in August 2002. In three seasons with Basingstoke Roach played 150 games and scored 57 goals before he rejected a new contract and signed for Conference South rivals Eastleigh. It was from Eastleigh that Roach joined Oxford on loan in November 2005, signed by Brian Talbot in a misguided attempt to revive a season that was rapidly going wrong and which ultimately ended in relegation from the Football League. Roach had just been transfer-listed by Eastleigh but he was unable to convince Talbot that he belonged with Oxford and he returned to Eastleigh in February 2006. He then went on loan to Maidenhead United, where he scored five goals in nine games. In June 2006 Roach returned to Basingstoke where he scored five goals in 28 games but he joined Maidenhead again on loan in January 2007 before signing permanently in April 2007. Roach had a loan at Harrow Borough and in September 2007 with Farnborough, who he joined permanently in October 2007. Roach had scored 13 goals for Maidenhead in 29 appearances spread over two spells. In January 2008 he moved to Uxbridge for the remainder of the season, and in the close season he returned to Oxfordshire to join Didcot Town. In July 2009 Roach signed for Hungerford Town and in December 2009 he joined Hartley Wintney. In May 2010 Roach took over as Hartley Wintney manager in the Combined Counties League Division 1.

ROBERTS, Dave

Centre-back
Born: 26 November 1949, Southampton
United debut: 20 February 1971 v Swindon Town (sub)
Final United game: 8 February 1975 v Manchester United
Appearances: 175+1
Goals: 8
Clubs: Fulham, Oxford United, Hull City, Chicago Sting (USA) (loan), Cardiff City, Tsuen Wan (Hong Kong)

David Frazer Roberts is arguably one of the best central-defenders ever to have played for Oxford. He joined Fulham as an apprentice and played 22 games for them between March 1969 and February 1971, when he joined United for £4,000. Roberts made his Oxford debut as a substitute (his only appearance from the bench) 12 days later in a 3–0 defeat at Swindon Town and made his full debut six days after that in a 2–0 defeat at Charlton Athletic. Roberts became club captain in 1973 and scored in United's only win at the County Ground, on 24 February 1973. His final appearance for the Yellows was on 8 February 1975, when Oxford beat Manchester United 1–0 in a Division Two game at the Manor. He was sold by United for £70,000 to Hull City, for whom he played 86 times, and in 1977 he joined NASL side Chicago Sting on loan, playing in 13 games for them. The following year he moved to Cardiff City for £50,000. Roberts played 41 games for the Bluebirds. When he retired in 1981 he became coach to Cardiff's reserves after a brief interlude playing for Tsuen Wan in Hong Kong. Roberts won his first full Wales cap in March 1973 in a World Cup qualifying game against Poland, which Wales won 2–0. He won a further five caps for Wales while with United, and went on to win 18 in total. He also won four caps for the Wales Under-23 side while with Oxford, the first in a 3–0 defeat by England in November 1972.

ROBERTS, Peter

Centre-forward
Born: 16 July 1925, Sherburn
United debut: 20 August 1949 v Hastings United
Final United game: 8 April 1950 v Gloucester City
Appearances: 24
Goals: 10
Clubs: Sherburn Hill Boys' Club, Newcastle United, Leeds United, New Brighton, Headington United

Peter Lorenga Roberts was an amateur with Newcastle United before he turned professional with Leeds in 1946. He did not play for the Leeds first team before moving to New Brighton two years later, where he made three Football League appearances. Roberts joined Headington United as a professional shortly before their first Southern League fixture in August 1949 and he scored the second of United's goals in their 5–2 defeat at Hastings United.

ROBERTSON, John

Right-back
Born: 28 March 1976, Irvine
United debut: 12 August 2000 v Peterborough United
Final United game: 5 May 2001 v Notts County
Appearances: 41+3
Clubs: Bonnyton, Stranraer, Ayr United, Oxford United, Ayr United, St Johnstone, Ross County, Hamilton Academical, Partick Thistle

John Alexander Robertson joined Oxford from Ayr United in the 2000 close season. However, he was a member of a defence that conceded 100 goals as the U's were relegated to the basement division. Robertson started his career with Stranraer, where he spent three seasons and won the 1996 Scottish Challenge Cup Final against St Johnstone before joining Ayr United in June 1997. He played 104 games for the Honest Men, scoring one goal, before his move to Oxford, which was his only venture south of the border. After his sole season with Oxford he returned to Somerset Park for a season, scoring four goals in 48 appearances. In 2002 Robertson moved to St Johnstone, where he played 58 games over two seasons before moving to Ross County for a year in June 2004. He played 33 games for the Staggies and then spent a season with Hamilton Academical, where he scored twice in 34 games. In August 2006 Robertson joined Partick Thistle.

ROBINSON, Les

Right-back
Born: 1 March 1967, Shirebrook
United debut: 5 May 1990 v Port Vale
Final United game: 6 May 2000 v Millwall
Appearances: 453+5
Goals: 6
Clubs: Chesterfield, Mansfield Town, Stockport County, Doncaster Rovers, Oxford United, Mansfield Town, Hednesford Town

Leslie Robinson arrived at Oxford from Doncaster Rovers in March 1990, making his debut in the final game of the 1989–90 season, a 0–0 home draw with Port Vale. He started as a junior with Nottingham Forest, joining Chesterfield in 1984, before moving to Mansfield Town in October 1984. In two years he played just 16 games for the Stags before joining Stockport County. He had made 77 appearances while at Edgeley Park when he moved to Doncaster for £20,000 in March 1988. He played 96 games at Belle Vue, scoring 13 goals, before Oxford paid £150,000 for him. Robinson started in central midfield, but dropped deeper to become a very accomplished right-back. He suffered with two long-term injuries after his arrival, but he managed to overcome them to get a regular place in the side. He was appointed club captain, a role in which he excelled with his committed tackling and organisational ability. Robbo continued playing for the U's until the end of the 1999–2000 season, after which he went to Mansfield

Town on a free transfer. His final Oxford game was a 1–0 defeat at Millwall exactly 10 years and one day after his United debut. After 91 games with the Stags, Robinson turned down the opportunity to sign for Notts County and Tamworth, instead moving to the Southern League Premier Division with Hednesford Town in July 2002. In September 2003 he returned to Oxfordshire to play for Banbury United, before age and injury caught up with him and he retired in 2005.

ROBINSON, Marvin

Striker
Born: 11 April 1980, Crewe
United debut: 1 September 2006 v St Albans City
Final United game: 20 September 2007 v Histon
Appearances: 15+18
Goals: 4
Clubs: Derby County, Stoke City (loan), Tranmere Rovers (loan), Chesterfield, Notts County, Rushden & Diamonds, Walsall, Stockport County, Lincoln City, Macclesfield Town, Oxford United, Cambridge United (loan), Kettering Town, Redditch United, Massey Ferguson FC, Nantwich Town, Hednesford Town

Marvin Leon St Clair Robinson joined United from Macclesfield on transfer deadline day in August 2006. United manager Jim Smith had handed Robinson his first start, at Derby County, where he scored one goal in 12 appearances, having previously played for England Under-18s while at school. In September 2000 he had a three-game loan spell with Stoke City in which he scored one goal, followed by seven games on loan to Tranmere in November 2002, where he bagged one goal. Robinson joined Chesterfield in September 2003; he played 35 games and scored seven goals in his year at Saltergate. In September 2004 Robinson signed for Notts County, but played just two games before moving to Rushden & Diamonds on a non-contract basis in November 2004. He scored one goal in four games for Rushden before signing for Walsall the following month, where he scored four goals in just 10 appearances. In March 2005 Robinson signed for Stockport County, where he managed just three games before joining Lincoln City at the start of the following season. He spent one season with the Imps, playing 39 games and scoring 11 goals before his move to Macclesfield. Robinson played just five games in his season at Moss Rose before he arrived at the Kassam Stadium. Unfortunately, Robinson was injured almost immediately, and missed most of the first half of the season. After his recovery, he was loaned for three months to fellow Conference outfit Cambridge United in September 2007. However, in October Robinson was seriously injured in a car crash, and so United agreed with Cambridge to end the loan prematurely. After supporting his recovery for a few months, his contract was ended by mutual agreement in January 2008. In November 2008 Robinson played a couple of games with Kettering as part of his recuperation and in January 2009 he joined Redditch United. He played for Massey Ferguson FC of the Midland Combination Premier at the beginning of the 2009–10 season, before joining Northern Premier League Premier Division side Nantwich Town in December 2009. In October 2010 Robinson signed for Southern League Premier Division side Hednesford Town.

ROBINSON, Matt

Left-back
Born: 23 December 1974, Exeter
United debut: 10 August 2002 v Bury
Final United game: 6 May 2006 v Leyton Orient
Appearances: 191+1
Goals: 4
Clubs: Southampton, Portsmouth, Reading, Oxford United, Forest Green Rovers, Salisbury City, AFC Totton, Swindon Supermarine

Matthew Richard Robinson joined Oxford from Reading on a free transfer in July 2002. He had an excellent reputation as an attacking full-back and soon showed himself to be the key to shoring up the defence. After four seasons, though, Robinson's pace had deserted him, and at the end of the 2005–06 relegation season he did not have his contract renewed. He started his career with Southampton, signing professionally in 1993 and making 17 first-team appearances before his £50,000 move to neighbours Portsmouth. At Fratton Park Robinson played 77 games and scored one goal before Reading paid £150,000 for him in January 2000. He played 75 games for the Biscuitmen without finding the net before he joined United. After his release by the U's Robinson joined Conference side Forest Green Rovers, for whom he scored one goal in 30 games, before leaving for Salisbury City in July 2007. While with Salisbury Robinson went part-time and trained to become a police officer, while making 51 appearances and scoring one goal for the Whites. Because of his police duties Robinson was unable to commit to playing and training regularly for Salisbury and he was released in February 2009, when he signed for AFC Totton. In July 2009 he moved to Swindon Supermarine and in February 2011 he became caretaker manager along with Gary Horgan.

ROGAN, Anton

Left-back
Born: 25 March 1966, Belfast
United debut: 14 August 1993 v Portsmouth
Final United game: 30 April 1995 v Swansea City
Appearances: 66+2
Goals: 3
Clubs: Cromac Albion (Northern Ireland), Distillery (Northern Ireland), Celtic, Sunderland, Oxford United, Millwall, Blackpool, Banbury United

Anthony Gerrard Patrick Rogan turned professional with Distillery, having been spotted playing for Amateur League Cromac Albion, who he joined after being a highly rated Gaelic Games player. In three seasons with Distillery Rogan played 72 games, scoring once, and caught the eye of Celtic, where he was due to have a trial in October 1984. However, he broke his leg in a League game and then broke it again as he was due to trial again with Celtic. The Bhoys did not lose interest in Rogan and offered him another trial in the summer of 1986, after which they signed him. Rogan made his Celtic debut in January 1987 and was a regular the following season as they won the League and Cup double in their Centenary year. In October 1987 he won the first of his 18 Northern Ireland caps. Rogan was also a Scottish Cup winner with Celtic in 1989 and a runner-up in 1990, when he missed a penalty in the shoot-out after a draw against Aberdeen. In October 1991

Rogan left for Sunderland for £350,000, having made 166 appearances for the Hoops and scored five goals. At the end of his first season the Rokerites reached the FA Cup Final at Wembley, where they lost 2–0 to Liverpool, but Rogan broke his leg again the following season and after 57 games and one goal he joined Oxford in August 1993 for £250,000. Although Rogan established himself as a solid left-back, United were relegated at the end of his first season and after missing out on promotion the following season he joined Millwall in August 1995. Millwall were also relegated at the end of Rogan's first season, but he remained for another year, playing 40 games in which he scored eight goals. He was released in May 1997 and signed for Blackpool, but suffered with injuries and after just 16 games in two seasons he retired from the professional game in May 1999. In July 2000 Rogan joined Banbury United and he later worked for Oxford City Council while occasionally turning out for charity games.

ROGET, Leo

Centre-back
Born: 1 August 1977, Ilford
United debut: 7 August 2004 v Boston United
Final United game: 22 April 2006 v Northampton Town
Appearances: 76+1
Goals: 5
Clubs: Southend United, Stockport County (loan), Stockport County, Reading (loan), Brentford, Oxford United, St Albans City, Harlow Town, Braintree Town, Rushden & Diamonds, Harlow Town

Leo Thomas Earl Roget first had a trial with Oxford in the summer of 2002, but Ian Atkins failed to take him on and he ended up moving to Brentford, a division higher. After almost two seasons at Griffin Park, where he played 33 games, he joined Rushden & Diamonds for six months, making 17 appearances, before coming to Oxford on a two-year deal. Roget was a solid centre-back who was once sent off when playing for Southend against Oxford, despite the actual culprit being white. His time at Oxford showed him to be occasionally prone to goal-conceding errors. When manager Brian Talbot arrived in the summer of 2005, he told Roget that if he was able to find another club then he could leave on a free transfer. Instead, Roget chose to prove to Talbot that he was worth a place, and after impressing in a League Cup defeat at Gillingham, Roget soon showed that he was a much-improved defender, and was in the running to win the Player of the Season award. However, his contract was not renewed at the end of the 2005–06 season after United were relegated to the Conference. Southend was Roget's first club, where he played 149 games and scored 10 goals before he joined Stockport County on loan in March 2001, playing eight games before signing permanently with the Hatters in May. Roget played 23 games for Stockport, scoring one goal before a one-game loan to Reading in February 2002. It was in April 2002 that he moved to Brentford. After leaving Oxford Roget did not sign for another club until he joined St Albans City in August 2007. He played three games for the Saints before being released and joining Harlow in January 2008. In July 2008 Roget had an unsuccessful trial with Gillingham before joining Braintree Town. Three weeks after joining the Iron he was released and signed for Rushden again, playing just one game before leaving the Diamonds in January 2009. In the summer of 2010 he rejoined Harlow Town but he left in July 2011 for personal reasons.

ROSE, Andrew

Defender
Born: 9 August 1978, Ascot
United debut: 4 April 1998 v Port Vale (sub)
Final United game: 20 March 1999 v Crewe Alexandra (sub)
Appearances: 2+4
Clubs: Oxford United, Harrow Borough, Maidenhead United

Andrew Mark Rose came through the ranks at Oxford, joining the YTS in 1995. He was a member of the side that won the Junior Floodlit Cup in May 1996 and signed as a professional in 1997. However, Rose failed to convince in his few senior appearances and was released in the summer of 1999. The defender joined Harrow Borough, moving to Maidenhead United in July 2001.

ROSE, Danny

Midfielder
Born: 21 February 1988, Bristol
United debut: 6 January 2007 v Morecambe
Final United game: 26 April 2008 v Ebbsfleet United (sub)
Appearances: 29+17
Goals: 2
Clubs: Manchester United, Oxford United (loan), Oxford United, Newport County

Daniel Stephen Rose arrived on loan from Manchester United, where he was reserve team captain despite being only 18 years old, during the January 2007 transfer window. He came with a reputation as a ball-playing midfielder, and his loan came as a direct result of the friendship between Jim Smith and Manchester United manager Sir Alex Ferguson. At the start of the 2007–08 season Rose was signed on a month-to-month contract after he had failed to land a deal with Bristol Rovers, and in January 2008 this was extended until the end of the season. Rose was released by United at the end of the 2007–08 season, having failed to establish himself in the side. In the summer of 2008 he signed for Newport County, with whom he won the Conference South in 2010 and was chosen for the Conference South Select XI that season. Rose won an England C cap in September 2010 in a 2–2 draw with Wales Under-23s.

ROUSE, Vic

Goalkeeper
Born: 16 March 1936, Swansea
United debut: 24 August 1963 v Chester City
Final United game: 19 September 1964 v Millwall
Appearances: 23
Clean sheets: 6
Clubs: Millwall, Crystal Palace, Northampton Town, Oxford United, Leyton Orient, Atlanta Chiefs (USA)

Raymond Victor Rouse started his career at Millwall, where he came through the ranks but left for Crystal Palace in 1956 without having made a first-team appearance. While at Selhurst Park Rouse set a then club record of 238 Football League appearances before he lost his place to Bill Glazier. Rouse became the first player from the Fourth Division to become a full international when he made his only appearance for Wales in their 4–1 defeat against Northern Ireland in April 1959. He was with Palace when they won promotion to Division Three in 1961 and moved to Northampton Town in 1963, although he did not play a League game for them before he joined Oxford in the summer of 1963. Rouse started the season as first-choice 'keeper, but lost his place through injury first to Mike Richards and then to Harry Fearnley and he played no part in that season's excellent FA Cup run. He regained his place when Fearnley was injured but lost it again and after spending most of his second season in the reserves he joined Orient in July 1965. After making 40 League appearances for the O's Rouse lost his place to Ron Willis and he moved to the States to play for Atlanta Chiefs, where he made 61 appearances over six years, the last three as player-manager. He was the Chiefs' goalie in 1968 when they won the NASL Championship after finishing first in the Atlantic Division. In 1972 Rouse returned to England to become manager of Metropolitan Police.

ROWDEN, Len

Centre-forward
Born: 31 May 1927, Swansea
United debut: 22 August 1956 v Dartford
Final United game: 22 August 1956 v Dartford
Appearances: 1
Goals: 2
Clubs: Plasmarl, Clydach, Swansea City, Llanelly, Headington United, Bangor City, Aberystwyth, Haverfordwest, Burton Albion

Leonard Albert Rowden almost certainly has the best goalscoring average of any United player, scoring twice in his only first-team appearance. He played for a couple of minor Welsh sides in Swansea before joining Swansea City in October 1953, making just one League appearance for the Swans, in a 0–0 draw with Leicester City. He also featured in Swansea's 1954 West Wales Senior Cup Final win before joining Llanelly in August 1955. Rowden won the Welsh League Cup with Haverfordwest in 1961 and had a spell with Burton Albion while teaching PE in Walsall, before returning to Wales to teach PE.

ROWSTRON, Bill

Centre-forward
Born: 21 March 1927, Foleshill
Died: November 1994
United debut: 30 September 1950 v Guildford City
Final United game: 1 March 1952 v Bath City
Appearances: 48
Goals: 31
Clubs: Coventry City, Headington United

William James Rowstron signed professional forms with Headington United aged 22. He lived in Coventry, next door to fellow Headington player Norman Aldridge.

RUSH, David

Striker
Born: 15 May 1971, Sunderland

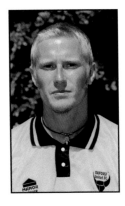

United debut: 24 September 1994 v Leyton Orient (sub)
Final United game: 14 December 1996 v Sheffield United (sub)
Appearances: 78+32
Goals: 24
Clubs: Notts County, Sunderland, Hartlepool United (loan), Peterborough United (loan), Cambridge United (loan), Oxford United, York City, Morpeth Town, Hartlepool United, Seaham Red Star, Barrow, Seaham Red Star

David Rush, although Sunderland born, actually started his career as a youth with Notts County before returning to Wearside in July 1989 to sign for his home-town club. As a youngster Rush played for the Sunderland Schools FA and the Durham County Schools FA Under-15s and Under-19s. Rush played 73 games for the Rokerites, including the 1992 FA Cup Final 2–0 defeat by Liverpool at Wembley, and he scored 13 goals before his £100,000 move to Oxford in September 1994. Meanwhile, in August 1991 Rush scored two goals in eight games on loan to Hartlepool, and he had a five-game loan spell with Peterborough United in which he scored twice in October 1993. Immediately before he joined Oxford Rush played two games on loan to Cambridge United. He made an instant impact at Oxford, coming off the bench for his debut against Leyton Orient and scoring a late winner. He struck up an instant rapport with the fans, as much for his laddish behaviour as for his goalscoring antics, and his goals in the climax of the 1995–96 season were integral to United's storming run-in to finish in second place and earn promotion to Division One. In the final game of the season, at home to Peterborough United, Rush made two and scored the fourth goal in a 4–0 win, despite being on the transfer list at the time. Rush moved back north in January 1997 when York City paid £80,000 for him, but he played just four games for the Minstermen before he was sacked amid rumours of behaviour involving illegal substances. After a period with Morpeth Town Rush joined Hartlepool again in September 1998, making 12 appearances without scoring. He joined Northern League side Seaham Red Star in May 1999 and in October 1999 he signed for Barrow, scoring on his debut against Gainsborough Trinity. He returned to Seaham Red Star in March 2000 and scored twice on his debut against Dunstan Fed. In May 2009 Rush was appointed manager of Hebburn Town, but he resigned from the Northern League Division Two side in September 2009 with the club at the foot of the table.

RUSSELL, Craig

Striker
Born: 4 February 1974, Jarrow
United debut: 12 February 2000 v Wycombe Wanderers
Final United game: 11 March 2000 v Colchester United (sub)
Appearances: 5+1
Clubs: Sunderland, Manchester City, Tranmere Rovers (loan), Port Vale (loan), Darlington (loan), Oxford United (loan), St Johnstone (loan), St Johnstone, Carlisle United, Darlington, Newcastle Blue Star, Jarrow Roofing

Craig Stewart Russell's parents were both keen Sunderland fans, and the striker claims that he was conceived following the Wearsiders' FA Cup Final win in 1973. He joined Sunderland, managed by Denis Smith, despite interest from Manchester United and was a member of the side that won the

Championship in 1996. Russell played 175 games, scoring 34 goals, before his £1 million move to Manchester City in November 1997 in a deal that saw Nicky Summerbee move the other way. For their money, City received a player who made just 36 appearances and scored two goals for them, spending more time out on loan to other clubs than he did at Maine Road. His first loan was at Tranmere in August 1998, where he played four games. Russell scored one goal in eight games at Port Vale in January 1999 and two goals in 12 games at Darlington in September 1999. He joined Oxford in February 2000, meeting up with Denis Smith again, but he was unable to find the net in his six games for the U's. The striker had a trial with Norwich City's reserves in February 2000 but he was not taken on by the Canaries. Russell's final loan move was to St Johnstone in March 2000; he made two appearances before returning to Maine Road with a hamstring injury, but he did enough to impress and in July the move was made permanent. In October 2002, after 41 games and three goals, Russell was allowed to leave the Saints by mutual agreement and in January 2003, after trials with Grimsby Town and Darlington, he signed for Carlisle. Russell scored two goals in 26 games for the Cumbrians before joining Darlington in January 2004 where he scored two goals in 41 appearances. Having completed a massage qualification, he was released in May 2005 and signed for Newcastle Blue Star while working as a masseur for Newcastle Falcons rugby union side. Russell moved to Jarrow Roofing in October 2005 and in August 2007 he joined South Shields. Meanwhile he had joined Newcastle United as a masseur before moving to the Stadium of Light in the summer of 2009 to provide the same role for Sunderland.

S

SABIN, Éric

Striker
Born: 22 January 1975, Sarcelles (France)
United debut: 2 September 2005 v Shrewsbury Town (sub)
Final United game: 6 May 2006 v Leyton Orient
Appearances: 34+1
Goals: 9
Clubs: Union Sportive du Robert (Martinique), Nîmes Olympique (France), Gazélec Ajaccio (France) (loan), ES Wasquehal (France), Swindon Town, Queen's Park Rangers, Boston United (loan), Northampton Town, Oxford United, AC Arles (France), Nîmes Olympique (France)

Éric Sabin was signed from Northampton on transfer deadline day in August 2005 on a two-year contract. As a youth he played in Martinique for US Robert, and in 1994 he started his professional career with Nîmes, where he scored seven goals in 39 matches, reaching the Coupe de France Final in 1996 and winning the French National Group B title the following season. After scoring one goal in four Champions League games, Sabin had a loan at Ajaccio, on the beautiful island of Corsica, before signing for Wasquehal, near Lille, in the French equivalent of Division Three. He stayed there for two years, scoring seven goals in 59 games, before he was spotted by Andy King, who signed him for Swindon in the summer of 2001. Sabin played 81 games for Swindon, scoring nine goals, before in July 2003 leaving for Queen's Park Rangers, where he played 16 games and scored just one goal. Sabin had a two-game loan to Boston United in March 2004, before he joined Northampton later that month. He played 65 games in just over a year at the Cobblers, scoring 15 goals and becoming a fans' favourite, although he was disappointed not to be offered a new contract at the end of the 2004–05 season, when he joined Oxford. Sabin started his Oxford career in the best possible way, scoring on his full debut in a 2–2 draw with Rushden. Initial impressions of Sabin were that he was very fast, and with a physical presence that other forwards at the club lacked. Unfortunately, and despite his two early goals, his finishing often let him down. Despite this, manager Brian Talbot indicated that he wanted to build his attack around Sabin, who scored in his final game for the club in the defeat by Orient that condemned the U's to relegation to the Conference. After being released by Jim Smith Sabin returned to France in July 2006 and joined Arles, with whom he won promotion to the National Division in 2007. After scoring 10 goals in 51 games over two seasons for Arles, Sabin returned to Nîmes at the start of the 2007–08 season, playing for their reserves side in CFA 2. In October 2008 Sabin won 3 caps for Martinique at the 2008 Caribbean Cup, scoring 4 goals, and in November he was recalled to the Nîmes first team as a substitute, playing in Ligue 2 for the first time since 2001. Sabin retired in 2009 to concentrate on his youth soccer project, while coaching part-time at Nîmes.

SALL, Abdou

Centre-back
Born: 1 November 1980, Dakar (Senegal)
United debut: 8 December 2002 v Swindon Town (sub)
Final United game: 14 December 2002 v Bristol Rovers (sub)
Appearances: 0+2
Clubs: Montauban FC Tarn-et-Garonne (France), FC Toulouse B (France), Kidderminster Harriers, Oxford United (loan), Nuneaton Borough, Revel, Cinderford Town, Kidderminster Harriers (loan), Forest Green Rovers, St Pauli (Germany), Altonaer Fußball-Club von 1893 e. V. (Germany)

Abdou Ahmed Sall had possibly the shortest Oxford career, in terms of game time, of any player. He joined United on loan from Kidderminster Harriers in November 2002, making his debut in Oxford's 1–0 FA Cup win over Swindon with just five seconds of stoppage time remaining. His second and final appearance for United was as a substitute against Bristol Rovers, where he played for the last five minutes, and in neither game did he touch the ball. Sall started his career with French side Montauban, joining Toulouse in 2000. It was from there that Sall joined Kidderminster in September 2001, scoring on his debut in a 4–1 defeat of York. After a bright start with the Harriers Sall was injured and he left Aggborough in February 2003, shortly after his loan with Oxford, following a falling-out with manager Ian Britton. He played three games with Nuneaton Borough and then had a brief spell in Saudi Arabia before rejoining Kidderminster in February 2004. In his total Harriers career, Sall played 56 games and scored three goals. In January 2005 he moved to Forest Green Rovers on a free transfer, scoring four goals in 26 appearances, before he joined German side St Pauli, based in Hamburg. Sall played just two League games for St Pauli in two seasons, before he joined Regionalliga Nord side Altona 93.

SALMON, Mike

Goalkeeper
Born: 14 July 1964, Leyland
United debut: 12 December 1998 v Birmingham City
Final United game: 12 December 1998 v Birmingham City
Appearances: 1
Clubs: Blackburn Rovers, Chester City (loan), Stockport County, Bolton Wanderers, Wrexham (loan), Wrexham, Charlton Athletic, Oxford United (loan), Ipswich Town, Tonbridge

Michael Bernard Salmon played just one game for Oxford while on loan from Charlton Athletic, at home to Birmingham City, but that game was United's worst home defeat in the Football League as the U's went down 7–1. Salmon began his career with Blackburn, where he played just one game although he enjoyed a lengthy 16-game loan with Chester City in October 1982. He joined Stockport County on a free transfer in August 1983 and went on to play 134 games for the Hatters over the next three seasons. In July 1986 Salmon joined Bolton, where he played 36 games before a 17-game loan spell with Wrexham in March 1987 that turned into a permanent move for £18,000. In the next two seasons Salmon made exactly 100 further appearances for the Red Dragons before Charlton Athletic paid £100,000 for him in July 1989. Salmon was with the Addicks for 10 years but due to injuries he played just 175 games for them. He moved to Ipswich in July 1999 as backup to England goalkeeper Richard Wright, but retired in 2002 without having turned out for their first team. Salmon became goalkeeping coach at Gillingham until 2004, while simultaneously coaching at the Arsenal Academy. In October 2007 Salmon moved to Vancouver, where he joined the Vancouver Whitecaps as goalkeeping coach.

SANDWITH, Kevin

Left-back
Born: 30 April 1978, Workington
United debut: 28 February 2009 v Torquay United (sub)
Final United game: 29 April 2010 v Rushden & Diamonds (sub)
Appearances: 31+10
Goals: 3
Clubs: Carlisle United, Barrow, AFC Telford, Doncaster Rovers, Halifax Town, Lincoln City, Macclesfield Town, Chester City, Weymouth, Oxford United, Mansfield Town

Kevin Sandwith joined United on a free transfer in February 2009 after being allowed to leave Weymouth following the Terras' inability to pay any of their players for over two months. Sandwith was unable to hold down a regular first-team place, and after being an unplayed substitute in the Conference Play-off Final he was released at the end of the 2009–10 campaign and signed for Mansfield Town, for whom he scored one goal in 33 games before being released by the Stags in May 2011. Sandwith started his career as a youth with Carlisle, making his debut in October 1997, but after just three games for the Cumbrians he joined Barrow in May 1998. Sandwith scored three times in 14 games for the Barrovians before joining Telford United in August 1999, where he scored once in 42 matches. He joined Doncaster in May 2001 but injury constrained his appearances to just 12 games, after which he moved to Halifax in November 2002. After three goals in 55 games Lincoln City paid £10,000 for him in March 2004 and in July 2005, after 45 games and two goals for the Imps, he moved to Macclesfield. In his year at Moss Rose Sandwith played 42 games and found the net five times before his move to Chester City in June 2006. He spent two seasons at the Deva, scoring three goals in 59 appearances, after which he turned down a new contract offer and signed for Weymouth in July 2008. Sandwith played 30 games for the Terras before he joined Oxford as a free agent.

SANGARÉ, Djoumin

Centre-back
Born: 16 December 1983, Dunkirk
United debut: 15 January 2011 v Bradford City (sub)
Final United game: 23 April 2011 v Chesterfield
Appearances: 2+2
Clubs: Wasquehal (France), Redbridge, Chelmsford City, Lewes, St Albans City (loan), Grays Athletic, St Albans City (loan), Stafford Rangers, Salisbury City, York City, Wydad Casablanca (Morocco), Oxford United, Kettering Town

Djoumin 'Jimmy' Sangaré started his career with the Dunkirk Academy before joining Wasquehal in the French Ligue 2. He moved to England to join Conference South side Redbridge in September 2004 while studying for a diploma in English. In January 2005 he moved to Chelmsford and thence to Lewes. At the start of the 2005–06 season Sangaré had five games on loan with St Albans and then joined full-time Conference National side Grays Athletic in August 2006. He made nine appearances for Grays before returning to Clarence Park on loan for the remainder of the season. In August 2007 Sangaré moved to Stafford Rangers after being released by Grays and in his season at Marston Road he scored two goals in 27 appearances. In August 2008 Sangaré signed for Salisbury City after scoring for them in a trial game when they beat Swindon Town and he scored two goals in 18 games for the Whites before joining Martin Foyle's York City in July 2009. Sangaré came on as a late substitute in York's Conference Play-off Final defeat by Oxford United, and the following season he left York in December 2010 to join Moroccan side Wydad Casablanca, managed by his former boss at Wasquehal. However, the manager left before his contract had been registered and the Moroccan champions agreed to rescind the offer, allowing Sangaré to return to England. He had a short trial with Lincoln City before Oxford nipped in to sign him. Sangaré, an athletic central-defender who was comfortable on the ball, impressed in his initial games, but he broke a metatarsal bone against Chesterfield and was released at the end of the season. In July 2011 Sangaré signed for Kettering Town.

SANTOS, Georges

Centre-back
Born: 15 August 1970, Marseilles
United debut: 6 January 2007 v Morecambe
Final United game: 23 January 2007 v Woking
Appearances: 5
Clubs: Toulon (France), Tranmere Rovers, West Bromwich Albion, Sheffield United, Grimsby Town, Ipswich Town, Queen's Park Rangers, Brighton & Hove Albion, Oxford United (loan), Chesterfield, Alfreton Town, Farsley Celtic, Fleetwood Town

Georges Santos started his career with Toulon, making 17 appearances for the French club before joining Tranmere in July 1998 and playing 54 games for them, scoring twice, before West Brom paid £25,000 for him in March 2000. Having helped save the Baggies from relegation Santos then joined Sheffield United in July 2000, spending two seasons at Bramall Lane. He played 68 games for the Blades, scoring six goals, before he was sent off in the 'Battle of Bramall Lane' against West Brom in March 2002, after which Neil Warnock did not select him again. He moved to Grimsby in December 2002, having already made his international debut for the Cape Verde Islands that September in their Africa Cup of Nations qualifier against Mauritania. The Mariners were relegated at the end of the season. Santos won their Player of the Season award, but he rejected a new contract in order to stay in the First Division and in July 2003 he moved to Ipswich. Santos scored one goal in 36 games for Ipswich before moving on to Queen's Park Rangers in July 2004. He stayed with Rangers for two seasons, scoring six goals in 77 appearances before Brighton signed him in August 2006, Santos having turned down an opportunity to return to Grimsby. Santos played 12 games for Brighton before his loan to Oxford, after which he was released by Albion and he joined Chesterfield on non-contract terms, but he did not play for them. After an unsuccessful trial with Rotherham Santos joined Alfreton in December 2007, but just over a month later he moved to Farsley Celtic. He made 17 appearances for the Leeds-based side before moving to Fleetwood in September 2008.

SAPPLETON, Ricky

Forward
Born: 8 December 1989, Kingston (Jamaica)
United debut: 1 January 2009 v Salisbury City (sub)
Final United game: 24 January 2009 v Crawley Town (sub)
Appearances: 2+3
Goals: 1
Clubs: Queen's Park Rangers, Leicester City, AFC Bournemouth (loan), Oxford United (loan), AFC Telford United (loan), Macclesfield Town (loan), Macclesfield Town

Reniel 'Ricky' Sappleton was a large, powerful striker who joined United on loan from Leicester City in January 2009, becoming manager Chris Wilder's first signing for the club. Sappleton scored on his debut against Salisbury City, but thereafter failed to impress and his loan was not extended. The Jamaican striker started as a youth with QPR, and after a trial he joined Leicester City in June 2007 after also having trials with Middlesbrough and Liverpool. Sappleton made just one substitute appearance for the Foxes, after which, in August 2008, he went on loan to Bournemouth, where he scored once in four games. After his loan to Oxford, Sappleton had a loan with Telford in March 2009, scoring one goal in seven games. In August 2009 he had an altogether more successful loan with Macclesfield Town, scoring six goals in 11 games and prompting the Silkmen to sign him permanently in January 2010. In March 2009 Sappleton was capped by Jamaica in the qualifiers for the Under-20 World Youth Cup in Florida. At the end of the 2010–11 season Sappleton was released by Macclesfield.

SAUNDERS, Carl

Striker
Born: 26 November 1964, Marston Green
United debut: 27 December 1993 v Crystal Palace (sub)
Final United game: 22 January 1994 v Stoke City (sub)
Appearances: 2+3
Clubs: Stoke City, Bristol Rovers, Middlesbrough (loan), Oxford United, Walsall, Sliema Wanderers (Malta), Hibernians (Malta)

Carl Stephen Saunders joined Oxford on non-contract terms after leaving Bristol Rovers. He had started his career with Stoke City, joining the Victoria Ground outfit in 1982 after leaving Washwood Heath School. Saunders was Stoke's top League goalscorer in 1986–87 with 19 goals and in his time with the Potters he scored 24 goals in 164 League appearances before he moved to Bristol Rovers in 1990. He played 142 League games for the Pirates, scoring 42 goals, and had a brief loan with Middlesbrough, before joining Oxford on non-contract terms in December 1993. Later that season Saunders played two games for Walsall before leaving for Malta, where he joined Sliema Wanderers, for whom he scored a record-breaking 18 goals in 17 games in the Maltese Premier League. In 1996 he joined fellow Maltese side Hibernians, but in 1998 he had to retire through injury and he became a community liaison officer with the Diversity Unit of the Avon and Somerset Constabulary.

SAUNDERS, Dean

Striker
Born: 21 June 1964, Swansea

United debut: 14 March 1987 v Liverpool
Final United game: 22 October 1988 v Blackburn Rovers
Appearances: 70+3
Goals: 33
Clubs: Swansea City, Cardiff City (loan), Brighton & Hove Albion, Oxford United, Derby County, Liverpool, Aston Villa, Galatasaray (Turkey), Nottingham Forest, Sheffield United, Benfica (Portugal), Bradford City

Dean Nicholas Saunders left Oxford in controversial circumstances. After United's Division Two game against Blackburn, Oxford boss Mark Lawrenson was informed by chairman Kevin Maxwell that Saunders had been sold to Robert Maxwell's Derby County for £1 million, despite prior assurances that he would not be sold during the season. Saunders started his career with his home-town club Swansea City, where he scored 12 goals in 55 games before being handed a free transfer to Brighton in August 1985, having completed a four-game loan spell with Cardiff in March that year. He was at the Goldstone Ground for 18 months, playing 86 games and scoring 26 goals before his £60,000 transfer to the Manor. In his short time with the U's Saunders became immensely popular with the fans with his lightning pace and his eye for goal, although his goals were not enough to prevent the club being relegated from the top flight in 1988. Saunders played 131 games and scored 57 goals for Derby, prompting Liverpool to pay an English record £2.9 million for him in July 1991 following the Rams' relegation from the First Division. However, Liverpool's patient passing game was not suited to Saunders' exceptional speed and he failed to prosper at Anfield, although he was a member of the 1992 FA Cup-winning side and the following season became the first Liverpool player to score four goals in a European game, against Finnish side Kuusysi Lahti in the UEFA Cup. After scoring 25 goals in 61 games he was sold on to Aston Villa for a club record £2.3 million in September 1992. Saunders was at Villa Park for three seasons, and his 49 goals in 142 appearances included a brace in a 3–1 win against Manchester United in the 1994 Coca-Cola Cup Final. In 1995 Saunders was voted the Supporters' Player of the Year but this did not prevent Villa from selling him to Turkish giants Galatasaray for £2.35 million. Saunders was in Turkey for one season, scoring 15 goals in 27 games, before returning to England when Nottingham Forest signed him for £1.5 million. He was at the City Ground for one season, scoring just nine goals in 51 games, with Forest getting relegated at the end of the campaign. In December 1997 Saunders joined Sheffield United on a free transfer. He was with the Blades for a year, scoring 22 goals in 57 matches and earning a £500,000 move to Benfica in December 1998. He was in Portugal for less than a season before manager Graeme Souness, who was also Saunders' boss in Turkey, got the sack and a change of personnel resulted in Saunders returning to England to join Bradford City, newly promoted to the Premier League, on a free transfer in August 1999. In his two seasons at Valley Parade Saunders scored six goals in 53 appearances before hanging up his boots and taking up a coaching role. In May 2003 he was appointed first-team coach at Blackburn and in September 2004 he again joined up with Souness when he became coach at Newcastle United. The whole management team was sacked in February 2006, and in June 2007 Saunders was appointed assistant manager of Wales, working under John Toshack. Saunders was appointed manager of Wrexham, alongside his Wales duties, in October 2008. During his career, Saunders' total transfer fees amounted to over £10.6 million, a record for an Oxford player. Saunders won Football League representative honours alongside his 75 Wales caps, of which six were won while he was at Oxford.

SAVAGE, Dave

Midfielder
Born: 30 July 1973, Dublin
United debut: 11 August 2001 v Rochdale
Final United game: 26 April 2003 v Scunthorpe United
Appearances: 95
Goals: 5
Clubs: Kilkenny City (Ireland), Brighton & Hove Albion, Longford Town (Ireland), Millwall, Northampton Town, Oxford United, Bristol Rovers, Rushden & Diamonds, Brackley Town, Oxford City

David Thomas Patrick Savage joined United in the summer of 2001, signed by Mark Wright just before the start of the first season at the Kassam Stadium following a successful trial. He joined from Northampton, where he had gained a reputation as being someone who was dependable but tended to be a 'Big Match' player. Savage started his career with Kilkenny City, scoring on his debut in October 1990 before he was signed by Brighton in March 1991. He had not played a game for the Seagulls before he returned to Ireland with Longford Town, although two years later he was back in England after Millwall paid £15,000 for him. Over the next three and a half years Savage played 152 games for the Lions, scoring 10 goals, before Northampton paid £80,000 for him in October 1998. He netted 18 times in 124 games for the Cobblers before he signed for Oxford. Savage was released by United in July 2003 and signed for Bristol Rovers, where he played 71 games and scored three goals in two seasons. In May 2005 Savage signed for Rushden & Diamonds, making 74 appearances and scoring three goals in two seasons. In May 2007 he was released and joined Brackley Town, moving to Southern League rivals Oxford City two years later. Savage finally retired from playing in May 2011. He won five Ireland Under-21 caps and five full Ireland caps.

SCOTT, Andy

Striker
Born: 2 August 1972, Epsom
United debut: 13 January 2001 v Walsall
Final United game: 4 October 2003 v Boston United
Appearances: 80+20
Goals: 25
Clubs: Sutton United, Sheffield United, Chesterfield (loan), Bury (loan), Brentford, Oxford United, Leyton Orient

Andrew Scott was signed from Brentford in January 2001 in a joint deal with Rob Quinn for £150,000 when he was the Bees' leading scorer. Scott's greatest asset was probably his pace although, for a forward, his finishing was lacking, especially in one-on-one situations. He also created a lot of goals for his strike partners, and his pace won the club a lot of penalties. After leaving United in March 2004 having broken his leg in his last game at Boston, he joined Orient, where it was discovered that Scott had a heart problem. He was forced to retire prematurely from playing the game, becoming a youth team coach for the O's, having scored 10 goals in 53 games for them. Scott started his career with Sutton United, from where he was signed by Sheffield United for £50,000 in December 1992. He scored 11 goals in 87 appearances for the Blades and had loan spells at Chesterfield in October 1996, where he scored three goals in five games, and at Bury in March 1997, where he played eight games. In November 1997 he moved to Brentford for £75,000 where he played 143 games and scored 37 goals before David Kemp signed him for Oxford. In May 2007 Scott was appointed Terry Butcher's assistant at Brentford, becoming caretaker when Butcher was sacked in December 2008 and taking over permanently the following month. Scott was sacked in February 2011 and appointed manager of Rotherham United in April 2011.

SCOTT, David

Goalkeeper
Born: 6 June 1918, Belfast
Died: December 1977
United debut: 20 August 1949 v Hastings United
Final United game: 16 September 1950 v Slough Town
Appearances: 32
Clean sheets: 6
Clubs: Linfield, Northampton Town, Headington United

David Perry Scott was one of Headington United's first professional players, signing from Northampton in August 1949 and making his debut in the club's first Southern League game, a 5–2 defeat at Hastings United. However, that was Scott's last first-team game until November 1949 as he lost his place to Jack Casley and then Gerry Woodward. Scott had made 11 League appearances for Northampton after joining them from Linfield.

SEACOLE, Jason

Forward
Born: 11 April 1960, Oxford
United debut: 7 September 1976 v Mansfield Town (sub)
Final United game: 31 March 1982 v Gillingham
Appearances: 113+21
Goals: 26
Clubs: Oxford United, Swindon Town, Witney Town, Wycombe Wanderers, Witney Town

Jason Paul Seacole was United's youngest ever first-team Football League player, making his debut on 7 September 1976 at the age of just 16 years and 149 days in a 3–0 home defeat by Mansfield Town. He is also the youngest United player to start a Football League game, on 2 October 1976 in a 1–1 draw with Tranmere Rovers, and the youngest United player to score in the Football League, his first goal coming in a 4–2 win over Shrewsbury Town on 1 March 1977. Seacole came through the youth team ranks at Oxford. He joined as an apprentice in 1976 and was promoted to the seniors in the same season, but he suffered through coming of age when the club was at its lowest ebb for many years. He also endured a serious injury that caused him to miss the whole of the 1978–79 season. He never regained his first-team place, making a handful of appearances in the next two seasons before being given a free transfer. Seacole was called-up for the England Youth squad to play in the 29th UEFA international tournament in Poland in May 1978. He joined Witney Town after a brief spell on Swindon's books, where he did not play a game. He was with Witney for five years and in 1986 joined Wycombe Wanderers, with whom he won promotion to the Conference. In December 1987 he rejoined Witney and he has since played cricket for Witney Swifts.

SELBY, Peter

Full-back
Born: 18 May 1940, Manchester
United debut: 28 December 1959 v Barry Town
Final United game: 30 January 1960 v Dartford
Appearances: 2
Clubs: Manchester City, Blackburn Rovers, Headington United

Peter D Selby played for Manchester Boys at the age of 14. He was signed by Manchester City when he left school and after playing for their colts and A teams he joined Blackburn as an amateur at the age of 16. He failed to progress beyond the Rovers A and B sides and when he was 18 he joined United.

SEMPLE, Ryan

Right-winger
Born: 4 July 1985, Belfast
United debut: 1 March 2008 v Forest Green Rovers (sub)
Final United game: 1 March 2008 v Forest Green Rovers (sub)
Appearances: 0+1
Clubs: Peterborough United, Farnborough (loan), Lincoln City, Chester City (loan), Rushden & Diamonds (loan), Oxford United, Brackley Town, Deeping Rangers, Haverhill Rovers, Gainsborough Trinity, Boston United

Ryan David Semple joined Oxford on non-contract terms at the end of February 2008, but he was released two weeks later because he was unable to prove his fitness. He started as a trainee with Peterborough United, but was hampered by a broken leg, going on loan to Farnborough in November 2003 to aid his recuperation. Semple scored two goals in nine games at Farnborough but even after recovery he failed to set the Posh alight and made just 52 appearances, scoring three goals, in four years at London Road. In July 2006 Semple moved to Lincoln City, where again he struggled for success, making just four substitute appearances for the Imps in his time at Sincil Bank. He had a six-game loan spell with Chester in November 2006 and four games on loan with Rushden & Diamonds in August 2007. In January 2008 his contract with Lincoln was cancelled and he tried his luck with Oxford on non-contract terms. After leaving United he joined Brackley Town, managed by his former Peterborough teammate David Oldfield. In May 2008 Semple was released by Brackley and after an unsuccessful trial with Boston United he joined Deeping Rangers in August 2008. In April 2009 Semple signed dual-registration forms, allowing him to play for Haverhill Rovers while remaining on Deeping's books. Semple scored 30 goals in 39 games for Deeping, making him joint top scorer in the United Counties League, before joining Gainsborough Trinity in June 2009. In March 2010 he signed for Boston United.

SHARMAN, Pete

Left-half
Born: 1924, Headington
United debut: 20 August 1949 v Hastings United

Final United game: 25 February 1950 v Bath City
Appearances: 25
Clubs: Oxford City, Headington United

Peter Leopold Sharman was, along with Cliff Nugent, the first semi-professional player to join Headington United following Harry Thompson's arrival. He was originally on Oxford City's books, where he had made his debut against Windsor & Eton in the Great Western Combination in September 1942. After playing 44 games and scoring one goal for City he played his final game for the Hoops in May 1949, and he then approached the Headington board in July 1949 to sign as a part-time professional. Sharman lived in Wolvercote and worked in Banbury at the time of his signing, making his debut in the club's first game in the Southern League, and he was a regular in the side until February 1950. However, he never adjusted to the pace of the Southern League and, after moving to live in Burford, he asked for his contract to be terminated in September 1950. He went on to be a sports teacher at Burford School.

SHAW, Paul

Midfielder
Born: 4 September 1973, Burnham
United debut: 1 September 2007 v Halifax Town
Final United game: 6 October 2007 v Droylsden
Appearances: 9
Goals: 2
Clubs: Arsenal, Burnley (loan), Cardiff City (loan), Peterborough United (loan), Millwall, Gillingham, Sheffield United, Rotherham United (loan), Rotherham United, Chesterfield, Oxford United, Ferencvaros (Hungary), Retford United, FC New York

Paul Shaw began his career with Arsenal in 1991 but spent much of his time on loan, first to Burnley, where he scored four goals in nine matches in March 1995, then to Cardiff City in August 1995, where he played six games, and finally to Peterborough United, where he scored five times in 14 appearances in October 1995. He made 13 first-team appearances for Arsenal, scoring two goals, before signing with Millwall for £250,000 in 1997, where he scored 31 goals in 125 matches. The attacking midfielder left Millwall in 2000, joining Gillingham for £450,000 and spending three and a half years at Priestfield, playing 151 games and scoring 29 goals. In January 2004 Shaw joined Sheffield United, scoring eight goals in 40 appearances before going on loan to Rotherham United in August 2004, where he scored twice in nine games. He signed permanently for the Millers in January 2006, playing a further 17 matches in which he scored four times, before moving to Chesterfield. He made 34 appearances for the Spireites in which he found the net on five occasions. After leaving Chesterfield by mutual consent Shaw signed for Oxford United, but before he could get established in the side he had the opportunity to move to Hungary to play for Ferencvaros between 2008 and 2010, scoring 21 goals in 48 games and helping the side return to the Soproni Liga after a three-year absence. Shaw returned to England and joined Retford United, where he scored three goals in 12 appearances before joining United Soccer League side FC New York as player-coach.

SHELTON, Gary

Midfielder
Born: 21 March 1958, Nottingham
United debut: 15 August 1987 v Portsmouth
Final United game: 13 May 1989 v Watford
Appearances: 73+6
Goals: 3
Clubs: Walsall, Aston Villa, Notts County (loan), Sheffield Wednesday, Oxford United, Bristol City, Rochdale (loan), Chester City

Gary Shelton joined Oxford from Sheffield Wednesday in July 1987 when Maurice Evans paid £150,000 to bring him to the Manor. However, United were relegated to the Second Division at the end of his first season and although Shelton looked more assured in the second tier he was transferred to Bristol City in August 1989 with future England manager Steve McClaren moving the other way. Shelton started his career with Walsall, where he was an apprentice, scoring one goal in his 29 appearances for the Saddlers. In January 1978 Aston Villa paid £80,000 for him, but in four years at Villa Park Shelton played just 27 games, in which he scored eight goals, plus an eight-game loan spell with Notts County in March 1980. He joined Sheffield Wednesday for £50,000 in March 1982 and was with the side two years later when they won promotion to the First Division. In over five years at Hillsborough Shelton played 242 games, scoring 24 goals and winning his solitary England Under-21 cap, before his move to Oxford. After his two years with United Shelton enjoyed another lengthy spell at Ashton Gate, making 180 appearances and scoring 27 goals over five seasons, and even being appointed joint caretaker manager for a while in 1992. At the end of his time in Bristol he played three games on loan to Rochdale in February 1994 before finishing his career at Chester City, where he signed in July 1994. The following year he was made player-assistant manager. He played 80 games for the Seals, scoring eight goals, before he retired from playing in 1998. In June 2002 Shelton left Chester and took up a coaching role with West Bromwich Albion.

SHEPHEARD, Jon

Centre-back
Born: 31 March 1981, Oxford
United debut: 11 January 2000 v Wycombe Wanderers
Final United game: 24 October 2000 v Wigan Athletic
Appearances: 10+1
Goals: 1
Clubs: Oxford United

Jonathan Thomas Shepheard joined United's YTS in 1997, joining the professional ranks two years later. He was released in April 2002 after suffering a bad injury 18 months earlier and then another injury midway through his comeback game for the reserves. His only goal for the club was in the League Cup against Wolverhampton Wanderers at the Manor.

SHEPHERD, John

Inside-forward
Born: 20 September 1945, Maltby
United debut: 4 October 1969 v Millwall

Final United game: 10 January 1970 v Middlesbrough
Appearances: 14+2
Goals: 1
Clubs: Rotherham United, York City, Oxford United, Hereford United, Reading

John Arthur Shepherd broke into League football with Rotherham, where he signed professionally in April 1966, playing in 24 League games in which he scored two goals. He joined York in September 1968, making just five appearances for the Minstermen before joining Oxford on a month's trial in September 1969. He did well enough to earn a full contract but after appearing in United's League Cup win at Nottingham Forest and quarter-final defeat at Carlisle and the FA Cup third-round defeat at Stoke he was given a free transfer to Hereford United and later had a non-playing spell with Reading.

SHERIDAN, Jimmy

Right-winger
Born: 31 May 1925, Glasgow
Died: 4 December 2002
United debut: 18 August 1951 v Worcester City
Final United game: 26 April 1952 v Cheltenham Town
Appearances: 37
Goals: 4
Clubs: Shettleston, Alloa Athletic, Headington United, Stenhousemuir, Boston United

James Killian Sheridan was a bricklayer by trade. He joined Headington from Alloa Athletic where he had scored seven goals in 35 Scottish League appearances. He spent one season at the Manor before returning to Scotland to play for Stenhousemuir, where he played just one Scottish League game. Sheridan, who won a Scottish Junior cap against Ireland, joined Boston United in 1953, scoring five goals in his 22 games for the Pilgrims.

SHERRATT, Brian

Goalkeeper
Born: 29 March 1944, Stoke-on-Trent
United debut: 6 November 1965 v Watford
Final United game: 18 December 1967 v Chelmsford City
Appearances: 52
Clean sheets: 6
Clubs: Stoke City, Oxford United, Nottingham Forest (loan), Barnsley, Colchester United, Clanfield, Gainsborough Trinity

Brian Sherratt was an apprentice with Stoke City, making just one League appearance for the Potters before joining Oxford in time for the start of the 1965–66 season. After taking over goalkeeping duties from Harry Fearnley he was United's first choice until the arrival of Jim Barron gave him competition. Sherratt played one game on loan to Nottingham Forest in October 1968 before leaving for Barnsley in June 1969. He played one season for the Tykes, making 15 League appearances, before his transfer in September 1970 to Colchester United where he played nine games. His next stop was Clanfield in April 1971.

SHIELDS, Jimmy

Centre-forward
Born: 26 September 1931, Derry
United debut: 30 March 1969 v Kidderminster Harriers
Final United game: 27 February 1960 v Poole Town
Appearances: 5
Goals: 1
Clubs: Crusaders (Northern Ireland), Sunderland, Southampton, Headington United, South Shields

Robert James Shields started with the Londonderry Boys' Club A team, where he was team captain in 1948 and 1949 when they won the Minor Cup and were runners-up in the Minor League. He signed for fledgling Irish League club Crusaders, with whom he won the Ulster Cup in 1953. He won an inter-league cap against the Football League in September 1953 and an amateur cap against Wales in January 1954, when he scored in a 3–2 win. Shields signed for Sunderland for £10,000 in March 1954, but he did not manage to get into their first team. He was signed by Southampton in July 1956, the £1,000 fee being paid for by the Southampton Supporters' Club. Shields scored on his Saints debut and his good form earned him a call-up for an IFA game against the British Army in October 1956, in which he scored, and a full Northern Ireland cap against Scotland in November 1956. In total Shields scored 21 goals in his 42 games for Southampton before he broke his left leg while playing for the reserves in September 1957, effectively ending his Football League career. He missed the entire 1957–58 season and played just three times the following season before joining Headington United in March 1959. In 1961 he returned to the North East where he played for South Shields while resuming his original career as a joiner.

SHIPPERLEY, Keith

Outside-left
Born: 14 June 1942, Brill
United debut: 26 March 1960 v Tonbridge
Final United game: 8 April 1961 v Gravesend & Northfleet
Appearances: 10
Goals: 3
Clubs: Headington United, Cheltenham Town, Banbury Spencer

Keith Walter Shipperley seemed destined for greatness while at school, attending Rycotewood College in Thame where he played in the team that won the Aylesbury and District Schools League and Cup. He captained the District Schools side and represented Berks, Bucks & Oxon Schools in November 1956. He was also the school's athletics champion for two years and represented them at both cricket and table tennis. He played for the Brill Minors team that swept all before them in two successive seasons in 1956 and 1957 before he joined Headington in 1958, when he also played for Oxon Youth. Shipperley turned professional in October 1959. In 1962 Cheltenham approached United with a view to signing Shipperley, but he turned it down because of the travelling until they came back with a much better offer. He received a cartilage injury playing cricket which was to come back and haunt him later in his career. Shipperley was scouted by Johnnie Crichton, then manager of Banbury Spencer, at a cricket match in 1966, but he again damaged his cartilage playing cricket and had to retire injured before he was able to play a game for Banbury.

SHOTTON, Malcolm

Centre-back
Born: 16 February 1957, Newcastle upon Tyne
United debut: 8 August 1980 v Southend United
Final United game: 22 August 1987 v Wimbledon (sub)
Appearances: 336+2
Goals: 15
Clubs: Leicester City, Atherstone Town, Nuneaton Borough, Oxford United, Portsmouth, Huddersfield Town, Barnsley, Hull City, Ayr United, Frickley Athletic, Barnsley

Malcolm Shotton started his career as an apprentice with Leicester City, where he played two League games before leaving for Atherstone Town, who played him at left-back. He then joined Nuneaton Borough while working as a dyer at a hosiery factory. Boro manager Roy Barry reverted Shotton to a central-defender, where he excelled. The following season he was selected for the FA XI and the England non-League squad. He was signed for Oxford for £15,000 by Bill Asprey, whose assistant was former Nuneaton boss Barry, who recommended Shotton to Asprey. Shotton earned the nickname Sheenie (after Barry Sheene) when he arrived for his first day of training on a motorbike, unaware that this mode of transport was proscribed to professional footballers. Shotton went on to write himself into United history, earning his status as a true club legend by captaining the club throughout the Glory Years of the early to mid 1980s, culminating in him lifting the Milk Cup at Wembley in April 1986. In November 1986 Shotton was injured and was out for the rest of the season, returning for the final game. In August 1987 Shotton made a final substitute appearance for Oxford before his £70,000 move to Portsmouth signalled the end of the greatest period in United's history. He played just 12 games for Pompey before leaving for Huddersfield in November 1987. Shotton scored one goal in his 18 games for the Terriers, leaving for Barnsley in July 1988 where he played 74 games, scoring six goals, before his move to Hull in February 1990. Shotton was with the Tigers until 1992, playing 67 games and scoring twice, before moving to Ayr United, where he was made captain and then player-coach. He scored three goals in 83 games for the Honest Men and then returned to Barnsley in 1994. Shotton played 11 games, scoring once, for the Tykes before hanging up his boots in 1996 and becoming Barnsley's coach. In January 1988, following a fans' campaign, Shotton was appointed manager of Oxford, saving the club from relegation in his first season in charge. In October 1999 he left United and joined Loughborough University as director of football. He later worked for Leeds United Academy and did some scouting for Leeds before becoming manager of Barnsley College Academy and then working in Huddersfield selling Mercedes cars.

SHUKER, Johnny

Defender/Midfielder
Born: 8 May 1942, Eccles
United debut: 29 August 1962 v Lincoln City
Final United game: 2 April 1977 v Peterborough United
Appearances: 529+5
Goals: 47
Clubs: Oxford United, Witney Town

John Shuker was playing junior football in his native Manchester when an Oxford scout spotted him and he was invited to the Manor for a trial. He was signed as an amateur in 1960 and played for United's Metropolitan League side initially, mainly as an outside-left. He moved to Oxford and took a job as a decorator and in June 1961 he became a part-time professional, becoming full-time at Christmas 1961. At the end of his first season with United Shuker was given a free transfer, but he won a last-minute reprieve following an excellent display at wing-half in an end-of-season friendly. Shuker made his first-team debut in August 1962 at Lincoln City in a 1–0 defeat, playing at centre-forward; he also played at inside-right and inside-left. That season, as well as scoring five League goals, he scored 17 goals for the reserves as they finished runners-up to Arsenal in the Metropolitan League. Shuker continued to play in a number of different positions; he was a left-half while captaining the reserves in 1964–65, and later also played in defence, where he brought style and imagination to the role, always still looking to attack. He became captain of the first team after Ron Atkinson left in 1971, and again after Dave Roberts' departure in 1975. Shuker holds the United all-time appearance record, having played 534 games for the club. In 1977 Shuker was released and he sued the club for wrongful dismissal, but an industrial tribunal ruled in the club's favour. Shuker earned his FA coaching badges and in 2001 became manager of Witney Academy, formed from the ashes of Witney Town, until it folded the following year. He had earlier, in 2000, been appointed as director of football at Milton United.

SILLS, Tim

Striker
Born: 10 September 1979, Romsey
United debut: 4 February 2006 v Rochdale
Final United game: 29 April 2006 v Wrexham (sub)
Appearances: 9+4
Goals: 1
Clubs: Camberley Town, Basingstoke, Staines Town (loan), Kingstonian (loan), Kingstonian, Aldershot Town, Oxford United, Hereford United, Torquay United, Stevenage Borough, Rushden & Diamonds (loan), Aldershot Town

Timothy Sills was signed for Oxford from Aldershot in the January 2006 transfer window. Sills had an impressive reputation as a goalscorer in the Conference, but he was unable to replicate that at United, and in the 2006 close season he was transferred to Hereford United. Sills started as a trainee with Millwall, but started his senior career with Camberley in 1997 where he scored 31 goals in 54 games. He moved to Basingstoke in 1999 where he combined playing with studying for a degree in sports science at Portsmouth University. In three seasons with Basingstoke Sills scored 37 goals in 115 games. He had a five-game loan spell with Staines in 2000 in which he scored eight goals, and he scored five goals in 16 games on loan to Kingstonian from January to April 2001. While with Basingstoke Sills played one game for the England C side, against Belgium in February 2003. In May 2003 Sills joined Aldershot, where his record of 46 goals in 111 games prompted Brian Talbot to bring him to Oxford. However, Sills struggled at the higher level and was released by Jim Smith after United's relegation to the Conference. His League goalscoring problems continued with Hereford, where he managed just two goals in 43 games, and he dropped back into the Conference when he signed for Torquay United in June 2007. Again Sills proved more than adequate at Conference level as he ended his first season as the Gulls' top scorer with 21 goals. The following season Torquay won the Conference Play-off Final against Cambridge United, with Sills scoring the second goal, but back in the Football League Sills again struggled to score and in January 2010 he returned to the Conference with Stevenage Borough. Sills had scored 41 goals in 127 games for Torquay, but just four in 24 games after promotion. Sills struggled to establish himself in the Stevenage side that was also on its way to promotion from the Conference, scoring one goal in 17 games before Borough's promotion, but none afterwards, and he was loaned to Rushden & Diamonds in September 2010, where he scored one goal in 11 appearances. Sills was released by Stevenage in January 2011 and he returned to Aldershot, where he scored twice in 19 games before being released at the end of the 2010–11 season.

SIMPSON, Billy

Centre-forward
Born: 12 December 1929, Belfast
United debut: 20 August 1960 v Worcester City
Final United game: 8 October 1960 v Bath City
Appearances: 11
Goals: 3
Clubs: Linfield (Northern Ireland), Rangers, Stirling Albion, Partick Thistle, Oxford United

William Joseph Simpson was signed by Rangers from Linfield for a Rangers and Irish League record £11,150 in October 1950, having scored 75 goals in 129 games for the Northern Irish side after making his debut in March 1947. Simpson scored a hat-trick on his Rangers debut and twice scored four goals in a game for the Gers. He stayed at Ibrox for nine years, during which time he won 12 Northern Ireland caps and scored five goals for his country, including the winner in a 3–2 victory against England in November 1957. He made 239 appearances and scored 163 goals for the Glasgow giants and is a member of the Rangers Hall of Fame. In March 1959 Simpson moved to Stirling Albion, where he scored one goal in seven Scottish League appearances, and the following season he moved to Partick Thistle, where he scored twice in six matches. Simpson joined Oxford from Partick Thistle but had to quit on medical advice after suffering a knee injury in a game at Bath City.

SIMPSON, George

Inside-forward
Born: 3 December 1933, Shirebrook
United debut: 7 September 1957 v Aylesbury United
Final United game: 30 September 1957 v Worcester City
Appearances: 3
Clubs: Mansfield Town, Cheltenham Town, Hereford United, Gillingham, Headington United

George Leonard Simpson was a Mansfield Town junior who made eight Football League appearances for the Stags before his move to Cheltenham Town in 1954. He joined Headington from Gillingham, for whom he did not play in the Football League, in the summer of 1957.

SIMPSON, Paul

Left-winger
Born: 26 July 1966, Carlisle
United debut: 2 November 1988 v Sunderland
Final United game: 15 February 1992 v Brighton & Hove Albion
Appearances: 162+6
Goals: 50
Clubs: Manchester City, Finn Harps (Ireland) (loan), Oxford United, Derby County, Sheffield United (loan), Wolverhampton Wanderers, Walsall (loan), Blackpool, Rochdale, Carlisle United

Paul David Simpson was given his chance by Manchester City while still an apprentice, becoming one of their youngest debutants in October 1982, aged 16. He had a brief loan spell at Irish side Finn Harps before returning to City for the end of the 1984-85 season, during which he scored six goals in 10 games to help City win promotion to the First Division. While at Maine Road Simpson won three England Under-18 caps and five England Under-21 caps, scoring in the 1987 Toulon Tournament. After 155 games for City, in which he scored 50 goals, Simmo joined Oxford United for £200,000 in October 1988. Over the next three and a half years Simpson scored 50 goals, including two hat-tricks. In his time at the Manor, Simmo proved to be an exciting attacking winger, and he was immensely popular with the Oxford fans both for scoring goals and for his many assists. In February 1992 Derby County paid Oxford £500,000 for him. Simpson was at Derby for over five years, playing 225 games and scoring 57 goals. He had a six-game loan spell at Sheffield United in December 1996 and eight games at Wolverhampton Wanderers in October 1997 in which he scored two goals before Wolves signed him permanently for £75,000 in November 1997. Simpson spent just under three years at Molineux, making a further 55 appearances and scoring five goals. He played 10 games while on loan to Walsall in September 1998, scoring once, and in August 2000 he moved on to Blackpool. He played 94 games for the Tangerines, scoring 13 goals, helping the side win promotion to the Second Division via the Play-offs, before moving on to join Rochdale in March 2002. His nine appearances and six goals helped Rochdale into the Third Division Play-offs at the end of the 2001–02 season, but they lost to Rushden & Diamonds. After the departure of John Hollins in May 2002, Simpson was appointed player-manager. However, his playing form dropped with the pressure of management, and despite a good FA Cup run he was released by Rochdale. In July 2003 Simpson joined Carlisle United as a player, before taking over the management duties from Roddy Collins. By this time Carlisle were suffering a transfer embargo and were 15 points adrift at the foot of Division Four. Carlisle lost the first 12 matches in which he was in charge, but he then fashioned a remarkable turnaround that almost saved the club from relegation to the Conference. However, they won promotion at the first attempt, via the Play-offs, and the following season Carlisle reached the final of the Football League Trophy and won a second successive promotion. He was named League Two Manager of the Year for 2006, and was statistically the best manager in the country. In June 2006, after 157 games in charge, Simpson shocked the Cumbrians by joining Preston North End. He led Preston to the top of the Championship, their highest League placing for 55 years, before an alarming slump saw the side miss out on the Play-offs. Simpson was sacked in November 2007 and went to manage Shrewsbury Town in March 2008. They reached the 2009 League Two Play-offs but lost to Gillingham and he was sacked in April 2010, becoming manager of Stockport in July, but a run of poor performances led to his dismissal in January 2011.

SIMS, John

Forward
Born: 14 August 1952, Belper
United debut: 28 September 1974 v West Bromwich Albion
Final United game: 9 November 1974 v Portsmouth
Appearances: 6+1
Goals: 1
Clubs: Derby County, Luton Town (loan), Oxford United (loan), Colchester United (loan), Notts County, Exeter City, Plymouth Argyle, Torquay United, Exeter City, Torquay United, Saltash United, Waldon Athletic

John Sims joined Oxford on loan from his first side, Derby County, in September 1974. Sims played just five games for the Rams, but also had loan spells with Luton in November 1973, Oxford, and then Colchester United in January 1975. In December 1975 Notts County paid £10,000 for him and he scored 13 goals in 61 Football League games. Sims moved to Exeter in December 1978 for £12,000, where his 11 goals in 34 League appearances earned him a £22,500 move to Plymouth in October 1979. Sims established himself at Home Park, playing 163 League games in which he scored 43 goals and being named Player of the Year in 1982. In August 1983 Sims moved to Torquay United, scoring eight goals in 30 League games before he returned to Exeter in February 1984. He played 25 League games for the Grecians, scoring six goals, before returning to Torquay in November 1984 as player-coach. He became manager of Torquay in August 1985, lasting 33 days before moving to Saltash United and then Waldon Athletic as player-manager, while running a pub in Torquay.

SKEEN, Ken

Inside-right
Born: 20 March 1942, Cheltenham
United debut: 19 August 1967 v Shrewsbury Town
Final United game: 23 April 1974 v Carlisle United
Appearances: 248+22
Goals: 40
Clubs: Trowbridge Town, Swindon Town, Oxford United, Cheltenham Town

Kenneth Albert Skeen was spotted by Swindon Town scouts while playing for a local Cheltenham side. He was a regular in Swindon's youth side when a camping accident left him with serious burns and out of the game for two seasons. Salvation came when he was offered a chance to play for Southern League Trowbridge, and it was after playing in a pre-season friendly against Swindon in 1964 that the Robins signed him on again. He made his debut as a striker in a 3–1 defeat against Crystal Palace, but initially found games hard to come by. He made only sporadic appearances over the next three seasons, and by the time he signed for Oxford for £3,500 in the summer of 1967 he had played just 22 games for Swindon, scoring six goals. Skeen's first game for United was a 2–0 defeat at Shrewsbury on 19 August 1967, and he went on to play in every position except left-back. He even featured in goal against Bristol City after an injury to Roy Burton in December 1971. He made 270 appearances for United in a seven-year period, scoring 40 goals, including a brace in his second game for the club in a 3–1 League Cup win over Swansea. He started at Oxford as an outside-right, but moved to inside-right shortly afterwards. After missing most of the start of the 1968–69 season, Skeen returned at centre-forward, but he dropped into the midfield after the signings of Nigel Cassidy and Derek Clarke. Towards the end of his time with United, his versatility often saw him used as a substitute. His penultimate goal for the club came on 6 September 1972, in the 2–2 League Cup draw with Manchester United. His last appearance for Oxford was a 1–0 home defeat by Carlisle United on 23 April 1974, and he was released at the end of that season, going on to sign for his home-town club, Cheltenham Town. Skeen also played cricket for Cheltenham and later worked as a reporter for the Press Association.

SKULL, John
Winger
Born: 25 August 1932, Swindon
United debut: 5 February 1955 v Kidderminster Harriers
Final United game: 23 April 1956 v Dartford
Appearances: 33
Goals: 14
Clubs: Wellington Town, Swindon Town, Wolverhampton Wanderers, Headington United (loan), Banbury Spencer, Swindon Town

Corporal John Skull arrived on loan at Headington United from Wolverhampton Wanderers in February 1955. He started his career as an amateur with Wellington Town before signing as an amateur for his home-town club, Swindon, where he scored two goals in six appearances before joining Wolves in June 1950. A qualified physiotherapist, Skull was a corporal with the Royal Army Medical Corps, stationed at Wheatley Military Hospital and playing for the U's by arrangement with Wolves. He joined Banbury Spencer after leaving Wolves and returned to Swindon in September 1957, scoring nine goals in 28 games in his one season with the club.

SLABBER, Jamie
Striker
Born: 31 December 1984, Enfield
United debut: 18 November 2006 v Gravesend & Northfleet
Final United game: 9 December 2006 v Rushden & Diamonds (sub)
Appearances: 2+1
Clubs: Tottenham Hotspur, Akademisk Boldklub Copenhagen (Denmark) (loan), Swindon Town (loan), Aldershot Town, Grays Athletic, Oxford United (loan), Stevenage Borough, Havant & Waterlooville, Grays Athletic, Woking, Eastleigh

A former Spurs apprentice, having previously had a trial with Norwich City, Jamie Andrew Slabber was signed from Grays Athletic on a one-month loan in November 2006, going straight into the side that played at Gravesend & Northfleet, and which suffered United's first Conference defeat of the season. Before Slabber's sole substitute appearance for Spurs he played for England Under-18s in June 2002 and he also represented the Under-19s. He went on loan to Danish Super League side AB Copenhagen in March 2004, playing four games, but after returning to Tottenham Slabber was unable to get into the first team and he went on loan again to Swindon in January 2005. He played 10 games without scoring and in April 2005 he was given a free transfer to Aldershot until the end of the season; in his four appearances Slabber scored one goal, in the Conference semi-final Play-off defeat against Carlisle. He was released in May 2005 and signed for Grays Athletic, where his impressive performances earned him a call-up to the England C side against Belgium in November 2005. Slabber played 44 games for Grays, scoring 15 goals before he left for Stevenage the month after his loan with Oxford came to an end. He made just four appearances for Boro before he was released in May 2007 and he moved to Havant & Waterlooville. Slabber scored four goals in his 41 games but was released in October 2008, having failed to impress, which was the story of his career so far. He rejoined Grays the following month, playing 40 games and scoring seven goals before leaving for Woking on his 25th birthday. In the summer of 2010 Slabber moved to Eastleigh.

SLATTER, Neil

Right-back
Born: 30 May 1964, Cardiff
United debut: 28 September 1985 v Manchester City
Final United game: 17 October 1989 v Swindon Town
Appearances: 112+3
Goals: 9
Clubs: Bristol Rovers, Oxford United, AFC Bournemouth (loan), Gloucester City

Neil John Slatter won his first Wales cap aged just 16, becoming the then youngest player to represent Wales. He started his career with Bristol Rovers where he made his debut in 1981, while still an apprentice. He played in 148 Football League games for Rovers, scoring four goals, and in July 1985 he became Maurice Evans' first signing for United, joining for £70,000. Slatter missed the Milk Cup Final through injury, but he became a regular, playing in both full-back positions as required until a bad knee injury ended his professional career. He retired to Cardiff while joining Gloucester City to play part-time, but he managed just 52 minutes for the Tigers before he was substituted and he never played for the club again. Slatter became a policeman in Cardiff.

SLOAN, David

Right-winger
Born: 28 October 1941, Lisburn
United debut: 24 February 1968 v Reading
Final United game: 24 February 1973 v Swindon Town
Appearances: 189+11
Goals: 33
Clubs: Bangor (Northern Ireland), Scunthorpe United, Oxford United, Walsall, Bridlington

David Sloan was an exceptional right-winger; small and quick, he was a tenacious player with plenty of skill and a fierce shot. He signed for Scunthorpe United from Northern Irish club Bangor in November 1963, aged 22, after losing his job as a shipyard worker. While at Bangor, Sloan won two amateur international caps. Both games were against England, in 1962 and 1963 – he scored the deciding goal in a 2–1 win in the latter game. He also won a youth international cap, also against England, in May 1960. At Scunthorpe, Sloan won an Under-23 cap for Northern Ireland, against Wales in February 1964. He made his League debut for the Iron at Swansea Town in January 1964, scoring with a long-range shot, and he also scored in his next two matches. He played 136 games for the Lincolnshire team, scoring 42 goals, before he signed for Oxford in February 1968. George Kerr went the other way, with his value of £7,000 supplemented by £2,500 in cash. Sloan's arrival proved the catalyst for Oxford to win the Third Division Championship. It was Sloan's goal in the last game of the season, a 1–0 win over Southport on 11 May, that clinched the title for the U's. The following season Sloan scored United's first goal in the Second Division, after just six minutes of the opening game against Bolton Wanderers in a 1–1 draw. He also scored the club's first away goal in Division Two, although United lost 2–1 at Millwall. On 24 September 1969 Sloan scored the only goal with a diving header as United knocked out League Cup holders Swindon Town in the third round of the competition. Sloan became the first player on Oxford's books to win a full international cap, being called-up to play for Northern Ireland against Israel in Tel Aviv on 10 September 1968 in a game that Ireland won 3–2. He won his second cap in Seville against Spain on 11 November 1970, where he played alongside George Best as Ireland lost 3–0. Sloan made a total of exactly 200 appearances for United, his last match being the famous 3–1 win at the County Ground, the only time Oxford have won in Swindon, on 24 February 1973, exactly five years after his debut. At the end of the 1972–73 season Sloan moved to Walsall, having turned down a move to Aldershot and the opportunity of playing in New Zealand. He played 49 games and scored three goals for the Saddlers. He then turned down the option of a third year at Fellows Park, instead returning to Scunthorpe to become a steelworker. He still turned out for Bridlington for a while.

SMART, Gary

Right-back
Born: 29 April 1964, Totnes
United debut: 24 September 1988 v AFC Bournemouth
Final United game: 8 May 1994 v Notts County
Appearances: 195+9
Clubs: Wokingham Town, Oxford United, Stevenage Borough, Chertsey Town, Chesham United, Hayes, Slough Town, Aldershot Town, Oxford City, Leighton Town, Windsor & Eton

Gary James Smart played for Oxford for six seasons without scoring. He lectured in PE at Abingdon College of Further Education, and initially played for Wokingham Town, featuring in the side that reached the semi-finals of the FA Trophy in 1988. He joined Oxford in July 1988 for £22,500 but did not establish himself in the first team until November 1988. Smart was an integral part of the side that found itself relegated to the Third Division in 1994 and he was released in May after the final game. After his release, Smart had a trial with Woking before he moved to Stevenage Borough. He stayed at Broadhall Way until December 1994, and he actually scored a goal, against Telford, in his 22 games. Smart's next club was Chertsey, and in March 1995 he moved to Chesham before joining Hayes and then Slough Town, where he again scored in his only League appearance, although he also played two FA Cup games. In June 1998 Smart joined Aldershot, making 35 appearances before joining Oxford City as player-coach in February 1999, replacing Kelvin Alexis, and in October 2000 he moved to Windsor & Eton in the top division of the Isthmian League, via Leighton.

SMILLIE, Jimmy

Winger
Born: 30 March 1933, Cumbernauld
United debut: 31 August 1955 v Worcester City
Final United game: 1 May 1957 v Tonbridge
Appearances: 75
Goals: 29
Clubs: Duntochter Hibs, Third Lanark, Headington United, Bedford Town, Dumbarton, Stenhousemuir

James Smillie joined Headington United from Scottish League side Third Lanark, where he scored one goal in 12 Scottish League appearances. He completed a very successful first season in 1955–56, being an ever present. A prolific goalscorer, he headed the wing men's total in the Southern League goalscorers' table. Smillie left for Bedford Town in the summer of 1957. In 1958 he returned to Scotland to play 11 Scottish League games for Dumbarton, scoring 13 goals. He later joined Stenhousemuir where he played eight Scottish League games, scoring one goal.

SMITH, Andy

Goalkeeper
United debut: 18 August 1956 v Yeovil Town
Final United game: 26 March 1958 v Dartford
Appearances: 70
Clean sheets: 16
Clubs: Easthouses Lily, Queen of the South, Headington United

Andy Smith was a Scottish goalie who made one Scottish League appearance for Queen of the South before he moved south to join Headington.

SMITH, Barry

Centre-forward
Born: 15 March 1934, South Kirkby
Died: February 2007
United debut: 17 October 1959 v King's Lynn
Final United game: 30 March 1960 v Kettering Town
Appearances: 14
Goals: 5
Clubs: Farsley Celtic, Leeds United, Bradford Park Avenue, Wrexham, Stockport County, Headington United, Oldham Athletic, Bangor City, Southport, Accrington Stanley

Joseph Barry Smith spent his entire career in the north except for the one season that he spent with Headington United. He started with West Riding youth team and appeared in Bradford Park Avenue's Northern Intermediate League side before signing for Farsley Celtic, giving up his job as an apprentice plumber to join Leeds United in October 1951, where he scored his only goal in his two Second Division appearances on his debut against Fulham. After completing his National Service Smith moved to Bradford Park Avenue in May 1955, where he played 64 League games, notching 38 goals. He joined Wrexham in June 1957, scoring 10 goals in 18 League games and in July 1958 Smith was signed by Stockport County where he made 17 League appearances, managing 10 goals before his move to Headington. After leaving the U's he returned to Lancashire with Oldham Athletic in August 1960, but he played just one game for the Latics. He left Oldham for Bangor City in 1961, and the same year he was also on Southport's books without playing for the Sandgrounders, and had a one-month trial with Accrington Stanley, for whom he played three times in that club's final season in the Football League before they were replaced by Oxford United. He then left football to become a plumbing equipment rep before starting his own company.

SMITH, Charlie

Inside-left
United debut: 31 January 1959 v Merthyr Tydfil
Final United game: 31 January 1959 v Merthyr Tydfil
Appearances: 1
Clubs: Headington United

SMITH, Dave

Midfielder
Born: 26 December 1970, Liverpool
United debut: 13 August 1994 v Hull City
Final United game: 2 January 1999 v Crewe Alexandra (sub)
Appearances: 232+7
Goals: 3
Clubs: Norwich City, Oxford United, Stockport County, Macclesfield Town (loan), Drogheda United (Ireland), Macclesfield Town

David Christopher Smith, known as Smudger, started his career as an apprentice with Norwich City in November 1987, turning professional in July 1989. He made 23 appearances for the Canaries before Oxford paid £100,000 for him in July 1994. Smith was a mainstay in the United midfield as the club won promotion in 1996, when he forged a strong partnership with Martin Gray. Smith was a steady if unspectacular player who, despite clocking up over 200 appearances for the U's, was hardly prolific. In February 1999 Smith was allowed to leave United and he signed for Stockport County, where he played 76 games, scoring three goals. Smith joined Macclesfield on loan in February 2002, playing eight games for the Silkmen, and on his return to Edgeley Park he was released, joining Drogheda United in Ireland. Macclesfield were keen to sign Smith again, but because he was based in Ireland they had to wait until the January transfer window, although he trained with the Silkmen for most of the season. He eventually returned to Moss Rose in January 2003, remaining at Macclesfield until his contract was not renewed in May 2004, having played 14 further games for the club.

SMITH, Jay

Midfielder
Born: 25 September 1981, Lambeth
United debut: 25 March 2006 v Peterborough United

Final United game: 6 May 2006 v Leyton Orient
Appearances: 5+1
Clubs: Aston Villa, Southend United, Oxford United (loan), Notts County (loan), Notts County, Eastwood Town, Tamworth

Jay Alexander Smith was one of five new players signed by Jim Smith immediately upon his arrival on transfer deadline day in March 2006, joining on loan from Southend United. Despite some strong and impressive performances in the centre of midfield, Smith was unable to prevent United's relegation to the Conference and despite Oxford wanting to sign him permanently he returned to Southend for another season. Smith had started as a trainee with Aston Villa, but he joined Southend, initially on loan, in August 2002 without playing for the Villains. He played 18 games, scoring once, before he signed permanently for the Shrimpers in November 2002. In November 2006 Smith joined Notts County on loan, scoring one goal in his 11 games, and he stayed at Meadow Lane after Southend released him in January 2007; he had played 61 games since his move to Roots Hall was made permanent, scoring nine goals. Smith scored six goals in 45 appearances for the Magpies before he was released in January 2009, suffering from a severe hamstring injury. With the help of Wigan Athletic's medical team Smith regained fitness and he signed a one-month deal with Eastwood Town in December 2009, during which he played four games, before moving to Tamworth in January 2010.

SMITH, Jim

Forward
Born: 23 October 1923
Died: June 2004
United debut: 2 April 1938 v Osberton Radiators
Final United game: 3 September 1955 v Chelmsford City
Appearances: 142 (from September 1949)
Goals: 22 (from September 1949)
Clubs: Oxford City, Headington United, Peterborough United

James Edward O Smith was the youngest player to represent Oxford Boys, at the age of 10, and he set another record three years later when he played for Oxford City in the Isthmian League. Smith joined Headington United when they were still in the Oxfordshire Senior League, making his debut in April 1938 at the age of 14 years and scoring in a 7–3 win over Osberton Radiators. He scored again three weeks later in a 3–1 win at Banbury Harriers as United finished second in the League. Smith did not feature much in the first team and when World War Two broke out in September 1939. He worked at the Radcliffe Infirmary before joining the RAF in 1940, during which time he spent two years as an amateur with Peterborough United in the Midland League. He returned to Headington after the war and played throughout the club's Spartan League days. After Headington United joined the Southern League, Smith opted to retain his amateur status. He missed the first five games of the club's first season at that level, coming back in to the side for a 1–1 draw with Worcester City in September 1949, in which he scored Headington's goal. Smith scored five goals in six games playing at outside-left, using his speed and his powerful shooting ability to full advantage. Smith was called-up for a trial with the England Amateur international side on 27 October 1951. By the time that Smith ended his playing career due to a knee injury he was the longest-serving amateur in the Southern League. Smith played a total of 142 Southern League games, scoring 22 goals. He had captained the Oxfordshire FA and at his testimonial in October 1956 against an All-Star XI a crowd of 10,000 turned out, with Stanley Matthews one of the players on show. After he finished playing Smith became an assistant coach at Headington United and then managed Witney Town for two years. He also played cricket, captaining Oxford Boys against Cambridge at Lord's in 1936 and becoming captain of Headington CC. Smith was awarded an MBE in 1980 for his work with Buckinghamshire Area Health Authority as an area supplies officer.

SMITH, Ken

Centre-forward
Born: 21 May 1932, South Shields
United debut: 22 August 1953 v Bath City
Final United game: 4 December 1954 v Exeter City Reserves
Appearances: 58
Goals: 32
Clubs: Sunderland, Headington United, Blackpool, Shrewsbury Town, Gateshead, Darlington, Carlisle United, Toronto Italia (Canada), Halifax Town, Trowbridge Town

Kenneth Smith joined Headington United from Sunderland in the summer of 1953, having scored two goals in five games for the Rokerites. Smith scored a hat-trick on his Headington debut in a 3–2 win at Bath City in August 1953 and he went on to score some significant goals for Headington, including the only goal of the game against Millwall in the FA Cup second round in December 1953 that gave the U's their first competitive victory against Football League opposition. Smith also scored against Bolton Wanderers in the 4–2 fourth-round defeat in the same Cup run. In October 1954 Smith scored four goals in an 8–2 win over Hastings United and his final goal before his £2,000 move to Blackpool was in a 4–2 defeat at Norwich City in the FA Cup first round in November 1954. Smith was not a success with the Tangerines, playing just six Football League games and scoring four goals in his three years at Bloomfield Road. He moved to Shrewsbury where he was far more prolific, scoring 20 goals in his 44 Football League appearances, and then to Gateshead where his record was 18 goals in 45 League matches. After seven goals in 24 League games for Darlington, Smith joined Carlisle, where he scored 12 times in 14 League appearances before he played for Toronto Italia, a Canadian side, in 1961. He returned to England the same year to join Halifax, where he made 27 League appearances, scoring six goals, before leaving for Trowbridge Town.

SMITH, Roy

Left-back
United debut: 6 September 1952 v Lovell's Athletic
Final United game: 23 April 1953 v Llanelly
Appearances: 26
Clubs: Headington United

SMITHERS, Tim

Left-back/Left-wing
Born: 22 January 1956, Ramsgate
United debut: 8 August 1980 v Southend United
Final United game: 13 May 1983 v Southend United
Appearances: 118+6
Goals: 7
Clubs: Atherstone United, Bedworth United, Nuneaton Borough, Oxford United, Nuneaton Borough, Bedworth United

Timothy F Smithers joined Oxford from Nuneaton Borough at the same time as Malcolm Shotton in May 1980, also costing £15,000. Smithers was a pacy left-back, equally at home on the left wing, who was an aircraft fitter while playing with Nuneaton. In fact it was Roy Barry, his manager at Nuneaton, who converted Smithers from a winger to a full-back after the player had appeared for Borough on the wing during their giant-killing win over Oxford in November 1977. When Ian Greaves took over he played Smithers on the wing again initially, but Jim Smith changed him back to left-back. After failing to get a first-team place at the start of the 1983–84 season Smithers decided to go part-time and he returned to Nuneaton, where he was selected for the England Non-League side.

SMITHSON, Rodney

Right-half
Born: 9 October 1943, Leicester
United debut: 23 October 1965 v Brighton & Hove Albion
Final United game: 5 November 1974 v Bristol City
Appearances: 174+6
Goals: 6
Clubs: Arsenal, Oxford United, Witney Town

In 1958 Rodney George Smithson was taken on as an apprentice by Arsenal, having already received schoolboy representative honours in his native Leicester and a call-up to the England Youth side (in which John Milkins also featured). He turned professional in 1962 and signed with Oxford United in the summer of 1964, after making only two appearances for the Gunners. He did not immediately gain a place in the side, but Smithson soon established a reputation as one of the best anchormen around, and by the time United reached Division Two in 1968 he was a regular in the side. Smithson was linked with a move to higher-placed clubs, but with his son Jeremy ill in hospital he opted to remain at the Manor. During the 1972–73 season, Smithson played only two games, one of which was in the Anglo-Italian Tournament in a 1–1 draw with Torino. The following season he again appeared just twice, and in his final season he played three games. This lack of first-team games meant that Smithson consolidated himself as captain of the reserves. He was granted a testimonial, against Swindon Town, in May 1975. After leaving Oxford, Smithson went on to be player-manager of Witney Town.

SODJE, Onome

Striker
Born: 17 July 1988, Warri (Nigeria)
United debut: 24 November 2009 v Forest Green Rovers (sub)
Final United game: 28 December 2009 v Salisbury City (sub)

Appearances: 2+3
Goals: 1
Clubs: Charlton Athletic, Welling United (loan), Gravesend & Northfleet (loan), Gravesend & Northfleet, York City, Barnsley, Oxford United (loan), FK Senica (Slovakia)

Onome Sodje grew up in Warri, in Delta State, Nigeria, before moving to England as an adolescent. He joined the Charlton Athletic Academy, where he scored 14 goals in 19 starts in the Under-17 FA Premier Academy League in 2003–04, and he progressed to the reserves. Sodje joined Welling United on work experience in March 2005, scoring one goal in the first of his six games. He joined Gravesend & Northfleet on loan in September 2005, scoring two goals in eight games in his first loan spell, and he returned to Stonebridge Road on a second loan in February 2006 when he scored once in six matches. He was released by Charlton in the summer of 2006 without having played a first-team game and he joined Gravesend permanently in August 2006. Sodje scored the only goal of the game for Gravesend against Oxford in November 2006, condemning United to their first defeat in the Conference. Sodje played 40 games for the Fleet, scoring nine goals, before moving to York City on a free transfer in June 2007 on a non-contract basis because the Nigerian did not have UK residency so could not sign a contract. Sodje came on as a substitute in York's 2–0 FA Trophy Final defeat by Stevenage Borough at Wembley in May 2009, but that was his last appearance for the Minstermen before he signed for Championship side Barnsley in June 2009, having scored 24 goals in 101 games for York. While with York Sodje was threatened with deportation to Nigeria but the club helped Sodje win his appeal and gain permanent residency in the United Kingdom in April 2009, on the promise that he would then sign a contract with them, which he reneged on. He made just one appearance for Barnsley before his loan to Oxford, and immediately after he returned to Oakwell he left for Slovakian Superliga side FK Senica, for whom he scored on his debut, but that was his only goal in his 13 games in the 2009–10 season.

SPEARING, Tony

Left-back
Born: 7 October 1974, Romford
United debut: 23 February 1985 v Blackburn Rovers
Final United game: 16 March 1985 v Brighton & Hove Albion
Appearances: 5
Clubs: Norwich City, Stoke City (loan), Oxford United (loan), Leicester City, Plymouth Argyle, Peterborough United, King's Lynn, Stalham, AFC Sudbury, Great Yarmouth, Wisbech Town

Anthony Spearing played for the Norwich City youth side that won the FA Youth Cup in 1983. He made his first-team debut in May 1984, but broke his leg at the start of the following season. As part of his recuperation he played nine games on loan with Stoke in November 1984, followed by his five games with the U's in Oxford's Division Two Championship season in February 1985. He eventually earned his place in the Norwich side and made 82 appearances before his £100,000 move to Leicester City in July 1988. Spearing scored one goal in 79 games for the Foxes before he moved to Plymouth in July 1991. He made 46 appearances for Argyle before moving to Peterborough in January 1993. Spearing was a regular with the Posh over the next four years, scoring two goals in 129 games, after which he joined King's Lynn in the summer of 1997. In May 1998 he was appointed player-manager of the Linnets, but in September he decided that he was not suited to management and stepped down to be solely a player. In 2000 Spearing was reappointed as King's Lynn manager and he was in charge for four and a half years before he was relieved of his duties in March 2002. He played briefly for Stalham before signing for AFC Sudbury, with whom he won the Jewson League and reached the Final of the FA Vase, losing 2–1 to Brigg Town in May 2003. That was his final game for Sudbury and the following season he played for Great Yarmouth, where he was voted Player of the Year, before joining Wisbech in August 2004, playing for them until he was released in October that year. Spearing became assistant manager of Cambridge United in the summer of 2005, but both he and manager Rob Newman were sacked in September 2006. He was appointed senior scout at Blackburn Rovers and in March 2008 he joined West Bromwich Albion as head of European recruitment.

SPELMAN, Ron

Outside-right
Born: 22 May 1938, Blofield, Norfolk
United debut: 1 September 1965 v Millwall
Final United game: 12 March 1966 v Bristol Rovers (sub)
Appearances: 18+1
Goals: 2
Clubs: CNSOBU, Norwich City, Northampton Town, Bournemouth & Boscombe Athletic, Watford, Oxford United, Wisbech Town

Ronald E Spelman signed professionally with Norwich City in August 1956, but made just two League appearances for the Canaries before his transfer to Northampton Town in November 1960. The Cobblers won promotion from Division Four at the end of his first season, but in March 1962, after scoring three goals in 34 League games, Spelman joined Bournemouth. He was with the Cherries until September 1963, making 28 League appearances and scoring four goals, when he joined Watford. Spelman was at Vicarage Road until his move to Oxford in the summer of 1965, playing 40 Football League games in which he scored three times for the Horns. Spelman failed to make the Oxford right-wing berth his own and he was given a free transfer at the end of his first season, after which he returned to Norfolk with Wisbech Town.

ST AIMIE, Kieron

Midfielder
Born: 4 May 1989, Brent
United debut: 1 November 2007 v Rushden & Diamonds
Final United game: 17 November 2007 v Ebbsfleet United
Appearances: 3
Clubs: Queen's Park Rangers, Oxford United (loan), Barnet, Grays Athletic (loan), Stevenage Borough (loan), Lewes (loan), Thurrock, Hitchin Town, Maidenhead United, Lewes, AFC Hornchurch, Kettering Town

Kieron Lloyd J. Minto St Aimie started his career with Queen's Park Rangers, signing professionally in the summer of 2007, having impressed playing for the reserves. St Aimie scored for the R's in a pre-season friendly against Celtic, and in October 2007 he joined Oxford on a two-month loan deal, but he failed to impress and returned to Loftus Road after just three weeks. In

January 2008 his Rangers contract was terminated by mutual consent; St Aimie had made just one senior appearance for the Super-Hoops, coming on as a substitute in a League Cup defeat by Leyton Orient in August 2007. He signed for Barnet later that month and in September 2008 he had a loan spell with Grays Athletic, in which he played six games and scored twice, both against Wrexham on his Grays debut. In November 2008 he went on loan to Stevenage but made just one substitute appearance, and in January 2009 he played five games on loan to Lewes. On his return to Underhill, where he had made 15 appearances, he was released by mutual consent, and in March 2009 he joined Thurrock, moving on to Hitchin the following month. St Aimie moved to Maidenhead in the summer of 2009 where he played in a variety of attacking roles, scoring eight goals in 24 games in his second season, until he was released in March 2011, rejoining fellow Blue Square South relegation strugglers Lewes later that week. He did not last long at Lewes, playing just half an hour for them before joining Hornchurch just a few days later. In April 2011 St Aimie joined Kettering Town, playing without pay in an attempt to earn a contract. He scored on his debut in a 1–1 draw with York and made five further appearances before the end of the season.

STABLES, Ian

Outside-right
United debut: 30 August 1958 v Boston United
Final United game: 22 November 1958 v Guildford City
Appearances: 6
Clubs: Balgownie, Dundee, Weymouth, Headington United, Kidderminster Harriers, Brechin City

Ian T Stables joined Headington in the summer of 1958, but he left for Kidderminster Harriers in January 1959 after failing to establish himself in the first team. The winger joined Dundee from Balgownie, scoring six goals in 26 Scottish League games in his four seasons at Dens Park before his move to Weymouth. After leaving Kidderminster Stables joined Brechin, where he played five League games.

STANDING, Michael

Midfielder
Born: 20 March 1981, Shoreham
United debut: 11 August 2007 v Forest Green Rovers
Final United game: 27 October 2007 v Merthyr Tydfil (sub)
Appearances: 3+4
Clubs: Brighton & Hove Albion, Aston Villa, Bradford City, Walsall, Chesterfield, Queen's Park Rangers, AFC Bournemouth, Oxford United, Grays Athletic, Lewes

After impressing while on trial during the 2007 pre-season friendlies, Michael John Standing signed for United on a non-contract basis. He left before the January transfer window, when he was snapped up by Grays Athletic. After starting as a trainee with Brighton he joined Aston Villa's youth squad. In March 2002 Standing was released by Villa and Bradford City swooped to sign him. He scored two goals in 32 appearances for the Bantams before signing for Walsall two years later. In July 2006 he left the Saddlers by mutual consent, having scored four goals in 61 appearances, and in October he signed for Chesterfield. Standing played just one first-team game for the Spireites, in the Johnstone's Paint Trophy, leaving shortly afterwards and then signing for QPR, for whom he did not play, on a non-contract basis in January 2007. In March 2007 Standing signed for AFC Bournemouth, for whom he made just one substitute appearance before signing for Oxford. After leaving the U's Standing played 16 games for Grays, scoring two goals, before he was released in the summer of 2008, when he signed for Lewes. He scored three goals in 36 games for Lewes before he was released and retired from playing, setting himself up as an agent.

STANTON, Sid

Wing-half
Born: 16 June 1923, Dudley
United debut: 20 August 1949 v Hastings United
Final United game: 5 May 1951 v Hastings United
Appearances: 51
Goals: 1
Clubs: Birmingham City, Northampton Town, Headington United

Sidney Horley Stanton made seven Football League appearances for Northampton before signing for £500 as a part-time professional with Headington in time for their first game in the Southern League. Originally with Birmingham City, he left St Andrew's without making a first-team appearance.

STEEL, Ronnie

Winger
Born: 3 June 1929, Newburn
Died: 2009
United debut: 23 August 1952 v Kidderminster Harriers
Final United game: 20 April 1955 v Gloucester City
Appearances: 131
Goals: 32
Clubs: Bishop Auckland, Darlington, Headington United, Bedford Town, Banbury Spencer, Witney Town

Ronald Steel played 66 Football League games for Darlington after he joined from Bishop Auckland in 1950. He joined Headington in the summer of 1952, but in 1955 he was one of four Headington players who left for Southern League rivals Bedford Town following a dispute over the non-payment of appearance money. Steel played 73 games and scored 15 goals for the Eagles over two seasons and next turned up at Banbury Spencer in 1958 and then at Witney in 1961.

STEELE, Lee

Striker
Born: 7 December 1973, Liverpool
United debut: 21 December 2002 v Exeter City (sub)
Final United game: 8 May 2004 v Rochdale (sub)
Appearances: 6+21
Goals: 4
Clubs: Bootle, Northwich Victoria, Shrewsbury Town, Brighton & Hove Albion, Oxford United, Leyton Orient, Chester City (loan), Chester City, Northwich Victoria, Barrow (loan), Oxford City, Ashton United, Oxford City

Lee Anthony Steele joined United during the summer of 2002, having earned himself an excellent reputation at Brighton. His start to the 2002–03 season was delayed due to suspension and a minor ankle injury, followed by an abdominal strain and other injuries. Steele scored on his eventual United debut against Exeter in December 2002, but just after breaking into the side a knee injury received in March 2003 kept him out of United's side until December. Steele started his career with Bootle, joining Northwich Victoria in March 1996. In August 1997 Shrewsbury paid £30,000 for Steele and over the next three seasons he scored 41 goals in 128 games for the Shrews before leaving for Brighton on a free transfer, denying Northwich a fee from a sell-on clause. Before his move to Oxford in July 2002 Steele played 70 matches and scored 12 goals. He was Albion's second-top scorer in their Division Two Championship season in 2002, despite only making 18 appearances. After leaving United he joined Leyton Orient, and it was while there that he scored the winning goal against Oxford that ensured the O's were promoted, while at the same time the U's were relegated to the Conference. He remained with Orient until October 2006, by which time he had made 86 appearances and scored 27 times, when he joined Chester on loan, the move being made permanent in the January 2007 transfer window. Steele scored three goals in 24 games before being released by the Seals in July 2007, upon which he returned to Northwich Victoria. In December 2007 Steele scored for the Vics in their win over Oxford United, repeating the feat in March 2008. His goalscoring rescued Northwich from relegation and earned him both the Players' and Supporters' Player of the Year awards. He played seven games without scoring on loan to Barrow in February 2009 before he left the Vics, having played 47 times and scored 16 goals, and returned to Oxford to play for City, commuting from Liverpool for the matches. Steele left City in June 2010 and signed for Ashton United, but he returned to Court Place Farm in November 2010.

STEIN, Mark

Striker
Born: 28 January 1966, Cape Town (South Africa)
United debut: 16 September 1989 v West Bromwich Albion (sub)
Final United game: 2 November 1991 v Barnsley
Appearances: 81+11
Goals: 18
Clubs: Luton Town, Aldershot (loan), Queen's Park Rangers, Oxford United, Stoke City (loan), Stoke City, Chelsea, Stoke City (loan), Ipswich Town (loan), AFC Bournemouth (loan), AFC Bournemouth, Luton Town, Dagenham & Redbridge, Waltham Forest

Earl Mark Sean Stein arrived from QPR in September 1989 as part of the deal that took David Bardsley to Loftus Road. Stein, who featured twice for England in the 1985 Under-20 World Cup in Azerbaijan, was a diminutive South African striker who started his career at Luton, alongside his brother Brian. He played 71 games for the Hatters, scoring 23 goals, and in January 1986 he scored once in two appearances on loan to Aldershot. Stein played for Luton in their 3–2 win over Arsenal in the Littlewoods Cup Final in 1988, having previously played in the semi-final win over Oxford, before joining Queen's Park Rangers for £300,000 in August 1988. He played 44 games and scored seven goals before moving to United. Stein was not really a success at the Manor, despite being with the club for over two years. In

September 1991 Stein played five games on loan with Stoke before joining the Potters permanently for £100,000 in November 1991, partnering Wayne Biggins in attack. While with Stoke, Stein scored the only goal as they beat Stockport County in the Autoglass Windscreens Trophy Final at Wembley in 1992. He scored 68 goals in 118 matches up to October 1993 when Chelsea paid £1.5 million for him. After failing to score in his first seven Chelsea games Stein then set a Premiership record by scoring in seven consecutive matches and he also played for the Blues in the 1994 FA Cup Final defeat by Manchester United. After losing his first-team place at the start of the 1995–96 season Stein played mainly for the reserves, although he scored four goals in 11 games on loan back to Stoke in November 1996 and three goals in 11 games on loan to Ipswich in August 1997. Stein's final loan from Chelsea was to Bournemouth in March 1998, where he scored four goals in 17 appearances, before he moved to Dean Court permanently in July 1998. In two years with the Cherries Stein played 99 games and scored 40 goals before he returned to Luton in July 2000, going on to play a further 36 matches and score four more goals for the Kenilworth Road club. In August 2001 Stein joined Dagenham & Redbridge. He made 79 appearances and scored 49 goals for the Daggers before finishing his playing career with Waltham Forest, for whom he scored three goals in eight games. After hanging up his boots he became a physiotherapist, plying his trade first at Barnet in June 2007 and then at Crawley in September 2010.

STEPHENS, Alf

Inside-left
United debut: 17 September 1949 v Hemel Hempstead
Final United game: 22 October 1949 v Weymouth
Appearances: 7
Goals: 1
Clubs: Headington United

Alfred Stephens had the misfortune to suffer a compound dislocation of a finger during his trial period with the club in 1949, preventing his selection for the side.

STEVENS, Mark

Centre-back
Born: 3 December 1977, Swindon
United debut: 28 August 1997 v Nottingham Forest (sub)
Final United game: 28 August 1997 v Nottingham Forest (sub)
Appearances: 0+1
Clubs: Oxford United, Ards (Northern Ireland) (loan), Bath City, Oxford City, Witney Town, Wantage Town, Cheltenham College, Calne Town

Mark Richard Stevens joined United's Youth Training Scheme as a part-timer in 1995, joining the senior squad in the summer of 1996. He was released midway through the 1997–98 season, however, having previously played two games on loan to Northern Irish side Ards in 1996–97. In February 1998 Stevens joined Bath City, where he played six games before being released, having been substituted at half-time against Crawley after conceding a soft penalty. In 2000 Stevens played three games for Oxford City, and he then moved to Witney Town before signing for Wantage.

STIRLING, Jude

Right-back
Born: 29 June 1982, Enfield
United debut: 20 August 2005 v Lincoln City (sub)
Final United game: 7 January 2006 v Shrewsbury Town
Appearances: 9+5
Clubs: Luton Town, Stevenage Borough (loan), Stevenage Borough, St Albans City (loan), Boreham Wood (loan), AFC Hornchurch, Dover Athletic, Tamworth, Grays Athletic, Oxford United, Lincoln City, Peterborough United, Milton Keynes Dons (loan), Milton Keynes Dons, Grimsby Town (loan), Barnet (loan), Notts County

Jude Barrington Stirling signed on non-contract terms at the start of the 2005–06 season after impressing while on trial during pre-season. He became an instant cult hero at the Kassam thanks to his unalleviated enthusiasm and prodigious throw-ins. Stirling's father Clasford ran the Broadwater Farm football academy, which is where Stirling learned his football before joining Luton Town as a junior. He became a professional with the Hatters in August 1999. He made 13 appearances for Luton before joining Stevenage on loan in February 2002, playing four games and signing permanently for Borough in March 2002. Stirling scored one goal in 22 games, joining St Albans City on loan in January 2003, playing four games. He then played 16 games on loan with Boreham Wood before leaving Broadhall Way and signing for Hornchurch in November 2003, scoring one goal in 15 appearances. Stirling joined Dover at the start of the 2004–05 season, scoring once in his nine games before signing for Tamworth in March 2005. He played four games for the Lambs and then joined Grays later that month, where he scored once in his four appearances. It was after leaving Grays that Stirling joined United, but his initial good impression was not maintained and he was released by the club in January 2006. He signed for Lincoln where he made six appearances, all as a substitute, before joining Peterborough in August 2006. He played 28 games for the Posh before his loan to MK Dons in January 2007, scoring once in 18 games for the franchise club before joining them permanently in August 2007. Stirling played regularly for the Dons as they won the League Two title in 2008 and also won the Johnstone's Paint Trophy at Wembley against Grimsby Town. He had a four-game loan with Grimsby in March 2010, and in March 2011 he joined Barnet on loan, helping them escape relegation to the Conference in his six appearances. At the end of the 2010–11 season, after 95 games and four goals, Stirling was released by the MK Dons and signed for League One rivals Notts County in June 2011.

STOCKLEY, Sam

Right-back
Born: 5 September 1977, Tiverton
United debut: 11 August 2001 v Rochdale
Final United game: 20 April 2002 v Darlington
Appearances: 42+2
Clubs: Southampton, Barnet, Oxford United, Colchester United (loan), Colchester United, Blackpool (loan), Wycombe Wanderers, Port Vale, Ferencvaros (Hungary), AFC Telford United, Droylsden, FC New York

Samuel Joshua Stockley-Phillips was brought to Oxford by Mark Wright before the start of the 2001–02 season for £150,000 from relegated Barnet, where he won the Player of the Season award and also got into the Division Three Team of the Season, having played 211 games and scored two goals in his four and a half years at Underhill. Stockley had joined Barnet from Southampton in December 1996, having been a trainee at the Dell without making a first-team appearance. Under Wright Stockley played as a right-wingback where his lack of pace often led to him underperforming. When Ian Atkins converted to 4-4-2 Stockley again found himself out of position on the right wing, and it was not until towards the end of the season that he played as right-back, where he belonged. He was loaned to Colchester in September 2002 where he really impressed, scoring once in 11 games. He had his loan extended for a second month with a view to a permanent move, but just when it looked as if he was on his way talks broke down after Oxford insisted on a sell-on clause, although he did eventually join Colchester, helping them to promotion to the Championship before leaving for Wycombe Wanderers in July 2006, having made 160 appearances and scored two goals. Stockley played seven games on loan to Blackpool in the interim in March 2006. In February 2008 Stockley had a trial with MLS side Dallas, but he remained with Wycombe, eventually making 65 appearances for the Chairboys in which he scored one goal before signing for Port Vale in July 2008. In November 2009 Stockley retired from playing on medical advice after an eye injury, although he came out of retirement in January 2010 to join Ferencvaros as a player-coach. He played 18 games for the Hungarian club, returning to England in January 2011 to play for Telford, but the following month Stockley moved to Droylsden after the Manchester side put in a seven-day notice for him. In April 2011 Stockley had yet another change of scenery, joining FC New York of the USL PRO.

STOTT, Ian

Centre-half
Born: 17 October 1955, Wallingford
United debut: 26 December 1977 v Swindon Town
Final United game: 1 December 1979 v Grimsby Town
Appearances: 30
Goals: 3
Clubs: West Ham United, Oxford United, Oxford City

Ian Stott joined Oxford as a non-contract player in July 1977 after failing to make the grade with West Ham, where he was an amateur. Stott immediately endeared himself to United supporters by scoring on his debut in a 3–3 draw with Swindon at the Manor. However, Stott was released in February 1980 after Joe Cooke's conversion from striker to centre-back. He then signed for Oxford City, for whom he made 11 appearances between March and May 1980.

STYLES, Alan

Right-half
United debut: 17 January 1959 v Wellington Town
Final United game: 30 March 1959 v Kidderminster Harriers
Appearances: 5
Clubs: Headington United

Local player Styles was promoted from the reserves to the first team by new Headington manager Arthur Turner in January 1959, but after just a handful of appearances he was released at the end of his first season.

SWEETZER, Jimmy

Midfielder
Born: 8 January 1960, Woking
United debut: 26 August 1978 v Swansea City (sub)
Final United game: 4 April 1979 v Brentford (sub)
Appearances: 1+8
Goals: 2
Clubs: Oxford United, Millwall, Wealdstone

James E Sweetzer became an Oxford United apprentice in the summer of 1976, becoming a professional later that season. He left Oxford for Millwall in November 1979 for £15,000, where he scored one goal in his three appearances. He was released in 1980 and joined Wealdstone, for whom he missed a penalty in their final game of the season against AP Leamington that saw the Stones relegated.

T

TAIT, Mick

Forward/Midfielder
Born: 30 September 1956, Wallsend
United debut: 22 February 1975 v Blackpool
Final United game: 29 January 1977 v Gillingham
Appearances: 65+4
Goals: 24
Clubs: Oxford United, Carlisle United, Hull City, Portsmouth, Reading, Darlington, Hartlepool United, Gretna, Hartlepool United

Michael Paul Tait became an Oxford United apprentice in the summer of 1972 at the same time as Les Taylor, with whom he came to the Manor from Wallsend Boys' Club after impressing in a game against Oxford Boys. Tait signed professionally in September 1974 and was a prominent member of the team that won the Midlands Youth League in 1975. Tait's debut was as a centre-back, but he was more successful when converted to a forward. Financial problems forced Oxford to sell Tait to Carlisle United in February 1977 for £60,000, then a record fee for the Cumbrians. He scored 22 goals in 120 games for Carlisle before Hull City broke their transfer record by paying £150,000 for him in September 1979. Tait did not spend too long at Boothferry Park though, playing 34 games and scoring four goals before Portsmouth paid £100,000 for him in June 1980. Tait was at Fratton Park for over seven years, scoring 33 goals in 282 appearances and featuring in the side that won the Third Division in 1983 and which finished second in Division Two in 1987. In September 1987 Tait joined Reading for £50,000, spending almost three years at Elm Park and playing 133 games, scoring 15 times, before joining Darlington on a free transfer in August 1990. He spent almost four years at Feethams, scoring twice in 91 appearances, before joining Hartlepool, where in his first spell he played 68 games, scoring twice, before joining Gretna in May 1994. However, Tait was back at Hartlepool in September 1994, going on to play a further 86 matches for the Pools, scoring twice, during which time he became player-manager in September 1994. He hung up his boots in May 1998 but continued to manage the club until January 1999, when he took over Sheffield United's reserves. In September 1999 Tait became manager of Blyth Spartans in the Unibond Premier League for the remainder of the season. In February 2001, after a brief spell out of the game, Tait was appointed assistant manager of Darlington, becoming caretaker manager in October 2002 until the end of that season, when he was awarded the position permanently. However, the permanency lasted just until October 2003 when he was relieved of his duties and stood down to become director of youth development. Tait left Darlington in 2007 and in December 2008 he took over as manager of Newcastle Blue Star before returning to manage Blyth Spartans in May 2009. In September 1998 he combined his duties as manager of Blyth by joining the Gateshead College Academy of Sport as a part-time coach. In May 2011 Tait resigned as Blyth's manager after being offered a full-time job with Northumbria University.

TAIT, Paul

Midfielder
Born: 31 July 1971, Sutton Coldfield
United debut: 16 January 1999 v Grimsby Town
Final United game: 13 April 2002 v Cheltenham Town
Appearances: 100+5
Goals: 3
Clubs: Birmingham City, Millwall (loan), Northampton Town (loan), Oxford United, Nea Salamis (Cyprus), Banbury United

Paul Ronald Tait joined Oxford from Birmingham City in January 1999. He came through the youth ranks at Birmingham, turning professional in the summer of 1988 and playing 211 games for the Blues, scoring 18 goals, including the first ever professional Golden Goal winner in the 1995 Auto Windscreens Shield Final against rivals Aston Villa, after which Tait revealed a T-shirt reading 'Shit on the Villa', for which he was fined two weeks' wages. In February 1994 Tait joined Millwall on loan but did not play for the Lions' first team, and in December 1997 he played three games on loan to Northampton Town. After leaving Oxford Tait played for Cypriot Division A side Nea Salamis, but his short stay ended in November 2002 following a disagreement with coach Takis Antioniou about being played out of position. In September 2004 Tait signed for Kevin Brock's Banbury United, but he quit after just three games, citing fitness and injury problems. After retiring Tait became head coach with Midland Soccer Coaching.

TALLANT, E

Centre-forward
United debut: 28 February 1952 v Gravesend & Northfleet
Final United game: 1 March 1952 v Bath City
Appearances: 2
Clubs: Headington United

TAPPING, Fred

Wing-half
Born: 29 July 1921, Derby
Died: 22 February 2007
United debut: 20 August 1949 v Hastings United
Final United game: 4 November 1950 v Lovell's Athletic
Appearances: 34
Goals: 7
Clubs: Chesterfield, Blackpool, Mansfield Town (guest), Derby County (guest), Leicester City (guest), Notts County (guest), Chesterfield, Headington United, Gresley Rovers

Frederick Harold Tapping played one game for Chesterfield during the 1942–43 wartime season. The following season he made 23 appearances as a guest player for Mansfield Town, scoring twice, and four appearances as a guest for Derby County. He also played seven games for Blackpool, scoring one goal in a 2–1 second-leg win over Manchester City that took Blackpool through to the Northern Cup Final, which the Tangerines lost to Aston Villa. In 1944–45 Tapping scored once in 10 games for Blackpool but also scored 10 goals in nine games as a guest for Derby, including a hat-trick against

Nottingham Forest in September 1944. He also scored two goals in seven guest appearances for Leicester City and two goals in nine games as a guest for Mansfield. The 1945–46 season was the final one before normal footballing conditions resumed and Tapping continued to play for Blackpool, scoring once in 11 games. He also made four guest appearances for Notts County, and scored two goals in three guest matches with Chesterfield, for whom he made his only Football League appearance the following season. Tapping joined Headington as a part-time professional in August 1949 and played in the club's first Southern League fixture at Hastings United. After losing his first-team place to Norman Aldridge in November 1950 Tapping dropped to the reserves, with whom he won the Metropolitan League Cup in 1951. He moved to Gresley Rovers in August 1951, scoring 43 goals in 86 appearances before leaving in May 1953. Tapping, who also made a name for himself as a local cricketer in Derby, was awarded an MBE.

TARDIF, Chris

Goalkeeper
Born: 20 June 1981, Guernsey
United debut: 7 August 2004 v Boston United
Final United game: 8 September 2007 v Altrincham
Appearances: 61+3
Clean sheets: 11
Clubs: Portsmouth, Havant & Waterlooville (loan), Newport (Isle of Wight) (loan), AFC Bournemouth (loan), Havant & Waterlooville (loan), Oxford United, Basingstoke Town, Maidenhead United, Farnborough, Bognor Regis Town, Worcester City, Winchester City, Maidenhead United, Basingstoke Town, St Martin's (Guernsey)

Christopher Luke Tardif arrived at Oxford from Portsmouth, where he had made six appearances, during the summer of 2004 as part of the massive squad-building exercise by manager Graham Rix. The Guernsey-born goalkeeper was one of a number of players who had been with Rix at Portsmouth, having also had a successful 15-game loan spell at Bournemouth in August 2002. Tardif had also been on loan to Havant & Waterlooville, for whom he played eight games in August 1999 and a further 5 games in October 2003, as well as a brief spell with Newport (Isle of Wight), for whom he did not make a first-team appearance. A series of Man-of-the-Match performances saw him established as Oxford's first-choice goalkeeper and he was voted both the Supporters' and Players' Player of the Year for 2004–05. However, the following season Tardif lost his place as automatic first choice to Billy Turley, but he nevertheless renewed his contract after United's relegation to the Conference at the start of the 2006–07 season, along with Turley. After only making one substitute appearance before Christmas, Tardif had a transfer request accepted, although no one came in for him. He eventually left United by mutual agreement, for him to get a full-time job out of football, in September 2007, joining Basingstoke Town in December 2007 following an unsuccessful trial with Eastleigh. He was released in February 2008 due to financial problems and the following month he signed for Maidenhead until the end of the season. In May 2008 Tardif joined Farnborough on a two-year contract, but he subsequently had a change of job that meant he could not commit to being available for training or matches and in August 2008, just a fortnight before the start of the new season, his contract was cancelled. The following month he joined Bognor Regis Town where he played until March 2009, at which point he left for Winchester City, but left a few days later for Worcester City while signing dual-contract forms to allow him to play for Winchester when not needed by Worcester. In June 2009 Tardif returned to Maidenhead where he remained until May 2010, when he rejoined Basingstoke. However, the peripatetic 'keeper left the Camrose in September 2010 and returned to Guernsey for family reasons, signing for St Martin's. The move allowed him to represent Guernsey in the annual Muratti Vase, in which they beat Alderney in the semi-final but lost on penalties to Jersey in the Final. Tardif had previously played for Guernsey in the Island Games tournament in Åland in 2009, winning a bronze medal. Despite being born in Guernsey, Tardif was also eligible to play for Northern Ireland, with whom he won youth honours.

TAYLOR, Geoff

Winger
Born: 22 January 1923, Henstead
United debut: 18 August 1956 v Yeovil Town
Final United game: 5 January 1957 v Hereford United
Appearances: 15
Goals: 4
Clubs: CNSOBU, Norwich City, Reading, Lincoln City, Brighton & Hove Albion, Stade Rennais (France), Bristol Rovers, SC Bruhl (Switzerland), Queen's Park Rangers, Guildford City, VFR07 Kirn (Germany), Headington United

Geoffrey Arthur Taylor joined Norwich City from the City of Norwich School Old Boys' Union (CNSOBU), but he made just one appearance for the Canaries, a 3–0 defeat to Notts County in 1946, before leaving for Reading, where his first-team career was equally brief. He left Elm Park for Lincoln, where again he played only a single first-team game, in November 1947, before he was on his way to Brighton. He managed to play twice for the Seagulls, leaving the Goldstone Ground to join Stade Rennais as player-coach in December 1949. He returned to England in September 1951 and signed for Bristol Rovers, where he made three appearances before venturing again to foreign climes, leaving for Swiss side SC Bruhl as player-coach in May 1952. Taylor spent 18 months with the St Gallen-based club before returning to England to join QPR in November 1953. He played just twice for Rangers before leaving for Guildford in August 1954, but then the lure of the continent again drew him overseas and he signed for German club Kirn in May 1955, again as player-coach. This sparked the beginning of a spell of coaching at a variety of clubs in Germany, including Sobernheim, Idar Oberstein, Weierbach, Bergen, Schwarzerden and Bundenbach. He interrupted his foreign coaching career with a brief interlude at Headington, signing in the summer of 1956. Taylor retired in 1984.

TAYLOR, Les

Midfielder
Born: 4 December 1956, North Shields
United debut: 31 March 1975 v Leyton Orient
Final United game: 4 November 1980 v Huddersfield Town

Appearances: 239
Goals: 16
Clubs: Oxford United, Watford, Reading, Colchester United

Leslie Taylor joined Oxford from Wallsend Boys' Club at the same time as Mick Tait, in the summer of 1972, having impressed in a game against Oxford Boys. Taylor signed professionally in December 1974, shortly after Tait, but he was in the same youth side that won the Midlands Youth League in 1975. Taylor stayed with United after Tait's departure and in 1978 he was named as Third Division Player of the Season by a Sunday newspaper. The following year Taylor was handed the Oxford captaincy, making him the youngest captain in the Football League at that time. After a spell at right-back Taylor became a dominant force in the midfield and there was little surprise when he was sold to Watford in November 1980 for a club record £100,000 (including Keith Cassells). Taylor won promotion to the top flight with the Horns in 1982 and two years later he captained the club to the FA Cup Final at Wembley, where they lost 2–0 to Everton. Taylor joined Reading in October 1986 and helped the Royals to win the Simod Cup two years later. He scored three goals in 75 League games for Reading before joining Colchester in 1989, playing for the Essex side until retiring in the summer of 1990. In 1992 Taylor returned to Oxford to coach the Under-16s and he remained with the club, eventually becoming the director of the Boys' Centre of Excellence.

TAYLOR, Matt

Striker
Born: 15 April 1991
United debut: 22 December 2007 v Aldershot Town (sub)
Final United game: 1 January 2009 v Salisbury City (sub)
Appearances: 0+11
Clubs: Oxford United, Woodstock Town, Oxford United, Abingdon United (loan), Cirencester Town (loan), Banbury United (loan), Brackley Town (loan), Didcot Town, North Leigh

Matthew Taylor came up through the Oxford United ranks, but was released at 16 years old. He played at Woodstock Town, where he impressed, and so United brought him back on trial in October 2007. In January 2008 he was offered a non-contract deal while studying at Oxford & Cherwell Valley College for a BTEC National Diploma in Performance & Excellence on their Football Development Centre Programme. In February 2008 Taylor joined Abingdon United on loan, moving to Cirencester in March. He signed a professional contract at the end of the 2007–08 season, and had a further loan with Banbury United in September 2008 followed by another loan to Brackley in February 2009. He was released at the end of the 2008–09 season and signed for Didcot Town in May 2009. In August 2010 Taylor moved to North Leigh, where his prodigious goalscoring exploits caught the eye and in May 2011 he had a trial with Cheltenham Town, playing against Yate Town in the Gloucestershire Senior Cup Final. He also won the North Leigh Players' Player of the Year award, along with the Manager's Player of the Year and Supporters' Player of the Year awards.

TETHER, Colin

Full-back/Wing-half
Born: 11 August 1938, Halesowen
United debut: 20 August 1960 v Worcester City
Final United game: 30 September 1961 v Gravesend & Northfleet
Appearances: 35
Clubs: Wolverhampton Wanderers, Oxford United

Colin Tether joined the Wolves ground staff on leaving school, aged 15. He was selected to play for the England Youth team against Scotland and to play in the International Youth Tournament in Italy. He signed professionally on his 17th birthday. He made one first-team appearance before his National Service, after which he joined Oxford playing regularly in United's Southern League Championship side.

THOMAS, Andy

Midfielder
Born: 19 December 1962, Eynsham
United debut: 6 September 1980 v Chesterfield (sub)
Final United game: 22 March 1986 v Liverpool (sub)
Appearances: 120+30
Goals: 45
Clubs: Oxford United, Derby County (loan), Fulham (loan), Newcastle United, Bradford City, Plymouth Argyle, Thame United, Oxford City

Andrew Mark Thomas started his career with Oxford United, signing apprentice forms in May 1979. He performed outstandingly in the reserves, and on 6 September 1980 he was rewarded with his first-team debut, coming off the bench in a 3–0 home defeat by Chesterfield. Thomas established himself in the first team at the start of the 1981–82 season, but at the start of the following season he found himself used more and more as a substitute and in the middle of the 1982–83 season he had short loan spells at Derby County, where he made one appearance, and Fulham, where he played four games and scored two goals. He was becoming an important player for Jim Smith's side in 1983–84, and scored a stunning goal in the 2–1 League Cup win over Newcastle United on 26 October 1983. However, Thomas' career took a turn for the worse on 2 January 1984 when, in a 3–1 defeat at Exeter City, he suffered a badly broken leg. Thomas did not return to first-team action until April 1985. He returned to regular football at the start of the club's First Division campaign the following season. However, he suffered an injury in December and did not play again until coming off the bench in February, and he only played two more games for Oxford, both as substitute in March. His last game for United was on 22 March 1986 in the side's then record 6–0 defeat by Liverpool at Anfield. Thomas was on the bench for the Milk Cup Final at Wembley, but did not get on the pitch. On 24 September 1986 Newcastle United came in for Thomas, who moved to St James' Park for £85,000 plus £25,000 after he had played 25 games. In two seasons Thomas played 31 League games for the Magpies, scoring six goals, before he moved to Bradford City for £80,000. He made 23 League appearances for the Bantams, finding the net five times, and from there he went to Plymouth Argyle, also for £80,000, in July 1989. In two seasons at Home Park, Thomas played 50 League games and scored 19 goals before retiring from professional football in July 1991 as a result of a serious back injury. After a brief spell at Thame United, Thomas became the player-manager at Oxford City, and he led the side to the FA Vase Final at Wembley in 1995, when they lost 2–1 to Arlesey Town. He later managed Brackley Town.

THOMAS, Johnnie

Outside-right
Born: 23 December 1926
United debut: 23 August 1952 v Kidderminster Harriers
Final United game: 1 October 1952 v Bath City
Appearances: 5
Goals: 1
Clubs: Everton, Swindon Town, Headington United, Chester City, Stockport County, Bath City

John Wilfred Thomas joined Headington from Swindon Town in the summer of 1952, having joined the Robins from Everton in February 1949 without appearing for the Toffees' first-team. Thomas scored three goals in 17 games for Swindon before his move to the Manor. After his brief spell with United Thomas joined Chester City, where he scored five goals in 29 League appearances prior to his move to Stockport County, where he played six League games. He then played 10 games for Bath City during the 1955–56 season.

THOMAS, Kevin

Goalkeeper
Born: 13 August 1945, Whiston
United debut: 3 March 1973 v Sunderland
Final United game: 31 March 1973 v Aston Villa
Appearances: 6
Clean sheets: 1
Clubs: Prescot Cables, Blackpool, Tranmere Rovers, Oxford United, Southport, Kettering Town (loan), Barrow, Workington

Kevin Anthony Thomas spent three years with Blackpool after joining them from Prescot Cables in June 1966, playing 16 games before joining Tranmere Rovers in September 1969. Thomas played 18 games for Tranmere, joining Oxford in July 1971, but spending most of his time at the Manor playing for the reserves. He moved to Southport in 1974, playing 67 games for the Sandgrounders, but then had a 14-month lay-off due to injury before joining Barrow, making his debut in August 1977 at Northwich Victoria. He played 317 games for the Barrovians, his last match coming at Trowbridge in April 1983, and he was rewarded with a testimonial match in 1984.

THOMAS, Martin

Midfielder
Born: 12 September 1973, Lyndhurst
United debut: 11 August 2001 v Rochdale
Final United game: 20 November 2001 v Leyton Orient
Appearances: 14+1
Goals: 2
Clubs: Southampton, Leyton Orient (loan), Fulham, Swansea City, Brighton & Hove Albion, Oxford United, Exeter City, Eastleigh, Winchester City (loan), AFC Totton, Eastleigh

Martin Russell Thomas was brought to Oxford from Brighton by Mark Wright in July 2001 and immediately installed as club captain. In this capacity he had the honour of leading the side out for the first game at United's new Kassam Stadium. Thomas started as a trainee with Southampton, turning professional in June 1992. He scored two goals in a five-game loan spell with Orient in March 1994 before joining Fulham on a free transfer in July 1994, without having featured for the Saints' first team. In four seasons with the Cottagers Thomas played 105 games and scored 11 goals, helping them to promotion from Division Three in 1996–97. In June 1998 he moved to Swansea where he made 110 appearances, scoring 11 times. Thomas helped the Swans qualify for the Division Three Play-offs in his first season and win that division's title the following year before joining Brighton in March 2001. Although he was with the Gulls for just three months, playing eight games, he was at the Withdean as Brighton won the Third Division Championship, Thomas' third promotion from that division in five years. At Oxford Thomas lost his place after Ian Atkins' appointment although he remained at Minchery Farm until May 2002, at which point his contract was cancelled and he joined Exeter City. At St James' Park Thomas suffered the disappointment of relegation to the Conference at the end of his first season, and he was released in June 2004, having played 40 games and scored three goals for the Grecians. Thomas signed for Eastleigh, where he played a key role in earning the Spitfires back-to-back promotions to the Conference South. However, in the 2006–07 season he found his chances limited and he finished the campaign on loan to Winchester. In June 2007 Thomas signed for AFC Totton, returning to Eastleigh in July 2008 to captain the reserves.

THOMPSON, Brian

Midfielder
Born: 9 February 1950, Kingswinford
United debut: 11 November 1969 v Bristol City (sub)
Final United game: 10 February 1973 v Millwall
Appearances: 56+5
Goals: 4
Clubs: Wolverhampton Wanderers, Oxford United, Torquay United (loan), Chelmsford City, Kettering Town

Brian Thompson joined Oxford from Wolverhampton Wanderers on trial in 1969, earning a full-time contract in the October, after his release by Wolves with whom he had signed professionally in 1967. Although he was a regular in midfield in his first season, thereafter he made only sporadic appearances and in March 1973 he had a nine-game loan with Torquay, scoring once. Upon his return to the Manor he was given a free transfer, joining Chelmsford City. He was later signed for Kettering by Ron Atkinson.

THOMPSON, Harry

Centre-half
Born: 29 April 1915, Mansfield
Died: 29 January 2000
United debut: 20 August 1949 v Hastings United
Final United game: 24 March 1951 v Chelmsford City
Appearances: 64
Goals: 1

Clubs: Mansfield Invicta, Mansfield Town, Wolverhampton Wanderers, Sunderland, York City (guest), Northampton Town, Headington United

Harold Thompson started his playing career with Mansfield Town juniors, signing as a professional in 1932, but he joined Wolverhampton Wanderers in 1933 without playing a game for the Stags. After 73 games and 17 goals Sunderland paid Wolves the then enormous sum of £7,500 for Thompson in 1937. He was at Roker Park when World War Two broke out, having played 11 games, scoring once, for Sunderland. During the war Thompson played for some top-class Army teams as well as guesting for York City while on Army duties at Marston Moor. In 1946, the resumption of League football saw Thompson sign for Northampton Town on a part-time basis. In the following three seasons he played 38 League games, scoring twice, for the Cobblers, having switched to playing centre-half. During the summers, Thompson coached Norwegian side Ranheim, based near Trondheim. In July 1949, Headington United secured the services of Harry Thompson as the club's first professional player-coach. At the end of the 1949–50 season Thompson was appointed player-manager, and was empowered to sign his own players. The side had finished fourth from bottom in their inaugural Southern League season, during which Thompson played 44 games, before an injury at Gillingham on 5 April ended his season. The following term United fared much better, finishing seventh, with Thompson playing 21 games and scoring once, in a 3–2 win at Torquay United Reserves in November 1950. Thompson's last game for the club was a 4–1 defeat at Chelmsford City on 24 March 1951, after which he decided to end his playing career. Thompson offered to resign if the club bosses decided they wanted to appoint another player-manager, but the board instead appointed him manager on an annual contract, with effect from August 1951. Under Thompson's guidance, United went from strength to strength, winning the Southern League and Southern League Cup in 1952–53, and finishing second the following season while retaining the Southern League Cup and reaching the fourth round of the FA Cup. He was eventually sacked in November 1958 after the side had lost seven consecutive Southern League games. His last game as manager was a 1–0 defeat at Guildford City in the Southern League Inter-Zone Competition. After leaving Headington United, Harry worked for Morris Motors and then Pressed Steel in Cowley. He died in Oxford on 29 January 2000, aged 84.

THOMSON, Andy

Striker
Born: 1 April 1971, Motherwell
United debut: 8 August 1998 v Bristol City
Final United game: 9 May 1999 v Stockport County (sub)
Appearances: 26+14
Goals: 7
Clubs: Jerviston FC, Queen of the South, Southend United, Oxford United, Gillingham, Queen's Park Rangers, Partick Thistle, Falkirk, Queen of the South

Andrew Thomson joined Queen of the South from Motherwell boys' club Jerviston in July 1989. In his 201 games Thomson scored 109 times, making him one of just three Queens players to score over 100 goals. In both 1991–92 and 1993–94 he was Scottish Second Division Player of the Year, and was also the country's leading scorer in the latter season. Queen of the South rejected a £150,000 bid from Aberdeen, but when Southend smashed their transfer record with an offer of £250,000 in July 1994 the Palmerston club was forced to accept, making Thomson their record sale. Thomson spent four seasons at Roots Hall, scoring 29 goals in 137 appearances, but in his final two seasons the club suffered successive relegations, finishing bottom of Division One in 1997 and Division Two in 1998. Thomson joined Oxford on a free transfer in the summer of 1998, but his goalscoring record was too inconsistent and he was allowed to leave at the end of his first season, moving to Gillingham for £25,000 in August 1999. At the end of his first season Thomson scored the winning goal for the Gills as they beat Wigan Athletic 3–2 after extra-time in the Play-off Final at Wembley. In March 2001, having scored 23 goals in 66 games for Gillingham, Thomson joined QPR on a free transfer, just in time to suffer relegation to Division Two with them. The following season he was Rangers' top scorer and in July 2003 he returned to Scotland with Partick Thistle; he had played 73 games and scored 30 goals for QPR. Thomson played just 23 games in his season at Firhill, scoring five times, before joining Falkirk in July 2004. The Bairns won promotion to the Scottish Premier League at the end of Thomson's first season, but he then lost his first-team place and in January 2006 he returned to Queen of the South after scoring 14 goals in 37 games for Falkirk. He scored a further five goals for Queens in his 29 games and in January 2007 he moved to Stenhousemuir, where he scored five goals in 19 appearances before hanging up his boots in March 2008.

THOMSON, Jim

Inside-forward
Born: 17 March 1931, Govan
United debut: 21 March 1959 v Nuneaton Borough
Final United game: 30 April 1960 v Gravesend & Northfleet
Appearances: 46
Goals: 12
Clubs: Beith, Raith Rovers, Southend United, Headington United

James Donaldson Thomson scored seven goals in 23 Scottish League appearances for Raith Rovers. He joined Southend in May 1956, playing 44 games in which he scored 13 goals, before his move to Headington in March 1959. He was a mainstay of the side the following season, but left the Manor in the summer of 1960.

THORNLEY, Barry

Winger
Born: 11 February 1948, Gravesend
United debut: 26 August 1967 v Bury
Final United game: 22 February 1969 v Preston North End
Appearances: 25+1
Goals: 4
Clubs: Gravesend & Northfleet, Brentford, Oxford United, Chelmsford City

Barry Edward Thornley started his career as a part-time professional with his home-town club of Gravesend & Northfleet before moving to Brentford in September 1965 and turning full-time. He played seven League games for the Bees in his first season and none in his second, joining Oxford on a free transfer in July 1967. After appearing regularly after his arrival he drifted out of the team, not helped by injuries, and after United's promotion to the Second Division Thornley rarely featured. In the summer of 1969 he left on a free transfer and joined Chelmsford, where he scored 31 goals in 210 games and became a Clarets legend.

TITCOMBE, Ken

Centre-half
Born: 30 October 1937, Swindon
United debut: 12 November 1960 v Hastings United
Final United game: 26 April 1961 v Yeovil Town
Appearances: 16
Clubs: Charlton Athletic, Oxford United, Wellington Town

Titcombe was an England Schoolboy international, playing against Wales in March 1953. He signed professionally with Charlton in December 1954, although he failed to play for their first team. He played regularly for United's Metropolitan League side but failed to earn a regular first-team place. After leaving United he joined Wellington in October 1961, but was released by them in December 1961 after just three appearances.

TODD, Colin

Centre-back
Born: 12 December 1948, Chester-le-Street
United debut: 28 February 1984 v Hull City
Final United game: 21 April 1984 v Bristol Rovers
Appearances: 12
Clubs: Sunderland, Derby County, Everton, Birmingham City, Nottingham Forest, Oxford United, Vancouver Whitecaps, Luton Town, Whitley Bay, Ashington

Colin Todd was one of the finest defenders in English football during the 1970s, and although by the time he arrived at the Manor he had lost much of his pace, he was still comfortable on the ball and had great ability to read the game, helping the U's over the finishing line as they won the Third Division title. He joined Sunderland as an apprentice in 1966 and was a member of the side that won the FA Youth Cup against Bimingham City in 1967. While with the Rokerites Todd scored three goals in 191 appearances, during which Sunderland were relegated from the top flight in 1970. In February 1971 Todd signed for Derby County for £170,000 and the following season the Rams won the Football League title, with Todd rewarded with the first of his 27 England caps in May 1972. Derby repeated the feat in 1974–75, with Todd imperious in the centre of defence, winning the PFA Footballer of the Year award. He remained at the Baseball Ground until joining Everton for £300,000 in September 1978, after 293 League matches with Derby in which he scored six goals. Todd failed to settle on Merseyside, being played out of position at right-back, and after 32 League games and one goal for the Toffees he joined Birmingham City for £275,000 in September 1979. He remained at St Andrew's until August 1982, playing 93 League games before his transfer to Nottingham Forest. Todd made 36 appearances for Forest before he joined Oxford in February 1984. By this time injuries were starting to take their toll and Todd made just 11 appearances with Vancouver Whitecaps after leaving the Manor. After playing two games for Luton in November 1984 Todd ended his professional career and returned to the North East to work for a brewery while ending his playing days with Whitley Bay and then Ashington. He joined Middlesbrough as Bruce Rioch's assistant in 1986, just before the club went into receivership, and became manager in March 1990 after Rioch's departure. He led Boro to the Second Division Play-offs before leaving for Bolton in June 1992, again as assistant to Rioch, taking over as manager in June 1995. Bolton were relegated from the Premiership at the end of Todd's first season, but he led them straight back up as champions with over 100 points. The Trotters only managed one season before being relegated again, but Todd took them to the Play-off Final in 1999, when they lost to Watford. He resigned in September 1999 and was out of work until May 2000, when he became Swindon Town's manager. His time at Swindon was unsuccessful and he left in November 2000 to become Jim Smith's assistant at Derby. Smith resigned in October 2001 and Todd succeeded him, but after just three months, in January 2002, he was sacked after poor results. In November 2003 Todd became Bryan Robson's assistant at Bradford City, following Robson into the hot seat in June 2004. He remained in charge until February 2007, when he was sacked, and in June 2007 he took charge of Danish club Randers, remaining there until January 2009. In May 2009 he replaced David Penney as Darlington's boss, bringing in Dean Windass as his assistant, but they both left in November 2009 after presiding over the club's worst ever start to a season. In November 2010 Todd joined BHP Sport as a consultant.

TOGWELL, Sam

Midfielder
Born: 14 October 1984, Beaconsfield
United debut: 23 October 2004 v Macclesfield Town (sub)
Final United game: 20 November 2004 v Rochdale
Appearances: 4+1
Clubs: Crystal Palace, Oxford United (loan), Northampton Town (loan), Port Vale (loan), Barnsley, Scunthorpe United

Samuel James Togwell joined Oxford on loan from Crystal Palace in October 2004, having already made his Palace debut, as part of his recuperation from a broken leg. He had another loan with Northampton, playing 10 games between March and May 2005, before playing his final three games for Palace prior to another loan with Port Vale from November 2005 until the end of the season. Togwell scored two goals in his 30 games for Vale, winning the club's Young Player of the Year award at the end of the season. However, Vale were unable to afford Palace's asking fee and in July 2006 he joined Barnsley for an undisclosed sum. Togwell played 73 games for the Tykes, scoring two goals, before joining Scunthorpe United in August 2008. At the end of his first season the Iron won the League One Play-offs, beating Millwall 3–2 in the Final.

*TONKIN, Anthony

Left-back
Born: 17 January 1980, Penzance
United debut: 16 January 2010 v Tamworth
Final United game: 7 May 2011 v Shrewsbury Town
Appearances: 61+2

Clubs: Yeovil Town, Stockport County, Crewe Alexandra, Yeovil Town, Grays Athletic (loan), Forest Green Rovers, Cambridge United, Oxford United

Anthony Richard Tonkin joined Oxford from Cambridge United in January 2010 and went on to be a vital component of the defence that won promotion from the Conference via the Play-offs in May 2010. He remained with the side as the main left-back in the first season back in the Football League. Tonkin began his career with Yeovil in December 1999, playing 107 games and scoring two goals for the Glovers, including playing in the side that won the FA Trophy Final against Stevenage Borough in May 2002. In September 2002 Tonkin moved to Stockport County for £50,000, playing 27 games before Crewe paid £150,000 to take him to Gresty Road in August 2003. Tonkin spent three seasons with Alex, playing 93 games, before returning to Yeovil in September 2006. However, he played just five games for the Glovers before going out on loan to Grays Athletic in March 2007, playing 13 games until the end of the season, at which point he was released by Yeovil, joining Forest Green Rovers two months later. Tonkin was at the New Lawn for one season, playing 41 games, before he was released and joined Cambridge in July 2008. In his year and a half at the Abbey Tonkin scored one goal in 66 games, impressing with his consistency, prompting Chris Wilder to sign him as a replacement for Kevin Sandwith.

TOULOUSE, Cyril

Right wing-half
Born: 24 December 1923, Acton
Died: March 1980
United debut: 18 March 1950 v Tonbridge
Final United game: 26 April 1954 v Llanelly
Appearances: 153
Goals: 20
Clubs: Brentford, Tottenham Hotspur, Guildford City, Headington United, Hastings United

Cyril Harvey Toulouse arrived at Headington United from Guildford City in March 1950. He was born in Acton on Christmas Eve 1923, and signed for his first club, Brentford, in January 1946. He played 10 times for the Bees in his first season, but was unable to prevent them being relegated to the Second Division. The following season he made three appearances before being transferred to Tottenham Hotspur in January 1947. Toulouse played just two games for Spurs before moving on to Guildford City. Headington acquired the wing-half for £150, with Toulouse signing an agreement that he would not leave the club before the end of the 1950–51 season. In the event, Toulouse stayed with the club until the end of the 1953–54 season. He was tall and described as 'unbeatable in the air'. He was also called the 'best pivot in the Southern League'. Despite being at the club for little over four seasons, he was granted a five-year testimonial, in accordance with Southern League rules, which was played against an 'All Star XI' in September 1954. Toulouse scored against Weymouth in the Southern League Cup Final second leg in April 1953, which United won 3–1 to take the trophy 4–3 on aggregate. Toulouse joined Hastings after leaving the Manor.

TOWNSLEY, Derek

Midfielder
Born: 21 March 1973, Carlisle
United debut: 9 August 2003 v Lincoln City
Final United game: 15 October 2003 v Rushden & Diamonds
Appearances: 12+2
Clubs: Gretna, Carlisle United, Queen of the South, Motherwell, Hibernian, Oxford United, Gretna, Workington, Newcastle Blue Star, Penrith, Annan Athletic

Derek Johnstone Townsley was a tall, gangly midfielder who scored a hat-trick against Moor Green in a pre-season friendly after signing from Hibs in June 2003, but he failed to live up to this early sign of promise. Townsley was a postman before becoming a professional footballer, playing with Gretna in the Northern Premier League. In August 1996 he joined Queen of the South, playing 75 games for them over three seasons and scoring 20 goals. He was with The Doonhammers as they lost the Scottish Challenge Cup Final to Falkirk in 1997. In May 1999 Townsley joined Motherwell, becoming a full-time professional, and scoring seven goals in 64 appearances for the Well before signing for Hibernian in July 2001. In two years at Easter Road Townsley played 52 games and scored nine goals before joining Oxford on the expiry of his contract. In February 2004 Townsley returned to Gretna, playing a central role as Gretna won promotion in successive seasons to reach the Scottish Premier League. They also reached the 2006 Scottish Cup Final, where they lost to Hearts in a penalty shoot-out after a 1–1 draw. Townsley appeared 102 times for Gretna, scoring 25 goals, before moving to Conference North side Workington Reds in January 2007. He started the following season with Newcastle Blue Star, joining Penrith just before Christmas 2007. In January 2008 he was signed by Annan Athletic as player-assistant manager, where he remained until hanging up his boots in July 2010.

TRAIN, Ray

Midfielder
Born: 10 February 1951, Nuneaton
United debut: 27 March 1982 v Chesterfield
Final United game: 22 February 1984 v Swindon Town
Appearances: 58+3
Clubs: Bedworth United, Walsall, Carlisle United, Sunderland, Bolton Wanderers, Watford, Oxford United, AFC Bournemouth (loan), Northampton Town (loan), Northampton Town, Tranmere Rovers, Walsall

Raymond Train joined Walsall as an apprentice from local side Bedworth United in 1967, having been rejected by Coventry City for being too small. He turned professional in November 1968, playing mainly as a winger and scoring 11 goals in his 75 League games before his £5,000 move to Carlisle in December 1971. Train was with the Cumbrians as the side won promotion to the First Division in 1974 and he was an ever present in that sole top-flight campaign. He scored eight goals in 155 League games for Carlisle, moving to Sunderland for £90,000 in March 1976, just before the Rokerites won the Second Division title. Train left for Bolton for £50,000 in March 1977 after making 32 League appearances and scoring once for Sunderland. He was with the Trotters as they won the Second Division title in 1978 and made 51

League appearances for them before moving to Watford for £50,000 in November 1978. Train scored on his Watford debut and the following season the side won promotion to the Second Division. He was with the Horns as they won promotion to the First Division in 1982; shortly after this he joined Oxford for £10,000. Train made his U's debut alongside fellow debutants Trevor Hebberd and George Lawrence and was made club captain until Malcolm Shotton took over that honour. Train rarely featured in United's Third Division promotion season of 1983–84 and midway through the season he had a loan spell with Bournemouth in which he played seven League games and also featured in their 2–0 FA Cup giant-killing against Manchester United, returning to the Manor in time to play against Everton in the Milk Cup fifth round. He had a loan to Northampton in March 1984, joining the Cobblers permanently in May and becoming club captain. Train scored once in 46 League games for Northampton before his move to Tranmere, where he played 36 League games prior to returning to Walsall in August 1986. Train played 16 League games for the Saddlers while also coaching the youth side, stepping up to become caretaker manager in December 1988 before returning to his previous role in January 1990. He moved to Middlesbrough as a coach early in 1990 after a brief spell as community officer at Fellows Park. He remained with Boro for 13 years, eventually becoming chief scout, before being released by Steve McClaren in November 2004 and going to scout for Portsmouth.

TRAINER, Phil

Midfielder
Born: 3 July 1981, Wolverhampton
United debut: 11 August 2007 v Forest Green Rovers
Final United game: 1 January 2009 v Salisbury City
Appearances: 66+3
Goals: 14
Clubs: Fordhouse Gala, Crewe Alexandra, Hyde United (loan), Hednesford Town (loan), Stalybridge Celtic (loan), Northwich Victoria, Halesowen Town, Tamworth, Moor Green (loan), Moor Green, Oxford United, AFC Telford United (loan), AFC Telford United

Philip Abbas Trainer arrived from Conference North outfit Solihull Moors (previously Moor Green) in July 2007, and had attracted interest from a number of League clubs. The qualified plumber was strongly recommended to manager Jim Smith by assistant manager Darren Patterson. However, when Chris Wilder took over in January 2009 it coincided with a loss of form for Trainer, and he went to Conference North side AFC Telford United on loan until the end of the season. He was released at the end of the 2008–09 season at which point he signed permanently for Telford, for whom he was influential in the centre of the field as the side won promotion to the Conference National in 2011, Trainer scoring the winning goal in their 3–2 Play-off win over Guiseley. Trainer was initially a product of the Crewe Academy after signing from Sunday League side Fordhouse Gala. He had a trial with the Mansfield youth team but Crewe offered him a two-year contract in June 2000, although he never played a first-team game for Alex. Trainer had an eight-game loan spell with Hyde in January 2001 in which he scored one goal, followed by four games and two goals on loan to Hednesford in November 2001. His final loan came in March 2002 when he played four games for Stalybridge, after which he was released by Crewe in

May 2002. Trainer joined Northwich Victoria in September 2002 but did not play for them before signing for Halesowen later that month. In February 2003 he had a brief loan spell with Willenhall before joining Tamworth in August 2003. Trainer made six appearances for the Lambs before joining Moor Green on a one-month loan in October 2003, joining permanently in November. Trainer was Moor Green's Player of the Year for 2004–05.

TREWICK, John

Full-back/Midfielder
Born: 3 June 1957, Bedlington
United debut: 24 January 1984 v Everton
Final United game: 1 September 1987 v Tottenham Hotspur
Appearances: 137+5
Goals: 4
Clubs: West Bromwich Albion, Newcastle United, Oxford United (loan), Oxford United, Birmingham City, Bromsgrove Rovers, Hartlepool United, Barnet, Gateshead, Hereford United

John Trewick joined United from Newcastle on loan for a month in January 1984, playing five games, before returning to the Manor permanently that summer. Trewick had joined Newcastle from West Brom, where he made his League debut in November 1974 and featured prominently in their promotion to Division One in 1976. He scored 11 goals in 96 League games for the Baggies before joining Newcastle for a Toon record fee of £250,000 in December 1980. Trewick settled in well for the Magpies, but in the opening game of the 1982–83 season he broke his leg and was out of action for almost a year and a half, his loan to Oxford being an aid to his return to fitness. After his return to Newcastle he helped the side win promotion to the First Division, after which he returned to the Manor on a free transfer, having scored eight goals in 87 appearances on Tyneside. Trewick was virtually an ever present in United's 1984–85 promotion season and he was a member of the 1986 Milk Cup winning side. All four of his goals for Oxford were penalties. He moved to Birmingham in September 1987, playing 37 League games before joining Bromsgrove in July 1988. He returned to the Football League with Hartlepool in October 1989, playing just nine games for the Pool before joining non-League Barnet. He made eight appearances for Gateshead in 1990–91 and became coach for West Brom in 1993. Trewick was youth team coach for the Baggies before taking over as first-team coach, and even had a spell as caretaker manager in 1997–98 before leaving to join Derby as coach in July 2001. He becames Wolves youth coach in 2003, becoming first-team coach at Hereford the following season. Trewick was appointed Hereford's manager after Graham Turner's resignation in April 2009, but in March 2010 Turner, who remained Chairman, sacked Trewick, who joined Shrewsbury as first-team coach to Turner in June 2010. Trewick made his debut for England Schoolboys in 1972 against Germany and scored the first goal in a 4–0 rout.

TURLEY, Billy

Goalkeeper
Born: 15 July 1973, Wolverhampton
United debut: 6 August 2005 v Grimsby Town
Final United game: 20 April 2010 v Wrexham
Appearances: 184+2

Clean sheets: 71
Clubs: Evesham, Northampton Town, Leyton Orient (loan), Rushden & Diamonds, Oxford United, Brackley Town

William Lee Turley joined United at the start of 2005–06, the first signing of Brian Talbot, his former manager at Rushden & Diamonds. He immediately displaced former Player of the Season Chris Tardif as first-choice 'keeper, despite concerns about his occasional errors. This was his first job back in football after he served a six-month ban for cocaine use. United offered him a new contract at the start of the 2006–07 season, which he signed despite offers from a couple of League clubs, and he then signed a further extension, until 2010, in January 2008. Turley was an immensely popular character with the United supporters, despite missing a penalty in the Conference Play-off semi-final shoot-out against Exeter City, and after leaving Oxford he joined Brackley Town. Turley started his career with Evesham in 1994 before joining Northampton in July 1995. He played 34 games for the Cobblers, and also had a 19-game loan spell with Orient between February and May 1995. In June 1999 Rushden paid £120,000 for him and in almost six years at Nene Park he played 249 games for the Diamonds, before his dismissal in December 2004 after testing positive for cocaine just two years after failing another drugs test for nandrolone.

TURNER, Arthur

Centre-forward
Born: 22 January 1922, Poplar
United debut: 10 September 1952 v Hastings United
Final United game: 8 April 1953 v Weymouth
Appearances: 22
Goals: 15
Clubs: Charlton Athletic, Colchester United, Headington United

Arthur Alexander Turner was an RAF officer who played part-time for Charlton Athletic, making a total of nine appearances in Charlton's run to the FA Cup Final in 1946, playing at centre-forward in the Final which they lost 4–1 after extra-time to Derby. Turner thereby became the only player to play in an FA Cup Final without ever playing a League game for his club. In 1947 Turner moved to Colchester, and scored Colchester's first Football League goal at Layer Road after the club's election from the Southern League. After scoring 15 goals in 45 League games Turner retired from football in the summer of 1951, before returning to play for Headington in their 1952–53 double-winning season.

TWIGG, Gary

Striker
Born: 19 March 1984, Glasgow
United debut: 11 August 2007 v Forest Green Rovers (sub)
Final United game: 26 December 2007 v Crawley Town (sub)
Appearances: 8+6
Goals: 3
Clubs: Derby County, Burton Albion (loan), Bristol Rovers (loan), Airdrie United, Oxford United, Hamilton Academical, Brechin City, Shamrock Rovers (Ireland)

Signed in the summer of 2007, Twigg started his career at Derby County when Jim Smith was also there, but he moved to Airdrie in August 2005 after making just nine appearances for the Rams, although he also had loan spells with Burton Albion, where he scored one goal in four games, and Bristol Rovers for eight matches. Twigg played 65 games for Airdrie, scoring 18 goals, before signing for Smith at Oxford. He scored his three Oxford goals in his first three matches for the club, before getting injured. Twigg left at the end of December 2007 because of his failure to settle in Oxford, partly due to his pregnant wife's homesickness, and signed for Hamilton. He played just four games for the Accies and had his contract cancelled at his own request in July 2008, when he signed for Brechin. In his time at Glebe Park Twigg scored 13 goals in 26 games, after which he moved to Shamrock Rovers in February 2009. In 2009 Twigg was the leading scorer in the League of Ireland, and he won the club's Supporters' Player of the Year award and the PFAI Player of the Year award. In October 2010 Twigg scored for the Dubliners in a 2–2 draw with Bray Wanderers that earned Shamrock the League of Ireland title.

V

van HEUSDEN, Arjan

Goalkeeper
Born: 11 December 1972, Alphen aan den Rijn (Netherlands)
United debut: 27 September 1997 v Bradford City
Final United game: 22 November 1997 v Norwich City
Appearances: 13
Clean sheets: 5
Clubs: Noordwijk, Port Vale, Oxford United (loan), Cambridge United, Exeter City, Mansfield Town, Torquay United, Rijnsburgse Boys, FC Lisse, sv ARC

Arjan van Heusden was an amateur with Dutch side Noordwijk when he joined First Division side Port Vale for £4,500 in August 1994 after a successful trial with the Valiants in December 1993. Van Heusden played 33 games over four seasons for Port Vale, during which he had his loan spell with Oxford between September and November 1997 that was a great success as he deputised for the injured Phil Whitehead. In August 1998 van Heusden moved to Cambridge United, starting as first-choice 'keeper before injury caused him to lose his place. After 53 appearances the Dutch goalie moved to Exeter City in August 2000, playing 81 matches for the Grecians before rejecting a new contract. He had a trial with Clyde in August 2002 but was unable to agree terms with the Scottish side and he returned to Exeter, who agreed to cancel his contract. Van Heusden joined Mansfield in September 2002, but made just five appearances for the Stags before joining Torquay on non-contract terms in November 2002. In April 2003 he signed a two-year contract with the Gulls at the end of which, after 52 games, he retired from professional football and returned to the Netherlands in January 2005. His first club back in his homeland was the amateur side Rijnsburgse Boys. In 2007–08 he joined FC Lisse, with whom he won the Dutch amateur Championship and two seasons later he was player-coach for his home-town club sv ARC.

VARADI, Imre

Midfielder
Born: 11 December 1972, Paddington
United debut: 23 January 1993 v Cambridge United (sub)
Final United game: 20 February 1993 v Wolverhampton Wanderers (sub)
Appearances: 3+2
Clubs: Letchworth Garden City, FC 75 (Hitchin), Sheffield United, Everton, Newcastle United, Sheffield Wednesday, West Bromwich Albion, Manchester City, Sheffield Wednesday, Leeds United, Luton Town (loan), Oxford United (loan), Rotherham United, Mansfield Town, Boston United, Scunthorpe United, Matlock Town, Guiseley, South Jersey Barons (USA)

Imre Varadi initially played for non-League side Letchworth while working as an asphalter but he was asked to leave in 1978 and had a spell with Hitchin Sunday League side FC 75 before he was signed by Sheffield United in April 1978. Varadi, who had Hungarian parents, scored four goals in 12 games before Everton paid £80,000 for him in March 1979. He played 35 games for the Merseysiders, scoring seven goals. Varadi was on the verge of joining Benfica in May 1981 but the deal fell through and he joined Newcastle for £100,000 in August 1981. He was on Tyneside for two years, playing 90 games and scoring 42 goals before he returned to Sheffield to sign for Wednesday for £150,000, where he remained for a further two seasons. Varadi played 94 matches for the Owls, scoring 40 goals before West Bromwich Albion paid £285,000 for him in July 1985. He was with the Baggies until October 1986, playing 41 games and scoring 13 times before his move to Manchester City for £50,000. It was while he was at Maine Road that supporters started the trend of bringing inflatable bananas to games as a pun on Varadi's surname, while the player scored 31 goals in 81 matches before he returned to Hillsborough for £50,000 in September 1988. Varadi's second spell with Wednesday was less successful than his first, as age was starting to catch up with him. He managed just 27 games, netting six times, before he was allowed to join Leeds United for £50,000 in February 1990. This was the third time that Howard Wilkinson had signed Varadi, but on this occasion he spent most of his time playing for the reserves, although he also played 29 first-team games, in which he scored six goals. He had a six-game loan with Luton in March 1992, scoring once, before he joined Oxford on loan in January 1993, where he failed to impress. Varadi left Leeds for Rotherham on a free transfer in March 1993, and was the Millers' leading scorer the following season, before losing his place the season after. He made 78 appearances and scored 29 goals in the Third Division before his move to Mansfield in August 1995, but after just one game he moved to Boston as player-coach. His stay at York Street was brief as his registration was cancelled as a cost-cutting exercise and in September 1995 he joined Scunthorpe United, for whom he made just two substitute appearances. In October 1995 he joined Matlock as player-manager but was sacked after relegation in the summer of 1996. After a brief spell as player-manager with Guiseley and then playing and coaching with South Jersey Barons in the United States, Varadi became part-time assistant manager at Stalybridge Celtic. He was then manager with Denaby and after setting up his own junior soccer school Varadi became a licensed agent in 2001, becoming a fully licensed FIFA agent in March 2004.

VARNEY, John

Centre-forward/Full-back
Born: 27 November 1929, Oxford
United debut: 27 December 1954 v Kettering Town
Final United game: 24 March 1956 v Bath City
Appearances: 17
Goals: 10
Clubs: Oxford City, Hull City, Lincoln City, Headington United

John Francis 'Frank' Varney was an Oxford lad who started with Oxford City, with whom he gained an England Youth cap in the 1947–48 season, having joined the club during World War Two. He joined Hull City in 1950, playing nine League games for the Tigers before signing for Lincoln City, making his debut in August 1951. He played 21 games for the Imps, scoring four goals before his final Lincoln game, against Leicester City in December 1952. Varney started with Headington as a full-back, but after Ken Smith left for Blackpool he played in the first team as centre-forward, but by the end of his time with the club he was featuring mainly at left-back again.

VEYSEY, Ken

Goalkeeper
Born: 8 June 1967, Hackney
United debut: 21 November 1990 v Bristol City
Final United game: 20 April 1992 v Plymouth Argyle
Appearances: 67
Clean sheets: 16
Clubs: Dawlish Town, Torquay United, Oxford United (loan), Oxford United, Sheffield United (loan), Reading, Exeter City, Dorchester Town, Torquay United, Plymouth Argyle, Taunton Town

Kenneth James Veysey started his career with Arsenal, despite being a Tottenham supporter and former ballboy, but he moved to Devon without playing a first-team game for the Gunners. After playing for Dawlish he moved to Torquay in November 1987 and on his League debut that month he saved a penalty against York City. Veysey was an ever present in the 1989–90 season and won the Player of the Year award. However, he lost his place the following season and in November 1990 he joined Oxford on a three-month loan. On his debut Veysey saved two penalties in the shoot-out against Bristol City in the Zenith Data Systems Cup and after his loan he signed for Oxford for £110,000, having played 90 games for the Gulls. Veysey had a loan to Sheffield United in December 1992 but did not play for the Blades, and he left Oxford after failing to get a first-team game during 1992–93, initially moving to Reading in August 1993, but in October he left for Exeter without having made a first-team appearance for the Royals. Veysey played 12 League games for Exeter before signing for Dorchester Town in 1994. While with Dorchester Veysey played against Oxford in the FA Cup first round in November 1995, conceding nine goals as the U's stormed to their best ever FA Cup win; the 9–1 scoreline could have been a lot heavier but for Veysey's goalkeeping. In August 1997 Veysey rejoined Torquay, initially on a part-time basis, but after making 48 appearances he was released and joined Plymouth in August 1999. He played nine games for Argyle, but was released in May 2000 and joined Taunton Town. After being goalkeeping coach with Exeter City he joined Torquay in a similar capacity in June 2007.

VICKERS, Keith

Inside-right
Born: 17 June 1940, Oxford
Died: 19 December 2003
United debut: 10 January 1959 v Hastings United
Final United game: 10 January 1959 v Hastings United
Appearances: 1
Clubs: Headington United, Bedford Town, Portsmouth, West Bromwich Albion, Gillingham, Margate (loan), Dartford

William Keith Vickers' only game for United was in new manager Arthur Turner's first home game at the club. After a brief spell in Ontario, Canada, Vickers returned to England in 1961 and joined Bedford Town, for whom he played 10 games. He was on Portsmouth's and West Brom's books without playing for either club, and also joined Gillingham, where he again failed to make a first-team appearance but did have a spell on loan with Margate, where he played seven games. After Gillingham released him, Vickers signed for Dartford in 1966, scoring 10 goals in 32 appearances over two seasons. After retiring from playing Vickers taught biology and PE at what is now Carterton Community College before starting up Vickers Hotel in Woodstock. He collapsed and died from a heart attack in December 2003 while trying to patch up an argument between customers at his restaurant.

VINTER, Mick

Striker
Born: 23 May 1954, Boston
United debut: 14 August 1982 v Reading
Final United game: 12 May 1984 v Rotherham United
Appearances: 93+3
Goals: 28
Clubs: Boston United, Notts County, Wrexham, Oxford United, Mansfield Town, Newport County, Gainsborough Trinity, Sutton Town, Matlock Town, Oakham United, Hucknall Town, Sneinton

Boston-born Michael Vinter started with his home-town club Boston United, managed at the time by Jim Smith, before joining Notts County in 1972. He scored 54 goals in 166 appearances for the Magpies and won the Supporters' Player of the Season award for 1977–78 before moving to Wrexham for a Notts County club record £150,000 in June 1979. Vinter made 101 League appearances for the Welsh side, scoring 25 goals, before Wrexham were relegated to Division Three and Oxford signed him for £25,000 in August 1982. Vinter was Keith Cassells' striking partner as United won the Third Division title in 1983–84, but after promotion he was released by Oxford and signed by Ian Greaves at Mansfield Town. He scored seven goals in 54 League games for the Stags, leaving for Newport County in August 1986 where he played 32 League games in which he managed six goals. Vinter's next move was to Gainsborough Trinity in the summer of 1987. He went on to play for a variety of lower league clubs in the East Midlands while working as an insurance salesman and then a lorry driver. In 1999 he coached the newly-formed Dayncourt Ladies FC, which later became Radcliffe Olympic Ladies, but in 2005 he was involved in a serious road accident. Vinter's life went downhill and in August 2007 he was found guilty of assault and ordered to serve an 18-month supervision order. He also had to complete a domestic violence abuse programme and have treatment for alcoholism for six months.

VIVEASH, Adi

Centre-back
Born: 30 September 1969, Swindon
United debut: 7 September 2002 v Torquay United
Final United game: 9 November 2002 v Rochdale
Appearances: 15
Clubs: Swindon Town, Reading (loan), Reading (loan), Barnsley (loan), Walsall (loan), Walsall, Reading, Oxford United (loan), Swindon Town, Kidderminster Harriers (loan), Kidderminster Harriers (loan), Aldershot Town, Cirencester Town

Adrian Lee Viveash joined Oxford on loan from Reading in September 2002 and performed a great job in shoring up a previously leaky defence. He started his career with home-town club Swindon in 1988 as a forward, although he had converted to the centre of defence by the time he made his debut in September 1990. Viveash failed to play for them during their sole season in the Premiership in 1993–94. In January 1993 he had his first loan spell with Reading, scoring once in six games for the Royals, and he had another six-game loan at Elm Park in January 1995. This was followed by a two-game loan with Barnsley in August 1995 in which Viveash scored once. In October 1995 Viveash played three games on loan to Walsall, signing permanently for the Saddlers the following month. Viveash was at the Bescot for almost five years, playing 237 matches and scoring 16 goals, winning the Player of the Year award in their 1999 promotion season before rejoining Reading, this time permanently, in July 2000. In his two years at the Madejski Viveash played 79 games and scored three times, and won promotion to Division One in 2002. With his loan to Oxford failing to result in a permanent move despite United's alleged desire to sign him and him being told he had no future at the Madejski, he returned to Reading. Viveash did eventually secure a move from the Royals, returning to Swindon in July 2003. After losing his first-team place Viveash had a seven-game loan spell with Kidderminster in March 2004 and he returned to Aggborough for another loan, again for seven matches, in August 2004. In December 2004 he agreed to have his contract cancelled and he moved to Aldershot, where he made seven appearances before being released in January 2005 to move to Cirencester Town. Viveash left Cirencester at the end of the following season to complete his coaching qualifications, and in May 2007 he returned to the Corinium as manager. In September 2008 he resigned from Cirencester to take up a coaching role with the Chelsea Academy.

W

WALKER, Ian

Goalkeeper
Born: 31 October 1971, Watford
United debut: 24 September 1990 v Port Vale
Final United game: 3 October 1990 v West Ham United
Appearances: 3
Clean sheets: 1
Clubs: Tottenham Hotspur, Oxford United (loan), Ipswich Town (loan), Leicester City, Bolton Wanderers

Ian Michael Walker signed on loan from Tottenham Hotspur in August 1990, some two years before his Spurs debut. He also went on loan to Ipswich in November 1990, but did not play for their first team. He stayed at White Hart Lane until July 2001, winning three England caps and a Worthington Cup medal after a 1–0 win over Leicester in March 1999, and making 314 appearances. He then signed for Leicester City in a deal worth up to £3 million, playing 156 games for the Foxes over four years and winning another England cap. In July 2005 Walker joined Bolton on a free transfer, playing just eight games, none in the League, up to December 2008, at which point he had his contract terminated by mutual consent. Walker was appointed manager of Bishop's Stortford in March 2011. In addition to his four England caps, Walker was also an England Youth international, won nine England Under-21 caps, and one England B cap.

WALKER, Richard

Striker
Born: 8 November 1977, Birmingham
United debut: 17 March 2004 v Cheltenham Town (sub)
Final United game: 17 April 2004 v Darlington
Appearances: 3+1
Clubs: Aston Villa, Cambridge United (loan), Blackpool (loan), Wycombe Wanderers (loan), Blackpool, Northampton Town (loan), Oxford United (loan), Oxford United, Bristol Rovers, Shrewsbury Town (loan), Burton Albion

Richard Martin Walker arrived in Oxford in March 2004 from Blackpool, initially on loan, but after just one substitute appearance he then signed a contract to take him to the end of the season. He started as a trainee with Aston Villa, turning professional in August 1995, making his debut in December 1997. In December 1998 he went on loan to Cambridge United, playing 24 games and scoring four goals, and he had a further loan spell with Blackpool in February 2001, scoring three goals in 18 appearances. Walker played 13 games on loan to Wycombe in September 2001, and after his return to Villa Park in December Blackpool paid £50,000 to take him to Bloomfield Road in December 2001. He had scored two goals in 10 matches for the Villains. Walker played 70 games while at Blackpool, scoring 15 goals, and while on the Seasiders' books he preceded his Oxford loan with 19 games at Northampton, in which he scored eight times, in October 2003. His time with Oxford was not a great success and at the end of the 2003–04 season he signed for Ian Atkins' Bristol Rovers. He was Rovers' top goalscorer in both the 2005–06 and 2006–07 seasons, but he lost his place the following season and in July 2008 he joined Shrewsbury on a year-long loan. Walker played 32 games for the Shrews, in which he found the net just six times, and after his return to the Memorial Ground he was released by the Pirates, having scored 62 goals in 176 matches. In July 2009 Walker signed for Football League newcomers Burton Albion, but he was released in May 2011 after playing 39 games in which he scored five goals.

WANLESS, Paul

Midfielder/Centre-back
Born: 14 December 1973, Banbury
United debut: 9 October 1991 v Portsmouth (sub)
Final United game: 7 May 2005 v Chester City
Appearances: 74+32
Goals: 7
Clubs: Oxford United, Lincoln City, Woking (loan), Cambridge United, Oxford United, Forest Green Rovers, Llanelli

Paul Steven Wanless rejoined the club where he began his career after seven seasons at Cambridge United, where he was club captain, at the start of the 2003–04 season. Wanless came through United's youth set-up as a YTS player in the summer of 1990, turning professional in December 1991. He was unable to establish himself in the side, and moved to Lincoln in the summer of 1995 having scored once in 35 games for the U's. Wanless played just eight games for the Imps and had a couple of months on loan at Woking before moving to Cambridge United in March 2006. He made 335 appearances for Cambridge, and scored 50 goals, before his surprising return to Oxford. He quickly established himself as a vital component of the U's midfield and immediately won the fans round for his committed performances, even after he was converted to centre-back as his pace deserted him. It was met with sadness by United fans when Brian Talbot's first act as manager was to release Wanless, who moved to Forest Green Rovers in July 2005. In two seasons at the New Lawn Wanless scored 10 goals in 38 Conference games and was voted Supporters' Player of the Year while becoming their top scorer. He had a brief spell as caretaker manager in August 2006 and then became player-coach under new manager Jim Harvey. Wanless was released by Forest Green in June 2007 when he moved to Llanelli, also as player-coach. He made seven appearances for the Welsh side before returning to Oxford to join Oxford City in June 2010, ostensibly on the coaching staff while still being registered as a player. However, just a month later he left City after being offered a scouting role with a Football League club.

WARD, Ron

Goalkeeper
Born: 29 March 1932, Walthamstow
United debut: 20 August 1955 v Gloucester City
Final United game: 20 March 1956 v Yeovil Town
Appearances: 17
Clean sheets: 3
Clubs: Tottenham Hotspur, Headington United, Darlington

Henry Ronald Ward joined Headington in the summer of 1955 from Tottenham, although he had never played a first-team game for the First Division side. At the end of the season he joined Darlington, with whom he played 26 Football League games.

WARRELL, Sam

Goalkeeper
Born: 16 January 1990, Oxford
United debut: 18 December 2007 v Tonbridge Angels
Final United game: 22 December 2007 v Aldershot Town
Appearances: 2
Clubs: Oxford United, Abingdon United, North Leigh, Didcot Town

Sam Mark Warrell came up through the Oxford youth team. He got his chance when regular goalie Billy Turley was suspended, but was released after completing his scholarship at the end of the 2007–08 season. After leaving United Warrell signed for Abingdon Town before moving to North Leigh and, in the summer of 2010, to Didcot Town.

WARREN, Mark

Centre-back
Born: 12 November 1974, Clapton
United debut: 26 December 1998 v Crystal Palace
Final United game: 16 January 1999 v Grimsby Town
Appearances: 4
Clubs: Leyton Orient, Oxford United (loan), Notts County, Colchester United, Southend United, Fisher Athletic, King's Lynn, AFC Sudbury, Parson Drove

Mark Wayne Warren arrived on trial from Leyton Orient at the same time as Mark Watson. Although he performed well, the superior Watson was chosen over him. Warren started his career with Orient, signing professionally in July 1992. He was the O's Player of the Year in 1997 and made 189 appearances for them, scoring eight goals, before he moved to Notts County for £30,000 immediately after his loan to Oxford expired in January 1999. He scored an own-goal for Notts County in Oxford's 1–0 win there in November 1999. Warren played 98 games for the Magpies, scoring one goal at the right end, and left for Colchester United in August 2002. He made 21 appearances before moving deeper into Essex when he joined Southend in June 2003. Warren was with the Shrimpers for one season, scoring twice in 39 games, before Fisher Athletic beat off competition from Hornchurch and Canvey Island to sign the out-of-contract defender. Warren spent two seasons with the Isle of Dogs side. He was a mainstay at the heart of the Fisher defence in his first season but this was followed by an injury-hit campaign in which he made only seven appearances, two of which were in the Play-offs at the end of the season. Warren joined King's Lynn in July 2006, staying with the Linnets for two seasons before he declined an offer to extend his contract. In September 2009 he played one game for AFC Sudbury but decided that injuries were taking their toll on his day job and he retired from regular football, although in October 2009 he joined Peterborough League side Parson Drove.

WASHINGTON, Lawrie

Right-half
Born: 15 October 1920, Headington
Died: March 2004
United debut: 24 September 1949 v Barry Town
Final United game: 24 September 1949 v Barry Town
Appearances: 1
Clubs: Headington United, Oxford City

Lawrence William Washington played for Headington United in the Oxfordshire Senior League shortly after the end of World War Two. He was a regular in the Spartan League side for the two seasons before the club joined the Southern League and he remained an amateur in the first season at the higher level. He left for Oxford City, making his debut for the Hoops in September 1950. Washington made 31 appearances, scoring one goal, finishing his career in April 1951.

WATERMAN, Dave

Midfielder
Born: 16 May 1977, Guernsey
United debut: 30 March 2002 v Hartlepool United
Final United game: 24 April 2004 v Cambridge United
Appearances: 43+10
Goals: 2
Clubs: Portsmouth, Oxford United, Weymouth, Gosport Borough, Bognor Regis Town

David Graham Waterman signed for Oxford from Portsmouth on transfer deadline day 2002, having played 88 games for Pompey, where he started as a trainee. Waterman also won 14 Northern Ireland Under-21 caps while at Fratton Park. He only made four starts in the remainder of his first season for Oxford, but featured more regularly thereafter. He struggled in midfield until his dismissal at Bournemouth in August 2002, after which he lost his first-team place. When he came back into the side in November, as the right-sided defender of a back three, Waterman was a revelation, despite a difficult personal situation with his young son, Oakley, suffering from cancer. Waterman's performances and commitment earned him the Players' Player of the Season award for 2002–03. In 2003–04 Waterman found it difficult to break back into the side until Graham Rix, his former boss at Portsmouth, replaced Ian Atkins. Rix's arrival heralded the appearance of Waterman at right-back, but at the end of the season Waterman left the club for Weymouth in order to play part-time and be closer to his son, who sadly died from cancer in August 2005, aged six years. He was released by Weymouth in January 2006 and the following month he signed for Gosport Borough where he scored one goal in 40 games before quitting the game to spend more time with his family. However, in July 2008 Waterman signed for Bognor Regis town, but he was released in September for budgetary reasons.

WATSON, Gary

Left-back
Born: 2 March 1961, Easington, County Durham
United debut: 14 October 1978 v Nottingham Forest
Final United game: 7 April 1980 v Swindon Town

Appearances: 25
Clubs: Oxford United, Carlisle United, Gretna, Arcadia Shepherds (South Africa), Newcastle KB United (Australia), Gretna, Workington, Penrith

Gary Watson was taken on as an Oxford United apprentice in 1977, in the same intake as Nick Merry. He was promoted to the seniors in November 1978, having already made his debut in the League Cup. A few weeks later he was the only Third Division player in the England Youth squad that finished fourth out of 18 in the Tournoi Juniors in Monaco. In May 1980 Watson was sold to Carlisle, at the same time as Hugh McGrogan, for £19,000. Watson played 18 League games for the Cumbrians before Bob Stokoe, who preferred more experienced players, came in as manager. In the summer of 1982 Watson was given a free transfer and moved to South Africa with Pretoria-based Arcadia Shepherds before a move to Newcastle, Australia. He returned to Cumbria and became a police officer, playing part-time with various local teams.

WATSON, Mark

Centre-back
Born: 8 September 1970, Vancouver (Canada)
United debut: 19 December 1998 v Stockport County
Final United game: 24 April 2000 v Bristol City
Appearances: 68+1
Clubs: Ottawa Intrepid (Canada), Hamilton Steelers (Canada), Montreal Supra (Canada), Vancouver 86ers (Canada), Watford, Vancouver 86ers (Canada), Colombus Crew (USA), New England Revolution (USA), Seattle Sounders (USA), Östers IF (Sweden), Walsall, Oxford United, Oldham Athletic, DC United (USA), Charleston Battery (USA), Vancouver Whitecaps (Canada), Charleston Battery (USA)

Mark Stewart Watson was a Canadian international defender who won 13 Canada Under-23 caps and 78 full Canada caps, scoring three goals for the national side, for which he featured in the 2000 CONCACAF Gold Cup winning team. Watson's career started with the University of British Columbia in the Canada University League in 1989 before he turned professional and played for a number of Canadian Soccer League sides. His first venture abroad took him from Vancouver 86ers to Watford in August 1993. Watson played 17 games in his first season at Vicarage Road but made just one appearance the following season, returning to his previous side in Canada for nine games and then joining Columbus Crew in the inaugural MLS season. In 1997 he joined Swedish side Östers, where he encountered Pål Lundin. Watson recommended Lundin for a trial with Oxford, and they shared a flat in Littlemore. Watson initially joined Walsall briefly, but did not play for them before his trial with Oxford. Malcolm Shotton wanted to offer Watson a three-year contract, but this was refused by Firoz Kassam and at the end of the 1999–2000 season Denis Smith failed to offer Watson a new contract because of concerns over the amount of time that he might spend on international duty. In September 2000 Watson signed for Oldham, but after just three games for the Latics he returned to the States with DC United in the MLS. In 2002 he joined Charleston Battery, with whom he won the League in 2003, and he was the A-League Defender of the Year and in the First Team All League in 2002. He became player-assistant coach with Battery in 2006, before moving into purely a coaching role in 2007. He finished the 2009 season with Charleston before spending the Play-offs with New England Revolution. Watson joined the San Jose Earthquakes in 2010 as an assistant coach. He had been an assistant for the Canadian national team system since 2004, coaching with the Under-20, Under-23 and senior national teams. He was also on the staff of the Under-23 team for the Olympic qualifying campaigns in 2004 and 2008 and also worked with the Under-20 team in qualifying for the 2009 FIFA Under-20 World Cup.

WAY, Mick

Midfielder/Right-back
Born: 18 May 1950, Oxford
United debut: 9 August 1969 v Huddersfield Town
Final United game: 12 February 1972 v Sunderland
Appearances: 16+2
Clubs: Oxford United, Thame United, Chipping Norton Town

Michael W Way became an Oxford United apprentice in 1967 after leaving Lord Williams's School in Thame, and playing a few games for Thame United while on Oxford's books. He turned professional two years later, just before making his Oxford debut. He started with the U's on the right wing, but was converted to a more conventional central-midfielder in the reserves. By the end of his Oxford career, curtailed by injuries in the summer of 1973, Way had dropped even deeper and was often first choice at right-back.

WEATHERSTONE, Ross

Centre-back
Born: 16 May 1981, Reading
United debut: 7 November 1999 v Reading
Final United game: 26 December 2000 v AFC Bournemouth
Appearances: 7
Clubs: Oxford United, Boston United, Nuneaton Borough, Farnborough, Stevenage Borough, Didcot Town, Woodcote

Younger brother of Simon, Ross Weatherstone started his United career in the YTS in 1997, turning professional in 1999. He made his debut with a strong performance at the back in a live televised win at Reading. Sadly, he was unable to replicate that excellent start, and his Oxford career pretty much came to an end after he was found guilty of racially abusing a taxi driver, although his conviction was overturned in June 2001. He went to Boston with Simon in February 2001 and was knocked unconscious on his debut. Ross was made available for transfer by the Pilgrims in May 2002, but it was not until March 2003 that he moved to Nuneaton Borough, having played 41 games and scored one goal for the Pilgrims. Weatherstone played nine games for Nuneaton before, in August 2003, he joined Farnborough, where he scored twice in 23 appearances before leaving the club by mutual consent and joining Stevenage in January 2004, remaining until July that year and playing four games. A knee injury kept Weatherstone out of action for most of the following season, and he trained with Slough Town in March 2005 to regain fitness, but he was not deemed fit enough for Slough to sign him on. In July 2006 Ross joined Didcot Town, where he featured at both right-back and on the wing, while when he played for Woodcote, where he arrived in 2009, he scored nine goals in 19 games playing up front in the 2010–11 season.

WEATHERSTONE, Simon

Midfielder
Born: 26 January 1980, Reading
United debut: 5 April 1997 v Port Vale (sub)
Final United game: 26 December 2000 v AFC Bournemouth (sub)
Appearances: 27+30
Goals: 4
Clubs: Oxford United, Boston United, Yeovil Town, Hornchurch, Stevenage Borough, Weymouth, Crawley Town, Eastbourne Borough

Simon Weatherstone, nicknamed 'Tintin', was on the bench as United won the Junior Floodlit Cup in May 1996, even though he was not part of the YTS intake until later that summer. Coach Mike Ford claimed that he had the best technique at the club and it was little surprise when he turned professional in March 1997. However, Weatherstone, who made his name when he scored four goals against Arsenal in a Football Combination game in March 1997, failed to get a regular first-team place and he left for Boston with his brother Ross and Jamie Cook in February 2001. Simon played 115 games for the Pilgrims, scoring 29 goals, leaving in January 2004 when Yeovil Town paid £15,000 for him. Weatherstone made 22 appearances, scoring one goal, for the Glovers before joining AFC Hornchurch for an undisclosed fee in August 2004. However, big-spending Hornchurch went out of business in October 2004 and Weatherstone moved to Stevenage Borough, where he scored just two goals in 41 games until he signed for Weymouth in June 2006. In two seasons with the Terras Weatherstone made 72 appearances and scored eight goals, earning him a move to Crawley in May 2008. In his second season at the Wessex Stadium he was made club captain and he led the club to Conference survival. He scored six goals in 39 matches for Crawley, signing for fellow Conference side Eastbourne Borough in July 2009. In the final game of his first season with the Sports Weatherstone scored a penalty against Oxford that saved Borough from relegation. He scored 10 goals in 63 appearances for Eastbourne, who released him in May 2011. Weatherstone won three England semi-pro caps while on Boston's books.

WEEDON, Ben

Full-back
Born: 30 March 1989, Kidlington
United debut: 28 January 2006 v Rushden & Diamonds (sub)
Final United game: 20 January 2008 v Exeter City
Appearances: 3+3
Clubs: Oxford United, Banbury United (loan), Abingdon United (loan), Cirencester Town (loan), Oxford City, Abingdon United, Kidlington

Benjamin David Weedon, born in Kidlington, was a first-year scholar in 2005, making his debut while still on his scholarship. However, his first-team opportunities were limited, and his progress was hampered when he suffered a cruciate ligament injury that ruled him out for most of the 2006–07 season. The club offered Weedon a three-month contract, later extended to six months, at the start of the following season to give him the opportunity to earn a longer-term deal. Weedon had a loan to Banbury in August 2007 and another loan with Abingdon United in February 2008, followed immediately by a month on work experience with Cirencester, where Adi

Viveash was manager. Despite all this he failed to stake his claim and was released at the end of the 2007–08 season. Weedon joined Oxford City, making his debut in August 2008, but after just seven games he left City and rejoined Abingdon United. In 2009 Weedon joined Kidlington, where he again linked up with his identical twin brother Chris.

WHATMORE, Neil

Forward
Born: 17 May 1955, Ellesmere Port
United debut: 16 October 1982 v Walsall
Final United game: 3 March 1984 v Bradford City
Appearances: 39+6
Goals: 16
Clubs: Bolton Wanderers, Birmingham City, Oxford United (loan), Bolton Wanderers (loan), Oxford United, Bolton Wanderers (loan), Burnley, Mansfield Town, Bolton Wanderers, Mansfield Town, Worksop Town, Eastwood Town

Neil Whatmore started his career with Bolton, where he scored twice on his League debut at Swansea in April 1973 while he was still an apprentice. Whatmore spent eight years with the Trotters, playing 277 League games in which he scored 102 goals. In August 1981 Jim Smith paid £350,000, a record Bolton sale, to sign him for Birmingham City. He again scored twice on his debut but after Smith was replaced by Ron Saunders Whatmore lost his place and he joined Oxford on loan in October 1982, scoring the first of his five goals in seven games on his debut against Walsall. In December 1982 Whatmore was loaned back to Bolton, scoring three goals in 10 matches, after which he signed for Oxford permanently in February 1983. He made up for not scoring on his debut by hitting a hat-trick against Bradford City in his second game. Whatmore found it difficult to get a regular spot in the first team in the 1983–84 season and in March 1984 he returned on loan to Bolton, where he scored twice in seven League fixtures. In August 1984 Whatmore left Oxford to join Burnley as part of the deal that brought Billy Hamilton to the Manor, but after just eight games, in which he scored once, he moved to Mansfield in November 1984. He played for the Stags as they beat Bristol City in the Freight Rover Trophy Final at Wembley in 1987, but in August of that year he left Mansfield and, yet again, joined Bolton. He failed to appear for Bolton's first team and in November 1987 he was back at Mansfield, playing four times for their first team but mainly coaching the reserves. He played for Worksop and Eastwood and then coached in South Africa before returning to Nottingham to coach Forest Town and Eastwood. In June 1993 Whatmore was appointed manager of Rainworth Miners' Welfare, where he remained until November 1994. In March 2001 he joined North Notts as reserve team manager.

WHELAN, Phil

Centre-back
Born: 7 August 1972, Reddish
United debut: 9 August 1997 v Huddersfield Town
Final United game: 6 May 2000 v Millwall
Appearances: 62+3
Goals: 3

Clubs: Ipswich Town, Middlesbrough, Oxford United, Rotherham United (loan), Southend United

Philip James Whelan was a towering central-defender, who joined Oxford from Middlesbrough in the summer of 1997 for £170,000. Whelan was at Manchester University studying for a degree in accountancy when Ipswich signed him, initially on trial, in July 1990. He finished his degree at the University of East Anglia. Whelan played 93 games for Ipswich, scoring two goals, before Middlesbrough bought him for £300,000 in March 1995. While at Ipswich he won three England Under-21 caps. Whelan failed to establish himself on Teesside and he played just 28 games, scoring twice, over two seasons before his move to Oxford. Towards the end of his time with Oxford Whelan suffered from a lack of pace and in March 1999 he was loaned to Rotherham for 13 games, scoring four goals in that time. He was released in the summer of 2000 and joined Southend United, going on to play 119 games for the Shrimpers, scoring eight goals, before hanging up his boots and taking up teaching.

WHITE, Archie

Midfielder
Born: 11 January 1959, Dumbarton
United debut: 7 May 1977 v Wrexham
Final United game: 12 January 1980 v Colchester United (sub)
Appearances: 10+18
Goals: 2
Clubs: Oxford United, Heart of Midlothian, Vale of Leven

Archibald White was in the squad when United won the Midlands Youth League in 1975, signing as an apprentice that summer and turning professional during the 1976–77 season. White was never able to establish himself in the first team and was tried in a variety of midfield positions without getting a regular run in any of them. Homesickness led United to sell him to Hearts for £15,000 in March 1980 and the Edinburgh side won the Scottish First Division title that season. He was released by Hearts in May 1981 and joined Vale of Leven.

WHITEHEAD, Dean

Midfielder
Born: 21 January 1982, Oxford
United debut: 7 December 1999 v Luton Town (sub)
Final United game: 8 May 2004 v Rochdale
Appearances: 101+35
Goals: 9
Clubs: Oxford United, Sunderland, Stoke City

Dean Whitehead was one of United's rising stars, coming through the youth team and reserves to the first team. Born in Oxford, Deano joined the YTS in 1998 and turned professional in 2000. He gave strength and vision to the midfield, playing mostly on the right where his accurate crossing was an important feature of United's game. Whitehead would probably have established himself in the United pantheon of homegrown greats, but he was signed by Sunderland before realising his potential at the U's. His appearances under Ian Atkins were initially limited to covering for the more experienced regulars. In the second half of the 2003–04 season Whitehead eventually made himself a regular in the midfield and was consistently United's best player. He was even captain for a day in United's final away game of the season at Macclesfield. He signed for Sunderland in June 2004 on a three-year contract on a Bosman transfer. Because he was under 23 years old the Rokerites had to pay compensation to Oxford, with the fee, determined by a tribunal, set as £150,000 plus: £15,000 for every 10 appearances up to 50, £100,000 on promotion, £50,000 on his first competitive international appearance, and 25 per cent of his fee should Sunderland sell him. Although he was relegated in his first season on Wearside, Sunderland won promotion back to the Premiership at their first attempt. Whitehead became a regular in the side, and went on to captain Sunderland in the Premiership. Whitehead played exactly 200 games for the Black Cats, scoring 14 goals before, in July 2009, he moved to Stoke in a £3 million deal, of which Oxford received 25 per cent. Whitehead came on as a substitute in the 2011 FA Cup Final that the Potters lost 1–0 to Manchester City at Wembley, having played 83 games and scored three goals up to the end of the 2010–11 season.

WHITEHEAD, Phil

Goalkeeper
Born: 17 December 1969, Halifax
United debut: 2 October 1993 v Grimsby Town
Final United game: 29 November 1998 v Norwich City
Appearances: 238
Clean sheets: 70
Clubs: Halifax Town, Barnsley, Halifax Town (loan), Scunthorpe United (loan), Bradford City (loan), Oxford United, West Bromwich Albion, Reading, Tranmere Rovers (loan), York City (loan), Tamworth

Philip Matthew Whitehead is considered by many Oxford fans to be one of the club's best goalkeepers. He played for United for almost exactly five years, during which time he cemented a reputation as not just a brilliant shot stopper, but also as a commanding and resilient character, who forged an excellent rapport with the crowd. Whitehead's career started at Halifax, where he played 52 games after making his debut in 1988. In March 1990 he was signed by near neighbours Barnsley for £60,000, but they immediately loaned him back to the Shaymen for a further nine games. He also had loan spells at Scunthorpe (twice) and Bradford City, clocking up a further 30 games, but meaning that he had only played 16 times for Barnsley when Oxford signed him for £75,000 in October 1993. He made his United debut on 2 October and kept his first clean sheet for the Yellows eight days later, when Oxford beat Stoke City 1–0. Whitehead was immediately established as Oxford's number one, replacing Paul Reece, but he was not able to prevent the U's being relegated to the Third Division. His last appearance for United was in a live TV game at Norwich City, which Oxford won 3–2. By this time the club was in dire financial straits, and Whitehead was one of several players sold in order to bring in some much-needed income. He went to Second Division rivals West Brom for £250,000, playing 28 games for the Baggies before being sold for the same amount to Reading just under a year later. He was with the Biscuitmen for almost four seasons, playing 108 games for them. He spent loan spells at Tranmere, where he played three games in September 2002, and an emergency seven-day loan with York City for two games in April 2003, before joining Tamworth in August 2003. However, after just 16 appearances he was forced to retire through injury. He became goalkeeping coach at AFC Bournemouth and also Brentford, a position he held for two years.

WHITEHURST, Billy

Forward
Born: 10 June 1959, Thurnscoe
United debut: 18 October 1986 v Liverpool
Final United game: 6 February 1988 v Luton Town (sub)
Appearances: 42+7
Goals: 6
Clubs: Hickleton Colliery, Retford Town, Bridlington Trinity, Mexborough Town, Hull City, Newcastle United, Oxford United, Reading, Sunderland, Hull City, Sheffield United, Stoke City (loan), Doncaster Rovers, Crewe Alexandra, St George-Budapest (Australia), Kettering Town, Hatfield Main Colliery, Goole Town, Stafford Rangers, Mossley, South China (Hong Kong), Glentoran (Northern Ireland), Frickley Athletic

William Whitehurst was possibly the hardest forward to have played for Oxford. His first club was Doncaster Senior League outfit Hickleton Colliery, where he was spotted by Retford Town's manager Keith Mincher. After a spell with Bridlington, Hull City signed him from Mexborough, where he played while working as a bricklayer, for £2,500 in October 1980. Hull were relegated to the Fourth Division at the end of his first season at Boothferry Park, but by the time he moved to Newcastle United in November 1985 they were in Division Two. Whitehurst made 231 appearances for the Tigers, scoring 62 goals before his move to St James' Park for £250,000, becoming Hull's record sale and Newcastle's record signing. The big striker scored seven goals in 31 appearances before he joined Oxford for £187,000 in October 1986. Whitehurst failed to set the Manor alight and did not contribute enough goals to establish himself in the first team, and in February 1988 he was sold to Reading for £122,500. Eight goals in 19 games was a decent return for the Royals, but in September 1988 he joined Sunderland for £100,000 where he played 18 games, scoring three goals, before returning to Hull at the start of 1989. Whitehurst netted seven goals in 40 matches in his second spell with Hull before he joined Sheffield United in February 1990, where he scored two goals in 23 games, plus a five-game loan with Stoke City in November 1990. In February 1991 Whitehurst signed for Doncaster, where he managed four goals in 26 appearances, before moving to his final League club, Crewe Alexandra, in February 1992. After 11 games without a goal Whitehurst's peripatetic career continued, taking in a variety of non-League clubs and spells abroad until he eventually retired in 1993 to run a pub in Sheffield. He then relocated to run another pub in Thurnscoe but after being given a probation order for fraudulent benefit claims in April 2005 he got a job on a building site in Nottingham.

WHITTINGHAM, Guy

Forward
Born: 10 November 1964, Evesham
United debut: 8 October 2000 v Swindon Town
Final United game: 8 October 2000 v Swindon Town

Appearances: 1
Goals: 1
Clubs: Oxford City, Waterlooville, Yeovil Town, Portsmouth, Aston Villa, Wolverhampton Wanderers (loan), Sheffield Wednesday, Wolverhampton Wanderers (loan), Portsmouth (loan), Watford (loan), Portsmouth, Peterborough United (loan), Oxford United (loan), Wycombe Wanderers, Newport (Isle of Wight), AFC Newbury

Guy Whittingham played for Oxford City while with the Army's Combined Services, scoring 20 goals in 29 games in the 1987–88 season. Whittingham was still in the Army when he joined Yeovil from Waterlooville. He was prolific for the Glovers, scoring 18 goals in 23 games in the 1988–89 season, prompting Yeovil to offer to buy him out of the Army. In the summer of 1989 he signed for Portsmouth, choosing them over Everton, and he spent the next four seasons at Fratton Park, scoring 104 goals in 188 games. In August 1993 Aston Villa paid £1.2 million for his services, but he featured just 33 times for the Villains, scoring six goals. Villa sent him for a 14-game loan with Wolves in February 1994, in which he found the net eight times, before he moved to Sheffield Wednesday for £700,000 in December 1994. Whittingham played 130 times for Wednesday, scoring 25 goals, but towards the end of his time at Hillsborough he went on loan to various clubs, starting with 10 games back at Wolves in November 1998 in which he scored one goal. He then scored seven goals in nine games for Portsmouth between January and March 1999 before a four-game loan to Watford in March 1999. Whittingham returned to Portsmouth on a permanent contract in July 1999, where he made 29 appearances and scored four goals, sandwiched by loans to Peterborough for six games and one goal in August 2000 and his one game for United in October 2000. He became an instant hero for the U's after caretaker manager Mike Ford signed him by scoring on his debut at Swindon. Sadly, United lost, but Whittingham was recalled by Pompey immediately despite Ford hoping for a longer deal. In March 2001 he left Pompey for Wycombe Wanderers, where he scored one goal in 13 games before the end of the season, which included the FA Cup semi-final defeat by Liverpool. In August 2001 he joined Newport (Isle of Wight) as player-coach, remaining until June 2003 when he moved to AFC Newbury as player-manager. Newbury then suffered badly from financial problems and after they were forced to start at the bottom of the Wessex League pyramid Whittingham quit in the summer of 2006. After six and a half years as the PFA's regional coach in the south-west Whittingham joined Portsmouth as development coach in 1999, signing a new two-year deal in March 2011.

WHYTE, Chris

Centre-back
Born: 2 September 1961, Islington
United debut: 4 March 1997 v Huddersfield Town
Final United game: 4 May 1997 v Barnsley
Appearances: 10
Clubs: Arsenal, Crystal Palace (loan), New York Express (USA), LA Lazers (USA), West Bromwich Albion, Leeds United, Birmingham City, Coventry City (loan), Charlton Athletic, Detroit Neon (USA), Leyton Orient, Oxford United, Rushden & Diamonds, Raleigh Capital Express (USA), Harlow Town, Hyvinkään Palloseura (Finland)

Christopher Anderson Whyte came in to shore up United's defence in March 1997. He started as an apprentice with Arsenal, going on to play 113 games for the Gunners, scoring eight goals, in over six years at Highbury. He also had 17 games on loan to Crystal Palace in August 1984. After leaving Arsenal in May 1986 Whyte had a spell in the States, playing in the Major Indoor Soccer League for New York Express, scoring 11 goals in 26 games, and then LA Lazers, where he played 77 games and scored 27 goals. He returned to England in August 1988 and signed for West Bromwich Albion, where he played 96 games and scored nine goals. In June 1990 Leeds paid £400,000 for him and in three seasons in the top flight he went on to make 174 appearances and score six goals for the Whites, including winning the League Championship in his second season at Elland Road. Whyte played in the European Cup for Leeds in 1992–93 and was integral to the side until Barry Fry took him to Birmingham City for £250,000 in August 1993. Whyte played 88 games for the Blues, scoring twice, and had a one-game loan to Coventry City in December 1995, before he joined Charlton Athletic on a free transfer in March 1996, playing 13 games in the remainder of that season before returning to the USA to play more indoor soccer with Detroit Neon. In January 1997 Whyte signed for Leyton Orient, but without playing for the O's he signed non-contract terms for Oxford the following month, becoming the then oldest United player to have featured in a competitive match. After he was released by Oxford at the end of the 1996–97 season Whyte signed for Conference side Rushden & Diamonds, going on to play 65 games, scoring once, over the next two seasons. After a spell with Raleigh Capital Express of the Atlantic Division in the USA, he joined Harlow Town in November 1999. In 2000 Whyte played for Finnish third division club *HyPS*, but soon returned to England. He then worked as a chauffeur and for a large supermarket chain. Whyte won four England Under-21 caps in the 1982 European Championships.

WILKIE, Alex

Left-back
United debut: 25 October 1958 v Gloucester City
Final United game: 7 February 1959 v Cheltenham Town
Appearances: 20
Clubs: Starks Park YC, Raith Rovers, Barry Town, Berwick Rangers, East Fife, Headington United

Alexander Wilkie joined Raith Rovers from local boys' club Starks Park in 1950, making 15 Scottish League appearances before he moved to Welsh side Barry Town in 1953. He returned to the Scottish League the following year with Berwick Rangers, playing 37 games before leaving for East Fife, where he made 29 League appearances before joining Headington in October 1958.

WILLEY, Alan

Inside-forward
Born: 16 September 1941, Exeter
United debut: 11 March 1961 v Yeovil Town
Final United game: 5 February 1966 v Shrewsbury Town
Appearances: 127+1
Goals: 48
Clubs: Bridgwater Town, Oxford United, Millwall, Durban City (South Africa), Banbury United, Witney Town

Alan Willey started out on the ground staff of his home-town club, Exeter City. He joined Bridgwater Town but, after impressing in an FA Cup second-round tie at the Manor in November 1960, which Oxford won 2–1, he was signed by United in the first week of December, despite interest from other teams. United paid £300 for Willey, who made just one appearance in his first season, but at the start of the following term Willey started getting regular outings. His first goals for United came in September 1961, when he scored twice as Oxford beat Tonbridge 4–1. His most prolific game came 28 days later when he hit four goals as United beat Gravesend & Northfleet 8–0. The following season Willey scored United's first home League goal when the side beat Lincoln City 2–1 in August 1962, and he then scored two in the following game as United beat Hartlepools 6–2. In April 1963 he scored his only League hat-trick in a 3–0 home win over Mansfield Town. In September 1965 Willey became United's first substitute following the introduction of the new rule allowing the use of a 12th man. In March 1966 he moved to Millwall, for whom he played 10 games. He then went to play for Durban City in South Africa before returning to Oxfordshire to play for Banbury United, before finishing playing at Witney Town.

WILLIAMS, Brett

Full-back
Born: 19 March 1968, Dudley
United debut: 29 February 1992 v Blackburn Rovers
Final United game: 1 April 1992 v Millwall
Appearances: 7
Clubs: Nottingham Forest, Stockport County (loan), Northampton Town (loan), Hereford United (loan), Oxford United (loan), Stoke City (loan), Arnold Town

Brett Williams started his career at Nottingham Forest, which is where he spent all his professional career apart from a number of loans, including his seven games at the Oxford, in which he made his debut at Blackburn in a rare Leap Day fixture (one of just two played by the club since its formation in 1893). His first loan was to Stockport, where he played twice in 1986–87, and the following season he played four games for Northampton Town. In 1989–90 he played 14 games for Hereford United and his final loan was for Stoke City in January 1993. On leaving Forest in May 1993, after making 43 League appearances, Williams joined Arnold Town, where he played 285 games. He went on to coach young players in the community for Kidderminster Harriers.

WILLIAMS, Michael

Forward
Born: 21 November 1969, Bradford
United debut: 26 March 1999 v Sheffield United (sub)
Final United game: 3 April 1999 v Bolton Wanderers (sub)
Appearances: 0+2
Clubs: Maltby Miners' Welfare, Sheffield Wednesday, Halifax Town (loan), Huddersfield Town (loan), Peterborough United (loan), Burnley, Oxford United, Halifax Town, Worksop Town

Michael Anthony Williams was signed in February 1991 from Maltby Miners' Welfare by Sheffield Wednesday, for whom he made 29 appearances, scoring one goal, in over six years at Hillsborough. During that time Williams had loan spells with Halifax, for whom he scored one goal in nine games from December 1992; in October 1996 he played twice for Huddersfield and he had six games for Peterborough in March 1997. In August 1997 Williams moved to Burnley on a free transfer, but in almost two seasons at Turf Moor he played just 22 games and scored one goal before his equally unsuccessful move to Oxford, where he played twice between March and May 1999. In November 1999 he joined Halifax, where he made just five appearances before the side's relegation to the Conference in May 2001, upon which he moved to Worksop.

WILLMOTT, Chris

Centre-back
Born: 30 September 1977, Bedford
United debut: 6 August 2005 v Grimsby Town
Final United game: 17 April 2009 v Burton Albion
Appearances: 107+8
Goals: 4
Clubs: Luton Town, Wimbledon, Luton Town (loan), Northampton Town, Oxford United, Brackley Town

Christopher Alan Willmott was signed from Northampton Town by Brian Talbot at the start of the 2005–06 season. A strong central-defender, he was the most consistent of a shaky back line during the relegation season, and a regular starter in the Conference until sidelined with an injury in December 2006. However, despite not playing again that season, his importance to the squad was emphasised by the club offering him a new contract in the summer of 2007, which he accepted. He was part of United's solid defensive performance during their good run in the second half of the 2008–09 season, after which he was released. Willmott started his career with Luton Town in August 1995. He played 14 games for the Hatters before Premier League Wimbledon paid £350,000 for him in July 1999, although the side was relegated at the end of Willmott's first season. He spent four seasons with the Dons, playing 59 games and scoring two goals, and in January 2003 he returned to Kenilworth Road on loan for 13 games. Willmott joined Northampton on a free transfer in June 2003 and went on to play 101 times for the Cobblers, scoring once, before he joined Oxford. After he was released by the U's he joined a large contingent of former United players at local side Brackley Town.

WILSON, Charlie

Left-half
United debut: 5 November 1949 v Bedford Town
Final United game: 18 March 1950 v Tonbridge
Appearances: 9
Clubs: Stockport County, Burnley (guest), Clapton Orient (guest), Gloucester City, Headington United

Charles Wilson played 12 games for Stockport County during the final year of World War Two, and 16 games for Burnley and one for Clapton Orient during the 1945–46 season. Wilson joined Headington from Gloucester in September 1949, becoming a stalwart in the wing-half position for United during much of the club's first season in the Southern League.

WILSON, Joe

Forward
United debut: 21 August 1954 v Bedford Town
Final United game: 8 April 1955 v Hereford United
Appearances: 33
Goals: 7
Clubs: Headington United, Banbury Spencer, Headington United

A local boy who left United when they were in the Oxfordshire Senior League to become a professional with Banbury Spencer. He returned to United in the summer of 1954. He was at home in practically any position in the forward line.

WILSON, Phil

Goalkeeper
Born: 17 October 1982, Oxford
United debut: 21 April 2001 v Bristol Rovers (sub)
Final United game: 5 May 2001 v Notts County
Appearances: 1+1
Clubs: Oxford United, Oxford City (loan), Stevenage Borough, Ford United, Maidenhead United, Sutton United, Carshalton Athletic, Dulwich Hamlet

Philip John Wilson joined United as a scholar in 1999 but at the end of his three-year scholarship he was released in 2002, finishing his time in Oxford with a six-game loan spell with Oxford City. He signed for Stevenage Borough in March 2002 as a backup 'keeper, playing six games for the Broadhall Way side before he was allowed by Graham Westley to leave for Ford United in March 2003. In July 2003 he moved to Maidenhead, followed by a spell with Sutton United. In July 2008 he joined Carshalton Athletic, moving on to Dulwich Hamlet in October 2009.

WILSTERMAN, Brian

Centre-back
Born: 19 November 1966, Paramaribo (Suriname)
United debut: 1 March 1997 v Crystal Palace
Final United game: 24 April 1999 v Norwich City (sub)
Appearances: 31+14
Goals: 2
Clubs: NEC (Netherlands), Go Ahead Eagles (Netherlands), Vitesse Arnhem (Netherlands), Dordrecht '90 (Netherlands), Beerschot (Belgium), Oxford United, Rotherham United, De Treffers (Netherlands)

Brian Hank Wilsterman was United's first Latin American, hailing from Paramaribo in the Dutch province of Suriname. He started his career with Second Division Dutch side NEC as an amateur, signing as a professional on his 18th birthday. After 66 games for NEC he spent a year with Go Ahead Eagles in the Dutch second tier, where he was voted 'Player of the Year' before moving on to Vitesse. Wilsterman then joined Dordrecht '90 who one season later merged with SVV to become SVV/Dordrecht '90. He remained with Dordrecht for five seasons, playing in both the Dutch Premier and Second Divisions. He moved to Belgian side Beerschot at the start of the 1996–97 season but the club got into severe financial difficulties and were keen to sell the giant centre-back, with Oxford paying £200,000 for him. Wilsterman had a nightmare debut for the U's as the club lost 4–1 at home to Crystal Palace, and he did not feature again until the following season. Wilsterman occasionally found it difficult to adapt to the English game and he was in the defence when the side recorded its worst home League defeat, going down 7–1 to Birmingham in December 1998. He also scored an own-goal in a 4–1 defeat at Swindon. In July 1999 he was released by Oxford and signed for Rotherham, who came second in the Nationwide League Division Three in his first season and second in Division Two the following season. Wilsterman's final game for the Millers was a 4–3 defeat at Oxford, after which he returned to the Netherlands, having scored four goals in 59 games for Rotherham. Wilsterman joined amateur club De Treffers, and later worked for Dutch housing association Portaal.

WINDASS, Dean

Striker
Born: 1 April 1969, Hull
United debut: 8 August 1998 v Bristol City
Final United game: 3 March 1999 v Queen's Park Rangers
Appearances: 38
Goals: 18
Clubs: North Ferriby United, Hull City, Aberdeen, Oxford United, Bradford City, Middlesbrough, Sheffield Wednesday (loan), Sheffield United (loan), Sheffield United, Oxford United, Bradford City, Hull City (loan), Hull City, Oldham Athletic, Darlington, Barton Town Old Boys, Scarborough Athletic

Dean Windass became Oxford's record signing when the club bought him from Aberdeen for £475,000 in the summer of 1998. He made his debut in the first game of the 1998–99 season at Bristol City, and he scored the first of his 18 Oxford goals in that 2–2 draw. A Humberside boy, Windass began his career with North Ferriby before joining Hull City in 1991, where he played 176 games, scoring 57 goals. He joined Aberdeen in December 1995 for £700,000, and played 95 games for the Dons, scoring 34 goals. While at Pittodrie he suffered the ignominy of being sent off three times in one game. Windass's stay at Oxford was not a particularly happy one, and although he finished the season as the side's leading scorer, when he heard that Bradford City were interested in signing him his Oxford performances declined. Oxford had already declined a £700,000 offer for him from Huddersfield when he joined Bradford for £950,000, rising to £1 million when the Bantams were promoted to the Premiership at the end of that season. The money received from Windass's sale enabled United to pay Aberdeen for his signing, as the Scottish club had not received any instalments from Oxford. He stayed at Bradford for almost exactly two years, playing 88 games and scoring 20 goals, including one against Liverpool that saved the club from relegation at the end of their first Premiership season. Middlesbrough then paid £600,000 for Windass, but he scored only three goals in 46 games for them over the next couple of years. He had loan spells at both Sheffield clubs, playing twice for Wednesday in December 2001 and scoring three goals in four games for United in November 2002, before joining the Blades on a free transfer in January 2003. At the end of the 2002–03 season, having scored three goals in 18 games, he rejoined Bradford, where he stayed for the next four seasons, playing 155 games and scoring 66 goals. He spent the latter half of the 2006–07 season on loan to Hull City, scoring eight goals in 18 games, and he joined the Tigers permanently in the summer of 2007 for a fee of £150,000, playing a further 48 games and scoring 17 goals. Windass joined Oldham on loan in January 2009, scoring once in 11 games. In June 2009 he joined Darlington as a player and assistant manager to Colin Todd, but he made just seven appearances before the pair left the club in October 2009. In August 2010 Windass signed for Barton Town and two months later he joined Scarborough Athletic, while also joining the Sky Sports team as a pundit.

WINTERS, Tom

Left-winger
Born: 11 December 1985, Banbury
United debut: 8 May 2004 v Rochdale (sub)
Final United game: 30 April 2005 v Rochdale (sub)
Appearances: 1+5
Goals: 1
Clubs: Oxford United, Brackley Town (loan), Brackley Town

Thomas Richard Winters came through the ranks at Oxford, becoming a first-year scholar in 2002 and turning professional in 2005. His exciting left-wing play was reminiscent of Joey Beauchamp, although he perhaps lacked the physique necessary for the lower tiers of English professional football. Winters made his first-team debut in the last game of the 2003–04 season, at home to Rochdale, where his running and willingness to shoot caught the eye. He failed to burst on to the scene in 2004–05, although he did score his first senior goal, against Exeter City in the LDV Vans Trophy. He was offered a professional contract at the start of the 2005–06 season, but was not able to secure a regular first-team place. He had a one-month loan at Brackley in December 2005, along with Jamie Brooks, both scoring in their final game. He was granted a three-month contract at the start of the 2006–07 season, but was released after two months. He later signed for Brackley Town, where he proved a great success, and he signed a new contract in May 2011.

WOLLEASTON, Rob

Midfielder
Born: 21 December 1979, Ealing
United debut: 7 August 2004 v Rochdale
Final United game: 3 January 2005 v Bury
Appearances: 16+6
Clubs: Chelsea, Bristol Rovers (loan), Portsmouth (loan), Northampton Town (loan), Bradford City, Oxford United, Cambridge United, Rushden & Diamonds, Farnborough Town, Weymouth

Robert Ainsley Wolleaston joined United from the virtually bankrupt Bradford City in June 2004, bringing with him the wildest hairstyle seen at the club since Brian Heron in the mid-70s. Wolleaston started at Chelsea, from where he knew Graham Rix, and scored a fantastic goal against United in a pre-season friendly at the Kassam Stadium in 2002. In March 2000 Wolleaston had a four-game loan at Bristol Rovers, and a year later he played six games on loan to Portsmouth. He joined Northampton on loan in July 2001, playing eight times for the Cobblers, eventually leaving Chelsea for Bradford City in July 2003. Wolleaston scored one goal in just 15 appearances for the Bantams before his move to Oxford. His first season at United was disappointing, the player himself declaring that he played 'rubbish'. Brian Talbot was unimpressed with his claims that he would do better in his second season, and Wolleaston also did not impress during his appearances for the reserves. He failed to make the first-team squad, and had his contract paid up in November 2005. In February 2006 he joined Cambridge United, initially on non-contract terms, and after a slow start he scored both goals as Cambridge beat Burton Albion 2–1 in the 2008 Conference Play-off semi-final, but they lost 1–0 to Exeter in the Wembley final. In June 2008, after exactly 100 games and 11 goals for Cambridge, Wolleaston moved to Rushden & Diamonds. He spent one season at Nene Park, scoring nine goals in 58 games, before signing for Farnborough in August 2010. He was at the Rushmoor Stadium for just one month before he moved to Weymouth.

WOOD, Brian

Outside-left
United debut: 9 April 1955 v Hastings United
Final United game: 27 December 1955 v Kettering Town
Appearances: 4
Clubs: Headington United

Brian Wood was a local player who could play in a variety of positions on the left side of the pitch.

WOOD, Steve

Centre-back
Born: 2 February 1963, Bracknell
United debut: 3 December 1994 v Brentford
Final United game: 30 March 1996 v Stockport County
Appearances: 17+1
Goals: 2
Clubs: Reading, Millwall, Southampton, Oxford United, Woking

Stephen Alan Wood joined Oxford on a free transfer from Southampton. However, he failed to break into the promotion-winning side of 1995–96. Indeed, when he was given his chance, at Stockport, the side lost 4–2 in their only defeat in the final 17 games of their season. Wood came through the ranks at Reading and spent over six years at Elm Park, playing 248 games and scoring nine goals before his £80,000 move to Millwall in June 1987. He made 134 appearances for the Lions without scoring, but that did not deter Southampton from paying £400,000 for him in October 1991. Wood scored one goal in 55 games for the Saints before his move to Oxford in July 1994. Wood went on to Woking, where he played seven games before an injury at Dover ended his career. He had already established a chain of soccer schools and he went on to become a specialist in sports law and then a players' agent.

WOODLEY, Aaron

Striker
Born: 13 October 1992, Oxford
United debut: 29 September 2009 v Crawley Town (sub)
Final United game: 20 April 2010 v Wrexham (sub)
Appearances: 0+3
Clubs: Oxford United, Oxford City (loan)

Aaron Russell Woodley came through the youth teams at Oxford. He made his debut while still just 16 years old, and signed a three-year deal when he turned 17. Woodley joined Oxford City on a one-month loan in September 2010. He won the Young Player of the Year award in 2010 and was nominated for the Football League Apprentice of the Year in 2011.

WOODMAN, Andy

Goalkeeper
Born: 11 August 1971, Camberwell
United debut: 19 January 2002 v Rochdale
Final United game: 24 April 2004 v Cambridge United
Appearances: 112
Clean sheets: 37
Clubs: Crystal Palace, Exeter City, Northampton Town, Brentford (loan), Brentford, Peterborough United (loan), Southend United (loan), Colchester United (loan), Colchester United, Oxford United (loan), Oxford United, Stevenage Borough, Redbridge, Thurrock, Rushden & Diamonds

Andrew John 'Woody' Woodman signed for United on transfer deadline day 2002 following a reasonably successful loan spell. He immediately made himself popular with the supporters and also helped to improve the atmosphere in the dressing room. His shot stopping and aerial presence gave United an added solidity at the back, although he was criticised for sometimes being too slow to get down to low shots, and he often failed to dominate his box and come for all but the easiest crosses. He was made club captain for the 2002–03 season because of his personality and desire to win. He published an autobiographical book with his best friend Gareth Southgate called *Woody and Nord* in autumn 2003. Woodman started as a youth with Crystal Palace, which is where he originally met Southgate, and was with them for five years without ever breaking through into the first team. He left for Exeter in July 1994 but played just 10 games for them, in which he received two red cards, and as a result he was allowed to leave for Northampton in March 1995. Woody made 200 appearances for the Cobblers before moving to Brentford, after a one-game loan at Griffin Park, in January 1999. He played 67 games over two years for the Bees, which included a number of loans; he went to Peterborough in March 2000 but failed to play for the Posh, and in August 2000 he played 19 games with Southend. On his return to Brentford in November he immediately joined Colchester for a seven-game loan that concluded with him signing a contract for them and playing 52 games before his move to Oxford. After leaving United Woodman joined Conference side Stevenage Borough but after playing 24 games he was transfer-listed by Graham Westley who did not want to enact an automatic contract extension, and Woodman's contract was then cancelled. He joined Redbridge, but made just one appearance for the Motormen before moving to Thurrock in February 2005 in controversial circumstances, with Redbridge making a formal complaint because Thurrock had failed to give a formal notice of approach. In the summer of 2005 Woodman joined Rushden & Diamonds as a player-coach but he played just four games for the Diamonds before an Achilles injury ended his playing career. He was appointed assistant manager in February 2006 but after Rushden's relegation to the Conference in May 2006 he was released and joined West Ham United as goalkeeping coach, following Alan Pardew to Charlton Athletic in the summer of 2007. In December 2010 Woodman was again united with Pardew when he moved to Newcastle United as goalkeeping coach.

WOODWARD, Gerry

Goalkeeper
Born: 22 April 1923
Died: July 1994
United debut: 1 September 1949 v Worcester City
Final United game: 20 January 1951 v Hastings United
Appearances: 36
Clean sheets: 2
Clubs: Oxford City, Headington United, Worcester City

Gerald Henry Hardcastle Woodward was previously on Oxford City's books, but although he was a regular in their reserves he failed to get into their first team. He became United's regular goalkeeper from January 1948, when he took over from Tommy Bott until the club joined the Southern League in August 1949. Thereafter he was largely used as a very capable backup to the more regularly preferred, usually professional, 'keepers.

WOOZLEY, David

Centre-back
Born: 6 December 1979, Ascot
United debut: 11 September 2004 v Rushden & Diamonds (sub)
Final United game: 26 February 2005 v Cambridge United
Appearances: 13+2
Goals: 1
Clubs: Crystal Palace, AFC Bournemouth (loan), Torquay United (loan), Torquay United, Oxford United, Yeovil Town (loan), Crawley Town, Farnborough Town, Staines Town, Carshalton Athletic, Windsor & Eton, Slough Town

David James Woozley joined Oxford from Torquay in the summer of 2004. For most of the following season Woozley was unable to break into the first team, and he was roundly criticised by many supporters for being too heavy and slow. This did not deter Yeovil, the League leaders taking Woozley on loan for a couple of months to cover for their defensive injuries, although Woozley only actually made one substitute appearance for the Glovers. Woozley was released by Brian Talbot shortly into the 2005–06 season. He first played for Crystal Palace, making his debut in March 1999 and playing 35 games for them. He had a six-game loan to Bournemouth in September 2000 and in August 2001 he joined Torquay United on loan, playing 13 games for the Gulls. He returned to Selhurst Park but was unable to break back into the Palace side and in March 2002 he moved permanently to Plainmoor. Woozley scored three goals in 65 games and was with Torquay as they won promotion from Division Three in 2004, although he did not play too often in the promotion-winning campaign and he was released at the end of the season before Graham Rix signed him for the U's. After leaving Oxford, Woozley dropped into the Conference, signing for Crawley Town in August 2005. He scored five goals in 76 games for the Red Devils and in October 2006 he was appointed joint player-caretaker manager with Ben Judge after John Hollins was sacked, remaining in the post until the end of that season and orchestrating the club's survival from relegation despite a 10-point deduction. He was released by Crawley in August 2007 and immediately signed for Farnborough Town while working part-time for the fire service. It was his commitment to his external work that led to him being released in May 2009, although he signed for Staines Town the following month. He moved to Windsor & Eton for the final two months of the 2009–10 season, making nine appearances and helping them win promotion to the Southern League Premier Division. Woozley became club captain and played 33 more games for the Royalists before their demise, which saw the club wound up. He moved to Slough Town in February 2011.

*WORLEY, Harry

Centre-back
Born: 25 November 1988, Lymm, Cheshire
United debut: 7 August 2010 v Burton Albion
Final United game: 7 May 2011 v Shrewsbury Town
Appearances: 44+2
Goals: 1
Clubs: Stockport County, Chelsea, Doncaster Rovers (loan), Carlisle United (loan), Leicester City (loan), Leicester City, Luton Town (loan), Crewe Alexandra (loan), Oxford United

Harry Jonathan Worley signed a three-year deal in July 2010 after a short trial, having been released by Leicester a few days earlier. Worley started as a nine-year-old with Stockport County, joining Chelsea as a first-year scholar in the summer of 2005 for a tribunal-determined fee of £150,000. In March 2007 he joined Doncaster Rovers on loan, playing 10 games, and at the start of the following season he had a month's loan with Carlisle United, making just one appearance. Worley played two games on loan with Leicester City in March 2008, joining the Foxes on a permanent contract after the loan expired, without having played for Chelsea's first team. He was a substitute in the 2007 Community Shield and was due to play but the final whistle blew before he could get on. He did not get to play for Leicester either, going on loan to Luton for eight matches in September 2008 for three months before joining Crewe Alexandra on a season-long loan in August 2009, scoring one goal in 24 appearances for the Alex. On his return to the Walkers Stadium he was released by Leicester and immediately snapped up by Oxford.

WOTTON, Paul

Midfielder
Born: 17 August 1977, Plymouth
United debut: 13 November 2010 v Rotherham United
Final United game: 4 December 2010 v Barnet
Appearances: 4
Clubs: Plymouth Argyle, Southampton, Oxford United (loan), Yeovil Town (loan), Yeovil Town

Paul Anthony Wotton was a defensive midfielder who joined Oxford on a two-month loan from Southampton in November 2010. He started with his home-town club, Plymouth Argyle, turning professional in 1994. He played in the Argyle side that was relegated from Division Two in 1998 and by the time the side was promoted with a record points total in 2002 he was club captain, and named in the PFA Division Three Team of the Year. In 2004 he was still captain as the side won Division Two and in 2005 he was named the Player of the Season for Plymouth. In the summer of 2006 an incident with his teammate Chris Zebroski left Wotton requiring over a hundred stitches in his head. A cruciate injury in December 2006 left him out for the remainder of the season, and he did not start another game until March 2008, with Wotton released by Argyle at the end of that season. He signed for Southampton in June 2008 having played 438 games for Plymouth, scoring 63 goals, and earning himself a place in the Plymouth Hall of Fame. It was while he was with the Saints that Wotton had his loan to Oxford, and this was followed in January 2011 with a six-game loan to League One side Yeovil Town, who he joined permanently at the end of the month on an 18-month contract.

WRIGHT, Tony

Midfielder
Born: 1 September 1979, Swansea
United debut: 18 April 1998 v Tranmere Rovers (sub)
Final United game: 2 January 1999 v Crewe Alexandra
Appearances: 5+3
Clubs: Oxford United, Swansea City (loan), Merthyr Tydfil, Llanelli, Cwmbran Town, Port Talbot Town, Cwmbran Town, Llanelli, Carmarthen Town, Llanelli, Garden Village, West End

Anthony Allan Wright joined Oxford's YTS in 1996 after a spell with the Norwich City Centre of Excellence at Chepstow, having been a former Liverpool trainee, turning professional in 1998. In March 1999 he joined Swansea city on trial, but was recalled by United later that month because of an injury crisis. He earned a cap for Wales B against Scotland B and also for Wales Under-21s against Belgium in October 1997, having earlier been capped for Wales at Under-17 and Under-19 levels. Wright was released in the summer of 1999 and played for Merthyr Tydfil on a non-contract basis, even having a trial with Swindon Town in August 1999 before joining Welsh Premier League side Llanelli. In two seasons with the Reds Wright scored eight goals in 49 WPL appearances before he moved to Cwmbran Town, where he played 24 games and scored eight goals. He had a brief, six-game spell with Port Talbot the same season before rejoining Cwmbran in 2002. He rejoined Llanelli in January 2003, having scored four goals in 20 WPL games, and he scored twice more in the remaining 15 games of the season before he left for Carmarthen Town in June 2003 after Llanelli's relegation. Wright played just five WPL games for Carmarthen before returning to Stebonheath Park to rejoin Llanelli. Over the next two seasons Wright scored one goal in 32 games. He then played for Garden Village before taking up a joint manager role with West End FC, while continuing as a player, in February 2008.

*WRIGHT, Jake

Centre-back
Born: 11 March 1986, Keighley
United debut: 16 January 2010 v Tamworth
Final United game: 30 April 2011 v Lincoln City
Appearances: 62+2
Clubs: Bradford City, Halifax Town (loan), Halifax Town, Crawley Town, Brighton & Hove Albion, Oxford United (loan), Oxford United

Jake Maxwell Wright joined Oxford on loan until the end of the 2009–10 season from Brighton. He was signed at the start of the January 2010 transfer window by Chris Wilder, and agreed a three-year deal in June 2010 on a free transfer. Wright started with Bradford City, turning professional in April 2005, but he joined Chris Wilder's Halifax on loan in August 2005, playing 14 games before returning to Valley Parade. After one substitute appearance for the Bantams Wright signed permanently for Halifax in June 2006. However, after the end of the 2007–08 season Halifax were declared bankrupt and demoted, but after 66 appearances and two goals for the Shaymen Wright was able to remain in the Conference when he signed for Crawley Town in June 2008. He played for Crawley for one season, playing 41 games, before League One side Brighton signed him on a two-year contract. He played eight games for the Seagulls before Gus Poyet was appointed manager and Wright lost his place in the side. He was loaned to Oxford and after playing in the side that won the Conference Play-offs in May 2010 he joined the U's permanently. Wright was appointed United's captain for the 2011–12 season.

WRIGHT, Mark

Centre-back
Born: 1 August 1963, Dorchester-on-Thames
United debut: 13 December 1980 v Plymouth Argyle
Final United game: 20 March 1982 v Lincoln City
Appearances: 10+2
Clubs: Oxford United, Southampton, Derby County, Liverpool

Mark Wright became a United apprentice in 1979, turning professional the following summer. The young centre-back impressed enough to be signed by Southampton in March 1982 along with Keith Cassells as part of the deal that brought Trevor Hebberd and £80,000 to the Manor. Wright won the first of his 45 England caps in May 1984 and went on to captain the international side once in 1991. He was a key member of the England side during the Italia 90 World Cup campaign, in which England reached the semi-finals. In August 1987, after 222 games and 11 goals for the Saints, Derby paid a record £760,000 to take him to the Baseball Ground. Wright was made captain for Derby, but after the departure of Robert Maxwell the side was relegated from the First Division and Wright, who had made 171 appearances and scored 10 goals for the Rams, was sold to Liverpool for £2.2 million in July 1991. In May 1992 he played for Liverpool's FA Cup-winning side that beat Sunderland 2–0 at Wembley in what would prove to be the only major honour of Wright's career. Wright played 212 games for Liverpool, scoring seven goals, hanging up his boots in August 1998. In December 1999 he was appointed manager of Conference side Southport, saving them from relegation in his first season and just missing out on the Play-offs in 2001. In June 2001, after Oxford's relegation to the bottom flight, he came back to Oxford as manager, becoming the club's first boss at the Kassam Stadium. However, he failed to get United challenging and after being suspended for alleged racist abuse against referee Joe Ross he left the club in November 2001. In January 2002 he took over at Chester City, saving them from relegation in his first season and guiding them to the Conference Play-offs the following year. In 2004 he won the Conference with Chester, but left the club in controversial circumstances in August 2004 before he could take charge of them in the Football League. Wright was not in management again until May 2005 when he joined Peterborough United, but in January 2006 he was suspended and then sacked for allegedly racially abusing a colleague, although Wright strenuously denied the allegations. He returned to manage Chester in February 2006 but again saved them from relegation to earn a longer-term contract. However, chairman Steve Vaughan sacked Wright just before the end of the 2006–07 season, although he was back in charge of the Seals in November 2008, this time lasting until June 2009 before he resigned.

Y

YATES, Harry
Inside-right
Born: 26 September 1925, Huddersfield
Died: 1987
United debut: 23 August 1952 v Kidderminster Harriers
Final United game: 30 April 1955 v Lovell's Athletic
Appearances: 102
Goals: 54
Clubs: Huddersfield Town, Darlington, Headington United, Bedford Town, Nuneaton Borough

Harold Yates started his career with his home-town club Huddersfield Town, playing just one Football League game before moving to Darlington in 1950. In the summer of 1952 he signed for Headington and played a prominent role as the club won the Southern League and Cup double in his first season, including scoring two hat-tricks. However, in September 1953 Yates was injured and was out of the side for six months, missing out on much of the historic FA Cup run. He returned as a regular for the 1954–55 season, but at the end of it he was one of a number of players involved in a dispute over non-payment of appearance money if players were unable to return to the team after injury and he left for Bedford Town along with Bobby Craig and Johnny Crichton. Yates scored 90 goals in 134 appearances for the Eagles, leaving them for Nuneaton Borough in 1957.

YOUNG, George
Inside-forward
Born: 2 November 1919, Dundee
Died: 1982
United debut: 18 March 1950 v Tonbridge
Final United game: 18 March 1950 v Tonbridge
Appearances: 1
Clubs: Hibernian, Watford, Headington United

George Young arrived in Watford just after the end of World War Two from Hibernian, without having made a Scottish League appearance for the Edinburgh side. He was with Watford for three seasons, playing 43 League games in which he scored five goals, before making his solitary appearance for Headington. He was described as a 'failure' and was only played because of injuries to all the club's recognised inside-forwards.

YOUNGMAN, Brian
United debut: 26 March 1958 v Dartford
Final United game: 26 March 1958 v Dartford
Appearances: 1
Clubs: Headington United

In December 1959 Gresley Rovers signed a left-winger named Brian Youngman, who scored two goals in four games for the Central Alliance Division One (North) side before leaving the following month. It would seem likely that this is the same player as made a sole appearance for Headington United in March 1958.

Z

ZEBROSKI, Chris

Striker
Born: 29 October 1986, Swindon
United debut: 21 March 2007 v Halifax Town
Final United game: 8 May 2007 v Exeter City
Appearances: 9+1
Goals: 2
Clubs: Cirencester Town, Plymouth Argyle, Millwall, Oxford United (loan), Torquay United (loan), Wycombe Wanderers, Torquay United (loan), Torquay United, Bristol Rovers

Christopher Matthew Zebroski signed on loan from Millwall just before the transfer deadline in March 2007. Zebroski was a quick striker but came with a dodgy reputation. He was on trial with United from Plymouth, where he was sacked before the start of the 2006–07 season, but Millwall nipped in to sign him before Jim Smith could nab him for the Yellows. Zebroski started his career with the Cirencester Academy, signing for Plymouth in August 2005 and turning professional in February 2006. He had made just five substitute appearances before he was dismissed because of an incident involving Paul Wotton, who required over a hundred stitches in his face following a fracas at a restaurant while the side was at a training camp in Austria, and he joined Millwall in September 2006. While on loan with Oxford, Zebroski played in both legs of the 2007 Conference Play-off semi-finals, missing the final penalty in the second-leg shoot-out against Exeter City. He made 32 appearances for Millwall, scoring three goals, before joining Conference side Torquay United on loan for the 2007–08 season. He scored 19 goals for the Gulls in 52 games, including a 1–0 defeat to Ebbsfleet United in the FA Trophy Final, and when his loan finished Millwall sold him to Wycombe Wanderers for £20,000. Zebroski made 55 appearances for the Chairboys, scoring nine goals, before returning on loan to Torquay, by then in League Two, in November 2009. Four goals in seven games convinced Torquay to sign him permanently in January 2010, and he played for them in their 1–0 defeat by Stevenage in the 2011 League Two Play-off Final. In June 2011 Zebroski handed in a transfer request and the following month he signed for Bristol Rovers for an undisclosed fee.

MANAGERS

Harry Thompson

Born: 29 April 1915, Mansfield
Died: 29 January 2004
Clubs played for: Mansfield Town, Wolverhampton Wanderers, Sunderland
Clubs managed: Headington United

Harry Thompson started his playing career with Mansfield Town juniors, signing as a professional in 1932, but he joined Wolverhampton Wanderers in 1933 without playing a game for the Stags. After 69 League games and 16 goals, in 1937 Sunderland paid Wolves the then enormous sum of £7,500 for Thompson, an inside-forward. He was at Roker Park when World War Two broke out, having scored once in 11 games for Sunderland. During the war Thompson played for some top-class Army teams as well as guesting for York City while on Army duties at Marston Moor.

In 1946, the resumption of League football saw Thompson sign for Northampton Town on a part-time basis. In the following three seasons he played 38 League games, scoring twice, for the Cobblers, having switched to playing centre-half. During the summers, Thompson coached Norwegian side Ranheim, based near Trondheim.

In July 1949, Headington United director Peter Smith reported to the club's first board meeting that he had secured the services of Harry Thompson as player-coach, with effect from 1 August 1949. Thompson was given a two-year contract, and was to be paid £550 a year, plus a match bonus of £2 a win and £1 a draw *while playing*. In addition, Thompson would receive an extra bonus depending on where the team finished in the Southern League. United were to provide Thompson with accommodation, eventually buying a house for him in Green Road, Headington. Thompson's duties were to assemble a squad by recommending players to the board, with Mr Smith negotiating the contracts, and to coach the players. Team selection was initially undertaken by a sub-committee, of which Thompson was a member.

At the end of the 1949–50 season Thompson was appointed player-manager, a decision that led board member HF Bradley to resign in protest, and Thompson was empowered to sign his own players up to a maximum wage bill of £130 a week. The side had finished fourth from bottom in their inaugural Southern League season, during which Thompson played 44 games, before an injury at Gillingham on 5 April ended his season. The following season United fared much better, finishing seventh, with Thompson playing 21 games and scoring once, in a 3–2 win at Torquay United Reserves on 11 November 1950. Thompson's last game for the club was a 4–1 defeat at Chelmsford City on 24 March 1951, after which he decided to end his playing career. Thompson was an honourable man, and offered to resign if the club decided it wanted to appoint another player-manager, but the board instead appointed him manager on an annual contract, with effect from August 1951.

Under Thompson's guidance, United went from strength to strength, winning the Southern League and Southern League Cup in 1953, and finishing second the following season while retaining the Southern League Cup and reaching the fourth round of the FA Cup. He was eventually sacked in November 1958 after the side had lost seven consecutive Southern League games. His last game as manager was a 1–0 defeat at Guildford City in the Southern League Inter-Zone Competition. After leaving Headington United, Harry worked for Morris Motors and then Pressed Steel in Cowley.

Thompson was described as a modest man, who was very fair. He talked common sense and would drop players who played badly, telling them why and treating everyone, whether full-time, part-time, or amateur, the same. Thompson was responsible, along with the board, for turning Headington from a part-time local team into a full-time professional side that was known nationally. He started from scratch, with no players, but built a team of good ball-players. He brought in players such as Geoff Denial, Johnny Love, Pat Quartermain, and Frank Ramshaw, all of whom would have lengthy and distinguished careers with United.

Arthur Turner

Born: 1 April 1909, Chesterton, Staffordshire
Died: 12 January 1994
Clubs played for: West Bromwich Albion, Stoke City, Birmingham City, Southport
Clubs managed: Southport, Crewe Alexandra, Birmingham City, Headington United

Arthur Owen Turner was born in Chesterton, a small former mining village on the edge of Newcastle-under-Lyme, Staffordshire. As a youth Turner played for Downings Tileries. Chesterton was part of the Wolstanton United Urban District, and Turner's next club was Wolstanton PSA. He left them in 1929, joining West Bromwich Albion as an amateur, leaving the following year for Stoke City, where he played as a centre-half, making seven League appearances in his debut season. Two seasons later Turner was an ever present, scoring five goals, as Stoke were promoted to the First Division and he continued as a regular for the Potters over the next four seasons, becoming Stoke's main penalty taker. By the time he moved to Birmingham City in 1938, Turner had played 290 League games for Stoke, scoring 17 goals, 10 from the spot. His first season at Birmingham ended badly, with the Blues relegated to Division Two with Turner playing 12 games. The following season Turner had played just two games before the season was halted early because of the outbreak of World War Two. During the war Turner played nearly 200 games for Birmingham, captaining them to the Championship of the wartime Football League South. In the first post-war season Turner played 27 games for Birmingham, who finished third in the Second Division, just missing out on promotion, and reached the semi-final of the first post-war FA Cup.

In January 1948 Turner was appointed player-manager of Southport, where he played 28 League games. He played his last game in October 1948, aged 39 years old, when he left to become manager of Crewe Alexandra. He was at Crewe for three seasons before returning to Stoke to become assistant manager to Bob McGrory and then Frank Taylor. In November 1954, Turner left Stoke to become manager of Birmingham City, leading them to the Second Division Championship in his first season, and then to sixth in Division One the following season. Turner resigned in September 1958 after finding out from the press that Pat Beasley, who he thought was appointed as his assistant, was in fact made joint manager.

Turner joined Headington United on New Year's Day 1959, when he became manager without a contract. On 2 April 1959 Turner was approached by First Division Leeds United to become their manager. Turner initially accepted the Leeds offer, but when Headington matched their terms he decided to remain in Oxford and signed a permanent contract. During what remained of the 1958–59 season, Turner managed to improve the side's results enough to ensure that they finished in the top half of the Southern League North Western Zone, albeit on goal average, thereby guaranteeing a place in the Southern League Premier Division the following season. The following season Headington were runners-up to Bath City, but in the next two seasons the club, now called Oxford United, won the Southern League Championship. In March 1962 Accrington Stanley resigned from the Football League after going bankrupt, and United were the obvious team to replace them.

The first season as a Football League club was one of consolidation, but the following season Oxford became the first Fourth Division side to reach the quarter-finals of the FA Cup, famously beating First Division Blackburn Rovers 3–1 in the fifth round before losing 2–1 to Preston North End. In 1965 United finished fourth in Division Four, earning promotion. Three seasons later Turner led United to the Third Division title and promotion to Division Two, just 10 seasons after becoming manager of the club that was in the bottom half of the Southern League. United struggled in their first season in the second tier and Turner resigned from team duties, becoming general manager in January 1969. Turner's time at the club ended on a sour note when he was sacked in the spring of 1972, having earlier been given a leave of absence, after United admitted that they could not afford to retain him despite having promised him a job until his retirement.

After leaving Oxford, Turner remained involved in football, scouting for Rotherham United and Sheffield Wednesday.

Ron Saunders

Born: 6 November 1932, Birkenhead
Clubs played for: Everton, Tonbridge, Gillingham, Portsmouth, Watford, Charlton Athletic
Clubs managed: Yeovil Town, Oxford United, Norwich City, Manchester City, Aston Villa, Birmingham City, West Bromwich Albion

Ronald Saunders joined Everton as a junior and made three League appearances for the Toffees in 1954–55; he also won England Youth honours while at Goodison. In July 1956 he joined Southern League side Tonbridge, and in his first season he equalled the club's record of 39 goals in a season, also scoring in the Southern League Cup Final. He returned to the Football League when Gillingham paid £800 for him in May 1957. Centre-forward Saunders was at the Gills for two seasons, scoring 20 goals in his 49 League appearances, before he became the first player to move from the Fourth Division to the First Division when Portsmouth paid £10,000 for him in September 1958. His 21 goals from 36 games failed to prevent Pompey's relegation, and two seasons later they were relegated again to the Third Division, despite Saunders scoring 20 goals, to add to the 17 he had scored the previous season. Saunders continued his impressive goals return the following season, scoring 32 from 42 games as Portsmouth won the Division Three Championship.

In 1964 Saunders moved to Watford, having played 236 League games and scored 145 goals. He was with Third Division Watford for one season, scoring 18 goals in his 39 games, before moving up a division to join Charlton Athletic, where he played 65 games, scoring 24 times. On 17 April 1967 Saunders became player-manager of Yeovil Town in the Southern League, but he left to join Oxford United on 19 February 1969, doubling his salary to £80 a week and becoming the first person to move from managing a non-League club to a Second Division side.

When Saunders arrived at Oxford, United were bottom of Division Two, with just 12 games of the season remaining. His first game in charge was a 1–1 draw at Bolton Wanderers, and over the next 11 games United lost only three and drew two to ensure their survival, thanks to a 1–0 win over Sheffield United on the last day of the season. They finished three points clear of relegated Bury, and eight points above Fulham. Considering Saunders' relative managerial inexperience this was a magnificent achievement and one that did not go unnoticed elsewhere. During the summer of 1969 Norwich City approached Saunders, and after United matched their initial offer they returned with a far better one that Saunders accepted, having been in charge at Oxford for just 12 matches.

In his third season at Carrow Road, Saunders led the Canaries to the Second Division title with an unbeaten home record. The following season Norwich survived in the First Division, finishing in 20th place. Norwich finished bottom the next season, but Saunders had already left the club in November 1973, taking over the reins at First Division Manchester City. Saunders was in charge at Maine Road for fewer than six months before being sacked, having won just six out of 24 games. He joined Aston Villa in the summer of 1974, taking them to second in Division Two in his first season. Their first season in Division One saw Villa finish 16th, but without an away win, and in 1977 Villa finished fourth. The next three seasons saw the Villains finish in the top half of the table and in 1981 Saunders led Villa to the First Division title. In February 1982, after more than 350 games in charge, Saunders left Villa to become manager of their arch-rivals Birmingham City, taking over from Jim Smith.

Saunders' first two seasons at St Andrew's were ones of struggle, with the Blues finishing in 16th and then 17th place. In the third season the Blues lost the struggle and finished 20th, in the third relegation place. Saunders got Birmingham back into the top flight the following season, as they finished second in Division Two, two points behind Oxford United. However, Saunders resigned from Birmingham in January 1986, with the Blues en route to relegation again, to join local rivals West Bromwich Albion, who were also doomed. That season West Brom finished bottom of Division One, to go down with Birmingham. He was sacked by West Brom in September 1987, with the Baggies struggling to avoid relegation to the Third Division. Saunders has not managed in football since leaving the Hawthorns.

Gerry Summers

Born: 4 October 1933, Birmingham
Clubs played for: Erdington Albion, West Bromwich Albion, Sheffield United, Hull City, Walsall
Clubs managed: Oxford United, Gillingham

Gerald Thomas Francis Summers' first professional club was West Bromwich Albion, whom he joined from Erdington Albion in 1951. He made his debut as a wing-half in 1955, playing 20 games in his debut season for the First Division side. He played just twice the following season, after which he joined Second Division Sheffield United. At the end of his fourth season with the Blades, for whom he played 260 games, scoring four goals, they won promotion to the top flight, and they finished fifth in the First Division the following year. In April 1964 Summers moved to Hull City of Division Three, where he scored one goal in 59 League games before moving to Walsall in October 1965. He played 44 League games for Walsall, scoring once, until he left Fellows Park in 1967. He then did some coaching at Wolves and was a coach on the staff of the FA before being appointed manager at the Manor in July 1969.

Summers' first game in charge was on 9 August 1969, a 2–1 home defeat by Huddersfield Town. During his first season he managed to consolidate the side in Division Two, and also reached the quarter-finals of the League Cup, losing 1–0 at Carlisle United in a replay after a 0–0 draw at the Manor. In September 1970 Summers took United to the top of the Second Division, the highest the club had ever been. However, they fell away from the top and ended the season in 14th place. United finished 15th the following season, but in 1973 they finished in their highest position yet, eighth in the Second Division. The following season was much tougher for United, who looked like they could go down until the final match of the season; a 0–0 draw at Millwall left Oxford in 18th place, just two points above relegated Crystal Palace. In 1974–75 United had another relatively successful season. They finished in 11th place, but for much of the season were higher than that. Summers' big signing in the close season was Peter Houseman from Chelsea, but United made a poor start and were bottom by the end of September. As a result attendances fell, and because of the club's precarious financial situation Summers was dismissed. Three weeks later he was appointed manager of Third Division Gillingham. In total, Summers had managed Oxford for 293 games, winning 93 and losing 111. His final game was a 3–2 home defeat by Charlton Athletic on 29 September 1975.

In his six seasons with the Gills, Summers' most successful was 1978–79, when they finished fourth, one point behind promoted Swansea City. He had 262 games in charge at Priestfield before being sacked at the end of the 1980–81 season. He went on to coach at West Bromwich Albion, Leicester City, and Derby County, becoming youth development officer with the Rams until his retirement in October 1998.

Mick Brown

Born: 11 July 1939, Dublin
Clubs played for: Hull City, Lincoln City, Cambridge City
Clubs managed: Oxford United

Michael J Brown started his playing career as a full-back with Hull City, whom he joined as a junior before becoming a professional in 1958. He played twice in his first season with the Tigers, who suffered relegation to Division Three at the end of the season. He played just six more games over the next two years before, in July 1967, he joined Lincoln City. He played 38 Fourth Division games for the Red Imps and then moved to Southern League side Cambridge United.

It was from Cambridge that Gerry Summers recruited Brown to help Ken Fish with training Oxford's reserves and A team in January 1970. Before the 1971–72 season Brown was made assistant manager, and when Summers was sacked in October 1975, with the side bottom of Division Two, Brown was made his successor. His first game, on 4 October, was a 2–1 win over Leyton Orient, and Brown's appointment led to a slight improvement in the team's results. They finished the season third from bottom, but still in the relegation zone. This was United's first relegation in the club's history.

Oxford initially struggled in the Third Division, finishing four points above the drop zone in each of the next two seasons. This was partly because Brown was forced to use many of United's youngsters as the club's financial situation worsened, and he also suffered through the sale of Derek Clarke, injury to Brian Heron, and Peter Houseman's death in a car crash. In 1979 United finished in 11th position, but at the end of that season Brown left to join Ron Atkinson at West Bromwich Albion as his assistant.

Atkinson and Brown were at West Brom until June 1981, after which Brown went with Atkinson to Manchester United. As a management duo the pair enjoyed huge success, twice winning the FA Cup, reaching the semi-final of the European Cup Winners' Cup, and reaching the League Cup Final, as well as finishing in the top four in each of the five years they were there. However, the absence of a League title led to the Old Trafford board dismissing Atkinson and Brown in November 1986. Three years later Brown became Phil Neal's assistant at Bolton Wanderers, where he remained until 1992, losing his job when Neal was sacked. In the summer of 1992 Brown was employed by the Pahang FA, in Malaysia, as a coach, before returning to England to become Coventry City's chief scout. Five years later Brown became Blackburn Rovers' chief scout, and a year after that he returned to Old Trafford to take up the same position for Manchester United. Upon reaching the age of 65 he was forcibly retired by the Manchester club, whereupon he rejoined West Brom as chief scout in 2005. Two years later Roy Keane brought him to Sunderland to perform the same function and in July 2010 he became chief scout at Tottenham Hotspur.

Bill Asprey

Born: 11 September 1936, Wolverhampton
Clubs played for: Stoke City, Oldham Athletic, Port Vale
Clubs managed: Oxford United, Stoke City

William Asprey joined Stoke City as a junior, signing as a full professional in September 1953. He had a slow start at Stoke, making just one appearance in his first season, three the next, and nine the one after, before breaking into the first team and becoming a regular in the defence. Before leaving the Potters for Oldham Athletic in January 1966, Asprey had made 341 appearances and scored 26 goals, and in 1962–63 he was an ever present as Stoke won the Second Division Championship. In his first season at Third Division Oldham, Asprey played 26 League games, scoring once. He went on to complete 80 League games and score four goals before signing for Port Vale in December 1967. He played 31 games for Vale without scoring, before hanging up his boots and joining the coaching staff at Sheffield Wednesday.

Between 1975 and 1978 Asprey was national coach in Rhodesia before joining Coventry City as Noel Cantwell's assistant. He was not at Coventry for long, joining Oxford United as a reserve team coach in the 1978 close season. After Mick Brown left to join West Bromwich Albion, Asprey was promoted to the role of first-team manager, starting with a League Cup game against Reading on 11 August 1979. This was not the most auspicious of beginnings, as United were hammered 5–1 at the Manor before losing the second leg 2–1 at Elm Park. Brown's first season was a relegation battle, the club eventually finishing the season 17th in Division Three. The following season started no better for Asprey, and with crowds plummeting (United recorded their lowest home League attendance of 2,526 against Chester City in November 1980) Asprey was sacked following a 2–1 defeat at Millwall that left Oxford third from bottom of the division, two points above bottom club Hull City.

After leaving the Manor, Asprey returned to Stoke as assistant to Richie Barker, becoming manager following Barker's dismissal in December 1983. He initially worked miracles to keep Stoke in the First Division, but the following season Stoke finished bottom, recording just 17 points, which at the time was a record low for the division. With just over a month of the season left Asprey resigned through ill health in April 1985, having already been suspended on full pay.

Ian Greaves

Born: 26 May 1932, Crompton, Lancashire
Died: 2 January 2009
Clubs played for: Manchester United, Lincoln City, Oldham Athletic, Altrincham
Clubs managed: Huddersfield Town, Bolton Wanderers, Oxford United, Wolverhampton Wanderers, Mansfield Town

Ian Denzil Greaves started his playing career at Buxton before moving to Manchester United in May 1953. He was a 'Busby babe', one of a number of young players given a chance by Man United manager Matt Busby, although he was never a regular at Old Trafford. In his first season Greaves played just once, at full-back, although he played 15 League games in 1955–56, winning a League Championship medal. He made just three appearances the following season, and 12 the next. On 6 February 1958 many Manchester United players were killed or badly injured in the Munich air disaster, and it is possible that, but for an injury, Greaves might also have been involved. However, the misfortune of others allowed him to secure a regular place in the first team, and he went on to play 34 League games that season as the side finished second in the League and runners-up in the FA Cup. The following season he played just twice before he moved to Lincoln City in December 1960. Greaves was at Sincil Bank for just five months, playing 11 games, as Lincoln were relegated to the Third Division, before he moved back to Lancashire to play for Oldham Athletic. He played 22 games for the Latics in the next two seasons and finished his playing career at Altrincham.

In 1964 Greaves joined Huddersfield Town as a coach, and became their manager in June 1968. He led the Second Division side to sixth in his first season, and the following year they won the Division Two Championship to earn promotion to the First Division for the first time in their history. They finished 15th in their first season, but were relegated the next season in bottom place. Greaves remained in charge despite a second successive relegation, and the next season the Terriers finished 10th in Division Three. In October 1974 Greaves replaced Jimmy Armfield as Bolton Wanderers' manager, and in his first season the side finished 10th in Division Two. The following two seasons Bolton finished fourth before Greaves led them to the

Second Division title and promotion in 1978. As at Huddersfield, though, Greaves struggled in the top flight as Bolton finished 17th in their first season and were relegated in bottom place in 1979. With the side struggling en route to a second relegation, Greaves was sacked in January 1980. He spent most of 1980 as assistant manager at Hereford United before joining Oxford United in December.

Greaves inherited a side that were second from bottom of the Third Division, with mounting debts and declining gates, and a sub-standard playing staff. His first game, on Boxing Day 1980, saw United incredibly beat top-of-the-table Charlton Athletic 1–0, and the following day they won 1–0 at Reading. After a brief stutter, United went unbeaten in their last 13 games and they finished 14th in the table. The 1981–82 season was United's most successful for 15 years, as they finished fifth in the Third Division and had decent runs in both cup competitions, getting knocked out of the League Cup by First Division Everton, and winning 3–0 at Division One side Brighton in the FA Cup. Throughout his time at Oxford Greaves had not signed a contract, and so it came as no great surprise when he left in February 1982 to take over at First Division Wolves. His last game in charge of Oxford was a 3–1 win at sixth-placed Walsall, which left United ninth in the table, and still in the FA Cup.

When Greaves took charge at Molineux Wolves were struggling to remain in the top flight, and he was unable to save them from the drop. In August 1982 Wolves were taken over by a consortium headed by Derek Dougan, and Greaves was dismissed. He left the game for a while before returning to manage Mansfield Town in January 1983. Relying mainly on a strong youth policy, Greaves took Mansfield up to the Third Division in 1986, and the following season the Stags won the Freight Rover Trophy Final, beating Bristol City on penalties at Wembley. He resigned in February 1989 and later had stints coaching at Bury and managing at non-League Emley before embarking on scouting work for a number of clubs in the north-west.

Roy Barry

Born: 19 September 1942, Edinburgh
Clubs played for: Heart of Midlothian, Dunfermline, Coventry City, Crystal Palace, Hibernian, East Fife
Clubs managed: East Fife, Nuneaton Borough, Oxford United (caretaker)

Roy Barry started his playing career with Musselburgh Athletic's juniors before joining Heart of Midlothian in 1961. He made his Hearts debut at centre-half in August 1961 and went on to play 178 games for the Edinburgh club before being sold to Dunfermline for £13,000 in September 1966. In April 1968 Barry was captain of the Pars when they beat Hearts 3–1 in the Scottish Cup Final. In October 1969 Coventry City paid £40,000 for Barry, who made 15 appearances in his first season for the Sky Blues. The following season Barry appeared only once before breaking his leg, but he went on to complete 83 appearances for Coventry, scoring twice, before Crystal Palace bought him for £45,000 in September 1973. He was at Palace for two seasons, playing 42 games and scoring once, before returning north of the border to sign for Hibernian. He was at Hibs for a season, playing 36 games, and then moved to East Fife to become player-manager. He made 12 appearances over the next one and a half years before retiring from playing.

After leaving East Fife, Barry worked for a while on the assembly line at the Leyland Triumph factory in Coventry, managing Nuneaton Borough on a part-time basis. He was appointed assistant to Bill Asprey at Oxford in March 1980, and when Ian Greaves left to manage Wolves, Barry stepped in as caretaker, although he made no secret of his desire to make the role permanent. Barry was in charge of Oxford for just seven games, including the 4–0 FA Cup fifth-round defeat at his former club Coventry. He started his reign with a 1–0 win over Reading on 3 February 1982, and ended it on 27 February with a 3–1 win over Chester City. After leaving Oxford, Barry left the game and worked in London for 25 years until his retirement in 2008.

Jim Smith

Born: 17 October 1940
Clubs played for: Sheffield United, Aldershot, Halifax Town, Lincoln City, Boston United, Colchester United
Clubs managed: Boston United, Colchester United, Blackburn Rovers, Birmingham City, Oxford United, Queen's Park Rangers, Newcastle United, Portsmouth, Derby County, Oxford United, Oxford United (caretaker)

James Michael Smith is an Oxford United legend. Smith has had three separate spells in charge of the club, and in all of them has made his mark in one way or another.

Smith began his professional playing career when signing for his home-town club Sheffield United as a trainee in January 1959, having previously played for Oaksfield. Smith never played for Sheffield's first team and he joined Fourth Division Aldershot in July 1961. Smith had four seasons at the Rec, playing 74 League games in midfield and scoring one goal. In July 1965 he joined Halifax Town, also in Division Four. In his first season at the Shay Smith played 45 games, scoring 4 goals, and by the time he left for Lincoln City in March 1968 he had played 114 games for the Shaymen, with seven goals to his name. Smith played 54 League games at Lincoln in the next 15 months, and then left to become player-manager at Boston United in the Northern Premier League in 1969.

In his first season at Boston Smith played 53 games and scored five goals as Boston finished third. He played 45 games the next season, scoring 11 times, and secured a fourth-place finish, and in 1971–72 he played a further 52 games, finding the net six times, taking the club up to second. In his final season with the Pilgrims, Smith played 19 games and scored one goal as Boston won the title. In addition to his player-manager duties, Smith also had to act as club secretary, run the club lottery, dig new drains, concrete the car park, and decorate the boardroom. During his time at York Street, Boston always finished in the top four and the side had gone unbeaten for 51 League games (a British professional record) when he left to join Colchester United in October 1972. Colchester were bottom of the Fourth Division when Smith joined, but he started to turn things around and won the divisional Manager of the Month award in his first month. At the end of the season Smith retired from playing, having managed eight games, as Colchester were re-elected to the Football League. The following season Smith turned Colchester around and the club finished third to earn promotion to Division Three, where the next season they finished 11th.

Smith's success at Colchester got him noticed by some bigger clubs, and in June 1975 he moved to Second Division Blackburn Rovers. In March 1978 Smith, disillusioned with the lack of money available to strengthen the team, moved to Birmingham City. At the end of the following season

Birmingham were relegated from Division One after finishing 21st, but Smith took them straight back up the following season with a third-place finish. After a mid-table finish the next season, Birmingham were struggling and Smith was replaced by Ron Saunders. Within two days of leaving St Andrew's, Smith had been contacted by Robert Maxwell and appointed to the vacant Oxford post.

United were still in with a chance of promotion when Smith took over, and they won his first game 2–0 at Bristol City on 6 March 1982. United were second on 1 May, but lost their last four games to finish fifth and miss out on promotion. This proved a blessing for Smith, who was able to rebuild the side. United finished fifth again the following season, but then Smith worked his magic and in 1983–84 United won the Third Division title at a canter, and also became the first side from Division Three to reach the fifth round of both the FA Cup and League Cup in the same season. The following season United became the first team to win consecutive Third and Second Division titles as Jim Smith took the U's into the top flight for the first time in the club's history. Smith was awarded the Bell's Scotch Whisky Second Division Manager of the Season award. Sadly, Smith was never to manage Oxford in the First Division as he had a dispute with Maxwell about a pay rise, and that summer Smith moved to Queen's Park Rangers.

In his first season at Loftus Road, Smith took QPR to the League (Milk) Cup Final, where they were beaten 3–0 by an Oxford side comprising mostly players who had played under Smith. Three seasons later, in December 1988, he moved to Newcastle United, who finished third in Division Two in Smith's first full season. On 26 March 1991 Smith resigned from Newcastle, claiming that the club was unmanageable, and he became boss of Portsmouth that June. He took them to the FA Cup semi-finals in 1992, and the following season they missed out on automatic promotion to the Premiership on goal difference, losing in the Play-offs. Two seasons later Smith was sacked from Fratton Park and then spent five months as chief executive of the League Managers' Association. In June 1995 Smith became manager of Derby County, getting them promoted to the Premier League in his first full season. Derby fared well in their first three seasons, but the following two campaigns saw the side struggling against relegation and Smith resigned in October 2001. Three months later Smith became Roland Nilsson's assistant at Coventry City, but the whole management team was sacked just three months later. Later in 2002 Smith became Harry Redknapp's assistant at Portsmouth, but they both resigned after the appointment of a director of football, which they considered to be a threat to their authority and control in team matters. Redknapp became the manager of Southampton and Smith was appointed his assistant a few weeks later, on 22 December 2004, having previously turned down the role of chief scout. However, when Southampton were relegated at the end of the season, Smith's contract was not renewed due to cost-cutting.

In March 2006 Smith was part of the Woodstock Partners Ltd consortium, with his neighbours and friends Nick Merry and Ian Lenagan, which bought Oxford United from Firoz Kassam for £1, taking on the club's £2 million debts, and Smith, now a director of the club, was installed as manager. Oxford were 18th, seven points above the drop zone, with seven games to play. Unfortunately, Smith was unable to halt the club's slide and a 3–2 home defeat to Leyton Orient in the final game of the season consigned the club to relegation to the Conference after 44 years in the Football League.

The next season Oxford set a Conference record by going unbeaten for their first 19 games. However, after their first defeat in November 2006 the club lost its way and eventually finished second to Dagenham & Redbridge. With just one automatic promotion place United had to take part in the Play-offs for the first time, but lost on penalties to Exeter City in the semi-finals. The following season Oxford started disappointingly, and after a 5–0 defeat at Rushden & Diamonds, Smith handed over the reins to Darren Patterson and resumed his directorial duties. After Patterson's dismissal in November 2008, Smith took on the caretaker manager role while a successor was appointed. United went unbeaten during the four matches that Smith was in charge to reverse the side's decline and set things up for new boss Chris Wilder. Smith stepped down as a director of the club in early 2009.

Maurice Evans

Born: 22 September 1936, Didcot
Died: 18 August 2000
Clubs played for: Reading, Andover Town, Shrewsbury Town
Clubs managed: Andover Town, Shrewsbury Town, Reading, Oxford United, Oxford United (caretaker)

Softly-spoken and mild-mannered Maurice George Evans provided a stark contrast to Jim Smith's more direct style when the Didcot-born former Reading player replaced Smith, initially in a caretaker capacity, in the summer of 1985.

Evans signed for Reading aged just 16, joining Elm Park as a ground staff junior. He played his first game for Reading in the 1955–56 season, in the Third Division South, and soon became a regular wing-half for the Biscuitmen. In his 12 seasons at the club Evans played 459 games, and it is a measure of his character that he was not booked once during that time. While at Reading, Evans completed his National Service, during which he won representative honours for the Army, and on his return to Elm Park he was also selected to represent the Third Division South in a game against the Third Division North. In 1967 Evans left Reading and became player-manager at Andover Town, but the following year he joined Shrewsbury Town as a player-coach, becoming their manager in 1972. The Shrews were relegated in 1974 and Evans left Gay Meadow to return to Reading as a coach and assistant to Charlie Hurley. When Hurley left in 1977 Evans was appointed as his replacement, initially as a caretaker. The following season Evans led Reading to the Fourth Division Championship and was awarded the divisional Manager of the Year award. Reading were relegated back to Division Four in 1983 after four seasons in the Third Division, and Evans was sacked in January 1984, despite the Biscuitmen being in third place, after Roger Smee became chairman.

After his departure from Elm Park, Evans joined Oxford United, initially as chief scout and youth development officer. Following Jim Smith's departure, Evans took over as caretaker manager, but after a successful start to their first season in the First Division, with United drawing their opening two games and then thrashing Leicester City 5–0, Evans became the side's permanent manager, although he refused to sign a contract. Using the side that Smith had built, with the addition of Ray Houghton, Evans led Oxford to their first major honour, a 3–0 triumph over Smith's QPR in the League Cup Final at Wembley. At this game Evans demonstrated his humility by sending long-serving trainer Ken Fish up the famous steps to receive Evans' winners' medal in his stead. However, Evans always faced a struggle to keep United in the top flight, especially given the injury to Billy Hamilton and the departures of Houghton and John Aldridge to Liverpool, and in March 1988, with United having just been eliminated from the League Cup semi-finals by Luton Town and not having won a League game since a 1–0 win over Coventry City on 7 November (when Oxford reached ninth in the First Division), Evans resigned. His last game in charge of Oxford was a 0–0 draw at Charlton Athletic on 26 March.

Despite stepping down from the job of team manager, Evans remained at the Manor, becoming the club's general manager, and again he found himself as chief scout and youth development officer. In 1993, following the departure of Brian Horton, Evans briefly became caretaker manager, looking after team affairs for just two games before Denis Smith was appointed. Oxford lost both matches. In January 1998, Evans was appointed to the board of directors, but on 5 November 1999 Evans resigned from the board and left Oxford to rejoin Reading as chief scout, having felt frozen out by the club after Fenton Higgins was appointed director of football and manager Malcolm Shotton stopped asking Evans for his advice.

Mark Lawrenson

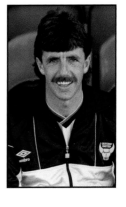

Born: 2 June 1957, Penwortham, Lancashire
Clubs played for: Preston North End, Brighton & Hove Albion, Liverpool, Thame United, Barnet, Tampa Bay Rowdies, Chesham United, Oxford City
Clubs managed: Oxford United, Peterborough United, Tampa Bay Rowdies, Corby Town

Mark Thomas Lawrenson's first club was Preston North End, his home-town team whom he joined when he was 17 years old in 1974. Two years later he won the first of his 39 Republic of Ireland caps. That same season he won Preston's Player of the Year award. In the summer of 1977, Brighton paid Preston £100,000 for Lawrenson, who had made 73 League appearances for the Deepdale club, scoring two goals. Lawro played 152 League games for Brighton, scoring five goals, including 39 games in the club's 1978–79 promotion season to the First Division. In the summer of 1981 financial problems led to Brighton having to sell Lawrenson to Liverpool for £900,000. Lawro was at Anfield for seven seasons, during which he consolidated his place in the Ireland side and established himself as a Liverpool legend. He won five League Championship medals and two runners-up medals, plus a European Cup winner's medal, an FA Cup winner's medal, three League Cup winner's medals, two Charity Shield winner's medals, and a number of runners'-up medals in all the above competitions, plus the World Club Championship in 1985. Lawrenson had played 332 games for Liverpool, scoring 18 goals, before he damaged his Achilles tendon in a career-ending injury in his final title-winning season in March 1988.

Lawrenson was a surprise choice by Oxford to succeed Maurice Evans, and he arrived to find the club in a state of disarray. Oxford were second from bottom of the First Division, having not won a League game for almost five months. In addition, United had just been knocked out of the League Cup at the semi-finals stage, and morale was rock bottom. His first game, at home to Arsenal on 30 March 1988, ended in a 0–0 draw, but that was as good as it got for the rest of that season, and Lawrenson did not see Oxford score until 23 March, when a Dean Saunders penalty rescued a point in a 1–1 draw with Everton. By that time United's relegation had already been confirmed and that was the last point they won before finishing bottom of the table. The following season Lawrenson had started to halt the decline and consolidate in mid-table in the Second Division. However, just after United had drawn 1–1 with Blackburn Rovers to leave the U's 10th in the table, he was told by chairman Kevin Maxwell that United had sold striker Dean Saunders to Derby County, managed by Kevin's father Robert Maxwell, for £1 million. He was then sacked by United (allegedly by Robert, not Kevin, Maxwell) in order to pre-empt his resignation.

After playing a handful of games for Thame United, and two games for Barnet, Lawrenson went to America to coach and play for Tampa Bay Rowdies, whom he took to the American Professional Soccer League title. On 6 September 1989, Lawrenson became manager of Fourth Division Peterborough United. His success there was limited and he left in November 1990 after the chairman ordered him to drop five first-team players because they could not afford to pay them the agreed appearance money. Lawro had a brief spell in charge of Corby Town in the Beazer Homes League, and in 1992–93 he played for Chesham United. He had by now turned his attention to the media, with a brief hiatus when he became Kevin Keegan's defensive coach at Newcastle United, becoming a regular for the BBC both on television and radio. He still occasionally played football, turning out for Oxford City for 21 games between 4 December 1993 and 7 May 1994. Meanwhile he was also landlord of the Eagle Tavern in Little Coxwell, near Faringdon in Oxfordshire, for several years.

Brian Horton

Born: 4 February 1949, Hednesford
Clubs played for: Hednesford Town, Port Vale, Brighton & Hove Albion, Luton Town, Hull City
Clubs managed: Hull City, Oxford United, Manchester City, Huddersfield Town, Brighton & Hove Albion, Port Vale, Macclesfield Town, Hull City (caretaker)

After a brief spell with Walsall's youth team Brian Horton joined his home-town club, Hednesford Town. In July 1970 Port Vale signed Horton, and he spent six years as a midfielder at Vale Park, playing 236 League games and scoring 33 goals. To the disappointment of Vale fans, he was sold to Brighton in March 1976 for £30,000, and it was at the Goldstone Ground that he played alongside Mark Lawrenson. At the end of his first full season Brighton were promoted to the Second Division, and two years later they achieved promotion to the top flight. Horton left Brighton after five full seasons, having played 217 League games, and having scored 33 goals. Luton Town signed him in August 1981 and in his first season at Kenilworth Road he captained the Hatters to the Second Division title. After two seasons in the top flight, and having played 118 games with eight goals, he moved to Boothferry Park to become player-manager at Hull City in July 1984. In his first season Hull finished third in Division Three and were promoted, with Horton playing in 22 League games. Horton continued to play sporadically for the next two seasons, hanging up his boots after playing 38 League games for the Tigers. After a good start to the 1987–88 season Hull started slipping down the table, and on 13 April Horton was sacked.

Horton's former teammate at Brighton, Mark Lawrenson, brought him to the Manor as his assistant in June 1988, and when Lawro was sacked in

October, Horton, who had offered to resign in support of Lawrenson, was appointed manager with Lawrenson's blessing. Horton's first game was a 1–0 defeat at Crystal Palace on 25 October, which began a run of four successive defeats and just one win in the next eight matches. Horton's first signing was Paul Simpson, whose arrival was pivotal to turning around the team's fortunes. Oxford finished 17th in Division Two at the end of Horton's first season, and in the same position the following year. Fortunes improved in 1990–91 as United finished in 10th place and beat First Division Chelsea 3–1 at Stamford Bridge in the FA Cup third round, but the following season was one of struggle, culminating in a dramatic last-day escape from relegation with a 2–1 win at Tranmere Rovers. The next season Horton again steadied the ship as United finished a respectable 10th, but the 1993–94 season had only just started when Manchester City surprised everyone by offering Horton the manager's job at Maine Road to replace Peter Reid. Horton's final game in charge of Oxford was a 3–1 defeat at West Bromwich Albion on 21 August 1993.

At the end of his first season in Manchester, City finished 16th in the Premier League, having been bottom in February. The following season City started off well, and they were sixth at the start of December, but a run in which they won just four of their remaining 25 League games saw them finish 17th, just four points above the drop zone, and Horton was sacked. He was then appointed manager of Huddersfield Town, taking them to eighth in the second tier in his first season. The following season, though, Huddersfield only just avoided relegation, finishing in 20th place, and he was sacked in September 1997 after a disappointing start to the season. Five months later Horton was appointed manager of Third Division Brighton, but he failed to make much of an impact at his former club, who finished second from bottom. Things improved the following season, but in January 1999 Horton left Brighton to become manager of Port Vale. They survived the drop in Horton's first season, finishing 21st in Division One, but the following season they finished just one place above bottom side Swindon Town and dropped to Division Two. In 2001 Port Vale won the LDV Vans Trophy at the Millennium Stadium, beating Brentford in the Final. In his sixth season as manager at Vale Park, Horton left by mutual consent after it was revealed that the board was considering reducing his contract as a cost-cutting measure. In April 2004, Horton was appointed manager of Division Three side Macclesfield Town. Horton was able to keep the struggling side away from relegation with a 20th-placed finish, and the following season he took them into the Play-offs, where they lost to Lincoln City in the semi-finals. They finished 17th the following season, but in 2006–07 the Silkmen failed to win any of their first 12 games and Horton was sacked with the side bottom of the League. On 23 May 2007, Horton was appointed assistant manager to Phil Brown at Hull City, and the following season the side won promotion to the Premiership for the first time. In March 2010 Horton was appointed joint caretaker manager of Hull and in January 2011 he joined Brown as his assistant at Preston North End.

Denis Smith

Born: 19 November 1947, Stoke-on-Trent
Clubs played for: Stoke City, York City (loan), York City
Clubs managed: York City, Sunderland, Bristol City, Oxford United, West Bromwich Albion, Oxford United, Wrexham

Denis Smith was an uncompromising centre-half in his playing days, becoming a Stoke City legend in the process. He joined Stoke in 1964 after leaving school, becoming a professional two years later, and making his debut in 1968–69. Over the next 14 years, Smith played 407 League games for the Potters, scoring 29 goals. In March 1982 he had a seven-game loan spell at York City, scoring once, before joining the Minstermen permanently in August that year. Smith played 30 games in his first season at Bootham Crescent, scoring four goals, before being appointed manager of the club the following season.

York finished seventh in Division Four in his first season, but the following year Smith took the club to the title and promotion to the Third Division, becoming the first club in the country to achieve 100 points in a season. The following year York beat Arsenal in the FA Cup and held Liverpool to a draw before losing the replay at Anfield. By the time Smith moved to Sunderland in 1987, he had been in charge of 258 York games. In Smith's first season at Roker Park he guided the club to the Third Division title with a record 101 points, and two seasons later Sunderland reached the Play-offs, where they were beaten by Swindon Town. However, Swindon were found guilty of financial irregularities and were demoted to Division Three, with Sunderland promoted to the First Division in their place. Sunderland struggled in the top flight, and were relegated on the last day of their first season. The following season Sunderland failed to make an impact and with the club in danger of relegation Smith was sacked in December 1991 and replaced by his assistant, Malcolm Crosby. He had been in charge of the Rokerites for 229 games. In March 1992 Smith became manager of Bristol City, but he resigned the following May having been unable to forge a decent working relationship with player-coach Russell Osman, and being unable to get on with the board.

Smith next applied for the vacant Oxford United post, and was appointed in September 1993. His first game, against former club Bristol City, ended in a 4–2 win for United and was a stormy affair, with Smith confronting City's new boss Osman in the tunnel after the game, blaming him for provocation for getting David Penney sent off. At the end of Smith's first season, Oxford were relegated to Division Three. The next season United started strongly and were three points clear at the top on Boxing Day after winning 4–1 at Peterborough United. However, in the next game United were beaten 2–0 at home by Wycombe Wanderers and that started a run of nine League games without a win, and United slipped out of contention for the Play-offs. In addition, the club had arguably the worst result in its professional history up to that point, losing 2–0 at Marlow of the Diadora League Premier Division in the FA Cup first round on 13 November 1994. The following season was a reverse picture, with Oxford starting slowly but having a storming finish to claim automatic promotion in second place, behind Swindon Town. Considering that United did not win their first away game until 30 January, and were 13th in mid-February, 12 points behind second-placed Crewe Alexandra, this was a fantastic achievement. In 1996–97 United finished 17th, but the following season was another one of under-achievement. With Oxford 16th following a 2–0 win at Tranmere Rovers, and the club under severe financial restraints, Smith resigned on Christmas Eve 1997, after 240 games in charge.

A few days after leaving Oxford, Smith was appointed manager of West Bromwich Albion. The Baggies finished 10th in Smith's first season and 12th the following year, but in July 1999 he was sacked. Smith, who still lived in

Cumnor on the outskirts of Oxford, was then out of work until February 2000, when he applied for the vacant job at Oxford United following Malcolm Shotton's departure. His first match back in charge was on 5 February, a 1–0 home defeat by Bristol City as Oxford battled relegation. They eventually secured Second Division safety with a 2–0 win over Scunthorpe United in the penultimate game of the season. United started the following season with four successive League defeats, and they were without a win in their first seven League games. The fans were disgruntled, and after a home defeat by Brentford on 26 August when they made their displeasure known, Smith strode over to the London Road end and held an impromptu fans' forum on the pitch, demonstrating the man's strength of character. However, this was not enough to save him and, with United at the bottom of the division, Smith resigned after a 1–0 home defeat by Bristol City on 30 September 2000.

Over a year later Smith was back in work, becoming manager of Wrexham in October 2001. Although the Welsh side were relegated at the end of that season, Smith took them straight back up to Division Two the following season. A mid-table finish in 2003–04 was followed by another relegation to the newly-renamed League Two (fourth tier) as Smith was hamstrung by chairman Alex Hamilton, who was trying to get the club evicted from the Racecourse Ground so he could sell it. In order to avoid paying creditors Hamilton had the club put into administration, becoming the first club to be docked 10 points under new League rules. Despite relegation, Wrexham won the LDV Vans Trophy. Wrexham finished 13th in League Two the next season, and in January 2007, with Wrexham in danger of relegation to the Conference, Smith was sacked. He was linked with the Oxford job again following Darren Patterson's dismissal in December 2008, and spent a lot of time promoting his autobiography *Just One of Seven*, published in October 2008.

Malcolm Crosby

Born: 4 July 1954, South Shields
Clubs played for: Aldershot, York City, Wrexham (loan)
Clubs managed: Sunderland, Oxford United (caretaker), Northampton Town (caretaker)

Malcolm Crosby's managerial career was for a long time inextricably linked with Denis Smith's. He started his playing career as an apprentice with Aldershot, joining in 1971 and making his debut that same season, coming on as a substitute. He became a professional at the end of that season and made just one appearance as the Shots won promotion to Division Three. It was not until the 1974–75 season that he became established as a regular in the Aldershot midfield, and he went on to make 294 League appearances, scoring 23 goals, before joining York City in November 1981. At York he played an important role in their record-breaking promotion season in 1983–84, and he played 103 League games, scoring four goals, for the Minstermen before Denis Smith, who became York boss in 1982, made Crosby his assistant. Crosby also had a brief loan spell at Wrexham in September 1984, playing five games and scoring once. After leaving York, he went to Kuwait for two years to do some coaching.

When Smith moved to Roker Park to become Sunderland's manager in 1987, Crosby followed him as youth team coach, before becoming reserve coach and then first-team coach. He even played a few reserve games for

Sunderland in the Central League. After Smith's sacking in 1991, Crosby was appointed caretaker manager while a replacement was sought. This took longer than anticipated, and in the meantime Crosby led Second Division Sunderland to the 1992 FA Cup Final, which they lost 2–0 to Liverpool. As a result, Crosby was offered the manager's job. However, the following season Sunderland continued to struggle in the League, and in February 1993 Crosby was sacked.

When Denis Smith was appointed manager of Oxford in September 1993, his first act was to bring in Crosby as his assistant. Crosby stayed with Smith throughout his tenure, moving to Cumnor village as Smith's neighbour. When Smith resigned in 1997, Crosby was appointed caretaker manager, his first game being a 1–0 defeat at Wolves on Boxing Day. After five games, which yielded just one point, Crosby decided that management was not for him and he stepped down to become first-team coach. His final game was a 2–1 home defeat by Charlton Athletic on 17 January 1998.

Almost immediately, Smith invited Crosby to become his assistant at West Bromwich Albion, and Crosby left for the Hawthorns. However, on 11 June 1999 the opportunity arose for Crosby to become Jim Smith's assistant at Premiership side Derby County, replacing Ray Harford. Crosby had been recommended to Smith by former Oxford player Steve McClaren, then assistant manager at Manchester United. On 15 February 2000 Crosby parted company with Derby with the agreement of Jim Smith, after a poor season saw the Rams languishing close to the Premier League relegation zone. On 4 May 2000 Crosby was appointed coach at Swindon Town, despite attempts by Denis Smith, now back at Oxford, to lure him back to the Manor. Crosby was initially under Roy Evans at the County Ground, but after Evans' resignation in December 2001, Crosby took over the first-team affairs for one game before Steve King was appointed and Crosby became his assistant. Crosby was at Swindon for four years before joining Middlesbrough as reserves coach in 2004, becoming Gareth Southgate's assistant two years later.

In June 2009 he was released by Middlesbrough and in September he became a coach at Northampton Town. In March 2011, following the sacking of Ian Sampson, Crosby was appointed caretaker manager of the Cobblers. However, he had yet to take charge of his first game when Gary Johnson was appointed manager and Crosby was made his assistant. In May 2011 Crosby left Northampton and he returned to Oxford as head of football development.

Malcolm Shotton

Born: 16 February 1957
Clubs played for: Leicester City, Nuneaton Borough, Oxford United, Portsmouth, Huddersfield Town, Barnsley, Hull City, Ayr United, Barnsley
Clubs managed: Oxford United

Former captain Malcolm Shotton became the first ex-Oxford player to become manager of the club when he was appointed in January 1998, following a campaign for his appointment led by Oxford supporter Neil Wakefield, and encouraged by Oxford's fanzine *Rage On*. Shotton initially joined Oxford from Nuneaton Borough in the summer of 1980, having previously been on the books of Leicester City, and by the time United experienced their 'Glory Years' of the mid-1980s, towering centre-half Shotton was the club captain. In August 1987 Shotton was sold to Portsmouth for £70,000. He played just 12 games for Pompey before

Huddersfield paid £20,000 for him in February 1988. His time at Huddersfield was only slightly longer as he played 18 games for the Terriers, scoring one goal, before moving to Barnsley in September 1988. He spent more time at Oakwell, playing 74 games and scoring six goals before Hull City paid £35,000 for him in February 1990. Shotton played 65 games for the Tigers, scoring two goals, before he moved north of the border to Ayr United. In his 22 months at Somerset Park Shotton made 83 appearances and scored three goals before returning to Barnsley in July 1994. In the 1994–95 season, Shotton played 11 games for the Tykes and scored one goal, in his final match, against Sunderland, after which he retired from playing and became Barnsley's reserve team coach and assistant to Danny Wilson.

In January 1998 Shotton was appointed manager of Oxford United, having earlier claimed that this would be his 'dream job'. At the time of his appointment Oxford were fifth from bottom of Division One, having just lost 2–1 at home to Charlton Athletic. Shotton's first game in charge was at home to Portsmouth, who were bottom of the table, and Oxford won 1–0. They followed this up with a 3–1 win at Nottingham Forest, and by the end of the season Shotton had steered the side to 12th place. The following season was a disappointing one as the club suffered financial problems that led to its near demise. The club was forced to sell its best players just to survive, and for two months in October and November the back-room staff, including Shotton and his assistant Mark Harrison, went unpaid, while the players had to be paid by a loan from the Professional Footballers' Association. Unsurprisingly, results suffered and United fell to their two worst defeats since turning professional in 1949, with a 7–0 reverse at Sunderland followed three months later by a 7–1 home defeat by Birmingham City, just one month after United had inflicted Birmingham's second home defeat of the season. The one chink of light came when Oxford were handed a home draw against Chelsea in the fourth round of the FA Cup, but with United leading 1–0 with less than five minutes remaining, Chelsea were awarded a controversial penalty to take the tie to a replay, which they won 4–2. Although Oxford won the final game of the season 5–0 against Stockport County, results elsewhere ensured that they had already been relegated. United started the following season badly, and on 25 October, following a 1–0 home defeat by Luton Town which left United fourth from bottom of Division Two, Shotton and Harrison left the club after coming to an agreement with chairman Firoz Kassam.

In June 2000, Shotton's former Huddersfield teammate Chris Hutchings was appointed manager of Bradford City, and his first move was to bring in Shotton as first-team coach, following Terry Yorath's departure. However, after a run of 10 games without a win that plunged City to second from bottom of the Premiership, Hutchings and Shotton were both dismissed. Shotton then dropped out of professional football, becoming director of football of Loughborough University's football team for several years. He later became a salesman for Mercedes cars in Huddersfield while managing the Barnsley College Academy side.

Mickey Lewis

Born: 15 February 1965, Birmingham
Clubs played for: West Bromwich Albion, Derby County, Oxford United, Banbury United, Oxford City, Des Moines Menace (USA)
Clubs managed: Oxford United (caretaker)

Michael Lewis was a popular player at Oxford, and his popularity continued after he joined the backroom staff. He started his playing days as an apprentice with West Bromwich Albion, signing professional forms in February 1982. After playing 33 games for the Baggies he moved to Derby County for £25,000 in November 1984. He played just 50 games between then and August 1988, scoring one goal, when he moved to Oxford as part of the deal that took Trevor Hebberd to the Baseball Ground.

Lewis, a tenacious midfielder who earned the nickname 'Mad Dog', made his Oxford debut on 27 August 1988, in a 1–1 draw at Leeds United, and he went on to play 351 games for the U's over the next 12 years, making his final appearance as a substitute in a 2–1 win over Chesterfield on 19 February 2000. This last appearance was an anomaly, though, as Lewis had effectively retired from playing at the end of the 1995–96 season. He then became United's youth team coach before being recalled to first-team duty in August 1999 as the result of an injury crisis. This came to an end in October 1999, after the 1–0 defeat by Luton Town that signalled the end of Malcolm Shotton's management, and Lewis was appointed caretaker manager. In that 1999–00 season Lewis had played in defence and in midfield, he had run the reserves and the youth team, driven the team bus to take the club's young players to matches, and even acted as physio in that season's game at Blackpool.

Lewis' first game in charge of the first team was a 3–2 first round FA Cup win over Conference side Morecambe. Lewis was to look after the team for over three months, culminating in a 4–0 home defeat by Preston North End, after which Denis Smith was reappointed as manager. Lewis remained in charge of the youth team, and continued adding his experience to United's reserves. In his time as manager Lewis had proven himself to be popular with the players and the fans. Lewis was appointed Denis Smith's assistant manager, and acted as caretaker for a 1–1 draw with Cambridge United when Smith was hospitalised with a blood infection. After Smith's resignation in October 2000, Lewis then acted as assistant to caretaker manager Mike Ford.

Lewis, who did not have a contract, was sacked by United in November 2000, while on loan to Banbury United, with whom he was playing on a non-contract basis. He played just one game for the Puritans, in a 2–1 defeat at Corby Town in September, before joining Oxford City as player-coach, eventually giving up the playing side to become assistant manager having had a spell as player-coach with Des Moines Menace in the summer of 2001. While at Court Place Farm, Lewis also became head coach to the Oxford University football team, leading them to three consecutive Varsity successes. Lewis left City in December 2003 following the resignation of manager Paul Lee. In January 2004 Lewis became coach at Slough Town in Ryman League Division One, and in July 2005 he became David Penney's assistant at Doncaster Rovers, leading the reserves to their League title. On 30 August 2006 Lewis and Penney both left Doncaster and Lewis returned to Oxford. He became a van driver while again coaching Oxford University, while also coaching at Southern League Abingdon United and working with Oxford United's Under-11s. On 10 May 2007 he became youth team coach at United, replacing Darren Patterson who had stepped up to become Jim Smith's assistant. When Patterson replaced Smith as first-team manager in November 2007, Lewis was made his assistant, continuing in that role after Chris Wilder's appointment in December 2008.

Mike Ford

Born: 9 March 1966, Brisol
Clubs played for: Leicester City, Devizes Town, Cardiff City, Oxford United, Cardiff City, Oxford United, Thame United, Didcot Town, Brackley Town
Clubs managed: Oxford United (caretaker), Brackley Town, Oxford City

Michael Paul Ford is the son of former Bristol Rovers player Tony Ford. Mike began his playing career at Leicester City, whom he joined as an apprentice before signing as a professional in February 1984. He did not make a first-team appearance for the Foxes and moved to Devizes Town in June 1984. Just three months later he was signed by Cardiff City, for whom he went on to make 167 appearances, scoring 13 goals. In the 1987–88 season Ford was Cardiff's Player of the Season, and Oxford bought him for £150,000 in June 1988. In the following 10 years he played 338 games for the U's, scoring 22 goals. Ford played in a variety of positions, starting as a midfielder, then a central-defender before becoming a left-back. In August 1998 he rejoined Cardiff, where he stayed for two seasons, playing 65 matches and scoring one FA Cup goal. In May 2000, Ford announced that he was retiring from playing after receiving a back injury.

At the start of August 2000, Ford returned to Oxford United, ostensibly as reserve and youth team coach. He played in just one first-team game, on 30 September, which United lost 1–0 to Bristol City. This was Denis Smith's last match in charge of United, and Ford was immediately chosen to act as caretaker manager while a replacement was sought. Ford's first game was a local derby at Swindon Town in a 2–1 defeat. Ford had six games in charge, in which United picked up just one point, before David Kemp was appointed in November. After Kemp's appointment, Ford was made youth team coach. When Kemp and his assistant Alan McLeary were sacked at the end of April 2001, Ford was again made caretaker manager for United's last two games of the season. Ford was still unable to find a win, earning a point against Port Vale in United's final match at the Manor, and then losing 2–1 at Notts County. Ford then became reserve team coach after Mark Wright became manager.

Following Wright's resignation and the appointment of Ian Atkins in November 2001, Ford was made Atkins' assistant. On 11 February 2003, Ford was sacked by United and a week later he joined Ryman League First Division club Thame United as a player. In August 2003, Ford signed for Didcot Town, managed by Peter Foley. At the end of the 2003–04 season Ford then moved to Brackley Town, newly-promoted to the Dr Martens League Division 1 West, as player-coach, becoming player-manager in October 2004. At the start of November 2006 Ford became assistant manager and coach at Oxford City, having by now given up playing. In August 2009 Ford was appointed manager of City following the resignation of Justin Merritt.

David Kemp

Born: 20 February 1953, Harrow
Clubs played for: Harrow Borough, Maidenhead United, Slough Town, Crystal Palace, Portsmouth, Carlisle United, Plymouth Argyle, Gillingham (loan), Brentford (loan), Edmonton Drillers (USA), Seattle Sounders (USA), San José Earthquakes (USA), Tulsa Roughnecks (USA), Chicago Sting (USA), Oklahoma City Stampede (USA)
Clubs managed: Norrköping, Plymouth Argyle, Slough Town, Oxford United

David Michael Kemp had a fairly peripatetic footballing career, beginning his playing days at Harrow Borough, before moving to Maidenhead United and then Slough Town. He signed for Crystal Palace in April 1975. As a forward, Kemp scored 10 League goals in 35 Division Three games for Palace before Third Division Portsmouth signed him in November 1976. Kemp was leading scorer in his first season, and followed that by being leading scorer the following season too, despite moving to Carlisle United in March 1978. He scored 30 goals at Fratton Park in 64 League games. Carlisle were also in the Third Division and Kemp played 61 league games for the Cumbrians, scoring 22 goals, before Plymouth Argyle paid a club record £75,000 for him in September 1979. Kemp scored 39 goals in 84 League games for Argyle, plus two goals in nine games while on loan to Gillingham and one goal in his three loan games at Brentford, before crossing the Atlantic in June 1982.

His first club in the NASL was Edmonton Drillers, for whom he played 16 games, scoring seven goals. The following season he played for Seattle Sounders, where he scored nine goals in 20 games, and the next season he joined Oklahoma City Stampede, of the United Soccer League, where he played 28 games. His first job as a manager was with Swedish side Norrköping in 1985. The following year he joined the coaching staff at Wimbledon, before becoming manager of Plymouth Argyle in March 1990. In 1992, after little success at Home Park, he left Plymouth to become manager of Conference outfit Slough Town. At the end of the 1992–93 season he joined Crystal Palace as assistant manager to Alan Smith. He followed Smith to Wycombe Wanderers at the start of the 1995–96 season, leaving at the start of the following season to become John Docherty's assistant at Millwall. His next post, in 1998, was as first-team coach at Wimbledon, under Joe Kinnear, before he returned to Millwall as first-team coach. Tony Pulis appointed Kemp as first-team coach at Portsmouth in December 1999.

Kemp was appointed Oxford manager at the end of October 2000, where he again met up with Kinnear, who was director of football at the Manor. His first game in charge was a 1–0 home defeat by Bristol Rovers and, despite two successive away wins in the next two games, things went downhill and United were relegated to the bottom flight with seven games still to play. Following huge protests by Oxford United fans Kemp was sacked by United with two games left of the 2000–01 season. Kemp's side had won just seven out of 31 games, and had lost 21 matches.

After leaving Oxford, Kemp was appointed chief scout at Leicester City in December 2001. Pulis made him first-team coach at Stoke City in August 2004, but he left Stoke the following June after Pulis was dismissed. He rejoined Pulis as assistant manager at Plymouth in September 2005, leaving in August 2006. That October he returned to Stoke as assistant manager, and stayed at the Britannia as Stoke won promotion to the Premier League in 2008.

Mark Wright

Born: 1 August 1963, Dorchester-on-Thames
Clubs played for: Oxford United, Southampton, Derby County, Liverpool
Clubs managed: Southport, Oxford United, Chester City, Peterborough United, Chester City

Mark Wright played his first game for Oxford United on 13 December 1980, aged 17, in a 3–0 FA Cup second-round defeat at Plymouth Argyle. His next appearance was not until 17 October 1982, when he played in a 1–0 win over

Bristol City. He went on to complete 12 games for United, without scoring, making his final appearance in a 2–1 defeat at Lincoln City on 20 March 1982. He was then sold to Southampton, along with Keith Cassells, with their joint value determined as £230,000 (£115,000 each, a record fee for Oxford), with Trevor Hebberd and George Lawrence coming the other way. In Wright's first full season for Southampton he was voted the club's Player of the Year, and the following season he earned his first England cap. In August 1987 Derby County paid a club record fee of £760,000 for the tall central-defender. He had played 222 games for the Saints, scoring 11 goals. At Derby, Wright was made captain, but financial problems following the departure of Robert Maxwell led to the club being relegated to Division Two at the end of the 1990–91 season. After 171 games for Derby, with 10 goals, Wright joined Liverpool in July 1991 for £2.2 million. Wright played for Liverpool until he retired in the summer of 1998. He had played 210 games, scoring nine goals, for Liverpool. He had also won 45 England caps, scoring one goal, which came against Egypt in the 1990 World Cup in Italy, becoming the only home-grown Oxford player to have represented England.

Wright took over as manager of Conference side Southport halfway through the 1999–2000 season. They were second from bottom when Wright arrived, and he led them to seventh place. The following season the Sandgrounders spent most of the time in the top three, eventually finishing fourth, after which Wright took over from David Kemp at Oxford United just after the season finished, giving him time to rebuild the side at newly-relegated United. Wright immediately brought the central-defensive duo of Phil Bolland and Scott Guyett from Southport and by the time the side kicked off in Division Four at the newly-built Kassam Stadium there were five new faces in the team, including captain Martin Thomas. Oxford lost that historic game 2–1 to Rochdale, and Wright's first season went from bad to worse as the side struggled to adapt to Wright's defensive tactics, despite the arrival of former Oxford striker Paul Moody in September. On 20 October United lost 1–0 at home to Scunthorpe, with two Oxford players and Wright being sent off by referee Joe Ross. In the aftermath, Wright was accused of making racist remarks to Ross, and United suspended him on full pay pending an investigation, while Ian Atkins was appointed director of football. Wright then resigned, followed shortly afterwards by his assistant, Ted McMinn.

Two months later, on 9 January 2002, Wright was appointed manager of Conference side Chester City. In his first full season Chester reached the Play-off semi-finals, where they lost to Doncaster Rovers. The following season Wright led them to the title and a return to the Football League. However, just two days before the start of the following season, Wright resigned from Chester following allegations that he was having an affair with a player's wife. After being out of the game for a whole season, Wright became manager of Peterborough United. He was at London Road from May 2005 until January 2006, at which point he was sacked for gross misconduct after allegedly making a racist comment to a member of staff; an allegation that Wright strenuously denied. A month later Wright rejoined Chester and saved the side from relegation to the Conference. Just before the final game of the 2006–07 season Wright was sacked with Chester struggling just above the relegation zone. To the surprise of many, Wright was again reappointed to the Chester post by Steve Vaughan in November 2008, joining on a non-contract basis. However, after Chester were relegated Wright resigned.

Ian Atkins

Born: 16 January 1957, Birmingham
Clubs played for: Shrewsbury Town, Sunderland, Everton, Ipswich Town, Birmingham City, Colchester United, Birmingham City, Cambridge United, Sunderland, Doncaster Rovers, Solihull Borough, Redditch United
Clubs managed: Colchester United, Cambridge United, Northampton Town, Chester City, Carlisle United, Oxford United, Bristol Rovers, Torquay United

Ian Leslie Atkins earned a reputation as a dour, defensive manager while at Oxford, whose preferred long-ball tactics worked initially but, once found out by opponents, quickly failed and who had no Plan B. This profile rather unfairly ignores the fact that he was probably United's most successful manager since Denis Smith's first time in charge.

Atkins' first club was Shrewsbury Town, who he joined in 1973 on leaving school. He turned professional two years later, and went on to stay with the Shrews until 1982. He made 279 appearances for the Shropshire club, scoring 58 goals, including 17 in his final season at the club in 1981–82. First Division Sunderland signed him in August 1982 for £80,000. In the next two seasons Atkins played 77 games for the Rokerites, scoring six goals, having by now turned from a midfielder into a defender. In November 1984 Everton paid £70,000 for him, but he failed to play regularly for the Toffees' first team, playing just seven games and scoring one goal. He moved to Ipswich Town for £100,000 in September 1985, and he established himself at Portman Road, playing 77 games and scoring three goals in the following three seasons. However, by the time that Birmingham City paid £50,000 for him in March 1988, Ipswich had been relegated to Division Two. Atkins played 93 games for the Blues, but suffered relegation to the Third Division with them in 1989. He scored six goals before moving to Colchester United as player-manager in 1990.

Atkins took Colchester to second place in the Conference, which was not enough to earn promotion, and he returned to St Andrew's in July 1991 as player-assistant manager. He had played 41 games at Layer Road. Atkins played eight games for Birmingham before he moved to Cambridge United as player-manager in December 1992. He played just two games for Cambridge, who were relegated from Division One at the end of that season, and in May 1993 he was sacked. He returned to Sunderland as a player but failed to make the first team, and in January 1994 he went to Doncaster Rovers, for whom he played seven games. After spells with Solihull Borough and Redditch United, Atkins went to manage Northampton Town in October 1994. In 1997 Atkins took Northampton into the Second Division via the Play-offs, and the following season Northampton again reached the Play-off Final, but this time they were beaten by Grimsby Town. In 1999 Northampton were relegated back to the bottom flight, and in October 1999 Atkins resigned. He became boss of Chester City in January 2000, but he was unable to save them from relegation to the Conference, despite coming close to saving the side that looked doomed when he took over, and he resigned in the 2000 close season. He became manager of Carlisle United in June 2000, and he helped them avoid relegation to the Conference despite having few resources at his disposal. In July 2001 Atkins became assistant manager to Alan Cork at Cardiff City, but when Mark Wright was suspended by Oxford United in November 2001 he was appointed as director of football at the Kassam

Stadium, taking charge of the first team and becoming manager following Wright's departure.

Atkins' first game in charge of Oxford was a highly encouraging 3–0 win over high-flying Cheltenham Town, but although the side improved they still finished 21st in the bottom division. The following season Oxford were challenging for promotion for much of the time, but were unable to put together a consistent run, and ended up finishing eighth, just behind Lincoln City, who occupied the final Play-off place. Oxford had a mini FA Cup run, beating Swindon Town 1–0 in the second round before narrowly losing to Arsenal at Highbury. They also beat Premiership Charlton Athletic on penalties at the Valley in the second round of the League Cup. United looked much stronger in the 2003–04 season, and by the turn of the year the side were top of the table. However, they were overtaken by Hull City and, following a 4–2 defeat at the KC Stadium, United started to slip out of contention. In March 2004 Atkins was controversially suspended by Firoz Kassam, allegedly for speaking to Bristol Rovers about their managerial vacancy. Kassam later claimed that he had offered Atkins to the Pirates, but the truth has never been established. Atkins was out of contract at the end of that season, and negotiations for a new contract had not started yet. Atkins' final game as Oxford manager was, like his first, a home win over Cheltenham Town. This time United won 1–0, on 17 March 2004.

After being sacked by Oxford, Atkins took over at Bristol Rovers on 26 April 2004, but he was sacked in September the following year after a poor start to the season. In April 2006 Atkins took over at Torquay United, with the club bottom of the League, five points adrift and with just six games remaining. Atkins took the Gulls on a magnificent run, the outcome of which saw Torquay safe for another season, while condemning Oxford to relegation to the Conference. He remained with Torquay until he was replaced by Lubos Kubik in November 2007, after which he did some media work before being appointed European scout by Sunderland.

Graham Rix

Born: 23 October 1957, Doncaster
Clubs played for: Arsenal, Brentford (loan), Caen (France), Le Havre (France), Dundee, Chelsea
Clubs managed: Chelsea (caretaker), Portsmouth, Oxford United, Heart of Midlothian

Graham Cyril Rix joined Arsenal in 1974, initially as an apprentice, and signed as a professional the following season. He scored on his debut in April 1977, and played 464 games as a left-winger for the Gunners, becoming captain in 1983, and scoring 51 goals. In 1980 Rix made his debut for England, and had won 17 caps by the time of his last appearance in 1984. Rix lost his place in the Arsenal team because of injury, and after playing six games on loan to Brentford in 1987 he was released. He went to France to play for Caen, where he played 89 games and scored nine goals, and then to Le Havre, where he made 12 appearances. He then moved to Scotland where he played 14 games and scored two goals for Dundee.

In 1993, Rix joined Chelsea as youth team coach, but an injury crisis led to his recall as a player and he played one game against Arsenal in 1995. In 1996 Ruud Gullit made him assistant manager and he remained in that position when Gianluca Vialli became manager. In March 1999 Rix was convicted of having sex with a 15-year-old girl and he spent six months of a 12-month sentence in prison. Upon his release he rejoined Chelsea, again as assistant manager. After Vialli was sacked in September 2000 Rix had a brief spell as caretaker manager before he also left the club. He became manager of Portsmouth in February 2001, but just over a year later he was sacked.

Following Ian Atkins' suspension by Firoz Kassam in March 2004, Rix was hired by United until the end of that season. His first game in charge was on 27 March, a 0–0 draw against leaders Doncaster Rovers. Surprisingly, after the end of the season Rix was offered a proper contract, despite the side only winning once in the nine games he was in charge. However, United fared little better at the start of the following season, and Rix was relieved of his duties in November 2004 after a run of eight defeats in nine games. His last game was a 2–1 defeat at Rochdale in the FA Cup on 13 November. Rix had managed Oxford for 29 matches. However, Rix was not sacked but instead made director of football, until he eventually left the club in March 2005.

In November 2005 Rix was appointed manager of Hearts, where he remained until March 2006, taking charge of just 19 games. Rix had an unhappy time at Hearts, where chairman Vladimir Romanov liked to meddle in team affairs. He was sacked in March 2006.

Darren Patterson

Born: 15 October 1969, Belfast
Clubs played for: West Bromwich Albion, Wigan Athletic, Crystal Palace, Luton Town, Preston North End (loan), Dundee United, York City, Oxford United
Clubs managed: Oxford United (caretaker), Oxford United, Bristol Rovers (caretaker)

Darren James Patterson started his playing career at West Bromwich Albion, who he joined in July 1988, but he left for Wigan Athletic in April 1989 without playing a game for the Baggies. Over the next three years Patterson played 124 games for Wigan, scoring 10 goals, which earned him a £225,000 move to Crystal Palace in July 1992. However, Patterson did not play for Palace until the 1994–95 season, by which time the club was in the Premiership. Patto played 32 games for the London club, including their FA Cup semi-final defeat by Manchester United, during which he and Roy Keane were sent off for fighting. Patterson, who had earned his first Northern Ireland cap in 1994, scored one goal in his time at Selhurst Park before Luton Town paid £230,000 for him. In his three seasons at Kenilworth Road, Patterson made 66 appearances without getting on the score sheet. He also had a two-game loan spell at Preston North End. In July 1998 he joined Dundee United, where he played 38 games and scored one goal. In May 2000, after injuries had curtailed his first-team chances, he left Tannadice Park by mutual consent, and in December he signed a three-month contract with York City. Towards the end of his contract, on 14 February 2001, Patterson joined Oxford United.

Patterson was signed for Oxford by David Kemp, for whom he had played while at Palace, and was Kemp's first signing as Oxford boss. Patto's first game for United was a 3–1 defeat at Bury on 17 February 2001, and he went on to play 20 games for the U's. He scored one goal, in a 1–1 draw with Stoke City in his second match, before finally hanging up his boots on 1 April 2002, following a 1–0 defeat at his previous side, York City. Injury had cut short his playing career, and at the end of the 2002–03 season Patterson left the club, his contract having come to an end. After featuring in a couple of pre-season friendlies, Patterson returned to Oxford on 3 September 2002 as youth team coach. On 14 November 2004 Patterson was appointed caretaker manager after Firoz Kassam relieved Graham Rix of his managerial duties.

Patterson was in charge for three games before Argentinian Ramón Díaz was announced as the new manager. United won one game, at Chester City, and lost the other two. After the arrival of Díaz, Patterson returned to coaching the youth team. In March 2006, after David Oldfield's departure, Patterson looked after the reserve team, and just a week later, when Brian Talbot was sacked, he was placed in charge of the first team and given a contract until the end of the following season. His first game was a 1–0 win over Bristol Rovers on 20 March, and relegation-threatened United drew their next two games before Nick Merry was installed as chairman and brought in Jim Smith as manager, with Patterson returning to his former job as youth team coach. In December 2006 Patterson was interviewed by Brentford for their managerial vacancy and he was offered the job, but he turned it down because of contractual issues. In 2006–07 he guided the youth team to the Puma Youth Alliance South West Conference title without losing a game, and in April 2007 Smith appointed him assistant manager following the departures of Andy Awford and Shaun North.

In November 2007, after a poor run of results had led to Smith stepping down as manager, Patterson was appointed to the post. His first game in charge was a 3–1 win over Northwich Victoria in the first round of the FA Cup. After a dip in form United's results picked up and they finished the season by winning nine of their last 11 games to finish ninth. The 2008–09 season started badly for United with two successive defeats and only two wins in their first 10 games. Although home form was good, Oxford struggled on the road and, with finances tight, a 2–0 defeat at Torquay United in the FA Cup on 29 November 2008 led to Patterson's dismissal. Patterson was appointed as head of the Bristol Rovers youth programme in May 2009 and he became assistant manager in May 2010. In December 2010 he was made caretaker manager for just under a month, until David Penney was appointed manager in January 2011, at which point Patterson returned to coaching the youth team. In June 2011 he was appointed Andy Scott's assistant at Rotherham United.

Ramón Díaz

Born: 29 August 1959, La Rioja (Argentina)
Clubs played for: River Plate (Argentina), Napoli (Italy), US Avellino (Italy), Fiorentina (Italy), Internazionale (Italy), AS Monaco (France), River Plate (Argentina), Yokohama Marinos (Japan)
Clubs managed: River Plate (Argentina), Oxford United, San Lorenzo (Argentina), Club América (Mexico), San Lorenzo (Argentina)

It was to the astonishment of just about everyone connected with football that Ramón Angel Díaz was appointed Oxford United manager on 11 December 2004. Díaz was one of the most successful managers and players in the world, and his arrival was totally unexpected, with the *Oxford Mail* that morning announcing Chris Turner as the new boss.

Díaz joined River Plate in 1978. He played in the same Argentina Under-20 side as Diego Maradona, winning the World Youth Cup in 1979, when they both scored in the Final against the Soviet Union. He played for Argentina in the 1978 World Cup, scoring against Brazil. He made his River Plate debut on 13 August 1978 and played 123 games, scoring 57 goals, before leaving for Napoli in the Italian Serie A. He had one season at Napoli, scoring three times in 27 games, and then spent three seasons at US Avellino, where he played 78 games and scored 23 goals. In 1986 he moved to Fiorentina, where he scored 17 goals in 53 games over two seasons. His final Italian club was Inter Milan, where he played 33 games with a return of 12 goals as he helped them win the Scudetto. In 1989 he signed for AS Monaco, who were managed by Arsene Wenger, playing 60 games over two seasons, and scoring 24 goals. He returned to River Plate in 1991, and over the next two seasons he played 52 games and scored 27 goals. His final club was Yokohama Marinos in Japan, where he spent two seasons, playing 75 games and scoring 52 goals, and he was the J-League's leading scorer in its inaugural season. He had also played 24 games for Argentina between 1979 and 1982, scoring 10 times for his country.

In 1995 Díaz was appointed River Plate's manager and over the next five years he won the Libertadores Cup and five Argentinian Championships. Díaz, who was being tipped to become Argentina coach, resigned as River Plate coach in 2002 in protest at club president David Pintado's austerity drive following the collapse of the Argentine economy.

In 2004, Monaco businessman Jean-Marc Goiran introduced Díaz to Firoz Kassam, and the eventual upshot was that Díaz agreed to manage United. Díaz brought with him a team of backroom staff, including Horacio Rodriguez, his former assistant at River Plate, and four others from their time at River Plate: Raul Marcovich, a coach; Pablo Fernandez, a physical trainer who worked with Saudi Arabia's 1994 World Cup squad; Rafael Giulietti, a doctor; and Giuliani Iacoppi, a translator. None of them were being paid by United, possibly because of work permit legislation, although Díaz was seeking an Italian passport (his wife was Italian and the family home was in Venice). Ramon's first game in charge was at home to Cambridge United on 11 December 2004, and United won 2–1. Results certainly improved for Oxford that season, but they came nowhere near challenging for promotion, finishing in 15th place. Díaz was absent for many of the 25 games for which he was nominally the manager, with the team being coached mainly by Rodriguez and, on a couple of occasions, David Oldfield. Rodriguez was absent for a fortnight in March 2005 to sort out the paperwork to allow him to stay in the country. The Argentine reign ended abruptly and in controversy when talks about a new contract for Díaz broke down at the end of April and he returned to France, although at the time it was announced that Rodriguez would remain. However, at United's last game of the season, at home to Chester City, Kassam took the extraordinary step of refusing to allow Díaz or any of his contingent to pay for admission to the stadium, leading to a fracas in the car park outside the ground while the game was being played. When the dust had settled the common opinion was that the appointment of Díaz and his entourage was no more than an unsustainable publicity stunt by Kassam, and that it was never going to work in the long term.

In 2007 Díaz was appointed head coach of Argentine side San Lorenzo, leading them to the Championship in his first season. In 2008 he moved to Mexican side Club América, where he was given a contract estimated to be worth $3.5 million a year. He was sacked by América in February 2009 and reappointed by San Lorenzo in August 2010 where he remained until announcing his resignation in March 2011.

David Oldfield

Born: 30 May 1968, Perth (Australia)
Clubs played for: Luton Town, Manchester City, Leicester City, Millwall (loan), Luton Town, Stoke City, Peterborough United, Oxford United, Stafford Rangers, Tamworth, Brackley Town
Clubs managed: Oxford United (caretaker), Brackley Town, Peterborough United (caretaker)

Midfielder David Charles Oldfield was playing for North Buckinghamshire village side Stoke Goldington when he was spotted by Luton Town, for whom he signed professionally at the age of 18 in 1986. He had played just 39 games for Luton, scoring eight goals, when Manchester City paid £600,000 for him in March 1989. He was at Maine Road for just 10 months, making 30 appearances and scoring nine times, before Leicester City signed him for £150,000 in January 1990. He was with the Foxes for four and a half seasons, playing 221 games and scoring 32 goals, with a brief 17-game (and six-goal) spell on loan at Millwall, before Luton Town bought him back for £150,000 in July 1995. He played 139 games for Luton, scoring 25 goals, before moving on to Stoke City in the summer of 1998. Oldfield played 74 games for Stoke, scoring just seven times, before leaving for Peterborough United in March 2000. Oldfield was at London Road for 15 months, playing 96 games and scoring five goals before he joined Oxford United, after a trial, in August 2002.

Oldfield's first game for Oxford was in the opening fixture of 2002–03 against Bury, on 10 August, which United won 2–1. When Mike Ford left United in February 2003, Oldfield assisted manager Ian Atkins with the coaching. At the end of the 2002–03 season Oldfield was out of contract, but was eventually re-signed in time for the start of the following season as a player-coach. Oldfield's last match for United was a 1–1 draw at Kidderminster Harriers on 30 August 2003, after which injury prevented him from playing for the first team again, although he was made assistant manager by Atkins. After Atkins was dismissed Oldfield was appointed caretaker manager, but the only game for which he was in charge before Graham Rix was appointed, away to Mansfield on 20 March 2004, was abandoned at half-time with the score 0–0, and it does not feature in official records. Oldfield's reputation as a coach was demonstrated when he was kept on by Rix and then Ramón Díaz. In March 2005, when both Díaz and his assistant Horacio Rodriguez were absent, Oldfield took charge of team affairs for draws at Scunthorpe United and against Leyton Orient. Following the departure of Díaz, Oldfield took charge of the team for the final game of the 2004–05 season, a 1–0 home defeat by Chester City. However, on 6 March 2006 Oldfield left United after being frozen out by manager Brian Talbot, who had told him that he did not want Oldfield to be involved on match days.

Oldfield signed for Conference side Stafford Rangers at the start of the 2006–07 season. He played 23 games as player-assistant manager before signing for Tamworth on 30 November 2007, making his debut the following day. Just four days after signing for the Lambs, Oldfield left to become manager of Brackley Town. In the summer of 2008 Oldfield left to become reserves and Under-18s manager at Peterborough United. In January 2011 Oldfield was caretaker manager for one game after Gary Johnson's departure.

Brian Talbot

Born: 21 July 1953, Ipswich
Clubs played for: Ipswich Town, Toronto Metros (loan), Arsenal, Watford, Stoke City, West Bromwich Albion, Fulham, Aldershot, Sudbury Town
Clubs managed: West Bromwich Albion, Aldershot, Hibernians (Malta), Rushden & Diamonds, Oldham Athletic, Oxford United, Marsaxlokk (Malta)

Brian Ernest Talbot was a much-travelled midfielder, who started his career with his home-town club, Ipswich Town, joining as an apprentice in 1968. In 1971 he spent two seasons on loan with Toronto Metros before returning to Portman Road. He went on to play 227 games for Ipswich, with whom he won the 1978 FA Cup. He was also capped five times for England while at Ipswich. In January 1979 he was signed by Arsenal for £450,000 and at the end of that first season he scored at Wembley as Arsenal beat Manchester United 3–2 in the FA Cup Final. The following season Talbot played 70 games for Arsenal, setting a new club record, and by the time he left Highbury in June 1985 he had made 327 appearances, scoring 49 goals. While at Arsenal, Talbot won his sixth, and last, England cap. In 1984 Talbot was elected chairman of the Professional Footballers' Association, a position he held for four years. After leaving Arsenal, Talbot signed for Watford for £150,000, playing 48 League games and scoring eight goals before a move to Stoke City in 1986. He played 54 League games and scored five goals before he joined West Bromwich Albion as player-manager in November 1988. He played 74 games for the Baggies but left in January 1991 after West Brom were beaten 4–2 by non-League Woking in the FA Cup. After a short five-game spell with Fulham, he ended an incident-packed career with 11 games at Aldershot in March 1991, before joining Sudbury Town.

In 1993 Talbot went to Malta to manage Hibernians, with whom he won the Premier League in 1993 and 1994, returning to England to become a coach at Conference side Rushden & Diamonds in 1996. He became manager in the summer of 1999 and, using chairman Max Griggs' fortune, he won the title and took the club into the Football League in 2001. They reached the Play-offs the following season but lost in the Final to Cheltenham Town, but in 2003 they were Third Division champions. Rushden started well the next season, but started to slip down the table as Griggs reduced his investment and, in March 2004, Talbot left and went to manage Oldham Athletic. Talbot secured Oldham's place in Division Two at the end of the 2003–04 season, but after 55 games in charge Talbot left the club at the end of February 2005.

Talbot was unveiled as Oxford United's next manager to the crowd before the final game of the 2004–05 season, taking his first game at the start of the following season, a 1–1 draw at Grimsby Town on 6 August. The season started well, and Oxford were sixth by the start of October. However, a slump soon set in and the side got progressively weaker and, after a 2–1 defeat at Stockport County on 11 March 2006, Oxford were third from bottom of League Two, just one point above the relegation zone. Talbot was sacked three days later, and Oxford were relegated on the last day of the season.

In April 2006, Talbot received a phone call from Mark Sciriha, chairman of Maltese club Marsaxlokk, offering him the manager's job. Talbot accepted, and in his first season he led the club to the Maltese Championship for the first time. In December 2008 Patrick Curmi was appointed coach of Marsaxlokk, with Talbot becoming technical director and adviser to the club's president.

Chris Wilder

Born: 23 September 1967, Sheffield
Clubs played for: Sheffield United, Walsall (loan), Charlton Athletic (loan), Leyton Orient (loan), Rotherham United, Notts County, Bradford City, Sheffield United, Northampton Town (loan), Lincoln City (loan), Brighton & Hove Albion, Halifax Town
Clubs managed: Alfreton Town, Halifax Town, Oxford United

Christopher John Wilder started his career at Southampton, for whom he signed as a trainee in 1982. He was released by the Saints in 1986 and in August that year he signed for Sheffield United. Wilder played 112 games for the Blades, scoring just one goal, over the next six seasons, and he also had short loan spells at Walsall, Charlton Athletic (twice), and Leyton Orient. In July 1992 Rotherham United paid £50,000 for him and he spent the next three and a half years at Millmoor. He played 158 games for the Millers, scoring 12 goals, before joining Notts County for £130,000 in January 1996. He played 53 games for the Magpies before Bradford City bought him for £150,000 in March 1997. Wilder was at Valley Parade for exactly a year, playing 45 games for the Bantams, after which he rejoined Sheffield United. He played 14 games and had loan spells at Northampton Town and Lincoln City before leaving in August 1999. Wilder's next club was Brighton, where he spent two months, playing 13 games. He then joined Halifax Town on 22 October 1999, going on to play 58 games and scoring one goal in the next two seasons. Wilder was appointed manager of Alfreton Town in October 2001 where he won four trophies in his only season in charge; the Northern Counties (East) League Premier Division, the League Cup, the President's Cup and the Derbyshire Senior Cup. In July 2002 Wilder became manager of Halifax, who had just been relegated to the Conference. In his 312 games in charge of the Shaymen, Wilder guided Halifax to the Conference Play-off Final in 2006, where they lost to Hereford in extra-time. He was always battling against the club's financial straits, and in June 2008 the club were demoted three divisions to Unibond Division One North after failing to get a Company Voluntary Arrangement passed after entering administration. As a result Wilder resigned from Halifax and joined League Two side Bury as assistant manager to Alan Knill.

Wilder applied for and was appointed to the Oxford United vacancy in December 2008, his first game being a 2–1 defeat at Salisbury City on Boxing Day. After missing out on the Play-offs by just four points at the end of his first season in charge, in which United were docked five points by the Conference for fielding an ineligible player before Wilder's appointment, he led United to the Conference Play-off Final at Wembley, where the U's beat York City 3–1 to confirm promotion back to the Football League.

OTHER NOTABLE
UNITED PERSONALITIES

Dr Robert Hitchings
Born: 28 December 1863, Headington
Died: 1943

Robert Hitchings qualified as a surgeon at the University of Edinburgh in July 1884 and was admitted to the Royal College of Surgeons of England in July 1886. In 1891 he was a general practitioner in Cowley Road, having initially worked for his father, whose practice was in Holywell Street. In June 1892 Hitchings got married and moved to Hill View, a new house in Windmill Road. In the summer of 1893 he was captain of Headington United Cricket Club and in October 1893 he called the meeting at the Britannia Inn at which Headington Football Club was inaugurated. Hitchings played in some of the club's earliest games, and is one of the club's first recorded goalscorers, registering Headington's third in a 3–3 draw with Victoria, the side's second recorded match. After his father's death in 1897 Hitchings took over the Holywell Street practice until he moved back to Headington, into a purpose-built surgery on the corner of Kennet Road and London Road, in 1908. Hitchings also wrote and produced plays for the Headington Drama Club. In 1930 Hitchings retired and moved into Abberbury Road in Iffley, although he continued as Headington's vaccinator until 1938.

Reverend John Holford Scott-Tucker
Born: October 1854, Kirby Muxloe
Died: 1917 or 1918

Born John Holford Scott, he entered Oxford University in October 1875 at St Mary Hall, but it took until 1883 for him to obtain his BA. In the interim he spent some time as a schoolmaster in Littleham, North Devon. Scott was married in Devon in 1884, having been appointed deacon in Falmouth the year before and ordained as a priest in the following year. In October 1886 he was elected Oxford diocesan secretary of the Church of England Temperance Society (CETS) based in Wellington Square and in May 1889 Scott was appointed vicar of Headington and chaplain of the Headington Union and he moved into the vicarage adjacent to St Andrew's Church in Headington. In 1891 Scott changed his surname by deed poll to Scott-Tucker. In the summer of 1893 Scott-Tucker played for Headington United Cricket Club and in October 1893 he became the first president of Headington Football Club. He is also the club's first recorded goalscorer, scoring the side's first two goals in a 3–3 draw with Victoria in the club's second recorded game. In 1900 Scott-Tucker was declared bankrupt following an episode in which he stood surety, in 1895, for the wife of his churchwarden, Colonel Kingscote. In 1899 Mrs Kingscote, who had borrowed over £50,000 from Lord Byron (a descendant of the famous poet), was declared bankrupt and fled to Switzerland, leaving Scott-Tucker and

George Moore (the vicar of Cowley, who had also stood surety) to face the music. In June 1899 Scott-Tucker was forced to resign as vicar of Headington, although he remained chaplain of the Headington Union Workhouse until 1901, at which time he was living in Divinity Road. Later in 1901 Scott-Tucker moved to South Africa where he was acting chaplain to the Forces for his first two years before becoming priest-in-charge of Rustenburg and then curate of St Alban's in Pretoria. He returned to England in 1905 and in 1907 he was appointed curate of St John the Evangelist in Westminster. The following year he changed his surname back to Scott and in 1911 he was recorded as living in Ely.

Major Lee

Born: October 1865, Bridport
Died: December 1955

William Lauriston Melville Lee was appointed head of PMS2 on its creation by MI5 in 1916, having reached the rank of Major in the British Army and, in 1901, written a history of the police in England. This was a very secret organisation created to spy on the British socialist movement. However, after a controversial court case in 1917 that resulted in convictions for three people accused of plotting to assassinate Prime Minister David Lloyd George, mostly on the evidence of a secret agent who did not appear in court, PMS2 was closed down and Lee retired to Stoke House, his home in Headington. Later that year he established and edited a journal called *Industrial Peace*, which circulated information on left-wing political organisations and individuals; this was printed in Oxford and published until 1928. In September 1919 Headington United held its first annual meeting following the end of World War One, and Major Lee was elected as the club's president. In this role he had the honour of performing the ceremonial kick-off before United's first game at the Manor, against Deddington in September 1925. In the summer of 1936, Lee stood down as the club's president.

1st Baron Elton

Born: 29 March 1892, Newport Pagnell
Died: 18 April 1973

Godfrey Elton was educated at Rugby School and in World War One he was wounded at the Siege of Kut-el-Amara and made a prisoner of war in Turkey between 1916 and 1918, having reached the rank of Captain. In 1919 he graduated from Balliol College with a BA and the following year he obtained an MA. Elton was expelled from the Labour Party in 1931 for supporting Ramsay MacDonald and in the same year he became a lecturer in modern history at Queen's College, Oxford. Elton lived at Greenways in Manor Road (later Osler Road). In January 1934 he was made the 1st Baron Elton of Headington and in the summer of 1936 he was made the president of Headington United, a post he retained until the club's first annual meeting after World War Two in 1946.

Vic Couling

Born: 27 September 1906, Oxford
Died: 27 March 1990

Albert Edward Victor Couling was a boxing promoter in Oxford who first got involved with United in July 1947, when he accepted an invitation from his friend, Headington United trainer Tom Webb, to attend the club's annual general meeting, at which he was elected president. Couling's first action was to apply for membership to the Spartan League as the club sought a higher level of football than the Oxfordshire Senior League. This was followed in February 1949 by Couling's proposal that the club accepted the principle of turning professional, and to this end Couling applied for membership to a proposed Southern League Second Division. However, in April 1949 the Southern League decided to postpone the creation of the Second Division after several prospective clubs withdrew their applications, although they did decide to expand the League from 22 to 24 clubs. After a lot of lobbying by Couling and other committee members the club was elected to fill one of these two new places and in August 1949, at the new club's first board meeting, Couling was elected as the first chairman of directors. Under his chairmanship Headington were one of the country's leading proponents of floodlit football, and he also oversaw the construction of a state-of-the-art stand along the Beech Road side of the Manor. He remained chairman until arthritis and time constraints took their toll and he resigned in November 1957, at which stage he was replaced by Ron Coppock, although Couling remained on the board, becoming de facto club secretary and editor of the matchday programme. Couling was the leading mover behind getting the club's name changed from Headington United to Oxford United, which was finally achieved in June 1960 and the following summer the club completed the purchase of the freehold of the Manor. United's transition was completed in June 1962 when Oxford were elected into the Football League. Couling eventually resigned from the board in June 1974 and in 1983 he published *Anatomy of a Football Club*, outlining his involvement with United from the Oxfordshire Senior League to the Second Division of the Football League.

Ron Coppock

Born: December 1909
Died: 1 January 1972

Ronald Stephen Coppock was one of the original members of Headington United's board of directors and he had been a United player in 1930–31, having previously played for their junior teams. In November 1952 Coppock was elected vice-chairman of the board, succeeding Professor George Keeton, and in November 1957 he replaced Vic Couling as club chairman. Coppock's first major achievement was appointing Arthur Turner to replace former manager Harry Thompson – Turner had recently left Birmingham City, who he had led to the FA Cup Final at Wembley two years earlier. This was followed shortly afterwards by beating an offer for Turner from First Division Leeds United to tempt him to their managerial vacancy. Coppock was chairman when the football club bought the freehold of the Manor and for Oxford's historic election to the Football League in June 1962. He also oversaw massive improvements to the ground, including new stands at the London Road and Cuckoo Lane ends and the erection of a new four-pylon floodlighting system. In April 1970 Coppock resigned from the board, having suffered ill health for some time and not being able to play as full a role as he would have liked, although he delayed his departure, feeling that the club was not stable enough for him to leave. He was succeeded as chairman by Peter Playford. Coppock died after a long illness on New Year's Day 1972.

Tony Rosser

Born: Oxford, approx 1940

Anthony Edward Rosser played football for Oxford City Colts and then Osberton Radiators in the Oxford Senior League. He had a serious motorcycle accident which ended his playing career, although he played cricket for Oxenford and had the odd game for Oxon over-50s. Together with his sons and Bob Hirons he started Summertown Stars boys' football team in 1973. He formed the Rosser Group in 1963, specialising in estate agencies and insurance brokerages, and commenced Techomes Ltd housebuilders in 1966. Rosser started Free Newspapers Ltd in 1972 and developed the first free newspaper – the *Oxford Journal* – in 1973. With his brother Colin he purchased Goodhead Press, also in 1973, and Free Newspapers continued to expand to include *Banbury Cake, Sheffield Journal, Bristol Journal, High Wycombe Observer, Henley Times, Marlow Times, Amersham and Chesham Times, Thame and Risborough Times, Aylesbury and Wendover Times, Cardiff Journal, Brighton Journal* and other papers in Manchester, Hull and west London. In 1981 Free Newspapers started a national paper called the *Sunday Journal*, which went on to become United's first shirt sponsor in 1981. Rosser joined Oxford United first as a director in 1973 and became chairman in 1974, leaving the club in October 1977. In November 1979 he was persuaded by Oxford City chairman Ray Barlow to take over City at their White House ground. In an effort to get better recognition for the club Bobby Moore, England's World Cup-winning captain, was appointed as manager and he persuaded his friend Harry Redknapp to come to City from America, where he was working at the time. Redknapp helped improve results, but the costs were too great and he was sacked and Moore left in 1983. Following difficulties with Citibank, the Rosser Group was sold in 1986. Rosser and his wife Cherry live in Cumnor, and their son Tim was an OxVox committee member for many years.

Robert Maxwell

Born: 10 June 1923, Slatinské Doly (Czechoslovakia)
Died: 5 November 1991

Robert Maxwell was born with the name Ján Ludvík Hoch to Jewish parents in an area that was then in Czechoslovakia, but is now in Ukraine. He fled the Nazis and arrived in England in 1940, aged 17. He was awarded the Military Cross in 1945 for his work with British Intelligence (who gave him the name Ian Robert Maxwell), and after the war he went into business, buying small publishers Pergamon Press and building them into a major publishing house. He was elected as Labour MP for Buckingham in the 1964 general election, but lost his seat in 1970. By this time he was already resident in Headington, attending occasional Oxford United games and even offering to loan the club money (an offer that the club declined). In 1981 Maxwell acquired the British Printing and Communication Corporation (BPCC) and in 1984 he bought Mirror Group Newspapers. In December 1981 Maxwell was alerted to the plight of United by one of his employees, whose son Bob Oakes worked for the club, and although on holiday in the West Indies, Maxwell managed to forestall Barclays Bank, who were threatening to have the club wound up if they were not repaid their overdraft of £150,000 (which United had already exceeded by £31,000). After returning from his holiday Maxwell studied the club's books and injected £121,000 into it, becoming chairman on 6 January 1982. Maxwell was hailed as a hero by the club's relieved supporters, but just 16 months later he was the villain after mooting the merger between Oxford and Reading. Many considered that this was a move to blackmail the local council into agreeing a site for a much-needed new stadium, but it failed, as did Maxwell with his promise that he would step down if the merger did not proceed. Maxwell then oversaw the two most successful seasons in the club's history as United became the first side to win the Third and Second Division titles in successive seasons and found themselves in the top flight for the first time. In the meantime, Maxwell had a bid for Manchester United of £10 million rejected, but he did buy Derby's Baseball Ground and cleared their debts, while installing his son Ian and daughter Ghislaine on the Oxford board, although Ian later left to become chairman of Derby, to be replaced by his brother Kevin. On 31 May 1987 Robert Maxwell resigned the chairmanship of Oxford to take over at Derby, with Kevin becoming United's chairman, at least nominally. Maxwell died in November 1991, when he fell overboard from his yacht, the *Lady Ghislaine*, in the Canary Islands. His body was found by a local fisherman shortly afterwards and Maxwell was buried at the Mount of Olives in Jerusalem, Israel.

Robin Herd

Born: 23 March 1939, Newton-le-Willows

Robin Herd was an Oxford graduate, achieving the university's second-best exam result with a double-first in physics and engineering. He worked on the Concorde project for four years, becoming a senior scientific officer at just 24 years old. He left to work for McLaren in 1965, moving to Cosworth three years later. In 1969 he co-founded March Engineering along with Max Mosley, Alan Rees, and Graham Coker (the name March was formed as an acronym of their surnames), setting up a factory in Murdock Road, Bicester. In 1986 he was awarded a CBE for his services to the motor racing industry. He sold March in 1989 and quit racing altogether six years later, when he bought Oxford United. Herd, advised by Keith Cox, was able to achieve planning permission for the Minchery Farm site, but when the finances ran out with the ground a mere skeleton, Herd stood down as chairman and later sold his shareholding to Firoz Kassam, two and a half years after taking over. In 1999 he formed March Indy International as he attempted to get back into the racing industry. In May 2006 Herd led a consortium looking to buy Liverpool FC for £180 million.

Firoz Kassam

Born: 1955, Musoma (Tanzania)

Firoz Kassam was one of five children, born in Tanzania of Indian parents. His father had a small confectionery business. His mother died when he was still a child and he had to share responsibility for his younger brothers and sisters. He came to Britain when he was 19, and found his first job working in an Indian take-away in south London, where he washed plates and cooking utensils. He opened his own successful fish and chip shop in Brixton and Kassam was able to borrow money to rent a building with 20 rooms in

Olympia in London. He operated a cheap 'bed and breakfast' hotel, but was unsuccessful. However, the local authorities were looking for cheap accommodation in London for homeless families and Kassam was able to oblige. The success of this venture enabled Kassam to obtain further loans to rent more properties and open other hotels. By the mid-1980s Firoz Kassam owned 18 cheap hotels in south London and was planning to build a luxury hotel. The recession of the late 1980s hit Kassam badly and many of his hotels were repossessed and his plans for the luxury hotel were abandoned. However, he was able to recover and his group of hotels developed through the 1990s. On 1 April 1999 he bought control of Oxford United Football Club from Robin Herd and reduced the club's debts. Kassam was able to negotiate the difficult obstacles to completing the abandoned shell of the half-built football ground in Minchery Farm that he later named after himself, along with the ancillary Ozone and Holiday Inn Express developments adjacent to the site. Kassam also bought Heythrop Park in Enstone in 1999 for £15 million and converted it into a luxury country hotel and conference centre. In 2005 he purchased Studley Castle in Warwickshire and had conferred an Honorary Fellowship by Oxford Brookes University. In 2006 he was foiled in his plans to redevelop Alexandra Palace and in March that year he sold his stake in Oxford United to Woodstock Partners Ltd. By this time Kassam had relocated to Monaco.

Kelvin Thomas

Born: 11 December 1972

Kelvin Brian Thomas' grandfather Bob played for Fulham and Crystal Palace, scoring 23 goals in Fulham's 1948–49 Second Division Championship season, and Thomas' cousin Geoff Pitcher spent three years at Watford after being a trainee at Millwall. Thomas was a player himself, mainly in the centre of defence or midfield. His first club was Dulwich Hamlet, but after only a few senior appearances he moved on to Croydon Athletic. It was at his next club, Banstead Athletic, where Thomas had most success, playing in the semi-final of the FA Vase in 1996–97 against Whitby Town. While a player Thomas also worked for Charlton Athletic and then Crystal Palace as a Football in the Community coach. After leaving Banstead, Thomas moved to the United States, where he played briefly for South West Florida Manatees in Division One (the level below the MLS). He remained in Florida, running a successful pest control business, until his appointment as a business adviser with United, supporting Nick Merry and Jim Smith as a director of WPL in 2006. After returning to Florida for a while, he was invited back to Oxford as chairman in October 2008, when he moved to Woodstock. Thomas was responsible for the appointment of manager Chris Wilder, and oversaw the club's return to the Football League via the Conference Play-offs.

Ken Fish

Born: 20 February 1914, Cape Town (South Africa)
Died: 4 August 2005

Kenneth Henry Albert Fish joined Oxford from Birmingham in 1964 to take on the role of trainer. He initially played for South African side Railway Association before moving to England and joining Aston Villa. He moved to Port Vale from Villa in November 1937. He became the first player to move from England to Europe for a fee when Vale sold him to Young Boys of Bern in October 1938. He returned to Vale shortly before World War Two, during which he played as a guest for Stafford Rangers, returning to Burslem as trainer in 1946. He was caretaker manager at Vale for a couple of months at the end of 1951, and in 1958 he moved to Birmingham as trainer-coach. Mr Fish, as he was known to everyone at United, was a strict disciplinarian and totally dedicated to serving the club; he took on numerous tasks, including masseur and kit launderer. He was rewarded for his time at the club with a testimonial against Leicester in May 1974 after 10 years' service, and at the Milk Cup Final in April 1986, when manager Maurice Evans sent Mr Fish up the famous Wembley steps to receive Evans' winners' medal. He retired in 1988 at the age of 74, and died in August 2005, aged 91.

ROLL OF HONOUR

Frank Webster
Gordon Clemson
Alan Galley
Jason Stafford
Steve Yates
Derek Brown
Cameron Stuart
Michael North
Alan J Stone
Paul Palgrave
Richard Lock
Graham Beacham
Alison Beacham
John Stoton
John Paul Stoton
Hugh Pudsey Dawson
Dr Kevin Stanton-King
Peter Hiscock
Roger Gascoigne
Henry Barrett
Peter Gordon
Ian Gordon
Jeremy G Dixon
Peter Harper
Roger Simmonds
Martin Halstead & Ralph Bates
Julian Dowdeswell
Andrew P Churchill
Stephen Kelly
David Reed
Dan Smith
Ian Norridge
Malcolm Norton
Pete Thoday
Philip Tanner
Anthony & Brenda Warne
Phil Malcolm
James East
Alex Ashmore
Mark Everett
Lawrence Ryan
Colin Morris
Andrew Wilmer

Colin Webster
Ron & Joan Kearley
Norman Foster MBE
Adrian Pledger
John Nicholls
Robert Gardner
Daniel House
Amanda Llewellyn
Jeffrey Wilkinson
JohnLindaEllenSophieWard
Peter Dixey
Matt Lambert
Jonathan Reddie
Barry Stayte
Bob Longden
Ian Faulkner
Ben Wyatt
Robert King
Alan Keep
Jeremy Cross
Keith Fletcher
Mark Blackwell
Mark Camilletti
Gary Gadsby
Steve Caron
James Caron
Matthew Caron
Daniel Caron
Wayne Paul Hawkins
Joel Jamie Hawkins
Alan & Joyce Stratton
Paul Seymour
Peter Camilletti
Gary Butler
Graham Knight-Whiddett
Trish Partlett
Mat Berry
Andrew Roper
Andrew Hack
Jonathan Hoad
JPG 'The Swot' Roberts
The McRae Family